Jews, Christians, and the Theology of the Hebrew Scriptures

SOCIETY
OF BIBLICAL
LITERATURE

SBL

SYMPOSIUM SERIES

Christopher R. Matthews, Editor

Number 8

Jews, Christians, and the Theology of the Hebrew Scriptures

edited by

Alice Ogden Bellis and Joel S. Kaminsky

Alice Ogden Bellis and
Joel S. Kaminsky, editors

Jews, Christians, and the Theology of the Hebrew Scriptures

Society of Biblical Literature
Atlanta

JEWS, CHRISTIANS, AND THE THEOLOGY OF THE HEBREW SCRIPTURES

edited by
Alice Ogden Bellis and Joel S. Kaminsky

Library of Congress Cataloging-in-Publication Data

Jews, Christians, and the theology of the Hebrew scriptures / Alice Ogden Bellis and Joel S. Kaminsky, editors.
p. cm. — (SBL symposium series ; no. 8)
Includes bibliographical references and index.
ISBN 0-88414-025-3 (pbk. : alk. paper)
1. Bible. O.T.—Theology. 2. Bible. O.T.—Criticism, interpretation, etc. I. Bellis, Alice Ogden, 1950– II. Kaminsky, Joel S., 1960– III. Symposium series (Society of Biblical Literature) ; no. 8.
BS1192.5.A1 J68 2000
221.6—dc21 00-061930

08 07 06 05 04 03 02 01 00 5 4 3 2 1

Printed in the United States of America
on acid-free paper

This book is dedicated in loving memory of:

Jayson David Kaminsky
12/18/1968–1/13/1996
May his life be bound up in the bundle of
life with the Lord your God.
והיתה נפש[ו] צרורה בצרור החיים את יהוה אלהיך
(1 Sam 25:29)

and

John Archie Haley
9/11/1927–10/10/1999
Uncle, Minister, Mentor, Friend
May the Holy One who kills and gives life,
sends down to Sheol and brings up to life
preserve you forever (adapted from 1 Sam 2:6)
יְהוָה מֵמִית וּמְחַיֶּה מוֹרִיד שְׁאוֹל וַיָּעַל

Joel S. Kaminsky
Alice Ogden Bellis

August 1, 2000
29 Tamuz, 5760

As editors of this project we learned much along the way from each other, and our task was facilitated greatly from many quarters. We wish to thank all the contributors who bore with us from the very beginnings until this project reached final publication, as well as the editorial staff at the Society of Biblical Literature, particularly Greg Glover and Gail O'Day, who initially encouraged us to pursue publishing this volume; Chris Matthews, the Symposium Series editor who gave us much good advice; Rex Matthews, who skillfully coordinated many aspects of this project; and Leigh Andersen and Bob Buller, who contributed to the final shape of the book. We both thank our spouses, Jody Rosenbloom and Douglass Bellis, for being patient through the many hours that we each devoted to this project. We also wish to express our gratitude to our home departments and institutions, the Department of Religion and Biblical Literature at Smith College and the Howard University School of Divinity, for providing each of us with a supportive environment that encouraged us to keep working on this important but often time-consuming project. Finally, Alice Ogden Bellis also wishes to thank the Wabash Center for Teaching Theology and Religion for the research grant that allowed her to work full time on this project during the summer of 1999.

CONTENTS

ABBREVIATIONS

ʿAbod. Zar.	*ʿAbodah Zarah*
AB	Anchor Bible
ABD	*Anchor Bible Dictionary,* ed. D. N. Freedman. 6 vols. New York: Doubleday, 1992.
ABRL	Anchor Bible Reference Library
ANET	*Ancient Near Eastern Texts Relating to the Old Testament,* ed. J. B. Pritchard, 3d ed. Princeton, N.J.: Princeton University Press
AnBib	Analecta biblica
AOAT	Alter Orient und Altes Testament
AThR	*Anglican Theological Review*
AUSS	*Andrews University Seminary Studies*
b.	Babylonian Talmud
B. Bat.	*Baba Batra*
BA	*Biblical Archaeologist*
BASOR	*Bulletin of the American Schools of Oriental Research*
BDB	Brown, F., S. R. Driver, and C. A. Briggs, *A Hebrew and English Lexicon of the Old Testament.* Oxford: Oxford University Press, 1907.
BEATAJ	Beiträge zur Erforschung des Alten Testaments und des antiken Judentum
Bib	*Biblica*
BJRL	*Bulletin of the John Rylands University Library of Manchester*
BTB	*Biblical Theology Bulletin*
BZAW	Beihefte zur Zeitschrift für die alttestamentliche Wissenchaft
Cant. Rab.	*Canticles (Song of Songs) Rabbah*
CBC	Cambridge Bible Commentary
CBQ	*Catholic Biblical Quarterly*
CCAR Journal	*Central Conference of American Rabbis Journal*
ChrCent	*Christian Century*
ConBOT	Coniectanea biblica: Old Testament Series
CRBR	*Critical Review of Books in Religion*
CRINT	Compendia rerum iudaicarum ad Novum Testamentum

CTA	*Corpus des tablettes en cunéiformes alphabétiques découvertes à Ras Shamra-Ugarit de 1929 à 1939,* ed. A Herdner
EncJud	*Encyclopedia Judaica*
Exod. Rab.	*Exodus Rabbah*
FCB	Feminist Companion to the Bible
FRLANT	Forschungen zur Religion und Literatur des Alten und Neuen Testaments
Gen. Rab.	*Genesis Rabbah*
HALOT	Koehler, L., W. Baumgartner, and J. J. Stamm, *The Hebrew and Aramaic Lexicon of the Old Testament,* trans. and ed. M. E. J. Richardson. 4 vols. Leiden: Brill, 1994–1999.
HBT	*Horizons in Biblical Theology*
HSM	Harvard Semitic Monographs
HTR	*Harvard Theological Review*
HUCA	*Hebrew Union College Annual*
IB	*Interpreter's Bible,* ed. G. A. Buttrick et al.
IBC	Interpretation: A Bible Commentary for Teaching and Preaching
IDB	*The Interpreter's Dictionary of the Bible,* ed. G. A. Buttrick. 12 vols. Nashville: Abingdon, 1952–1957.
IDBSup	*Interpreter's Dictionary of the Bible: Supplementary Volume,* ed. K. Crim. Nashville: Abingdon, 1976.
Int	*Interpretation*
JAAR	*Journal of the American Academy of Religion*
JAOS	*Journal of the American Oriental Society*
JBL	*Journal of Biblical Literature*
JECS	*Journal of Early Christian Studies*
JFSR	*Journal of Feminist Studies in Religion*
JJS	*Journal of Jewish Studies*
JNES	*Journal of Near Eastern Studies*
JQR	*Jewish Quarterly Review*
JR	*Journal of Religion*
JSOT	*Journal for the Study of the Old Testament*
JSOTSup	Journal for the Study of the Old Testament Supplement Series
JSS	*Journal of Semitic Studies*
JTS	*Journal of Theological Studies*
KTU	*Die keilalphabetischen Texte aus Ugarit,* ed. M. Dietrich
Lev. Rab.	*Leviticus Rabbah*
LSJ	Liddell, H. G., R. Scott, and H. S. Jones, *A Greek-English Lexicon*

LXX	Septuagint
m.	Mishnah
Meg.	*Megillah*
Mek.	*Mekilta*
Midr. Tanḥ.	*Midrash Tanḥuma*
MT	Masoretic Text
NIB	*The New Interpreter's Bible*
NJPS	*Tanakh: The Holy Scriptures: The New JPS Translation according to the Traditional Hebrew Text*
NRSV	New Revised Standard Version
NTS	*New Testament Studies*
Num. Rab.	*Numbers Rabbah*
OBO	Orbis biblicus et orientalis
OBT	Overtures to Biblical Theology
OTL	Old Testament Library
OTS	Old Testament Studies
OtSt	*Oudtestamentische Studiën*
PAAJR	*Proceedings of the American Academy of Jewish Research*
Pesiq. Rab.	*Pesiqta Rabbati*
Pesiq. Rab. Kah.	*Pesiqta de Rab Kahana*
Pirqe R. El.	*Pirqe Rabbi Eliezer*
QD	Quaestiones disputatae
Qidd.	*Qiddušin*
Šabb.	*Šabbat*
Sanh.	*Sanhedrin*
SBLDS	Society of Biblical Literature Dissertation Series
SBLMS	Society of Biblical Literature Monograph Series
SBLSCS	Society of Biblical Literature Septuagint and Cognate Studies
SBLWAW	Society of Biblical Literature Writings from the Ancient World
SBS	Stuttgarter Bibelstudien
SBT	Studies in Biblical Theology
ScrHier	Scripta hierosolymitana
SJT	*Scottish Journal of Theology*
SSN	Studia semitica neerlandica
SWBA	Social World of Biblical Antiquity
t.	Tosefta
TAPS	Transactions of the American Philosophical Society
TDNT	*Theological Dictionary of the New Testament*, ed. G. Kittel and G. Friedrich, trans. G. W. Bromiley. 10 vols. Grand Rapids: Eerdmans, 1964–1976.

TDOT	*Theological Dictionary of the Old Testament,* ed. G. J. Botterweck and H. Ringgren, trans. J. T. Willis et al. 10 vols. Grand Rapids: Eerdmans, 1974–.
TLZ	*Theologische Literaturzeitung*
TRu	*Theologische Rundschau*
TS	*Theological Studies*
VT	*Vetus Testamentum*
VTSup	Supplements to Vetus Testamentum
WBC	Word Biblical Commentary
Yad.	*Yadayim*
Yebam.	*Yebamot*
ZAH	*Zeitschrift für Althebräistik*
ZAW	*Zeitschrift für die alttestamentliche Wissenschaft*

Introduction

Joel S. Kaminsky and Alice Ogden Bellis

Over the last several decades dialogue between Jews and Christians has occurred on several fronts. While this conversation first began sometime in the 1960s, it is fair to say that in many ways the impetus for this discussion was the Shoah or Holocaust and particularly the realization that there was a connection between the *adversus Judaeos* tradition that runs so deeply throughout much of Christian theological history and the flourishing of modern anti-Semitism, or more bluntly, Jew hatred. Because this dialogue originated in the wake of the Shoah, some areas of discussion have received much greater attention than others. Thus a survey of the literature published in this rapidly expanding field reveals that an immense amount of scholarly effort has been put into clarifying issues such as, Does the New Testament contain anti-Semitic/anti-Judaic language, or in what ways was Hitler's anti-Semitism related or indebted to earlier Christian forms of anti-Judaism/anti-Semitism?[1] Because the earliest participants in this dialogue were attempting to overcome the vast chasm that seemed to have grown between these two religions as most powerfully symbolized by the events of the Holocaust, they frequently stressed what Judaism and Christianity had in common rather than focusing upon their differences.

As the second and perhaps now even the third generation of scholars have joined this dialogue, it has moved into areas that are not as focused on the question of Christian culpability for the Holocaust, and it appears that those now engaged in the dialogue are more willing to acknowledge and explore the significance of the deep and abiding differences in each tradition's theological outlook. Thus Jews and Christians are no longer simply trying to tame old hatreds; rather, they are now striving to reach a

[1] For bibliography on the field as a whole up until 1988, see Michael Shermis, *Jewish-Christian Relations: An Annotated Bibliography and Resource Guide* (Bloomington: Indiana University Press, 1988). For more recent scholarship, see Jeremy Cohen, ed., *Essential Papers on Judaism and Christianity in Conflict: From Late Antiquity to the Reformation* (New York: New York University Press, 1991); and Marvin Perry and Frederick M. Schweitzer, eds., *Jewish-Christian Encounters over the Centuries: Symbiosis, Prejudice, Holocaust, Dialogue* (New York: Peter Lang, 1994).

clearer understanding of each other's religious worldview through respectful but candid conversation.

The fruits of these rather recent developments in Jewish-Christian relations can be seen in many areas including the field of Hebrew Bible, especially in work that is focused on questions of biblical theology. While one might have thought that discussions between Jewish and Christian Hebrew Bible scholars would have developed early in the dialogue process and that there would be an extensive publication list of works demonstrating how these scholars engage the text of the Hebrew Bible in similar and different ways, this is not the case. A few seminal books have indeed been published in the last few years,[2] and many other important articles have appeared in various anthologies and academic journals.[3] However, the field is in many ways quite young and still developing. It seems that this particular area of Jewish-Christian dialogue took a while to come into its own not only because much of the early focus was on the Holocaust, but also because Jewish biblical scholars have only recently begun to enter the field in larger numbers. That the latter phenomenon is relatively recent stems at least in part from the fact that the field was dominated for so long by certain Christian, particularly Protestant, biases.[4] In any case, it is clear that interest in this specific area of interreligious dialogue is growing, both inside and outside of the academy, and many new voices can now be heard, even as many senior participants continue to make valuable contributions to this area. This anthology brings together some of the leading Jewish and Christian scholars of the Hebrew Bible, both older and younger, in the process of reflect-

---

[2] The most prominent examples are Roger Brooks and John J. Collins, eds., *Hebrew Bible or Old Testament? Studying the Bible in Judaism and Christianity* (Christianity and Judaism in Antiquity 5; Notre Dame: University of Notre Dame Press, 1990); Jon D. Levenson, *The Hebrew Bible, the Old Testament, and Historical Criticism* (Louisville: Westminster/John Knox, 1993).

[3] A few particularly noteworthy examples are Joseph Blenkinsopp, "Old Testament Theology and the Jewish-Christian Connection," *JSOT* 28 (1984): 3–15; John J. Collins, "Is a Critical Biblical Theology Possible?" in *The Hebrew Bible and Its Interpreters* (ed. W. Propp, Baruch Halpern, and D. N. Freedman; Winona Lake, Ind.: Eisenbrauns, 1990), 1–17; M. H. Goshen-Gottstein, "Tanakh Theology: The Religion of the Old Testament and the Place of Jewish Biblical Theology," in *Ancient Israelite Religion: Essays in Honor of Frank Moore Cross* (ed. P. D. Miller Jr., P. D. Hanson, and S. D. McBride; Philadelphia: Fortress, 1987), 617–44; and several of the essays in *Biblical Studies: Meeting Ground for Jews and Christians* (ed. L. Boadt, H. Croner, and L. Klenicki; Mahwah, N.J.: Paulist, 1980).

[4] Jon D. Levenson, "Why Jews Are Not Interested in Biblical Theology," in *Judaic Perspectives on Ancient Israel* (ed. J. Neusner, B. A. Levine, and E. S. Frerichs; Philadelphia: Fortress, 1987), 281–307; repr. in idem, *Hebrew Bible,* 33–61.

ing on the ways in which their respective religious commitments affect their scholarship as well as exploring how the ongoing Jewish-Christian dialogue has affected modern critical reflection on the theological study of the Hebrew Bible.

The idea for this anthology grew out of a well-received meeting of the Theology of the Hebrew Scriptures Section of the Society of Biblical Literature, a section Alice Ogden Bellis previously chaired and then co-chaired with Joel S. Kaminsky, who continues in this role, that took place in November 1996 in New Orleans. This particular session focused upon papers by two Jewish (Tikva Frymer-Kensky and Marvin Sweeney) and two Christian thinkers (Walter Brueggemann and Jorge Pixley), followed by a lively discussion among the panelists themselves, as well as between the panelists and various audience members. Building on the foundation of these four contributions, we solicited essays from additional Jewish and Christian Hebrew Bible scholars representing a range of perspectives and utilizing a variety of methodological approaches to the biblical text. Some of the essays offer broad reflections on the state of the field as a whole, while others engage in close exegetical readings of particular biblical passages. In two cases we asked one Jewish and one Christian scholar to write an exegetical piece on the same biblical text in order to get a clearer sense of the ways in which scholars' religious commitments inform their scholarly work. These paired essays are quite illuminating because they concretize many of the very issues raised in the abstract in the more broadly reflective pieces. We also pair Jewish and Christian thinkers in two scholarly exchanges on liberation theology, one between Jon Levenson and Jorge Pixley, and a second between Levenson and John J. Collins.

The book is organized in two large parts. Each major part is further subdivided into sections that group a related set of essays together. To mirror the ongoing process of Jewish-Christian dialogue, the essays within each section generally alternate between Jewish and Christian contributors. If one section begins with a Jewish contributor, the following one will begin with a Christian one. The organization of the book is intended to aid the reader in gaining a clearer understanding of both the similarities and the differences between Jewish and Christian approaches to the Bible, to guide the reader through the complex issues that have arisen in the field of biblical theology, and to allow easy access to those areas of greatest interest to individual readers. However, while these divisions give structure and coherence to the overall shape of the book, readers should be aware that many of the essays share common concerns with other essays beyond the boundaries marked by the sections.

Part 1 consists of essays that begin from a variety of abstract approaches to the field, but also frequently explore how a specific approach might bear fruit in the act of interpreting certain concrete biblical texts and themes. The first section of part 1 opens with an essay by Joel S. Kaminsky entitled "Paradise Regained: Rabbinic Reflections on Israel at Sinai." Kaminsky begins by mapping out the current state of Jewish-Christian dialogue from a Jewish perspective. He notes that the dialogue has now reached a point where Jews cannot simply criticize problematic Christian texts, theologies, and historical reconstructions, but rather must learn from the insights of their Christian counterparts and be willing to be critical of problematic Jewish texts, theologies, and historical reconstructions. The bulk of this essay is devoted to carefully unpacking an important but frequently neglected rabbinic perspective, that Israel recovered immortality at Mount Sinai only to lose it once again with the sin of the golden calf. Kaminsky argues that these rabbinic theological musings about Israel's immortality are a potential avenue for a renewed relationship and a deepened dialogue between Jews and Christians.

The second contribution to this section is Johanna W. H. van Wijk-Bos's "Writing on the Water: The Ineffable Name of God." In this provocative piece, van Wijk-Bos argues against the European and American Christian scholarly custom of vocalizing the Tetragrammaton (YHWH). She traces this questionable practice to certain anti-Jewish prejudices. This alone might be enough to discourage continuing the tendency to vocalize God's name, but van Wijk-Bos points out additional problems from both scholarly and Christian vantage points to bolster her case. These include the hypothetical nature of any attempted vocalization, the division between church and academy that the vocalization tends to exacerbate, and the illusion it fosters that humans can name God, thereby capturing God's essence. Van Wijk-Bos notes that the common practice of translating YHWH as LORD is also troublesome because of its masculine and domineering connotations as well as the difficulty that many contemporary Westerners have relating to the term. By utilizing insights of Martin Buber and Franz Rosenzweig that emphasize the relationality of God, she attempts a solution to this translation conundrum that preserves the unknowable and unnameable qualities of God as well as God's dynamic presence, without identifying God exclusively with one gender.

Murray H. Lichtenstein's "An Interpersonal Theology of the Hebrew Bible," the third essay in this section, argues that to look at the Hebrew Bible in traditional theological terms may itself be a mistake. In many ways it is more apt to say that the Hebrew Bible presents a psychology of God rather than a description of God's attributes. Although the Bible moves toward a depiction of God that avoids physical and mythological elements, it also portrays a God who is passionately and emotionally involved with creation and who attempts to carry out various divine agendas through different modes of direct and indirect personal involvement with humans. In spite of God's deep entanglements with humans, the Hebrew Bible characterizes God as quintessentially lonely and needy.

The fourth and final contribution to the opening section of the book is Ellen F. Davis's thoughtful "Losing a Friend: The Loss of the Old Testament to the Church." This is an eloquent personal reflection on the growing unimportance of the Bible in general and the Old Testament in particular to many Christians today. Davis argues not so much for a critically informed knowledge of the Hebrew Bible as a means to further academic theology and ethics, but for a more basic, if not more profound, appreciation of Scripture, or as she describes it, intimacy with the text.

The second section of part 1 contains essays that map out the current state of the field and suggest possible new directions. It opens with Walter Brueggemann's "Biblical Theology Appropriately Postmodern," which epitomizes his groundbreaking recently published *Theology of the Old Testament*.[5] Recognizing the multiplicity of both the voices in the Hebrew Bible and of contemporary readers and the difficulty of finding a single overarching theme that would guide the theological interpreter, Brueggemann opts to focus on process. He views the theological substance of the Hebrew Bible as an open-ended interaction between the Holy One and humanity. His hermeneutical claim is that "dialogic transactions" offer a promising alternative to Cartesian positivism. Brueggemann uses juridical language to argue that the text is a witness to various transactions, thus bracketing out both claims of ontology and history. The result is a call for Christian interpretation to resist the pressure for closure and a plea for all of us to listen to each other, not in order to achieve some new synthesis or harmony, but to create a human community in which all readings may be honored, even as alternative readings mutually challenge each other.

Tikva Frymer-Kensky's "The Emergence of Jewish Biblical Theologies" highlights some of the same points that Brueggemann does, but reflects on such matters from a Jewish point of view. She argues that the discoveries of modern biblical studies have led to Jewish approaches to biblical ideas that are at least partially independent of traditional rabbinic interpretation. The most important change has been the creation of a core of Jewish scholars who have not "moved on" to the Talmud, as previous generations of scholars did, but have remained focused on the Bible. Until recently, modern biblical scholars, including Jewish ones, shared with their predecessors the desire for a single, objective, correct reading of biblical texts that could claim authority. In the last twenty years, the authority claimed by scholarship has been subverted by both the recognition of the multivocality of the text and the plurality of competing interpretive communities—Christian, Jewish, third world, feminist, and so forth. This multivocality of the text is not a problem, but rather a reminder that the

---

[5] Walter Brueggemann, *Theology of the Old Testament: Testimony, Dispute, Advocacy* (Minneapolis: Fortress, 1997).

Bible is so rich and complex that only God can understand it fully. Frymer-Kensky rejects any new version of absolutism on the one hand or nihilism on the other, and embraces the concept that revelation and the sacred rest not in any particular word but in the process of engaging the text in order to wrest new meanings from it.

The third essay in section 2 of part 1, S. David Sperling's "The Law and the Prophet," is concerned with how the concept of Scripture originated. He suggests that while this concept may not have fully blossomed until sometime in the Persian period, its roots reach back to passages such as Num 12, in which the resolution of the conflict between Moses and Miriam and Aaron was accomplished in such a way that Moses became the prophet par excellence and all others were viewed as speaking in riddles. This claim to authority paved the way for the Torah, considered Moses' book, to be viewed as Scripture. Gradually other materials, including the Prophets, began to be viewed as Scripture. This in turn led to the cessation of oral prophecy. The end of oral prophecy marked the beginning of the Rabbinic period in which contemporary prophecy was replaced with interpretation of existing texts. New Testament authors, of course, also interpreted these same texts, albeit in a fulfillment mode. Sperling believes that the common goal of Jewish and Christian biblical scholars is first to discover the range of meanings the Scriptures had for their original audiences and then to disseminate information about what they meant in different postbiblical communities.

This section concludes with Rolf Rendtorff's "A Christian Approach to the Theology of Hebrew Scriptures," which surveys the history of European biblical theology with regard to its attitudes toward the Old Testament and Judaism. In harmony with elements of Sperling's argument, Rendtorff believes that the first task of both Jewish and Christian scholars is to understand and explain the Scriptures within their historical and social context. Furthermore, Rendtorrf notes that any attempt to understand early Christianity and how it grew out of and eventually separated from its Jewish milieu will call for a closer cooperation between Hebrew Bible and New Testament scholars than has been the case in the past.

The essays of the third section of part 1 focus particularly upon the ethics of engaging in the study and production of biblical theology and demonstrate some of the ways in which various ideological biases have distorted the biblical text, consequently allowing it to be used by some to oppress and harm others. The opening essay in this section, Marvin A. Sweeney's "Reconceiving the Paradigms of Old Testament Theology in the Post-Shoah Period," explores the shape of biblical theology in light of the Holocaust. He emphasizes the important role that humans play within the text's theological vision. To make his point he focuses on the books of Amos and Esther. In the case of Amos he deconstructs the usual Christian reading of this book as a universal call for justice, instead seeing Amos's Judahite roots as one of the primary factors behind the prophet's scathing critique of Israel. His reading of Esther highlights the necessity of human initiative in a world where God is hidden. In both books, the human protagonists Amos and Esther take actions in order to establish justice. In light of the Shoah, the biblical text's frequent emphasis upon the responsibility incumbent upon human beings for bringing justice into the world deserves greater emphasis by those engaged in the field of biblical theology.

Jorge Pixley's "Christian Biblical Theology and the Struggle against Oppression," also explores the relationship between interpreting the Bible and creating a more just world. Working from an evangelical, liberationist perspective in the context of the Latin American struggle for a better life, Pixley does not view theology as something primarily found in the Bible; rather, he sees it as something that occurs as faithful people reflect critically on the power struggles documented in the Bible. The task of biblical scholars, according to Pixley, is to serve popular movements seeking justice, which are in tune with the deepest forces governing the universe.

The final essay in this section rounding out the first half of the book is Baruch Halpern's "YHWH the Revolutionary: Reflections on the Rhetoric of Redistribution in the Social Context of Dawning Monotheism." Halpern begins by pointing out two opposing tendencies within biblical studies: (1) the appeal to congenial ancient biblical theologies as justification for contemporary ideological commitments; and (2) the rejection of repugnant biblical theologies. The first tendency is displayed, he argues, by liberation theologians; the second, by those concerned with issues of slavery and patriarchy. More sympathetic treatments—dealing with the ancients on their own terms—exist, according to Halpern, but do not find wide appeal. Halpern points out the naive and selective use of texts in liberationist readings and suggests an alternative perspective: in the end the God of the Hebrew Bible abdicates responsibility, requiring humans to take responsibility for their own situation, which includes reading the biblical text in a nuanced and critical fashion.

The second half of the book contains essays that take up important biblical texts and move from interpretations of these texts to larger reflections on the field of biblical theology. The first section in part 2 presents a series of essays that explore the legitimacy of recent attempts to marshal the biblical text in the service of contemporary sociopolitical movements, with particular attention to liberation theology's use of the exodus story. Jon Levenson's seminal 1991 article on "Liberation Theology and the Exodus" criticizes liberation theologians for ignoring central emphases of the biblical text, especially the chosenness of Israel. Using Jorge Pixley's commentary on Exodus as an example, he suggests that Pixley's ideological commitments blind him to many of the features of the text, including the particularity of the people God chose to free. Levenson also notes that even though Pixley considers himself an evangelical, he is forced to reject important features of the text in favor of a reconstructed version of biblical history in order to overcome the Bible's emphasis on the Jewish people. According to Levenson, Pixley needs to obscure the story's particularistic features so that he can more easily utilize the story to bolster Marxist-based revolutionary movements in Latin America. Levenson finds it ironic that Pixley wants to allow the Bible to speak anew today, while his interpretation of the exodus overlooks its subtle message of redemption and service, thereby silencing much of the text's profundity.

Jorge Pixley's "History and Particularity in Reading the Hebrew Bible" responds to Jon Levenson by faulting both his own Exodus commentary and Levenson's article for employing a confrontational style typical of the Cold War, which is now over. But he repudiates the notion that his reading of Exodus from the perspective of the poor negates the Jewish reading of the liberation of ethnic Jews. Finally, he defends the necessity of historical reconstruction as essential to seeing the sacred within contemporary struggles and defending marginalized peoples today.

Levenson continues the dialogue in his "The Perils of Engaged Scholarship" by applauding Pixley's humanitarian concerns and the courtesy with which he approaches the contentious issues, but nevertheless arguing that it is not legitimate to ignore the chosenness of Israel in preference of a reading that focuses only on the liberation of a group of enslaved people. He once again questions why reconstructed history should trump the theology of the text. While Levenson acknowledges that no reading is totally objective, he insists that objectivity is an important goal. In Levenson's opinion, Pixley's reading derives more from his political commitments than from a careful, critical exegesis of the text.

The issues at stake in this debate are further clarified in a subsequent interchange between John J. Collins, who comes to the defense of liberation theology in his "The Exodus and Biblical Theology," and Levenson's "The Exodus and Biblical Theology: A Rejoinder to John J. Collins." Collins contends that Levenson has oversimplified the position of most liberation theologians as well as the wider biblical portrayal of the exodus story. Looking to texts like Amos 9:7, Collins notes that the process of universalizing the exodus event is one found already within the confines of the biblical text. Collins concludes that the range of valid interpretations is limited, but that there is a legitimate diversity of ways in which the Bible can be read. Thus no one has a monopoly on biblical authority.

Levenson acknowledges Collins's point that the text can indeed be read in different ways. He recognizes the legitimacy of activists and preachers like Martin Luther King Jr., who reinterpret texts for use in new contexts; however, he asserts that historical critics like Pixley have allowed their ideological commitments to interfere with their responsibility to exegete the full text in its historical context, leading to subjective readings that claim the authority of objective scholarship. With regard to Amos 9:7 he contends that Amos may have been trying to shock his audience by telling them that they were no different from other nations. If his words were intended to be more rhetorical than literal, Levenson suggests that using this text as support for the exodus being universalized is questionable. Levenson's primary concern is with the liberation theologians' lack of attention to what he calls the familial-national aspects of the text.

The second section of part 2 offers close readings of some important biblical passages, which are presented in canonical order. The first two contributions comprise a set of paired readings on Gen 27, Terence E. Fretheim's "Which Blessing Does Isaac Give Jacob?" reflecting the perspective of a scholar teaching at a Christian seminary, and the other by David Marcus, a professor at a Jewish seminary, entitled "Traditional Jewish Responses to the Question of Deceit in Genesis 27."

In considering not only Gen 27 but also other texts closely connected to it, Fretheim argues that neither Isaac's commendation of Jacob to God nor God's oracle to Rebecca predetermine God's choice to bless Jacob. Isaac's "blessing" is more of a wish than an automatically effective word. In fact, some textual evidence indicates that Jacob's position declines in the immediate aftermath of his deception of Isaac. If this is the case, then the Bible may even be criticizing Jacob's actions by noting how they impeded God's plan, rather than endorsing his deceit.

Marcus surveys a variety of traditional Jewish approaches dealing with the deception of Isaac in Gen 27. Some shift the blame from Jacob, either to Rebecca, who is defended as trying to carry out God's will as expressed in the oracle given to her in Gen 25:23, or alternatively to Isaac, who allegedly allowed Rebecca to overhear a crucial conversation with Esau and supposedly only pretended not to recognize Jacob. Another strategy acknowledges that Jacob is the responsible party but claims that he did not actually lie or that the deception is legitimate because Jacob had become the legal Esau by virtue of Esau's selling him the birthright. In certain ways, these classical Jewish interpretations anticipated the results of modern scholarship, which views Jacob as a clever trickster whose trickery is understood to have been evaluated positively by the original audience.

The next essay is Esther Fuchs's thought-provoking exegesis and personal reflection, "A Jewish-Feminist Reading of Exodus 1–2." Fuchs reconstructs the "immasculating" process in which women are depicted according to male-constructed myths ("mythogynies") and in which female readers tend to identify with the masculinist ideology of the text. She points out that women are valorized in Exod 1–2 in their maternal roles when they ensure a patrilineal genealogy; however, they are also ambiguated and constricted in various ways, keeping them on the margins. The presentation of women in Exod 1–2 sets the stage for the exclusion of women from meaningful roles in the religious and national construction of the Israelite story, and elements of this marginalization are also present in the modern Israeli nationalist, male-centered narrative.

The section continues with a second paired set of Jewish and Christian readings on a single text: Brooks Schramm's "Exodus 19 and Its Christian Appropriation," and Marc Zvi Brettler's "The Many Faces of God in Exodus 19." Schramm focuses on the divergent ways in which the Jewish and Christian communities have evaluated the significance of the giving of the law at Sinai. Acknowledging the difficulty of isolating sources, Schramm focuses instead on theological issues. What is distinctive about Sinai is not that it involves a conditional covenant unlike the supposedly unconditional Abrahamic covenant and not that Israel here becomes God's elect (they already were), but rather that at this point, having experienced God's liberating activity in the exodus, Israel comes of age as a liberated people tied to a liberating God, for the sake of the world. This is particularism within a universal perspective. However, the golden calf incident tests the limits of the relationship. If it were not for Moses' invocation of God's promise to Abraham, Israel would have been destroyed. This means that Israel's disobedience cannot, in the end, thwart God's grace toward Israel, but neither does God's mercy ensure Israel's obedience. In Neh 9 the Abrahamic and Sinai covenants are conceived as one, with the Abrahamic part ensuring endurance while the Sinaitic aspect energizes the relationship. Paul severs the relationship between the two aspects of the unified covenant, by viewing the Abrahamic in a positive light and the Sinaitic negatively. While his concern was to maintain the identity of the God who was at work in the gospel among the Gentiles, once that concern was lost, negativity toward Sinai easily slipped into total negation, creating a theological rift between the Old and New Testaments.

Brettler, like Schramm, demonstrates the difficulty of applying traditional source criticism to Exod 19. Rather than spending energy on the possibly futile task of isolating the exact extent of each possible source and attempting to explain this chapter's redactional history, he seeks to understand the multiple ideologies that are present in the text. He suggests that the "messiness" of this text in which multiple images sometimes conflict, creating paradox, could be an intentional attempt to recreate the human experience of encountering the divine. Scholars trained in rational, scientific methodologies should keep in mind that they are engaged in interpreting religious texts that may resist attempts to be fully rationalized because they have been purposefully obscured to mirror the most profound elements of the human religious experience.

Finally, the collection as a whole concludes with Alice Ogden Bellis's "Habakkuk 2:4b: Intertextuality and Hermeneutics," in which she focuses on a pivotal text for Christians, literally "the just shall live by his (its) faith(fulness)." She argues that a triple entendre may be involved. In the face of impending crisis: (1) the just shall live—in the sense of surviving—because of his, that is, God's faithfulness, or its, that is, the divine vision's trustworthiness; (2) the just shall live—in the sense of being able to maintain his religious identity—by his own faith (in God's faithfulness); and (3) the just shall live, meaning that he will have the ability to conduct his life, in spite of the crisis, faithfully. Following Mark Nanos she further argues that the citations of this text by Paul and the author of the letter to the Hebrews are not as radically reinterpretive as is often believed, since all three of these meanings may be present in the New Testament readings and not just the second one, as is usually thought. Although Bellis suggests that the New Testament appropriations of Hab 2:4b are creative, responsible interpretations, she is much less sanguine about popular Protestant Christianity's use of these New Testament passages.

In assessing the contributions to this volume, a few preliminary conclusions may be drawn. Jewish and Christian scholars of the Hebrew Scriptures have much in common, most importantly the same array of scholarly tools and the same passion for the text. We also have some obvious differences deriving from our different religious and cultural traditions. Jewish scholars are much more likely than Christian ones to draw on rabbinic insights, though some Christian scholars are investigating this important area. Christian scholars have been formed by the New Testament texts in ways in which Jewish ones have not, even if many Jewish scholars are far more knowledgeable of the New Testament and Christian tradition than most Christians are with postbiblical Jewish tradition. As we become more familiar with each other's rich histories, we may come to understand and even celebrate these differences rather than view them as a source of acrimony.

While the reader will probably not find it surprising that Jewish and Christian biblical scholars read the Hebrew Bible differently, it is the contention of this anthology that these differences are potentially more instructive than disruptive and that interreligious dialogue among thinkers, as illustrated in this volume, is of immense value to the field of biblical studies as a whole. Such dialogue illuminates the theological content of the Hebrew Bible as distinct from later Jewish and Christian traditions, clarifies the processes by which each tradition grew out of and uniquely appropriated the Hebrew Bible, and forces a rethinking of the classic stereotypes that each religion has about the other, as well as those idealized images each religion has about itself. An additional benefit of such open discussion is that sometimes seeing one's own tradition through the eyes of the other highlights important theological ideas that those inside a given tradition had forgotten or underemphasized.

By entering into the kind of sustained dialogue represented by this volume, we have the opportunity to reflect on the ways in which we have been religiously shaped which, in turn, may open our eyes to new realities we could not see alone. With this point in mind, we have selected a line from Gen 43:3 as an epigraph for this book: "You shall not see my face unless your brother is with you." In the Joseph story, the term *brother* is not used generically, but refers to an actual brother. We are appropriating this text and using it in a different way, not only in terms of gender, but also with regard to whose face is to be seen. In a similar fashion we might invoke 1 Cor 13:12a, "Now we see through a glass, darkly; but then face to face."

Part 1:

Theoretical Perspectives

Section 1:

Primary Propositions

Paradise Regained: Rabbinic Reflections on Israel at Sinai[1]

Joel S. Kaminsky

Introduction

As noted in the introduction to this volume, while the fruits of recent Jewish-Christian dialogue have been many, vastly more critical attention has been focused on Christianity than on Judaism. This can be seen in the multitude of publications, public lectures, and panel discussions devoted to Christian portrayals of Judaism, which attempt to assess and critique Christian triumphalism and supersessionism.[2] On the other hand, comparatively little ink has been spilled on potentially analogous issues within Judaism. This imbalance is quite understandable in the light of the long history of Christian anti-Judaism and anti-Semitism and the disturbing ways in which certain Christian theological ideas appear to have contributed to the events culminating in the Shoah. Nevertheless, now that discussions have progressed well beyond their initial stages, Jewish scholars, heeding the canons of critical scholarship and intellectual fairness, are beginning to critique widespread Jewish stereotypes of Christianity, as well as their own tradition's idealized self-images.

One much-needed area of attention is the rather common tendency of many Jewish people to assume that Judaism is quite closely associated with the theology of the Hebrew Bible, while viewing Christianity as a tradition that reads the Hebrew Bible through a lens that is totally alien to it.[3] Thus

---

[1] The initial research for this paper was done with the help of the National Endowment for the Humanities (Summer Seminar: "Adam and Eve in Jewish and Christian Tradition," Hebrew University, Jerusalem, 1996). I am indebted to Gary Anderson, Michael Stone, and other members of the seminar for their support and their many helpful contributions to this project. I also wish to thank Professors Jon D. Levenson, John J. Collins, and Gregory Spinner for reading various drafts of this paper, making many helpful suggestions and providing much encouragement along the way.

[2] One can see this concern in the contributions to this volume by Brueggemann, Levenson, Rendtorff, Schramm, and Sweeney.

[3] This attitude can even be found among certain Christian thinkers who wish to counter the Christian tendency toward supersessionism. Thus Rolf Rendtorff, in his

Judaism is portrayed as the mother religion and Christianity as a headstrong daughter who went off in a new direction. While it is true that Christianity grew out of some form of preexisting Judaism, this portrait ignores the fact that rabbinic Judaism, the religion we know today as Judaism, and Christianity "were born at the same time and nurtured in the same environment."[4] Thus there is a growing scholarly consensus that the relationship between Judaism and Christianity is better described as a sibling rivalry. While this brotherly competition has led each tradition to claim to be the true heir of the religious worldview found in the Hebrew Bible and to discount or dismiss totally the other sibling's claims to the same effect, recent scholarship has demonstrated that both traditions frequently read parts of the Hebrew Bible in ways that creatively subvert the plain meaning of the text.[5]

This new understanding of early Jewish-Christian relations begs for contemporary Jewish scholars to reappraise the persistent and relatively pervasive tendency to (mis)represent early Christianity as an illegitimate religion and consequently to exaggerate the differences between Christianity and rabbinic Judaism. Such reevaluation is urgent not only because it might create greater harmony between these two religions, but also because it will facilitate the recovery of important pieces of the Jewish theological tradition that such stereotyping regularly ignores or dismisses.

A clear example of the propensity to draw a simplistic set of distinctions between Jewish and Christian interpretations of the Hebrew Bible can be found in the way that certain popularly read Jewish authors contrast Jewish versus Christian treatments of Gen 2–3. While it may be true that Judaism gives less theological weight to the story of Adam and Eve than does Christianity, statements like the following, versions of which I have heard repeated countless times, seriously misrepresent the classical Jewish tradition.

contribution to this very volume, states that "Christian theologians often forget that Christianity grew out of Judaism and that therefore Christian interpretation of the common Hebrew Holy Scriptures is always the second in order. Judaism has its own interpretation, which is in some senses much closer to the Hebrew text, while Christian interpretation is mediated through another collection of writings, the New Testament" ("A Christian Approach to the Theology of Hebrew Scriptures," 144–45).

[4] Alan Segal, *Rebecca's Children* (Cambridge: Harvard University Press, 1986), 1.

[5] I am in agreement with the following quote from S. David Sperling's contribution to this anthology: "The result is that even sections of Scripture that were reasonably clear to their original target audiences have become overlaid with meanings inconceivable to their authors. Contemporary Christians and Jews must reckon with the theologically significant fact that their religious beliefs and practices are hardly based on plain-sense interpretations of Scripture" ("The Law and the Prophet," 135).

> In the Haggadah of the Rabbis the scenes and characters of the Genesis paradise saga appear not infrequently.... However, no doctrinal consequences were ever drawn from the Garden of Eden legend for Judaism as was the case for Christianity.... Primal Myths have nothing to do with the history of the Jewish people.... The Genesis myths were in no way decisive for the theology of Judaism.[6]

The most likely explanation for the popularity of this sentiment is that it manages to paint Judaism as a rational religion that is in accord with a variety of modern religious assumptions. Such an apologetic approach downplays Jewish sources that speak of otherworldly redemption or any type of immortality or resurrection and overemphasizes those sources that see humans as fundamentally good creatures who have the ability to freely choose their own destiny. Another widely read book not only proclaims that "Judaism has no room for anything resembling the Christian doctrine of 'original sin'" but that "there is virtually nothing in *authoritative* Jewish belief (of course, there are popular superstitions) that is contrary to reason and the laws of nature."[7] While the intent of these authors to help Jews understand their distinctive religious heritage is to be commended, their relegation of vast portions of the rabbinic corpus to the category of "popular superstitions" that are "in no way decisive for the theology of Judaism" misrepresents Judaism and leaves the reader with an oversimplified portrait of the similarities and differences between Judaism and Christianity.

The purpose of this article is to begin to provide a more nuanced reading of the theological importance of the Adam and Eve material within rabbinic Judaism and thus argue that, contrary to popular belief, Judaism does indeed contain something akin to the Christian notion of the "fall." While the rabbis do not affirm the full complement of theological ideas that the early church derived from the notion of humanity's fall, some of their readings of the Adam and Eve story have a stronger resemblance to early Christian readings of Gen 2–3 than is commonly acknowledged. In any case, both early Jewish and early Christian readings of these materials share more features with each other than either one shares with a plain-sense reading of the biblical text. Because these Jewish materials are not

---

6 Abba Hillel Silver, *Where Judaism Differed: An Inquiry into the Distinctiveness of Judaism* (Philadelphia: Jewish Publication Society of America, 1957), 165–66. It is clear that this book has been popular since it was first written in 1956 and has gone through numerous reprintings, with a recent reprint currently available in hardback by Aronson.

7 Trude Weiss-Rosmarin, *Judaism and Christianity: The Differences* (1943; repr., New York: Jonathan David, 1972), 48, 39 [emphasis is Weiss-Rosmarin's]. The copy I quoted from is a seventh printing, but this book has once again been reprinted by the same publisher in 1997 as a hardback.

widely known, the bulk of this paper will be devoted to analyzing a variety of rabbinic texts that touch upon this mythic complex. Toward the end of the paper I will briefly compare these Jewish texts to a few early Christian texts and conclude by exploring the relevance of these rabbinic texts to the ongoing task of Jewish-Christian understanding.

The Rabbinic Evidence

One might assume that if Judaism does contain some type of fall myth, it would be located in the midrashic sources on Gen 2–3. But one of the greatest difficulties with the rabbinic materials on any subject is that they are rarely presented in a systematic or easily accessible manner. Thus it is helpful to find a motif or series of motifs and begin to collect the texts in which these motifs recur. As will be seen shortly, the majority of the materials that will be examined in this paper are generated by the rabbinic attempt to link the Adam and Eve narrative (Gen 2–3) to the story of Israel at Mount Sinai before and after the sin of the golden calf (Exod 19–34). Unfortunately, any attempt to discuss all the relevant texts on even this more limited subject would require at least a book-length monograph. Still, it can be useful to investigate one particular locus in rabbinic literature that explores the relationship between Gen 2–3 and Exod 19–34.

The easiest way to narrow the field of potential passages is to find a proof-text that frequently occurs in close relationship to the motifs under discussion and use that prooftext as a method to collect and analyze a particular theological complex. This investigation will focus upon a selection of seven rabbinic texts that make use of Ps 82:6–7 ("I said: You are gods, all of you the sons of the Most High; nevertheless you will die as mortals, you will fall like one of the princes"), a passage that the rabbis read as an epitome of Israel's Sinai experience, and the ways in which this experience resembled Adam and Eve's in Eden.[8]

Israel Is Granted Temporary Immunity from Death

The first text I will examine is from the *Mekilta of Rabbi Ishmael,* a collection of legal, as well as some haggadic (narrative) midrashim[9] on the book of Exodus. This collection is commonly dated to a second-century

---

[8] Inasmuch as it would be impossible to discuss every rabbinic passage that cites Ps 82:6–7 within the confines of a single paper, I carefully chose passages that complement each other and mutually illuminate certain often-neglected aspects of rabbinic thinking. Furthermore, because there is no single rabbinic approach to the Bible, an additional criterion in the selection process was that the rabbinic texts come from a wide range of locales and historical periods.

[9] Midrashim is the plural of midrash.

C.E. Palestinian context, although it is likely that certain pieces may be older and others quite a bit younger. The *Mekilta* records the following tradition on Exod 20:19, a verse in which the Israelites who are overwhelmed by the Sinai theophany say to Moses, "speak to us and we will listen; but do not let God speak to us, or we will die."

> This tells us that they did not have the strength to receive more than the Ten Commandments, as it is said: *If we hear the voice of the Lord our God any more, then we shall die* (Deut 5:22 [Eng. Deut 5:25]). . . . R. Jose says: It was upon this condition that the Israelites stood up before mount Sinai, on condition that the Angel of Death should not have power over them. For it is said: *I said you are like godlike beings,* etc. (Ps 82:6). But you corrupted your conduct. *Surely you shall die like men* (ibid., v. 7).[10]

This midrash contains only a few hints at the larger complex of materials that other midrashim, cited further below, address in much greater detail. But it is a useful place to begin both because its brevity will make it easier to unpack and because its undeveloped form may reveal that this *mythos* grew in complexity over time. On the surface this passage only appears to link Exod 19–20 to Ps 82:6–7, and even this connection is quite cryptic. The corruption mentioned toward the end of the passage surely refers to Exod 32, but its exact meaning is far from clear to the uninitiated reader. Genesis 2–3 appears nowhere in plain sight. The text implies that under normal circumstances Israel would not have been able to endure receiving the Ten Commandments and therefore they received at least a temporary grant of immunity from the Angel of Death.[11] The proof-text that Rabbi Yose uses to substantiate his exegetical point is Ps 82:6–7.

---

[10] *Mekilta de-Rabbi Ishmael* (trans. J. Z. Lauterbach; 3 vols.; Philadelphia: Jewish Publication Society of America, 1949), 2:270–72 (בחודש ט). In general, I have opted to use the standard English translations of the midrashic texts under discussion so as to allow the reader to access the complete text with ease. The reader should be aware that many of the collections of midrashim have not yet been published in critical editions. For more background on these texts and translations, see Hermann L. Strack and Günter Stemberger, *Introduction to the Talmud and Midrash* (Minneapolis: Fortress, 1992). I have left all translations of biblical verses that occur within midrashic translations as is; however, I have opted to standardize how they are marked off from the surrounding midrashic expansions by italicizing all such quotes. Translations of biblical verses from the Hebrew Bible elsewhere in the paper are my own, while those from the New Testament are from the NRSV.

[11] A similar motif, in which Israel dies each time God speaks a word and is then resurrected after each spoken word, is found in *b. Šabb.* 88b. In some sense the biblical text itself hints at Israel attaining at least a temporary suspension from death inasmuch as all the Israelite firstborn are spared from the tenth plague.

To grasp Rabbi Yose's point, one must understand why he thought Ps 82:6–7 contained a cryptic hint of Israel's experience at Mount Sinai. Before entering into a fuller discussion of this rabbinic interpretation of Ps 82:6–7, however, it is important to note that Ps 82 as a whole was bound to catch the eye of the ancient interpreter. A straightforward reading of Ps 82 indicates that the psalmist openly accepts the notion that God is the ruler over a pantheon of other deities.[12] It may be true, as has been argued cogently by M. Tsevat, that Ps 82 signals a change from a polytheistic toward a more monotheistic understanding of religion in ancient Israel.[13] Nevertheless, the psalm clearly speaks of God's taking "his place in the divine assembly" and giving judgment "in the midst of the gods" (Ps 82:1).

Obviously this is not the way the rabbis read the psalm. In fact, the rabbis tended to be troubled by all references to other gods and thus they developed readings, sometimes a bit forced, to fit these texts into their monotheistic worldview. For example, the rabbis creatively re-read the word "gods" in the commandment, "You shall have no other gods before me" (Exod 20:3), in a variety of ways, including "those which others call gods" and gods "who act like strangers towards those who worship them."[14] Similarly, they interpret the divine assembly language found in Ps 82:1 as referring to judges and do the same for Exod 22:8. "Hence the verse 'He is a Judge among Elohim' [Ps 82:1] is to be read 'He is a Judge among judges,' as in the verse 'The cause of both shall come before the judges (*Elohim*)' (Exod 22:8)."[15] So when this psalm uses language that implies the existence of many gods, the rabbis interpret it as referring to humans in an exalted state.

When readers turn from the psalm as a whole to verses 6–7 in particular, initially they may be mystified as to how the rabbis could think that the statement, "I said: 'You are gods, all of you the sons of the Most High; nevertheless you will die as mortals, you will fall like one of the princes,'" had anything to do with the Israelites at Mount Sinai. However, on closer inspection several textual links can be discerned between Ps 82:6–7 and the Sinai materials, as well as a rather cryptic connection to Gen 2–3.

---

12 Hans-Joachim Kraus, *Psalms 60–150: A Commentary* (trans. Hilton C. Oswald; Minneapolis: Augsburg, 1989), 153–57.

13 Matitiahu Tsevat, "God and the Gods in Assembly: An Interpretation of Psalm 82," in *The Meaning of the Book of Job and Other Biblical Studies: Essays on the Literature and Religion of the Hebrew Bible* (New York: Ktav, 1980), 131–47.

14 *Mekilta de-Rabbi Ishmael,* 2:239 (בחודש ו).

15 *The Midrash on Psalms,* vol. 2 (trans. William G. Braude; Yale Judaica Series 13; New Haven: Yale University Press, 1959), 59. Also see the *Mek.* on Exod 22:8 and *b. Sanh.* 6.

To begin with, the rabbis, as noted above, were not inclined to read the reference in verse 6 to "gods, children of the Most High" as referring to other heavenly beings but assumed it referred to a group of earthly beings who had been in an exalted state. Additionally, the mention of the sons of the Most High may have called to mind Deut 14:1, in which Moses, reporting for God, tells Israel, "you are sons of the Lord your God." And even more to the point, the reference to Ps 82:7 describes the rather quick loss of this exalted state by using the phrase, "you [plural] will die כאדם—like humans" (or reading with the rabbis "like Adam").

The use of the word אדם, which can be translated generically as humans or specifically as referring to Adam the first human, creates an excellent exegetical link between the fate of Adam and these other exalted beings mentioned in Ps 82:6–7. The rabbis had already decided these exalted beings were humans who experienced a closeness to God similar to Adam's and like Adam quickly fell from grace. It is thus possible to see one reason why they thought that Ps 82:6 speaks of Israel in her exalted state after having just received the law,[16] while verse 7 speaks of her fall after the sin of the golden calf. As will be seen further below, many other verbal, thematic, and mythic associations led the rabbis to homologize the Adam and Eve story to the Sinai–golden calf narrative.

Before proceeding to the next midrash, a quick summary of this midrash is in order. Its major point is that God granted Israel temporary immunity from death in order to help her survive the danger posed by encountering God and receiving the Ten Commandments.[17] However, this midrash's reference to Ps 82:7 hints at an idea that is a central concern of this paper: Israel's experience at Sinai directly parallels Adam's in the garden of Eden, as each had a chance at permanent immortality but lost it through committing a sin.[18]

God Intended Israel, Like Adam, to Have Immortality

The next midrash, *Exod. Rab.* 32:1 on Exod 23:20, "I am going to send an angel in front of you... ," explicitly draws a variety of close correspondences between Exod 19–34 and Gen 2–3.

---

[16] The tendency to link Ps 82 to the giving of the law at Sinai also appears to be hinted at in John 10:31–39, as noted by A. Hanson, "John's Citation of Psalm LXXXII," *NTS* 11 (1964–1965): 158–62.

[17] The idea that encountering God can be dangerous is common in the Hebrew Bible, as indicated by passages such as Gen 32:22–32; Exod 4:24–26; 19:12, 21–23; etc.

[18] I am not claiming that the biblical text supports the notion that Adam had immortality and then lost it but that the rabbis did indeed believe that Adam had been granted immortality and then lost it. This contention will receive extensive support below.

> Thus it is written, *I said: Ye are godlike beings* (Ps 82:6). Had Israel waited for Moses and not perpetrated that act, there would have been no exile, neither would the Angel of Death had any power over them. And thus it says, *And the writing was the writing of God, graven* (חרות) *on the tables* (Exod 32:16). What is the meaning of חרות? ... R. Judah says: Free (חירות) from captivity; and R. Nehemiah says: Free from the Angel of Death. When Israel exclaimed: *All that the Lord has spoken will we do, and hearken* (24:7) the Holy One blessed be He said: "If I gave Adam but one commandment that he might fulfill it, and I made him equal to the ministering angels, for it says *behold the man was one of us* (Gen 3:22)—how much more so should those who practice and fulfill all the six hundred and thirteen commandments—not to mention their general principles, details and minutiae—be deserving of eternal life?" This is the meaning of *And from Mattanah to Nahaliel*—נחלו (Num 21:19); for they had inherited [through the Torah, given as a gift], from God eternal life. As soon, however, as they said, *This is thy god, O Israel* (Exod 32:4), death came upon them. . . . Since you have followed the footsteps of Adam, *Nevertheless ye shall die like men*. What is the meaning of *And fall like one of the princes*? R. Judah said: Either as Adam or as Eve. Another explanation. . . . God said to them: "You have brought about your own downfall. In the past, you were served by direct inspiration; now however, you will be served only by an angel"—as it says, *Behold, I send an angel before thee*.[19]

This is a much more complex passage than the one previously considered; thus it will be necessary to treat it at length. First, one must understand why Exod 23:20 sets off this negative train of thought about Israel's disobedience. As is clear from the end of the passage, the rabbis read the sending of an angel as an indication that Israel had fallen from a higher status that she once had attained. While they do not explicitly cite Exod 33:1–3 here, it seems highly probable that they believe these two texts describe the same event. Inasmuch as Exod 33:1–3, in its current canonical placement, implies that God would send an angel rather than accompany the people himself because he is angry over the sin of the golden calf,[20] they read Exod 23:20 as carrying the same negative connotation. It is also possible that the motif of sending an angel brought to mind the Angel of Death, a character who receives some attention here.

The text begins by drawing an implicit comparison between the consequences of Israel's sin at Mount Sinai and the rabbinic understanding of the results of Adam's sin. Just as Adam's sin led to the loss of immortality and his banishment from Eden, so too in Israel's case, her sin led to the

[19] *Midrash Rabbah: Exodus* (trans. S. M. Lehrman; London: Soncino, 1939), 404–5.

[20] Precisely this association is made in *Exod. Rab.* 32:8, by Rashi in his comment upon Exod 23:20, as well as by Brevard Childs, *The Book of Exodus: A Critical, Theological Commentary* (OTL; Louisville: Westminster, 1974), 588.

loss of the immortality she had just acquired, as well as to the eventual banishment from her paradisiacal situation in the land of Israel.

The rabbis support this point exegetically by citing a widely used pun on Exod 32:16 in which they playfully substitute the Hebrew word חירות, meaning freedom, for the word חרות, meaning engraved. Frequently this pun is used to make the point that true freedom is found by living in obedience to God's law revealed at Sinai. Here the rabbis use it as proof that Israel at Sinai had attained a state of perfection closely analogous to Adam's, one that included both immortality and its counterpart, life in God's garden/land. Unlike the *Mekilta,* this text implies that such immortality was indeed potentially eternal.

The passage then uses an a fortiori argument to explain why God felt obliged to grant Israel the same immortality that Adam had once been given. If Adam received such a reward for his reception of a single divine commandment, how much more should Israel's acceptance of the 613 commandments entitle them to eternal life.

The rabbis further bolster their argument by creatively rereading Num 21:19. In a plain-sense reading this verse simply transmits a series of locations in Israel's wilderness wanderings, while in this rabbinic interpretation it contains a cryptic code of Israel's spiritual wanderings. The location Mattanah is interpreted as shorthand for the giving of the law, which Jews even today call *mattan* Torah, the gift of the law. And Nahaliel is split into two words נחלו (they inherited) and אל (God), which in this midrash is understood to mean that Israel inherited eternal life from God through the gift of the Torah. This reading builds upon the rabbinic understanding of Prov 3:18. While this verse describes wisdom as "a tree of life to those who lay hold of her," in the rabbinic mind wisdom is just another name for Torah. Thus Torah becomes associated with the tree of life and the gift of immortality.[21] Then the last location of Num 21:19 receives exegetical attention. Bamoth is also split into two words and understood as בא מות (death came), when Israel committed idolatry in Exod 32:4.

The correlation between Israel and Adam is then driven home by citing Ps 82:7, whose last word should be translated here as "like Adam" and not, as the Soncino translation suggests, "like men." The midrash closes by

---

[21] The synagogue liturgy surrounding the reading of the Torah on Sabbath morning makes these connections quite explicitly. Thus Prov 3:18 is sung as part of the liturgy of returning the Torah scroll to the ark after the weekly Torah reading. Furthermore, each participant called to the Torah recites a blessing, after his or her reading is completed, that blesses God as the one "who has given us the Torah of truth and planted eternal life in our midst." These prayers testify to the way in which the rabbis drew a complex set of connections between Torah, wisdom, the tree of life, and immortality.

giving attention to Ps 82:7b, "you will fall like one of the princes," a text that receives no mention in the other midrashim cited in this paper. In one of the two interpretations offered, the rabbis make yet another attempt to link Israel to Adam and Eve. However, it is likely that this verse fragment receives attention here because the second explanation given allows the midrashist to link his exegesis back to Exod 23:20 by showing that Israel needed an angel because she fell from her own angelic state.

This midrash uses a variety of texts to explore the links between Israel's experience at Mount Sinai and Adam and Eve's in the garden of Eden. Much of the discussion grows out of and further reinforces the rabbinic belief that both attained immortality but lost it through disobedience. But it is important to see that even as the rabbinic discussion moves far beyond the biblical materials, it builds upon and sheds light on a number of thematic and verbal links between the two biblical stories. In general terms, each story begins with humans in close proximity to God and the requirement of obedience to God's commandment(s). Both stories include an act of human disobedience that results in a fractured relationship between the humans and God.[22] Finally, neither story ends with God completely severing all relations with the humans who disobeyed him. Many other less obvious correspondences can also be discerned. For example, it is odd that the punishments in both narratives are similarly complicated in two opposing ways: first, each narrative tends to include a multiplicity of punishments, and second, God never executes the expected, more severe punishment. Thus, in the Adam and Eve narrative, while it is frequently assumed that the loss of innocence is the first punishment, a close reading indicates that the loss of innocence flows immediately from eating the fruit rather than from any specific action taken by God (Gen 3:6–7). Later, God does indeed impose punishments upon the snake, the woman, the man, all their posterity, and on the ground as well (Gen 3:14–19). Finally, almost as an afterthought, Adam and Eve are driven from the garden of Eden and thus lose the possibility of eating from the tree of life and attaining immortality (Gen 3:22–24). But in any case, the harsher predicted punishment of imminent death proclaimed by Gen 2:17 never comes to pass.

In the golden calf episode, Moses smashes the tablets (Exod 32:19), thus depriving Israel of God's revelation and probably indicating that the covenantal relationship has now been terminated.[23] Then he forces the

---

[22] This trope is explored at length in a brilliant midrash in *Gen. Rab.* 19:9 that makes much of the fact that God's question to Adam in Gen 3:9, "where are you?" and the first word in Lamentations share the identical consonants, איכה.

[23] Weinfeld, drawing on other ancient Near Eastern parallels, reaches the following conclusion: "The violation of the commandments, validated by the covenant, made the covenant document void, and the breaking of the tablet-

Israelites to drink water with the dissolved calf in it (Exod 32:20), an act most likely meant to function as some type of trial by ordeal similar to the one concerning the suspected adulteress (Num 5:11–31). Next, quoting a divine command, Moses orders the Levites to purge the camp of sinners by killing them with their swords (Exod 32:25–29). While chapter 32 ends with God's agreeing to forgive the people, he not only announces that he will punish Israel at some future point but also sends a plague among the people (Exod 32:30–35). Furthermore, chapter 33 seems to involve the additional, at least temporary, punishment that God distances himself from Israel (Exod 33:3), as well as orders the people to remove their ornaments (Exod 33:5). It should also be noted that the expression "in the day" that occurs in the description of Israel's future punishment in Exod 32:34 is reminiscent of the two uses of this expression in Gen 2:17 and 3:5.[24] Finally, both stories contain attempts by one party to shift the blame to a different party. Thus both the argument between God and Moses (Exod 32:7–14) and the one between Moses and Aaron (Exod 32:21–24) sound quite similar to Gen 3:12–13 in which Adam blames Eve, who, in turn, blames the snake. While not all of these textual connections are explicitly invoked, it is quite probable that many of them, along with a host of other mythic connections that will receive attention further below, do indeed contribute to the rabbinic belief that these two complexes are not only quite similar, but actually homologous.

Israel's Immortality Is Linked to the Crowns of Glory Bestowed at Sinai

The third passage comes from a much later, rather eclectic collection called *Pirke de Rabbi Eliezer,* and it adds another rich level of mythic ideas that assists the rabbis in interweaving Israel at Sinai with Adam in Eden.

> Rabbi Elazar, son of Arakh said: When the Holy One, blessed be He, descended upon Mount Sinai to give the Torah to Israel, sixty myriads of the ministering angels descended with Him, . . . and they crowned the Israelites with the Ineffable Name. All those days whilst they had not done that deed, they were as good as (or some mss. read, better than) the min-

---

document was the proper sign for it" (Moshe Weinfeld, *Deuteronomy 1–11* [AB; New York: Doubleday, 1991], 410).

24 R. W. L. Moberly, *At the Mountain of God: Story and Theology in Exodus 32–34* (JSOTSup 22; Sheffield: JSOT Press, 1983), 59. Moberly points this out in reference to an argument about whether Exod 32:35 belongs to the action begun in verse 34. Another more obscure verbal connection noticed by the rabbis in *Gen. Rab.* 18:6 is that both stories use different, but equally rare, forms of the root בוש (both look like they might derive from בשש rather than בוש) in a context immediately preceding the sin-punishment sequence (Exod 32:1; Gen 2:25).

> istering angels before the Holy One, blessed be He. The Angel of Death did not hold sway over them and they did not discharge any excretions like the children of man; but when they did that deed, the Holy One blessed be He, was angry with them and He said to them: I thought that you would be like the ministering angels, as it is said, *I said, you are angels, and all of you are the sons of the Most High*. But now, *Nevertheless you will die as men....* In that night the same sixty myriads of ministering angels descended and they severally took from each one of them what they had put upon them, and they became bare [ערמים], not according to their own wish, as it is said, *And the children of Israel stripped themselves* (Exod 33:6).[25]

The centerpiece of this midrashic excerpt is the claim that when the people of Israel received the law at Mount Sinai they attained angelic status, which included immortality and the cessation of normal bodily excretions.[26] This midrash implies that God intended to grant this angelic status to Israel forever. However, God withdrew this gift on account of the sin of the golden calf. Once again Ps 82:6–7 is read as an epitome of this rabbinic interpretation of Exod 19–34.

This passage also refers to an important mythic connection between Gen 2–3 and Exod 19–34, the motif of the "garments of glory." The rabbis believed that Adam and the Israelites were each clothed in garments of glory before they sinned but subsequently were stripped of these garments.[27] As Gary Anderson makes clear, several exegetical problems help generate this motif in the garden of Eden story.[28] These include: (1) the duplication of the making of the garments, once by humans and once by God (Gen 3:7 and 3:21); (2) the rabbinic belief that the second making of

---

[25] *Pirke de Rabbi Eliezer* (1916; repr., trans. Gerald Friedlander; New York: Sepher Hermon, 1981), 367–68 (the beginning of chap. 47).

[26] Other midrashim have Israel as free from diseases for a time as well. Thus *Num. Rab.* 7:4 on Num 5:2 says that Israel was once leprosy free and cites Ps 82:6 as proof. Perhaps this idea is generated by the various biblical texts that proclaim that obedience to God and his commandments will result in freedom from the diseases God brought upon the Egyptians (Exod 15:26; Deut 7:15).

[27] In fact, the rabbis describe Israel after the stripping of the ornaments at Sinai as ערמים "naked," the same word used in Gen 2:25 and 3:7.

[28] Gary Anderson, "The Garments of Skin in Apocryphal Narrative and Biblical Commentary," in *Studies in Ancient Midrash* (ed. James Kugel; Cambridge: Harvard University Press, 2000), 101–43. Also note the excellent discussion of Stephen N. Lambden, "From Fig Leaves to Fingernails: Some notes on the Garments of Adam and Eve in the Hebrew Bible and Select Early Postbiblical Jewish Writings," in *A Walk in the Garden: Biblical, Iconographical and Literary Images of Eden* (ed. Paul Morris and Deborah Sawyer; JSOTSup 136; Sheffield: JSOT Press, 1992), 74–90.

garments by God may have been displaced from its original location at the end of chapter 2,[29] a belief supported by the fact that 3:20 contains a second naming of Eve, indicating that the interrupted narrative at the end of chapter 2 has now been resumed;[30] and (3) the language used in describing God's making of these garments leads the rabbis to associate the word עור (skin) with the word אור (light), and claim that the text is hinting at the idea that God clothed Adam and Eve in garments of light, which were removed when they sinned.[31] In addition to these exegetical issues in Gen 2–3, there is the text of Ezek 28:14, which implies that Eden was filled with fiery stones. This latter text no doubt contributed to the popular mythic idea that Adam and Eve had nail-like skin before they sinned.[32]

In Exod 33:4–6 a similar motif can be seen in the removal of the ornaments after Israel's great sin. The ambiguity regarding whether the Israelites stripped themselves (Exod 33:4, 6) or were prohibited by God from putting on their ornaments (Exod 33:5) resembles the duplication of the making of garments by humans and then by God in Gen 3.[33] While

---

[29] This rabbinic belief is found in *Gen. Rab.* 18:6; 85:2 and is discussed in detail by Rashi in his comment on Gen 3:20.

[30] An additional factor is that both the rabbis and the church fathers seem to have been hesitant about the possibility that humans were really naked in the garden and that eating the fruit only resulted in a change in their perception but not in their actual physical/spiritual state.

[31] This interpretation is found in *Gen. Rab.* 20:12.

[32] This motif is clearly stated in *Pirqe R. El.* 14, as well as implied in the popular belief that the ritual of holding one's fingernails up to the light cast by the havdalah candle after Sabbath is done as a symbolic reminder that the fingernails are the last remnant of Adam's "horny" skin. For references, see Louis Ginzburg, *The Legends of the Jews* (7 vols.; Philadelphia: Jewish Publication Society of America, 1913–1938), 5:113; and the Byzantine source *Shoshan Sodot* 77a: "One gazes on the nails to arouse compassion, for prior to Adam's sin, his garment was made [of nail]," cited in Elliot K. Ginsburg, *The Sabbath in the Classical Kabbalah* (Albany: State University of New York Press, 1989), 281 n. 29. Additionally one wonders whether the blunting of Adam's teeth described in *Pirqe R. El.* 13 is connected to the loss of these protective garments.

[33] I have not found many of the same links in the church fathers between Eden and the Sinai–golden calf stories, but Gregory of Nyssa does use the removal of the ornaments in Exod 33:4–6 to connect these two stories. "At the first entrance of sin the advice to disobey the commandment removed the earrings. The serpent was regarded as a friend and neighbor by the first mortals when he advised them that it would be useful and beneficial to them if they transgressed the divine commandment, that is, if they removed from their ears the earring of the commandment" (Gregory of Nyssa, *The Life of Moses* [trans. Abraham Malherbe and Everett Ferguson; New York: Paulist, 1978], paragraph 213). The motif of the first sin involving the use of the ear is taken up in a variety of interesting exegeses that see

this seems like a slender basis for importing this motif into the Sinai materials, the many thematic similarities between the two narratives discussed above, along with a host of other mythic ideas (see below), support the possibility that Israel at Sinai, like Adam in Eden, once had garments of glory. Of particular importance is the notion that those close to God require some type of protection because proximity to the divine can be dangerous or fatal (Exod 33:20; Lev 10:4; Isa 33:13–16).[34] Exodus 19 is filled with images of the potential danger posed by God's proximity to the people of Israel. One must also remember that Sinai symbolizes the cosmic mountain or mountain of the gods and that some images of Eden evoke cosmic mountain symbolism.[35] Furthermore, the biblical text draws interconnections between the temple, paradise, and Mount Sinai. Thus Ps 29 links much of the Sinaitic pyrotechnics with God's presence in his holy temple, and other texts like Ps 46:5 and Ezek 47:1–12 imagine the temple with Edenlike[36] fertility images. That the tabernacle design, which also includes a detailed description of the garments worn by those who approach God, is inserted in the middle of the Sinai–golden calf episode no doubt further contributed both to the idea that Israel must have worn special garments during the Sinai encounter (note Exod 19:10), as well as to the growing propensity to homologize Sinai and the Jerusalem temple.

Mary's conception of Jesus through her ear as an undoing of this first sin. I am indebted to Nicholas Constas for sharing his insightful unpublished paper, "The *Conceptio per Aurem* in Late Antiquity: Observations on Eve, the Serpent, and Mary's Ear."

[34] The Isaiah reference is particularly germane to our subject. In it God is portrayed as a consuming fire, but righteous behavior acts as a protection against being consumed by God. A rabbinic extension of this idea is found in *b. Šabb.* 88b in which Moses is fearful of being consumed by the fiery breath of the ministering angels until God spreads the divine presence over him as a kind of protection.

[35] Ezekiel 28:14–17 clearly connects the images of Eden and the mountain of the gods. For a good discussion of this motif in biblical and apocryphal literature, see Gary Anderson, "The Cosmic Mountain: Eden and its Early Interpreters in Syriac Christianity," in *Genesis 1–3 in the History of Exegesis: Intrigue in the Garden* (ed. Gregory Allen Robbins; Lewiston, N.Y.: Mellen, 1988), 187–224. General background on this motif in the Hebrew Bible and its ancient Near Eastern setting can be found in R. J. Clifford, *The Cosmic Mountain in Canaan and the Old Testament* (Cambridge: Harvard University Press, 1972). For an investigation of this motif focused specifically on the biblical text of Gen 2–3, see Howard N. Wallace, *The Eden Narrative* (HSM 32; Atlanta: Scholars Press, 1985), 65–99.

[36] On this motif, see Jon D. Levenson, *Theology of the Program of Restoration of Ezekiel 40–48* (HSM 10; Missoula, Mont.: Scholars Press, 1976), 7–53; and Michael Fishbane, "The 'Eden' Motif/The Landscape of Spatial Renewal," in *Text and Texture* (1964; repr., New York: Schocken Books, 1979), 111–20.

The connection between paradise, temple and Sinai can be found in texts such as *2 Bar.* 4, which dates from sometime shortly after 100 C.E.

> It is not this building that is in your midst now; it is that which will be revealed, with me, that was already prepared from the moment that I decided to create Paradise. And I showed it to Adam before he sinned. But when he transgressed the commandment, it was taken from him—as also Paradise.... Again I showed it to Moses on Mount Sinai when I showed him the likeness of the tabernacle and all its vessels. Behold, now it is preserved with me—as also Paradise.[37]

It cannot be conclusively proven that all these mythic themes are operative in this one midrash; however, it should be noted that the rabbinic attempt to link Adam's prelapsarian garments to those worn by Israel at Sinai is just one item in a large inventory of homologies that the rabbis drew between Gen 2–3 and Exod 19–34.[38] The citation of a proof-text does not necessarily mean that the rabbis deduced an idea on the basis of a particular verse. Such a citation may simply be providing further support for an already widely held rabbinic belief. The rabbis were probably firmly convinced that the Sinai and Eden episodes were linked together in innumerable ways. Hence, they presumably set off in search of scriptural clues that would enable them to ground their extrascriptural beliefs in the biblical text.

Israel's Experience at Sinai Parallels Adam's in Eden

The next passages to be considered are two midrashim from *Eccl. Rab.* 8:2–3 that comment on Eccl 8:1, "Who is like the wise man? And who knows the interpretation of a thing? Wisdom makes one's face shine, and the hardness of one's countenance is changed."[39]

---

[37] J. H. Charlesworth, ed., *The Old Testament Pseudepigrapha* (2 vols.; Garden City N.Y.: Doubleday, 1983, 1985), 1:622. The translation and estimated date are from A. F. J. Klijn.

[38] While this paper focuses on the ways in which the rabbis see Israel's experience at Sinai as similar to Adam's in Eden, the homology can work in the reverse as well. There is evidence of an ancient Jewish propensity to import the revelation at Sinai back into Eden, as indicated by texts like Sir 17:11–13. For a more in-depth discussion of this issue, see John J. Collins, "Wisdom, Apocalypticism and the Dead Sea Scrolls," *Jedes Ding Hat seine Zeit...* (ed. Anja Diesel et al.; Berlin: de Gruyter, 1996), 21–26.

[39] There is an almost identical set of midrashim that use Eccl 8:1 in a similar manner in *Pesiq. Rab Kah.* 4:4, *Pesiq. Rab.* 14:10 and in *Midrash Tanḥuma* חקת נז ב. (The latter two start from Num 19:2.)

> Another interpretation of *Who is as the wise man?* This alludes to Adam of whom it is written, *Thou seal most accurate, full of wisdom . . . thou wast in Eden the garden of God* (Ezek 28:12ff.). *And who knoweth the interpretation of a thing?* Because he gave distinguishing names to all things. *A man's wisdom maketh his face to shine:* his beauty made his face shine. R. Levi said: The ball of Adam's heel outshone the sun. . . . And after all this glory, *Dust thou art and unto to dust shalt thou return* (Gen 3:19). *And the boldness of his face changed:* When the Holy One, blessed be He, said to him, *Have you eaten of the tree?* (Gen 3:11), the anger of the Holy One, blessed be He, caused the boldness of his face to change and He expelled him from the Garden of Eden.[40]

> Another interpretation of *Who is as the wise man?* This alludes to Israel of whom it is written, *Surely this great nation is a wise and understanding people* (Deut 4:6). *And who knoweth the interpretation of a thing?* Because they knew how to explain the Torah.... You find that when Israel stood at Mount Sinai and said, *All that the Lord has spoken we will do, and obey* (Exod 24:7), there was granted them something of the lustre of the Shechinah[41] of the Most High. [They are commenting on how wisdom makes the face shine, although this verse fragment is not cited explicitly.] When they sinned, however, they were made haters of the Holy One, blessed be He, as it is written *And the boldness of his face changed,* and the anger of the Holy One, blessed be He, changed the words applied to them into what is written, *Nevertheless you shall die like men* (Ps 82:7).[42]

The first midrash, which attempts to read Eccl 8:1 as a short history of Adam, is reasonably accessible, even to the untutored reader. After all, Adam was in the garden of Eden and did eat of the tree of knowledge. Furthermore, the notion that the first man was perfect in wisdom and beauty is amplified in the quote from Ezek 28, which describes the king of Tyre's rise and fall in mythic terms that reflect a variant form of the Eden story. The midrash then turns to the expression, "wisdom makes a man's face shine," which uses the Hebrew word אדם, evoking the image of Adam clothed in garments of light, a symbol of his angelic/divine status as well as of his immortality (Ezek 28:11–14; Dan 12:2–3).[43] Finally, the rabbis

40 *Midrash Rabbah, Ecclesiastes* (trans. A. Cohen; 3d ed.; London: Soncino, 1983), 213–14.

41 The Shechinah is the rabbinic term for the presence, glory, or indwelling of God.

42 *Midrash Rabbah, Ecclesiastes,* 214–15.

43 Morton Smith persuasively argues that ancient Jews believed the light associated with certain exalted human beings indicated their divine status ("The Image of God," *BJRL* 40 [1958]: 473–512).

proceed to the end of the verse, which in their mind describes how God changed (here reading an active tense rather than the Bible's passive one) Adam's "bold face" and expelled Adam from Eden.[44] On the one hand, the change in Adam's face is linked to its loss of light, signaling a loss of his immortality. On the other hand, the rabbinic attempt to link Adam to the expression עז פנים "bold of face," a term that elsewhere carries the connotation of pride, arrogance, or insolence (Prov 7:13 and perhaps Deut 28:50; Dan 8:23), may suggest that the church fathers were not the only ones who thought that Adam's sin was one of hubris.[45]

In a strikingly similar fashion the next midrash applies this same midrashic reading to Israel at Sinai before and after the sin of the golden calf. However, several variations at the end of this passage are worth highlighting. In this midrash the rabbis are troubled by the final א in the last word rather than the expected ה. Thus the rabbis are led to repoint the שׁ as if it were a שׂ and translate the word יְשֻׁנֶּא as if it were from the root שׂנא "hate," rather than שׁנה "change." Their reading of the verse is probably best translated as "he who is bold of face is hated [by God]." However, they still pun on the meaning "to change" by indicating that God changed the words applied to the people of Israel.

While they never indicate which words God had originally applied to Israel, it is quite probable that it was Ps 82:6, a verse that the *Mekilta* offers as proof that Israel had once attained immortality at Sinai. And of course Israel's fall from her state of sharing in the light of the Shechinah and the immortality it implies is supported by citing Ps 82:7. The fact that the rabbis apply Eccl 8:1 to both Adam in Eden and Israel at Sinai reveals how deep their propensity is to homologize Gen 2–3 and Exod 19–34. While the application of the various aspects of Eccl 8:1 to the whole people of Israel at Sinai at first seems a bit forced or farfetched, once again, one must bear in mind that the rabbis are working from a rich network of thematic and mythic associations.

On the thematic side, both Adam and Israel have access to a type of special knowledge, the names of animals and the laws of Sinai, respectively; yet each misused their knowledge and rebelled against God. On the mythic side, it is evident that the belief that Israel at Sinai, like Adam before her, had been clothed in garments of light symbolizing her immortal status facilitated the rabbis in applying Eccl 8:1 to Exod 19–34. It is this belief that allows the rabbis

---

44 *Genesis Rabbah* 11:2 is surely in the background of the exegetical move to link Adam's changed face to his immediate expulsion from Eden. In this midrash, Job 14:20 is read as if it said, "you changed his countenance and then sent him away."

45 A biblical basis for the understanding of Adam's sin as pride can be found in the expression, "your heart was proud" (lit. "lifted up"), which occurs in Ezek 28:17 in a description—replete with Edenic imagery—of the fall of the king of Tyre.

to claim that the verse fragment, "a man's wisdom makes his face shine," indicates that Israel was clothed in the Shechinah and granted immortality.

Israel's Lost Immortality Will Be Regained in the Messianic Era

One also finds the motif of the crowning of Israel at Mount Sinai and its counterpart, Israel's godlike status, in the following passage from the *Tanna Debe Eliyyahu:*

> R. Ishmael ben Eleazar said: When Israel accepted the Holy One's sovereignty and said, *All that the Lord said we will do, and we will obey* (Exod 24:7), sixty myriads of ministering angels came down and set two crowns upon the head of each and every one in Israel—one for saying *we will do,* and one for their saying *we will obey*—two crowns like Adam's crown, as is said, *Ye shall be unto me a kingdom of priests, and a holy nation* (Exod 19:6). But when Israel acted abominably in making the calf, one hundred and twenty myriads of angels of destruction came down and took away the crowns from Israel, as it is said, *And the children of Israel were stripped of their ornaments* [set upon the head of each one in Israel] *at Horeb* (Exod 33:6). Lest you think they were taken away forever, it is also said, *The ransomed for the Lord shall return, and come singing unto Zion, because the joy of long ago shall be upon their heads* (Isa 35:10)—not "the joy long ago in their hearts," *but upon their heads.* We are thus taught that the Holy One will restore all of Israel's crowns in the days of the Messiah and in the time-to-come: hence *the joy of long ago . . . upon their heads.* And what thought had been in the Holy One's mind [from the beginning]? It was this: that each and every nation and kingdom would come and accept the Torah and so live and endure forever and ever and ever, as is said, *The tables were the work of God, and the writing was the writing of God, graven upon the tables* (Exod 32:16). Read not, however, חרות "graven," but חירות "freedom"—freedom from death, that is, for no man is truly free unless the angel of death has no power over him. Hence, we are to read the verse *From Mattanah to Nahaliel; and from Nahaliel to Bamoth* (Num 21:19) as follows: After the giving (*mattan*) of Torah, Israel possessed themselves of a false god, and because they worshiped a false god, the angel of death came upon them. Thus, at first God said [to Israel], *Ye are godlike beings* (Ps 82:6), but after their deeds became corrupt, God went on to say, *Surely, ye shall die like men* (Ps 82:7).[46]

Many motifs that have already been discussed above recur here with only slight variation. These include the crowning of Israel by the angels[47]

---

[46] *Tanna Debe Eliyyahu* (trans. W. G. Braude and I. J. Kapstein; Philadelphia: Jewish Publication Society of America, 1981), 382–83. This corresponds to *Eliyyahu Zuta* 179.

[47] *Pesiq. Rab.* 21 indicates that this motif is at least partly influenced by a creative rabbinic reading of Ps 68:18, a verse that mentions God's arrival at Sinai with myriads in his retinue.

(here with two crowns), the removal of the ornaments (here requiring twice as many angels as the crowning), the חירות-חרות motif, the reading of the itinerary in Num 21:19 as a spiritual geography (however this time נחלו אל is understood as "they [Israel] inherited a god," that is worshiped the golden calf),[48] and the use of Ps 82:6–7 to summarize Israel's experience of immortality gained and lost.

In addition to these motifs, many innovations can be found here, including the comparison between Israel's crowns and Adam's, the idea that Israel's crowns will eventually be restored (as suggested by the exegesis of the verse from Isa 35), the notion that all nations were to have received the Torah and the immortality with which it came, and the statement that humans are not truly free as long as they experience death. These particular innovations provide the reader with insight into how the rabbis understood the relationship between Adam, Israel, and the redemption of the world. Connecting the double crowning of Israel to Adam's crown implies that Israel reached or perhaps even surpassed Adam's exalted status, inasmuch as Israel received two crowns to Adam's one. This crowning symbolizes Israel's royal and priestly status, as well as her reattainment of Adam's lost immortality. The fall created by Adam's disobedience was indeed remedied with the giving of the Torah at Sinai. The reference to the restoration of these crowns in the messianic future suggests that it is God's full intention to restore Israel's lost immortality at some point in the messianic future. It also indicates that the rabbinic concept of redemption is centered around the restoration of Israel to the state she had attained at Sinai, rather than being focused on undoing the consequences of Adam's sin—because in many ways, Adam's sin had already been undone. Inasmuch as God's initial intent for all the nations to receive the Torah is left unfulfilled, the place of the nations in God's redemptive plans remains somewhat unclear. Will only Israel be redeemed, or will Israel somehow mediate the Torah to others?

The Temple As a Means for Reattaining Israel's and Adam's Lost Immortality

The next set of midrashim provides yet further insight into how the rabbis aimed at trying to recover the immortality that Israel once possessed but lost through sin. These passages from *Lev. Rab.* 11:1 and 11:3 are built around Prov 9:1–4, but occur in comments upon Lev 9:1, "And it was on the 8th day Moses summoned Aaron and his sons. . . . "

---

[48] Interestingly enough, in *m. ʾAbot* 6:2 the rabbis interpret this same cryptic verse as evidence of a wholly positive spiritual journey, rather than one that began well and ended in disaster.

> *She hath sent forth. . . . She calleth her servants* (Prov 9:3a) alluding to Adam and Eve. *On the wing*[49] *of the heights of the city* (Prov 9:3b) means that the Holy One, blessed be He, enabled them to fly and designated them as deities, as it is written, *you shall be as God* (Gen 3:5).[50] . . . After all this excellence . . . since they neglected the wishes of the Holy One, blessed be He, and conformed to the wishes of the serpent. Because he [Adam] thus *lacketh understanding, she said to him* (Prov 9:4): *For dust thou art, and to dust shalt thou return* (Gen 3:19).[51]

> *She hath called her attendants* refers to Israel. *On the wing of the heights of the city* refers to the fact that the Holy One, blessed be He, enabled them to fly, and attributed to them divine qualities, as it is said, And I said: *Ye are godlike beings* (Ps 82:6). Now after all these favours . . . They forsook the will of the Holy One, blessed be He, and said of the golden calf, *This is thy god, O Israel*. For this reason, *She said to him: One who lacketh understanding* (Prov 9:4), *Indeed ye shall die like men* (Ps 82:7).[52]

These excerpts come from the middle of each midrash. Thus the reader needs to know that both midrashim manage to link Prov 9:1–4 to Lev 9:1 by playing upon the fact that Prov 9:1 associates wisdom with the number seven, while Lev 9:1 speaks of the eighth day. *Leviticus Rabbah* 11:1 proceeds by assuming that when Prov 9:1 speaks of wisdom building her house with seven pillars, it is an allusion to the seven days of creation in Gen 1:1–2:3 and to wisdom's participation in creation.[53] When the midrashist arrives at Prov 9:3–4, he reads these verses as an epitome of the rabbinic interpretation of Gen 2–3. Thus Prov 9:3 indicates that Adam and Eve had become deities and could fly, while 9:4 is associated with Adam and Eve's downfall when they disobeyed God.

The second midrash, presuming the association between wisdom and Torah discussed above, sees Prov 9:1–4 as containing a summary of Israel's Sinai experience. In this midrash, "She hath called her attendants" refers to

---

49 Proverbs 9:3b is read as if it were written in rabbinic rather than biblical Hebrew, thus the rabbis understand נפי as wings, rather than heights, or elevation (*Midrash Rabbah, Leviticus* [3d ed.; trans. Judah J. Slotki; London: Soncino, 1983], 135 n. 6).

50 Ibid., 136 n. 3 indicates that one should probably insert Ps 82:6 here.

51 Ibid., 135–36.

52 Ibid., 137–38.

53 The notion that wisdom, which in the rabbinic mind is equivalent to Torah, participated in creation receives biblical support from texts like Prov 3:19–20 (cited by this midrash but not included in the excerpt above), and especially Prov 8:22–31 (used in the famous opening midrash in *Gen. Rab.* 1:1).

Israel. "On the wing of the heights of the city" means that God enabled Israel to fly and gave them divine qualities until they committed the sin of the golden calf. While only the second midrash explicitly mentions Ps 82:6–7, the structure of both passages is so closely parallel that the note in the English translation suggests emending the text of *Lev. Rab.* 11:1 so as to include Ps 82:6 in place of Gen 3:5. Once again, one sees the tendency to link Adam and Eve's state before and after their disobedience to the state of the Israelites at Sinai before and after their fall from grace. One might argue that the flying motif originated with the second midrash in that Exod 19:4 describes God's carrying Israel on eagles' wings.[54] Regardless of where it originated, the idea that at one point both Adam and Eve as well as Israel could fly suggests that they not only attained immortality but something approaching divinity itself, as indicated by the use of the expression וקרא אותן אלהות (lit., he attributed to them divinity) found in both midrashim.[55] The fact that these passages occur in the opening midrashim on Lev 9 is also quite significant, inasmuch as it demonstrates once again that the rabbis are not only interested in such matters in relation to certain past events but also envision recovering this lost state of nearness to God. After all, Lev 9 describes the inauguration of the Israelite cultus and ends with the glory of the Lord appearing before the people, who also see a fire sent by God devouring the sacrifice and then respond by falling down to worship. It should come as no surprise that in the rabbinic mind one major avenue for recovering Israel's lost immortality and undoing the consequences of human sinfulness is through the eventual restoration of the temple cult.[56]

Torah As the Way to Immortality Here and Now

The last text to be considered is from the *Sifre* on Deuteronomy §306. This passage contains a variety of comments on Deut 32:2, a verse from Moses' Song that begins, "May my teaching drop like the rain."

> Rabbi Simai said: all creatures that are created from heaven, their souls and their bodies are from heaven. All creatures that are created from earth, their souls and their bodies are from earth. Except this Adam (or man) whose soul is from heaven and his body from earth. Therefore if

---

[54] *Midrash Rabbah, Leviticus,* 137 n. 8.

[55] M. Margulies, *Midrash Vayyikra Rabbah: A Critical Edition Based on Manuscripts and Genizah Fragments with Variants and Notes* (5 vols.; Jerusalem: American Academy of Jewish Research, 1953–60), 1:220, 222.

[56] This point is further reinforced by the fact that the second and fourth midrash in this same series (*Lev. Rab.* 11:2, 4) link Prov 9:1–4 to the messianic era and the original dedication of the sanctuary, respectively.

> man does Torah and fulfills the will of his father in heaven, behold he becomes like one of the creatures from above, as it says, *I have said: You are gods, all of you sons of the Most High* (Ps 82:6). But when man does not do Torah and fulfill the will of his father in heaven he becomes like one of the creatures from below, as it says, *Nevertheless, you will die like an earth creature* (Ps 82:7).[57]

This midrash is interesting on several counts. Like the *Mekilta,* it comes from a Tannaitic compilation, and it too seems more restrained in linking the giving of the Torah at Sinai to the attainment of permanent immortality.[58] Furthermore, this midrash does not expend much effort searching for exegetical and thematic connections between Eden and Sinai. However, it does explore a central theological premise that undergirds the rabbinic drive to link these two motifs.

One of the greatest questions raised by the material under investigation in this paper is why the rabbis wished to argue that the Israelites at Sinai reached the Adamic state, or perhaps even higher (note the double crowning in the passage from the *Tanna Debe Eliyyahu*), when they knew that Israel had quickly fallen from this exalted state by worshiping the golden calf and thus committing perhaps an even greater sin than Adam's. Several factors may be at work. The rabbis probably wished to elevate Israel's Sinai experience to the level of Adam's prelapsarian state in order

---

57 The translation is my own from the critical edition of the *Sifre on Deuteronomy* (ed. Louis Finkelstein; New York: Jewish Theological Seminary of America, 1993), 340–41 (פיסקא ש"ו). The standard English translation is *Sifre: A Tannaitic Commentary on the Book of Deuteronomy* (trans. Reuven Hammer; Yale Judaica Series 24; New Haven: Yale University Press, 1986), see page 307.

58 I recognize that both the *Mekilta* and the *Sifre* may contain later materials placed into the mouths of various Tannaim. But in any case these collections "present us with the earliest traditions assigned to tannaim" (Irving Mandelbaum, "Tannaitic Exegesis of the Golden Calf Episode," *A Tribute to Geza Vermes* [ed. Philip Davies and Richard White; JSOTSup 100; Sheffield,: JSOT Press, 1990], 220 n. 4). Interestingly enough, Mandelbaum finds substantial differences between the Tannaitic discussions of the golden calf episode and those attributed to amoraic sources. In particular, he sees the Tannaitic sources as much more critical of Israel's idolatrous behavior while the amoraic midrashim introduce a variety of mitigating explanations that function in an apologetic manner. This may indicate that the rabbis softened their approach to this material in reaction to early Christian claims that the golden calf story demonstrated that the relationship between God and Israel had been totally abrogated. For fuller argumentation on this possibility, see Leivy Smolar and Moshe Aberbach, "The Golden Calf Episode in Postbiblical Jewish Literature," *HUCA* 39 (1968): 91–116; and Arthur Marmorstein, "Judaism and Christianity in the Middle of the Third Century," in *Studies in Jewish Theology* (ed. J. Rabbinowitz and M. S. Lew; London: Oxford University Press, 1950), 179–224.

to claim that the rift created by Adam's fall was indeed healed by the giving of the Torah. While a new fall was created when Israel worshiped the golden calf, any future redemption is now focused on Israel as a corporate body, rather than on Adam and Eve. These ideas flow from the rabbis' belief that the people of Israel are central to God's redemption of the world. In addition, while the rabbis acknowledge that Israel's sin opened a new rift between humanity and the divine, they also affirm that the benefits of God's giving the Torah to Israel at Sinai are not completely erased by Israel's sin. Thus the people of Israel, as well as humanity in general, are in a far better position after the golden calf episode than either Adam or anyone else was after Adam's sin. This is so for four reasons:

1) The observance of the commandments issued at Sinai provide a previously unavailable remedy to Adam's sin. Thus Torah in general is described as an antidote to the evil inclination that is first exhibited in Adam's disobedience.[59] Furthermore, certain specific commandments are understood to counteract the curses placed upon Adam and Eve and their descendants. For example, "a wife lights the Sabbath candles as a task enjoined on her as an antidote to the 'curse of Eve' (*Gen. Rab.* 17:8)."[60] Other commandments hint at the future restoration of the Jewish people to Adam's exalted state. "The daily morning prayers begin with the hope of life to come in the Garden of Eden, the donning of the tallit (prayer shawl) symbolizing the future divine robe of the soul."[61] So, in the rabbinic imagination, this daily ritual adumbrates the restoration of the garments of glory that both Adam and Israel had, but lost.

2) Living within the law gives one access to the immortality that Israel attained at Sinai, as indicated by the midrash from *Sifre* §306. The idea is not simply that paradise was lost and will be regained in the messianic future. Rather, this midrash implies that even in the present it is still possi-

---

[59] The *Sifre* on Deuteronomy §45 punning on the first word in Deut 11:18 ושׂמתם, speaks of the words of Torah as the "elixir (lit., the spice) of life" בסם חיים. *b. Qidd.* 30b makes a slightly better pun by calling the words of Torah a "perfect remedy" סם תם. This latter passage goes on to describe God as saying to Israel "my son, I have created the evil impulse, but I have created the Torah as its antidote" (lit., spice) תבלין. The identical expression can also be found in *b. B. Bat.* 16a. A related set of puns on the word תבלין that connects Torah to the land of Israel occurs in the *Sifre* §37.

[60] Paul Morris, "Exiled from Eden: Jewish Interpretations of Genesis," in *A Walk in the Garden: Biblical, Iconographical and Literary Images of Eden* (ed. Paul Morris and Deborah Sawyer; JSOTSup 136; Sheffield: JSOT Press, 1992), 118. A possible Christian parallel to this tradition is 1 Tim 2:15, a verse that may indicate that women can undo the results of Eve's sin through childbearing.

[61] Ibid.

ble to partake of immortality and once more live in close proximity to the divine by means of Torah observance. Psalm 82:6–7 is not something that only applied to Adam, nor only to the generation that stood at Sinai, but to all subsequent Jews who either obey or disobey the Torah. Thus the rabbis view the law as having a proleptic quality.

3) Observing these commandments might possibly hasten the dawning of the messianic era. Even while it is true that the rabbis sometimes assert that one should not force God to bring the messianic era before its time (commonly citing Song 2:7),[62] they also proclaim that keeping the commandments is a way to hasten the coming of the messianic era. Thus some rabbinic texts speak of Israel's ability to bring on the messianic era by observing Sabbath properly even once, or by fully repenting.[63]

4) Those who experienced the Sinai revelation, which in the rabbinic mind included the soul of every Jewish person ever to be born,[64] have less powerful urges toward certain types of sinful behavior than their gentile counterparts do, as indicated by the following rabbinic comment:

> Why are idolaters lustful? Because they did not stand at Mount Sinai. For when the serpent came upon Eve he injected lust into her. [As for] the Israelites who stood at Mount Sinai, their lustfulness departed; the idolaters who did not stand at Mount Sinai, their lustfulness did not depart.[65]

All four of these points inform the rabbinic mind-set, and, more importantly, they regularly are intertwined in a rather complex fashion, as can be seen from the way in which the *Targum Neofiti,* a fourth-century C.E. Palestinian text, comments on Gen 3:15 and 24.

> *And it will come about that when her sons observe the Law and do the commandments they will aim at you and smite you* on your head and *kill you. But when they forsake the commandments of the Law* you will aim

---

[62] The notion of not rushing the messianic era can be found in *Cant. Rab.* 2:7.

[63] The reference to observing the Sabbath properly occurs in *Exod. Rab.* 25:12 and in *b. Šabb.* 118b. For the notion that repentance can quicken the arrival of the messianic era, see *Exod. Rab.* 25:12 as well as *b. Sanh.* 97b–98a. I disagree with Scholem, who argues that the rabbis did not actually believe one could do anything to hasten the arrival of the Messiah, but only made these statements to enhance "the moral value of the suggested conduct" (Gershom Scholem, "Toward an Understanding of the Messianic Idea in Judaism," in *The Messianic Idea in Judaism* [New York: Schocken Books, 1971], 11).

[64] Ginzburg, *Legends of the Jews,* 3:97, based on *Exod. Rab.* 28:6 and *Pirqe R. El.* 41.

[65] *The Babylonian Talmud, Tractate Shabbath,* vol. 2 (trans. H. Freedman; London: Soncino, 1972), 145b–146a. This same idea is mentioned in *b. Yebam.* 103b and *b. ʿAbod. Zar.* 22b.

> and *bite him* on his heel *and make him ill. For her sons, however, there will be a remedy . . . since they are to make appeasement in the end, in the days of King Messiah*.[66]
>
> *He had prepared the garden of Eden for the just that they might eat and delight themselves from the fruits of the tree, because they had kept the precepts of the Law in this world and fulfilled the commandments. . . . For the Law is a* tree of life *for everyone who toils in it and keeps the commandments: he lives and endures like* the tree of life *in the world to come. The Law is good for all who labor in it in this world like the fruit of the tree of life*.[67]

These passages clearly proclaim that a residue of the original grace that Israel received from encountering God at Sinai remains active and opens the possibility of removing the damage done through Adam's sin and thus of reattaining Adam's lost state of immortality through keeping the commandments. While some parts of this text imply that the fractured relationship between God and the human community will only be fully healed in the messianic era, other parts stress that the means for overcoming this fractured relationship are available now and in this world, if Israel will only live in obedience to the commandments given at Sinai.

Theological Reflections

In what ways does the existence of this material lead to a reconceptualization of rabbinic Judaism and one's understanding of the differences between rabbinic Judaism and early Christianity? To answer this question with some accuracy it should be remembered that the ancient rabbis pursued a variety of different tropes in their quest to illuminate their understanding of God and his relationship to the people of Israel in particular and to all human beings in general. Certain tropes are sometimes in tension with, or even occasionally contradict, the logic of other tropes that are pursued just as forcefully. Thus one cannot draw a definitive picture of rabbinic Judaism solely from the religious ideas found in the midrashim explored above. Nevertheless, the pervasiveness of the motifs discussed in these midrashim demands that one give them a fair hearing, even while acknowledging that other texts present very different views on the effects of Adam and Eve's sin.[68] This said, the texts explored throughout this

---

[66] *Targum Neofiti 1: Genesis* (trans. Martin McNamara; Collegeville, Minn.: Liturgical Press, 1992), 61. The italicized text indicates the way the targum has expanded the biblical text.

[67] Ibid., 64.

[68] Thus Fraade's important study of the different ways that Jewish and Christian thinkers interpreted the pre-Abrahamic materials reveals a strain of rabbinic

paper indicate that a strong stream of rabbinic thinking maintains that Adam's sin did indeed cause humanity to fall from the immortal state God had originally intended for them.[69] This fall was remedied through Israel's acceptance of the Torah at Sinai. While the sin of the golden calf caused a new fall that would not be completely cured until the arrival of the messianic era, the revelation of the law at Sinai and its observance left a variety of residual positive effects, including remedying Adam's sin, providing access to the immortality that Israel attained at Sinai, possibly hastening the dawning of the messianic era, and leaving those who experienced the Sinai revelation with less powerful urges toward certain types of sinful behavior.

While this religious outlook is by no means identical to that found in various texts from early Christianity, it does share certain affinities with some of these texts. For example, in Rom 5:12–21 Paul sees Adam's sin as resulting in a state in which humans are alienated from God. This state is characterized as one of sin leading to death. Of course, Jesus Christ provides the cure for this state, and belief in him gives one access to eternal life.

> If, because of the one man's trespass, death exercised dominion through that one, much more surely will those who receive the abundance of grace and the free gift of righteousness exercise dominion in life through the one man, Jesus Christ. Therefore just as one man's trespass led to condemnation for all, so one man's act of righteousness leads to justification and life for all. . . . So that, just as sin exercised dominion in death, so grace might also exercise dominion through justification leading to eternal life through Jesus Christ our Lord. (Rom 5:17–18, 21)

While Paul does not see a second fall as the rabbis do, he does believe that even though Christ has remedied the consequences of Adam's sin, the full effect of this remedy will only be realized at Christ's second coming.

> But in fact Christ has been raised from the dead, the first fruits of those who have died. For since death came through a human being, the resurrection of the dead has also come through a human being; for as all die in Adam, so all will be made alive in Christ. But each in his own order: Christ the first fruits, then at his coming those who belong to Christ. Then

thought that sought to deemphasize the notion of an original sin committed by Adam and Eve by reading all of Gen 3–11 as a history of human (and perhaps even divine) failure (Steven D. Fraade, *Enosh and His Generation: Pre-Israelite Hero and History in Postbiblical Interpretation* [SBLMS; Chico, Calif.: Scholars Press, 1984]).

69 Of course, there are other rabbinic texts that view death positively and thus not necessarily as an evil (see *Gen. Rab.* 9:5). The ancient rabbis did not have a systematic approach to these complex issues.

comes the end, when he hands over the kingdom to God the Father, after he has destroyed every ruler and every authority and power. For he must reign until he has put all his enemies under his feet. The last enemy to be destroyed is death. (1 Cor 15:20–26)

That rabbinic Judaism and Christianity share somewhat similar readings of Adam's sin is less shocking once one realizes that many of these ideas already occur in various Hellenistic Jewish texts that probably influenced both traditions. Thus Sir 25:24 notes that "from woman sin had its beginning and because of her we all die."[70] Similarly *4 Ezra,* a pseudepigraphic book from around 100 C.E., states: "O Adam, what have you done? For though it was you who sinned, the fall was not yours alone, but ours also who are your descendants" (7:118).[71]

Recognizing that both traditions grew out of a common heritage and continue to share much in common is not to deny that each tradition developed its own unique theological insights. Still, the theological similarities are striking. Both traditions have a strong investment in the notion that humans were created to live forever, both affirm that human sin in some way foiled God's original plan, and both believe that God then created a new way to restore this lost immortality, which will only become fully manifest in the messianic era. At the same time, a serious argument between the two traditions over whether the new path toward immortality was created at Sinai and is accessible through the observance of the commandments, or whether it was made available through the events of Jesus' life, death, and resurrection, still divides Judaism and Christianity.

It is also important to note that even while both of these positions grew out of careful readings of the Hebrew Bible, both are greatly at odds with a plain-sense reading of the biblical text. Genesis 2–3 does not directly say that Adam had immortality and then had it taken from him as a punishment for his disobedience. Furthermore, the various authors of the

---

[70] Jack Levison has argued that Ben Sira was not referring to Eve here ("A Contextual Analysis of Sir 25:24," *CBQ* 47 [1985]: 617–23). However, I agree with John Collins, "that there can be no doubt that Sirach 25:24 . . . is the earliest extant witness to the view that Eve was responsible for the introduction of sin and death" (*Jewish Wisdom in the Hellenistic Age* [OTL; Louisville: Westminster/John Knox, 1997], 67). Sirach also contains other statements that indicate that Adam and Eve's sin is much less problematic, such as 15:14–17. For some interesting reflections on these tensions within Sirach and other Jewish texts produced during the Hellenistic era, see Collins, *Jewish Wisdom,* 80–96 and idem, "Wisdom, Apocalypticism and the Dead Sea Scrolls," 19–32.

[71] Charlesworth, *Old Testament Pseudepigrapha,* 1:622. The translation and estimated date are from B. M. Metzger. Again one can find the opposite sentiment in *2 Bar.* 54:15, a passage likely written around the same period.

Hebrew Bible apparently did not spend great amounts of energy discerning how immortality might be regained or bemoaning the existence of death when it occurred after a full life span.[72] Thus not only did rabbinic Judaism and early Christianity grow from the same Jewish-Hellenistic soil and end up sharing many of the same metaphysical assumptions about the connection between human sin and the loss of immortality, but also both religions reshaped the biblical text in a similar manner using many shared techniques of exegesis. All of these facts indicate

> that the relationship, usually characterized as one of parent and child, is better seen as a rivalry between two siblings. Judaism and Christianity are both, in substantial measure, midrashic systems whose scriptural base is the Hebrew Bible and whose origins lie in the interpretive procedures internal to their common Scripture and in the rich legacy of the Judaism of the late Second Temple period.[73]

Acknowledging that the two traditions are better described as siblings is not only important for the sake of historical accuracy; it also has implications for Jewish self-understanding as well as for Jewish-Christian relations today. As long as Jewish people continue to see themselves as the only legitimate biblical tradition, they will view Christianity and its complex of theological ideas as utterly alien to that tradition. This not only impoverishes contemporary Judaism by flattening out and homogenizing the Jewish theological landscape, but it also cuts off new possibilities for deepening Jewish-Christian understanding and cooperation. The widespread tendency to strip Judaism of its powerful mythic ideas by portraying it as a rational religion while viewing Christianity as its number one enemy was likely based on the rather optimistic premise that modernity and Judaism were totally compatible. This situation was no doubt fueled by the historic enmity that Christianity had displayed toward Judaism in combination with the liberal Jewish wish to fit into the modern democratic state that seemed willing to enfranchise Jews fully, so long as they presented themselves as individuals and not as members of the Jewish community. While modernity has brought about many positive changes, more recently it has also given birth to a variety of troubling trends, including a deeply antireligious secularism, a tendency toward extraordinarily vapid forms of personalized spirituality, as well as occasionally exhibiting disturbing nihilistic impulses.

---

[72] These points are mapped out in detail in James Barr, *The Garden of Eden and the Hope for Immortality* (Minneapolis: Fortress, 1992), 1–56.

[73] Jon D. Levenson, *The Death and Resurrection of the Beloved Son: The Transformation of Child Sacrifice in Judaism and Christianity* (New Haven: Yale University Press, 1993), 232.

If Jews hope to resist, or better yet, reshape the larger culture in which they live, they will need to recover those transcendent elements of their own tradition that have been marginalized by the attempt to argue that Judaism and modernity complement each other perfectly. Inasmuch as many of these marginalized ideas reveal the theological similarities between Judaism and Christianity, once these elements are reintegrated into current expressions of Judaism, Jews may recognize that Christians are their spiritual siblings as well as their potential allies in bringing about positive societal change. While Judaism and Christianity do indeed disagree over much, it is essential to undercut those stereotypes that distort either tradition or exaggerate the differences between them. Overcoming these misrepresentations will not only help Jews and Christians recognize many family resemblances between the two traditions that are currently overlooked or obscured, it will also help each tradition articulate its distinctive traits with greater accuracy and clarity. This in turn will deepen the level of dialogue and mutual understanding and allow for greater cooperation between the two communities as they each face the difficult task of creating religious communities that offer a transcendent alternative capable of resisting and transforming the contemporary cultural landscape. With their distinctive identities intact they might strive to realize the words of the psalmist:

הנה מה טוב ומה נעים שׁבת אחים גם יחד

"Indeed, how good and pleasant it is for brothers to dwell together" (Ps 133:1).

Writing on the Water: The Ineffable Name of God

Johanna W. H. van Wijk-Bos

The Beetle and the Poet

In a famous Flemish poem of my youth, the poet is engaged in questioning a small insect that pirouettes above the water surface of small streams and creeks, the so-called whirligig beetle. This insect, the Latin *gyrinus natans,* is called the "little writer" in Flemish and Dutch. The poet, intrigued by the small animal's industrious motion, wants to know what it is actually writing about since nothing it writes can be discerned by the human eye. As he observes: "You write and 'tis gone, 'tis erased." Numerous subjects for the "little writer's" activity occur to the questioner, who finally receives an answer, with some indignation expressed on the part of the beetle that the poet would be so dense as not to recognize what is being written on the water. There is, so says the "little writer," only one lesson they were given to write, only one lesson their teacher taught them: "We write and rewrite and write yet again, / the most holy name of God."[1]

This poem, aptly entitled "The Little Writer," composed by the Belgian Roman Catholic poet Guido Gezelle in the 1850s, hints at some profound truths concerning God's name. This name is indiscernible, the poet's eye cannot make it out; it is unutterable, what cannot be read cannot be said; and it is ungraspable, it comes and goes on the water, its lines are barely set down and they must be traced all over again. The "little writer" therefore writes what is indescribable, ineffable. Yet, the setting down of this name is worth a constant effort, as a lesson to be repeated; it is the one lesson necessary for learning. While the name cannot be seen or read or said, it must be written and rewritten on the water; it is worth the industrious attention spent on it by the little writer beetle and all his sisters and brothers.[2] But as

---

[1] Guido Gezelle, "Het Schrijverke (*Gyrinus Natans*)" in *Een Nieuwe Bundel (vierde deel) Bloemlezing van Nederlandse Poëzie: Achtiende en Negentiende Eeuw* (ed. K. H. de Raaf and J. J. Griss, as revised by F. W. van Herikhuizen; Rotterdam: W. L. & J. Brusse Uitgeversmaatschappij, 1958), 353.

[2] The whirligig beetle is a member of the most numerous species of the animal kingdom. (When asked what he had concluded from his studies, the noted biologist

tenacious and hard-working as this animal seems to be, its labor is not that of a plodder; rather, its activity is that of a dancer and poet, one who knows that the truth of God's name, if it can be caught at all, remains fleeting and out of reach even as it finds shape and articulation. The whirligig, who has learned its lesson, teaches it to the poet, and it seems an appropriate lesson with which to begin this deliberation about the name of God in Christian understanding and practice.

Practices of Writing

Rather unlike the whirligig, Christian scholars of Scripture in the European-American context of the past 150 years or so hardly seem to be engaged with the name of God at the point of its ineffability. The full spelling of the Tetragrammaton is in fact so prevalent in Christian circles that one is hard put to find resources on the Old Testament[3] that do not use it. If one teaches introductory classes in Hebrew language and Scripture, and if one discourages students from pronouncing the name of God with vocalization of the Tetragrammaton, as my colleagues at Louisville Presbyterian Seminary and I do habitually, it is especially confusing for the student when the secondary materials used for instruction do not exhibit the same scruples that their teachers demonstrate. In fact, the name of God is splashed across the pages of almost every contemporary North-American Christian commentary, introduction, or other hermeneutical work on the Hebrew Bible.[4]

J. B. S. Haldane noted that he had observed that the Creator had a special fondness for beetles (see Brian Farrell, "Inordinate Fondness Explained: Why There Are So Many Beetles," *Science* 281 [1998]: 555). The whirligig has some marvelous capacities, as being able to look both under and above the surface of the water at the same time, on account of the division of its compound eyes into two parts. Also, these insects are capable of diving and staying under water for a long time by trapping air under their abdomens, in a type of underwater lung phenomenon. The hind legs of the whirligig beat sixty times per second to whirl them over the water's surface. All these feats are performed by an insect that at its largest is fifteen millimeters.

[3] The text of the Jewish Bible is called the Old Testament in traditional Christian terminology. This term carries with it all the negatives that accompany the word "old" in North American culture. It is, on the other hand, not easy to find an adequate alternative. I have opted for Hebrew Bible at times, even though the term is not completely accurate; at other times I have used Old Testament, especially when indicating the work of scholars who use this term in their work.

[4] Since I partake to some degree of the scruples about the vocalized Tetragrammaton that exist in a Jewish context, I have tried to avoid using the vocalized name of God in my discussion and also in bibliographical references. Where the author used the vocalized Tetragrammaton in a resource, I have substituted a dot for each vowel in the citation.

For example, the most recent work by Walter Brueggemann, *Theology of the Old Testament,* spells out the Tetragrammaton on almost every page.[5] Another recent arrival on the theological scene, Bernhard Anderson's *Contours of Old Testament Theology,* shows some insight into the hesitancy with which the name should be approached but nevertheless continues with full vocalization of the Tetragrammaton.[6] Neither should these two scholars be singled out for reproach since they participate in an overwhelming Christian cloud of witnesses. As Brueggemann observes "It is conventional among Christian interpreters to vocalize the tetragrammaton (YHWH)."[7] First, I propose to trace the roots of this usage as it accompanies Christian anti-Jewish prejudice; second, I will examine the problems the usage creates for the Christian context itself; and third, I will put forward a suggestion for an appropriate rendering of God's name into English in a Christian context within a feminist-liberationist perspective.

Traces of a Habit

Any statement about convention among Christian interpreters, quoted above, should probably receive some geographical definition rather than be identified as generally Christian.[8] I speak of the vocalization of the Tetragrammaton with a geographic origin in Western Europe, from which

---

[5] Walter Brueggemann, *Theology of the Old Testament: Testimony, Dispute, Advocacy* (Minneapolis: Fortress, 1997), passim. Brueggemann relegates his awareness of the problem and his "uneasiness" at the vocalization of the Tetragrammaton to one sentence in a footnote (21 n. 52).

[6] Bernhard W. Anderson with Steven Bishop, *Contours of Old Testament Theology* (Minneapolis: Fortress, 1999), 51.

[7] Brueggemann, *Theology of the Old Testament,* 21 n. 52.

[8] In his essay, "Funding Postmodern Imagination" (*Texts onder Negotiation: The Bible and Postmodern Imagination* [Minneapolis: Fortress, 1993]), Walter Brueggemann argues that in this post-Enlightenment era knowledge and truth claims have become, among other things, contextual rather than universal. In making his argument, he observes, "It is clear ... that the old modes of knowing that are Euro-American, male, and white, no longer command respect and credibility as objective and universally true.... We are now able to see that what has passed for objective, universal knowledge has in fact been the *interested claim of the dominant voices who were able to pose their view and to gain either assent or docile acceptance from those whose interest the claim did not serve.*" (8–9, italics mine) When Brueggemann states in his *Theology of the Old Testament,* "It is conventional among Christian interpreters to vocalize the tetragrammaton (YHWH)" (21 n. 52), I suggest that this remark represents such an interested claim as described by Brueggemann in his earlier essay.

it spread to North America, and which is now more prevalent in the United States than in the places of its origin. How did this happen?

The current vocalization of the name of God as it occurs more than six thousand times in the Bible in the form of the four consonants usually identified as the Tetragrammaton arose simultaneously with the rise and flourishing of the school of biblical historical criticism in Germany and the rest of Western Europe during the last half of the nineteenth century. Both Kuenen and Wellhausen, the developers of the source theory for the composition of the Torah, use a vocalization of the Tetragrammaton.[9] These two scholars make no observations about Jewish taboos, either positive or negative, and since one can hardly assume that they were not aware of these, we must conclude that they ignored Jewish scruples regarding the name of God.[10] Wellhausen in his *Prolegomena* made overtly denigrating comments about the development of the religion of ancient Israel[11] and thereby implicitly of Judaism. In his case an implicit lack of respect for Jews is accompanied by an explicit lack of respect for God's name.[12] Wellhausen's understanding of the religion of ancient Israel as evolving from primitive animism to the "ethical" religion of the prophets, to the

---

9 Although there is, even today, little agreement among scholars of what the vocalization of YHWH should be, the insertion of the vowels *a* and *e* is the most common practice in translations and reference works that do not deal directly with the subject of God's name.

10 The same cannot be said, unfortunately, for John Calvin, who declared the Jewish taboo on the pronouncement of the name of God a "foul superstition" (John Calvin, *Commentaries on the Four Last Books of Moses: Arranged in the Form of a Harmony by John Calvin* [Grand Rapids: Eerdmans, 1950]: 1.127).

11 There are a number of ways to refer to the people by whom and for whom the text of the Hebrew Bible was composed. The designation "Israel," a conventional Christian way of naming this group in the North American Christian context, is for several reasons not desirable. Even though a confusion with the modern-day state and people of the same name is not very likely, this designation, wittingly or unwittingly, contains an implicit disregard for the reality of contemporary Israel. I have chosen the name ancient Israel to indicate the community out of which and on whose behalf the text of the Hebrew Bible was initially created.

12 The following remark is representative of Wellhausen's view of the status of ancient Israel's religion from the exile on: "The Creator of heaven and earth becomes the manager of a petty scheme of salvation; the living God descends from His throne to make way for the law. The law thrusts itself in everywhere; it commands and blocks up the access to heaven; it regulates and sets limits to the understanding of the divine working on earth. As far as it can, it takes the soul out of religion and spoils morality" (*Prolegomena to the History of Ancient Israel with a Reprint of the Article Israel from the Encyclopaedia Brittanica* [Cleveland: World Publishing, 1957], 509).

dead legalism of postexilic convictions cast a long shadow over biblical scholarship of the entire Bible in every area where historical criticism was embraced in the Christian context. Thus, Christian anti-Jewish impulses always present in Christian biblical interpretation were provided with new impetus during the rise of the historical-critical school on the European continent. In the European Christian context of that time, a way of reading and understanding the Old Testament that took seriously that this text was and is, first and foremost, the Jewish Bible had not yet emerged.[13] The so-called historical-critical school of biblical research did nothing to bring this simple truth to light.

In addition, the Wellhausian school promulgated the belief that "objective" historical, scientific research would uncover the true process of the composition of the biblical text. Vocalizing the Tetragrammaton then was one element in the scientific approach to Scripture, divorced from the context of the believing, worshiping community. The "great" Christian German scholars of the first fifty years of the twentieth century, whose works were studied everywhere in the Euro-American context, from Gunkel to Eichrodt to von Rad, all used the vocalized Tetragrammaton.

During those first fifty years of the twentieth century the Holocaust or Shoah occurred in the same lands where Old Testament scholars had propagated their anti-Jewish perspectives by their reading and understanding of the Hebrew Scriptures as a part of the Christian Bible. There were certainly connections, whether directly causal or not, between the theologically motivated animosity toward Jews and anti-Semitism of Christian scholarship and the events of the Shoah. I suggest here that the full vocalization of the Tetragrammaton partakes of the "teaching of contempt" that is an aspect of the hatred of the Jews that made the Shoah possible.

American scholarship of the Hebrew Bible among Christians is indebted deeply to its German predecessors. For both Brueggemann and Anderson, in the works cited above, basic theological points of reference are formed by Eichrodt and von Rad. While the North American schools of

---

[13] To a great degree this lack of awareness still prevails in many Christian contexts. See, for example, the following telling remark by Rolf Rendtorff (*Canon and Theology* [Minneapolis: Fortress, 1993], 43): "The crucial point is the theological acceptance or, first of all, even awareness, of the existence of contemporary Judaism as a living religion which uses the Hebrew Bible as its Holy Scripture. Christian theologians, Old Testament scholars included, have never been taught to realize that. I myself during more than ten years of teaching Old Testament was never aware of this problem.... As far as I can see, there are still very few Christian biblical scholars who are aware of all this." Rendtorff made this remark originally in a lecture delivered in English at the 1989 University of Notre Dame Conference on "Hebrew Bible or Old Testament? Studying the Bible in Judaism and Christianity."

biblical interpretation of an earlier period shared a negative appraisal of the eventual outcome of the faith of ancient Israel, hence of Judaism, this is less clearly true of a scholar like Brueggemann. And yet, I suggest that any theological articulation on the part of Christians that in essence is disrespectful of the convictions and beliefs of Jews is inherently anti-Semitic and "breathes that same air of the 'teaching of contempt'" toward the Jews mentioned above.[14]

"We Write and Rewrite and Write Yet Again..."

When I was young and learned Hebrew in high school in the Netherlands, I learned to read *Adonai* where the Tetragrammaton occurred in the Hebrew text. When I went to the university and continued Hebrew studies, the same habit prevailed, both in the liberal-arts faculty and the theological faculty. My teacher in high school was a Christian with right-of-center convictions, my professor in the liberal-arts faculty was entirely secular, and my Old Testament professor in Leiden was Piet de Boer, whose convictions were far left-of-center on the Christian spectrum. In other words, these teachers did not share the same perspective, not even the same belief system, yet they taught us the same habit of reading *Adonai,* which amounted to avoidance of pronouncing God's name. When I came to the United States I had occasion to be glad for good habits learned young, as I continued my Hebrew studies at Columbia University in an all-Jewish context. But I was shocked to learn that the same habits did not prevail at the Christian seminary where I did my doctoral studies or in any American Christian scholarly circles of my acquaintance then or later.[15]

My teachers in the Netherlands, with all their varied backgrounds, had much the same experience. The disaster that Jews call the Shoah had taken place in our Christian lands, and Christian responsibility for this event had heightened awareness of anti-Jewish attitudes and practices. As to what happened in the United States, one can only speculate that theologically motivated anti-Jewishness was not as easily recognized because the events of the Shoah were relegated to another period and another place without

---

[14] My observation is a translated paraphrase of a remark made by the writers of a contemporary German introduction to the Old Testament (Erich Zenger et al., *Einleitung in das Alte Testament* [Stuttgart: Kohlhammer, 1998], 18) in which they note previous models for reading and interpreting the Old Testament that were prevalent in Christianity: "Atmen, gewollt oder ungewollt, den Atem jenes 'teaching of contempt,' der ein Aspekt jener fatalen theologischen Jüdenfeindschaft ist, die *einer* der Auslöser des rassischen Antisemitismus war."

[15] A notable exception is Louisville Presbyterian Theological Seminary where it is the practice in the Old Testament area to avoid writing and speaking the vocalized Tetragrammaton.

the impact on North American Christian consciousness that was shared on the Western European continent. It is an astonishing phenomenon that very few Christian introductions, commentaries, or theologies of the Old Testament from the United States context are available that take the Shoah into account in terms of how it might affect Christian reading and understanding of the Bible. Sometimes this subject is taken up in works that specialize on the subject, but generally there is in the secondary materials on the Bible a thundering silence in terms of the Holocaust. Ironically, then, today one has to look to Europe to find works that proceed from the perspective that previous models of Old Testament interpretation are deeply flawed because of their participation in hostile attitudes and practices toward the Jews and their possible connections to the events of the Shoah. Similarly, one has to look toward Germany for an introductory work on the Old Testament that is respectful toward God's name.[16] Silence about the Shoah, accompanied by a chorus of voices pronouncing the ineffable name of God, is what one encounters in the North-American context today among the vast majority of Christian Bible scholars.

Farewell to Innocence and Arrogance[17]

The awareness, the "shock," of the potential outcome of anti-Jewishness among Christians, also among Christian biblical scholars, through the events of the Shoah, makes it incumbent upon us to set aside

[16] See, for example, Zenger's *Einleitung* (17), where three common models of reading and understanding the Old Testament in a Christian context are discussed and rejected for a variety of reasons, among them the reason that they contribute to "disastrous theological hostility toward the Jews." In some form each of these models, separate or in combination, are very much operative in standard American Christian biblical interpretation today. The authors of this introduction maintain that the shock caused by the Shoah occasioned an (all-too-slowly) reached insight into the connections between theologically motivated hostility against the Jews and anti-Semitism, and therefore demands also a *new Christian way of dealing with the First Testament* ("Die im Erschrecken über die Schoa [viel zu] langsam gereisste Erkenntnis der Zusammenhänge zwischen theologisch motivierter Jüdenfeindschaft und Antisemitismus fordert auch einen *neuen christlichen Umgang mit dem Ersten Testament*" [18, italics mine]).

[17] In his book *Farewell to Innocence: A Socio-Ethical Study on Black Theology and Power* (Maryknoll, N.Y.: Orbis Books, 1977) the South African author and theologian Allan A. Boesak discusses the notion of innocence as a suspect virtue that can be discarded in a situation of inequality. For a similar discussion in an Asian American feminist context, see Rita Nakashima Brock's essay, "Dusting the Bible on the Floor: A Hermeneutics of Wisdom," in *Searching the Scriptures: A Feminist Introduction* (ed. Elisabeth Schüssler Fiorenza; New York: Crossroad, 1993), 64–75.

"innocence." Innocence, as discussed by the South African theologian Allan Boesak in his work *Farewell to Innocence,* can be a destructive force when it "blocks off all awareness and therefore the sense of responsibility necessary to confront the other as a human being." As Boesak maintains, this kind of innocence kept the status quo of inequality intact in the context of the power dynamics and racism of South Africa of the 1970s.[18] When we apply this insight to the subject of our concern, it appears that innocence prevents Christian interpreters of Scripture from facing the implications of a continued use of the vocalized Tetragrammaton as the name of God in the Hebrew Bible. In "innocence" Christians confess ignorance of the Jewish taboo regarding God's name;[19] in "innocence" we miss the connections between the silence surrounding the Holocaust/Shoah and the spokenness of God's name.

Arrogance on the other hand would maintain that it is, after all, a universal practice to vocalize the Tetragrammaton;[20] arrogance makes Christians proclaim that the taboo on pronouncing God's name is due to superstition;[21] arrogance holds that the Jews lost the name of God and Christians found it.[22] In his essay "On Translating the Divine Name" David S. Cunningham observes that "bodies are important to Christians, and the effects that words have upon bodies are also important.... Ultimately ... our words should not maim or injure, they should heal."[23] This remark, made in the context of advocacy for greater nuances in the context of inclusive language for God,

---

[18] Boesak, *Farewell to Innocence,* 4

[19] See, for example, David Clines, "Y.hw.h and the God of Christian Theology," *Theology* 83 (1980): 323.

[20] So D. N. Freedman and M. P. O'Connor, "יהוה (YHWH)," *TDOT* 5:501.

[21] So Gottfried Quell suggests in "κύριος," *TDNT* 3:1058–81. Dropping the use of the name, Quell observes, "was the result of a revival of the primitive dynamic conceptions of paganism," (1070). The preface to the ASV states that "the American revisers, after a careful consideration, were brought to the unanimous conviction that a Jewish superstition, which regarded the Divine Name as too sacred to be uttered, ought no longer to dominate in the English or any other version of the Old Testament." Cf. also Walter Lowrie, "The Proper Name of God," *AThR* 41 (1959): 245–52.

[22] R. Laird Harris begins his article, "The Pronunciation of the Tetragram," (in *The Law and the Prophets: Old Testament Studies Prepared in Honor of Oswald Thompson Allis* [ed. J. H. Skilton; Nutley, N.J.: Presbyterian & Reformed, 1974] 215–224) bemoaning the loss of the name of the God of Israel and goes on to say that "Not to use the name of God seems to profane it just as the coarse use of the Name would have done" (215). See also David Clines ("Y.hw.h and the God of Christian Theology," 323), who remarks, "Somewhere between the fifth and the second centuries B.C. a tragic accident befell God: he lost his name."

[23] David S. Cunningham, "On Translating the Divine Name," *TS* 56 (1995): 438.

we may well apply to the issue at hand. In the end, it is perhaps simply a question of the intention of the Christian body vis-à-vis the Jewish body. If Christians truly intend to end the maiming and injury of the past, to repent of past hostility, of arrogance and innocence, and if we hope for a mended relation with Jewish sisters and brothers, can we afford to go on using an appellation for God that is offensive to the other side?

The Beetle and the Scholar

So far, I have considered problems created by the use of the vocalized Tetragrammaton in terms of Jewish-Christian relations. I turn now to problems created inside Christian contexts by this usage. I touch here on three areas of concern. The first is the hypothetical nature of the common vocalization. The claim that something is "universally accepted" should perhaps always cause suspicion. Thus Freedman would have one form of the vocalized Tetragrammaton be "accepted almost universally."[24] Apart from the Christian arrogance embedded in this claim, we may consider whether it is true. Unlike the whirligig beetle, who abides in the ineffability of God's name, Christian Old Testament scholars have been trying to nail down the vowels of the Tetragrammaton with great industry. The result of all the motion, beyond the superficial acceptance of one type of vocalization, is that little agreement exists today on what the name of God actually should be. Various hypotheses, all brought forward with solid argumentation, suggest at least three if not four viable alternative spellings.[25] Nothing is certain in this terrain, not the utterance of the name, nor its meaning, but we, not content with writing on water, persist in our attempts at finding what eludes our grasp.

---

[24] D. N. Freedman and M. P. O'Connor, "יהוה (YHWH)," 5:501.

[25] Compare, for example the well-argued discussions of G. R. Driver ("The Original Form of the Name Y.hw.h: Evidences and Conclusions," *ZAW* 46 [1928]: 7–25), B. D. Eerdmans ("The Name Jahu," *OtSt* 5 [1948]; 2–29), and Sigmund Mowinckel ("The Name of the God of Moses," *HUCA* 32 [1961]: 121–33) on the one hand, with those of Elias Auerbach (*Moses* [Detroit: Wayne State University Press, 1975]); Martin Buber (*Moses: The Revelation and the Covenant* [New York: Harper & Row, 1958], 50), and Franz Rosenzweig ("'The Eternal': Mendelssohn and the Name of God," in *Scripture and Translation* [trans. Lawrence Rosenwald with Everett Fox; Bloomington: Indiana University Press, 1994], 109), on the other, and both of these different vocalizations with the arguments from D. N. Freedman, ("The Name of the God of Moses," *JBL* 79 [1960]: 151–56), and Gottfried Quell ("κύριος," 3:1058–81) to get an idea of the complexities involved. For an overview of various suggestions, see also G. H. Parke-Taylor, "יהוה," in *Y.HW.H: The Divine Name in the Bible* (Waterloo, Ontario: Wilfrid Laurier University Press, 1975), 79–96.

The second area of concern pertains to the division between the academy and the church, between scholars and lay persons. Let us assume that the Christian biblical scholar who is also at work on the historical level has an obligation to retrieve if possible the earliest theological convictions embedded in the biblical text. This obligation then could drive such scholarly endeavor to uncover the name of God. The assumption underlying this task is that the vocalized Tetragrammaton provides information about God, about God's relation to God's people, ancient Israel, and that people's understanding of God. The vocalized Tetragrammaton, however, hardly does that; in fact, one could say, it precisely does not do that. The Tetragrammaton with vowels does not lead to enlightenment in any of these areas. Even if there were scholarly agreement on the meaning of the name of God, and there is not, the vocalized name would hardly convey this meaning. The name remains alien and opaque, used in the Christian context only by some when they do their work outside of a context of worship. The already-existing divisions between the world of scholarship and the church become even larger in this way than they are ordinarily. Sometimes such divisions cannot be forestalled, although we should probably always be at work to overcome them, but in the case of the vocalized Tetragrammaton the division is an unnecessary and potentially dangerous one, whereby an aura of erudition and scholarship hides the limits of what can be learned.[26]

Even if this particular division were overcome, a more serious one lurks down the road. Let us assume for a moment that the vocalized Tetragrammaton would become the familiar way in which the Christian believer spoke about the God of ancient Israel. Would such a habit not underscore the different ways in which God is revealed as related in the two Testaments, would it not reinforce the Christian tendency to view the Testaments as witnessing to two different gods, the God of ancient Israel, and the God of Jesus Christ, with only one of these the real God for Christians?

---

[26] David Clines ("Y.hw.h and the God of Christian Theology," 324) argues that it is the very alien quality of the vocalized Tetragrammaton that will guarantee the personhood of God and prevent Christian christomonism. He observes, "It is a foreign name, quite un-English.... The very awkwardness of addressing a god whose name is not native to one's language in itself alerts us to the alienness of Y.HW.H to every god created in our image." Second, the name of God would safeguard God's personhood, according to Clines's understanding, and prevent a transformation of God into a "philosophical abstraction" (326). It is questionable, however, whether foreignness in itself is of any use in naming God and certainly there are enough personal adjectives and titles available in naming God that we need not worry about "philosophical abstractions." The question is whether naming God with the vocalized Tetragrammaton with vowels is less of a philosophical abstraction than naming God Father or Mother.

The third concern is a most important one for it concerns the insight that in the end human beings do not have the capacity to name God, that in speaking of God and writing of God we always write on the water as it were: we write and 'tis gone, 'tis erased. Yet, like the whirligig beetle we must speak of God and write of God, and it is crucial that we give to this task all our attention. The insight that arose first in the community that created the Hebrew Bible, that the name of God must not be pronounced, rests not on superstition, but on the correct insight that there is power in naming and that a human being cannot exert this power over the one it considers most holy.[27] To leave the one holy name of God shrouded in mystery may remind us of this limitation in calling to mind that all our speaking and writing of God is inaccurate as well as accurate, that we always have it wrong as well as right. The only "wrong" naming of God is that which is sure of having it "right."[28] The greatest danger of our landing on the vocalized Tetragrammaton as God's "true" name is that we would think exactly this, that now we have it right.

The Most Holy Name of God

Where do we go from here? How can Christians solve the problem that we must speak of God while the name always eludes our grasp? One direction we could take is to adopt the custom of reading and speaking *Adonai* or *Hashem* where the name occurs in the Hebrew text. Either one of these options is appropriate when we read the text in Hebrew. But how do we render God's name in Bible translations or reference works?[29] A common Christian practice of the past has been to translate Adonai with "LORD" following Christian Greek and Latin renderings of the Tetragrammaton with *kurios* and *dominus,* respectively.[30] I will take up objections to this rendering below.

[27] For a discussion of this issue see Johanna van Wijk-Bos, *Reimagining God: The Case for Scriptural Diversity* (Louisville: Westminster/John Knox, 1995), 28–30.

[28] See Elizabeth A. Johnson, *She Who Is: The Mystery of God in Feminist Theological Discourse* (New York: Crossroad, 1992), 105. See also van Wijk-Bos, *Reimagining God,* 95.

[29] I follow the practice of reading *Adonai* or placing the Tetragrammaton without vowels in my translations of biblical texts throughout *Reimagining God.*

[30] It is probable that early versions of the Septuagint did not translate the Tetragrammaton with κύριος, as is generally assumed. For an illuminating discussion on this issue, see George Howard, "The Tetragram and the New Testament," *JBL* 96 (1977): 63–83. After careful consideration of the manuscript evidence, Howard sums up as follows: "In pre-Christian Greek manuscripts of the Old Testament, the divine name normally appears not in the form of κύριος, as it does in the great Christian codices of the Septuagint known today, but either in the form of the Hebrew

Franz Rosenzweig and Martin Buber, in essays and letters explaining their choice for the representation of the Tetragrammaton in their Bible translation, argued strongly for a translation of the name of God. Untranslated, the name of God is meaningless, according to them. For Buber and Rosenzweig the name of God is above all a "bearer of meaning" and becomes meaningful only when translated appropriately.[31] Thus Buber observed:

> That name (i.e. the Tetragram) alone among the divine epithets in the Bible is entirely a name and not a concept; but it is a name in which biblical consciousness perceives a meaning, or rather *the* meaning, that meaning that is disclosed in revelation, in the Burning Bush.[32]

I propose to follow the direction laid down by Buber and Rosenzweig in looking for an appropriate translation of the Tetragrammaton.[33] "Lord" was an unsatisfactory translation for Buber because it replaces a name with a title, or a concept, where one must rather read an attribute that describes

---

tetragram (written in Aramaic or paleo-Hebrew letters) or in the transliterated form of ΙΑΩ" (71). One witness to this practice is Origen, who wrote the Tetragram in the Greek versions used in the Hexapla, including the Septuagint, which may testify to early Christian habits.

[31] "The Tetragrammaton ... is name and name of an attribute in one. Vocalizing the Tetragram in expressions such as 'They shall know that I am YHWH,' 'YHWH is a war hero,' and 'YHWH is his name,' makes no sense at all and becomes meaningful only when one somehow renders the name as a bearer of meaning." This is Barbara Galli's translation of this passage from Franz Rosenzweig's essay ("Der Ewige: Mendelssohn und der Gottesname" in Rosenzweig, *Gesammelte Schriften. Zweistromland: Kleinere Schriften zu Glauben und Denken* [Dordrecht, 1984], 812) in her "Rosenzweig and the Name for God," *Modern Judaism* 14 (1994): 79). Rosenzweig's essay was published in German in a number of different sources, the original version in 1929 (*Gedenkbuch für Moses Mendelssohn* [N.p.: Verband der Vereine für jüdische Geschichte und Literatur]). It is available in its entirety in English translation as "'The Eternal': Mendelssohn and the Name of God," in *Scripture and Translation: Martin Buber and Franz Rosenzweig* (trans. Lawrence Rosenwald with Everett Fox; Bloomington: Indiana University Press, 1994) 99–113. In this volume, see also Martin Buber's "On Word Choice in Translating the Bible: In Memoriam Franz Rosenzweig" (originally published in 1930), 79–89, and Rosenzweig's "A Letter to Martin Goldner" (dated June 27, 1927), 189–92.

[32] Buber, "On Word Choice," 87.

[33] The reading "Adonai" or "Hashem" in translations partakes after all of the same objections that I have outlined above in terms of the divisions between academy and church and of the separating of the two Testaments in a Christian context, in terms of how they speak of God. See p. 54. This argument goes against my own practice in *Reimagining God,* which I would handle differently if I were writing today.

adequately what is disclosed in the name.[34] Rosenzweig, who voiced some guarded approval of the translation "Lord" for the Tetragrammaton, also finally rejected it because he considered YHWH to reveal a God who is above all relational, and "Lord" is the word of "a false relation, a ruling and not a helping, an overseeing and not an assisting."[35]

Rosenzweig's conviction about "Lord" being a term of "false relation" fits well within a feminist-liberationist framework. From such a perspective "Lord" is a problematic title for God within the framework of a search for language for God that offers an alternative to exclusively male imagery and that is yet rooted in Scripture. Within such a framework "Lord" is a difficult metaphor to maintain for God, because it is a masculine term and does not connect to contemporary experience, at least in the North American context. The first difficulty entails that "Lord" presents an exclusively male image of God and the second problem pushes the imagery into literalism.[36]

For Buber and Rosenzweig the name of God expresses above all God's being in relation. God is present—with but in God's own way, in "continual and unpredictable renewal." Buber rejects, therefore, a possible translation of the name as "the one-who-is-there" or "the one-who-is-present," since this rendering would not preserve the unpredictable quality, the mystery of the disclosure of the name.[37]

Another important point that enters into their reflections concerning the name of God is the quality of spokenness of the Bible that must be emphasized as much as possible, in Buber and Rosenzweig's opinion. "The translator must elicit from the letter of the Hebrew text its actual auditory form," declares Buber. The spokenness of the Bible is thus awakened every time "an ear biblically hears the word or a mouth biblically speaks it."[38]

These considerations led Buber and Rosenzweig to translate the Tetragrammaton with three different personal pronouns, for in this way the "Name in its full presence leaps forth with the explosive force of orality from the always past speech of the book into the present."[39] They chose the pro-

---

[34] Buber ("On Word Choice," 87). Rosenzweig ("The Eternal") says that rendering the Tetragrammaton as "the Lord" replaces "the reality with fiction" (106).

[35] Rosenzweig, "The Eternal," 106. Rosenzweig expresses, however, that "'the Lord' was in one sense a better rendering of the name than 'the Eternal,' insofar as it had in itself not a limited meaning but one pointing beyond itself" (106).

[36] For a discussion of the function and usefulness of metaphors in language for God and the difficulties with the metaphors "king" and "lord" for God, see van Wijk-Bos, *Reimagining God,* 35–41.

[37] Buber, "On Word Choice," 87.

[38] Ibid., 75

[39] Rosenzweig, "The Eternal," 105. In the context he remarked: "To the narrative context, then, the only justifiable translation is one that makes prominent not God's

nouns "I" and "MY" for the Tetragrammaton when God is speaking; "YOU" and "YOUR" when God is spoken to; "HE" and "HIS" when God is spoken of. Exodus 3:14–15 reads as follows in the Buber/Rosenzweig translation:

> God said to Moses:
> I will be there as I will be there.
> And he said:
> So you shall say it to the sons of Israel:
> I AM THERE sends me to you.
> And further God said to Moses:
> So you shall say it to the sons of Israel:
> HE,
> the God of your fathers,
> the God of Abraham, the God of Isaac, the God of Jacob,
> sends me to you.[40]

The choice of the threefold personal pronoun offers new possibilities insofar as it keeps intact both the mystery and promise of presence contained in the name of God. The third masculine pronoun, however, suffers a similar liability as the title "Lord," in that its patriarchal overtones make it a word of "false relation, a ruling and not a helping, an overseeing and not an assisting." Also, and in line with Buber's emphasis on the importance of the spokenness of the Bible, today, at least in the North American context, the masculine pronoun spelled in capital letters underlines maleness rather than divinity, masculinity rather than relationality.

My suggestion is to retain the Buber/Rosenzweig rendering in part and to use the first pronoun when God is speaking and the second pronoun when God is spoken to. In this way, we retain something of the "explosive force of the orality" of which Buber spoke. When God is spoken about, a fitting translation of the Tetragrammaton may be "the Holy God" or "the Holy One" when it is combined with another word indicating deity. The word *holy* preserves both the unnameable and unknowable qualities of God and the nearness of God to God's people and God's creation. Holiness when paired with God points to God's otherness and elicits praise and awe from human beings as in the familiar text from Isaiah:

---

being eternal but his being present, his being present for and with you now and in time to come. I have shown elsewhere how in the rendering of the thus clarified name this fact can be condensed into the three dimensions of the personal pronoun: the speaker, the one spoken to, the one spoken of. Only in the pronoun is the meaning of the One who is present in one of three ways, the One who is present in one of three sorts of presence, concentrated into a single word" (105).

40 My translation from Martin Buber and Franz Rosenzweig, *Die fünf Bücher der Weisung: Fünf Bücher des Moses* (Cologne: Jacob Hegner, 1968).

Holy, holy, holy!
Holy God of Hosts!
Filled is the earth with his glory. (Isa 6:3)

God's name remains a mystery, it is unknowable, ungraspable, unsayable; it is a holy name. At the same time this Holy God is present with the community of God's love precisely as the Holy One. This presence is strongly promised in the revelation at the burning bush and is embedded in the disclosure of God's name. A text that witnesses to this understanding of God's holiness in the midst of the ancient covenant community is Hos 11:9:

For I am God and not a man
in your midst the Holy One;
I will not come in anger.

Baruch Levine has pointed out that God's holiness is not intended to describe God's essential nature but rather how God is manifest: "The statement that God is holy, means ... that God acts in holy ways: God is just and righteous."[41] Buber claims that the holiness of God denotes not "a static but a dynamic concept, not a condition but a process."[42] Taken together, these two insights show that the rendering "the Holy God" for the Tetragrammaton points to the notion of God's presence and at the same time to the dynamic nature of that presence.

The holiness of God also lays claim on the human community to be manifest in holiness as God is manifest in the midst of them, that is, with acts of forgiveness, justice, and righteousness. "Be holy, for I, the Holy One your God, am holy" reiterates the text in Lev 19 (v. 2 and passim).[43] In translating the Tetragrammaton with "the Holy God," we are reminded that we as Christians are also called to a life that manifests this holiness. In addition, when we translate the Tetragrammaton with "Holy God," both God's mystery and God's presence are maintained. Finally, calling to mind that the truth of God's name remains fleeting and out of reach, even as we give it shape and articulation, that we too write on the water as it were, I offer this rendering not so much as a conclusive solution to the problem of how to articulate God's name appropriately, but as a step on the way, in an attempt to remain faithful to the notion of the "continual and unpredictable renewal" also embedded in God's name.

---

[41] Baruch Levine, *The JPS Torah Commentary: Leviticus* (Philadelphia: Jewish Publication Society of America, 5749/1989), 256.

[42] Buber, "On Word Choice," 79.

[43] See also van Wijk–Bos, *Reimagining God,* 31–33.

An Interpersonal Theology of the Hebrew Bible

Murray H. Lichtenstein

One of the few abstract theological formulations crystallized by ancient Israelites and left for their posterity avers that "YHWH is one" (Deut 6:4). As biblical usage makes clear, there is more than one possible meaning to this singular statement: one in number, unique, uniform, and more. But, surely, the unequivocal identification of YHWH, and YHWH *alone,* as God elsewhere in the writings of the Deuteronomist (Deut 4:35, 39; 32:39; 1 Kgs 8:60) leaves little room for such sublime ambiguities. It is, therefore, remarkable that, as actually depicted in the Hebrew Bible, this quintessentially lone being never remains alone for very long. Soliloquies, solo appearances, and, above all, any prolonged state of isolation, splendid or otherwise, constitute the rarest of exceptions to a rule; God is conceived of not so much as a being in and of itself, but rather as a presence realized in the presence of one or more "others." From "the beginning" of the first chapter of Genesis, God is depicted in the act of creating, manipulating, naming, and evaluating the merits of something or someone other. Indeed, the very etymology of the divine name vocalized as "Yahweh" suggests a deity understood, first and foremost, in terms of one characteristically "bringing (another) into existence." It would almost seem as if God's observation that "it is not good for the human being to be alone" (Gen 2:18) was more a projection of the divine psyche than a reflection on the human condition. With no divine helpmate of its own, no progeny, and no pantheon of divine colleagues, the God of Israel must look elsewhere for company and, as it were, for personal fulfillment.[1]

[1] There doesn't seem to be much substance or depth to the relationship between the God of Israel and the "celestial family" provided by Canaanite mythology. Thus the "sons of El" appear in perfunctory roles as mostly silent or mindlessly acquiescing members of the divine assembly (e.g., Job 1–2; Ps 29:1), and they may be summarily dismissed from their more important functions at will (as in Ps 82). So too, extrabiblical inscriptions do not show "YHWH's Asherah" doing anything beyond joining in YHWH's blessing of some fortunate individual. Only personified "Wisdom" seems to provide YHWH with any "quality time" company to speak of, and even that ends up having to be shared with her human constituency (Prov 8:30–31).

Arguably the most distinctive and original religious conception of the Israelites remains that of "covenant," a metaphor rooted in the regulation of international relations and interpersonal relationships. The biblical record presents the whole sweep of Israelite history in terms of the succession of a series of covenants, from the universal covenant with Noah, and the individual covenants with the patriarchs, through the national covenants at Sinai, Moab, and Shechem, and the royal Davidic covenant, to the covenantal reforms of King Josiah, and the "new covenant" envisioned by the prophet Jeremiah. The biblical medium of choice for the actualization of the divine presence in history is thus fully consistent with the image of a deity insistent upon becoming and remaining involved, engaged, and interactive with Israel, and so the world.[2] As such, it may well be inappropriate, and more than a little artificial, to seek "theology" in the Hebrew Bible (that is, systematized knowledge of the nature of God), when Scripture itself offers, quite differently, a "psychology" of divine interpersonal relations.

[2] I cannot concur with the recent challenging of the uniqueness and overarching significance of the Israelite covenant metaphor, especially on the basis of the usage detected in the Arslan Tash amulet, for which see S. David Sperling, "Israel's Religion in the Ancient Near East," in *Jewish Spirituality from the Bible through the Middle Ages* (ed. Arthur Green; New York: Crossroad, 1986), 25, citing that author's detailed, and otherwise exemplary, study of the text in S. David Sperling, "An Arslan Tash Incantation: Interpretations and Implications," *HUCA* 53 (1982): 1–10. Thus, the clearly apotropaic function of the divine pact said to have been effected with those under the protection of that amulet, is surely more consistent with the illicit (and promptly invalidated!) "covenant with Death" in Isa 28:15, 18, but bears no resemblance whatsoever either to the scope or the intent of the patriarchal and national (!) covenants attested in the Hebrew Bible. On the cultic level, the metaphor of covenant effects the radical replacement of "image" with "imagery" in the divine throne room of the Israelite holy of holies, and, in an equally radical way, it further becomes the *Leitmotiv* of an entire historiographic literature, developments unattested elsewhere in the ancient Near East. These functions sharply distinguish the biblical covenant concept from the clearly limited figure of speech attested in both Isa 28 and the Arslan Tash amulet. Indeed, in the thought world of magic, divine powers often extend highly specific and limited kinds of immunity to their clients, offering a solemn oath as guarantee, and such an oath, or modified divine nonaggression pact, is what the Arslan Tash amulet is all about (compare, for example, Lilith's oath on the Jewish amulets protecting the newborn, for which see James A. Montgomery, *Aramaic Incantation Texts from Nippur* [Philadelphia: The University Museum, 1913], 259–64). By the same token, the mere attestation of political treaty terminology in an ancient Near Eastern religious text is, by itself, clearly not to be equated with the patriarchal and subsequent national covenants of the Hebrew Bible, which both reflect and effect a comprehensive and highly nuanced personal *relationship* between the deity and an entire people throughout its history.

The above observations are certainly not new. Rather, there is a long-lived Jewish exegetical tradition behind them, extending from the pseudepigrapha and rabbinic haggadah, through medieval poetry and the Kabbalah, all the way to Martin Buber's *I and Thou,* Abraham Joshua Heschel's *God in Search of Man,* and beyond. My own contribution in these pages is toward a renewed emphasis and reflection on this interpersonal view of God, especially as applied to the reading of biblical narrative, an approach that, to me, offers a most helpful and potentially productive resource for the formulation of "biblical theology."

The image of God presented in the creation stories of Genesis is a useful starting point for these reflections. I have long followed the scholarly custom of distinguishing the P and J accounts of creation in terms of the transcendent view of God in the former, as opposed to the immanent view of God in the latter. Yet, as is clear to me now, there is more at issue here. In their present order in the text, the J creation account seems bent on developing the interpersonal view of God just hinted at in the preceding version of P, which for all its divine transcendence, is not content to leave "God in his heaven." Nothing is said in P of the celestial realm, nor of the nature of the deity itself, beyond the act of creating an "other" reality, the motivation for which is left emphatically unexplained. In the J account, the deity moves from the mode of commanding the others to a more dynamic mode of interaction with the last-named creation of the first account, humankind. There, the latter is successively commanded, warned, mused upon, installed in its own specially planted garden, maneuvered into the process of naming the animals, put to sleep, operated upon, and presented with a mate. Yet movement toward this interpersonal mode begins in the P account itself, in which first the animate creatures, and then humankind, are directly addressed and imparted blessings, not just impersonally commanded. Humankind's blessing repeats the motif of fertility granted to the animal world ("Be fruitful and multiply, and fill up . . . " Gen 1:22), to which is added the motif of sovereignty ("subdue and hold sway over," 1:28). There is little qualitative difference between the content of this divine-human interaction and the one described later on in Gen 22:17, in the likewise twofold blessing of Abraham, "I will surely bless you, multiplying your offspring as the stars of heaven and the sands on the seashore; and may your offspring inherit the towns of their enemies." Indeed, the same may be said of the blessing of Rebecca by her family in Gen 24:60. "Our sister, may you become thousands of myriads, and may your offspring inherit the towns of their foes." A third generation of patriarchs receives the double blessing as Isaac unwittingly bestows it upon Jacob, posing as the elder Esau: "May God give you of heaven's dew and earth's fatness, with abundant harvest of grain and grape; may peoples serve you, and nations bow before you" (Gen 27:28–29). In this sense, the creation accounts do not merely precede, but are a prologue to, the patriarchal narratives, in which patterns of divine interaction are both mirrored and developed.

Intervening between the creation accounts and the patriarchal narratives are other programmatic texts of the primeval history. In its barest essentials, the latter, from Eden to Babel, is the story of God, who doesn't so much act as *react* to the behavior of human others: punishing here, rewarding there, as well as anticipating and preventing any undesired acts. As the rabbis never tired of observing in a myriad of specific instances, the nature of divine reaction was neither arbitrary, general, nor impersonal, but rather followed a uniquely personalized poetic justice, and such is decidedly the case in the primeval history. As others have observed, to one degree or another, in the Eden narrative of Gen 3, the words "tree" (עץ) and "fruit" (פרי) and "eat" (אכל) are repeated again and again in the initial divine prohibition and subsequent indictment, so that by the time punishment is prescribed one is prepared for the outcome: having prompted others to eat fruit, the serpent is itself destined to eat (אכל) the dust (עפר). The woman and the man having both eaten from the tree (עץ) are both punished by discomfort (עצבון), and it is in the latter state, accompanied by "the sweat of the brow," that humankind will eat (אכל) its food. Like the serpent, the man's punishment in the matter of the fruit (פרי) is linked to the similar sounding "dust" (עפר), to which he is bound to return in death. So, too, in Gen 4, Cain's having spilled his brother's blood on the earth (אדמה) results in banishment from sedentary life and from successful cultivation of the earth (אדמה); in Gen 6, the deluge is a divine ruination (שחת) of the land in accord with its having been ruined (שחת) by humankind; in Gen 11, the builders of the tower proposed "Let us build" (הָבָה נִבְנֶה), so YHWH disposed, "Let us descend and there confound (their speech)" (הָבָה נֵרְדָה וְנָבְלָה), with the result that they are punished with dispersion, the very condition that they had sought to avoid by their act of hubristic defiance. In short, nothing is actually done by God for God alone; everything that takes place in these episodes is in reference to other persons, and everything done by them is accorded a swift, direct, and highly personalized divine response.

Nor is the dynamic of divine interpersonal relations in the primeval history restricted to reward and punishment. Rather, we encounter here a number of intriguing and suggestive instances of rapport between the deity and humankind. Thus, in the garden, the interplay goes far beyond a simple case of human action and divine response. Consider the dramatically calculated questions posed to the man and woman: "Where are you?... Who told you that you were naked?" (Gen 3:9, 11). Of the same kind are YHWH's leading questions to Cain: "Why are you so irritated and dejected?" and "Where is Abel, your brother?" (Gen 4:6, 9). These questions are intentionally designed to elicit a particular anticipated response, which in turn will be addressed by appropriate instruction or rebuke, as warranted. To me, at least, these stylized verbal interactions speak less of divine omniscience, as a theological tenet, than they do of parental or pedagogical ploys. That is, the questions reveal an intimate rapport with the subjects, and a finely tuned familiarity with their customary thought patterns, evasions, and defenses. Once again, the primeval history serves as prologue to subsequent narratives, especially in terms of similarly rhetorical questions posed, for example, to Elijah ("What prompts your coming here?" 1 Kgs 18:9, 13) and Jonah ("Are you really so very distraught?" 4:4, 9). There is a depth of divine concern in these pointed interrogations, as well as a personal stake and involvement on the part of the deity, that far transcends abstract philosophical categories such as "omniscience."

And what of Enoch and Noah, both of whom "walked with God" (Gen 5:22, 24; 6:9)? A perusal of biblical usage suggests that the infrequent Hebrew idiom התהלך את האלהים bespeaks an unusual degree of identification and shared interests, as, for example, the close working relationship that grew between Nabal's herdsmen and David's band as the former accompanied the latter, their protectors (1 Sam 25:15).[3] The relationship seems to go beyond, for example, that connoted by התהלך לפני, which suggests pious obedience toward the deity rather than genuinely intimate rapport as such (Gen 17:1; 24:40; 48:15). The special degree of closeness implied here is confirmed, of course, by the unique destinies of Enoch and Noah at God's hand. The biblical passage concerning Enoch piques our curiosity about the implications of such divine-human identification by employing the idiom "to walk about with God" twice, first in what is clearly a metaphorical sense ("to enjoy close rapport with the deity"), and then in the literal sense of physically accompanying the deity to some removed place, so that "he was not." This artful repetition suggests a cause-and-effect nexus, whereby Enoch's unique "translation" is directly attributable to his equally unique relationship to the deity. But is this simply a case of a divine reward for human devotion, as, for example, the Mesopotamian

[3] The biblical idiom התהלך את האלהים depicting the relationship of both Enoch and Noah to the deity has been compared lexically and morphologically to the use of Akkadian *ittanallak itti* in a Mesopotamian omen text (Ephraim A. Speiser, "Ancient Mesopotamia," in *The Idea of History in the Ancient Near East* [ed. Robert C. Dentan; New Haven: Yale University Press, 1955], 71 n. 97). Idiomatically, however, the parallel is inexact, in that in the Akkadian text it is the god who "ever accompanies" the pious human devotee, and not the reverse, as in our biblical passages. The difference between the two is in the resulting images: one of a conscientiously ubiquitous divine patron, and the other of a worshipfully ubiquitous human client. In 1 Sam 25:15, as in Gen 5 and 6, the ones who are dependent on the superior power and good will of another "ever accompany" their protective benefactor, human or divine, as the case may be.

hero Atrahasis-Utnapishtim is rewarded by Enlil at the behest of his divine patron, Ea-Enki? Or is there also, perhaps, the suggestion of a divine unwillingness to part with a special favorite, a divine desire, or even a need, to "take" Enoch, as the text has it?[4] The same may be asked concerning the prophet Elijah, who is "zealous" for YHWH and who hears the deity's "soft, sobbing sound," and is likewise "taken" by God. Such emotional vulnerability is surely unthinkable for "the God of the philosophers," but the same cannot be said of the God of Israel.

Taken together, the various portrayals of the deity in the primeval history of Gen 1–11 lay the conceptual groundwork for the patriarchal and Mosaic narratives that follow, and most especially the covenant motif that informs them. That is, by the time one reaches Gen 12, all of the logical preconditions for a covenantal mind-set have been duly established and put in place. First, Gen 1 establishes the existence of the all-powerful deity, whose will is unchallenged and is thus in a position to dictate binding and reliable terms. Second, the same account tells of a divinely exalted humankind, created "in the image of God," to which sovereignty is granted over the creatures inhabiting its world. We have thus been introduced in short order to "the party of the first part" and "the party of the second part," respectively. In the well-known terms of ancient Near Eastern treaty language, there is now a great king presiding over an empire and a quasi-autonomous vassal prince exercising legally defined powers over his own smaller territory. Being a vassal means being subordinate to one who is greater, but it also means being reckoned important and potentially valu-

---

[4] The hero of the Mesopotamian flood stories is not rewarded by being taken to abide with his divine patron, Ea-Enki, but rather is sent elsewhere (and to quite a remote "elsewhere"!), and even that reward seems designed less to elevate the human being and more to humiliate the god's own divine rival, Enlil. The special bond between the divine Ea-Enki and the human Atrahasis-Utnapishtim is actually stressed only in the fragment of the Atrahasis text from Ugarit, where the hero claims *ina bīt ea bēliya ašbāku,* "I resided in the house (i.e., temple) of my lord Ea." In the Atrahasis epic itself (1:366–367, in a restored passage) the divine-human relationship seems to be expressed exclusively in terms of an ongoing dialogue between the two, whereby Atrahasis keeps Ea informed of what transpires (W. G. Lambert and A. R. Millard, *Atra-ḫasīs* [London: Oxford University Press, 1969], 66–67 and 132–33). The admittedly romantic reading of the translation of Enoch offered here, that is, as motivated out of some personal divine desire for his company, or at least his continued proximity, is anticipated in a text belonging to the early Jewish *hekhalot* literature, where God acknowledges: "this (human being) whom I took from among them was the choicest of them all, equal to the whole lot of them in faithfulness, righteousness, and proper deeds; this one I took is My reward from the world beneath the heavens" (Adolph Jellinek, *Bet ha-Midrash* [in Hebrew] [3d ed.; 1872; repr., Jerusalem: Wahrmann Books, 1967]: 5:173).

able enough to merit having been accorded the privileged status of vassal by the great king, as opposed to being annexed outright. Third, Gen 2–3 introduces rules of conduct dictated by God and then, together with the remainder of the primeval history, firmly establishes humankind's accountability before God through stories of precisely, even poetically, meted out divine rewards and punishments (mostly the latter!), even as any royal vassal would bear direct responsibility for his actions vis-à-vis the great king. In the denouement to the biblical flood story, unlike that of any of its ancient Near Eastern analogues, formal precedent is given for the divine initiation of a solemn "covenant" with humankind, repeatedly labeled as such, some seven times in the course of ten verses (Gen 9:8–17). That ancient Israel chose to conceptualize the establishment of divine-human interaction through a metaphor drawn from the living context of contemporary international law and diplomacy offers eloquent testimony as to the vital importance and weighty significance that they and, as they believed, their God accorded to such interaction.

With the patriarchs, especially Abraham and Jacob, the deity's perceived capacity and desire for interpersonal relations with humankind is depicted in more fully developed instances and in more significantly intensified modes of interaction. The calling of Abraham to his destiny in Gen 12, like the creation account before it, is presented as a bald fact, a given, with no hint as to why the deity has initiated the action. We are not told why it was "Abram," and not another, who was called, and, more to the point, why an all-powerful and presumably self-sufficient divine being should choose to choose any human being at all. Yet, in those instances in which it is a human being who makes a demand upon God, as when Abraham seeks some physical sign of confirmation for the divine promise of progeny (Gen 15:8), or when the patriarch intercedes on behalf of Sodom (Gen 18:23–33), the deity generously provides a full and detailed response. Indeed, some glimmer of insight is afforded by God's private musings ("private" from Abraham, but not private from us!) on the imminent destruction of that city:

> Should I really be concealing what I am about to do from Abraham? Abraham, after all, is surely destined to become a great and numerous people, and all the peoples of the earth will be invoking his lot as the very blessing they would seek for themselves. *For I have made him an intimate of mine* [lit., "known him" MT] *so that he would command his offspring, his entire posterity, that they should meticulously follow YHWH's own behavior, by their practicing what is right and just, that I (YHWH) might fulfill for him all that I have promised concerning him.* (Gen 18:17–19)

The above statement of purpose advances the notion that YHWH becomes so involved in human affairs out of the need and/or desire to actualize divine norms of behavior, that which is "right and just" (צדקה ומשפט). The very same divine priority as articulated at the beginning of Israelite history is repeated in connection with the new beginning envisioned for the imperiled Judean kingdom not long before it, in fact, comes to an end:

> The time is coming, says the Lord, when I will establish for David
> a rightful scion, a king who will rule with intelligence,
> and practice *justice and right* in the land. (משפט וצדקה; Jer 23:5)

Leaving aside the precise nature of the divine imperative, the statement of intentions concerning Abraham suggests that, like many a parent, the deity would seem to be intent upon fashioning "chips off the old block," ones who would serve as extensions of the parent and provide gratification by perpetuating parental values. Further, in Gen 18, YHWH's intimacy with Abraham, "knowing" him, not only promotes and predisposes him toward the desired behavior, but helps assure the rewards attendant upon it, revealing a blend of divine self-interest and altruism. By the same token, having been "known" by YHWH and then failing to actualize the divine norms of justice and right brings upon one an especially severe reckoning: "It was you alone, of all the families of the earth, that I have made my intimates [lit., "known"], and so I will hold you to strict account for all your transgressions" (Amos 3:2).

But how far will YHWH go to make sure that human favorites do not disappoint divine expectations and miss out on their reward or, conversely, that those for whom punishment is intended do not evade it by some rapid change of heart? The second part of the question is clearly the more difficult. It is easier for us to accept a kindly deity, ever solicitous for the success of human charges, who stretches the rules just enough to ensure human success, than a deity who will just as actively sabotage human chances for averting disaster. But *both* interventions constitute violations of human free will, a condition for which humankind opted long ago in the garden of Eden and for which we were made to pay a price. In fact, the biblical narrative knows of more cases of divine sabotage than it does of human beings divinely programmed with the *in*-capacity to fall short. Surely the most well-known instance of the former is YHWH's "hardening the heart" of Pharaoh, so that the Israelites would not be released from their bondage at Moses' first requests and that the power of the God of Israel might be revealed to one and all in its awesome might (Exod 7:3–5). Clearly, Pharaoh is being compelled to act against his own best interests, even as Absalom (2 Sam 17:14) and Rehoboam (1 Kgs 12:15) were locked into self-defeating courses of action by a deity determined to bring them to grief. So, too, the Canaanites have their "resolve hardened" by YHWH, so that they would irrationally persist in military encounters that would be sure to spell their doom (Josh 11:20; cf. Deut 2:30), just as Israel and Judah would later be placed in that same unenviable position (1 Kgs 22:19–23). Even something as personal as Samson's preference for Philistine women is likewise stated to have been "from YHWH," in this case being a matter of God's "seeking a pretext against the Philistines" (Judg 14:4). That is, for the rather pleasure-bent, self-centered and patriotically uninspired Samson ever to realize his divinely assigned destiny "to save Israel from the power of the Philistines" (Judg 13:5), he first had to be maneuvered into a situation in which he had a personal animosity toward them and a significant personal score to settle with them; given his special physical prowess, the rest would then take care of itself. Then, there are Hophni and Phinehas, the two sons of Eli the priest, who do not heed the warnings of their father to change their ways "because YHWH desired to bring about their deaths" (1 Sam 2:25). And how disconcerting it must have been for the prophet Isaiah to be ordered to "desensitize (lit., "fatten the heart/mind of") this people, impair their senses (lit., "make heavy their ears and confound their eyes"), so that they can neither see with their eyes, nor comprehend with their ears, nor understand with their mind, lest they reform, and their sorry state be improved" (Isa 6:10). These, and more, are clearly not ideal instances of mutual interaction but rather of unilateral manipulation.[5] The latter is, nevertheless, a regular feature of interpersonal relations anywhere and everywhere, and the deity's acts constitute no exception. But none of these instances of YHWH's having stolen the wits of others is arbitrary, capricious, or personally self-serving. Rather, in most cases, they clearly serve the interests of other human "others."[6] The emphasis in these narratives would thus seem to be less on the deviousness of divine interaction than on the no-holds-barred fervor with which the interests of the deity's beneficiaries are pursued. Once again, theological pronouncements on the

[5] In 2 Sam 24:1 God incites David, against his own better judgment (and that of his ever-shrewd general, Joab), into conducting a census, thus incurring the divine wrath upon the people. The Chronicler, however, seemingly embarrassed by the ethical implications of that manipulation, retells the story with a "Satan" replacing YHWH as the perpetrator of that deception (1 Chr 21:1).

[6] On the motif of the gods' calculated use of externally induced delusions in ancient Greek literature, see now the penetrating analysis in Ruth Padel, *Whom the Gods Destroy* (Princeton, N.J.: Princeton University Press, 1995), which, regrettably, refrains from any comparative discussion of potentially illuminating parallel or contrasting phenomena attested in earlier or contemporary ancient Near Eastern and biblical texts. For a brief, but at times quite suggestive, comparative treatment of this subject, see Robert H. Pfeiffer, "Hebrew and Greek Sense of Tragedy," in *The Joshua Bloch Memorial Volume* (ed. Abraham Berger et al.; New York: The New York Public Library, 1960), 54–64.

inherent nature of the deity are not so much the point here as is the historical depiction of the deity interacting as loyal and concerned covenant partner.

There are, however, a far greater number of biblical instances of less blatant forms of psychological-emotional coercion, which straddle the line between human free will and divine predestination with rather intriguing subtlety. These represent some of the finest achievements of biblical literary art and, in the present connection, some of the most telling texts for the formulation of an interpersonal theology of the Hebrew Bible. For our purposes, it will suffice to consider the dynamics of some of the divine interpersonal relationships in the patriarchal narratives of Genesis. We begin with Sarah and her much-discussed difficulties with her Egyptian maid Hagar. On two separate occasions, this resolute, some would say heartless, matriarch effects Hagar's departure from the household, leaving the latter to suffer a perilous exile in the wilderness. The first such incident, related in Gen 16, provides the opportunity for a divine oracle announcing to Hagar her destiny and, more to the point, the destiny of Ishmael, the son she will soon bear to Abram. The oracle assures the survival of that son and the proliferation of his progeny, but it goes on to depict a future for him that is utterly inconsistent with what one would expect of the heir whom God had earlier promised Abram. Ishmael is destined to be a rough and ready, free spirit of a man, who, like the onager of the steppe, spurns the comforts, and especially the constraints, of civilization.[7] His lot will be one of continual contention, as he takes up life on the margins of society, "facing" (i.e., confronting) his kin, not joining with them. This tenuous and precarious kind of existence is surely not appropriate for the offspring who is to multiply and take full possession of the land as promised. Moreover, the fulfillment of this divine oracle necessarily involves the future estrangement of Ishmael from his kin, the family of Abraham. Yet Hagar is told to return to Abraham's household, where her son is to be born. Obviously, something must take place there that will yield the results that have been foretold, although the precise mechanism for achieving that end is left unspecified.

---

[7] See the delightful vignette in Job 39:5–8, highlighting the carefree existence of the wild ass, to be viewed alongside the contrasting drudgery of its "city cousin," the domesticated donkey, as depicted in Gen 49:14. Yet the "Babylonian Theodicy" singles out the onager for its careless self-indulgence at the expense of others and foresees it as inevitably coming to a bad end (W. G. Lambert, *Babylonian Wisdom Literature* [London: Oxford University Press, 1960], 72–75; cf. 144–145:22, 28). And so, too, Jer 2:24 portrays the wild ass as a sexual hedonist with neither scruples nor self-restraint. In short, Ishmael's having been likened to such a creature is hardly a vote of confidence for an heir apparent.

In Gen 21, after the birth and maturation of Ishmael, Sarah takes even more aggressive steps to expel Hagar together with "her son" (Sarah does not even refer to the boy by name), thus ensuring that her own son, Isaac, will be his father's sole heir. Here, too, a divine oracle speaks reassuringly to Hagar of divine deliverance and blessing. Viewed in succession, and by themselves, these two discrete episodes present contrasting portraits of Sarah and the deity. The deity is depicted as benevolent and solicitous, while Sarah appears as a rather vindictive, self-centered, and callous individual, single-mindedly bent on the undoing of poor Hagar. But, unlike some latter-day readers, the decidedly nonmelodramatic biblical narrator has interposed between the two episodes a scene in Gen 17 critical for understanding Sarah less simplistically—and critical for understanding the dynamics of divine interpersonal relations. In this pivotal scene the deity reveals to (the newly renamed) Abraham that a son to be borne by (the likewise newly renamed) Sarah, and not Ishmael, will become the patriarch's true heir. Conspicuously absent from this scene between God and Abraham, as from the scene between God and Hagar in the wilderness, is Sarah, who (in Gen 21:10) has, nevertheless, arrived at the same position as that ordained by God. That position is first hinted at in the content of the divine oracle of Gen 16:12, then more explicitly stated by the deity in Gen 17:19, and, finally, presented as a divine seconding of Sarah's own words in Gen 21:12: Isaac alone will inherit. Significantly, it is as a direct result of Sarah's behavior that the conditions of the oracle to Hagar (the estrangement of Ishmael from his kin and from "civilized" society in general) as well as the oracle to Abraham (the naming of Isaac as heir) come to be met.

The deity has thus worked *through* the adamant personality of Sarah to actualize the oracles delivered to Hagar and Abraham. The depiction of Ishmael in the oracle of Gen 16:12 as a most unlikely heir to the patriarchal covenant follows, affirms, and, perhaps, justifies Sarai's first attempt to sabotage Hagar's future role as the mother of Abram's future heir. Just so, a divine statement follows, affirms, and now more explicitly justifies her second attempt. There is no indication whatsoever in Gen 21 that God had made Sarah hypersensitive to Ishmael's behavior toward Isaac, behavior that is left so vague (by the use of the multi-purpose root צחק in the D conjugation) that it is clearly not the cause, only a pretext, for Sarah's extreme response. Quite the contrary, Sarai already exhibited the same hypersensitivity back in Gen 16 with respect to the "attitude" of the newly pregnant Hagar, leaving one to conclude from the twofold repetition that this was how and who Sarai/Sarah was. Rather, here is a case where divine and human wills coincide in one and the same result, and the divine will has been put into effect through the actions of a clearly unwitting human agent. Here, God does *not* manipulate the person but rather exploits the existing and perceived situation, so that, just by being herself, Sarah accomplishes a divine objective that she, in fact, believes to be hers alone.

Another instance of employing an oracle to announce divine intention, only to have it realized through what are depicted as clearly independent human actions, presents itself in the story of the even more adamant and resourceful matriarch Rebecca and her own favored son, Jacob. In Gen 25:23, a distraught Rebecca, suffering a rather difficult pregnancy, and characteristically having taken it upon herself to seek a direct oracle from God, is told: "Two peoples are in your womb, two nations will separate out from within your body; one nation will prove stronger than the other, the elder will come to serve the younger." In short order, we are shown the younger twin, Jacob, wresting the birthright from his elder brother. After a brief interval, mother and son, working in concert, succeed in duping Isaac into bestowing the patriarchal blessing intended for the elder Esau upon the younger Jacob. Thus, the divine oracle is well on its way towards fulfillment. And yet, there is no evidence of divine manipulation of any of the human principals in this at once domestic, national, and cosmic drama, causing them to behave differently than they would have otherwise. Prior to the fateful act itself, both Rebecca and Jacob had already revealed themselves as self-assertive individuals, used to taking matters into their own hands. Indeed, Rebecca's innate capacity for independent thought, resolve, and action is several times underscored in the portrayal of her life in Haran, even as she takes it upon herself to inquire of the Lord as the wife of the more passive Isaac.[8] On the other hand, Isaac is incapacitated by old age, although his preference for Esau over Jacob, based as it is on purely gastronomic considerations, suggests that his shortsightedness is something more than simply physical blindness. Esau, likewise a slave to his appetite, had earlier displayed a crudely impetuous nature, coupled with utter disdain for his birthright (Gen 25:34), discrediting him

[8] In Gen 24, Rebecca not only volunteers to water Eliezer's camels, conforming to the prearranged sign he had asked of God (vv. 19, 46), but again independently volunteers what Eliezer has not requested, offering straw and fodder for the animals, as well as accommodations for his spending the night with the family (v. 25, omitted from Eliezer's rehearsal of the events to Laban). So, too, Rebecca is directly consulted on the proposed marriage to Isaac (vv. 57–58), formally blessed by her family (v. 60), and, upon arrival in Canaan, proceeds to conduct herself according to social protocol, alighting from the camel and covering herself with a veil, without need of anyone else's instruction or prompting (vv. 64–65). Thus, her display of initiative in personally seeking a divine oracle (25:22) and her spontaneous formulation and execution of a ruse (down to the smallest details of disguise) to obtain the patriarchal blessing for her favored son, Jacob, are entirely consistent with the depiction of her previous behavior and do not reflect any external control on the part of the deity.

as a fit vehicle for the covenantal legacy, and this well before Rebecca forges her ruse. So, as with Sarah, a matriarch's private determination to advance her son's interests falls neatly in line with a divinely ordained plan and actually effects its realization. Did Rebecca remember the oracle she received during her pregnancy so long ago, or, for that matter, did its true meaning even register in her distracted mind at the time she received it? Yet, it is remarkable that, while we were told precisely why Isaac favored Esau, the narrator shrewdly omitted any such explanation for Rebecca's preference for Jacob, leaving open the possibility of some hidden motivation, hidden even from the matriarch herself (Gen 25:28).

A third oracle account serves to frame the entire patriarchal saga and so bring it to a dramatically as well as a theologically self-consistent conclusion. In Gen 15, Abram receives an initially ambiguous oracle, like the ones operative in the accounts of Sarah and Rebecca, all the more similar in that all three historically decisive divine revelations come not as unilaterally volunteered divine pronouncements, but as direct responses to some manner of petition or posed question. The patriarch is informed that his future progeny will be alien residents in some unspecified land not their own, and there they will be worked and subjugated for some four hundred years, after which their former tormentors will be held to account, while they themselves will take their leave, greatly enriched. The how, what, when, where, and who of this oracle are, of course, to be clarified only at the time of its fulfillment. In Gen 37, some three generations later, the process of fulfillment begins, and the narrator not only refrains from any reference to the oracle itself but engages in a marvel of literary sleight-of-hand, employing indirection and distraction so effectively that one would not even suspect that the long-awaited denouement is at hand.

Implementation of the divine plan for history as revealed to Abram in the oracle of Gen 15 necessitates, first and foremost, a geographical move by Abraham's progeny to "a land not their own." Since the game plan involves moving all of the players from "square A" to "square B," the narrator of Gen 37 obliges with a convoluted but single-minded tale accounting for the eventual relocation of Jacob and his entire family (Abraham's "progeny" as mentioned in the oracle) to Egypt (the "land not their own"), again, never once referring directly to the oracle of Gen 15. As in the two previously discussed cases of oracular fulfillment, *human personality* works hand in hand with a *divine plan,* producing history. But in the more dramatically and conceptually developed narrative of the Joseph stories, we discern more clearly a facilitating factor, *divine providence,* which exerts its own unique influence decisively, if at times almost imperceptibly, over the critical point at which divine and human wills converge. Thus, in the remarkably short space of ten verses (37:2–11) the narrator engages in a kind of motivational overkill, providing more than enough reasons for Joseph's brothers to have reached the point of lethal rage toward their younger brother: (1) tension between brothers who are sons of different mothers; (2) Joseph's having informed on his brothers to his father; (3) Jacob's overtly preferential treatment of Joseph, including the gift of a special garment; (4) Joseph's twice-repeated dreams of preeminence over his brothers, and even over his parents. This veritable school of "red herrings" serves admirably as a distraction from the words of the divine oracle in Gen 15, highlighting the human factor in Joseph's (and, more importantly, Israel's) destiny to the seeming exclusion of any divine input whatsoever.

Yet, still and all, dreams are held to be divine in origin, and while Joseph was not compelled by the deity to share their content with his family, the dreams did, nevertheless, provide the ultimate pretext for the murderous rage of his brothers (Gen 37:19–20). Further, when Joseph is sent by his father to find his brothers, they are only located by means of a rather improbable coincidence: an unidentified man just happened to be in earshot as the brothers reached their decision to move on to another grazing area, and the same man just happened to be on hand when Joseph arrived at their original location and began looking for them. When Joseph finally catches up with his brothers, they might well have acted on their violent impulses and done him in, if not for the timely intervention of another one of those coincidences that are just too convenient to have really been a "coincidence." Thus, the arrival on the scene of a caravan bound for Egypt, just as the brothers are ready to dispose of Joseph, allows for his deliverance and brings the oracle of Gen 15 one step closer to realization. And so Joseph goes down to Egypt, later to be followed by his brothers in response to yet another "act of God," a famine in the land.[9] First Simeon is held in Egypt as a hostage, then Benjamin is on the verge

[9] The symmetry in the Joseph narrative between dreams and famine as hallmarks of the divine participation in human affairs is apparent from the equally lavish verbal repetition accorded to the *Leitwort* of each motif. Thus, verbal and nominal forms of the root חלם, "to dream," appear some twelve times in Gen 37, nine times in chapter 40, and eighteen times in chapter 41. The term רעב, "famine," is repeated no less than thirteen times in chapter 41 alone. A similar coupling of motifs integrates the three "wife-sister" stories, where Gen 12 and 26 feature "famine," while Gen 20 employs a divine dream sequence. So, too, Gen 12 and 20 employ the device of divinely imposed physical disability, while 26 opts for the use of the functionally equivalent motif of "coincidence," whereby King Abimelech just happens to be looking out the window at the very moment that Isaac and Rebecca are visibly engaging in some obviously nonbrotherly and nonsisterly activity. In the book of Ruth, once again, the narrator has recourse to the motifs of famine (1:1, 6) and coincidence (see especially 2:3, lit., "her 'happening-upon' happened upon the portion of the fields belonging to Boaz, a kinsman of Elimelech").

of being held there as a prisoner, which prompts Judah to volunteer to take his place there, and finally, with Joseph's dramatic revelation of his true identity, Jacob joins the remaining brothers in journeying there to take up residence. All the players—the progeny of Abraham—being in place, one now waits for their scheduled servitude and liberation.

So one may well ask, how do Joseph, his brothers, and his father all end up in Egypt, or, more broadly, how do the progeny of Abraham get to "a land not their own," in conformity with the *divine plan?* The insensitivity of Jacob toward his less-favored sons, the indiscretions and self-importance of a young Joseph in dealing with his older half-brothers, the propensity towards violence characterizing the brothers (excluding Reuben and Benjamin)—these are the proximate causes attributable to the autonomous, idiosyncratic workings of *human personality*. The critically timed dreams, coincidences, and famine—these are the settings, the living context, for human behavior afforded by *divine providence*. The integrity of the human personality is preserved intact, free from coercion or manipulation, while the inviolability and inevitability of the divine plan are likewise left uncompromised. What the divine oracle has determined is only the "bottom line," while human character provides the precise means through which that result is obtained, and divine providence facilitates by creating impeccably timed events, opportunities, and challenges in which the two might come together as one.

With respect to the independent workings of human personality, the various mechanisms of divine providence often supply a "turn of the screw," intensifying the situation and raising the stakes, as it were, so that one's true nature will reveal itself, as it often does in crises, "natural" or otherwise. What the famine was to Jacob and his sons in the Joseph stories, it had already been to Abraham and Isaac (Gen 12 and 26), and it would come to be to the family of Elimelech and Naomi (Ruth 1), namely, a divinely employed mechanism to bring about a change in someone's physical location. Famine, the result of the deity's having withheld the rains, serves to move people to the right place, at the right time, so that the right things could happen in fulfillment of a divine promise or plan, even as the people involved react to that crisis in their own distinctively individual ways. The famine in the Joseph stories allowed for Jacob to overcome his patent selfishness in forbidding a return trip to Egypt, even at the cost of Simeon's life, the physical survival of the entire family, and so the realization of God's covenantal promises to the patriarchs. The famine was also the catalyst that ultimately allowed for the expression of Judah's moral regeneration and of Joseph's perception of a divine plan that gave new meaning and coherence to the chaotic, seemingly random events of his earlier life. Thus, the geographical movement occasioned by the famine is directly correlated with biographical movement, that is, psychological, ethical, and/or spiritual growth in the family of the patriarchs, growth that is not forced, but rather allowed to happen.

A striking parallel between divine and human styles of personal interaction is afforded by Joseph's own artificial creation of crises, in the course of which the ethical and moral character of his family is transformed, or allowed to emerge. Thus, Joseph's behind-the-scenes manipulations of the situation (but not of the individuals!) by trumping up charges, taking hostage, and planting incriminating evidence results in the brothers making two trips to Egypt, even as God's famine produces two such journeys. Indeed, Joseph, like God, is in the position of alternately granting and withholding sustenance. The narrator of these stories never explicitly tells us why Joseph is so intent upon seeing his brothers in their true selves, stripped of all that prevented them from being just and right. We may surmise that he needed to know if his brothers had changed, or could change, from what they had been, before revealing his identity to them and effecting both a reunion and a reconciliation. Obviously, the same may be said for the deity, who is said to scrutinize humankind in order to determine whether reward or punishment, rapport or distance, is warranted. Indeed, the symmetry in this narrative between the respective acts of Joseph and the deity imparts a measure of irony to Joseph's earnest protestation: "Am I in God's stead?" (Gen 50:19).

The extent of his own (unwitting) collaboration and identification with the deity notwithstanding, there is still much that Joseph does not understand, even as he undertakes to explain the workings of divine providence to his brothers: "So, it wasn't you who sent me here, but rather God, positioning me as 'father' to Pharaoh, master of his household, and ruler over all of Egypt" (Gen 45:8). But, it *was* Joseph's brothers, and his father, and Joseph himself, who, just by being themselves, made history happen *together with* the deity, the One who rarely works alone but rather works in conjunction with others as "one." As we have seen, it was the individual, characteristic behavior of Joseph, Jacob, and his brothers, in concert with the timely "coincidences" wrought by divine providence, in line with a larger, overarching divine plan, that *together* sent Joseph to Egypt. So, too, it was Joseph's own ethical refusal of Mrs. Potiphar's advances (combined with her lust and her husband's rashness) that landed him in jail, while a "coincidence" wrought by divine providence ensured that it was the right jail, at the right time, so that Joseph might gain access to the corridors of political power in Egypt and thus play a part in the fulfillment of the divine covenantal promise to his ancestor, Abraham. In short, this highly convoluted narrative, like the simpler tales that precede it, consistently understands human beings to be an integral, necessary, even indispensable part of the process whereby divine covenantal promises attain realization.

A much simpler narrative prefiguring the ultimate fulfillment of the Gen 15 oracle is afforded by the story of Jacob. Just as envisioned for the progeny of Abraham in the oracle, Jacob goes to (what is to him) a foreign land, Haran, where he toils in servitude for another, only to leave there greatly enriched by family and possessions. Indeed, the proliferation of Jacob's offspring during this epoch of his life represents the first flowering of God's promise to Abraham. The latter had but one son through whom the covenantal promise might be fulfilled, and, in turn, that son, Isaac, had but one son, Jacob, from whom a great nation might descend. But the birth of Jacob's twelve sons marks the true beginning of the arithmetic process itself, and, like the fall and rise of Joseph, those births manifest the quintessentially biblical intersection and interaction of divine and human wills. For the deity, there is the "bottom line" of multiple births to enlarge the family of Jacob and so to execute the covenantal promise initially made to Abraham. But for the members of Jacob's family, there exist no such overarching, intergenerational, cosmic concerns. For the wives of Jacob there is only the single-mindedly private and personal consideration of competing for, winning, and retaining the favor of their jointly held husband through their own fertility and that of their respective personal maids. The self-centered perspective and objective of the two sisters, Leah and Rachel, thus work unawares toward the realization of the more broadly conceived divine agenda, and what seems, on the human level, to be a rather negative and personally demeaning race to reproduce is, on the divine level, a positive and constructive step along the way to fulfillment. The deity did not turn the two sisters into, at times, bitter rivals, nor was it the deity who "programmed" Jacob's personal preference for Rachel over Leah (unlike the case of Samson and his Philistine women), which initially gave rise to their reproductive rivalry. But so intimate was the divine knowledge of, concern for, and personal stake in this human family, that the most private details of their domestic life could be effectively appropriated and made to serve as the scenic backdrop for a process at once more ambitious and consequential.[10]

---

[10] In the Ugaritic legend of Keret (or Kirta), a divine oracle pronounced at the hero's wedding reception provides that the youngest daughter (and probably the youngest son as well) will ultimately be accorded the legal status of firstborn. Later on, in their young adulthood, the pronounced devotion of the youngest son and daughter and their heartfelt concern for the well-being of their ailing father, as well as the blatant selfishness and even treasonous disloyalty of the eldest son, all work toward ensuring the fulfillment of El's decree, as in our biblical instances of the divine-human partnership in history. It is equally clear, however, that, unlike the case of the Israelite YHWH, the personal stake of the Canaanite god El in this "historical" process is, at the very least, imperceptible. Beyond a touching paternal concern and compassion for his royal client, El seems to have no grand plan in store for the king, nor for his specially elevated offspring, no discernible long-range national-political program, and certainly no cosmic moral vision (as in Gen 17:19). Rather, what we find in the oracle of the Keret legend is more akin to the enigmatic

These selected observations bring us to the end of the book of Genesis, which, in its present position in the canon, functions, in effect if not necessarily by original design, as a programmatic and ideological prologue to the larger biblical story, in which the drama of divine interaction plays out in ever-diversified extrapolations to other eras, events, and personalities. The exodus and wilderness narratives, as well as the Deuteronomistic History, move from the divinely sanctioned (or accommodated) behavior of the patriarchs and matriarchs to a more harshly critical consideration of liberated Israel on its way to the promised land. God's more overt effusions of love and/or outbursts of rage in these subsequent texts may be all the more readily assimilated to an initially established psychological profile of the deity as passionately engaged and concerned with a too-often noncompliant humankind. Further, the intense emotionalism of the prophetic portrayals of the deity, especially as the wronged lover in Hosea and Jeremiah, would be well-nigh impossible for one to accept, even as metaphor, without the kind of intellectual and experiential preparation afforded by the divine-human interactions in Genesis, as subtle, understated, and indirect as they are. With no foreknowledge of the deity as one profoundly and intimately involved with Israel, and so humankind, the whole gamut of divine emotional responses to the people envisioned and represented by the prophets—disbelief, frustration, resentment, rage, regret, pain, chagrin, nostalgia, hope, and more—would appear at best bewildering, at worst madly irrational. So, too, when Lady Wisdom appears in Prov 1, 8, and 9, alternately threatening, reasoning, and cajoling humankind to seek out, accept, and love her, we encounter a figure very much the alter ego of God, for which, once again, we have been prepared by the psychological understanding of the deity implicit in Genesis and its subsequent application in the legal, historical, prophetic, and hymnic texts that now follow it. That psychological understanding posits a divine persona that is scarcely conceivable without active, continual, and emotionally charged interpersonal involvement with humankind, which exists not merely as a habit but as an acutely felt and variously experienced *need* for personal acceptance, vindication, and fulfillment.

Underlying the Genesis narratives is a question begging to be addressed, if not answered, concerning that of divine motivation. Why did the deity create the world of humankind; and why was the subsequent behavior of humankind scrutinized so meticulously; and why was humankind rescued

---

or seemingly inescapable birth prophecies of fairy tales and folklore, ancient and modern alike, with the important difference that the level of religious vision in the Ugaritic composition never rises much beyond that of a royal family drama, on either the personal or dynastic level. For the Keret (Kirta) legend, see now the fine edition and translation by Edward L. Greenstein in *Ugaritic Narrative Poetry* (ed. Simon B. Parker, SBLWAW; Atlanta: Scholars Press, 1997), 9–48.

from possible oblivion in the deluge; and why was one individual, Abram, chosen, together with his offspring, and the nation of Israel, and their Davidic king, to bear the benefits and obligations of an eternal divine covenant? It isn't very difficult to understand why human authors, tracing their descent—be it biological or spiritual—to a son of Noah, and later to Abraham, would want to create and perpetuate stories about their ancestors entailing divine concern and even election. But propaganda, self-justification, and self-gratification aside, what are those authors saying about the nature of God in the process? One traditional answer, of course, appeals to the notion of חסד, or, as it has become better known through the theological lexicon of Christianity, *grace*. However, in light of the manifestly interpersonal nature of God in the Hebrew Bible, so purely unilateral an explanation is clearly insufficient. (I won't go so far as a former student of mine, a ninety-year-old Quaker lady, who confided, "Sometimes I think Grace is just a gal's name.") Biblical literature leads one to the inevitable and inescapable conclusion that the deity, like humankind, is indeed a "social being," and without the society of humankind the deity would remain (like Lady Wisdom in Prov 1, 8, and 9) pure, absolute, infinite potential. Finite and corporeal to a fault, it is only humankind that is suited to "embody" divine norms and intentions and so translate them into actuality.[11] On this point, I cannot refrain from quoting from the stunning "mashal" of my former teacher, Yochanan Muffs, whose inspired insights and gifted sensitivities I have never appreciated more than I do now, some thirty-three years later:

> Once there was a great playwright, the cosmic Shakespeare. And once He saw His whole essence in a play. And the need to bring this play into fruition was an unbearable urge, an expression of His innermost being. But unfortunately, the platonic idea of the play cannot turn into reality without a stage, lights, actors, and an organization.... The play has begun, the actors have appeared, and the dramatist still haunts the wings of the theater, desperately worried about the fate of His play.... Humanity is indeed a partner in this play, for when they observe the Torah, they become partners with God in the act of creation."[12]

---

[11] The eloquent words of Abraham Joshua Heschel are right to the point: "To fulfill the will of God in deeds means to act in *the name of* God, not only for *the sake* of God [emphasis Heschel's]; to carry out in acts what is potential to His will. He is in need of the work of man for the fulfillment of His ends in the world. Life consists of endless opportunities to sanctify the profane, opportunities to redeem the power of God from the chain of potentialities, opportunities to serve spiritual ends" (*God in Search of Man* [1955; repr. Cleveland: World Publishing and Jewish Publication Society of America, 1963], 291).

[12] Yochanan Muffs, *Love and Joy* (New York: Jewish Theological Seminary of America, 1992), 45–46. The mashal, quoted here in part, was originally published

The notion of divine need and human capacity as inextricably bound up together in the historical process survived the biblical epoch and became a recurrent theme in classical rabbinic theological speculation and early biblical interpretation.[13] Indeed, these later incarnations of the idea in Judaism present us with formulations that might well strike the contemporary reader as audacious, if not downright blasphemous. In *Pesiq. Rab Kah.*, Piska 25, Rabbi Azariah (in the name of Rabbi Judah bar Rabbi Simon) proposes that when humankind does the will of God, their actions actually strengthen the deity, while, conversely, failure to do so has just the opposite effect. Indeed, Rabbi Yudan discerns in Num 14:17 the suggestion that divine strength, like that of humans, increases only with exercise, so that, presumably, without the opportunities offered by humankind, God's strength would never, and could never, increase.[14] Elsewhere in the same rabbinic collection (Piska 12), Rabbi Shimeon ben Yohai, explaining (the clearly misdivided MT of) Isa 43:12, goes so far as having God say: "(Because) you are My witnesses, (therefore) I am God," that is, "When you are my witnesses, then I am God; when you are not my witnesses, then, so to speak, I am not God."[15]

So, too, the divine need for human affirmation finds bold expression in *Gen. Rab.* 30:10, as Rabbi Yohanan and Resh Laqish seek to interpret the phrase "the God before Whom our ancestors walked" (Gen 48:15).[16] Rabbi Yohanan compares the deity to a shepherd who stands behind the flock so as to keep a protective watch over them, stressing the human need for the divine presence. Quite to the contrary, Resh Laqish compares the deity to royalty, before whose procession walks an entourage of notables (lit., "elders"), stressing the divine need for a suitably worthy human presence. Thus, according to the one view, by their having "walked before God," the

---

in Hebrew in 1984, but I had the good fortune of hearing it in person in 1965–1966 in one of his uniquely exhilarating classes at the Teachers Institute of the Jewish Theological Seminary. Clearly, my indebtedness to Dr. Muffs's approach in this paper goes far beyond the quoted passage itself.

[13] For a more comprehensive conceptual discussion of some of these and related midrashic passages, see Solomon Schechter, *Aspects of Rabbinic Theology* (1909; repr. New York: Schocken Books, 1961), 33, 80–86, 97–101.

[14] *Pesikta de-Rab Kahana: R. Kahana's Discourses of Sabbath and Festal Days* (trans. William G. Braude and I. J. Kapstein; Philadelphia: Jewish Publication Society of America, 1975), 386–87.

[15] *Pesikta de-Rab Kahana,* 232–33.

[16] Moshe Aryeh Mirkin, *Bereshit Rabbah* (in Hebrew) (Tel-Aviv: Yavneh, 1957), 2:15–16, Parasha 30:10 (end). Note, in the same passage, an interpretation opposite to the one advanced here, viz., that התהלך את represents a less intimate or prestigious rapport (as experienced by Noah) than התהלך לפני (as experienced by Abraham).

patriarchs basked in the divine glory that extended to them, while, according to the other view, it was the deity who basked in the reflected glory of the patriarchs. The editorial juxtaposition of these two contrasting interpretations in the midrash offers, in turn, a third view, pointing the way toward a theology of divine and human interdependence and shared need. Perhaps a more recognizably biblical way of expressing this at once humanistic and theistic insight is suggested by the following reading of Lev 10:3: "It is (only) through (ones who act as) My intimates that My holiness may become manifest, and it is (only) in the presence of all of the people that My splendor may become a reality."

Radical biblical thinkers sought to liberate the God of Israel from all of the physical needs that characterize both mythic and human existence, but they scrupulously left the emotional needs intact and in force, if not intensified by way of compensation: "YHWH is an impassioned God." And being, for the most part, "one" and alone in the divine realm, gratification of God's need for emotional expression, interaction, and fulfillment fell to the lot of humankind, if only by default. It may be spiritually uplifting and edifying to some to see this development as an unqualified affirmation of human worth, even a kind of early "Hebrew humanism." As much as I would like to take my leave of the subject of biblical theology on that happy note, I must confess to seeing, in addition, a darker, more psychologically nuanced side to the matter. If ancient Israel did indeed create God in its own image, then the biblical view of the deity that it advanced, namely, a lone "*one*" ever engaged in a more often than not unsatisfied search for a personally fulfilling "help-meet," offers a sobering, disquieting commentary on the human condition. Some brave Israelite souls once dared look into the abyss of human alienation and disaffection and saw there the face of the living God. Or, perhaps, they dared look into the face of the living God and beheld in it their own unrelieved pain over a congenitally flawed humanity living in an intrinsically imperfect world. To have seen God as essentially alone and in seemingly ever-present emotional need, working through some master plan with human partners not always up to the task, and sometimes in open rebellion, be it out of ingratitude or out of ignorance, requires the vision of a suffering servant, "one rejected and isolated from the company of others, one much pained and an intimate of affliction" (Isa 53:3). Such a vision of God *is not* simply "biblical theology." It is also a profound, albeit unconscious, attempt to confront and wrestle with the less-than-cosmic, all-too-human experience of frustrated visions and failed ideals. Ancient Israelite speculation about God depicts the various attempts of the deity to actualize divine norms and agendas in human history and, indeed, steadfastly insists upon the possibility of their successful realization through any number of different modes of God's direct and indirect personal involvement—in, with, around, and through *others*. But, in telling that story, the Hebrew Bible can hardly avoid telling of the quintessential loneliness and needfulness of being . . . *One*.

Losing a Friend: The Loss of the Old Testament to the Church[1]

Ellen F. Davis

The problem I wish to consider is the functional loss of the Old Testament in the church. Many Christians, both ordained and lay, view the Old Testament as a historical document that is impenetrably complex and morally problematic. Even in evangelical traditions, few pastors, teachers, or preachers feel confident in drawing upon it for theological insight and guidance for their lives. In a word, the Old Testament is ceasing to function as Scripture in the European-American mainstream church with which I am most familiar.

Two "interests" have taken its place, at least in the academies of the church. The first is an antiquarian interest in the religion, social structure, and literary practice of ancient Israel; the second, a political interest in how that society's biases (e.g., its patriarchal character) have, through the medium of Scripture, continued to affect us—the implication being that this is a problem that can be cleared up in our own day. Both the antiquarian and the political interests are valid; yet if that is where our interest in the Old Testament stops, then the text never leaves the academy, and the preacher is rendered mute. And so it is that there is very little serious teaching or preaching from the Old Testament in the (broadly speaking) liberal Protestant, mostly Anglo church.

I do not consider this in the first instance a loss of biblical authority, although that is how the problem is most often discussed (among those who see it as a problem). More fundamentally, it is a loss of intimacy. For many Christians, profound friendship with the Old Testament is no longer a live possibility.[2] This is a metaphor with critical value; it enables us to come to some critical estimation of the kind of influence the Old Testament might exercise on the lives of Christians. Serious friendship (including mar-

---

[1] This is a slightly altered version of an address delivered to the Academy of Homiletics on December 4, 1998, and is forthcoming in *Pro Ecclesia*.

[2] For the metaphor of friendship as a way of conceiving our relationship to a text, I am indebted to Wayne Booth, *The Company We Keep: An Ethics of Fiction* (Berkeley and Los Angeles: University of California Press, 1988).

riage) has the most far-reaching ethical consequences of any interpersonal activity in which we engage, except probably the parenting of young children. Inevitably the choices we make about friendship shape our characters for good or for ill: choices about the people with whom we spend our discretionary time and how we spend it, what we think and talk about, the attitudes we adopt in each other's presence, the confessions we make or the secrets we withhold, the things we hope and work for together. Because of the amount of time and the degree of concentration involved, literary critic Wayne Booth argues that reading books is an ethical activity analogous to time spent with friends.

Booth offers an ethics of fiction. I wish to apply his basic insight to the subject of reading the Old Testament as an ethical activity—in other words, to the subject of befriending the text. What effort would a serious friendship with the Old Testament require of us? What might we gain from cultivating such a friendship? In the second part of this essay, I will look at specific texts in order to illustrate what one might call an "intimate" reading. I give special attention to the pulpit as the primary place where such friendship can be fostered in the church and the first place where the deterioration of that friendship is widely felt. While I believe that the academy, and my own biblical guild in particular, bears grave responsibility for the deterioration, I am not confident that the fire of affection will be rekindled from within the Society of Biblical Literature. So I address these remarks chiefly to those who locate their work within the church, as preachers and teachers.

Willing Readers

It was a comment made to me after I climbed down from the pulpit that marked a nodal point in my own thinking about what is involved in teaching and preaching from the Old Testament. Perhaps eight or nine years ago, as a guest preacher, I preached on the image of Aaron's breastplate of judgment in Exod 28. What I said is in this context less interesting than what the priest who regularly serves the parish said to me when I had finished: "I am so glad you preached on the Old Testament lesson! I never do—I've forgotten too much."

"I've forgotten too much." That speaks volumes about what this woman took away from her biblical education (and she is an honors graduate of a very fine seminary). "I've forgotten too much" to preach from the Old Testament. The implication is that the prerequisite for preaching is a certain kind of knowledge about the Bible, the kind of knowledge you learn for an exam and then forget in the normal course of events (for instance, is this passage J, E, or P?). For the approach I propose here, it is crucial to recall that virtually all the people who have through the centuries regularly, indeed eagerly, preached from the Old Testament have had a quite different idea of what one needs to know in order to do that responsibly. In this group I include some with a very fine historical-critical sense, such as George Adam Smith, Gerhard von Rad, Walter Brueggemann. Almost universally, the good and the great biblical preachers would have said that one must know the Bible directly, through slow and repeated reading, through steady work of teaching and preaching. You learn to preach the Bible truly and well by doing it.

In other words, the Bible is more like a person than an academic subject. You learn about it as you learn about a person with whom you aspire to a deep and profitable relationship: by spending time, a lot of time, listening and taking in a way of being. While you know a certain number of facts about your friend, those facts remain in the background of your awareness most of the time. You can represent your friend responsibly to others because of what you have absorbed, through prolonged exposure, at mostly unconscious levels. You can call to mind and evoke for others a certain characteristic way of looking at the world, of thinking and speaking. And is not just this the preacher's task: to represent the Bible responsibly to the church, to evoke its way of looking at the world in ways that engage the imagination of Christians? We need not worry about convincing anyone it is true; the Bible, if well represented, will take care of that. Our job as preachers is rather to enable people to hear the language of Scripture with comprehension and interest. We must give them a chance to fill their minds with the images of Scripture, its claims and promises and demands.

So, if the preaching task is to represent our friend well, then what is involved in cultivating a friendship with the Old Testament? I suggest that it requires of us three kinds of willingness:

—willingness to risk being "taken in"
—willingness to change
—willingness to deal with the extreme difficulty of the text.

(Probably all I have to say about these three things applies to friendship with the New Testament also, but I confine my examples to the Old Testament.)

Willingness to risk being taken in: by this I mean willingness to enter into a new imaginative world whose presuppositions we do not initially share, some of which are startling and offensive to us. The reason this is required is because in the Old Testament we are dealing with an imaginative construction of reality. Not a false construction— indeed, I am convinced that on all essential points the biblical construction is reliable. But we can enter into this way of seeing the world only through vigorous exercise of the imagination, which is how we must relate to all that is strange and not fully known to us. Another way of putting this is to say that the Old Testament is throughout a poetic text. It uses language to delineate realities not otherwise accessible to us. As C. S. Lewis observes, "No poem will give up its secret to the reader who enters it regarding the poet as a potential deceiver, and determined not to be taken in. We must risk being taken in, if we are to get anything."[3] Lewis was pointing to an aspect of the educational climate that has only become more pronounced in the forty years since he wrote, namely, the tendency to view every book through the lens of other books. We are educated to be critics to the degree that we lose the primary experience of reading: the risky, potentially life-changing experience of entrusting our imaginations for a time to a text. "Criticism," viewed as a style of reading, is a guarded, derivative experience of the text. The opposite disposition toward the text might be termed "generosity." "There must be something in it for me!"—thus George Steiner characterizes the attitude of a generous reader, one who is open to receiving something new and unexpected from the text.[4]

I think it is obvious that this sort of generosity toward the text is only possible where you can be pretty sure that what is in it for you is not abuse and humiliation. Here the important point for teaching and preaching is that if we are to encourage others to befriend the Old Testament, then we must treat it in such a way as to convey respect, by which I mean primarily the text's respect for its hearers. For all its infamous harshness, I believe that the Old Testament accords its readers respect. As evidence for that, I would point first of all to the shape of the canon itself. The Old Testament presents, not a monolithic argument, but rather a multivoiced witness to the nature of Israel's intimacy with God. This is a witness that shows changes in perspective and strong differences in viewpoint, that utters vehement protest even against God. The Old Testament canon does not give us pat formulae for holiness—not even in the much-maligned Priestly material, as we shall see. Rather, the canon, viewed as a whole, forces us to exercise discretion, to test the spirits. The best way to convey the Old Testament's respect for its readers, and also their own obligation of discernment, is to preach and teach widely. Work with texts with which you feel comfortable and those with which you do not, texts that comfort and texts that hurt, texts that bring to the surface deep disagreements within Israel's own understanding of God and the holy life—disagreements the canon does not bother to hide from us.

If the preacher succeeds in making the canon's respect for its hearers felt, then there should follow the second form of willingness that friendship with the Old Testament requires: willingness to change, to think and act differently in response to what we hear from our friend. The New

---

[3] C. S. Lewis, *An Experiment in Criticism* (Cambridge: Cambridge University Press, 1961), 94.

[4] George Steiner, *After Babel: Aspects of Language and Translation* (London: Oxford University Press, 1975).

Testament term for this is, of course, *metanoia,* "repentance," literally "a change of mind." The word denotes the fundamental rethinking of our position that is the practical consequence of being "taken in" by the imaginative world of the Bible and, further, the consequence of learning to read it "against ourselves." This latter phrase is Dietrich Bonhoeffer's. In August 1932, he addressed a church conference in this way:

> We come together to hear Christ. Have we heard him? I can only put the question; each man must answer for himself.... And should some of us now have to say in all honesty: we have heard nothing, and others perhaps equally honestly say: we have heard no end of things, let me express to both groups a great concern which has been bearing down on me with growing heaviness throughout the whole conference; has it not become terrifyingly clear again and again, in everything that we have said here to one another, that we are no longer obedient to the Bible? We are more fond of our own thoughts than of the thoughts of the Bible. We no longer read the Bible seriously, we no longer read it against ourselves, but for ourselves. If the whole of our conference here is to have any great significance, it may be perhaps that of showing us that we must read the Bible in quite a different way, until we find ourselves again.[5]

So we find ourselves, paradoxically, by reading the Bible against ourselves. Reading "against ourselves" happens when we become so vulnerable to the text that it overpowers our natural way of reading. We naturally seek to read the Bible in our own immediate interest, to consolidate our present position; the common term for this is "proof-texting." But the witness of the Bible is that the possibility of a relationship with God depends entirely upon our acquiring the discipline of regularly subverting that first impulse to read "for ourselves." The basic text here perhaps is Josh 24:22: "And Joshua said to the people [at Shechem], 'You are witnesses against your own selves, that you yourselves have chosen for yourself the Lord, to serve him.' And they said, 'Witnesses.'" As Walter Brueggemann has recently shown in a compelling way, the covenant ceremony at Shechem is paradigmatic for how we always stand before God when we read the covenantal text. We stand as potential witnesses against our own selves, as those who confess their own need and will to change, individually and (even more) as a community of faith.[6]

The implication for preaching is grave. If we are preaching effectively from the Bible, then we are steadily, week by week, placing the people

---

[5] Dietrich Bonhoeffer, *No Rusty Swords: Letters, Lectures and Notes 1928–1936* (London: Collins, 1965), 185–86.

[6] Walter Brueggemann, *Theology of the Old Testament: Testimony, Dispute, Advocacy* (Minneapolis: Fortress, 1997).

we serve in a position of extreme vulnerability. We are helping them become alienated from ways they have learned to cope with the world, to cope with their own weaknesses and limits; and that is terrifying. Obviously, inducing such alienation is a genuine service only if we can show them that "the strange new world" (to use Karl Barth's descriptive phrase) that the Old Testament opens up to them is more spacious, ultimately more gracious and forgiving, than the world in which they have hunkered down. Effective teaching and preaching should demonstrate that there are more exciting possibilities for genuinely human life on the other side of a change of mind.

Preachers must make it clear—and stay with the text until they are sure themselves—that willingness to change does not preclude disagreement, questioning, protest, fierce articulations of doubt that may or may not issue directly in the embrace of new possibility. We see the range of freedom of faithful speech especially in the full-blown poetry of the Old Testament: in the Psalms, Job, Jeremiah, Isaiah, also in Ecclesiastes. In each of these books, we see that openness to God involves the confidence to dismiss pious assurances, to challenge God's "M.O." directly. At the same time, taking these books as a whole, we see Israel's acceptance of a challenge coming from God's side, and this makes possible previously unwelcome change: the embrace of new hope or responsibility, the critique of an old position now seen to be inadequate.

The third kind of willingness requisite for friendship with the Old Testament is the willingness to contend with the relentless difficulty of its language. I do not mean Hebrew, at least in the first instance, but rather poetic language—the kind of language that predominates in the Old Testament, including in its narrative portions. Poetic language is necessarily difficult, as George Steiner has brilliantly argued,[7] because it is the business of those who write poetically to traffic in obscurities and uncertainties. In contrast to discursive writers, "poets" (in the broad sense) push us into new ways of thinking by stretching language to its limits, playing with ambiguities, bringing what was hidden to the light and casting a shadow of doubt over what previously seemed obvious. One may express this in traditional theological terms: By means of language the Holy Spirit, who—as John Donne saw—is a poet, moves us to repentance, *metanoia,* to open up new mental space.

But now the question of Hebrew does come in, simply because many difficulties and ambiguities are not evident in translation. The problem here may be more acute with the Old Testament than with the New. I am inclined to think that Greek translates into English with less remainder than

---

[7] George Steiner, "On Difficulty," in *On Difficulty and Other Essays* (New York: Oxford University Press, 1978), 18–47.

does Hebrew, although any translation of a poetic text involves the loss of fruitful ambiguities. At any rate, the advice I give to aspiring biblical preachers is to study both languages, because that is the surest way to gain a sense of the intense excitement of biblical faith, of how the whole canon endlessly begets interpretations that are new, fresh, and good. Here is one small example from my first-year Hebrew class. Genesis 11:1, the first line of the tower of Babel story, reads: "Now all the earth *was* one language and one set of words." I don't know any translation that reproduces that; they all say "*of* one language, *had* one language." But the Hebrew is stranger than that, as one of my students noticed. "The earth *was* one language... "—that is a *reductio ad absurdum,* underscoring the ludicrous consolidation of human population and power in the land of Shinar, a consolidation that God first mocks, then shatters and scatters. The very first phrase tells the story of impossible human pride, if you are moving slowly enough over the text to see it. This example depends on reading the text in Hebrew, but in many cases what you might call the "productive difficulty" of the text is fully evident in English (I'll give an example of that shortly). Yet we customarily read so quickly that we miss it. So I would advise those who do not have the opportunity to work in Greek and Hebrew to memorize some of the texts on which they preach—again, for the sake of slowing down. "Chew the words," as the monastic commentators of the Middle Ages advised. For the words of Scripture are like grains of spice. We must chew them until they release their full savor and sweetness.

Of course, the three categories of willingness I have set forth are not discrete. In the practice of reading the Old Testament, one leads almost imperceptibly to another. I may be struggling with a linguistic or structural problem in the text, sometimes in a highly intellectual frame of mind. Then suddenly I find that I have fallen in deep, that my way of being in the world is called radically into question, or a possibility I never imagined has opened before me. Following are three examples that have surfaced in the last few years of my own reading and have occasioned for me fairly drastic new ways of thinking.

Intimate Readings

The first example is Gen 1:28, the first commandment to the newly minted human beings: "And God blessed them and God said to them, 'Be fruitful and multiply, fill the land [or "earth"] and conquer it, and exercise dominion over the fish of the sea....'" I know of no published translation that does not soften that verb "conquer" (כבשׁ), although the most common use of this verb is in the "conquest narrative" in the book of Joshua. The reason for softening it here is obvious: This is an offensive verse, especially to our ecologically conscious age. People are increasingly aware that this verse has in the last three centuries been used as a proof-text to underwrite wholesale human exploitation of the whole nonhuman creation. We are rightly outraged, but the verse did not make people read it that way. Greed made them do it, and the verse was interpreted in a convenient way. Proof-texting is typically bad exegesis, for it ignores the literary context. Genesis 1 as a whole leaves us in no doubt about God's exacting interest and delight in the whole creation.

The word "conquer" can be misinterpreted, yet it is no mistake. Rather, I want to argue that the Priestly writer is taking a calculated risk. The word is meant to arrest attention and push us to another level of understanding. Consider the whole phrase, verb and noun: "conquer the land, ארץ"—the same Hebrew noun can designate what we would call the planet earth, but more often it refers to a specific territory, usually the land of Israel. "Conquer the land"—that phrase instinctively locates us at the beginning of the history of the people Israel in the land. As the Deuteronomistic Historian tells it, Israel was sent into the land with the "book of the Torah" in hand and mouth (Josh 1:8), to instantiate the divine kingship. Yet that historical "conquest" was no better than a qualified failure. From the second chapter of Joshua, the biblical account is an almost uninterrupted record of Israelite fear, failure, and unfaithfulness to God, told with bitter irony and sometimes just plain bitterness. Israelites in the land regularly look worse than Canaanites; it is telling that there is in fact not a single story of Canaanite wickedness executed in the land. So in Pogo's words, "We have met the enemy, and he is us."

The echo between Genesis and the Deuteronomistic History is unmistakable, when it is translated correctly; and verbal echoes are the means by which the biblical writers regularly correlate events. With the phrase "conquer the land," the Priestly writer is deliberately recalling that sad history of Israel in the land, which had already reached its tragic climax in exile by the time the "book of the Torah" achieved its final form, with this first chapter at its head. Always we must read the Bible backwards and forwards to get an accurate perspective. So here already there is an intimation of self-serving failure at the very moment the human being is created. Like Israel in the land of Canaan, we may fail miserably to make God's benevolent dominion visible in the world.

I suspect the irony in this verse is sharper for us than for any previous generation of Bible readers. From our present historical vantage point, we recognize that the human being created in the image of God has come to look more like a chaos monster. We are, as Rosemary Radford Ruether says, "the rogue elephants of the world," wreaking havoc upon all creation. "Today this Scripture is fulfilled in your hearing" (Luke 4:21). Maybe we need to reassess the Priestly writer, who is normally considered a humorless pedant obsessed with calendars and other cultic matters. Could it be that P stands for

Prophet? For here the P source does what the prophets, including Jesus, always do—namely shock us into seeing our behavior and situation as they really are, seeing ourselves as God must. In a word, then, what a difference it makes if we read the verse over against ourselves, as a dire warning, rather than reading it for ourselves, as a warrant for free exercise of our greed.

A second example of an "intimate" reading of an offensive text: Gen 22, the "sacrifice" or "binding" of Isaac. In my listening experience, the most common way that preachers and teachers attempt to subdue this text is to read it as an etiological narrative of Israel's repudiation of the pagan practice of child sacrifice. The problem with this approach is that in the story itself there is no repudiation of human sacrifice as a grisly abomination. To the contrary, although Isaac is spared this time, God specifically commends Abraham's willingness to sacrifice his darling son. Listen: "And [the angel] said, 'By myself I swear—an utterance of the LORD—just because you have done this thing and have not held back your son, your only one—I will surely bless you and greatly multiply your seed like the stars of the heavens'" (vv. 16–17). The text does not share our scruples; it refuses our offer to rescue it on those "humane" terms. I once saw a preacher, who was honest enough to recognize the problem, throw up his hands and say, "I'm glad I don't worship the God of Abraham!" Another approach is to say that this story is about Abraham's obedience only; we are not meant to read in it anything about God's character. But Genesis is a relentlessly theocentric book. To speak of Abraham here and not of God is to see only half the story, and not even the most important half.

So what might we learn about God from this story? I remember the moment when that dimension of the text opened up for me. My homiletics colleague, Richard Ward, and I were doing a teaching session together, and he recited Gen 22 from memory. In the freshness of that new medium, I heard a verse I had always passed over before, although I do not recall his giving it any special emphasis. Again, the angel of the LORD is speaking: "Do not stretch out your hand to the lad and do not do a single thing to him, for *now I know that you are a God-fearer*, and you did not withhold your son, your only one, from me" (v. 12). If we take those words seriously—and in this narrative not a word is wasted—then we have to believe that there is something God now knows for the first time. (For all its theocentricity, the book of Genesis gives little comfort to the doctrine of divine omniscience.) What God knows now is so crucial that this most terrible "test" (v. 1) was devised, in order to show whether in fact Abraham cares for God above everything and everyone else—even above Isaac, his son and his own slender hope for fulfillment of God's promise.

I spoke earlier of cultivating generosity toward the text, if we are indeed to befriend it. Generosity toward the Old Testament must mean this at least: accepting the text on its own terms, literally, working seriously with the language it offers us. The advantage of this present reading is that it is directed by the words of the passage rather than by an extraneous idea—the immorality of child sacrifice, the omniscience of God—however valid that idea might be in another interpretive situation.

This reading also coheres with the larger narrative context, to which the very first words of the chapter point us: "After these things, God tested Abraham." After what things? Where are we in the history of salvation? At this point, all God's eggs are in Abraham's basket, almost literally. Recall that after the tower of Babel, God gave up on working a blessing directly upon all humankind and adopted a new strategy: channeling the blessing through Abraham's line (Gen 12:3). Our story takes account of that new divine strategy: "And all the nations of the earth will find blessing through your seed, because you heeded my voice" (22:18). God, having been badly and repeatedly burned by human sin throughout the first chapters of Genesis, yet still passionately desirous of working blessing in the world, now consents to become totally vulnerable on the point of this one man's faithfulness. But the narrative has just cast a shadow of doubt over Abraham's total faith in God. Remember those two episodes in which Abraham has Sarah pass herself off as his sister? In Egypt and again in Canaan he lets his beautiful wife go into a king's harem, rather than trusting God to protect them on their sojourn (Gen 12:10-17 and 20:1-18). "After these things, God tested Abraham." After all that, we can begin to understand why God must know for sure whether the single human thread upon which the blessing hangs will hold firm.

Further confirmation of this reading comes from two sources outside the Old Testament, but ones that are helpful for the preacher and teacher to bear in mind. First, it is congruent with what we know of the lives of saints. Those upon whom God most depends for the dissemination of blessing have more difficult lives—there is a lot of evidence for that (among recent examples, Nelson Mandela comes to mind). They must always be prepared to sacrifice what is most dear to them in this world, for that which is dearer yet. A second source of confirmation is liturgical usage. The church has always seen in the binding of Isaac an adumbration of Jesus' passion; the passage is commonly appointed as a Good Friday reading. It is at least doubly appropriate to that occasion: first, as a story of total human faithfulness to God; second, as the story of the father's willingness to sacrifice the "only" son. But if indeed this story testifies to God's extreme vulnerability to human unfaithfulness, then it is triply appropriate. For in Christ on the cross we see the ultimate cost of total faithfulness to God, joined with God's own terrible wounding by human sin.

A third and final example is from the Song of Songs, the ultimate "intimate read" in the Bible. Yet our notion of intimacy has changed in this matter. It is now almost universally agreed that the Song is celebrating human sexuality, intimacy and mutuality between woman and man; and traditional mystical readings are dismissed. Notions that the Song is about the love between God and Israel, as Jews have said, or the love between Christ and the church, are generally regarded as arbitrary with respect to the text and repressive with respect to the audience. Yet consider this: the Song as traditionally understood once generated more preaching, more theological commentary than perhaps any single book of the Bible. Indeed, this reading of the Song was foundational for Christian preaching and biblical interpretation altogether: The first Christian commentary ever written was Origen's *On the Song of Songs,*[8] and his sermons on the Song are among the earliest sermons preserved. The medieval church produced hundreds of commentaries, probably thousands of sermons, inspired by the Song. Now it is virtually never preached; its general usage is to provide a few licit erotic lines at wedding ceremonies. If we have finally found the right interpretation, how is it that we have lost so much preaching ground?

I suggest that the sexual interpretation of the Song, while not wrong, accounts for only a small part of the data. And the data here are, of course, linguistic: the words of the text. One striking thing about the Song is its use of erotic language. Equally striking is the fact that the Song is in large part (erotica included) a tissue of quotes from other parts of Scripture. Phrases from the Prophets, Torah, Psalms abound—and not just scattered words but in many cases connected phrases, vivid images, and terms too specific for their other contexts to be forgotten by those familiar with biblical language. The Song is like an echo chamber, and modern commentators have not taken that seriously enough. We need a more generous interpretation of the Song, one that takes full account of this remarkable resonance. Accordingly, we need a style of interpretation that allows the text to say more than one thing—a truism to the medieval preachers, but strangely lost to us.

I have tried to offer that kind of reading of the Song in a commentary.[9] Here I sketch the basis for the kind of multileveled reading to which I believe the Song is directing us. Of particular note is the fact that much of the Song's memorable imagery, especially the blooming garden, is drawn in language that elsewhere in the Bible describes Jerusalem and the temple. Although this initially seems odd, it is not hard to make the connection when you think about the symbolizing habits of the biblical writers. For the Jerusalem temple is itself designed as a garden. Its ornamentation—cherubim, lilies, pomegranates, flowers—show that this is the stylized garden of God. Moreover, the language of the Psalms (e.g., Ps 36:7) confirms that the temple is Eden revisited, and pilgrimage to the temple is a return to the gar-

---

8 Origen, *The Song of Songs: Commentary and Homilies* (trans. R. P. Lawson; Ancient Christian Writers Series 26; Westminster, Md.: Newman, 1957).

9 Ellen Davis, *Proverbs, Ecclesiastes, the Song of Songs* (Westminster Bible Commentary; Louisville: Westminster/John Knox, 2000).

den from which we were first exiled. In all of the Old Testament, there are only these three prominent gardens: Eden, the temple, and the garden where the lovers take joy. And through the medium of language, the lovers' garden enfolds the other two. The last garden—the Song is a late entrant into the Hebrew Bible—reclaims the others and thus imaginatively reverses untold damage, both primeval and historical. When the poet of the Song evokes the mythos and symbolism of the Jerusalem temple, the Babylonian destruction and the exile are undone. Reaching much further back, when lovers have joy in the garden, all the ruptures that occurred in Eden are healed. Remember, the first disobedience in Eden disrupted the created order at several levels. It made hostile divisions between man and woman, between humanity and nonhuman creation, between God and humanity. Following the path laid down by the language of the Song, we experience each of those ruptures as healed. Man and woman now meet in full mutuality. Most obviously, there is a reversal of the primeval curse: "Toward your husband will be your desire, but it is he who will rule over you" (Gen 3:17). Now we hear the Shulammite (Song 7:1) exult in almost identical terms: "I am for my darling, and toward *me* is *his* desire!" (Song 7:11). At another level of healing, the soil that once sprouted "briars and thorns" (Gen 3:18) now brings forth flowers and fruit with an inhibition that mirrors the lovers' own. As for the rupture between God and humanity—I believe the Song testifies strongly, albeit obliquely, that through the medium of the Song, we may meet God as Lover, as the mystics have always known. This is finally how we must understand such extensive use of language that normally attaches to Zion and its temple. We are meant to see here the healing of the rupture between God and humanity, for the temple is above all the place where heaven and earth meet and are reconciled, where paradise is restored. When the lovers, having overcome external opposition and also their own ambivalence, meet in the garden, then every terrible exile, from Eden and Jerusalem, is reversed.

I have some hope—flickering hope perhaps—that preaching may yet prove to be the vehicle whereby the fuller sense of the Song is restored to the church. This is why I have hope: A colleague of mine, a very fine Old Testament scholar, recently took on the task of preaching the Song of Songs—at a wedding, I believe. He began with the standard critical assumption about the meaning of the Song. Yet to his surprise, he discovered that he could not help speaking, not only about human love, but also about the love between God and Israel. How are we to account for that? In my view, the simplest and best explanation is the traditional one: this is the work of the Holy Spirit inspiring the preacher, opening to him the *sensus plenior* ("fuller sense") of the text in response to his generosity, his own openness and desire to be "taken in" to its imaginative world. May his tribe increase.

Part 1:

Theoretical Perspectives

Section 2:

Mostly Methods

Biblical Theology Appropriately Postmodern

Walter Brueggemann

Even so classic a scholar as Horst Dietrich Preuß can begin his Old Testament theology with this personal disclaimer, surely unthinkable in an earlier generation:

> Each effort to set forth an overview carries with it some of the personal idiosyncracies or peculiarities of the author. This means that the present investigation contains my own peculiarities and weaknesses and reflects both the character and the limits of my knowledge.[1]

A New Context for Theological Interpretation

Such a disclaimer is representative of a quite new situation in Scripture interpretation, which reflects what may be conveniently termed a "postmodern context."[2] By that I mean simply the loss of hegemonic privilege among Christian interpreters or, alternatively, among the "ruling class" of critical scholars. This new post-hegemonic situation both permits and requires biblical theology to be done differently.

On the one hand, it requires Christian interpreters to notice for themselves a new interpretive position that no longer claims the field. Jon Levenson has well documented the supersessionist triumphalism of Christian Old Testament theology in times past.[3] The primary models of Gerhard von Rad and Walther Eichrodt are not the most offensive examples of supersessionism, but they do roughly participate in the Euro-Christian assumptions of transcendence, and with it the capacity to set forth a singular, comprehensive model for Old Testament theology that serves both the theological and cultural interests of

---

1 Horst Dietrich Preuß, *Old Testament Theology* (2 vols.; Louisville: Westminster/John Knox, 1995), 1:1.

2 See my discussion of the problems and possibilities of a new interpretive context, Brueggemann, *Texts under Negotiation: The Bible and Postmodern Imagination* (Minneapolis: Fortress, 1993).

3 Jon D. Levenson, "Theological Consensus or Historicist Evasion? Jews and Christians in Biblical Studies," in *Hebrew Bible or Old Testament? Studying the Bible in Judaism and Christianity* (ed. Roger Brooks and John J. Collins; Christianity and Judaism in Antiquity 5; Notre Dame: University of Notre Dame Press, 1990), 109–45.

Christian domination. My impression is that Childs's canonical perspective seeks to continue that enterprise, but with only limited success.[4]

Any Christian biblical theology in this new depositioned locus must, in my judgment, lower its voice in order to recognize that it is one of many closely contexted participants in a quite open interpretive conversation, and may expect to be instructed by many other voices, not only Jewish, but other Christian interpreters in other social locations. I do not expect for myself or others to give up a Christian locus of interpretation, nor to cease to claim Hebrew Scriptures as authoritative for Christian faith, but I do expect that our long-standing assumption of privileged or dominating interpretation to be abandoned.

Conversely, the dislocation of Christian privilege in interpretation may permit renewed participation in a shared conversation of Jewish voices in what passes for biblical theological interpretation. Jon Levenson has made clear "Why Jews Are Not Interested in Biblical Theology."[5] I take Levenson's summary to be a fair representation of a mode of biblical theology that has prevailed in times past. And none can fault the negative conclusion Levenson draws of that enterprise. A new interpretive situation, however, may permit Jews back into common interpretive enterprise, as is evidenced in the judgment of M. H. Goshen-Gottstein.[6] Clearly such a participation, represented now in powerful ways by Levenson himself, does not proceed according to the long-privileged categories of Christian dogmatics, but more nearly permits the categories of interpretation to arise from the text itself.[7]

The depositioning of Christian interpretation and the renewed entry of Jewish interpreters into a shared interpretive conversation may be based in a now widely shared recognition that the text of Hebrew Scriptures is pro-

---

[4] See my comments in a review of Carl E. Braaten and Robert W. Jenson, eds., *Reclaiming the Bible for the Church* in *Theology Today* 53 (1996): 349–53.

[5] Jon D. Levenson, "Why Jews Are Not Interested in Biblical Theology," in *The Hebrew Bible, the Old Testament, and Historical Criticism* (Louisville: Westminster/John Knox, 1993), 33–61.

[6] M. H. Goshen-Gottstein, "Tanakh Theology: The Religion of the Old Testament and the Place of Jewish Biblical Theology," in *Ancient Israelite Religion: Essays in Honor of Frank Moore Cross* (ed. Patrick D. Miller Jr., P. D. Hanson, and S. D. McBride; Philadelphia: Fortress, 1987), 617–44.

7 Levenson's writings are impressive examples of biblical theology, albeit not in the conventional categories of the conventional Christian discipline. See *Sinai and Zion: An Entry into the Jewish Bible* (New York: Winston, 1985); *Creation and the Persistence of Evil: The Jewish Drama of Divine Omnipotence* (San Francisco: Harper & Row, 1988); and *The Death and Resurrection of the Beloved Son: The Transformation of Child Sacrifice in Judaism and Christianity* (New Haven: Yale University Press, 1993).

foundly plurivocal and does not admit of settled, enforceable larger categories.[8] This reality in the text of course has long been recognized in Jewish interpretation that proceeded—since the ancient rabbis—by way of commentary, as distinct from a Christian propensity to systematization. This plurivocal quality intrinsic to the text is now deeply reflected in pluralism in interpretation: a plurality of methods, a plurality of interpreting communities, and a plurality of provisional grids of interpretation, all of which are reflected in the work of the Society of Biblical Literature. The plurality is reflected in Preuß's opening disclaimer, which would have been unthinkable in the high days of Christian hegemony.

Leo Perdue has nicely suggested that the departure from hegemonic interpretation (my formulation, not his) is evidenced in a departure from *history* as the controlling category of interpretation.[9] It is, moreover, clear that the mesmerization of history is a peculiarly *modern* commitment, in which Christians have been deeply implicated.[10] The departure from "history" reflects a departure from modernist domination and, as Perdue makes clear, opens the way for other perspectives, notably hermeneutical enterprises concerned with narrative, metaphor, imagination—all inviting open-ended playfulness. The cruciality of such "playfulness" is that it does not insist upon conformity and leaves room for conversation among those who share much but who differ greatly.

Interpretive Themes Endlessly Processive

Acknowledging the plurivocal quality of the text, and consequently of the interpretive enterprise, one must nonetheless recognize that "theology of Hebrew Scripture" is in some way—hopefully a self-aware and self-critical way—engaged in the process of thematization. Thematization is an attempt to notice claims (truth claims, normative claims, substantive claims) that are larger than the individual text.[11] There is no doubt that any thematization runs the risk of reductionism, and no doubt that thematization is a greater propensity for Christian interpreters than it is for their Jewish coun-

[8] See Mark Coleridge, "Life in the Crypt or Why Bother with Biblical Studies," *Biblical Interpretation* 2 (1994): 139–51.

[9] Leo G. Perdue, *The Collapse of History: Reconstructing Old Testament Theology* (OBT; Minneapolis: Fortress, 1994).

[10] On the decisive role of memory in a Jewish notion of history, see Yosef Hayim Yerushalmi, *Zakhor: Jewish History and Jewish Memory* (Seattle: University of Washington Press, 1982).

[11] Jon D. Levenson ("The Eighth Principle of Judaism and the Literary Simultaneity of Scripture," in *Hebrew Bible,* 62–81) has presented a study of Jewish modes of thematization that is closely paralleled to what Brevard Childs terms a "canonical" perspective.

terparts.[12] Having recognized both of these factors, "theology of Hebrew Scripture" in my judgment is an enterprise of thematization, and it is such thematization that evokes not only the problematic of this volume but also the interest, inventiveness, and interplay that enlivens the discipline.

At the same time, every thematization is bound to fail because the text finally refuses thematization. The text is saturated with disjunctions and contradictions that mark it as an endlessly deconstructive enterprise, and therefore our thematizations are likely to be quite local and quite provisional. Indeed, my judgment is that past thematizations pose problems precisely because these past interpreters rarely notice the local and provisional character of their work and come to regard such work as universal and enduring. It is easy to see, for example, that Eichrodt's thematization around the theme of covenant was pertinent to a time and place preoccupied with national socialism in Germany, but we have more recently had to unlearn much of covenant. Von Rad's thematization is of course more open to an ongoing dynamic of the traditioning process, but in his own final work, *Wisdom in Israel,* von Rad himself has had to recognize the inadequacy of the thematization of historical traditions on which he had spent his primary energy.[13]

As with Eichrodt and von Rad, so much more so with some lesser attempts. In my own effort at theological interpretation, I have concluded that it is impossible to find a substantive thematization that is sufficiently comprehensive.[14] Either the thematization is so specific that it omits too much, or it is so inclusive as to be meaningless.

The primary interpretive move I have made, as a result, is to decide that the interpretive thematization I will pursue is not *substantive* but *processive.* That is, the theological substance of Hebrew Scripture is essentially a theological process of vexed, open-ended interaction and dialogue between the Holy One and all those other than the Holy One.[15] In this dialogic transaction it is not possible to specify in large categories much substantive about the Holy One, though one may enumerate the usual inventory of actions and attributes. Conversely not much can be said in

---

[12] David R. Blumenthal, *Facing the Abusing God: A Theology of Protest* (Louisville: Westminster/John Knox, 1993), has most unambiguously offered an example of reading *seriatim,* an approach at the greatest remove from any "canonical" reading.

[13] Gerhard von Rad, *Wisdom in Israel* (Nashville: Abingdon, 1972).

[14] Brueggemann, *Old Testament Theology: Testimony, Dispute, Advocacy* (Minneapolis: Fortress, 1998).

[15] To speak of "interaction and dialogue," of course, is not far removed from classic notions of covenant, except that my terms mean to suggest a much more open and less structured I-Thou relation that is filled not only with attentiveness of each partner to the other but also with abrasion and disjunction.

large categories about the other party to the transaction (variously Israel, creation, human persons, the nations). The most one can do is to notice, in particular texts, the processes there underway between the parties. In large, the *hermeneutical claim* that interests me is that *dialogic* transactions offer a crucial alternative to Cartesian positivism.

More specifically, I have adopted the juridical language of testimony to suggest that the text is *witness* to that rich and varied transaction. The witness, a category that brackets out all questions of being (ontology) and all questions of happening (history), proceeds in a dialectic of *core testimony* and *counter testimony*. By "core testimony" I refer to the articulation of basic claims made for the Holy One that are characteristic over time and through the text that in general are affirmative. But as in any serious juridical struggle for "truth," that core testimony is immediately under scrutiny and assault in cross-examination ("counter testimony"), whereby fresh evidence and new probing questions are put that expose the core testimony as not quite so full, so sure, or so compelling as at first glance.

I suggest three rubrics that I would pursue in this dialectic process of testimony:

1. *Covenant and Exile*. The covenant, rooted in either the ancestral narratives or in the Sinai materials, attests to an enduring relationship between a trustworthy God and a responsive community.[16] There are of course variations in the articulation of covenant. The Abrahamic covenant appears to be "less conditional" than the Mosaic, the Noachic more comprehensive than either that of Abraham or Moses.[17] But in all cases and in each case, the relationship is demanding and reassuring.

The pivotal focus of the Hebrew Scripture on exile, however, destabilizes the assurances of covenant. Even if we regard the exile as a partisan, fictive construct rather than a historical event, it is clear that exile—which may be seen as punishment or as enraged abandonment—poses deep questions for covenant. And while enormous theological assurances arise from within exile, it is evident that the texts are not so sure or so simple or so neat as if the exile had not "happened."

2. *Hymn and Lament*. It is clear that the hymnic traditions, reaching all the way back to the Songs of Moses and Miriam, set out the base-line of Israel's faith. Indeed, these sweeping doxologies, rooted in particular trans-

---

[16] For a fine theological summary of the significance of covenant, see Ernest W. Nicholson, *God and His People: Covenant and Theology in the Old Testament* (Oxford: Clarendon, 1986).

[17] On the cruciality of the Noah covenant for biblical theology, see Patrick D. Miller, "Creation and Covenant," in *Biblical Theology: Problems and Perspectives* (ed. Steven J. Kraftchick et. al.; Nashville: Abingdon, 1995), 155–68.

formations, constitute Israel's core testimony about the goodness, fidelity, and power of Yahweh.[18] But every interpreter of Scripture knows that the core testimony of hymns is endlessly accompanied by lament and complaint, which subvert the great doxological claims. Indeed, Israel's relentless tradition of complaint finds a way of destabilizing every grand positive claim.

On the one hand, it is evident that these witnesses refused to lie in order to protect the Holy One, or to deny their own experiences of negation. They insisted not only on their experiences of negation as the truth of their life. But they also insisted that the Holy One must be drawn into and subjected to the circumstance of suffering and negation. Indeed, Jacques Derrida goes so far as to suggest that justice—in the world and from God—is undeconstructable and therefore more ultimate than God.[19] The vigor of the complaints suggests that God is held to a norm of justice by ancient Israel.

On the other hand, in biblical interpretation and in theological reflection, Christians have much for which to answer in their disregard and refusal of this aspect of biblical disclosure and this aspect of human reality. Indeed, Christians are much more inclined to lie and to deny for the sake of "protecting God." It is my judgment that recent attention to complaints and laments in Christian interpretive conversations is both required and permitted by the end of cultural hegemony.[20]

It is beyond doubt that such a posture of "counter testimony" undermines and destabilizes the seemingly safe claim of the hymns. And therefore I suggest that the dialectic of hymn-complaint, as a mode of core and counter testimony, is a characteristic process of biblical theology.

3. *Presence and Theodicy*. In yet a third way I identify the governing dialectic of this material. There is no doubt that the presence of the Holy One is decisive for Israel's faith. This is evident in the promise of accompaniment of Abraham. It is the source of dispute with Moses in Exod 33, and it is the assumption of Israel's temple traditions.[21] This is none other than "The Holy One in your midst." In a variety of ways these texts bespeak presence. A more systematic extrapolation makes a parallel

---

[18] On doxology as data for biblical theology, see Walter Brueggemann, "Praise and the Psalms: A Politics of Glad Abandonment," in *Psalms and the Life of Faith* (Minneapolis: Fortress, 1995), 112–32.

[19] On the judgment of Derrida, see John D. Caputo, *Demythologizing Heidegger* (Bloomington: Indiana University Press, 1993), 201–2.

[20] See the discerning study of Patrick D. Miller, *They Cried to the Lord: The Form and Theology of Biblical Prayer* (Minneapolis: Fortress, 1994).

[21] See Walter Brueggemann, "The Crisis and Promise of Presence in Israel," *HBT* 1 (1979): 47–86; and Tryggve Mettinger, *The Dethronement of Sabaoth: Studies in the Shem and Kabod Theologies* (ConBOT 18; Lund: Gleerup, 1982).

point about creation, for God is, as Eberhard Jungel asserts, "The Mystery of the World."[22]

There is no doubt that God's presence is problematized in Hebrew Scripture. Samuel Terrien had recognized this in his modifier "elusive." Indeed Terrien's splendid discussion is permeated with the recognition that the God of Israel is *Deus Absconditus*. In his first page, Terrien asserts, "Indeed, for most generations of the biblical age, Israel prayed to a *Deus Absconditus*."[23] But of course even that acknowledgement does not go far enough. Israel is given finally to theodicy, to the question of God's reliability, God's presence, God's willingness to be connected to Israel. The issue surfaces in many places, but of course most dramatically and powerfully in the book of Job. It is clear, moreover, that the resolution of the Joban question in 42:6 is fogged at best, perhaps a characteristic move in this tradition of affirmation.[24]

It is my judgment that in these several ways—*covenant and exile, hymn and lament, presence and theodicy*—and in many other ways that could be named, we are able to see the characteristic and definitional processes about which this testimony is concerned. And because there is this endless destabilizing—required by the bodied truth of lived experience—no large claim for the Holy One of Israel can be made except locally and provisionally. The classic tradition of Christian interpretation has been uneasy with such a disclosure and so has felt obligated to skew the evidence.

Interpretation That Refuses Closure

It seems clear to me—and definitional—that this way of testifying to the Holy One of Israel is endlessly dialectical. As soon as one voice in Israel says it is so, another voice, or the same voice in a second utterance, is sure to counter the claim. What I think is most important for future shared work in Jewish and Christian interpretation is the recognition that the Christian tradition of interpretation has a deep propensity to give closure, to end the dialectic, to halt the deconstruction, and to arrive as quickly as possible at affirmation. Thus, characteristically, *covenant* is an enduring claim through and in exile, complaint characteristically ends in *doxology,* and *presence* will always trump theodicy. Well, yes and no. Yes, one can make such a case. But

---

[22] Eberhard Jüngel, *God As the Mystery of the World: On the Foundation of the Crucified in the Dispute Between Theism and Atheism* (Grand Rapids: Eerdmans, 1983).

[23] Samuel Terrien, *The Elusive Presence: Toward a New Biblical Theology* (San Francisco: Harper & Row, 1978), 1.

[24] On the verse, see Jack Miles, *God: A Biography* (New York: Knopf, 1995), 425 n. 324.

no, one cannot clearly make the case. And even if one could, the lived reality of the interpreting community knows better. The community has always known better, even if the decisive learning for us all now is the Shoah.

Church interpreters of Hebrew Scripture, in my judgment, must resist the Christian propensity to closure. I am not clear why the pressure to closure is so strong a Christian propensity. It is perhaps the drive to Constantinian hegemony, which cannot tolerate instability and openness. Or it is perhaps the reasonableness of the Hellenistic traditions of interpretation, which refuses ambiguity. But now Christian interpreters are increasingly emancipated from the needs of political and intellectual hegemony. We have known for a long time, moreover, that this tradition of testimony sits ill at ease with Hellenistic reasonableness.

Thus, postdomination interpretation of Hebrew Scripture is now situated to proceed without undue or premature closure. The closures to which we are tempted are of two kinds. First, it is to give closure that is *affirmative:* Finally God is gracious. All is well and all will be well. This temptation is enhanced by "therapeutic culture." Second, it is to give closure that is *christological:* Jesus fulfills all.

If, however, it is definitional in this material to resist closure, then Christian theology of the Hebrew Scriptures cannot afford innocent affirmation because neither text nor life is like that. If it is definitional in this material to resist closure, then Christian theology of the Hebrew Scriptures cannot be afforded an innocent, triumphal run to Jesus. As an alternative to that, interpretation in my judgment must attend to the endless dialectic of affirmation and negation, and must attend to the ways in which the text is open to a Jesus-reading as it is open at the same time to other faithful, responsible readings. A Christian theology of Hebrew Scriptures may present the materials for Christian reading, but only an offer and not a direct hookup.

It is clear to me that the deconstructive dialectic of the Hebrew Scriptures is indeed characteristically and intransigently Jewish in its openness to ambiguity and contradiction, as is reflected in midrashic interpretation, in Freudian depth psychology, and in the haunting interface of modernity and Shoah.[25] More than that, it is clear to me that a dialectic deconstruction belongs to the quality of the truth that is revealed here to which Israel testifies. The Only One of Israel is not innocently "omnipotent, omnipresent, and omniscient," as too much Christian theology has insisted, but is a God present with and absent from, a God to be praised in full adoration and assaulted as an abuser.[26]

---

[25] On the linkage of the Shoah and modernity, see Zygmunt Bauman, *Modernity and the Holocaust* (Ithaca, N.Y.: Cornell University Press, 1989).

[26] On this dialectic in the character of God, see Blumenthal, *Facing the Abusing God.*

The loss of hegemony in Christian theology invites a deep Christian rethink in these matters.[27] I suspect that what is to happen in the Christian connection is the recovery of the cross as *a symbol and mode of deconstruction* that is the pivot of faith and that lives in ongoing, unresolved tension with Easter. It is clear that in Christian reflection Easter does not put Friday to rest. And therefore a serious reader of Christian faith makes the deconstructive dialectic of Hebrew Scripture an inescapable habit.

By accenting such a deconstructive dialectic, I mean to give no comfort to dismissive skeptics who have given up on the theological seriousness of the Hebrew Scriptures. One would end in such easy skepticism if the deconstruction were only one step toward negation. But of course it never is only one step in Hebrew Scriptures. Because in turn the negation is also regularly deconstructed with new affirmation. And it is the full dialectic that Israel endlessly enacts in its testimony.

Contextual Readings amidst Large Common Crises

I do not wish to minimize or deny the divisions and distinctions that separate Jews and Christians in our interpretive responsibility. Least of all do I want to minimize the historic asymmetry of Christian domination and Jewish suffering. It is my judgment that, important as they are, most of these differences and divisions stem from cultural, historical, and political realities propelled by Christian hegemony and domination, which has produced not only anti-Semitism and supersessionist interpretation but also a serious misconstrual of our own tradition.

If it is the case, as I have suggested, that the Hebrew Scriptures are plurivocal and refuse closure, then conventional Christian closure (or any responding Jewish closure as a means of defense) is unfortunate and beyond the allowance of the text. I do not then concede to Childs that Jews and Christians read different Bibles, nor do I grant the same point when made from a Jewish perspective by Levenson.[28]

My own angle on interpretation is that we read together a testimony to the Elusive One who is endlessly rendered and rerendered, around whom has gathered a rich inheritance of testimony, consisting in image, metaphor, and narrative—acts of imaginative construal that admit of no single reading but that generate many possible futures.

---

[27] See the important study of R. Kendall Soulen, *The God of Israel and Christian Theology* (Minneapolis: Fortress, 1996).

[28] See Brevard S. Childs, *Biblical Theology of the Old and New Testaments: Theological Reflections on the Christian Bible* (Minneapolis: Fortress, 1992), 25–26. See Levenson, "The Eighth Principle," 80 and passim, from where I understand him to be in essential agreement with Childs.

Like every interpreter, I read locally and provisionally. I read with certain habits and interests, as a tenured, white Christian male. All of my companion readers also read locally and provisionally. No apology for local, provisional reading. Apology is to be made for the cultural seduction of forgetting that our reading is local and provisional and imagining it is total and settled. That seduction, very strong in hegemonic Christianity, leads me to read only in isolation or in the company of other readers like myself. Precisely because the text advocates, sponsors, and insists upon many readings, my local, provisional reading must perforce be done in the presence of other serious readings—not white, not male, not tenured, not Christian—that endlessly subvert my own preferred reading.

Such a process, which evidently goes on within the text itself, does not lead to a new theological synthesis or harmonization. It leads rather to a human community in which every reading may be heeded and valued, but done in endless jeopardy, knowing that another text, another testimony, another reading will question my best truth.

I do not believe for an instant that critique of Christian supersessionism is misguided. I do not believe, moreover, that canonical reading in the Christian community is the wave of the future precisely because it continues old hegemonic assumptions. But I also do not believe that Christian reading by definition is wrong reading. A Christian claim of an exclusively right reading (like any exclusive Jewish claim of right reading) fails to take into account the elusiveness that is at the heart of the disclosure. And therefore it is my judgment that Jews and Christians may indeed read together as we wait together. I anticipate no easy overcoming of long habits of abuse and exclusivism. But I am sure that our sense of waiting matters to how we read. Martin Buber has said so well of our waiting:

> What is the difference between Jews and Christians? We all await the Messiah. You believe He has already come and gone, while we do not. I therefore propose that we wait Him together. And when He appears, we can ask Him: Were You here before? And I hope that at that moment I will be close enough to whisper in his ear, "For the love of heaven, don't answer."[29]

Finally, however, my concern is not simply that Jews and Christians may make common cause in reading. In the end, I believe the risk of our reading-while-we-wait is situated in a much larger crisis. Our larger cultural crisis suggests that the reference point for theological interpretation of Hebrew Scripture concerns the biblical chance for humanness of a dialec-

---

[29] Quoted without citation by Elie Wiesel, *Memoirs: All Rivers Run to the Sea* (New York: Knopf, 1995), 354–55.

tical kind that stands over against the flat, one-dimensional option of technological society. The intramural differences among us Jews and Christians in our several reading traditions are as nothing when set in the context of the loss of humanity that issues in uncurbed brutality. No doubt the Hebrew Scripture is about the Holy One of Israel, but there issues from it a chance for humanness given nowhere else, albeit mediated through post-Hebrew Scripture literatures of Jews and of Christians. And that should summon us to our shared, disputed reading.

In my judgment George Steiner has it right when he takes the deconstructive moments of Friday and Sunday and links them to the larger human crisis:

> There is one particular day in Western history about which neither historical record nor myth nor Scripture make report. It is a Saturday. And it has become the longest of days. We know of that Good Friday which Christianity holds to have been that of the Cross. But the non-Christian, the atheist, knows of it as well. This is to say that he knows of the injustice, of the interminable suffering, of the waste, of the brute enigma of ending, which so largely make up not only the historical dimension of the human condition, but the everyday fabric of our personal lives. We know, ineluctably, of the pain, of the failure of love, of the solitude which are our history and private fate. We know also about Sunday. To the Christian, that day signifies an initiation, both assured and precarious, both evident and beyond comprehension, of resurrection, of a justice and a love that have conquered death. If we are non-Christians or non-believers, we know of that Sunday in precisely analogous terms. We conceive of it as the day of liberation from inhumanity and servitude. We look to resolutions, be they therapeutic or political, be they social or messianic. The lineaments of that Sunday carry the name of hope (there is no word less deconstructible).
>
> But ours is the long day's journey of the Saturday. Between suffering, aloneness, unutterable waste on the one hand and the dream of liberation, of return on the other. In the face of the torture of a child, of the death of love which is Friday, even the greatest art and poetry are almost helpless. In the Utopia of the Sunday, the aesthetic will, presumably no longer have logic or necessity. The apprehensions and figurations in the play of metaphysical imagining, in the poem and the music, which tell of pain and of hope, of the flesh which is said to taste of ash and of the spirit which is said to have the savour of fire, are always Sabbatarian. They have risen out of an immensity of waiting, which is that of man. Without them, how could we be patient?[30]

---

[30] George Steiner, *Real Presences* (Chicago: University of Chicago Press, 1989), 231–32. The Friday-Saturday-Sunday sequence is decisive for the theology of Hans

Ours is a Saturday work. I suggest that, before this irascible One embedded in this elusive text, all our reading is Saturday reading.

Urs von Balthasar, *Mysterium Paschale: The Mystery of Easter* (Edinburgh: T&T Clark, 1990). Von Balthasar characterizes the three days as 1. "Going to the Cross," 2. "Going to the Dead," and 3. "Going to the Father."

The Emergence of Jewish Biblical Theologies

Tikva Frymer-Kensky

At one time, not too long ago, writing on "Jewish biblical theology" would have been considered unthinkable. It was a truism that Jews don't do theology, and the long roster of distinguished Jewish theologians of the twentieth century, Hermann Cohen, Martin Buber, Franz Rosenzweig, Abraham Joshua Heschel, Mordechai Kaplan, and Emanuel Levinas (to name only the most prominent), did nothing to dispel this axiomatic understanding. Somehow, each of these theologians was considered an aberration and, at any event, more a "philosopher" than a "theologian." Jews, after all, didn't do theology.

As strange as the concept of Jewish theology may have seemed, at least there were some writers who wrote "Jewish philosophy." The enterprise made some sort of sense, and the negative Jewish reaction to the concept of Jewish theology was mostly an issue about the definition of "theology." Theology was narrowly understood as the study of God, and writing about God was not considered a Jewish activity. But Jews did write about the religious dimensions of life and had a long history of serious contemplation of the universe, life, and humanity. Most Jews preferred to call such contemplation "Jewish philosophy" or even מחשבת ישׂראל, "Israel's thinking," but there was a tradition of reflection on such issues. On the other hand, Jewish biblical theology was simply incomprehensible. The Bible was simply not the axis around which "Israel's thinking" revolved.

The Bible plays an enormous role in Jewish ritual life. Many psalms from the book of Psalms have been incorporated into the synagogue liturgy, forming an essential component of the regular daily, Sabbath, and festival services. A group of Psalms forms the core of the special service for Sabbath eve (קבלת שׁבת), and another group of Psalms is the core of the additional celebration on festivals and new moons (the הלל). On Jewish festivals, entire books of the Bible are read aloud as part of the service: the Song of Songs on Passover, Ruth on Pentecost, Lamentations on the Ninth of Ab, Jonah on the Day of Atonement, Ecclesiastes on Tabernacles, and Esther on Purim.

But the main ceremonial use of the Bible in Jewish worship involves the Torah (the Pentateuch), for the Torah is at the ritual center of the Sabbath morning prayer service. The architecture of a synagogue entails an "ark," an ornamental, ceremonial cupboard at the front of each synagogue, on the eastern wall, usually upon a raised platform. This ark houses at least one Torah scroll, a scroll that contains the first five books of the Bible, carefully inscribed on parchment with a quill pen. Every Saturday morning, the Torah is taken out of the ark and promenaded around the synagogue, touched and kissed and loved by the congregation. The Torah is then "undressed," for the scroll normally wears a velvet cloak, with a silver breastplate over the cloak. Even the wooden poles around which the scroll is wrapped are ornamented, for they wear either a crown around the two or individual caplets, רמונים (pomegranates), on each pole. After the procession and the unveiling, the Torah is ready to be read. Individual members of the congregation receive the honor of being "given an *aliyah,*" being called up to the Torah to bless God for granting the Torah to Israel. A portion of the Torah is then chanted aloud. In traditional services, seven such honors will be awarded. The portions to be read are consecutive, so that each year the entire Torah will be read aloud from Gen 1:1 to Deut 34:12. An alternate tradition allows three years for the reading of the entire Torah, but in this tradition also, the entire Torah is chanted from start to finish. When each Torah reading is complete, the individual being granted the honor will once again offer blessings of thanksgiving. After the seven readings, a companion piece is chanted. This piece, called the haftarah, is a selection from the prophetic books that tradition decrees complements the Torah portion. When the readings are finished, the Torah is dressed and adorned once more and is conveyed back to the ark in ritual procession. A minor version of this service takes place on Monday and Thursday mornings. At that time, three people are called up, only the first section of the week's portion is read, and there is no haftarah. A macro version of the Torah service takes place once a year, on the festival of Simḥat Torah, "Rejoicing in the Torah." All the Torahs in the ark are taken out for procession; there are seven processions; each procession is an occasion for dancing and song; and most of the people present take turns dancing with the Torah scrolls. On this holiday, everyone in the congregation is given the honor of being called up for the blessings of thanksgiving. Some congregations call the people up to the Torah in seven groups; other congregations call each person up, one by one, for as long as it takes. In this latter case, in order to speed up the action, several people may chant from different Torah scrolls simultaneously. The final section of the Torah is read, and then the Torah is begun again with a special ceremonial chanting of Gen 1.

In all these liturgical ceremonies, the Torah is the central icon of the long relationship between God and Israel and a visual symbol of the regal nature of God the king. Through participation in these rituals, Jewish worshipers receive a deep sense of the awe and the joy of the

Torah. At the same time, this centrality of the Torah is more symbolic than real, more celebrated than maintained. The liturgical and symbolic centrality of the Torah functions strongly on an emotional level. But in many respects, the Torah, and indeed the whole Bible has been marginalized in Judaism. Symbolically central to the faith, the Bible has been placed on a pedestal in Judaism. But being placed on a pedestal has its negative aspect, for it entails a certain degree of isolation: the Bible is not directly involved in matters of halakah, Jewish practice and law. Authority in halakah lies in a chain of tradition that begins with the rabbis of the Talmud. The Bible is the source of halakic authority, but it does not function on its own and is not an independent source of authority in traditional Judaism. A new reading of the Bible has never had the power to upset rabbinic laws or attitudes. The rabbis turn to biblical passages to legitimate and give great weight to rabbinic concepts or provisions. The Bible is of paramount importance as a source of legitimation. But it does not have the power to delegitimate or to invalidate rabbinic provisions. One cannot argue that the rabbinic reading of a biblical passage is misguided and expect that this argument will uproot the practices that were based on that rabbinic reading. New readings of the Bible do not change old customs. In traditional Judaism, the Torah, regal as it is, is not sovereign. It is yoked to a rabbinic system that it serves. In effect, the Torah was (and is, in most traditional circles) a king or queen in captivity. It is well known that the Christian church was explicitly "supersessionist." It showed honor to and interest in the Hebrew Bible and claimed it as its heritage, but it considered the New Testament as its foundational Scripture and drew its behavioral conclusions from there. Judaism was almost equally supersessionist, but it did not make its supersessionism apparent. It behaved ritually as if the Torah was the central facet of Judaism, but it dictated the way that the Torah should be read. In effect, Jewish tradition subordinated and domesticated the Bible. Rabbinic readings declare the sense of Scripture. These rabbinic readings of biblical passages are rarely judged wrong or misguided. They have so much weight in tradition that new readings are not only extraneous and irrelevant—they are practically unthinkable or inconceivable. The traditional readings overlay the biblical text so extensively that they obscure the readers' view of it. The Queen on her pedestal is hidden by veils.

This domestication of the Bible had ramifications in the way the Bible was taught and was in turn reinforced by Jewish religious pedagogy. The Bible was taught as an entry-level book. Little children learned their Bible, mostly concentrating on the Torah. But children would "graduate" from the Bible to higher forms of Jewish learning. By the time they were eight or ten, they would be studying the Mishnah, a Jewish law book that was produced around 200 C.E. When a little older, they would enter the world of

Talmud study, which they would continue to study in adulthood, later perhaps also studying mystical or philosophical literature. Grown-up children did not come back to the Bible with more sophisticated eyes. They had learned their Bible and were expected to know it. But the Bible they had learned remained the text of their childhood and of ritual.

There is a form of Bible study that continues into adulthood in traditional Judaism, a semiritual form of study in which the portion of the Torah read aloud that week is studied as a devotional activity. In this study, the Torah portion is augmented by the comments that medieval teachers wrote about it. Of these commentators, the most important was Rashi, who lived in the eleventh century. He was a master educator with an important goal: he wanted to enable people to continue to study the Bible. To this end, he distilled the bewildering array of postbiblical study of the Bible and the legends attached to it into a simple line-by-line commentary. Rashi's eyes became the lens by which Jews read the Bible. His commentary became so authoritative that Jews often did not distinguish between what the Bible says and Rashi's interpretation. Later readers and commentators built new ideas and commentaries on top of the foundation that Rashi laid, but they very rarely went beneath his commentary into the biblical text to find alternate readings.

As time went on, the "Rashi lens" with which Jews looked at the Bible was joined by a translation lens. Most Jews read the Bible in English, or French or German, alongside their Hebrew. But all translation is interpretation, and modern translations are in the tradition of the great translations of the Renaissance/Reformation, in which one of the goals of the translation was to remove ambiguity from the text in the interests of opening the Bible to the masses. Like Rashi, the translators streamline and simplify the Bible to make it easier to read. With two such lenses "helping" the reader to see the Bible, the actual text could easily be simplified and amplified into almost total invisibility. The Queen on the pedestal had even more veils.

Things have changed. The many discoveries of modernism have had an enormous impact on our knowledge of Judaism. They have revealed the existence of many different streams of Judaism in antiquity and later, thus removing the impression that rabbinic choices were the only possible Jewish choices. There have also been enormous changes in the way we read the Bible. The modern disciplines of biblical studies have increased our knowledge of biblical Hebrew and have led to approaches to biblical ideas that are at least partially independent of the classic traditional ways of reading the Bible. Ancient Near Eastern studies and Assyriology have given us perspectives on the Bible that come from times prior to the Bible and contemporary with it. These and other avenues of approach to the Bible have been added to the traditional "vertical" approach that descended chronologically to the Bible through the layers of later tradition.

At the same time, the modern development of Jewish studies has led to an explosion of our knowledge of ancient texts from Qumran and from the Cairo Genizah. Ancient Jewish magical texts have been discovered, and there has been a reawakening of interest in Kabbalah. All of these discoveries and methodologies have multiplied our resources for the study of Bible. The growth of contemporary philosophy and literary theory have also given Jews a new appreciation for the plurifold approach of midrash, which declared that there were seventy facets to the Torah and that everything could be found in it. Perhaps the most significant impact of biblical and Judaic studies has been the creation of a core of highly educated Jewish scholars who have not "moved on" from Bible to Talmud but have remained focused on the Bible, applying their reading of the Bible to everything else they learn.

These modern developments were not always caused by modernism itself. Modernism challenged the validity of certain biblical claims, often juxtaposing biblical claims with scientific knowledge. But it very rarely looked to see whether the "biblical claims" it challenged were actually the Bible's claims. In fact, modernism often increased the simplified approach to the Bible that tradition generated. The trajectory of reading in the modern period has been to achieve a single authoritative reading of the biblical text. Modernism, with its belief in univocal objective truth, intensified the expectation that there could be ever more exactness in the one true reading. Early biblical scholarship, imbued with the attitudes of modernism, sought to use philology, historical criticism, and scientific data in order to achieve ever more precision in reading. With scientific precision, modern scholars "corrected" old readings and challenged the authority of traditional commentators by undermining faith in the accuracy of their traditional readings. But the modernist scholars shared with the medieval commentators the effort to determine a clear and unequivocal reading of Scripture that could command the allegiance and submission of its readers. Authority demands submission, but one must know to what one is expected to submit. So authority must present a clear, unambiguous statement to which allegiance is required. The text cannot be allowed to have a rich texture of multiple meanings, or how would people know to what meaning one is required to submit? Modern biblical scholarship displaced the source of authority from the traditional clergy and medieval traditions to the scholar and the new modern traditions. But the approach of scholarship, like the approach of the religious traditions, was to claim authoritative readings and understandings. A new approach to reading the Bible, and a new understanding of its theological significance, had to wait for the collapse of the authority of the same modernism that had itself challenged the authority of the old approaches.

The last twenty years have witnessed a collapse of all the old certainties, the demise of modernist ideas about objectivity and even about rationality.

Much more attention is now paid to the impact of the researcher in science, the interpreter in history, the reader in literature. Contemporary students of texts or events know that the texts and events acquire much of their meaning through the interaction of events, objects, or written documents with the person studying them. The interests and agenda of those doing the reading always affect the results of their reading process, sometimes unconsciously and sometimes with full intention. This new attention to the mutable and subjective nature of knowledge pervades much contemporary thinking. But it is especially strong in biblical scholarship, which has not only learned these contemporary principles from contemporary theory, but has also come to realize them empirically through the inclusion in dialogue about the Bible of groups who had been on the margins. This dialogue revealed that different groups had different readings of the text, different readings influenced by the presuppositions and agendas of those who were doing the reading. Jews had their traditional authoritative readings that were sometimes quite different from traditional Christian readings. The poor read with their own experiences in mind, the Third World readers with their own experience of marginalization and colonization, and groups of women in turn read the Bible with eyes conditioned by their own experiences. Dialogue among these groups began to highlight the great amount of interpretive content that lay underneath interpretations that masqueraded as simple reading.

The ongoing reinterpretation of biblical texts and the dialogue about interpretation and about these texts have made it clear that there was nothing essentially "true" about the traditional religious or scholarly readings. They were "hegemonic readings," readings that depended for their authority on the hegemonic power of those doing the reading, the authority of the church or the academy. The church or academy spread their interpretations by the power of their position. At the same time, the demands of power and the interests and agenda of the readers in power helped shape the particular content of these traditional readings. The traditional readings reflected the experiences of men of power. These hegemonic readings, it became clear, made choices in interpretation, and other people could make other choices. Today, the hegemonic readings continue to hold their authority within authority-driven circles, but within the world of scriptural studies and more open environments, the inclusion of new voices in the wider interpretative community has created a climate in which the old hegemonic readings have collapsed.

The collapse of hegemonic authoritative readings has resulted in a liberation of the text itself. Instead of being forced into the straitjacket of the "one true truth," a biblical passage can now demonstrate its complexity and ambiguity. The contemporary babble of views has begun to reveal the multivocality of the Bible, its complexity and ambiguity. Knowing that many different interpretations of the text have in fact existed and held authority has caused us to carefully examine the nature of biblical writing that makes multiple readings possible. We have begun to gain understanding of the literary techniques of the biblical story, in particular the technique of "gapping," the most important tool of ambiguity in the Bible, leading us to see how the biblical authors created a story that changes with different reading communities. The gapped writing of the biblical story makes the interpreter or interpretative community fill in the gaps according to their presuppositions. As presuppositions change, the way that communities fill in the gaps also changes, so that the text begins to have many different variations, allomorphs of the biblical story.

We have begun to recognize other biblical modes of complexity, other techniques that allow the biblical story to change with its readers even more than literature usually does. One such technique involves intertextual allusion. Biblical stories are often written intertextually, so that situations and key words in one story draw allusion to another story. Paying attention to intertextual allusions shows us how stories and laws relate to each other and cluster in discourses. The story or law has meaning when read by itself but adds another layer of meaning as part of a discourse that may present a whole spectrum of ideas about any given topic.

Another source of ambiguity is contained in the oracular nature of biblical rhetoric. Famous statements, long "understood," like ורב יעבד צעיר (Gen 25:23) and שׁלח־נא ביד תשלח (Exod 4:13) turn out to be much more problematic than once believed. Does Rebekah's oracle declare that "the elder will serve the younger" or "the elder, the younger will serve"? Rebekah chose the first reading and acted to make it so. But is that understanding required by the oracle? And Moses' statement is translated "send someone else." But the words mean, "Send by whomever you send." Moses has learned to speak as cryptically as God, and God gives him his own prophet, Aaron, to interpret him.

The Bible begins with an enigmatic construction: בְּרֵאשִׁית בָּרָא. The traditional translation, "in the beginning," ignores the ungrammatical nature of this phrase. The word בְּרֵאשִׁית is a noun in construct, "the beginning of," and a construct should be followed by a noun: "the beginning of something." Rashi emends the vowels, reading בְּרֵאשִׁית בְּרֹא, "at the beginning of God's creating." But the text says, "At the beginning of—he created." Assyriologists point to the Akkadian *awāt iqbû,* a grammatical construction in which a construct is followed by a verb. *Awāt iqbû,* which literally means "the word of—he spoke," is a way of forming a relative clause with the meaning "the word that he spoke." Thus perhaps בְּרֵאשִׁית בָּרָא should be translated as "when God began to create (the heaven and the earth)." In support of such an understanding, the two major Babylonian creation myths both begin with a "when" clause. The *Enuma Elish* begins "When on high the heavens had not yet been formed," and the Atrahasis Epic begins "When the Gods, like men, (had to work)." There are enormous theological implications to such a change in translation. "In the beginning" speaks of the beginning of all things, the start of God's activity. Earth and humanity are the first entities that God created. In this translation, the Bible is profoundly geocentric and anthropocentric. Nothing existed before our own cosmos, God did nothing before God created us. A translation, "when God began to create," on the other hand, says nothing about the beginnings of God's activities, nothing about events before the six days of creation, nothing about the primacy of our world. There is time before the creation of our space, space before our own. In this translation, the Bible is picking up the story at the beginning of our universe, but in *medias res* in the story of God, and says nothing about the beginning of time or the primacy of this or other worlds. For these reasons, I prefer this translation. But it is not certain. בְּרֵאשִׁית בָּרָא is not exactly an *awāt iqbû* formation. This formation occurs once in the Bible, תְּחִלַּת דִּבֶּר־יְהוָה בְּהוֹשֵׁעַ, ("When God began to speak to Hosea," Hos 1:2). The true *awāt iqbû* formation in Gen 1:1 would be רֵאשִׁית בָּרָא. Why does it have an extra ב (*bêt*)? And as for Mesopotamian parallels, the few Sumerian tales about creation start with the words *u-rí-a,* or *u-úl-la,* meaning *in illo tempore,* "at that time," in other words, "in the beginning."

The composers of the first chapter of Genesis knew Hebrew at least as well as I do. They could say something clearly when they wanted to. Moreover, the beautiful litany is carefully, poetically constructed. They were not being sloppy or racing for deadline when they wrote בְּרֵאשִׁית בָּרָא. The ambiguity of the phrase must be purposeful. The two possible translations reflect our own uncertainty and lack of clarity about our role in the wider cosmos. An intentionally ambiguous phrase mirrors the mystery of creation. People who do not know whether eternity preexists creation and creation preexists terra can refrain from writing in such a way that would reflect a certainty that is not there. The ambiguity is also a foreshadowing and a tip-off about things to come in the Bible. The world the Bible considers is complex, and the text reflects the world: different voices compete and clash, claim and disclaim.

It is difficult to talk about the intentionality of authors, divine or human, but the more we look at the Torah, the more oracular it seems, and the more Delphic in its oracularity. The very word *torah,* after all, means "divine instruction." It is related to the Akkadian term *tertu,* divine instruction by means of oracles, a word that ultimately became specialized as a technical term for instruction through liver omens, the chief way in which the Babylonians received their divine instruction. In Israel, the term *torah* originally referred to a specific teaching. By the time of Ezra, the people sought divine instruction within the written tradition of Israel, and

Torah became the term for the entire collected Pentateuch. People could "seek out" revelation within the book precisely because the book is complex, ambiguous, and difficult. Like the world itself, like historical events, the book in which divine instruction was sought was full of riddles wrapped in enigmas.

The God of the Bible is not easily known. First Genesis, then the pentateuchal narrative in Exodus through Numbers and the narratives that follow in the historical books trace a trajectory in which the God who once walked the garden in Gen 3 and actively spoke to Abraham removes the divine presence from human affairs. God remains to be sought in sacred space and time and in the sacred word. But God remains to be sought, not confronted simply and unambiguously. Even the high priest in the holiest section of the holiest place, on the holiest day of the year, could not confront God directly. He experienced a God who was doubly veiled, obscured first by the cloud in which God hovers, then by the cloud of incense the priest created, a cloud of incense that prevented him from even glimpsing the divine cloud. God is experienced through veils, experienced through visions and glimpsed through events. And God's presence can be felt through the writings that record these experiences and consider these events. But these writings cannot be simpler or more obvious than the God they represent.

The complexity and multivocality of Scripture need not deter those who read it. Nobody has to understand the full meanings of the text: indeed, the text, like life, can be so multivocal and complex that only the mind of God can fully comprehend it. There is no obligation to understand, no demand to spend one's life looking for fuller, deeper, more comprehensive meaning. One can live, Deuteronomy tells us, with only the simple truths: that God made us God's people and that we owe God the behavior appropriate to God's people. A life lived in accord with a simple truth is a simple life, and there is great ease, beauty, and peace in a simple life. When our lives become more complex, we may react by longing for simple truths and simple lives, or we may be led to look for more complex truths, to seek fuller meanings and more understanding. It is then that we begin to "seek" the text, and when we do, we find that the simple truths no longer look as true or as simple.

There are yet other reasons that the Bible was written with such complexity and ambiguity. First, the Bible is a text, a written document, and written documents from the ancient world were not "records" in our present sense of the word. A text was a witness to an event, not a complete or accurate recording of events or ideas. The very *sight* of the stela, or tablet, or scroll, as much as their content, served as witness to the reasons they were written. Even as a witness, the text was limited: it could not be entered as evidence in a law dispute unless there were witnesses to attest to what was on it. The text could not stand by itself. To use it in law, you had to have witnesses; to use it in study, you had to have interpreters The texts are written laconically and often need explication. In the Near Eastern and biblical law collections, two cases will differ from each other by at least two variables. Oral discussion is needed to discuss which variable is determinative and what the result will be if only one change takes place. The written text will never replace the interpreter. And the rights of interpreters depend on their authority, their ability to convince others to listen and be convinced by their interpretation.

The authority of interpreters depends on their power, but the vagaries of history, not the logic of inevitability, determine who will have such power over the text. The biblical text does not itself determine who will be the authorized leaders. In fact, the Bible finds its final shaping under the impact of the collapse of all biblical systems of authority. Judah had a monarchy that claimed divine election and privilege. There had been antimonarchic forces in Israel, which claimed that with God as king, there was no need for the apparatus of state. But the book of Judges invalidates the antimonarchic point of view even as it presents it, arranging the stories to show the utter collapse of premonarchic society. The book of Kings does not like the monarchy of the northern kingdom of Israel, holding it tainted by the religious and political acts of the first king Jeroboam, foundational acts that determined the nature of the kingdom. But the book of Kings ultimately loses faith in the Davidic dynasty of Judah as well and blames its kings for the destruction of the kingdom. Even the other basic tenet of Judah, the Jerusalem ideology that considered Jerusalem God's inviolate city, lost its power as God allowed Jerusalem to be destroyed. The Davidic promise and its ideology were destroyed along with the Judahite state. Much later, the Davidic king and Jerusalem became the centers of messianic and eschatological hopes, and that language is still used today. But that development came later. The disillusionment at the destruction of Judah was so great that, Haggai's wishes to the contrary, the monarchy was not restored when Israel was returned to its land.

The other sources of authority in Israel, the priests and the prophets, also lost their authoritative aura and their hegemonic power by the time of the destruction. The longstanding prophetic critique of the priesthood and its sacrificial system was compounded by the priestly failure to ensure that God continued to dwell in the temple. Nor was prophecy the answer. The ability of the prophets to determine policy was always somewhat problematic. The prophet Elisha was active in instigating the revolt of Jehu against the Omride dynasty—but the prophet Hosea clearly disliked Jehu's actions. The biggest problem with prophecy is the veracity of the prophets and their reliability. Whom can you believe? Deuteronomy demands that the people listen to prophets and insists that signs and wonders are not a good indicator—Deuteronomy claims that God might send prophets with signs in order to test the steadfastness of the people. The true indicator, says Deuteronomy, is the content of the message: the prophet must be telling hearers/readers to stay faithful to God (13:2–6). But this standard is only helpful when the false prophet advises abandoning God: when the issues are subtle and complex, how can the people know what action constitutes staying faithful? Deuteronomy considers this problem, "And if you question in your heart, 'How will I recognize the matter which YHWH has not spoken to him?,' the prophet who speaks in the name of YHWH and the matter does not come to pass—that is the matter which YHWH did not speak to him" (Deut 18:21–22). But history cannot be the test of a true prophet. It cannot determine what to believe now, only what should have been believed then. Moreover, the book of Jonah argues that the best result a true prophet can hope for is to have his prediction made false by inspiring repentance. During Jeremiah's blasphemy hearing, elders recalled that in the days of Hezekiah, Micah prophesied that Zion and the temple would be destroyed, but Hezekiah feared YHWH and YHWH relented and did not destroy the city (Jer 26:17–19). At that time, those who prophesied the Isaianic message, peace on Jerusalem, were proved right. But Jeremiah denounced as false prophets those who delivered that message in his day—and the destruction proved him right.

The Bible relates stories that illustrate the danger of following a false prophet and the great difficulty in understanding when a prophet is false. Even a prophet cannot always tell. At the time of Jeroboam's revolt, a Judahite prophet went to Bethel on a mission to denounce Jeroboam's religious innovations. As he returned home, an elderly prophet invited him to eat and drink. The traveling prophet declared that God had demanded that he fast till he get home, but the other prophet replied, "I too am a prophet, like you," relating that an angel instructed him to have the first prophet eat. But when the first prophet sat to eat, the word of YHWH informed him that he had disobeyed and as a result would not receive proper burial. A lion then dismembered him on his way home (1 Kgs 13:11–25). The old prophet was not evil; when he heard what had happened he buried the remains of the traveling prophet and asked to be buried with him. The old prophet may not even have known that he was inducing a prophet to rebel against God's word; he may have believed his own prophecy about his duty to show him hospitality. This is the core problem with prophetic authority: even prophets do not know when they are not speaking a true prophecy. The story of Micaiah's vision (1 Kgs 22:2–26) dramatically illustrates this problem. King Ahab wants Jehoshaphat king of Judah to join him in battle for Ramoth-gilead. Jehoshaphat wants a prophecy, and Ahab brings out four hundred court prophets who predict victory. Jehoshaphat wants still another prophet, and

Ahab sends for Micaiah even though "he never prophesies good about me." Micaiah comes and tells Ahab to go, but Ahab is suspicious and demands that he tell him only truth. Micaiah then prophesies doom and relates his vision: he has seen the heavenly court, with God on his throne asking for someone to entice Ahab to battle so that he can die in battle. A spirit volunteered. When God asked how the spirit would do this, the spirit declared, "I will be a lying spirit in the mouth of his prophets," and God sent him to do so. Zedekiah, the head of the court prophets, is horrified at this story; he strikes Micaiah on the cheek, declaring, "How is it that the spirit of God passed from me to speak to you?" Zedekiah is convinced that he is a true prophet; Micaiah is convinced that God has deceived Zedekiah. In the face of such deception, nobody can tell what to believe. By the time of Ezekiel, the people have lost faith in prophets, and Ezekiel records a proverb, "the days are prolonged and every vision fails" (Ezek 12:22).

The destruction discredits all the old systems of authority. As Zephaniah says (3:3–4), "Her princes in her midst are raging lions, her judges are wolves ... her prophets are reckless men of treachery and her priests have polluted the holy and turned the Torah into lawlessness." It is no wonder that people seek the will of God in a book rather than turn to their leaders. But even the law is somewhat problematic. Allegiance to laws of debt and debt slavery, declared Amos, is שׁד וחמס, criminal lawlessness and brigandry, and because Israel collects debts and holds debt-slaves, they are worthy of destruction. Jeremiah shows us that the child sacrificers in the Valley of Hinnom really believed that God had commanded them to sacrifice their children. To Jeremiah, God says, "I didn't command it; it didn't enter my mind" (Jer 7:31; 19:5)—but they believed they were commanded by God. Even more horrifying, Ezekiel tells us that God really did command them, that some of the laws are booby traps intended to doom the people (Ezek 20:25).

The written law depends for its authority on Moses, for it is the "Torah that Moses commanded," but Moses himself is subtly undermined by the narrator on at least two occasions. In one, the people are at Sinai, and the narrator shows us two dialogues: God's command to Moses to tell the people to prepare for revelation, and Moses' charge to the people. There is a significant difference between them, for when Moses commands the people, he adds, "Do not approach a woman," a command never given by God (Exod 19:15). Moses, on his own, without God's command, has introduced the separation of sex from sanctity into Israel's law and gender inequality into Israel's congregation. And the narrator, the anonymous voice of Torah, shows the reader that God never commanded this. Another story is equally serious. The people have angered God by attaching themselves to Baal Peor, God has brought a devastating plague, and God now commands Moses to "take all the leaders of the people and impale them for YHWH before the sun" in order to stop the plague (Num 25:4). But Moses never relays this message; instead he tells the leaders to search out and punish the guilty parties. Moses has rejected the idea of the vicarious punishment of leaders and substituted individual responsibility and retribution. And the narrator has shown that that important principle of law is from Moses, not God.

If some laws are from God, but shouldn't be followed, and other laws are from Moses rather than from God, there is no room for legal positivism. Every law has to be examined on its own merits; no law can simply rest on its own authority as "God's word." The written word has no more unquestionability than the priests who teach it, the prophets who proclaim it, or the state authorities who enforce it. This lack of trust in any given authority contributes to the complex multivocality of the Bible.

The Torah was completed during a time of complexity and new horizons. The rest of the Bible was finished in yet another period of complexity, the Roman era. To deal with a complex, shifting world, we need a complex text, and the Writings and the Prophets abound in diverse opinions and contradictory thoughts. Much of the complex variety has been simplified or ignored during the eons since the composition of the Bible by authorities who have claimed hegemonic power to determine the interpretation of Scripture. Now, however, the world is once again exploding with new horizons, and the old hegemonic authorities have come under suspicion. Indeed, the very idea of hegemonic power clashes with some of our contemporary approaches to reality. The genie and genius of indeterminacy have come out of the bottle, and the multiple facets of the Bible are once again compelling attention. Indeed, in our contemporary world, this very negotiating between voices gives the Bible a new centrality in Jewish religious thinking. The new interpretations of the Bible show that the rabbinic interpreters made choices and that other choices can be made. By presenting alternative voices in the central iconic text in Judaism, the study of the Bible helps undermine the authority of any single biblical voice, any one particular biblical reading. Biblical theology presents an alternative source of authority to rabbinic thinking and creates a very fertile opportunity for dialogue between biblical and rabbinic ideas. The Bible offers us an ability to triangulate our contemporary sensibility with two major systems of our past. Above all, the Bible offers us a model of how to react to the collapse of old hegemonies. It shows us that we need not fly into a new absolutism or to nihilistic despair, but should proceed with a determination to keep faith and an understanding that revelation and sacrality do not lie in any particular written word, but in the very process of sifting and negotiating and wresting. This is the process of Torah.

The Law and the Prophet

S. David Sperling

The most significant question related to the theology of Scripture is the standing of Scripture itself within Judaism and Christianity. The present essay attempts to show how the concept of Scripture originated within the Bible. It is well known that both the canon of the Old Testament and the New Testament[1] represent the final stages of processes of collection and selection.[2] Within the present OT and NT we see how some late authors commented explicitly on those earlier literary productions that were already Scripture for them. For example, the exilic or postexilic author of Josh 8:30–31 takes pains to show that Joshua built an altar on Mount Ebal in conformity with the regulations of "the book of the law of Moses":

---

[1] The designations "Old Testament" (OT) and New Testament (NT) carry theological implications. According to one NT writer the divine word to Jeremiah (31:31) that God would in the future make a "new testament" or "new covenant" (Hebrew: ברית חדשה) with Israel was a prophecy that Christianity would supersede Judaism: "By speaking of a new testament He has pronounced the first one obsolete; and anything that is becoming obsolete and growing old will surely disappear" (Heb 8:13). By the end of the second century OT and NT had become literary terms to distinguish the earlier, originally Jewish, collection from the later specifically Christian writings. (See Clement of Alexandria, *Stromateis* 1.28.2; 3.71.3. I thank my colleague Prof. Adam Kamesar for these references.) In recent years some Jewish and Christian scholars have attempted to replace OT and NT with other terminology. Some prefer the acronym "Tanak," formed from the initial Hebrew letters of the threefold Jewish division *Torah* = Gen–Deut, *Nevi'im* = Josh–Mal, and *Ketuvim* = Ps–2 Chr, but this designation seems a bit recherché. "Older Testament" and "Newer Testament" are occasionally heard, but they are too cute. In addition, "Newer Testament" (along with "New Testament," which used to pass muster with virtually all Jews) is unacceptable to many Jews because they reject the sacred character of these writings. Another proffered solution has been to refer to the OT as "Jewish Scriptures," denying the historical fact that they are Christian as well. Similarly, to call the NT "Christian Scriptures" as some Jewish writers have recently begun doing is confusing to many Christians and other Gentiles who designate the OT and NT collectively as "Christian Scriptures." In light of the above I have chosen to retain "Old Testament" and "New Testament" as convenient literary terms long sanctioned by usage.

[2] See James A. Sanders, "Canon, Hebrew Bible," *ABD* 1:837–52; and Henry Gamble, "Canon, New Testament," *ABD* 1:852–61.

> At that time Joshua built an altar to Yahweh the God of Israel on Mount Ebal. The altar was of blocks of unhewn stone on which no iron tool had been used, as Moses the servant of God had commanded the people of Israel, as it is written in the book of the law of Moses, "an altar of unhewn stones, upon which no man has lifted an iron tool"; and they offered on it burnt offerings to Yahweh, and sacrificed peace offerings.

In this instance the author of Josh 8:30–31 shows how Joshua followed the law of Moses, by making specific reference to that which was written in the "book of the law of Moses," in Deut 27:1–8.[3]

Another late author, the writer of Neh 13:1–3 takes a further step:

> On that day they read from the book of Moses in the hearing of the people; and in it was found written that no Ammonite or Moabite should ever enter the assembly of God; for they did not meet the children of Israel with bread and water, but hired Balaam against them to curse them—yet our God turned the curse into a blessing. When the people heard the law, they separated from Israel all those of mixed descent.

The reference to what was read in the book of Moses is to Deut 23:4–6, verses that prohibit marriage with two specific groups for very specific reasons. Yet the reaction to the law is to separate *all* people of mixed descent from Israel.[4]

Nehemiah 8, likewise set in the fifth century B.C.E,[5] takes us into the realm of legal exegesis or legal midrash:[6]

> On the second day the heads of fathers' houses of all the people, with the priests and the Levites, came together to Ezra the scribe in order to study the words of the law. And they found it written in the law that Yahweh had commanded by Moses that the people of Israel should dwell in booths during the feast of the seventh month, and that they should pub-

---

[3] See Samuel Ahituv, *Joshua: Introduction and Commentary* (Jerusalem: Magnes, 1995), 141–43.

[4] On the specific exegetical strategies involved here, see Michael Fishbane, *Biblical Interpretation in Ancient Israel* (Oxford: Clarendon, 1985), 114–28.

[5] Possibly the setting is the fourth century if Ezra's activity is dated in the reign of Artaxerxes II. On the chronological problems, see H. G. M. Williamson, *Ezra, Nehemiah* (WBC 16; Waco, Tex.: Word Books, 1985), xxxix–xliv.

[6] With the following cf. Fishbane, *Interpretation,* 109–13; Cf. further, H. G. M. Williamson, "History," in *It Is Written—Scripture Citing Scripture: Essays in Honour of Barnabas Lindars, SSF* (ed. D. A. Carson and H. G. M. Williamson; Cambridge: Cambridge University Press, 1988), 29–30.

> lish and proclaim in all their towns and in Jerusalem,[7] "Go out[8] to the hills and bring branches of olive and wild olive, myrtle and palm and other leafy trees to make booths, as it is written. So the people went out and brought them and made booths for themselves, each on his roof, and in their courts and in the courts of the house of God, and in the square at the Water Gate and in the square at the Gate of Ephraim. And all the assembly of those who had returned from the captivity made booths and dwelt in the booths; for from the days of Jeshua the son of Nun to that day the people of Israel had not done so. And there was very great rejoicing. And day by day, from the first day to the last day, he read from the book of the Torah of God. They kept the feast seven days; and on the eighth day there was a solemn assembly, according to the ordinance. (Neh 8:13–18)

The source text that they found "written in the law" is apparently Lev 23:39–43:

> On the fifteenth day of the seventh month, when you have gathered in the produce of the land, you shall keep the feast of Yahweh seven days; on the first day shall be a solemn assembly, and on the eighth day shall be a solemn assembly. You shall take for yourselves on the first day the fruit of goodly trees, branches of palm trees, and boughs of leafy trees, and willows of the brook; and you shall rejoice before Yahweh your God seven days. You shall keep it as a feast to Yahweh seven days in the year; it is a statute for ever throughout your generations; you shall keep it in the seventh month. You shall dwell in booths for seven days; all that are native in Israel shall dwell in booths, that your generations may know that I made the people of Israel dwell in booths when I brought them out of the land of Egypt: I am Yahweh your God.

The question facing the author of Neh 8 was the connection between the command to dwell in booths in Lev 23:42 and the command to collect the materials in 23:40. The author's solution is to use the materials in constructing the booths. But the activity in which Ezra and his contemporaries were engaged is more important than the particular solution at which they arrived. According to Neh 8:13 the Jews assembled "to study the words of the Law." The Hebrew verb לְהַשְׂכִּיל, which we translated idiomatically as "study," in context literally means "look at," "gain insight

---

[7] The LXX reads: "and that they should sound with trumpets in all their cities and in Jerusalem."

[8] LXX reads: "Esdras said 'go out…'." This appears to be a better reading because it is difficult to derive the command to go out to the mountains from Lev 23:40. For a different solution, see Williamson, *It Is Written,* 30.

into," and "seek."[9] It is especially significant that in at least one biblical passage[10] the verb is a synonym of דרש, which likewise means "seek," "look at." In the OT דרש often takes a divinity or object of worship as its direct object with the technical or mantic sense "to inquire of a divinity."[11] In the book of Ezra, however, the same verb is used with the direct object "torah";[12] the use of the synonym להשכיל points to the same activity, the direction of mantic activity to a document rather than to a divinity.[13] "For Ezra had set his heart to study [Heb.: דרש] the law [Heb.: תורה] of the LORD, and to do it, and to teach his statutes and ordinances in Israel" (Ezra 7:10).

The above examples illustrate the legal application of earlier tenets by later writers. At least equally significant is the application of earlier prophecy to the situation of the later reader. A good example is provided by the author of chapter 9 of the book of Daniel:

> In the first year of Darius the son of Ahasuerus by birth a Mede, who became king over the realm of the Chaldeans—in the first year of his reign, I, Daniel, was studying in the books the number of years which, according to the word of Yahweh to Jeremiah the prophet, must pass before the end of the desolations of Jerusalem, namely, seventy years. (Dan 9:1–2)

In this instance the writer of these verses has been studying "the books" (Hebrew: ספרים) that contain the words of the prophet Jeremiah. "Daniel" expects that once the prophetic word has been uttered, it must ultimately find fulfillment. In the words of Deutero-Isaiah (40:8), "the word

---

[9] See the study by Moshe Weinfeld, "שׂכל, עין, דיק: A Semantic Analysis," *Tehillah le-Moshe: Biblical and Judaic Studies in Honor of Moshe Greenberg* (ed. Mordechai Cogan, Barry L. Eichler, and Jeffrey H. Tigay; Winona Lake, Ind.: Eisenbrauns, 1997), 101–6 (in Hebrew section).

[10] Ps 14:2 = Ps 53:3.

[11] E.g., Gen 25:22; Exod 18:15; Deut 18:11; 1 Sam 9:9; 2 Kgs 1:3, 16.

[12] This is the beginning of a process that is carried further in the Dead Sea Scrolls in which דורש התורה, "explicator of the torah," appears and that reaches its culmination in rabbinic מדרש, a word from the same root. Cf. Itamar Gruenwald, "Midrash and the 'Midrashic Condition': Preliminary Considerations," in *The Midrashic Imagination* (ed. Michael Fishbane; Albany: State University of New York Press, 1993), 9. In rabbinic midrash the biblical text is viewed as an "independent entity ... which can be interrogated to answer religious questions." See Moshe Idel, "Midrashic versus Other Forms of Jewish Hermeneutic: Some Comparative Reflections," in *Midrashic Imagination,* 49.

[13] Note that in another postexilic source "the great torah hymn," Ps 119, the object of דרש may be a synonym of תורה. Thus in Ps 119:45, 94 the object is פקודים, "commands," while in Ps 119:155 the object is חקים, "laws."

of our God will endure forever." This notion "was deeply rooted in the primary mantic character of prophecy in Israel"[14] already in preexilic times, for, after all, the criterion for determining that an individual was a true prophet was that the words spoken by that prophet materialized.[15] In the preexilic period, however, most prophecy was directed to the near future rather than to some time far off and distant. In addition, and no less significant, most prophecy reached its audience orally rather than in writing.[16] For reasons both technical and ideological, matters changed considerably beginning in the exilic period. First, only the written prophecies of the preexilic period survived, presumably those which had been "authenticated" by history. Second; the exilic and later prophets, notably Deutero-Isaiah, turned to the fulfillment of earlier prophecy as proof that Yahweh alone was divine: "The fact that only the Word of Yahweh of Israel has come true proves that he is the only true god."[17] Paradoxically, the availability of prophetic statements in written form centuries after their original utterance valorized the notion of "Scripture" at the expense of live prophecy. In the exilic period the notion developed that "every true prophecy is to be fulfilled in due time."[18] Inasmuch as true prophecy was to be found in

---

[14] See Alexander Rofé, "How Is the Word Fulfilled? Isaiah 55:6–11 within the Theological Debate of Its Time," in *Canon, Theology and Old Testament Interpretation: Essays in Honor of Brevard S. Childs* (ed. Gene Tucker et al.; Philadelphia: Fortress, 1988), 246; I. L. Seeligmann, "The Understanding of Prophecy in Deuteronomistic and Chronistic History," in *I. L. Seeligmann Studies in Biblical Literature* (ed. Avi Hurvitz et al.; Jerusalem: Magnes, 1992), 205–28.

[15] See Deut 18:21–22; cf. Rofé, "How Is the Word Fulfilled?" 250–51.

[16] These two phenomena are closely related. Oral prophecies would normally not survive as long as written ones. At the divine command Jeremiah committed his prophecies to writing, but these written words were meant for oral delivery to Jeremiah's contemporaries rather than for an audience of later readers. (See Jer 36:1–8 and contrast William Holladay, *Jeremiah 2: A Commentary on the Book of the Prophet Jeremiah, Chapters 26–52* [Hermeneia; Philadelphia: Fortress, 1989] 254–55.) Note that God tells Jeremiah to put sale documents in a pottery vessel "so that they might be preserved for many days" (Jer 32:14). He does not command Jeremiah to do the same for his prophecies.

[17] Rofé, "How Is the Word Fulfilled?" 251; see also Zech 1:4–6; 7:8–14.

[18] Rofé, "How Is the Word Fulfilled?" 251. For the different terminologies expressing the concept, see n. 17. An anonymous teaching cited in *b. Meg.* 14a distinguishes between scriptural prophecy and nonscriptural prophecy: "Many prophets arose for them—the Israelites—twice as many as those (Israelites) who left Egypt. Prophecy which was necessary for future generations was written down but prophecy which was unnecessary [for future generations] was not written down." On this understanding all scriptural prophecy remains relevant and ultimately applicable.

Scripture, once there was a Scripture it was difficult for a living prophet to compete with it. But where did the notion of Scripture as true prophecy originate? I suggest that the source of that notion is Num 12:1–8:

> Miriam and Aaron spoke against Moses because of the Cushite woman whom he had married, for he had married a Cushite woman; and they said, "Has Yahweh indeed spoken only through Moses? Has he not spoken through us also?" And Yahweh heard it. Now the man Moses was very meek, more than all men that were on the face of the earth. Then suddenly Yahweh said to Moses and to Aaron and Miriam, "Come out, you three, to the tent of meeting." And the three of them came out. Then Yahweh came down in a pillar of cloud, and stood at the door of the tent, and called "Aaron and Miriam"; and they both came forward. And he said, "Hear my words: If there is a prophet of Yahweh among you, I make myself known to him in a vision, I speak with him in a dream. Not so with my servant Moses; in all my household he alone is reliable.[19] With him I speak mouth to mouth, clearly, and not in riddles; and he beholds the form of Yahweh. Why then were you not afraid to speak against my servant Moses?"

Numbers 12:6–8 is often compared to Deut 34:10–12, which likewise stresses the uniqueness of Moses, but the two pericopes have a rather different message, a point that becomes clear by juxtaposing them. Deut 34:10–12 reads:

> And there never again arose in Israel a prophet like Moses, whom Yahweh knew face to face, none like him for all the signs and the wonders which Yahweh sent him to do in the land of Egypt, to Pharaoh and to all his servants and to all his land, and for all the mighty power and all the great and terrible deeds which Moses wrought in the sight of all Israel.

What is emphasized in Deut 34 is the power of the prophet Moses to perform signs, wonders, and mighty deeds.[20] That these signs and wonders were done in the sight of the entire people and had the effect of freeing the people from the power of Pharaoh distinguished Moses from all subsequent prophets. Yet according to Deut 34 the fact that Moses was more intimate with Yahweh than were other prophets did not result in prophecies that were qual-

---

[19] So approximately NEB and REB.

[20] It has been argued that the end of Deuteronomy may have the political intent of contrasting Moses' (= Deuteronomic) opposition to syncretism with those prophetic teachings that legitimated certain forms of syncretism in the cult of Yahweh. See Jeffrey Tigay, "The Significance of the End of Deuteronomy (Deuteronomy 34:10–12)," in *Texts, Temples, and Traditions: A Tribute to Menahem Haran* (ed. Michael Fox et al.; Winona Lake, Ind.: Eisenbrauns), 137–43.

itatively better or more reliable—the validity of prophecies uttered by prophets other than Moses was not called into question.

In contrast, Num 12 undermines the validity of all non-Mosaic prophecy. The writer begins by seconding what is commonly acknowledged by prophets, namely that they receive dreams[21] and visions from Yahweh. But in the continuation the writer observes that only Moses is a reliable prophet because Yahweh speaks to him "mouth to mouth." The additional information that to him alone Yahweh speaks "clearly, not in riddles" means only one thing: that to all other prophets Yahweh speaks unclearly and in riddles. The rhetorical strategy employed by the writer is not less than brilliant.[22] There is no opposition to the claim of Miriam and Aaron that Yahweh has not spoken through Moses alone (v. 2). The writer concedes that Yahweh has indeed spoken through other male and female prophets. Unfortunately, none of them is reliable because Yahweh's speech to them was in riddles, thereby leaving room for faulty interpretation. In contrast, the prophecy of Moses leaves nothing to the imagination. But if that is the point of the narrative, what are its implications?

It has become increasingly clear since the 1970s that nothing in the narrative of the Pentateuch is historical.[23] Although the events related in the Pentateuch are set in a period before the rise of the Israelite states, it can now be said with confidence that this temporal[24] setting is fictitious. I have suggested elsewhere that all of the pentateuchal narrative should be categorized as "allegorical."[25] That is, stories about such fictitious characters as

---

[21] Jeremiah does not accept the validity of dreams, but he does appear to believe that a genuine prophet could stand in the divine council and have access to reliable prophecy. See Jer 23:22, 25–28. On dreams, cf. Zech 10:2.

[22] A similar strategy is employed by the writer of Deut 18:16–19, who provides an etiology of prophecy in Israel. He admits that all Israelites heard the divine voice at Horeb. But the Israelites themselves requested never again to hear the voice of Yahweh directly lest they perish. That Yahweh ever since that time speaks to Israel only through prophetic intermediaries is not to be seen as prophetic self-aggrandizement but as Yahweh's acquiescence to Israel's request.

[23] See conveniently, Neils Lemche and William Dever, "Israel, History of," *ABD* 3:526–58.

[24] Often this holds for the spatial setting as well. It is now clear that Israel arose through some kind of political realignment within Canaan. Archaeology has falsified the biblical claims that Israel was enslaved in Egypt, trekked through the Sinai desert, and conquered the promised land. See William Dever, "Israel, History of (Archaeology and the Israelite 'Conquest')," *ABD* 3:545–58. This means that stories set in Egypt and in the desert before the "conquest" are allegorical both temporally and spatially. (See the following note.)

[25] For an attempt to apply allegory systematically as a hermeneutical tool in interpreting the narratives of the Pentateuch, see S. David Sperling, *The Original*

Abraham, Isaac, Jacob, Esau, Moses, Miriam, and Aaron refer allegorically to characters in the historical period between 1100–400 B.C.E. To take a well-known example, the "discovery" by "Jacob" in Gen 28 that Bethel is a holy place, a perfect site for a sanctuary, is a transparent legitimation of the designation of Bethel as a holy site by Jeroboam I.[26] As such, a story about the competing prophetic talents of Moses, Miriam, and Aaron should be read not simply as a statement about prophetic worthies of a fictitious past but as an ideological statement made by a writer attempting to influence an audience in a matter of contemporary importance. Viewed from that perspective the story in Num 12, which bears the message that all prophecy other than that of Moses is unreliable,[27] must emanate from a time in which the prophecy of Moses could be measured against all other prophetic competition. The historical period that fills that requirement is the Persian period (539–331 B.C.E.).[28] According to the book of Ezra-Nehemiah it was on the authority of the Achaemenids that the Jews were given the opportunity to live by their own laws.[29] Taking advantage of this opportunity the

---

Torah: The Political Intent of the Bible's Writers (New York: New York University Press, 1998).

[26] See Sperling, *Original Torah,* 95–97.

[27] The biblical authors did not unanimously praise prophecy or the holders of the prophetic office. See David Marcus, *From Balaam to Jonah: Anti-Prophetic Satire in the Hebrew Bible* (Atlanta: Scholars Press, 1995). It will be recalled that in 1 Kgs 22:22–23 the possibility is raised that Yahweh himself might permit a deceitful spirit to mislead prophets and thus deceive their audiences. For the 1 Kgs 22 passage and others, see J. J. M. Roberts, "Does God Lie? Divine Deceit As a Theological Problem in Israelite Prophetic Literature," in *Congress Volume: Jerusalem 1986* (ed. J. A. Emerton; VTSup 40; Leiden: Brill, 1988), 211–20; cf. Alexander Rofé, *Introduction to the Prophetic Literature* (Jerusalem: Academon, 1992), 55. The story in 1 Kgs 22 may be late (Rofé, *Introduction,* 61); Hans Barstad argues that the book of Deuteronomy holds a negative view of prophecy ("The Understanding of the Prophets in Deuteronomy," *SJT* 8 [1994]: 236–51), but contrast Knud Jeppesen, "Is Deuteronomy Hostile Toward Prophets?" *SJT* 8 (1994): 252–56.

[28] Cf. Philip J. Budd, *Numbers* (WBC 5; Waco, Tex.: Word Books, 1984), 138: "Mosaic revelation has a unique and supreme authority and thus it paved the way for the 'Mosaic law' of the post-exilic period. Miriam and Aaron appear together to represent the claims of prophetic inspiration.... Even prophetic revelation is subordinate to Mosaic religion." Budd dates Num 12 to the seventh century but views the chapter as paving the way for postexilic thinking.

[29] See Ezra 7:25–26. The Jews were not treated uniquely in this respect. For a parallel treatment of Egyptians under Achaemenid rule, see Eduard Meyer and Franz Altheim, cited by Michael Fishbane, *Biblical Interpretation,* 37 n. 53; Joseph Blenkinsopp, "The Mission of Udjahorresnet and Those of Ezra and Nehemiah," *JBL* 106 (1987): 409–21; see further Kenneth G. Hoglund, *Achaemenid Imperial*

Jews assembled their earlier literature, including prophecies that had been verified by the events of history. What was to be the relation between the prophecies of the past, which were now available in written form, and the prophetic word of living prophets? The author of Num 12 answered the question by writing a story in which the legitimacy of living prophecy was not directly questioned.[30] Instead, that prophecy was described as flawed because it was like a riddle that needed to be solved. In contrast, the prophecies of Moses were to be found in the Torah, which, it is claimed, was straightforward and did not need to be solved.[31]

According to Num 12, then, there is no conflict between law and prophecy.[32] Rather, the Torah of Moses is the highest form of prophecy. Only in the Torah is the divine word available in clear and reliable form. Gradually this notion was extended to other writings, some of these produced within the very circles of prophecy denigrated by the author of Num 12. By the late first century C.E. Josephus could describe the Jewish sources on which he relied for the details of his people's doings in remote antiquity as the writings of prophets who learned what to write from "God himself by inspiration."[33] Subsequently, Jewish rabbinic tradition asserted that the canonical writings of the second and third divisions of the OT,[34] the Prophets (*Nevi'im*) and the Writings (*Ketuvim*), were produced under the

Administration in Syria-Palestine and the Missions of Ezra and Nehemiah (Atlanta: Scholars Press, 1992).

30 Numbers 12 may have some bearing on Neh 6:14, a verse in which Nehemiah mentions a certain "Noadiah the woman prophet [Heb.: נביאה] and the rest of the prophets who were used to intimidating me." Possibly, "Miriam" of Num 12 is an allegorical representative of this Noadiah of whom nothing is otherwise known. Note however that the Peshitta and other ancient versions reflect here the masculine form נביא. See David Marcus, "Is Nehemiah a Translation from Aramaic?" in *Boundaries of the Ancient Near Eastern World: A Tribute to Cyrus H. Gordon* (ed. Meir Lubetski et al.; JSOTSup 273; Sheffield: Sheffield Academic Press, 1998), 107–8.

31 In contrast, classical rabbinic Judaism sometimes expressed the opposite opinion: Rabbi Yannai (third century C.E.) said, "The words of the Torah were not given as clear-cut decisions" (*Midr. Pss.* 12:4, cited from David Weiss Halivni, "From Midrash to Mishnah: Theological Repercussions and Further Clarifications of 'chate'u yisrael,'" *Midrashic Imagination,* 30).

32 Contra Budd, *Numbers,* 138.

33 In *Against Apion* 1.7 Josephus uses the term ἐπίπνοια, "breathing upon," "inspiration" (See LSJ, 652).

34 On the development of the threefold division, see Avi Hurvitz, "On the Borderline between Biblical Criticism and Hebrew Linguistics: The Emergence of the Term ספר־משה," in *Tehillah le-Moshe: Biblical and Judaic Studies in Honor of Moshe Greenberg* (ed. Mordecai Cogan, Barry L. Eichler and Jeffrey H. Tigay; Winona Lake, Ind.: Eisenbrauns, 1997), 42 n. 18 (in Hebrew section).

influence of the holy spirit (Heb.: רוח הקדש).[35] Thus Rabbi Simeon b. Menasia (second–third century C.E.), who considered Song of Songs canonical, said:

> The Song of Songs defiles the hands [= is canonical] because it was uttered by means of the holy spirit. Qoheleth does not defile the hands [= is not canonical] because it is of Solomon's [own] wisdom.[36]

But in Jewish thinking this same holy spirit had ceased to operate directly through persons in the Persian period: "With the death of the last prophets, Haggai, Zechariah and Malachi, the holy spirit departed from Israel."[37]

Similarly, citing Dan 11:3, "a great king shall arise," the *Seder Olam Rabbah*[38] comments:

> He is Alexander of Macedonia who reigned for twelve years. Until then the prophets used to prophesy by means of the Holy Spirit. [Heb.: רוח הקדש][39] From this time forth:[40] "Incline your ear and obey the words of the sages." [Prov 22:17][41]

---

[35] On רוח הקדש, see Alan Unterman, *EncJud* 14:364–66. As Unterman observes, the phrase occurs in the Bible (e.g., Isa 63:10), but its technical meaning is post-biblical. In biblical Hebrew the רוח, "breath," of Yahweh (Num 11:29; 2 Sam 23:2) or Elohim (Num 24:2; 1 Sam 10:10) may confer the gift of prophecy. In rabbinic sources הקדש, "the Holy," served as a euphemism for the older Hebrew names for God. Consequently, the biblical term רוח הקדש could be reinterpreted as "spirit of God = prophecy."

[36] For a recent study on the connection between canonical books and ritual impurity, see Shamma Friedman, "Holy Scriptures Defile the Hands," in *Minḥah le-Naḥum: Biblical and Other Studies Presented to Nahum M. Sarna in Honour of his 70th Birthday* (ed. Marc Brettler et al.; JSOTSup 154; Sheffield: Sheffield Academic Press, 1993), 117–32; the connection between canonicity and defilement of the hands is challenged by Shneur Zalman Leiman, *The Canonization of the Hebrew Scriptures* (Hamden: Archon, 1976), 102–28.

[37] *B. Sanh.* 11a. Rabbi Joshua b. Korhah (second century C.E.) identified Malachi with Ezra. See *b. Meg.* 15a.

[38] For the text, see Moshe Weinstock, ed., *Seder Olam Rabbah Ha-shalem* (Jerusalem: Torat Hesed, 1961), 3:466–67.

[39] In later sources some distinction is made between רוח הקדש and prophecy. See Halivni in Fishbane, *Midrashic Imagination,* 40 n. 13.

[40] Cf. *t. Yad.* 2:13. Cf. further Josephus, *Against Apion* 1.8: "For we have not an innumerable multitude of books among us, disagreeing from and contradicting one another, [as the Greeks have,] but only twenty-two books, which contain the records of all the past times; which are justly believed to be divine; and of them five belong to Moses, which contain his laws and the traditions of the origin of mankind

Rabbinic tradition saw the period of Ezra as the beginning of rabbinic Judaism because the rabbis accepted the notion that the Torah was Mosaic. For them the cessation of prophecy was coeval with the beginning of rabbinism, not with the compilation of the Pentateuch. Ironically, nineteenth-century biblical criticism, largely a Protestant enterprise, agreed that the law and its Pharisaic-rabbinic application had put an end to prophecy.[42] Functionally of course this was true, but, in theory, prophecy survived in a new medium, that of Scripture.

Jewish scriptural thinking found its successor in Christianity. For example, 2 Tim 3:16–17 reads:

> All Scripture is inspired by God [Gk.: θεόπνευστος; lit., "God-breathed"] and beneficial for teaching, for reproving, for setting things straight, for disciplining in righteousness that the man of God may be fully competent, completely equipped for every good work.

But the daughter religion differed with its mother in two significant ways. First, and not without controversy,[43] classical Christianity accepted the Old Testament as Scripture, while rabbinic Judaism rejected the New

---

till his death. This interval of time was little short of three thousand years; but as to the time from the death of Moses till the reign of Artaxerxes king of Persia, who reigned after Xerxes, the prophets, who were after Moses, wrote down what was done in their times in thirteen books. The remaining four books contain hymns to God, and precepts for the conduct of human life. It is true, *our history hath been written since Artaxerxes very particularly, but hath not been esteemed of the like authority with the former by our forefathers, because there hath not been an exact succession of prophets since that time;* and how firmly we have given credit to these books of our own nation is evident by what we do; for during so many ages as have already passed, no one has been so bold as either to add any thing to them, to take any thing from them, or to make any change in them; but it is become natural to all Jews immediately, and from their very birth, to esteem these books to contain Divine doctrines, and to persist in them, and, if occasion be willingly to die for them" (emphasis added).

[41] In rabbinic chronology there is not much difference between the talmudic source and *Seder Olam Rabbah* because the latter source allotted only thirty-four years between the rebuilding of the temple (516/515 B.C.E.) and the reign of Alexander. See *EncJud* 14:1092.

[42] For references, see U. F. W. Bauer, "Anti-Jewish Interpretations of Psalm 1 in Luther and in Modern German Protestantism," *Journal of Hebrew Scriptures* (Electronic) 2 (1998): 1–27, esp. 12. The irony is that for the classical rabbis the end of prophecy was a positive development, divinely sanctioned.

[43] The best-known opponents of the OT as Christian Scripture were the Marcionites and the Gnostics.

Testament.[44] Second, when it came to the manner of interpretation, much of the NT interprets the OT very narrowly in what is often referred to as "fulfillment exegesis." For these writers OT Scripture was a coded prophecy predicting what would happen in the end of days in which they perceived themselves to be living.[45] Accordingly, these writers viewed all of OT Scripture as a prediction of what would happen to them and their contemporaries. Here is a well-known example from the second chapter of Matthew:

> Now when they had departed, behold, an angel of the Lord appeared to Joseph in a dream and said, "Rise, take the child and his mother, and flee to Egypt, and remain there till I tell you; for Herod is about to search for the child, to destroy him." And he rose and took the child and his mother by night, and departed to Egypt, and remained there until the death of Herod. This was to fulfill[46] what the Lord had spoken by the prophet, "Out of Egypt have I called my son." (Matt 2:13–15)

In contrast, the rabbis, who probably were a subgroup within the larger Pharisaic community,[47] read expansively. They applied to Scripture the same kinds of methods that Hellenistic[48] and Mesopotamian[49] scholars had brought to their texts. By inference from minor to major, inference by analogy, extension of a regulation found in one biblical passage to another passage, derivation of laws from apparently superfluous words, and the

---

[44] The NT writings do not "defile the hands" according to *t. Yad.* 2:13. There was some rabbinic controversy about whether the fact that NT books (presumably owned by Jewish Christians) contained the name of God obligated Jews to attempt to rescue them from a blaze. See *t. Šabb.* 13:5 (ed. Lieberman, 58).

[45] The roots of fulfillment exegesis are in the OT itself as may be seen in the example of Dan 9 cited above. Two other good examples are 1 Kgs 2:27 and 2 Chr 36:22. The tendency is especially pronounced in the pesher literature of the Qumran community. See Devorah Dimant, "Pesharim, Qumran," *ABD* 5:244–51.

[46] The Greek verb employed here, πληρόω, "make full," (LSJ, 1419–20) is the same used by the Septuagint to translate Hebrew כלה, "bring to an end," "complete," and מלא, "fill up," when these verbs connote "fulfill a prophecy." See 1 Kgs 2:27; 2 Chr 36:21; and 2 Chr 36:22; See further Gerhard Delling, "πληρόω," *TDNT* 6:286–98; Charles Moule, "Fulfill," *IDB* 2:327–38; Gene Tucker, "Exegesis," *IDBSup* 296–303; G. Stanton, "Matthew," in *It Is Written,* 205–19.

[47] For recent bibliography on rabbinic origins, see Hermann Strack and Günter Stemberger, *Introduction to Talmud and Midrash* (Edinburgh: T&T Clark, 1991), 1–2.

[48] See Saul Lieberman, *Hellenism in Jewish Palestine* (New York: Jewish Theological Seminary of America, 1950), 47–82.

[49] See Stephen Lieberman, "A Mesopotamian Background for the So-Called Aggadic 'Measures' of Biblical Hermeneutics?" *HUCA* 58 (1987): 157–225.

use of word play,[50] the rabbis made it possible to derive new laws from the ancient texts as well as to find support in the biblical text for traditions that had arisen independently of Scripture. By opening up the Torah in this manner, rabbinic Judaism laid the foundations for the forms of Judaism that were to survive until the end of the eighteenth century.

With the close of the NT, Christian exegesis became more complex. Hirshman observes that we can identify many more genres of written exegesis in Christian sources of late antiquity than in Jewish writings of the same period.[51] Nonetheless, because Christian polemics were often based on the desire to demonstrate that the Jews had failed to interpret their own Scripture correctly,[52] Christian reading of Scripture continued (and continues) to bind the OT and NT much more closely than Jewish reading bound the OT to rabbinic tradition.[53] Martin Luther, who spearheaded Christianity's return to Scripture, was committed to the exegetical principle that in interpreting OT texts, "the *sensus literalis* is at the same time the *sensus propheticus,* that is, refers to Jesus Christ."[54]

The adversarial history of Judaism and Christianity over the centuries has falsified the claim of Num 12. If the prophecy of Moses was clear and "not in riddles," succeeding generations have found matters a good deal more complicated. A live prophet may be interrogated by an audience and required to clarify a prophetic utterance. In contrast, once prophecy survived only in written texts, it became open to ever-constant reinterpretation. The result is that even sections of Scripture that were reasonably clear to their original target audiences have become overlaid with meanings inconceivable to their authors. Contemporary Christians and Jews must reckon with the theologically significant fact that their religious beliefs and practices are hardly based on plain-sense interpretations of Scripture. Our

---

[50] See the chapter on rabbinic hermeneutics in Strack and Stemberger, *Talmud and Midrash,* 17–34; for detailed studies, see David Weiss Halivni, *Peshat and Derash: Plain and Applied Meaning in Rabbinic Exegesis* (New York: Oxford University Press, 1991); idem, "Reflections on Classical Jewish Hermeneutics," *PAAJR* 62 (1996): 21–127.

[51] See Marc Hirshman, *A Rivalry of Genius: Jewish and Christian Biblical Interpretation in Late Antiquity* (trans. B. Stein; Albany: State University of New York Press, 1996), 21.

[52] See Reidar Hvalvik, *The Struggle for Scripture and Covenant: The Purpose of the* Epistle of Barnabas *and Jewish-Christian Competition in the Second Century* (Tübingen: Mohr Siebeck, 1996) and the review by Robert F. Hull Jr., *JECS* 6 (1998): 325–27.

[53] See Jon D. Levenson, "Why Jews Are Not Interested in Biblical Theology," in *Judaic Perspectives on Ancient Israel* (ed. Jacob Neusner, Baruch A. Levine, and Ernest S. Frerichs; Philadelphia: Fortress, 1987), 281–307, esp. 286.

[54] Bauer, "Psalm 1," 5.

respective Judaisms and Christianities would have made little sense to Moses, Miriam, Mary, or Jesus. It appears to me that Jewish and Christian biblicists should be prepared to affirm publicly that our common goal is to recover the range of meanings that the different components of Scripture had for their audiences, even when the scriptural texts have been assigned far different meanings by the church and synagogue. Surely there is no longer any need for Christian readers to find the Holy Ghost of the Trinity in the רוח אלהים of Gen 1:2 any more than for Jews to force monotheism into the verse, "let us make humans in our image" (Gen 1:26). But we should be sharing a second common goal: the dissemination of what Scripture has meant within the faith communities even when those meanings have resulted from radical recontextualization. It is probably fair to say that most Jews and Christians are largely unaware of each other's interpretative traditions. As such it may be the task of the next generation of Bible scholars to adopt the medieval model of multiple senses of Scripture in the following way. We should encourage the continuing uses of "mainstream" biblical scholarship to recover what the NT and OT might have meant to their earliest audiences. Alongside this enterprise we should encourage the compilation of a series modeled on the Christian *glossa ordinaria* and the Jewish מקראות גדולות in which biblical texts are surrounded by commentaries from within the respective traditions.[55] That way Christian readers of Exod 17, for example, would learn that when Moses raised his hands against Amalek, they were raised in prayer. Jewish readers would learn on the same page that with his raised hands Moses made the sign of the cross. The interreligious activity of combining what have been for the most part separate academic disciplines could prove most salutary.

---

[55] I thank Arthur Samuelson for suggesting in another context the notion of an interfaith project incorporating the insights of the great precritical Christian and Jewish commentators.

A Christian Approach to the Theology of Hebrew Scriptures

Rolf Rendtorff

The Hebrew Scriptures As Christian Bible

Looking at the history of theological interpretation of the Old Testament, it seems rather surprising to speak of a theology of Hebrew Scriptures. In a 1992 volume on *The Flowering of Old Testament Theology* only one Jewish scholar, Jon D. Levenson, is included. He is quoted from a 1985 publication saying, "the sad fact, however, is that the endeavor known as 'Old Testament theology' has been, as its name suggests, an almost exclusively Gentile affair."[1] Gentile obviously means Christian, in particular Protestant. In 1987 Levenson published an essay entitled "Why Jews Are Not Interested in Biblical Theology."[2] In this essay he explores why there is no Jewish equivalent of Walther Eichrodt's or Gerhard von Rad's well-known works.

Obviously the situation has changed. Now Jewish and Christian scholars are invited to speak about their specific approaches to a theology of Hebrew Scriptures. The terminology is striking: Instead of *Old Testament* the term *Hebrew Scriptures* is used. Of course, although commonly used in different contexts, Old Testament is an exclusively Christian term. There can only be an "Old" Testament if there is also a "New," and only both Testaments together form the Christian Bible.

What is the origin of the term *Hebrew Scriptures?* One of the traditional names for the Jewish Bible is כתבי הקדש, "the Holy Scriptures," which were written in Hebrew anyhow. So Hebrew Scriptures seems to be a specifically Jewish term. But this is only half the truth. The term "the Scripture," ἡ γραφή, or "the Scriptures," αἱ γραφαί, appears frequently in the New Testament, referring to the Bible of the writers and readers of the New Testament, that is to the Jewish Bible, the Hebrew Scriptures, the Holy Scriptures (e.g., Rom

---

[1] B. C. Ollenburger, E. A. Martens, and G. F. Hasel, eds., *The Flowering of Old Testament Theology: A Reader in Twentieth-Century Old Testament Theology, 1930–1990* (Winona Lake, Ind.: Eisenbrauns, 1992), 429.

[2] In Jacob Neusner, B. A. Levine, and E. S. Frerich, eds., *Judaic Perspectives on Ancient Israel* (Philadelphia: Fortress, 1987), 281–307.

1:2). In whatever language they might have used their Bible, it is obvious that "Scriptures" is a term common to Jews and Christians.

The first Christians were Jews, Jesus included. They quoted from their Bible, that is from the Jewish Bible. But after the separation of the Christian community from the majority of the Jews the Christian Bible was no longer simply the Jewish Bible. It became something else, finally a two-part Bible whose first part was more or less in accordance with the Jewish Bible. At this point our specific problem begins. First, both parts of the Christian Bible were written in Greek. The Hebrew Scriptures for the Christians were no longer in Hebrew! Of course, the majority of Jews in the world of late antiquity lived in Greek-speaking contexts, so the language must not have been a reason for conflict or antagonism. Ever since the Christians had adopted the first Greek translation of the Hebrew Bible, the Septuagint, many Jews ceased to use this translation. So the Septuagint became the first Christian Old Testament.[3] One of the main consequences was that both parts of the Christian Bible were written in the same language, in Greek. So it seemed to be really *one* Bible.

Later in the Western churches the Latin translation, the Vulgate, dominated. It is still in liturgical use in the Roman Catholic Church. The Reformation turned to the study of the original languages of the Bible. One very important result of this change was that from now on Old Testament and New Testament appeared to be two different books, written in two different languages. The consequences are obvious, in particular when after the Enlightenment theologians concentrated more and more on the biblical texts in their original languages. The final step was the almost complete separation of Old Testament and New Testament studies in the academic world.

One might imagine that at this point the scholarly study of the Hebrew part of the Bible would have become a common effort of Jewish and Christian scholars. Obviously this was not the case, and for different reasons. Here one very important aspect of naming the Scriptures common to Jews and Christians the "Old Testament" becomes visible: Jewish scholars were *de facto* excluded from the academic study of their own Bible because these studies were exclusively executed as Old Testament studies in the framework of confessional Christian theological faculties.[4] On the other hand, the kind of scholarly Bible studies done in "mainstream" institutions

---

[3] See Emanuel Tov, "The Septuagint," *Mikra: Text, Translation, Reading and Interpretation of the Hebrew Bible in Ancient Judaism and Early Christianity* (ed. M. J. Mulder; CRINT 2.1; Assen: Van Gorcum; Philadelphia: Fortress, 1988), 163.

[4] For these developments, see in particular M. H. Goshen-Gottstein, "Christianity, Judaism and Modern Bible Study," *Congress Volume Edinburgh 1974* (ed. G. W. Anderson; VTSup 28; Leiden: Brill, 1975), 69–88.

did not belong to the main interests of Jewish studies, so that even in Jewish scholarly institutions in the nineteenth and early twentieth century little endeavor in the field of modern critical biblical studies was undertaken.

Reflecting on the reasons why things have now changed, one of the actual causes may be that the center of biblical studies moved from Europe to North America, with its different system of higher education. Here Bible studies and Bible teaching are now executed in a great variety of different universities, schools, seminaries, and the like, most of them in one way or the other involved in the development of "the modern secular university ... in the United States."[5] The opportunities for Jewish students to study Bible in a modern context that is not identified as Christian are much better than ever before, and likewise the chances for Jewish scholars to get teaching positions in this field.

The second important development is the gradual change of Christian-Jewish relations. Today many Christians, in particular Christian Bible scholars, are aware of the fact that the first part of their Bible had been the Jewish Bible before Christianity came into being, and still *is* the Jewish Bible. Through the centuries much too often Christian theologians even denied any Jewish claim upon the Old Testament after Christ. Since at least the majority of Christian Bible scholars have given up this kind of supersessionism, there is now room for new reflections. Recently, Christians who are engaged in Christian-Jewish relations have been discussing the use of terms other than *Old Testament* because some feel that even the term *Old Testament* itself includes an element of expropriating the Bible from the Jewish people. Some prefer the term *First Testament* in order to avoid the word "old," which could be—and often is—understood as outdated. Others speak about the *Jewish Bible* or *Israel's Bible*. In any case, since among Christian Bible scholars the idea of having a monopoly on the Old Testament, called by whatever name, is no longer accepted, it is much easier to use common terminology such as *Hebrew Bible* or *Hebrew Scriptures*.

Now, however, we are back to our original question: In what sense are the Hebrew Scriptures part of the Christian Bible? The problems are well known. Along with the problem of the different languages, the structure of the canon also presents difficulties. The different versions of Christian Bibles do not reflect the tripartite canon of the Hebrew Bible, the Tanak. The main change is the position of the prophetic books at the end of the Christian canon; furthermore, the positions of certain books such as Ruth, Chronicles, Ezra-Nehemiah, Esther, Threni, and Daniel are different; and finally the Apocrypha (deuterocanonical books) is included in the Roman Catholic canon. Whatever the particular reasons for those changes might

---

[5] E. S. Frerichs, "Introduction: The Jewish School of Biblical Studies" in *Judaic Perspectives on Ancient Israel,* 5.

have been, in any case the theological message of the canon(s) of the Christian Bible(s) seems to be different from that of the Hebrew Bible.

What does this mean for the approach of Christian scholars to the Hebrew Scriptures? Surprisingly enough, the majority of Christian Bible scholars who concentrate in the first Testament actually work in the framework of the canon of the Hebrew Bible. This is particularly evident with the classical introductions to the Old Testament by Otto Eissfeldt,[6] Rudolf Smend,[7] Brevard S. Childs,[8] and others, my own included.[9] These scholars arrange their books according to the tripartite Hebrew canon, even using the Hebrew titles Torah, Former Prophets, Latter Prophets, and Writings. Here it becomes evident that notwithstanding the divergent theological traditions the textual basis for the studies of Jewish and Christian scholars is actually the same. This is also evident in the common use of the *Biblia Hebraica,* first *Kittel* and then *Stuttgartensia,* presenting the text of the Hebrew Bible according to the Jewish Masorah, worked out by German Protestant scholars.

So far there is a broad and solid textual basis for common scholarly work of Jews and Christians on the Hebrew Scriptures. In many fields of exegesis, philology, history, and the like, a fruitful interchange between Jewish and Christian scholars developed in the last decades, in many cases even without any consideration of religious or confessional background.

Present Christian Approaches

The moment we enter the field of theology, complications arise. The first reason for that is the fact that "theology" is a central Christian term while it is not in use in Jewish religious tradition. "Therefore it has been frequently asserted that Judaism has no theology."[10] In 1987 Moshe Goshen-Gottstein published an article "on the possibility and necessity of a hitherto nonexisting area of academic study in the field of biblical religion: the theology of Tanakh."[11] In this respect on the Jewish side a shift

---

[6] Otto Eissfeldt, *The Old Testament: An Introduction* (trans. Peter R. Ackroyd; New York: Harper & Row, 1965).

[7] Rudolph Smend, *Die Entstehung des Alten Testaments* (4th ed.; Stuttgart: Kohlhammer, 1989).

[8] Brevard S. Childs, *Introduction to the Old Testament As Scripture* (London: SCM Press, 1979).

[9] Rolf Rendtorff, *The Old Testament: An Introduction* (trans. J. Bowden; Philadelphia: Fortress, 1986).

[10] *EncJud* 15:1103.

[11] M. H. Goshen-Gottstein, "Tanakh Theology: The Religion of the Old Testament and the Place of Jewish Biblical Theology," in *Ancient Israelite Religion:*

is taking place, as is demonstrated by this very volume. What can be said about Christian theology of the Old Testament? Is it as close to Jewish studies as are many of the other fields of biblical studies?

Of course not. It is sometimes disturbing to realize that the same Christian Bible scholars using the Hebrew Scriptures daily in their exegetical work turn in a totally different direction of thinking the moment they speak about theology of the Old Testament. A recent example comes from the well-established *Jahrbuch für Biblische Theologie*. Its 1997 volume included an article by Hermann Spieckermann on "Die Verbindlichkeit des Alten Testaments" (The Normativity of the Old Testament). The summarizing series of theses begins, "Theology of the Old Testament is a Christian discipline." The third thesis begins, "Both Testaments bear witness to Jesus Christ, each according to their own ways.... The basis of cognition (*Erkenntnisgrund*) of the one truth of both testaments lies in the New Testament." The author does not even mention the existence of a Jewish religious community whose Bible is the same as the Christian Old Testament. It is obvious that for this kind of Christian theologian the Old Testament has no other theological message than a Christian one. In other words, the Old Testament has no distinctive message at all because there is only "one truth" witnessed by both Testaments.[12] This is just one quite recent example of a long Christian tradition of a total theological monopolizing of the Old Testament.

A much more differentiated position is presented by Brevard Childs.[13] He is also aware of the opinion that it is the "fundamental goal" of biblical theology "to understand the various voices within the whole Christian Bible, New and Old Testament alike, as a witness to the Lord Jesus Christ, the selfsame divine reality."[14] The way he chooses to explain this understanding, however, concedes much more theological relevance to the Old Testament.

The first part of his book, covering more than one hundred pages, is dedicated to "The Discrete Witness of the Old Testament."[15] The second part treats "The Discrete Witness of the New Testament," and finally the third part offers "Theological Reflection on the Christian Bible." This third part deals with a number of thematic topics, all of which lead up to dog-

---

Essays in Honor of Frank Moore Cross (ed. Patrick D. Miller Jr., P. D. Hanson, and S. D. McBride; Philadelphia: Fortress, 1987), 617–44.

[12] Hermann Spieckermann, "Die Verbindlichkeit des Alten Testaments: Unzeitgemäße Betrachtungen zu einem ungeliebten Thema," *Jahrbuch für Biblische Theologie* 12 (1997): *Hermeneutik* (Neukirchen-Vluyn: Neukirchener, 1998), 46, 47, 49 (25–51).

[13] Brevard S. Childs, *Biblical Theology of the Old and New Testaments: Theological Reflection on the Christian Bible* (Minneapolis: Fortress, 1992).

[14] Ibid., 85.

[15] Ibid., 95–207.

matics. Even in this part, each of the individual chapters begins with a paragraph on the Old Testament witness on specific topics such as "the identity of God," "God the creator," and so forth. So the voice and message of the Old Testament in its own right is heard throughout the book, even if it is finally included in the common testimony to Jesus Christ.

Childs's book highlights two basic elements in this kind of Christian biblical theology. First, in this context there is no independent theology of the Hebrew Bible or Old Testament because the theological reflection on the Old Testament is from the outset part and parcel of a Christian biblical theology that embraces both parts of the Christian Bible. This is true even if some authors use the term "Old Testament theology."[16] Secondly, Old Testament theology is finally part of Christian dogmatics. This becomes quite clear from the overall structure of Childs's book. This is of particular interest because almost every account of the history of biblical theology begins with Johann Philipp Gabler's famous *oratio* from 1787 about the distinction between biblical and dogmatic theology.[17] This has always been taken as the beginning of the liberation of biblical theology from dogmatic preconditions and of the development of an independent biblical theology. Now Childs explicitly revokes this separation, pleading for "a return to a pre-Gabler position"[18] and leaving the final word to dogmatics.

This is only one side of the present situation in the field of Christian Old Testament theology. The well-known theologies by Walther Eichrodt and Gerhard von Rad were far from any supersessionist attitude and also did not concede any role for dogmatics in unfolding the theology of the Old Testament. Of course, von Rad in particular was fully aware of the fact that the Old Testament is only one part of the Christian Bible. Therefore in the last part of his *Old Testament Theology* he very carefully drew some lines from the Old Testament to the New, but he did so only after he had finished his explication of the message of the Old Testament in its own right.[19] In general, the same could be said about the majority of other works on Old Testament theology in the period before and after von Rad. Most of the authors do not subjugate the Old Testament to theological criteria taken from Christian theology, be it the New Testament or dogmatics. Some do not even deal explicitly with the relations of the Old Testament to Christianity (e.g.,

---

16 Childs himself did so in his earlier book, *Old Testament Theology in a Canonical Context* (Philadelphia: Fortress, 1986).

17 See now Rolf Knierim, "On Gabler," in *The Task of Old Testament Theology: Substance, Method, and Cases* (Grand Rapids: Eerdmans, 1995), 495–556.

18 Childs is here quoting an earlier essay by Gerhard Ebeling, "The Meaning of 'Biblical Theology,'" in *Word and Faith* (Philadelphia: Fortress, 1963), 79–97.

19 Gerhard von Rad, *Old Testament Theology* (trans. D. M. G. Stalker; 2 vols.; New York: Harper & Row, 1962, 1965).

Eichrodt,[20] Köhler,[21] Zimmerli,[22] Preuß,[23] and Schreiner[24]) or just briefly in a historical review (e.g., Jacob[25]). Others (e.g., Vriezen,[26] Fohrer,[27] Terrien,[28] Westermann,[29] Schmidt,[30] and Brueggemann[31]) treat these problems more explicitly. All of them emphasize the independent theological relevance of the Old Testament, even as they reflect upon its relationship to the New Testament in different ways.

Nevertheless, one can still find some very recent publications on Old Testament theology that explicitly deny the independent value of the Old Testament for Christians. Gunneweg declares that only the New Testament could be the criterion for the adoption of the Old Testament as a book of the Christian church. Only where the Old Testament "measures up" to the New Testament criteria can it be adopted in a Christian way.[32] Kaiser repeats the earlier positions of Emanuel Hirsch and Rudolph Bultmann that the Old Testament can only be understood in its "failing" (*Scheitern*) as promise for Christians.[33] While it is obvious that this kind of old-fashioned

---

[20] Walther Eichrodt, *Theology of the Old Testament* (trans. J. A. Baker; 2 vols.; Philadelphia: Westminster, 1961–1967).

[21] Ludwig Köhler, *Old Testament Theology* (London: Lutterworth, 1957).

[22] Walter Zimmerli, *Old Testament Theology in Outline* (Atlanta: John Knox, 1978).

[23] H. D. Preuß, *Old Testament Theology* (2 vols.; Louisville: Westminster/John Knox, 1995–1996).

[24] Josef Schreiner, *Theologie des Alten Testaments* (Würzburg: Echter, 1995).

[25] Edmond Jacob, *Theology of the Old Testament* (London: Hodder & Stoughton, 1958).

[26] Th. C. Vriezen, *An Outline of Old Testament Theology* (Oxford: Blackwell, 1958; 2d ed., 1970).

[27] Georg Fohrer, *Theologische Grundstrukturen des Alten Testaments* (Berlin: de Gruyter, 1972).

[28] Samuel Terrien, *The Elusive Presence: Toward a New Biblical Theology* (New York: Harper & Row, 1978).

[29] Claus Westermann, *Elements of Old Testament Theology* (Atlanta: John Knox, 1982).

[30] W. H. Schmidt, *Alttestamentlicher Glaube* (8th ed.; Neukirchen-Vluyn: Neukirchener Verlag, 1996).

[31] Walter Brueggemann, *Theology of the Old Testament: Testimony, Dispute, Advocacy* (Minneapolis: Fortress, 1997).

[32] A. H. J. Gunneweg, *Biblische Theologie des Alten Testament: Eine Religionsgeschichte Israels in biblisch-theologischer Sicht* (Stuttgart: Kohlhammer, 1993), 36.

[33] Otto Kaiser, *Der Gott des Alten Testaments. Theologie des Alten Testaments 1: Grundlegung* (Göttingen: Vandenhoeck & Ruprecht, 1993), 86, 87.

conception and outdated theological position is still voiced, in my estimation these views cannot be taken as representative of a large number of Old Testament theologians in Germany today.[34]

Looking back at this whole field of Old Testament theology, it is obvious that on the one hand the only specific issue for Christians that properly goes beyond the Old Testament itself is the question of the relationship between the Old and New Testaments, while on the other hand very few Christian biblical theologians even mention the original and continuing Jewish character of the Hebrew Bible. Therefore, the question inherent in the title of this volume could only be answered by most of these theologians: There is no relationship between Christian and Jewish approaches to the Old Testament. Moreover, the Jewish character of the Old Testament is not felt to be a matter of relevance for Christian theologians.

Changing Views

Of course, this cannot be the last word in this discussion. Some years ago I had the chance to discuss these questions with Jewish and Christian Bible scholars at the 1989 University of Notre Dame Conference, "Hebrew Bible or Old Testament? Studying the Bible in Judaism and Christianity."[35] I would like to draw the lines from that discussion a step further. At the outset I want to state that the basic precondition for a fruitful working together of Christians and Jews toward a theological reading of the Hebrew Scriptures is the full acknowledgment by the Christians that these Scriptures are the Holy Scriptures of Judaism as well as of Christianity. Therefore it would be impossible to speak about the theological relevance of the Hebrew Scriptures exclusively in terms of a Christian perspective. The majority of Christian Bible scholars have given up the traditional Christian supersessionism when they are operating as biblical scholars. Unfortunately, when speaking about theology many of them fall back into a kind of exclusivism. They probably would not explicitly deny the theological relevance of the Hebrew Scriptures for Judaism, but they are not interested in this question because they do not see its relevance for themselves.

In my view, the problems lie still deeper. Christian theologians often forget that Christianity grew out of Judaism and that therefore Christian

---

[34] See my review: "Recent German Old Testament Theologies," *JR* 76 (1996): 328–37.

[35] Roger Brooks and J. J. Collins, eds., *Hebrew Bible or Old Testament? Studying the Bible in Judaism and Christianity* (Christianity and Judaism in Antiquity 5; Notre Dame: University of Notre Dame Press, 1990). My own contribution in this volume is "Toward a Common Jewish-Christian Reading of the Hebrew Bible," 89–108.

interpretation of the common Hebrew Holy Scriptures is always the second in order. Judaism has its own interpretation, which is in some senses much closer to the Hebrew text,[36] while Christian interpretation is mediated through another collection of writings, the New Testament. The question is how this mediation works and what the consequences are for a Christian understanding of the theology of the Hebrew Scriptures.

I believe that at this point the traditional Christian interpreters of the Bible are making a serious mistake. Usually the New Testament is taken as the starting point for comparing the two Testaments and for asking the question of the relevance of the Old Testament for Christian belief. By this procedure only a very small sector of the message of the Hebrew Scriptures comes in view. But such an approach is "highly misleading and one-sided in the extreme," because in the early church

> the Jewish scriptures were held as the authoritative voice of God.... The problem of the early church was not what to do with the Old Testament in the light of the gospel, which was Luther's concern, but rather the reverse. In the light of the Jewish scriptures which were acknowledged to be the true oracles of God, how were Christians to understand the good news of Jesus Christ?[37]

I am quoting Childs because he himself could have contributed to such a misleading view by saying just before that "it is basic to emphasize that something totally new began with the resurrection, and this sharp discontinuity in Israel's tradition is rightly reflected in the formation of two separate and distinct testaments. The old came to an end; the new began."[38] Then, however, he shows in many details the fundamental relevance of the Old Testament for Christian belief. Let me just refer to one basic point: the understanding of creation and of God as creator. Here, "it is apparent that the Old Testament's understanding of God as creator was simply assumed and largely taken for granted as true.... In a word, large portions of the New Testament reflect an unbroken continuity with the Old Testament trajectory of creation traditions."[39] And for Christians the first article of the

---

[36] It is not my task here to speak about the relevance of postbiblical interpretation of Scripture for Judaism. I think that my rather general formulation "much closer" will do justice to the relation between Jewish and Christian interpretation of Scripture.

[37] Childs, *Biblical Theology,* 225–26. Childs is here referring to Hans von Campenhausen, *The Formation of the Christian Bible* (Philadelphia: Fortress, 1972), 64ff.

[38] Childs, *Biblical Theology,* 225.

[39] Ibid., 391.

Apostles' Creed, that speaks about God the creator, is only understandable on the basis of the witness of the Hebrew Scriptures.

Other authors admit the important role of Old Testament theological topics, if even just on the fringes. Gunneweg, for example, writes that the church from the beginning used the Old Testament only "by selection," but that this selection

> complements the Christian message, because the latter [the early Christian community] from the beginning presupposes it and therefore doesn't explain it any more. One only need mention monotheism, belief in creation, the notion of election, the idea of the people of God among the nations, selections from the Psalter as the prayerbook of Christianity.[40]

This is indeed an impressive number of topics that the Christians took as an "addendum" to their own belief, and it could easily be expanded, in particular by including the message of the prophets. It would be more meaningful, however, to turn the argument the other way around: fundamental elements of the early Christian religious thinking and belief were Jewish. To them new elements were added, which finally gave the whole system of thinking another direction. But nevertheless, from the beginning basic elements of the message of the Hebrew Scriptures have been unquestioned and undisputed ingredients of Christian thinking and belief.

A New Departure Is Necessary

What does this mean for a Christian approach to the Hebrew Scriptures? First of all, there is no reason to approach the Hebrew Bible from a specific Christian point of view. The custom of many Christian theologians of approaching the Hebrew Bible backwards from the New Testament or Christian dogmatics fails to do justice to the actual relevance of many theological topics of the Hebrew Bible for Christian thinking and belief. That God is *one,* and that there is no other God, early Christians knew from their own Jewish tradition, and they "continued as good Jews ... to worship the one God of the Old Testament,"[41] that is, of their own Bible. The same is true for other topics such as God the creator and the whole understanding of human life within the creation, including the responsibility of humans for the preservation of the created world. This is a particularly important point today, when many Christians are reflecting on ecological problems. While they will not find much help in the New Testament on these concerns, the Hebrew Bible is more helpful.

[40] Gunneweg, *Biblische Theologie,* 36.

[41] Childs, *Biblical Theology,* 365

Another important field is the book of Psalms. Nowhere in the whole Bible will the Christian reader find so much guidance and instruction for prayer, individually and in common, as in the Hebrew Scriptures. Even more importantly, Christian worship is not imaginable without the Psalms. At very specific points of Christian liturgy certain psalms are indispensable as, for example, Ps 103 for unfolding God's merciful behavior toward sinful humans. Few Christian pastors or priests would tell their congregations that they should understand what they are praying or hearing in the words of the Hebrew psalms in a specifically Christian way that is different from the original meaning of the words. That God is merciful and that humans could not live without being conscious of that is one of the fundamental elements of the message of the Hebrew Scriptures from its very beginning.

I could continue to name basic elements of the Hebrew Scriptures that are obvious Jewish contributions to Christian thinking and belief. Of course, there are also many other concepts that only emerge upon deeper reflection. The concept of divine election is an important example. The election of Abraham and his descendants meant first of all the separation of one group of humans for the exclusive service of the *one* God. All those who were participating in this service of the one God were included in this election. In a more specific sense the election of Abraham meant the election of the Jewish people. At this point a problem arose for the Christian community. At the beginning, the followers of Jesus were a group of Jews who adhered to a peculiar messianic belief but remained members of the Jewish people. Later more and more Gentiles joined this group and finally became the majority. From that point on the now so-called Christians (see Acts 11:26) progressively became a community different and separated from the Jewish people. From a theological point of view the question arose whether and how this new community could claim to be included among the adressees of the divine promises given in the Hebrew Scriptures to the people of Israel.

Unfortunately, "something went wrong in the beginning,"[42] because this problem was not handled in a way that did justice to both sides. Instead, the Christians declared themselves to be the only legitimate heirs of Abraham's election. They not only took over terms like "people of God" and "the chosen people," but even called themselves the new Israel or the true Israel and the like. It is important to realize that this had not yet happened in New Testament times. In particular the Apostle Paul clearly spoke about Israel in its original sense, even emphasizing his own membership in this people (Rom 11:1; cf. 9:3). Nevertheless, the Christian approach to

---

[42] Krister Stendahl, "Judaism and Christianity II: A Plea for a New Relationship," *Harvard Divinity Bulletin*, NS 1 (1967): 2–9; repr. in idem, *Meanings: The Bible As Document and As Guide* (Philadelphia: Fortress, 1984), 224.

this matter developed in the wrong direction. Therefore, as we learn from Krister Stendahl and others, what we need now is a new departure. Certainly, something has been achieved in the last few decades, but the examples from recent publications cited above show clearly that we are still far from a commonly accepted, nonsupersessionist Christian position.

No False Polarization

Christian-Jewish relations as such are not the topic here. The main question is how Christians should deal with the traditions of the Hebrew Scriptures. In the previous sections I tried to clarify some of the preconditions. The complexity of the problem thus became evident. First, for Christians the Hebrew Scriptures are part of their Bible. This basic fact should always be the starting point. That means that at the outset the Christian interpreters need not justify their use of these Scriptures. They stand in a long tradition of reading this part of the Bible, which includes a broad spectrum of theological and social implications that shape contemporary Christians' approaches. At this point I am not speaking about more specific Christian implications like christology but rather about the broader theological milieu in which the Christian theological interpreter lives.

Second, the Christian interpreter of the Hebrew Scriptures should always be aware that there is another approach from the Jewish side. This awareness should include the realization that this part of the Bible has been written and composed at a time and in a context when Christianity did not yet exist and that the Jewish interpretation is much more immediate to the Hebrew Scriptures. This awareness should not necessarily influence or alter the Christian way of reading and interpreting the Hebrew Scriptures; but it should function as a kind of warning sign to avoid using certain elements of Christian interpretation that could have developed only after the closing of the canon of the Hebrew Scriptures.

Third, particularly problematic for Christians are those traditions in the Hebrew Scriptures that are specifically addressed to the Jewish people. Of particular relevance are the ideas of Israel's divine election and of God's covenant with the people of Israel as well as the promise of the land. In these fields Christians have to be particularly careful not to utilize these ideas in a way that results in expropriating them from the Jewish people. By such an interpretation Christians would put themselves in the wrong, even if there has been a long Christian tradition of this kind of interpretation. These points are of particular relevance for a new self-identification of Christianity toward Judaism. The relationship of the Christian church to the Jewish people in view of the biblical ideas of election and covenant are in my view among the most important topics to be considered by Christians as they attempt to relate themselves theologically to the religious world marked by the biblical traditions. Little theological energy has been expended on this important topic.[43]

Fourth, in a number of areas Christian theology developed ideas that explicitly go beyond the Hebrew Scriptures. The obvious example is, of course, the matter of messianism. I do not feel that this must be a really controversial field as long as Christian interpreters make a clear distinction between the words of the Hebrew Bible and its later Christian interpretation. A few texts in the Hebrew Bible express a messianic expectation. Others include certain elements that could be interpreted in a messianic way, though the interpretation is controversial. All these texts speak about the future, however, by expressing promises, expectations, and hopes. Christians say that certain of these promises are fulfilled in the appearance of Jesus Christ. Neverthless, Christians should never claim that such a Christian interpretation is *the* correct or the only possible interpretation. Even less should they argue that the texts of the Hebrew Bible themselves speak about Jesus Christ. Here things must be clearly separated. The pattern of promise and fulfillment in this field can only be a Christian one, which goes beyond the exegesis of the Hebrew Scriptures.

In other areas greater problems face us. The topics of sin and atonement are sad examples. The Hebrew Bible presents a full system of cultic performances for atonement, while one of the basic elements of Christian theology is the idea that through Jesus Christ the sin of believers is forgiven once and for all. This characterization, however, is an oversimplification of the problems, because in both contexts the presentation of sin and atonement is more subtle and nuanced. The Hebrew Bible includes a wide range of texts speaking about divine forgiveness of sins in a noncultic way, beginning in the primeval history and continuing through the Sinai story and later texts in Isaiah, Psalms, and elsewhere. All these texts are open to Christian interpretation and adoption. On the other hand, in the Christian tradition many elements of cultic or quasi-cultic handling of atonement and forgiveness can be found that are, of course, different from the handling of these matters in the Hebrew Bible, though not fundamentally contradictory.

I could continue speaking about the often-declared antithesis of law and gospel. Here the same is true as in the matters of sin and atonement. The usual oversimplification and polarization fail to do justice to both the Hebrew Bible and Christian belief. The Hebrew Bible is full of gospel, and Christian tradition, not only Catholic but also Protestant, is far from being without law. Here we are entering a complex field of theological interpretation that is beyond the focus of this paper.

---

[43] In Germany this discussion began in the last few years, among others in the journal *Kirche und Israel* since 1991.

Steps to Be Taken

It is my conviction that the Christian Bible scholar first of all should interpret the Hebrew Scriptures in their own right. This includes explaining the theology of these Scriptures. One could argue, as Jon Levenson has,[44] that such an approach would compel the interpreter to step outside of his or her religious context and "to bracket their traditional identities."[45] Therefore Levenson calls this meeting ground of Jews and Christians a "neutral ground." In a sense this is true. But it is also true, as Levenson adds, that such bracketing has not only its limitations but "can have great value." I would like to add that it is highly necessary that Bible scholars read and interpret the Hebrew Scriptures very carefully before going beyond these Scriptures into the realm of their respective religious traditions. I believe that the task of biblical scholars is to understand and explain the message of the Hebrew Scriptures within their own historical and social context.

The next step then will be very different for Jewish and Christian scholars. For the Jewish scholar the wide field of midrashic and halakic interpretation of biblical texts presents itself. In the Christian tradition nothing is quite comparable. In particular, almost no methodological reflection on the reception and interpretation of "the discrete witness of the Old Testament" (to use Childs's terminology) can be found in early Christianity. Above I spoke about the error of looking only at those elements of the Old Testament tradition that are explicitly present and interpreted in the New Testament. In addition, while the question of what a biblical theology of the Old and New Testaments should look like has been widely discussed, Brevard Childs was the first one actually to present such a work. Unfortunately he tried to take two steps at the same time: from the Old Testament to the New and from the Christian Bible to dogmatics. He himself explained how difficult the second step must be: "The problem is complex and controversial because the concept of dogmatic theology is presently as much in flux as is Biblical Theology."[46] While Childs himself has a clear idea of his dogmatic position, based on his studies with Karl Barth, in my view his concept cannot be taken as a widely acceptable approach to a biblical theology.

What is necessary is a close cooperation between scholars of the Hebrew Bible and of the New Testament who are strongly committed to understanding and to explaining the biblical religion of the early Christians,

---

[44] Jon D. Levenson, "Theological Consensus or Historistic Evasion? Jews and Christians in Biblical Studies," in *Hebrew Bible or Old Testament?* 109–45.

[45] Ibid., 144.

[46] Childs, *Biblical Theology,* 89.

namely, their being rooted in their Jewish Scriptures, be they in Hebrew or Greek. Only through such cooperation would it be meaningful to point out the divergences of certain Christian views and beliefs from the common Jewish understanding of the Scriptures. The evaluation of those differences and their developments, however, would look different from such a starting point than from the starting points of the past, when Jews and Christians were not cooperating with each other. Recently some scholars from different backgrounds emphasized the Jewishness of Christianity. Norbert Lohfink, a well-known Roman Catholic professor of Old Testament in Germany, entitled a book *The Jewish Element in Christianity*.[47] David Flusser, the famous Jewish scholar in Jerusalem, went even further with the title of his book *Christianity: A Jewish Religion* (literal translation of German original).[48] In both cases the title is a kind of signal within a wider context. I mention these titles in order to show that there is a certain movement, after a much too lengthy history of antagonism and mutual misinterpretation, towards a reflection on the common ground on which both Jews and Christians stand.[49] It is in this framework that I understand my own endeavors toward a theology of Hebrew Scriptures.

---

[47] Norbert Lohfink, *Das Jüdische am Christentum: Die verlorene Dimension* (Freiburg: Herder, 1987).

[48] David Flusser, *Judaism and the Origins of Christianity* (Jerusalem: Magnes, 1990).

[49] I am aware of the complexity of the term *Jewish*. Levenson ("Theological Consensus or Historistic Evasion?" 143) takes it in a strict sense when he declares that the novelty of the situation in biblical studies "lies in the recovery of the Hebrew Bible as opposed to the *Tanakh* and the Old Testament affirmed by rabbinic Judaism and Christianity, respectively." The authors of the last-mentioned books are taking it in a broader sense including the Hebrew Bible. While the first connotation is more precise, the latter is often intended in the framework of Christian-Jewish relations.

Part 1:

Theoretical Perspectives

Section 3:

Engaging Evil

Reconceiving the Paradigms of Old Testament Theology in the Post-Shoah Period[1]

Marvin A. Sweeney

The Breakdown of the Enlightenment Consensus

The field of Christian Old Testament theology, and indeed biblical exegesis in general, is currently undergoing a major methodological paradigm shift as it makes the transition from the "Age of Enlightenment" to the "post-modern" world. In his recently published survey of the field, Leo Perdue characterizes this methodological shift as "the collapse of history," which in his understanding refers to the general assault now being mounted by scholars who are dissatisfied with the historical paradigms that have dominated biblical exegesis and theological discourse for the past two to three centuries of the "Age of Enlightenment."[2] To be sure, Perdue does not argue that historical criticism has become "passé, impossible, or insignificant for modern Old Testament scholarship and Old Testament theology," although many scholars maintain that such is precisely the case.[3] Rather, he points to the breakdown of the dominant scholarly consensus that posits a unified epistemological worldview based upon historical positivism and that promotes historical critical exegesis as the only legitimate means by which to arrive at an authoritative interpretation of the Bible. In an increasingly pluralistic climate that acknowledges the great diversities in the means by which human beings perceive their world and establish truth claims, historical criticism has now become not the exclusive means to establish legitimate interpretation of the Bible, but one among an ever-growing number of reading strategies that are employed to interpret the Bible, such as liberation and feminist hermeneutics, new literary and reader-response criticism,

---

[1] This is a slightly revised version of a paper published in *Biblical Interpretation* 6 (1998): 142-61. I would like to thank E. J. Brill publishers for granting permission to republish the essay in the present volume. It is based on the lecture I presented at my installation as Professor of Hebrew Bible at the School of Theology of Claremont, January 23, 1996.

[2] Leo Perdue, *The Collapse of History: Reconstructing Old Testament Theology* (OBT; Minneapolis: Fortress, 1994).

[3] Ibid, 4.

canonical hermeneutics, and others. One can no longer speak of a single "normative" method for engaging the field of Old Testament theology.

In discussing the reasons for this change, Perdue points to a variety of factors, such as the methodological diversity that appears in the field of theology at large and the need to engage the Hebrew Bible text with the constructive concerns of contemporary theology and culture. In short, he describes the character of the debate largely in terms of the proper exegetical and theological methods employed in biblical interpretation. But in order to understand the full dimensions of the debate, the methodological changes now taking place in Old Testament theology must be considered in relation to the political, social, and economic changes that have played major roles in bringing about this paradigmatic shift and in influencing its character and directions.[4] Indeed, the universalist, monolithic, or "normative" assumptions that informed the worldview of Enlightenment scholarship also played a role in determining who might participate in theological discourse. Although the rhetoric of the Enlightenment spoke of universal human reason as the essential criterion by which "objective" truth claims might be measured, in practice the historical progressive elements in Enlightenment thought combined with its relatively introspective and chauvinistic character to define the Western European, liberal Protestant, heterosexual male as the normative model of the human being capable of exercising reason in the modern progressive Enlightenment world.[5]

In this regard, the epistemological claims of the Enlightenment must be viewed in relation to at least three underlying socioeconomic, political, and religious factors: (1) the political, economic, and religious ascendancy of Western European powers that were able to dominate much of the rest

[4] For a full discussion of the impact on theological exegesis of the social, political, and economic changes that have taken place in the Western world since World War II, see Robert Morgan with John Barton, *Biblical Interpretation* (Oxford Bible Series; Oxford: Oxford University Press, 1988).

[5] For an example of this contradiction in Enlightenment German society, see Paul Lawrence Rose, *Revolutionary Antisemitism in Germany from Kant to Wagner* (Princeton, N.J.: Princeton University Press, 1990). Rose's study points to the continuation of the anti-Semitic mentality in early Enlightenment German society, which advocated the emancipation of Jews while simultaneously demanding that they give up their distinctive cultural and religious identity that set them apart from their Gentile counterparts. In effect, the emancipation of Jews in eighteenth-century Germany functioned as a call for their assimilation into the German "mainstream" or their disappearance as a distinctive social entity within German culture. See Lucy S. Dawidowicz, *The War against the Jews 1933–1945* (New York: Holt, Rinehart & Winston; Philadelphia: Jewish Publication Society of America, 1975), 23-47, who traces modern German anti-Semitism and the roots of the Shoah into the eighteenth-century Enlightenment.

of the world; (2) the early industrial revolution that changed the socio-economic fabric of preindustrial culture by giving the male much greater power and autonomy than he had possessed before; and (3) the constitutive influence of Protestant Christianity that, because of its inherent interests in theological repristinization and renewal and its role as the major religious voice in most of the Western European powers, was able to dominate and define theological discourse during the Enlightenment. All three of these factors played major roles in defining the "objective," "empirical," "historical," and "universal" character of Old Testament theology during the Enlightenment period.

In light of changes in the character of each of these factors since World War II, many modern critics have successfully argued that no fully objective interpretation of the biblical text can be achieved, because biblical interpretation is not simply a description of the concerns of the biblical text. More properly, biblical interpretation must be understood as the product of the interaction of the text and the subjective concerns, perspectives, and biases of the reader.[6] Thus, subjective constructive theological concerns in fact enter into the supposedly "objective" historical-critical reconstructions of the past, in that historically oriented scholars have been insufficiently aware of or concerned with their own theological and social biases and the role that these biases play in historical exegesis. In this respect, historical-critical exegesis has frequently served as a means to legitimate the theological perspectives and socio-theological standing of its practitioners. Several examples demonstrate the point. The emphasis placed upon the spiritual vitality of iconoclastic and individualist prophecy over against that of the institutionally oriented priesthood and temple reflects Protestant Christianity's separation from the Roman Catholic Church. The relative disinterest in the feminine or nurturing qualities of G-d as opposed to the role of G-d as warrior, king, and judge who righteously takes land from less progressive pagans and gives it to his religious elect reflects both the male-dominated character of the western European social structure and its interest in colonizing much of the non-European world. The interest in YHWH's universal relationship to the nations as opposed to the "sinful" people Israel, who transgressed the Mosaic covenant and thereby prepared the way for YHWH's revelation to the Gentiles, reflects Christianity's ascendancy over Judaism and its rejection of Judaism's theological legitimacy in the aftermath of the Second Temple's destruction.

---

[6] Reader-response criticism is especially influential in these perspectives. For a brief overview and bibliography, see Bernard C. Lategan, "Reader Response Theory," *ABD* 5:625–28. See especially, Stanley Fish, *Is There a Text for this Class? The Authority of Interpretive Communities* (Cambridge: Harvard University Press, 1980).

World Wars I and II, as well as other factors, have provoked the relative diminution of Western European political, economic, and religious power in the world at large, and the emergence of the postindustrial revolution has enhanced the social and economic roles of women relative to men. As a result, the dominance of the white, Anglo-Saxon, heterosexual, Protestant male in theological discourse is now facing increasing challenges. The years since the World Wars have seen the emergence of an increasingly pluralistic world in which growing numbers of national, social, and religious groups have been able to assert their views and roles within the larger world. Thus, contemporary Old Testament theology sees the influence of a great variety of voices and perspectives, such as those of women, Africans, Asians, Latinos, Roman Catholics, Jews, gays and lesbians, and others, who were marginalized in the past because they stood outside the "normal" social paradigms for those who were considered to be eligible to engage in "legitimate" theological discourse. The result is greater attention to areas of specific interest to these constituencies that were routinely ignored or devalued in the past. Examples include the role of women in the Hebrew Bible, the social and literary dimensions of legal literature, the role of the priesthood and temple in Judahite society, and the role of ethnicity within ancient Israel and Judah. The concerns of both past and present scholarship demonstrate that methodological discourse is as much the product of the identities of those taking part as it is of a concern to articulate the message of the Hebrew Bible itself. This does not mean, however, that historical criticism must come to an end. It simply means that those who engage in historical-critical exegesis must be aware of and account for their own biases and the ways in which they shape the character and results of theological exegesis.[7]

The Impact of the Shoah on Old Testament Theology

It is against this background that the topic "Reconceiving the Paradigms of Old Testament Theology in the Post-Shoah World" must be understood. The Shoah, or Holocaust as it is more popularly but inappropriately known,[8] is an especially important perspective by which to understand the changes that are now taking place in the field of Christian Old

---

[7] See, for example, John J. Collins, "Is a Critical Biblical Theology Possible?" in *The Hebrew Bible and Its Interpreters* (ed. William Propp, Baruch Halpern, and D. N. Freedman; Winona Lake, Ind.: Eisenbrauns, 1990), 1–17.

[8] For a discussion of the issues concerning the terms *Shoah* and *Holocaust,* see Zev Garber and Bruce Zuckerman, "Why Do We Call the Holocaust 'The Holocaust?' An Inquiry into the Psychology of Labels," *Modern Judaism* 9 (1989): 197–211; repr. in Zev Garber, *Shoah: The Paradigmatic Genocide* (Studies in the Shoah 8; Lanham, Md.: University Press of America, 1994), 51–66.

Testament theology, in that it points to the contradictions inherent in the supposedly objective and universalist claims of Enlightenment thought that have been expressed in the field. The attempted murder of the entire Jewish people in Europe during World War II was influenced in part by theological premises articulated within Christianity and identified as universal or normative during the Enlightenment. Christian theologians in many quarters have come to recognize the role that the *adversus Judaeos* tradition played in denigrating Judaism and the Jewish people in the history of Christian theology and biblical interpretation and in bringing about the reality of the Shoah.[9] As a result, Christian theology has begun to confront an element of evil within itself that was brought about by an exclusivist and self-legitimizing worldview that failed to value the existence and theological validity of others. Both Jewish and Christian theologians, such as Emil Fackenheim, Paul Van Buren, Rolf Rendtorff, and others, have argued that the Shoah has forever changed the way in which the Hebrew Bible is to be read theologically.[10] The supersessionist models of the past that denied theological legitimacy to Judaism and the Jewish people in Christian theology must be rejected as morally and theologically bankrupt.[11] This is not to say that Christian theology as a whole is even now

---

[9] See, for example, John T. Pawlikowski, "Christology, Anti-Semitism, and Christian-Jewish Bonding," in *Reconstructing Christian Theology* (ed. R. S. Chopp and M. L. Taylor; Minneapolis: Fortress, 1994), 245–68; Rosemary Radford Ruether, *Faith and Fratricide: The Theological Roots of Anti-Semitism* (New York: Seabury, 1974); Clark M. Williamson, *A Guest in the House of Israel: Post Holocaust Church Theology* (Louisville: Westminster/John Knox, 1993); Paul Van Buren, *A Christian Theology of the People Israel 2: A Theology of the Jewish-Christian Reality* (New York: Seabury, 1983).

[10] Emil L. Fackenheim, *The Jewish Bible after the Holocaust: A Re-reading* (Bloomington: Indiana University Press, 1990); Paul Van Buren, "On Reading Someone Else's Mail: The Church and Israel's Scriptures," in *Die Hebräische Bibel und ihre zweifache Nachgeschichte* (ed. Erhard Blum, Christian Macholz, and E. W. Stegemann; Festschrift R. Rendtorff; Neukirchen-Vluyn: Neukirchener Verlag, 1990), 595–606; Rolf Rendtorff, "The Impact of the Holocaust (Shoah) on German Protestant Theology," *HBT* 15 (1993): 154–67; idem, "Toward a Common Jewish-Christian Reading of the Hebrew Bible," *Canon and Theology: Overtures to an Old Testament Theology* (OBT; Minneapolis: Fortress, 1993), 31–45.

[11] See the introduction to *Hebrew Bible or Old Testament? Studying the Bible in Judaism and Christianity* (ed. Roger Brooks and John J. Collins; Christianity and Judaism in Antiquity 5; Notre Dame: University of Notre Dame Press, 1990), 1–11. See Walter Brueggemann, *Theology of the Old Testament: Testimony, Dispute, Advocacy* (Minneapolis: Fortress, 1997), which represents a legitimate attempt to engage Judaism theologically on its own terms while asserting a Christian theological perspective.

entirely free of anti-Jewish bias. For example, recent studies of elements within liberation and feminist theology point to the continued polemical use of Jewish theological stereotypes to convey models of unacceptable behavior and viewpoint.[12] Likewise, the antagonism to modern Zionism in many Christian circles is informed in part by a monolithic view of Judaism only as a religious entity, and a victimized or dependent one at that, when in fact Judaism is a combination of religious and national identities.[13] Nevertheless, the extensive interest in this question on the part of Christian theologians demonstrates a major effort on the part of the church, or churches, to rethink its/their relationship to Judaism and the Jewish people in light of the Shoah.

A reexamination of the role of Judaism and the Jewish people in Old Testament theology, both as it has been conceived in the past and how it might be conceived in the future, is therefore crucial to the interpretation of the Hebrew Bible in Christianity.[14] A great deal of modern Old Testament theology presupposes Wellhausen's historical-theological axiom that preexilic prophecy represents the earliest spiritual and universal core of the Hebrew Bible, whereas cultic matters and legal concern represent the degeneration of pristine Israelite religion into a spiritually vacuous and ritualistic Judaism during the postexilic period. The Protestant theological

[12] See, for example, Jon D. Levenson, "Exodus and Liberation," *The Hebrew Bible, The Old Testament, and Historical Criticism: Jews and Christians in Biblical Studies* (Louisville: Westminster/John Knox, 1993), 127–159; Katharina von Kellenbach, *Anti-Judaism in Feminist Religious Writings* (American Academy of Religion Cultural Criticism Series; Atlanta: Scholars Press, 1994).

[13] See Leonard Dinnerstein, *Anti-Semitism in America* (New York: Oxford University Press, 1994), 230–32; Norman Solomon, "The Christian Churches on Israel and the Jews," in *Anti-Zionism and Anti-Semitism in the Contemporary World* (ed. Robert S. Wistrich; New York: New York University Press, 1990), 141–54. On the continuity of the Jewish people from biblical times to the present as a distinct civilization, see now S. N. Eisenstadt, *Jewish Civilization: The Jewish Historical Experience in a Comparative Perspective* (Albany: State University of New York Press, 1992). Eisenstadt characterizes the Jewish people as a "civilization" because of the limits of both religious and national definitions. Eisenstadt's understanding of civilization combines elements of culture, ontology, and social dynamics and "entails the attempts to construct or reconstruct social life according to ontological visions that combine conception of the nature of the cosmos, or transmundane and mundane reality, with the regulation of the major arenas of social life and interaction" (13). For a full discussion of his understanding of civilization, see pp. 5–21, esp. pp. 13–17.

[14] See Joseph Blenkinsopp, "Old Testament Theology and the Jewish Christian Connection," *JSOT* 28 (1984): 3–15; Rendtorff, "The Impact of the Holocaust (Shoah) on German Protestant Theology"; idem, "Toward a Common Jewish-Christian Reading of the Hebrew Bible"; Brueggemann, *Theology of the Old Testament*.

agenda in such a conception is clear, as is the polemical interest in depicting Judaism and the Jewish people as irrelevant to the true religious core of the Hebrew Bible, namely, the Jewish people (and the Roman Catholic Church) sinned by not recognizing the truth of G-d's intended purposes and thereby relegated themselves to theological subservience to Protestant Christianity. As Jon Levenson has shown, past Old Testament theology has been severely hampered by Christian scholars who devalue and marginalize Judaism, Jewish concepts, and the Jewish people in their assessments of the theology of the Hebrew Bible.[15] Eichrodt's identification of Judaism's "torso-like appearance ... in separation from Christianity" underlies his efforts to denigrate a great deal of Israelite religion as legalistic and unsuited to the new covenant of Christianity. Von Rad's *heilsgeschichtliche* model likewise enables him to ignore the reality of postbiblical Judaism by arguing that Israel's history of redemption, expressed especially by the eighth-century prophets, led inexorably to its fulfillment in Jesus Christ. Although Judaism and the Jewish people do play roles in these theologies, their roles are defined especially by the theological stereotype of Israel as a monolithically sinful people that failed to recognize G-d's truth and thereby stand in judgment as foils to Christianity.

To be sure, scholars have been giving increasing attention both to the role that postbiblical Judaism and the Jewish people play in continuity with the articulation of theological ideas and practice in the Hebrew Bible and to the theological legitimacy of such ideas and practice. The Wellhausenian distinction between prophetic Israelite religion and postexilic, legalistic Judaism is now beginning to break down as scholars recognize the constitutive role of the temple as the center of creation and religious and national life in Judah's worldview and the source of its moral order expressed as Torah.[16] The commands to respect life, both human and animal, are rooted in priestly conceptions concerning the treatment of blood that underlie the kosher dietary laws, and the commands to respect and renew the land during the

---

[15] Jon D. Levenson, "Why Jews Are Not Interested in Biblical Theology," in *Hebrew Bible,* 33–61.

[16] Jon D. Levenson, "The Temple and the World," *JR* 64 (1984): 275–98; cf. idem, "The Jerusalem Temple in Devotional and Visionary Experience," in *Jewish Spirituality: From the Bible to the Middle Ages* (ed. A. Green; New York: Crossroad, 1988), 32–61; Marvin A. Sweeney, "The Book of Isaiah As Prophetic Torah," in *New Visions of Isaiah* (ed. R. F. Melugin and M. A. Sweeney; JSOTSup 214; Sheffield: JSOT Press, 1996), 50–67; Richard D. Nelson, *Raising up a Faithful Priest: Community and Priesthood in Biblical Theology* (Louisville: Westminster/John Knox, 1993); John G. Gammie, *Holiness in Israel* (OBT; Minneapolis: Fortress, 1989). Concern with the relevance of the Israelite cult to Old Testament theology was anticipated in John L. McKenzie, *A Theology of the Old Testament* (Garden City, N.Y.: Doubleday, 1974).

Sabbath and the Temple Sabbatical and Jubilee years entail care for both the land and the poor who live in it and underlie Judaism's long tradition of social and ecological responsibility. Likewise, scholars are paying greater attention to the social dynamism and theological creativity expressed within the Hebrew Bible. One such example is the Deuteronomistic History (DtrH) in the books of Joshua through Kings. The DtrH does not reflect a historical account of "sinful" Israel's demise, but a theological reflection on the causes of evil in which the authors address the problem of theodicy by choosing not to argue that G-d is evil, but that responsibility for evil lies instead within the people. As a result, Christian theologians are now coming to grasp the full theological significance of this issue: Judaism and the Jewish people are a theologically legitimate reality in their own right. They stand in continuity with the Hebrew Bible, which functions in two distinctive forms as the Tanak of Judaism and as the Old Testament, a component of the sacred Scripture of Christianity. Consequently, Judaism, the Jewish people, and the Hebrew Bible must be evaluated theologically both independently in and of themselves and in relation to Christianity.[17] They stand as the legitimate subjects of the Hebrew Bible and as its legitimate interpreters.

Such interaction in modern theological reflection is crucial to the well-being of both Christianity and Judaism. For Christianity, it provides the opportunity to address a moral problem that has been manifested in Christian theology in general and in Old Testament theology in particular, namely, the Christian rejection of Judaism and the Jewish people as theologically relevant in their own right. It also provides the opportunity for Christianity to continue its examination of the Old Testament as a component of the sacred Scriptures of the church, to reappropriate it as sacred Scripture that is theologically valid in its own right, and to read it as such without distorting its message in relation to the New Testament. For Judaism, it provides the opportunity to articulate a distinctive theological understanding of the Hebrew Bible over against that of Christianity, so that Judaism does not function merely as a stepping-stone to the New Testament within the larger context of Christian biblical theology. For both Christianity and Judaism, such interaction provides the opportunity to reconstruct their relationship in a manner that recognizes their common roots in the Hebrew Bible and at the same time respects the distinctive theological identity of each.[18]

---

[17] For discussion of major issues posed by reading the Hebrew Bible in its own right and in continuity with Christian tradition, see Roland Murphy, "Tanakh—Canon and Interpretation," in *Hebrew Bible or Old Testament?* 11–29; Brueggemann, *Theology of the Old Testament,* 1–114.

[18] A common Jewish-Christian reading of the Hebrew Bible has its place in Jewish-Christian dialogue, in that it points to the common roots of both Jewish and

The Task of Old Testament Theology in a Post-Shoah World

One must now ask what this means for the theological interpretation of the Christian Old Testament. During the years since World War II, Christian theological scholarship has increasingly turned its attention to the literary character and ideological perspectives of the books of the Hebrew Bible and to the social, political, and economic dimensions of the people of Israel who are presented in and who produced those books.[19] In both cases, these efforts represent to a large extent attempts to overcome the theological biases of the past. Literary critics have developed exegetical approaches that are less theologically selective, insofar as they have shown greater efforts to interpret the literature of the Hebrew Bible in its entirety as theologically relevant. Likewise, social-scientific approaches represent attempts to come to grips with the social reality of the people of Israel/Judaism as a living people in all of its socioeconomic, political, and ideological diversity, not as a stereotypical and monolithic theological construct.[20]

Nevertheless, the result has been somewhat of an impasse in Old Testament theology in that scholars, beginning especially with von Rad, have discovered that the books of the Hebrew Bible do not express a sin-

---

Christian traditions in the Hebrew Bible, but a common theology of the Hebrew Bible for both Judaism and Christianity as proposed by Rendtorff ("Toward a Common Jewish-Christian Reading of the Hebrew Bible," *Hebrew Bible or Old Testament?* 89–108; repr. in *Canon and Theology,* 31–45) is problematic because it threatens the theological legitimacy of each by collapsing their individual identities. See the comments by Jon D. Levenson ("Theological Consensus or Historicist Evasion? Jews and Christians in Biblical Studies," *Hebrew Bible or Old Testament?* 109–45; repr. in *Hebrew Bible,* 82–105) and David Levenson ("Different Texts or Different Quests? The Contexts of Biblical Studies," *Hebrew Bible or Old Testament?* 153–64).

[19] For an introduction to this discussion, see the essays collected in R. E. Clements, ed., *The World of Ancient Israel: Sociological, Anthropological, and Political Perspectives* (Cambridge: Cambridge University Press, 1989).

[20] Various scholars, on the other hand, have argued that the portrayal of Israel in biblical literature represents an artificial construct of the postexilic Jewish community that attempted to establish its identity by a retrospective projection of its own self-image into the past (e.g., P. R. Davies, *In Search of Ancient Israel* [JSOTSup 148; Sheffield: JSOT Press, 1992]; Thomas L. Thompson, *Early History of the Israelite People: From Written and Archaeological Sources* [Leiden: Brill, 1992]). Although such studies correctly raise a methodological issue of the extent to which later authors project their own self-understandings into the past, they must recognize that all historical writing is inherently retrojective. This does not negate the reality of the history that is written; it merely requires a certain sense of critical control on the part of scholars in that history must be read in light of the biases of its writers, to the extent that such biases can be identified.

gle coherent theology that can be identified throughout the Hebrew Bible and characterized as the theology of the Old Testament.[21] Rather, the Hebrew Bible expresses a variety of theological viewpoints that presuppose various social settings, both within and among the books contained therein, concerning the character of G-d, the people of Israel and Judah, the nations, and the cosmic dimensions of the world at large, that defy attempts at systematization.[22] Fundamentally, one might even ask whether theology is the all-encompassing standpoint from which to interpret the Hebrew Bible in view of the fact that the Hebrew version of the book of Esther does not even mention G-d, nor does it presuppose divine activity.[23] The issue has been further complicated by the insights of canonical criticism that point to the diverse conceptions of the Bible itself, insofar as different canons, often containing different sacred books, as well as different arrangements and versions of sacred books, appear within the various communities of faith, whether Christian or Jewish.[24] In short, there is no single Old Testament, nor is there a single theology that encompasses the entire Old Testament. Rather, the Hebrew Bible, whether conceived as the Christian Old Testament or the Jewish Tanak, and the theologies or ideologies that are contained therein are the products of the people who wrote and assembled the books that comprise the Hebrew Bible.

This has tremendous implications for conceiving Christian Old Testament theology because it points so clearly to the centrality of the human or Jewish role in articulating the theologies or ideologies that appear within the Hebrew Bible. In this respect, it points especially to the particularity and subjectivity of Old Testament theology, not only on the

---

[21] For an overview of the discussion concerning the "center" of Old Testament Theology, see Gerhard Hasel, *Old Testament Theology: Basic Issues in the Current Debate* (4th ed.; Grand Rapids: Eerdmans, 1991), 139–171.

[22] See Rolf P. Knierim, "The Task of Old Testament Theology," *HBT* 6 (1984): 25–57; revised edition published in idem, *The Task of Old Testament Theology: Substance, Method and Cases* (Grand Rapids: Eerdmans, 1995), 1–20; cf. John Goldingay, *Theological Diversity and the Authority of the Old Testament* (Grand Rapids: Eerdmans, 1987).

[23] See Levenson, "Why Jews Are Not Interested in Biblical Theology"; Marvin A. Sweeney, "Why Jews Should Be Interested in Biblical Theology," *CCAR Journal* 44 (Winter 1997): 67–75.

[24] See James A. Sanders, "Adaptable for Life: The Nature and Function of Canon," *Magnalia Dei: The Mighty Acts of G-d* (ed. F. M. Cross, W. Lemke, and P. D. Miller Jr.; Festschrift G. E. Wright; Garden City, N.Y.: Doubleday, 1976); idem, "Canon, Hebrew Bible," *ABD* 1:837–52; Marvin A. Sweeney, "Tanakh versus Old Testament: Concerning the Foundation for a Jewish Theology of the Bible," in *Problems in Biblical Theology* (ed. H. T. C. Sun and K. L. Eades, with G. I. Moeller and J. M. Robinson; Festschrift Rolf P. Knierim; Grand Rapids: Eerdmans, 1997), 353–72.

part of the Old Testament's modern interpreters, but on the part of its ancient writers (and interpreters) as well. Whatever one might posit concerning the universal reality or absolute character of G-d, Old Testament theology must account for the fact that G-d, and all worldly reality and experience influenced by G-d, is presented in the Hebrew Bible, and indeed in the New Testament as well, from particular human standpoints. This applies both to the canonical forms of the Hebrew Bible and to the individual books or groupings of books that appear within its canonical forms. The distinctive canonical forms of the Hebrew Bible as Old Testament and Tanak and the general means by which each has been shaped by and by which each expresses the distinctive and particularistic theologies and worldviews of Christianity and Judaism, respectively, have been treated elsewhere.[25] The present discussion will focus on the human, or more specifically the Israelite or Jewish, role in writing the individual books of the Hebrew Bible and the implications of this insight for Christian Old Testament theology.

First and foremost, one must begin with the fact that the Old Testament comprises all of its books, that is, no books may be dismissed as theologically irrelevant, nor may portions of books, such as those written by "later redactors," likewise be dismissed. Books such as Leviticus, Ezekiel, Nahum, Haggai, Proverbs, Esther, and Ezra-Nehemiah all have their place in the Old Testament canon, as do the priestly writings of the Pentateuch, the final form of the book of Isaiah, including all of its later redactional expansions, and the Chronicler's reworking of the Deuteronomistic History. Second, all of the books or writings that comprise the Old Testament in Christianity were written by Israelites, or more properly Judahites or Jews, in various historical periods and social settings. The writings of the Old Testament thereby reflect various theological or ideological viewpoints concerning the nature and character of G-d, as well as the nature and character of the world and human experience of G-d and the world, that were articulated within Judaism and amongst the Jewish people. Even when G-d speaks in the Hebrew Bible, the interpreter must recognize that G-d's word is presented by the author or authors of the text, and it reflects the particular understanding of G-d or human experience articulated by the authors within the text. The interpreter of the Bible cannot therefore assert definitively that any given text in the Hebrew Bible portrays G-d in G-d's absolute or universal character; rather, the texts of the Hebrew Bible present the author's or authors' perspectives on G-d and the nature of human experience within the world. The same must be said of the New Testament, which presents particular Christian perspectives on G-d and human experience. Third, the writings of the Hebrew Bible do not

---

25 Sweeney, "Tanakh versus Old Testament."

monolithically reflect only the theological concerns of ancient Jews; they reflect the social, economic, and political concerns of the people as well. Thus, the theological concerns expressed in the Hebrew Bible must be weighed in relation to such factors as the political character of the ancient Israelite and Judahite states and the means by which the religious conceptions of the Hebrew Bible function in relation to the political and economic realities of ancient Israel and Judah. For example, Gen 15, understood in Christian exegesis to express the theological principle of Abram's/Abraham's justification by faith, promises that the patriarch will become a great people with a land whose borders coincide with those defined later as the boundaries of the Davidic state. In other words, the promise to Abraham is presented in relation to the political interests of the later Davidic monarchy.[26] In short, the books or writings of the Old Testament are the product of the Jewish people and as such reflect the concerns of a living people who developed and expressed their views on G-d, the character of the world and the states in which they lived, and their own role in it, in relation to the diverse factors that characterize any living human society. Insofar as the Old Testament functions as sacred Scripture in Christianity, those specifically Jewish perspectives form a component of Christian revelation and theological reality.

A Post-Shoah Reading of Amos and Esther

It is therefore crucial for the Old Testament theologian to recognize the theological significance of the particular Jewish nature of the presentation of G-d and human experience in the Hebrew Bible. Theologians have certainly recognized this issue but in general have proceeded to identify as authoritative for Old Testament theology the supposedly universal aspects of G-d's character and human experience as expressed in the Hebrew Bible and to exclude from consideration, or at least to devalue, those elements that were considered to be particularistic. And yet one must ask whether such a distinction is possible; just as one never experiences the ideal universal representation of reality in Platonic thought but only particular representations of the ideal, so one never experiences the ideal universal representation of G-d and human experience in the Hebrew Bible, but only its particular Jewish expressions.

With this in mind, discussion may turn to an examination of two major texts, Amos and Esther, that have some bearing on understanding the role

---

[26] See Ronald E. Clements, *Abraham and David: Genesis XV and Its Meaning for Israelite Tradition* (SBT 2.5; London: SCM Press, 1967); Marvin A. Sweeney, "Form Criticism," in *To Each Its Own Meaning: An Introduction to Biblical Criticisms and Their Application* (ed. Steven L. McKenzie and Stephen R. Haynes; rev. ed.; Louisville: Westminster/John Knox, 1999), 58–89.

of the Jewish people, in all of its social reality, in composing the writings of the Hebrew Bible and in articulating their theological and ideological viewpoints. In each case, the text presents a particular perspective on divine activity and/or human experience that reflects partisan viewpoints concerning the nature of G-d and human experience or attempts on the part of the authors to wrestle with the problems posed by G-d and experience in the world. The book of Amos is chosen because it is generally taken to be representative of the universalist moral concerns of biblical prophecy, and the book of Esther is chosen because it is frequently dismissed as lacking in theological significance or moral perspective. Both examples demonstrate that universal and particular perspectives cannot be so neatly separated in articulating the theological interpretation of the Old Testament. Rather, Jewish perspectives constitute the universal significance of the Old Testament and must be accepted as such in Christianity.

Christian theological interpretation generally identifies Amos as the paradigmatic prophetic representative of G-d's universal values of social justice and the pure, unmediated individual human encounter with the deity that prompts the prophet to stand alone in condemning his own nation as sinful and announcing its destruction.[27] The grounds for interpreting Amos in this fashion include the oracles against the nations in Amos 1–2 that culminate in the prophet's condemnation of Israel; the oracles of judgment against Israel throughout the book that focus on socioeconomic abuse of the poor by the wealthy ruling class; the vision sequence in Amos 7–9 in which G-d appears to Amos to deliver the divine message of judgment; the narrative concerning Amos's confrontation with the high priest Amaziah in Amos 7:10–17 in which Amos declares that he is not a professional prophet; and the conclusion that the oracle concerning the restoration of the fallen booth of David in Amos 9:11–15 is a postexilic addition and therefore irrelevant to the message of the prophet.

Nevertheless, various elements of the book of Amos point toward a more nuanced interpretation of the book and the presentation of the prophet contained therein.[28] First, Amos is Judahite, a herdsman and dresser of sycamore trees from the Judean village of Tekoa, located south of Jerusalem.

---

[27] For modern critical treatments of the book of Amos, see Hans Walter Wolff, *Joel and Amos* (Hermeneia; Philadelphia: Fortress, 1977); James L. Mays, *Amos: A Commentary* (OTL; Philadelphia: Westminster, 1969); cf. B. E. Willoughby, "Amos, Book of," *ABD* 1:203–12.

[28] For a more detailed treatment of Amos in relation to the methodological issues that are now influencing the interpretation of prophetic books, see Marvin A. Sweeney, "Formation and Form in Prophetic Literature," in *Old Testament Interpretation: Past, Present, and Future* (ed. J. L. Mays, D. L. Petersen, and K. H. Richards; Festschrift G. M. Tucker; Nashville: Abingdon, 1995), 113–26.

This identity is confirmed by his visions, all of which represent the common experience of a Judahite agriculturalist, and by his consistently Judahite viewpoint, which portrays YHWH's roaring like a lion, the symbol of the tribe of Judah. Second, Israel and Judah are two politically distinct kingdoms in which Judah, under the rule of King Uzziah/Azariah ben Amaziah, was forced to serve as a vassal state to Israel, under the rule of King Jeroboam ben Joash. Third, the nations enumerated in the oracles against the nations were all subject to or allied with the northern Israelite empire established by Jeroboam ben Joash. Fourth, Amos condemns the leadership of Israel for abusing the poor who are unable to support themselves and thus lose their land or possessions to the wealthy. Fifth, Amos is present at Beth El, the royal sanctuary of the northern kingdom of Israel, during a time of sacrifice or the presentation of offerings, and his oracle condemning the Beth El sanctuary in Amos 9:1–10 appears immediately before the call for the restoration of the fallen booth of David in Amos 9:11–15.[29]

One must ask why he is at Beth El and how all of these various elements relate to the message that the book presents. When one nation is subject to another in the ancient world, it is required to pay some form of tribute to the suzerain nation. For an agriculturally based economy like that of Judah in the eighth century B.C.E., such tribute generally constitutes a share of the country's produce. Whether it is regarded as a tax or as tribute, produce is collected by ancient governments through their sanctuaries, where it is dedicated to the gods and employed for use by the sanctuary and the government.[30] In the case of a suzerain country such as eighth-century Israel, the tribute presented by vassal states such as Judah would have been presented at the royal sanctuary at Beth El. It would appear that Amos is at Beth El in his role as herdsman and dresser of sycamore trees to present a share of the Judahite tribute to Israel.

Several aspects of his message thereby become clear. First, his references to the plight of the poor, including the locust plagues and fires that followed the king's mowings (see 7:1–6), speak to the plight of Judahite farmers such as himself, who must bear the brunt of Judah's tribute obligations to Israel. Second, his condemnation of the nations culminating in Israel does not present a universal scenario of divine judgment but points to the subjugation of nations to northern Israel as a means to point ultimately to the fall of Israel for abusing its vassals and allies. Third, Amos does not condemn the leadership of his own nation, but that to which his nation was subjected. In this regard, the call for the restoration of the fallen booth of David following Amos's call for the destruction of the Beth El altar

---

[29] For a treatment of Amos 9:11–15 that assigns the pericope to the prophet Amos, see Shalom Paul, *Amos* (Hermeneia; Minneapolis: Fortress, 1991).

[30] See Moshe Weinfeld, "Tithe," *EncJud* 15:1156–1162.

must be seen from the perspective of the above considerations. It does not represent a postexilic hope for national renewal or messianic redemption, but Amos's call for the downfall of northern Israelite rule and the restoration of Judean independence and rule over the northern tribes of Israel as it had once existed under David and Solomon.

In short, the kingdom of Judah and the Jewish people stand at the center of Amos's prophetic message. Amos's call for judgment of the nations and of Israel does not represent a universalist demand for worldwide justice and proper treatment of the poor, but a partisan demand that speaks from the interests of an individual Judean who was part of a living nation with its own political, economic, and religious interests, perspectives, and identity. Amos's call for justice does not represent a theological condemnation of his own nation; rather, it constitutes an attempt to speak for the interests of both his nation and himself. In short, Amos is a Judean nationalistic prophet who calls for justice for his own people. In evaluating the theology and message of Amos, Old Testament theologians must take this partisan view into account as theologically legitimate. In calling for justice and speaking on behalf of G-d, prophets do not uniformly condemn their own nation; they also speak on its behalf. More fundamentally, prophets are not only concerned with theology, nor do they withdraw from worldly affairs, but they engage as partisans in the political, social, and economic issues of their time. Even more fundamentally with respect to issues posed by the Shoah, they recognize the responsibility to speak up when they see evil, rather than to remain silent when evil manifests itself in the world, thereby allowing it to take its course.

The second example is the book of Esther.[31] Both Christian and Jewish theological interpretation of Esther generally views it as a problematic book with questionable or unclear theological significance.[32] One reason for this viewpoint is the complete absence of G-d or direct divine activity in the Hebrew version, generally conceded to be earlier than the extant

---

31 For detailed treatment of the issues discussed, see Marvin A. Sweeney, "Absence of G-d and Human Responsibility in the Book of Esther," in *Reading the Hebrew Bible for a New Millennium: Form, Concept, and Theological Perspective*, vol. 1, *Theological and Hermeneutical Studies* (ed. Deborah Ellens et al.; Harrisburg, Penn.: Trinity Press International, 2000).

32 For modern critical treatments of the book of Esther, see Bernhard W. Anderson, "Esther; Introduction and Exegesis," *IB* 3:821–74; Carey A. Moore, *Esther* (AB 7b; Garden City, N.Y.: Doubleday, 1971); Jon D. Levenson, *Esther: A Commentary* (OTL; Louisville: Westminster/John Knox, 1997); cf. C. A. Moore, "Esther, Book of," *ABD* 2:633–43. For discussion of Esther in medieval Jewish interpretation, see Barry Dov Walfish, *Esther in Medieval Garb: Jewish Interpretation of Esther in the Middle Ages* (Albany: State University of New York Press, 1993).

Greek versions. A particular point of contention is the fact that Jews take vengeance on their enemies in the aftermath of Haman's failure to destroy the Jewish people in the Persian Empire. In the view of some Christian interpreters, such so-called nationalism and bloodthirstiness on the part of the Jews justifies the punishment and humiliation that they have suffered by rejecting Jesus Christ.

In order to understand the significance of the book of Esther, particularly in the aftermath of the Shoah, it is important to consider several key features of the book and the situation that it presents. First, it is Holy Scripture in both communities and deserves to be taken seriously as such, since it conveys theological truth that both Christianity and Judaism should hear. Second, it portrays Jews as subject to a foreign power, in this case the Persian Empire, which dominated the Near Eastern world from the sixth to the fourth centuries B.C.E. Jews are thereby depicted in a precarious social and political position. Third, it presents Haman, a high-ranking official in the Persian government, as the source of an official government program to exterminate the Jews. No one in the Persian government or elsewhere in the empire questions this action. Certainly, the death of his Jewish subjects did not seem to be of great concern to King Ahasuerus. Fourth, the only means to counter this attempted extermination was in the hands of the newly married Jewish Queen Esther, whose identity as a Jew was not made known; perhaps it would have worked against her in the Persian Empire. Furthermore, Esther had seen her predecessor Vashti banished on the slightest whim of the king, who was angered when she refused to dance for his cronies. Fifth, G-d does not appear or intervene in a time of overwhelming crisis for the Jewish community. Jews must take matters into their own hands in order to save themselves; there is no one else, not even G-d, who will help. Sixth, it is the enemies of the Jews who are attacked and killed because they present a continuation of the threat posed by Haman. The death of Haman would likely not end this threat, but magnify it. And Esther, recognizing her own precarious situation in relation to the king, might not have the opportunity to act at a later time when the king tired of her presence.

With these considerations in mind, the charges against Jews made by theological interpreters of Esther ring very hollow, especially in light of contemporary discussion concerning attempts to blame the victims of crime (e.g., she asked for it; they deserved it). The book of Esther does not advocate wanton killing or revenge; rather, a fundamental issue of justice is at hand—the basic right of self-defense in the face of threat. From a theological perspective, this must be understood not only in relation to the principle of divine justice, but in relation to the responsibilities of human beings in the world. When G-d is absent or chooses not to intervene, humans must act to counter evil.[33] A similar message is apparent in the book of Amos: when G-d is present, humans must also act to counter evil. This is a lesson not to be lost either by Jews or by Christians, particularly in light of the Shoah. It was not lost on the Jews of the Warsaw Ghetto, who died in a failed attempt to resist the Nazi aggression because no one else would help them,[34] or Jews from Mandate Palestine who fought the Nazis as part of the British Army in North Africa during World War II and later became the core of the Israel Defense Force; nor was it lost on "righteous Gentiles," such as the German pastor Dietrich Bonhoeffer, who died as a martyr at the hands of the Nazis, or King Christian and the people of Denmark, who chose to don the yellow star identifying one as a Jew rather than hand over Danish Jews to the extermination camps.[35] But it was lost on countless numbers of people in Europe, the Middle East, and the Americas, including many common citizens who had little to do with the Nazis and many at the highest levels of government and church, who failed to raise their voices or to act for any number of reasons, such as fear of retribution, a refusal to believe the full scope of Nazi intentions, or a sense that somehow, the Jews deserved it.[36] Both Amos and Esther tell us that G-d demands justice, and we, both Christians and Jews, are obligated to bring it about, not only in the social world in which we live but in the interpretation of the religious traditions and Scriptures that guide us.

Concluding Reflections

Obviously, much more can be said on this issue. The recognition of the significance of Judaism and the Jewish people in Christian Old Testament theology clearly has tremendous implications for a variety of issues, includ-

---

33 See Eliezer Berkovitz, *Faith after the Holocaust* (New York: Ktav, 1973), who develops the notion of "the hidden face of G-d" as a means to emphasize the role of human responsibility in confronting evil.

34 See Gerald Reitlinger, *The Final Solution: The Attempt to Exterminate the Jews of Europe 1939–1945* (Northvale, N.J.: Aronson, 1987), 272–81.

35 For an overview of Danish efforts to resist Nazi efforts to exterminate Denmark's Jews and the successful smuggling of Danish Jews into Sweden, see Reitlinger, *The Final Solution,* 345–51. For a detailed treatment of this issue, see Leni Yahil, *The Rescue of Danish Jewry: Test of Democracy* (Philadelphia: Jewish Publication Society of America, 1969). See also Nechama Tec, *When Light Pierced the Darkness: Christian Rescue of Jews in Nazi-Occupied Poland* (New York: Oxford University Press, 1986).

36 See, for example, Daniel Jonah Goldhagen, *Hitler's Willing Executioners: Ordinary Germans and the Holocaust* (New York: Knopf, 1996); David S. Wyman, *The Abandonment of the Jews: America and the Holocaust, 1941–1945* (New York: Pantheon, 1984).

ing not only the interpretation of the Old Testament within Christianity, but the relationship between the Old Testament and the New Testament within the larger context of the Christian Bible and the overall relationship between Christians and Jews. In conclusion, a saying of Rabbi Hillel from the Mishnah is particularly pertinent to the concerns of this paper:

אם אין אני לי מי לי? וכשאני לעצמי מה אני? ואם לא עכשו אימתי?

"If I am not for myself, who will be for me? And if I am for myself alone, what am I? And if not now, when?" (*m. 'Abot* 1:14).

Christian Biblical Theology and the Struggle against Oppression

Jorge Pixley

In Latin America in the last forty years the Bible as the word of the God of the poor has been discovered. This discovery came out of the confluence of several major factors. First, no doubt, was the inspiration of the successful Cuban Revolution. In addition the Latin American contact with North American Christians as a result of the inflow of Catholic missionaries responding to Pope John's call for mission to Latin America and of a new wave of evangelical missionaries, Pentecostals and others, played a role. The Second Vatican Council invited the churches in the diverse regions to become regional churches with the blessing of Rome. The older Protestant churches were also ready to be present in the construction of a new Latin America. A qualitative change in the Christian situation in Latin America resulted. Along with the upsurge of revolutionary consciousness among the poor, including poor Christians, came an explosive interest in the Bible, to the surprise of most pastors and theologians. No longer was the Bible read only as the road to personal salvation nor conceded to church authorities to be studied and interpreted only by the clergy and the theologians. It became God's word to be studied by ordinary Christians because the revolution was God's work for the salvation of the Latin American poor people who felt themselves to be God's people.

What I wish to do here is to look at what this has meant for biblical scholars and more specifically for the theology of the Hebrew Scriptures. At the outset I must admit that for us in poor Christian Latin American communities this way of posing the issue is somewhat artificial, since in our fundamentally Christian context the Bible is understood as the Christian Old Testament, usually including the Greek books of the broader Roman Catholic canon, and is read together with the Christian New Testament. It is artificial also to ask about biblical *theology*. Theology for us is not something that believing people who seek guidance for their struggles expect to find *in the Bible*. Theology as a second step, as reflection on the faith of the people and the word of God, emerges out of the interaction of critical analysis of the current conjuncture, an equally critical analysis of the social struggles of Israel, and the tactics for the daily practice of the struggle for liberation in the nitty-gritty of building schools and clinics, carrying out strikes, fumigating against mosquitoes and vaccinating children, supporting women who face violence, and a myriad of other tasks. In these tasks the word of God is basic guidance. Theology, though important, comes later.

When as scholars and teachers we think about the theology of the Hebrew Scriptures, we start looking for a body of doctrine that can be organized and transmitted to students, a body of teaching that is somehow to be found "in" the texts. Such a body of doctrine is of very little importance to the communities of faith for whom I speak. There is, of course, some basic teaching that is perceived as the revelation of the God who created the universe and who liberated the people of Israel from their Egyptian bondage. But for us systematizing a body of theology of the Scriptures is unimportant.

Beginning with the knowledge of the true and living God, what is important is to receive God's marching orders for the struggles being planned, both on a broad scale to challenge the global market and on a small scale where life is defended by volunteers carrying out vaccinations or women studying to be more effective midwives. The preaching of the prophets about the social problems of their day, the problems faced by Moses in guiding, feeding, and defending the people in the desert, the struggles of Naomi and Ruth fighting to survive, the efforts of Nehemiah in building the defenses of the city and confronting the debt burden on the poor, the words of Jesus confronting the petty ambitions of his followers and facing up to the exploiters in the temple—it is in such places that our people look for the word of God for us today.

The starting point that makes this whole exercise useful is the revelation that the true God who created and governs the universe is a God who opts for the poor for the sake of the salvation of all. This is biblical theology in that it is a theme of the Hebrew Bible. The exodus is the fundamental paradigm, for the exodus is (correctly) perceived in the Latin American Christian community as the foundational text of the Bible. God responds in this text to the cry of the oppressed. As a result, for us, being for the poor becomes an option, a conscious choice, even for those who are poor out of necessity. One has to perceive one's poverty as the result of historical oppression and assume the struggle to change the social conditions that produce this poverty. This God of the oppressed becomes the touchstone for reading other biblical texts. The ambiguous texts about Solomon reveal the hand of scribes who represent both the ruling classes and also the interests of the classes who were oppressed by the royal families and their retainers. In such texts the true God is the one who incites Jeroboam to rebel against Solomon more than the one who blesses Solomon's grand temple.

The book of Psalms is a book dominated by the supplications of persons who are persecuted and oppressed. The psalms serve to confirm the God of the exodus as the true God and poverty as above all else the result of oppression. Qohelet is a book that can be read and is read in our communities as a rejection of the "novelties" of a culture that was claiming to be superior due to the new and better ways of the Greeks for conducting educational, business, and military matters. The affirmation of the Preacher that there is nothing new under the sun is a call for the oppressed people of the Hellenistic empires to resist the fascinations of the dominant culture. Qohelet was less certain about what culture he (or she) could affirm, and so are we. But Qohelet was not impressed with Greek wisdom and technology.

These quick observations on Qohelet can serve to introduce a major aspect of the faith and theology of these relatively new Christian communities in Latin America, mostly Catholic and some Protestant. The Bible is a field for training in social analysis. This social analysis will look for the mechanisms of oppression behind what are presented in the Bible or by contemporary spokespersons as "natural" wisdom or laws. More important than knowing the threats to Israelite culture from Hellenistic cultural invasion is recognizing the threats to native American culture from European and Euro-American cultural invasion. All of the activities surrounding the five-hundredth anniversary of what we called the "Resistance of Black, Native, and Popular Peoples" have served to heighten sensibilities to these issues. This increased sensibility both deepens our reading of the Bible and is improved by our reading of the Bible.

Mention of the five-hundredth anniversary brings up a fundamental issue, that of the role of religion in the struggle for liberation. The struggle of Yahweh versus Baal is read among us as basically the ideological side of a class struggle between the Israelites, who saw their national identity as that of a people who affirmed a new egalitarian way of existing in the land of Canaan, versus the city-states ruled by kings who lived from the tributes collected from peasants. In our times the Canaanites correlate with the struggle of rich Christians to dominate the native populations, to steal their natural resources, to use their labor to grow the crops and raise the cattle needed to maintain their colonial enclaves, and to destroy the self-respect of native peoples by breaking their sacred places and images, which are labeled instruments of devil worship. Thus for us the struggle against idolatry in the Hebrew Bible is the religious expression of the struggle against exploitation. The Hoseanic denunciation of Baal worship on the part of the Jehuite dynasty is a model for resisting religious polemic that provides cover for oppressive political and economic behavior. This supposedly truly Israelite (or Christian) rhetoric masked the real exploitative functions of the religious tradition.

The discovery that the religious struggle represented, for instance, by the papal visits to Latin America to strengthen the authority of archbishops who see themselves as allies of governing elites is correlative with the struggle between social classes, the exploiters and the exploited. This situation leads to the class analysis where Marxist thinkers are our main teachers. The class analysis that interprets the dynamics of the lives we live is also useful in reflecting on the dynamics of Israelite society. Religious conflict in the Bible, as in our world today, is often a reflection of class conflict.

I have tried to describe the scene in which the Bible is read in Latin American Christian communities as the word of the living God who makes an option for the poor. A profoundly religious vision is at work here: Jeremiah may end up in the dungeon and Jesus on the cross, but the God of Jeremiah and Jesus is in the end the God who created the world, who governs the world, and who wills to redeem the world. This vision we believe is an appeal to resist the siren calls of those spokespersons for the global market who say there is no other way to organize the economy than the laws of the market, which have built-in mechanisms for increased social differentiation.

Now we must ask what the academic guild of biblical scholars can contribute to this biblical revival. First of all, we must recognize that we are no more than learned assistants. The main action is elsewhere than in our classrooms and our studies. The Bible becomes God's word in the communal debates of those who are seeking survival for themselves and a transformed world for their children. It is here that God speaks more than in our classrooms or through our books. If we want what we teach and write to be helpful, we have to be in tune with these popular discussions.

Second, however, because the struggle requires that we read the Bible as the record of the struggle of poor people for their liberation, *critical analysis of the text is necessary*. Unless there is the accompaniment of biblical scholars to guide this analysis, the popular reading of the Bible may quickly go awry. One frequent response of poor people to the Bible is to cultivate a life of prayer and fasting in the hope that the powerful God who destroyed Pharaoh's army will also destroy the global market.

This reading must be seen as a temptation, which like all temptations must be rejected. The only protection against this pervasive temptation is a critical reading of (1) society, (2) religious communities, and (3) the Bible. For the first task we need social scientists, for the second we need theologians, but for the third we need biblical scholars who listen to people who read the Bible to guide them in their struggle for life and who offer their scholarship as an aid and who listen to the critical analysis of social scientists. Fortunately, even in the "First World" some biblical scholars of this sort are now active.

Biblical scholars are expensive to train and expensive to sustain with all the resources we need to function. This cost factor exposes us to the temptation to sell out to those who have the most financial resources to train scholars for our discipline, regardless of their social commitments. In order to keep the supply of the type of scholars needed to sustain our popular reading of the Bible, we must believe that the God who makes an option for the poor is the true God who creates the world, sustains and redeems it. We must be convinced that our scholarship at the service of the popular movement is in tune with the deepest forces governing the universe. Otherwise, we would go where the heavy sponsorship is found. Having struggled all my adult life against the accusation of disbelief, I surprise myself by sounding so pious, but for the kind of biblical scholarship that makes a difference I do not see any other way. We believe and support with our critical interpretations a movement that is biblically motivated, or we give up and do innocuous biblical tinkering.

I was invited as a Christian to contribute to this volume, and this way of understanding the theology of the Hebrew Bible *is* Christian. I don't believe it is anti-Jewish. The ordinary, everyday Christian God in our context is, unfortunately, the God who assisted in the genocide of the native peoples of Latin and British America. That is not our God in the popular movement. Thus I represent a *critical* Christian biblical theology.

YHWH the Revolutionary: Reflections on the Rhetoric of Redistribution in the Social Context of Dawning Monotheism

Baruch Halpern

Contemporary Understandings of the Theology of the Hebrew Bible: Problems and Prospects

If economics is the dismal science, theology is that of human aspiration. For just that reason, however, even historical theology, as much as systematics, is given to wish fulfilment—manifested, for example, in a proselytizing zeal for policy rather than analysis. In biblical theology, scholarship vacillates between two poles: appeal to congenial ancient theologies for reinforcement of an ideological commitment to action and rejection of repugnant theologies in our sources. Those succumbing to the former impulse, treated below, wield the Bible's social authority to advance their agenda. Their counterparts, concerned perhaps with slavery or patriarchy, seek to undermine that authority. Occasionally, it may therefore seem that in theology, as in history, battles are being fought over the dignity of Scripture. More sympathetic readings, concerned to understand the ancients in their own terms, certainly do emerge in the pages of scholarship.[1] But these do not attract the attention of a public so readily as studies with more transparent contemporary applications.

From the 1960s into the 1990s, a piercing chorus in the theory of Israelite religion has been that of leftist, or seemingly leftist, theologians. The reasons for their warm reception among scholars, who for the most part lean liberal, are not far to seek.[2] The work of these scholars could therefore be regarded as the outgrowth of a particular social moment, and it is probably for that reason that it has not been subject to a searching his-

---

[1] See esp. Moshe Greenberg, *Ezekiel 1–20* (AB 22; Garden City, N.Y.: Doubleday, 1986). This essay is dedicated to Moshe Greenberg: ממשה למשה ממשה.

[2] J. M. Sasson, "On Choosing Models for Recreating Israelite Pre-Monarchic History," *JSOT* 21 (1981): 3–24.

torical critique. On the other hand, the scholarship itself deserves attention for the lessons it has to teach, positive as well as negative.

Two major overtures to the theological implications of biblical texts characterize these approaches. The first is that adopted emblematically by George E. Mendenhall in the early 1960s.[3] Mendenhall reconstructed premonarchic Israel as an ideal community embodying authentic Mosaic precepts. These included a social "covenant," the antiquity of which Mendenhall defended at length. Unfortunately, the defense did not include advertence either to the genres of biblical literature or to the attestations of the treaty ("covenant") genre in the period of the biblical texts. Still, the Mosaic vision was one of egalitarianism, in which all Israelite parties were subject alike to the law. It prescribed ecumenism, in the reception of new coreligionists into the community of the faithful. The result, as has long been observed (see n. 2), was an Edenic graft of Protestant religiosity and American constitutionalism. Mendenhall's Mosaic social blueprint justified the Reformation and, less explicitly, American jingoism. By getting at the alleged prehistory of the Israelite community, Mendenhall extracted from the text's now-explicit views on ethnicity and social stratification a "pristine" revelation, before those Israelite backsliders mucked it up. He could reject biblical Israelite culture—whatever it represents—yet find in the prehistory of that culture sufficient authority to justify his emotions and religion. In a way, Mendenhall's prescriptive reconstruction inverts an older scholarly strategy. Finding, thus, that some pentateuchal narratives attributed to YHWH feelings and actions offensive to later, especially modern, sensibilities, Otto Eissfeldt relegated these to an "L (lay) source," separated out from and earlier than J (though now incorporated into it). This was yet another way to rusticate from the exegete's "essential" canon elements unfit for canonization.[4]

---

[3] G. E. Mendenhall, "The Hebrew Conquest of Palestine," *BA* 25 (1962): 66–87; idem, "Biblical History in Transition," in *The Bible and the Ancient Near East. Essays in Honor of William Foxwell Albright* (ed. G. E. Wright; Garden City, N.Y.: Doubleday, 1965), 27–58; idem, *The Tenth Generation* (Baltimore: Johns Hopkins University Press, 1973); idem, "Ancient Israel's Hyphenated History," in *Palestine in Transition: The Emergence of Ancient Israel* (ed. D. N. Freedman and D. F. Graf; SWBA 2; Sheffield: Almond Press, 1983), 91–103. Mendenhall articulated his program in nuce in "Ancient Oriental and Biblical Law," *BA* 17 (1954): 26–46; and "Covenant Forms in Israelite Tradition," *BA* 17 (1954): 49–76.

[4] See esp. D. R. Hillers, "Palmyrene Aramaic Inscriptions and the Bible," forthcoming (in *ZAH*) on the crudity of YHWH in these materials; for analysis, see O. Eissfeldt, *The Old Testament: An Introduction* (New York: Harper & Row, 1965), 194–99. I am indebted to Professor Hillers for sharing with me this and other material cited here in advance of its publication. On Mendenhall's agenda, see Halpern, "Sociological Comparativism and the Theological Imagination: The Case of the

The second sort of overture to the texts is best represented in the work of Walter Brueggemann.[5] Brueggemann, the brother-in-law of Patrick D. Miller Jr., operates in diametric opposition to Mendenhall, despite reaching related conclusions. Instead of invoking the authority of (pre)history to trump that of the Bible, instead, indeed, of stratifying early and degenerate "secondary" text, Brueggemann identifies broad thematic corpora. Sinai, thus, is the conditional covenant restricting the power of the elite to oppress the bulk of Israelites—it is in effect revolutionary. Zion, conversely, is the divine ratification of the elite's hegemony. This perspective, in its assignments of values within a classically Pauline dichotomy, is anti-Pauline, a point that seems to have escaped Mendenhall in his embrace of a similar position. It is also the case that it concerns itself only with Israel as a model, not as an antecedent, of modern social organization. Unlike Mendenhall's attempts at finding a bejeweled reality behind the veil of the sources, then, Brueggemann's work concerns itself with finding the reality reflected by the sources; it respects the integrity of the phenomena under discussion in our texts. The reconstruction does not suffer from the defects of triumphalism and ethnic and religious supersession that characterize Mendenhall's oeuvre.

These two paradigms are not incompatible, despite their methodological variance: Norman K. Gottwald effectively combines the two.[6] In his work on premonarchic Israel, Gottwald defended from a Marxian vantage point the idea that Israel was born out of a peasant rejection of Canaanite stratification. In his work on the prophets, conversely, Gottwald treats monarchic Israel with greater balance than does Mendenhall, arguing the survival of egalitarian ideologies of earlier periods. Without such survivals, of course, no evidence would support Mendenhall's views; its presence makes nonsense of most of his vilification of the monarchy as an unadulterated oriental despotism, a position that does nothing more than reproduce Wellhausen, himself a pro-Junker Bismarckian, almost a century later.

Conquest," in *"Sha'arei Talmon" Studies in the Bible, Qumran, and the Ancient Near East Presented to Shemaryahu Talmon* (ed. Michael Fishbane and Emanuel Tov; Winona Lake, Ind.: Eisenbrauns, 1992), 53–67.

[5] Walter Brueggemann, *In Man We Trust* (Richmond: John Knox, 1972); idem, "A Convergence in Recent Old Testament Theologies," *JSOT* 18 (1980): 2–18; idem, "Trajectories in Old Testament Literature and the Sociology of Ancient Israel," *JBL* 98 (1979): 161–85; idem, "A Shape for Old Testament Theology, 1: Structure Legitimation," *CBQ* 47 (1985): 28–46.

[6] See Norman Gottwald, *The Tribes of Yahweh* (New York: Orbis Books, 1979); idem, *The Hebrew Bible: A Socio-Literary Introduction* (Philadelphia: Fortress, 1985); idem, "The Participation of Free Agrarians in the Introduction of Monarchy to Ancient Israel: An Application of H. A. Landsberger's Framework for the Analysis of Peasant Movements," *Semeia* 37 (1986): 77–106.

But Gottwald is able to knit together both a programmatic perspective on the historical reconstruction of pristine Israel and a more balanced view of the social complexities of the monarchic era.

What all three of these disparate scholars share is both a merit and a defect. The merit is that they take language very seriously. The language of law, implicitly egalitarian (chattels excepted), resonates for them. Prophetic language, too, speaks meaningfully to them, and to others on the Left:[7] texts such as Amos, Isaiah, and Micah exhibit a notorious concern for justice, for marginal social elements. Moreover, as Brueggemann is at pains to observe, these and other biblical materials, such as Psalms and Deutero-Isaiah, and, indeed, even the national "epic," feature motifs compatible with social revolution. Thus several standard morphemes of biblical folklore, the birth of a child to the barren wife (Sarah, Rachel, Hannah, Samson's mother) and the inheritance of the last-born in place of the first (Isaac, Jacob, Joseph, David), overturn the expectations of a traditional society. The image of the razing of the high places and the raising of the low, a program metaphor in Isa 40–55, of humbling the proud and exalting the humble (common in Psalms especially), indeed, of raising up leaders from shepherds, youths and those who do not know how to speak,[8] all represent for these scholars a revolutionary ethic in the religious establishment. To have heard this, to have understood it, to allow the rhetoric to penetrate and speak directly to the modern reader, is a great hermeneutical achievement. So is the synthesis of all these strands into a single fabric with the theology of covenant generally, and of fealty to YHWH, to the exclusion of secular powers in conflict with the god.

And yet, the problems with this view have not been cast up in its face. In some respects, these theologians resemble the Communist Party members of the 1930s to 1950s, and the even more radical members of the academy in the 1960s to 1980s. The comparison is not ideological—Mendenhall rejects leftism, though his positions on Zionism (which he equates with racism) and on Judaism (in his view, a fossil religion, in contrast to Lutheranism) coincide with those of less-principled elements of the Left. Rather, the affinity is in an approach to language.

Western Stalinists were sometimes cynical. But far more often, they and their fellow travelers fervently believed the words, the ideas, the slogans,

---

[7] E.g., Marvin Chaney, "Ancient Palestinian Peasant Movements and the Formation of Premonarchic Israel," in *Palestine in Transition. The Emergence of Ancient Israel* (ed. D. N. Freedman and D. F. Graf; SWBA 2; Sheffield: Almond Press, 1983), 39–90, deducing widespread eighth-century social stratification from anecdotal evidence in the early literary prophets.

[8] For motifs in the myth of Israelite leadership, see Baruch Halpern, *Constitution of the Monarchy in Israel* (HSM 25; Chico, Calif.: Scholars Press, 1981), 111–48.

and the cliches of Soviet or other Marxist establishments. In this patois, the witch hunts, the purges, the repression, the deliberate impoverishment, and mass murder, "The Great Terror," coupled in the Soviet Union with rampant racism, and elsewhere with unrestrained xenophobia, were all minor glitches in a noble resistance, especially to American capitalist imperialist ambition. Now it is one thing to develop a rhetorical strategy, and even possibly to believe the words one uses. It is another altogether to listen to another party's rhetoric and not to ask first about the use to which it is put, then about the correlation between the language and reality. This is an error we excuse in an electorate, which after all does elect politician after politician on the basis of legislative projects destined never to come to any semblance of genuine fruition. It is why simplistic, half-baked, and often counterproductive solutions to social or ecological problems win widespread support—banning elephant-hunting, for example, instead of converting it into so valuable a resource as to induce careful management by the hunters.[9] But it is the error of a historical naif and is thus almost inexplicable in a scholar dealing with his or her specialized field.

Revolutionary Religious Rhetoric and the Powerful Elite

There is no question that the *rhetoric* of the passages to which the theologians point carries a high ideological charge. Specifically, the trope on which they focus is that of the reversal of expectations, and especially the reversal of status, motifs that are also invoked to reconstruct a Jesus in revolt against proto-rabbinic Judaism (probably, originally by the gospel writers) especially in Q studies. This is typically the theology of divine election throughout the Bible and is often enough signaled with the introduction of a new, and now fitting, nomenclature.[10] The most familiar cases involve the patriarchs: at the receipt of the divine promise of the land and especially of progeny, Abram's name becomes Abraham; Sarai's, Sarah; on his wrestling with an angel, Jacob's name becomes Israel. In the Priestly source, Joshua's name is changed from Hosea to include the theophoric element, YHWH. And of course Solomon is (re)named Jedediah by the prophet Nathan.

These and like renamings express the transformative power of divine election. Similarly, the Israelite leader is conventionally incapable of saving

---

9 See "Sustainable Argument," *Economist* 343.8022 (June 21, 1997): 83. A perfect example was the death in 1982–1983 of 65 percent of spotted owls tagged by environmentalists with transmitters: the extra weight prevented them from catching their normal rodent prey.

10 For what follows, see Baruch Halpern, "The New Name of Isaiah 62:4: Jeremiah's Reception in the Restoration and the Politics of 'Third Isaiah,'" *JBL* 117 (1998): 623–43.

even himself, let alone a nation, from present threat: Moses, Gideon, Saul, and other figures in the historiography both of Kings and of Chronicles, as well as of Judges (Barak, Jephthah), are portrayed as marginal in social standing, talent, or personal charisma before their divine designation. Joshua must be "magnified" by YHWH before assuming Moses' role as leader. David was a mere shepherd, and his father's youngest, when YHWH catapulted him into Saul's court. Even the literary prophets appropriated the motif of a protest of inadequacy at their vocation—in some cases, as that of Isaiah, of impurity; in others, as in the case of Amos, of a lack of professional training; in some, as in the case of Jeremiah, of an inability to withstand aggressive opposition. The same attitude surfaces toward royal election in Jotham's fable, in Judg 9; the lowly bramble, not the vine or the olive tree, accepts kingship (and similarly the motif underlying Herodotus 2.172, for example, on the kingship of Amasis).

YHWH's revisionist activity also extends to other realms. He punishes sin and, in the case of repentance or the completion of one's punishment, purges sin. Thus Hosea applies the theme of renaming also to Israel (and then undoes the names) to signify punishment and rehabilitation; Isaiah renames Judah; Jeremiah and Deutero-Isaiah, Jerusalem, among other things. Indeed, any divine intervention alters the mundane by definition. The transformation is not necessarily revolutionary, as distinct from reactionary. But the justification is always cast in the language of sympathy for the oppressed and righteous (newly so or not) and stern but deserved chastisement for the evil, portrayed as oppressors.

Here is a difficulty occasioned by the theologians. YHWH's every intervention can be regarded as revolutionary. But, as a brief consideration will show, the contexts of intervention—the humbling of the mighty, the empowerment of the despised—are those reinforcing and even sanctifying the status quo. In theory, one might exempt the prophetic literature from this verdict. The prophets, after all, are the iconic figures of religious traditions derivative from the Jerusalemite cult—not just in Judaism, but also in Christianity, where Paul and Reformationists follow the Gospels in affirming the predestination of events the prophets predict, and again in Islam and Bahai. All the same, to appeal directly to the text is to finesse the question that must be directed at all our sources before their interrogation for historical information. How did the material survive? Why do we have it? What was the nature of prophecy in its context? Our texts themselves attest prophetic competition in antiquity; prophecy was variegated. Yet the codification of prophecy in writing, then in a canon, should arouse our deepest suspicions about claims as to its revolutionary character. To judge from this diagnostic, the prophets were not unrelenting opponents of the state. On the contrary, they served the central elite, which, after all, preserved, coopted, and disseminated their written words. The scholarly obsession with unearthing some less statist, or antiestablishment, seed-kernel from beneath the rotting fruit of transmissional editing (usually for programmatic purposes) merely betrays a velleity, namely, that "the" prophets should shine forth as the avatars of moral purity, that is, of our own values and integrity. In reality, there were prophets enough for the establishment to *choose* its own men and texts, so that relatively little domestication of their ideas and words would be required: as a doctrine of political economy, sustainable use is no modern invention. The idea of "the prophets" as somehow independent, other-worldly, free radicals is a fiction that the ancient establishment *intended* to perpetrate. It maintained the pretense—or at least did not dispel the ambiguity—that it itself was monolithic and identical with the elements under attack: this made the prophetic critique all the more "daring" and thus effective. A *seeming* other-worldliness is what made the prophets whose work or words we have politically useful and, indeed, politically canny. As Ghandi makes a great screen saint, so "the" prophets made wonderful icons for Jewish and Christian doctrine and for medieval and Renaissance art. We *are,* says the canonizer, the prophets.

Specifically, our "revolutionary" rhetoric indulges a habit of turning up in contexts expressing the most establishment vantage points. The texts, codified and transmitted by the central elite in Jerusalem, are anything but representative of a social spectrum. On the contrary, they emerge from a royal and perhaps priestly complex with a profound interest in advancing its own regimen of taxation, organization, and ideological justification.

Take, for example, the covenant. The idea of law based on a divine covenant may in name be late.[11] This changes nothing for the purpose of a synchronic overview. What can be made theologically of the covenant as a whole—namely, the subjection of authorities to YHWH and the rule of law—does not inhere in its detailed regulation of reality, nor indeed in the specifics of our legal sources. The "stipulations," thus, of the "covenant" define the way Judahite society was to run: the "covenant" laws are in fact ruling-class implements. And the ordinances derived from some combination of elite strata, probably divided by party.[12]

---

[11] But see recently the important study of Norbert Lohfink, "Bund als Vertrag im Deuteronomium," *ZAW* 107 (1995): 215–39. For covenantal models already in the Song of Deborah, see the author's "Center and Sentry," in *Megiddo III* (ed. I. Finkelstein, D. Ussishkin, and B. Halpern; Tel Aviv: Institute of Archaeology, 1999).

[12] Mendenhall's evasive strategy is to assign the "covenant" to the premonarchic era. See further Frank Crüsemann, *The Torah* (Philadelphia: Fortress, 1996), 109–200, against which Eckart Otto, "Die Tora in Israels Rechtsgeschichte" *TLZ* 118 (1993): 903–10. Even were this reversion to the antique notion of an "amphictyonic ideal" correct, the expedient would not imply either a vulgar or a revolutionary origin for the material: laws are not enforced by the powerless.

The state, after all, enforced the legislation of the "covenant." A possible exception is the juridical oversight of overarching "ethical" principles, such as "honor your father and mother" in the classic Decalogue (Exod 20; Deut 5). Such injunctions were typically actuated in more specific legislation (e.g., Exod 21:17; Deut 21:18–21), whatever the temporal relation between the formulations. Moreover, where they were not, the "covenant," or rather the stipulation, was not a mechanism of concretized answerability but merely the displacement of that answerability into another dimension. In other words, where the penalty for abrogation of a provision is YHWH's curse, the situation is little different than in the case of the displacement of recompense into the afterlife of the individual from the corporation of one's descendants; the latter had the merit of making cultural sense. Further, each provision's content was determined by those who deposited it in writing, namely, the elite. Why, after all, does the applied theology, so to speak, of Israelite law make enforcement of norms a collective responsibility, their neglect a collective liability? This imposition of terror—of YHWH's curse—on the population at large was an ideological mechanism for enlisting them in policing compliance.

The texts presenting the covenant, in sum, actually represent a means to inculcate the status quo, except when the elite chose to revolutionize this (as in the case of Deuteronomy).[13] This much we should perhaps have deduced simply from the fact that no covenant in the Bible can be contracted either without the consent of the parties to it (as the Sinai covenant, to which Israel must formally subscribe) or without the political leadership. One need hardly add that the laws' ubiquitous concern with protecting immoveable and chattel property bespeaks an alliance with monied classes. In sum, to make the covenant, as an idea, the implement of revolution, one must empty it of its specific ("secondary"?) content and regard it merely as a theory of social contract. Likewise, the liturgical materials that contain the tropes identified by theologians as revolutionary need to be considered first in their context before one can know how seriously, or indeed how at all, to take their words.

The psalms, thus, are the deposit of ritual in the Jerusalem temple. This structure was situated in the palace compound of the Davidic dynasty, and its priesthoods were appointed by and served at the pleasure of the kings, as indicated by the expulsion of Abiathar (1 Kgs 2:26-27) and even the incomplete enfranchisement of hinterland Levitical priests under Josiah (2 Kgs 23:8-9). To the extent that the temple liturgy indicted the king, therefore, it also delegitimated the priesthood; to the extent that it affirmed the

[13] On the dating of the (original) Deuteronomic code, see recently Eckart Otto, "Treueid und Gesetz: Die Ursprünge des Deuteronomiums im Horizont neuassyrischen Vertragsrechts," *ZABR* 2 (1996): 1–52.

king's divine right, it conferred legitimacy on the specialists who molded and preserved it. In the circumstances, it is not at all surprising that most of the psalms mentioning the human king do so favorably (as Ps 45): the king is the recipient of a promise of dynasty from YHWH (Pss 89; 132), is even the god's son (as Pss 2; 89). The liturgy had many ideological connections but was both commissioned and controlled by the royal house.

In the simplest terms, the implication is that any "revolutionary" language in Psalms is conventional in nature. Its function, rather than overt meaning, was conditioned by a performative context. That is, the message of the psalms is not to be grasped in the exegesis of an isolated exemplar but in an understanding of the ritual and ideological contexts in which the psalm was rendered, actualized, realized.[14]

Some details deserve consideration. First, the Mesopotamian New Year involved a ritual humiliation of the king: the kingship was theoretically in abeyance before the latter could resume his station. Likewise, the court officials divested themselves of and then assumed their insignia. This is not materially different from the treatment of the chief god in this festival; at the outset of the New Year, chaos threatens, and Marduk (later, in Assyria, Asshur) must be found and in some versions of the ritual even rescued in order to restore the cosmos.[15] Thus, the New Year's ritual, in one of the most hierarchical and authoritarian societies in the ancient Near East, involves a "revolutionary" reversal of status. Jerusalemite employment of the same motifs need have no more antiroyal content than the Mesopotamian.

Like the protest of inadequacy during a call narrative, the ritual reversal of status has a distinct theological function. Specifically, it avers that it is YHWH (or, in Mesopotamia, the high gods) who exalts the humble. Without YHWH's imprimatur, the king and officials would be unworthy and impotent in the face of insecurity. But this very affirmation carries the implication, obvious to the ancient observer, that YHWH has elected those who are in power.

It is not, the text tells us, by their own accomplishment or might that they have succeeded, but through divine favor. This is a motif with a long history in the Near East, appearing not just in typical royal inscriptions and in the Sargon myth, but also in the "confession" to the pharaoh of Abdi-Hepa, sometime around 1360 B.C.E:

---

[14] See esp. Sigmund Mowinckel, *The Psalms in Israel's Worship* (New York: Abingdon, 1967).

[15] See the ritual text in *ANET* 331–34. See Francois Thureau-Dangin, *Rituels accadiens* (Osbarück: Otto Zeller, 1975), 127–54; cf. 86–111; K. F. Müller, *Das assyrische Ritual I. Texte zum assyrischen Königsritual* (Leipzig: J. C. Hinrichs, 1937), 4–58.

> Neither my father nor my mother set me over (Jerusalem), but the strong arm of the king (set me over my father's house).[16]

Though the seigniorial estate of Jerusalem was hereditary, it was only by the overlord's confirmation that the local ruler served.

The point is that no inherent quality makes a leader or a prophet. Only election can do so. And here the conventions of the text fall into a logical place, in contexts in which king or country might be portrayed as suffering, desperate. These plights might perhaps be real; but much more often, they must have been conventional, dramatic, real emotionally, real relatively—in relation to imagined earlier prosperity and peace—but not urgent politically. One could argue that subjectively the votaries experienced the repetition of despair occasioned by earlier events. Regardless, in the course of the ritual, the participants longed to escape morbidity. Only when the worshipers are *in extremis* and sufficiently chastened to humble, humiliate, and deprive themselves by fasting, pleading, mutilation, and the immolation of loved ones, can YHWH act on their behalf: any amelioration at all, ritual or real, is a function of a need, and the more pressing the need, the more radical the intervention, the greater the glory of YHWH. The reversal of status is a necessary precursor to YHWH's demonstration of power. The demonstration overturns the standing both of those on whose behalf and of those against whom YHWH takes action. In all this, nothing implies an ethic of revolution, a program for revolutionizing society. Instead, the claim is that the social order itself represents such a revolution, over against the chaos, or the oppression, that preceded. We are, the rhetoric proclaims, a community of the liberated, the saved. A more Pauline or Diocletianic perspective on the social order can hardly be imagined.

To what do we owe this far-from-perfunctory genuflection in the direction of social justice and redistribution? For that is what psalmodic and prophetic rhetoric proclaims. The state is the agency of redistribution, the guarantor of justice—not just in Israel, of course, but across the Near East—and is the defender of the helpless. And this is the role the state assumes in our poetic and prose rhetoric (as Nathan's parable); it is the agency policing predation by the wealthy on the insolvent. The state poses, that is to say, as the party restraining the enfranchised citizenry, not just from exploiting but from illegally, immorally, undeservedly subjugating and enslaving marginal social elements.

The fact that this—to modern eyes, laughable—imposture of compassion stretches back to the dawn of civilization suggests that its roots are deep, probably already manifest in band behavior earlier still. The instinct

---

[16] J. A. Knudtzon, *Die El-Amarna-Tafeln* (Vorderasiatische Bibliothek; Aalen: Otto Zeller, 1964), 286:9–13; 287:25–28; 288:13–15.

of caring for the helpless, after all, is sociobiologically programmed from infancy; it can be parsed as a strategy for the preservation of one's gene pool. But the attitude was no doubt extended by the rise in the Early Bronze I-II of debt-enforcement mechanisms newly equated with the earlier use of force. In Israel, before the rise of the state,[17] there are no indications of administration, taxation, or social hierarchy external to the kinship structure. The introduction of state expropriation of wealth, including time and labor, in the Iron Age (IIA) also explains why the prophetic rhetoric, and the folklore motifs of status reversal, are as they are. These project a message, a subtext, that reality, life, the world, and therefore YHWH is revolutionary, redistributionist. YHWH in this sense is identical with the state.

So, too, is the human king: unworthy of honor, he is magnified by YHWH's designation, the ethic of redistribution incarnate. The bramble in Jotham's fable, thus, undertakes governance from a sense of obligation that is not shared by the olive or vine, both of which are productive and thus wealthy and uninterested in restricting their own class's latitude. No false consciousness here! The true elite, says the fable, the elite engaged in primary production, spurns power as an encumbrance. It takes little talent for *Realpolitik* to read between these lines: for shirking the distractions of responsibility, the producers must *pay* for state consumption.

With this chord, the repeated advertence to ultimogeniture and to YHWH's fertilitizing the barren in our folklore rings in harmony. Here are two motifs that are widely distributed (not just in Israel) and that have engendered variants such as the resurrection of the son of the Shunammitess in Kings (2 Kgs 4:8-37: she was barren, then fertilized, then bereaved and refertilized, so to speak) or the rejection of David's firstborn by Bathsheba ultimately in favor of Solomon. They also relate to the legitimation narratives of such characters as Moses, but also Sargon and several other Mesopotamian kings, plus the whole postexilic temple community.[18]

---

[17] The existence of prestate Israel, while disputed, is attested in the identification of the southern state with David (Tel Dan, Mesha), the northern with Omri (Mesha and neo-Assyrian sources), plus Shalmaneser's identification of Ahab as "the Israelite"; not until annexation is the state identified with the capital alone. The Merneptah Stela, early biblical poetry and historiography, and the archaeological record reliably document the prestate era. See, latterly, Baruch Halpern, "How Golden Is the Marshaltown, How Holy the Scripture?" *JQR* 87 (1997): 1–16.

[18] See, latterly, Baruch Halpern, "A Historiographic Commentary on Ezra 1–6: Achronological Narrative and Dual Chronology in Israelite Historiography," in *The Hebrew Bible and its Interpreters* (ed. W. H. Propp, Baruch Halpern, and D. N. Freedman; Biblical and Judaic Studies from the University of California, San Diego; Winona Lake, Ind.: Eisenbrauns, 1990), 81–142, arguing that Samarian rejection of

And in no case ever does the language of reversal have future reference. In every case, it is historical or present in character, antedating the achievement of the present state of the universe. Shemaryahu Talmon has therefore suggested that the folklore served as a "steam valve" for the state.[19] These topoi represent outlets for a standing fear of failure, or disgruntlement, mitigating stigmas potentially attaching to abnormal or misprised status and thus relieving social tension. Like revolutionary Israelite rhetoric about leadership—the leader as one raised from impotence by the god—this affirmation of the transformed qualities of society represents the appropriation in the state cult (Psalms) and culture of schemes of legitimation based on social justice rather than on social order. It is from the classes of the unproductive (Jotham's fable), from the marginal (David, Saul, Gideon), and the expelled (Moses, Jephthah, Levi) that the leadership classes of *this day* have arisen.

Though interpreted as evidence of a revolutionary biblical ethic sanctioning the "liberation" of the "oppressed," this same language is deployed in ritual in cultures anterior to and later in contact with Israel. Its function, as in Israel, is never a call to revolution; rather, it either affirms the divine election of the king and thus the state or recalls a community of landed citizenry to shared ethical norms. In either case it relieves the contradictions of the relations of production and preserves, rather than subverts, the existing social order. Notably, the language is absent from premonarchic Israelite texts, from the very period to which Mendenhall appeals: its introduction, under the monarchy, reassures the citizenry that the existing order is already revolutionary, redistributive. Again, this is no surprise. It is, after all, the courtly version of the folklore that has made its way into our canon, not some tract of class consciousness. And it is precisely the state that needed to assert its preservation of such continuity with the culture of a kinship-based hinterland.

The folklore motifs and the prophetic insistence on social justice (one thinks of Isa 10:1-4, for example, or Mic 2:1-2) are two sides of a

---

the temple's rebuilding is modeled on Nabonidus's explanations for the delay in the construction of Sin's Haran sanctuary. Note likewise Ps 118:22, "the stone the builders had rejected has become the cornerstone; it is from YHWH that this comes." On the Sargon myth, see, latterly, J. G. Westenholz, *Legends of the Kings of Akkade: The Texts* (Mesopotamian Civilizations 7; Winona Lake, Ind.: Eisenbrauns, 1997), 38:1–40:13.

[19] Shemaryahu Talmon, "*Har* and *Midbār*. An Antithetical Pair of Biblical Motifs," in *Figurative Language in the Ancient Near East* (ed. M. Mindlin, M. J. Geller, and J. E. Wansbrough; London: School of Oriental and African Studies, 1987), 124; idem, "Literary Motifs and Speculative Thought in the Hebrew Bible," *Hebrew University Studies in Literature and the Arts* 16 (1988): 150–68.

single coin.[20] The latter had the desired effect not only on the ancients, but also on modern interpreters, who focus on, rather than pierce, the veil of rhetoric. To quote Roscoe Conklin, "Reform is the final refuge of a scoundrel."

Prophetic Critique As a Social-Control Mechanism

How was the prophetic appeal to social norms useful? It is no coincidence that prophetic literature was codified in the late eighth century, probably under Hezekiah, just when the kings of Judah needed most urgently to beat down centers of resistance in the countryside.[21] The literary prophets do indeed criticize the state, but they serve the state's interests in doing so; in fact, their criticism is directed primarily at powers, such as those charged with local jurisdiction, who operated with the support, but also under the constraints of, central authority. This is why the prophets' words (or those of their epigones) survive at all. And this very survival, whatever amendments one imagines were introduced by later transmitters, is inextricably bound up with the circumstance that characters such as Isaiah, Jeremiah, and Ezekiel clearly enjoyed the patronage of at least one party at the court. One can even make this argument in the case of Amos, the most trenchant, plangent bulwark of the "poor." Amos's connection to the Judahite establishment is not just transparent but is also inferred by the Israelite establishment in one of the book's narratives: "Hie yourself to the land of Judah, *and eat bread there, and there prophesy,*" says the priest Amaziah (see Amos 7:12-17). Amos is to join Judahite festivals and earn his living among his sponsors.

The sense of the literary prophets' social addresses is simple: the poor, the widow, and the orphan must be protected against landowners' abuses. The same ethic as that reflected in law or legal homily on the unfortunate is present here. But who assumes the role of protector? The only possible agent is the state. The calls for social justice are in other words invocations to the state to act as it should, on the norms it traditionally articulates,

---

[20] For some passages in Amos, Micah, and Isaiah, see J. A. Dearman, *Property Rights in the Eighth Century Prophets* (SBLDS 106; Atlanta: Scholars Press, 1988); for the seventh century, Mayer Sulzberger, *The Status of Labor in Ancient Israel* (Philadelphia: Dropsie College, 1923), which, despite outdated assumptions, reflects a model methodological and philological scruple.

[21] D. N. Freedman, "Headings in the Books of the Eighth-Century Prophets," *AUSS* 25 (1987): 9–26; Baruch Halpern, "Sybil, or the Two Nations? Archaism, Kinship, Alienation and the Elite Redefinition of Traditional Culture in Judah in the 8th-7th Centuries B.C.E.," in *The Study of the Ancient Near East in the 21st Century* (ed. J. S. Cooper and G. M. Schwartz; Winona Lake, Ind.: Eisenbrauns, 1996), 311–12, 334–35 n. 115.

namely, as the restraint on legalized bullying by the propertied. These wield local power, especially in economic affairs, against their inferiors, but are by their nature the only genuine potential threat to state impositions.[22] Here, the state is again identified with the humble, the lowly, the poor; it becomes, in effect, the poor in its own eyes, much like the Jerusalem Church in primitive Christianity, or the Communist Party in Lenin's dictum that the Party is the workers, and must—of all the workers—be the best and first preserved.

The prophets, so called, are of course revered in the Western religious traditions and even function as theoretical role models for their exegetical heirs. So a deconstruction of their social role is not emotionally congenial. All the same, nothing in the nature of prophecy insulated it either against the temptations of expediency, particularly payment and patronage, or against political co-option either in advance or after the delivery of an oracle. In their textual manifestations, the literary prophets act principally in the service of the state; they advance an agenda of restricting the centers of wealth, on the theory that this serves the interest of the indigent; it is easier to enlist sympathy for the latter (and encourage the socialization of a false consciousness) than it is to justify the state's appropriation of resources by any other strategy. Notably, 1 Sam 8 represents the introduction of kingship as a means for the creation of a professional soldiery and thus for the primitive accumulation of capital through conquest. In the language, if not the mentality, of the Near Easterner, plundering others is indistinguishable from the defense of capital accumulation from conquest. This trope represents *all* of Israelite society as "poor" or "oppressed," in need of succor. It deflects to the external sphere, as do the books of Judges and 1 Samuel generally, the accusations of exploitation reserved for domestic elements in the prophetic literature (and in Nathan's parable concerning Uriah, and in the Naboth story, and, indeed, in the tax revolt of 1 Kgs 12). Conversely, foreign conquerors in the prophetic literature are typically portrayed as being YHWH's implements of retribution, up to a point (at which they themselves incur the onus of retribution). "Oppression" or "grievance" as a category of discourse is a stock-in-trade of Near Eastern culture, and the party speaking or writing is *always* in his or her own view aggrieved.

Like the "revolutionary" morphemes of the folklore, the literary prophets, then, are in Talmon's sense steam valves for the state (not unlike the professoriate!). They facilitate royal inroads on the landed, particularly

---

[22] Against Dearman's view (*Property Rights*) that the prophets attack state officials. No one in Israel or Judah held power (as distinct from influence) without state acknowledgment—as was the case in the localities of the Ottoman Empire. But it is an error to identify local powers with the central hierarchy directed from the capital.

on countryside corporations, the clan sections.[23] That the court should incline to such a policy is neither surprising nor unique, any more than is the philosopher's Machiavellian advice to the Sicilian tyrant: "Cut down the high grain." Of course, the state could attach domestic wealth only from the landed citizenry, and evasion of the state's claims was no doubt rampant. Hence the portrayal of the Solomonic schism (1 Kgs 12) and of Samuel's public diatribe against kingship (1 Sam 8) as a concern with taxation; hence also the curbs on the royal prerogative of personal aggrandizement in the "Law of the King" (Deut 17:14-20; cf. 1 Sam 10:25) and in the tonic of the Uriah and Naboth stories. Such "abuse" is the flip side of the prophetic rhetoric, which urges the nurturing of the needy *against* such characters but, both narratives imply, within the bounds of justice. So the true value of the prophetic texts is to justify the state's hinterland agenda: squashing the resistance of the clans; taxing those with means, or anything one might label means; imposing a universal standard of top-down justice and conflict resolution on a much more varied and distributed population. Bluntly put, the literary prophets are codified because they supply a Morton's Fork for feasting at the court.

A word on the "Law of the King" (Deut 17:14-20) is apposite here. Many commentators have argued that this cannot reflect a courtly milieu because its demands are impractical. Gösta W. Ahlström, for example, projects the law into the postexilic era on the grounds that its utopian character would make it unworkable in the Iron Age.[24] This is hardly an argument to any date at all; the impossible is impossible at all times. But the law accomplishes an ideological task: the king does not accrue wealth, concentration of which is evil in Israel's zero-sum universe—*public* property is theft. Thus, the king can pour resources into the cult, can collect and redistribute them. But the proclamation exculpates the court of extracting from society at large any surplus for its own luxury. This is now a late Judahite law; it prohibits the assembly of a large chariot force, something not seen in Judah in the late eighth and seventh centuries, but places no limitation on fortress garrisons or professional infantry. Furthermore, the injunction against multiplying foreign wives, rather than taking them, reads, as many have noted, as a reference to the indictment of Solomon in 1 Kgs 11 (esp. vv. 1–3), a passage that can be traced without much question to Josiah's repudiation of Solomonic policy in the Deuteronomistic

---

[23] See Baruch Halpern, "Jerusalem and the Lineages in the 8th–7th Centuries BCE: Kinship and the Rise of Individual Moral Liability," in *Law and Ideology in Monarchic Israel* (ed. Baruch Halpern and D. W. Hobson; JSOTSup, 124; Sheffield: Sheffield Academic Press, 1991), 11–107; "Sybil."

[24] G. W. Ahlström, *The History of Ancient Palestine* (JSOTSup 146; Sheffield: JSOT Press, 1993), 43.

History (the Josianic portions of which, such as Judg 1–2, are also concerned with local intermarriages). So the law fits the Josianic milieu characterizing both Deuteronomy and the Deuteronomistic History and like them invokes social justice in order to veil the realities of power politics. The king, who is the state, is identified in every respect with the poor, the humble, the oppressed.

The power elite's surface rhetoric favors redistribution. And perhaps this is even sincere, although to what degree is disputable. "No man's wife or property is safe," the apothegm dictates, "when Congress is in session." Again, the "revolutionary" claims of the text are those of the state, and the effect, whatever the intention, is conveniently to camouflage the inefficiencies of redistribution as fairness and natural sympathy for the unfortunate. Like applied Marxism, this is nothing more than the platform of an oligarchy immune from the custody of its constituencies.[25]

Overall, the question as to the nature of Israelite society and ideologies is not to be answered on the basis of what our texts say. Rather, the issue must be how and in what contexts they functioned and especially how they promoted "false consciousness." That said, there is even less question once the sociology of the preservation of our texts is taken into account, as well as that aspect of the texts that represents their surface expression (the overturning of order or expectation being always in the past): the valence is consistently to the service of the state. Far from being revolutionary, the texts are bulwarks of the existing power structure.

YHWH's Identity in Essentialist and Functional Views

The conservative function of ancient redistributionist rhetoric is predictable. It dovetails neatly with the theories offered in Israel as to the innermost, essentialist nature of the state high god, YHWH. The following considerations address the issue of stasis in our textual theologies—again, against old-style liberation theology's attempt to conscript YHWH in the service of its own ends. Simultaneously, they lay out an intellectual contribution of Israelite religion to Western tradition.

Robert Ingersoll, the agnostic Yankee answer to the European poet-courtier tradition, once paid a visit to the celebrated "Bible"-pusher, Henry Ward Beecher—so the story goes. He particularly admired Beecher's globe, depicting the constellations and planets. "Why, Henry," Ingersoll exclaimed, that's just the sort of thing I've been looking for. Who made it?" Ward Beecher replied, "No one, Robert. It just happened."

---

[25] See esp. Reuven Yaron, "Social Problems and Policies in the Ancient Near East," in *Law, Politics and Society in the Ancient Mediterranean World* (ed. Baruch Halpern and D. W. Hobson; Sheffield: Sheffield Academic Press, 1993), 19–41.

The contrast to this anecdote comes from Julian Huxley. To adapt it to the preceding account, Beecher's counterpart taxes Ingersoll's: "A philosopher is like a blind man in a dark room looking for a black cat that isn't there." "That may be so," replies the Ingersoll equivalent, "but a theologian would have found it."

These two vignettes illustrate the polarity of theological discourse. Beecher appeals to the principle of Aquino-Maimonidean faith in an ultimate prime mover—it's not "turtles all the way down" after all. The Ingersoll position denies faith altogether, affirming that theologians, like the House Ethics Committee, study something that does not exist. The modern mind conceives of the two approaches as diametric opposites. Oddly, at a philosophical level, the elite religion of ancient Israel, at least in late monarchic apologetic, spans the yawning chasm.

This is not to say that biblical, let alone Israelite, religion is somehow unified in any sense at all. The Bible, famously, is an anthology, theological as well as literary, no doubt produced by negotiations as complex as those at Nicea, and a great deal more complex than those of the "Jesus Seminar" at the Westar Institute, with its caucuses over the authenticity of sayings in the canonical Gospels. The myth of a canonizing conclave at Yavneh in the vicinity of 100 C.E. is probably exaggerated, if not altogether incorrect.[26] All the same, the iterative winnowing process was stiff; this is a selection of texts and doctrines that suited successive generations of Judah's elite. The result, for the purpose of understanding the religions of Israel, is at best a set of fossils, from which reconstruction of the great beasts themselves must begin, but to which the reconstruction must not be limited. Discussions of monotheism, after all, tend to blur the distinction between theology and religion. Non-Western religion is a matter of behavior, of assimilation into a culture. Theology, by contrast, superimposes on custom cohesive philosophical speculation, although this can be compartmentalized within an individual myth or other rhetorical product.

Under the circumstances, despite frequent quests after the "unique" characteristics of Israelite and, more often, biblical religion, one of the few durable achievements of critical scholarship has been the recognition that the Israelite pantheon, even among the elite, early contained various gods. Exodus 15, one of the oldest lyrics in the Hebrew Bible, marks off one of its stanzas with the question, "Who is like you among the gods, YHWH?" (15:11). Psalm 29 begins, "Ascribe to YHWH, O sons of gods. . . , " addressing an assembly of gods among whom YHWH "takes his place" in Ps 82:1 to render judgment.

---

26 Jack Lightstone, "The Formation of the Biblical Canon in Judaism of Late Antiquity: Prolegomenon to a General Reassessment," *SR* 8 (1979): 135–42.

Traditionally, scholars have taken a theological and prescriptive approach to the issue of Israelite and Near Eastern monotheism. From this perspective, monotheism is the conviction that only one god exists; no others need apply. But this conviction is absent from broadly socialized Near Eastern cultures, including that of Israel. Egyptian, Mesopotamian, Hittite, Greek, and Ugaritic and Canaanite myths all present developed pantheons. All share myths in which the divine succession, usually involving a generational shift just as among humans, entails war among the gods. In Mesopotamia, the creation of the universe results from this conflict. And the focus in Mesopotamia, Hatti, and Canaan is on the defeat of the sea-god by the storm-god, who then administers the cosmos (the motif, ill-adapted to conditions in Egypt, is transformed there). In all these cultures, the common thread is the succession of a patriarchal high god's royal son, that is, the birth of monarchy among the gods.

These pantheons, thus, all have a high god, under whose benign administration the other gods—of rain or pestilence or astral bodies—act, though often independently. The high god, in the Near East, is the god of the state. Probably in some cases, the state pantheon subsumed local high gods of towns or regions in the empire. Thus, different states may share essentially identical pantheons but identify different figures as the high god: in Babylon, for example, the high god from the mid-second millennium forward was Marduk; the Assyrian high god was Asshur. Sennacherib, Assyria's king at the end of the eighth century, actually rewrote the Babylonian creation epic to accord Marduk's role in it to Asshur. Yet the supporting cast of "great gods," and most of the minor deities, were identical in the two realms.

With Canaan, Mesopotamia, and, less formally, Greece (kingship having waned there), Israel shared the notion of a divine council presiding over human affairs.[27] Job 1–2 predicate the idea, as do 1 Kgs 22:19–22 and Isa 6. Indeed, the claims of Judges and Kings, reinforced by the rhetorical hyperbole of Jeremiah, make it clear that "other gods" were never regarded as heterodox before the cult reforms especially of the late seventh century.[28] And excavation has yielded votive figurines in sufficient quantity to

[27] So H. L. Ginsberg, *The Writings of Ugarit* (in Hebrew) (Jerusalem: Bialik, 1936); further, Otto Eissfeldt, "El and Yahweh" *JSS* 1 (1956): 25–37; esp. F. M. Cross, *Canaanite Myth and Hebrew Epic* (Cambridge: Harvard University Press, 1973), 112–44 with extensive bibliography.

[28] Judg 2:11–19; 3:7, 12; 4:1; 6:1; 10:6, etc; 1 Kgs 11:1–8; 2 Kgs 23:13; 1 Kgs 17–19; 2 Kgs 8:18, 27; 16:3–4; 21:3–7; Jer 11:13; 2:8; 7:1–8:3; 14:15; 23:13; 27:15. In Jeremiah, any heterodox activity is the worship of "other gods" or "baal." For the indigenous origins of these gods, see Baruch Halpern, "Jerusalem and the Lineages"; idem, "Sybil"; idem, "'Brisker Pipes Than Poetry': The Development of Israelite Monotheism,"

dispel any question about the limitation of such practice to isolated circles: every expanded family in monarchic Israel had at least one such *female* icon in its housing compound.[29] The worship of subsidiary deities in Israel, deities in YHWH's "suite" to use Yehezkel Kaufmann's locution, was a going commercial concern.

Some have argued that YHWH so dominated the subordinate gods of the Israelite pantheon as effectively to be omnipotent and alone.[30] As many scholars have observed, however, a similar view emerges from the Babylonian creation epic, the *Enuma Elish,* in which the attributes of the entire pantheon are ascribed to the chief god, Marduk. The date of the text is disputed, but the prologue to the Code of Hammurabi (seventeenth century B.C.E.) presupposes such a myth. In the same texts, Marduk is installed as king over all the (surviving) gods. Not unrelated is the fact that Mesopotamian literature is replete with pleas to gods and goddesses, such as Ishtar of Arbela, Ishtar of Nineveh, or Shamash, or Adad (Hadad, Haddu); in such prayers, the god under address is the only active divinity, so that, at a local level, devotion is exclusive. The state myth did not reflect the subjective experience of a worshiper during his or her devotions.

Scholars used to refer to this phenomenon as "affective henotheism," devotion to one god without denial of others' potency. This principle, as readers of Freud and Velikovsky know, was supposedly elevated to state policy in Egypt under the fourteenth-century pharaoh, Amenhotep IV (Akhenaten). Akhenaten channeled resources into the cult of the solar disk (Aten) at the expense of other temple establishments. He supposedly propagated the heresy that the solar disk (Aten) was prepollent among all deities and without human representation. This is no doubt a caricature of Akhenaten's own position,[31] but even if it represents the polemic of Akhenaten's posthumous opponents, it indicates that the limitation of devotion to a single being was conceived of as a possibility in the Egypt

---

in *Judaic Perspectives on Ancient Israel* (ed. Jacob Neusner, Baruch Levine, and Ernest Frerichs; Philadelphia: Fortress, 1983), 77–115; "The Baal (and the Asherah) in Seventh-Century Judah: Yhwh's Retainers Retired," in *Konsequente Traditionsgeschichte. Festschrift für Klaus Baltzer* (ed. Rüdiger Barthelmus, Thomas Krüger, and Helmut Utzschneider; OBO 126; Freiburg: Universitätsverlag, 1993), 115–54.

[29] See especially J. S. Holladay, "Religion in Israel and Judah under the Monarchy: An Explicitly Archaeological Approach," in *Ancient Israelite Religion: Essays in Honor of Frank Moore Cross*. (ed. P. D. Miller Jr., P. D. Hanson, and S. D. McBride; Philadelphia: Fortress, 1987), 275–80.

[30] Paradigmatically, Yehezkel Kaufmann, *The Religion of Israel: From Its Beginnings to the Babylonian Exile* (New York: Schocken Books, 1960).

[31] D. B. Redford, *Akhenaten, the Heretic King* (Princeton, N. J.: Princeton University Press, 1994).

of the time. A later attempt to install a god atop a state pantheon—under Nabonidus, king of Babylon at the end of its resurgence (556–538 B.C.E.)—exhibits similar characteristics, with many divine statues concentrated in the capital, possibly to ensure countryside resistance to the Persian invaders.[32] Possible Judahite influence on Nabonidus has not been explored, nor his policies' relation to the philosophical monotheism of Second Isaiah. Nevertheless, his reform, like Akhenaten's, proved abortive.

Precisely these failures, however, show that the line between monotheism and polytheism should not be too precisely drawn. Akhenaten and Nabonidus focused the cult on their own gods. But the "monotheistic" traditions of Judaism, Christianity, and Islam are no different. All these traditions admit the existence of subordinate immortals—saints, angels, even demons, and, in the case of traditional Christianity, the devil, an eternal evil principle almost equipollent with the high god. Monotheism, in short, as the modern monotheist imagines it, was neither original to nor practiced in the historical Israel of the Bible.

These limitations on the exceptional character of Israel have long been acknowledged. George Ernest Wright was one of the most successful respondents to them, stressing instead the distinctiveness of Israel's religion as a "historical" one. In Wright's scheme, YHWH's claim to allegiance derived primarily from actions that humans might have witnessed. In this sense, YHWH was a real god, unlike the mythic agents of Mesopotamia and Canaan.[33]

Wright's attempt to salvage Israel's god from comparison to contemporary congeners was rejected, especially by the Assyriological community, which stressed that Mesopotamian gods, too, intervened in history.[34] Even at Ugarit, El and Haddu direct human affairs in the Keret epic. Indeed, it is difficult to imagine that any people, "pagan" or not, would worship gods unable to manipulate mundane reality; one does not worship impotence. This is why traditional language about "fertility gods" or "cults" is often misleading; there is no such thing as a sterility cult. Like the idea of a "wisdom tradition," the existence of which would be news to ancient authors writing in the "stupidity tradition," the nomenclature is sufficiently absorbent and flexible to induce slovenly thinking. The same is true of facile characterizations of monotheisms and polytheisms.

More diachronic approaches to the literature have also been common. In a bellweather study, Albrecht Alt distinguished the "god(s) of the fathers"

---

[32] For a slightly different view, P.-A. Beaulieu, "An Episode in the Fall of Babylon to the Persians," *JNES* 54 (1993): 241–61.

[33] See G. E. Wright, *God Who Acts: Biblical Theology As Recital* (London: SCM Press, 1952).

[34] As J. J. M. Roberts, "Myth *versus* History" *CBQ* 38 (1976): 1–13.

from YHWH. The patriarchal deities (the god of Abraham, the fear of Isaac, the stallion of Jacob), according to E and P, were identified with YHWH only in Moses' time. Alt, assuming the antiquity of this tradition, identified the patriarchal gods with prehistoric nomadic groups.[35] His approach, like that which fell into disuse in the nineteenth century of reading ancient myths to extract their coded but—to the individual exegete—all too transparent historical content, had widespread influence. The resulting damage to the reconstruction of early Israelite history has been little short of disastrous.[36]

Frank Cross sophisticated Alt's analysis into a systematic reconstruction of the history of Israelite religion. Cross argued that Alt's patron deities were, like the gods (he maintained) in Amorite personal names, originally active in the personal lives of their client-votaries. But neither Amorite nor later Arabic deities were the anonymous lares posited by Alt; they were, rather, major gods, named by epithets. The epithets underscored the personal relationship with the gods' clients, and the onomastica of Moab, Ammon, and Edom, which seem to *name* only one, national god, suggest that the ethnic dynamic there was the same as Israel's.

Cross contrasted the personal aspect of the patriarchal god with that of the creator. Canaanite El, Babylonian Marduk, and YHWH, like Zeus (and Haddu in Canaan), presided over or participated in epic primordial battles against primal powers. This, Cross suggested, is the godhead of pure myth, of eternity. The patriarchal gods, however, were placed in historical time.

Cross thus characterized Israelite religion as a synthesis of the personal with the cosmic aspects of the god, in which the client relationship of the patriarch to the god metamorphosed into a client relationship between the nation and the god. In his reconstruction, the synthesis also transformed YHWH's nature; the cosmic god was now one who acted in history. Like the patriarchal deities, the new god acted in full view of humanity, but on such a grand scale as to dwarf the common embellishments of legend. And, while the patriarchal god might influence or even decide events, his power was circumscribed by the puissance of other divinities. The now-personalized cosmic god intervened with finality. Formerly mythic, the cosmic god was in Israel defined primarily by his behavior on earth, in the way he shaped history.[37]

Even were this overture correct, Israel's religion would not stand out from her neighbors'—which, after all, is why one distinguishes Western monotheism from other religions. As noted above, Israel did not spurn

---

[35] Albrecht Alt, *Der Gott der Väter* (Stuttgart: W. Kohlhammer, 1929).

[36] See, for example, Roland de Vaux, *The Early History of Israel* (Philadelphia: Westminster, 1978), 161–287 and passim for use of late traditions about prehistory as though they were reliable.

[37] Cross, *Canaanite Myth,* 3–75.

gods different from YHWH, though we can only surmise, not know, that the worshiper did not apprehend those gods as YHWH's competitors. Likewise, in Homeric epic Athena and other gods act in both the cosmic and mundane spheres, which are in ancient thought closely related. And while El and Baal never wreak the sort of natural havoc that YHWH is—in Cross's treatment—thought to specialize in, they do act as personal gods to a king while nevertheless retaining their full-blown cosmic significance. YHWH is neither the only, nor even the first, god to have bridged the gap between myth and legend.

In fact, the gods of the patriarchs are "personal" because the patriarchs impersonate the nation. So almost none of the criteria mooted as distinctive features of Israelite religion passes a rigorous scrutiny.[38] Even the covenant is not so unusual as essentialism might suggest. True, the idea of a contract with a god (with or without the term) pertains in the main to royalty in Mesopotamia, and in the case of one Sumerian king is explicit. But the covenant is merely metaphoric for a reciprocal relation with the deity;[39] this reciprocity is present all over the ancient world. Offending Poseidon leads to Odysseus's loss of self. Neglecting Marduk leads to a shambles in Babylon. Propitiating the gods brings reward. These ideas are so common as to be obvious, whatever the metaphor for them. Gods and priests must be appeased. Whether one calls the relationship contractual is a semantic, not substantive, quibble.

Yet despite these strictures, Israel's religion *can* be said to have had distinctive elements and especially combinations of elements. These are encoded in the definition of YHWH's nature. Here the contrasts are not Alt and Wright, but nuances in the chiaroscuro of unsystematic theology. Specifically, Israel's "historical" god, the earth-shaker, is far from unique in that respect. What makes him unique is the degree to which his "historical" nature has led his worshipers away from the genre of myth in their conceptualization of the cult, in their strategies for the socialization of religious ideologies, and, indeed, in their whole definition of cyclic time.

Signal in this respect is the character of Israel's festivals. It is an unshaken scholarly tenet that the major holy days, Passover (Pesach), Booths (Sukkot) and Weeks (Shevuot), originated as agricultural celebrations. They coincided with holidays on the Canaanite calendar, assumed to

---

[38] See Peter Machinist, "The Question of Distinctiveness in Ancient Israel: An Essay," in *Ah, Assyria...: Studies in Assyrian History and Ancient Near Eastern Historiography Presented to Hayim Tadmor* (ed. Mordechai Cogan and Israel Ephʿal; ScrHier 33; Jerusalem: Magnes, 1991), 196–212. Machinist concludes that Israel's claims of distinctiveness arose from identity formation. The persistence of that concern suggests the operation of other processes as well.

[39] So Lohfink, "Bund."

be purely agricultural *and* mythic.[40] Yet to varying degrees, Israel reduced them to re-creations of national history. Thus, the Canaanite autumn harvest festival probably involved rehearsal of Haddu's triumph over Mot, "Death," a myth sometimes regarded as "Baal's resurrection."[41] In Israel, traces of this background remained.[42] Over time, however, the reinterpretation took hold that the celebration commemorated Israel's wanderings after the exodus in "booths."

Sukkot's divorce from agriculture was slow. The same is true of Shevuot, though as a wheat festival it was less festive, less well appointed. Even in modern times, neither has shed the trappings of the harvest feast. Pesach, however, seems to have been different. Although the corresponding spring New Year's festival in Babylon commemorated Marduk's victory over the Salt-Sea, Tiamat, Israel's Passover attached from early on to the nation's rescue from Egypt (as Exod 15). Israel's "historical" experience replaced what in Mesopotamia, and probably Canaan, was a cosmogonic myth. This transition was eased by the calendrical location of Passover—the festival of the green wheat poking up from the clods, long in advance of the harvest. To be sure, its focus was agrarian (pastoralism aside), but it never celebrated the enjoyment of produce—it was a festival of expectation—and that is also its character in its historical transmogrification, of liberation from Egypt *before possession of the land*. It exalted the end of oppression, by winter and by Egypt. This made it so dominant in religious consciousness that P had to shift the calendar to place the New Year in the seventh month and link a separate New Year's festival to Sukkot: for P, possession is the object of celebration (Josh 5), and this may be more authentic, as a theology, than the mock-revolutionism of the JED tradition (while the focus on the *consumed* but still apotropaic lamb is also atavistic).

Pesach is not the only festival in which history replaced myth as a program. No Near Eastern religion had a festival like Purim, for example, commemorating an alleged escape from genocide, or like Hanukkah, traced to the rededication of the temple during the revolt against the Seleucids. Over time, history so supplanted myth that Judaism absorbed new ritual princi-

---

40 Classically, Julius Wellhausen, *Prolegomena to the History of Ancient Israel* (Cleveland: Meridian, 1957), 83–120. For linkage to the ancestors, see A. M. Cooper and Bernard Goldstein, "The Festivals of Israel and Judah and the Literary History of the Pentateuch," *JAOS* 110 (1990): 19–31; idem, "Exodus and Matsot in History and Tradition," *Maarav* 8 (1992): 15–37; idem, "The Cult of the Dead and the Theme of Entry into the Land," *Biblical Interpretation* 1 (1993).

41 *CTA* 23:8–11, with 2; 4; 6; *KTU* 1.23; 2; 4; 6.

42 Mowinckel, *Psalms,* 1:106–92; *Der achtundsechzigste Psalm* (Oslo: Jacob Dybwab, 1953).

pally as historical moments (the Fast of Gedaliah, the 9th of Av); the trend toward "historicization" of the cult went further in Israel than elsewhere. Sacralized reminiscences—and the assumption of mythic function makes history mythic in character, as in the division of the Reed Sea[43]—so came to predominate in Israel's consciousness over the timeless myths that the very "cyclical" holy days of the agricultural year took on the raiment of Israel's past. The relation of the spring New Year's festival to liberation from "bondage" in Egypt is the emblem of this impulse. But the impulse rears its head in other arenas of Israelite religion as well.

The cultic calendar was never wholly divorced from myth. Though the Decalogue of Deut 5:6-21 links the Sabbath to Egyptian corvée, that of P (Exod 20) associates it with the creation. Already Isaiah, around 700, compared the contemporary prospect of Israel's return from Assyria both to the exodus from Egypt and to the defeat of the sea-monster, Leviathan (Isa 11:11–16; cf. *CTA* 5:1:1-3). The typological equation of the exodus with YHWH's cosmogonic victory over chaos (cf. Job 40:6–32) suggests the likelihood of connections in the cult.

Writing 170 years later, the author of Isa 40–55 embellishes the same equation in connection with the Judahites' return from Babylon. For him, the primordial salvation from sea, the exodus, and the contemporary restoration all cohere (as Isa 51:9–11; also 44:24–28; 52:7–12; cf. 63:1–14; 42:5–16). His reveries invoke a mythic heritage to comment on historical cult myths. So First Isaiah testifies to the historicization of cult myths in Israel by equating the primordial defeat of sea with the cosmogonic exodus as models for an anticipated return from Assyria. Second Isaiah shows how deeply historical consciousness has supplanted myth in the elite religion. One characterizes the historical by allusion to the mythic. The historical experience is real, programmatic, the overt referent. Myth furnishes a metaphorical language with which to describe it; the event casts no light on the myth, but the myth provides insight into the event.

The use of history as cult myth is not unique. Islam celebrates the Prophet's mundane achievements. Moreover, historical or not, a myth is a myth. From no religious viewpoint can one differentiate Jesus' resurrection as a program for Easter from Israel's exodus as a program for Pesach. Israelite religion is, however, further imbued with history. It is peculiarly historical in its approach to prophecy. Prophecy, speaking for the god, is one of the few ways to divine divine intent (other than technical divination or necromancy by nonspecialists) in the religion. Its moorings, like those of other mantic arts, are supernal.

In seventh-century Judah, a simple rule was developed, or promulgated, for determining whether one should trust a prophecy:

---

[43] For the development of this historical myth, see Cross, *Canaanite Myth,* 122–44.

> Should you say in your heart, "How can I know the oracle that YHWH has not spoken?" What the prophet says in the name of YHWH—and that oracle does not come to be nor come to pass—that is the oracle that YHWH did not speak. (Deut 18:21–22)

Bismarck could not have designed a more pragmatic text. The prophecy that is realized, by definition, is correct. That belied by events is uninspired. (The logic is that of a Boolean truth table.) Many exegetes differentiate true from false prophets; the text affords no such ground.

The distinction is between a prophecy and a prophet. Thus, though inspired, Ahab's prophets (1 Kgs 22:19–23) deliver false oracles. They are misled by the inferior medium of aural, rather than visual, revelation; the story lionizes Micaiah more like Ezekiel than like Jeremiah in the typology of word versus vision prophecy. Again, Micah's prophecy of Jerusalem's destruction need not be realized, certainly not right off (Jer 26). It was forestalled by repentance, to be brought on by renewed sin. Yet Jeremiah's appendix on applied prophecy (chs. 26–29) makes much of the timeliness of a prediction's materialization. One might even suspect that this, and not sedition, was the basis for the indictment of Jer 26. The narrative, which contextualizes Jer 7, is dated to 609, after all, and might be redated arguably as late as 598, a decade before the temple's destruction. Does it explain Jeremiah's ambivalence toward Zedekiah, his "YHWH our vindication"? The prophecy's accomplishment comes much later and yet is implicitly viewed by our narrator as Jeremiah's own vindication, despite his erring in matters such as the treatment of Jehoiakim's corpse. Prophecy is deucedly flexible.

Prophecy exposes YHWH's will; one can identify true prophecy, however, only through events, after the fact. As inconvenient as this is for the audience of competing prophets, the test is tangible. As in the case of the Pesach myth, the Israelite elite here makes history the ultimate referee, the last court of appeal. This perspective also actuates the polemic and its historical documentation in the Deuteronomistic History (DtrH), which extends the tradition of the historical explanation for suffering found earlier in 2 Samuel, in the treatment of the sin of Sargon, and in Mesopotamian Chronicles (as P) to indict a culture as ancient as human memory.

The Name YHWH and History

The apotheosis of history, as a program for festivals, as a measure of revelation, finds another reflex in the most direct definitions the biblical materials offer of the god. This god has an unusually bewildering variety of names, אלהים, "the pantheon"; אל, "god"; אל שדי, probably "the god of the mountain"; אל עליון, "the most high god"; and so forth. But all the evidence, oblique and direct, concurs on one proper name par excellence. That name is יהוה.

Scholars sometimes claim to identify evidence of this name outside Israel. Thirteenth-century Egyptian topographic lists mention a "land of the pastoralists of *yhw*³," somewhere in the eastern Sinai. More dubious have been attempts to find reference to YHWH in Amorite names of the early second millennium or at Ebla in the later third millennium B.C.E.[44] Today's evidence for extra-Israelite familiarity with the name is spotty.[45]

Still, sentiment is asymptotic to a consensus on the name's meaning. As early as 1909, when Paul Haupt, W. F. Albright's teacher, published "Der Name Jahweh" in the *Orientalische Literaturzeitung,* critics have translated, "He causes to be." Haupt derived יהוה as a causative (Hiphil) from Hebrew הוי, "to be." Several writers apply the rendition to Exod 3:14, אהיה אשר אהיה, "I am that I am," a formulation that less rapid students identify with "Popeye the Sailor-Man." Cross suggests a reconstruction, *yahwi du yahwi,* "He creates what he creates."[46]

In biblical Hebrew, three objects govern the name YHWH. No contemporary method can determine which of these formulations is most antique or even whether all are secondary to the plain designation, YHWH. Matters are clearer if YHWH does mean "he causes," as a socialized Israelite interpretation of the form, based on the assumption of a (southern?) dialectal variant. For the historical period, only Israelite etymologies are relevant. History, after all, addresses development, not origins, because in time, in succession, there is no natural or complete chapterization, no stops and starts. No historical era is Kublai Khan's garden, with walls and towers girded round. Each must, however, be studied on its own terms, its own evidence.

In Israel, the most abundantly attested version of YHWH's name is יהוה צבאות, AV "LORD of Hosts." This Jerusalem favorite, tied by its literature to the ark (1 Sam 4:4; 2 Sam 6:2; 22:11; Pss 80:2; 99:1), means perhaps "he causes armies to be." Its transparent reference is to the forces of the heavens, the stellar army, the gods. Importantly, P reinterprets "YHWH's Hosts" to mean Israel and depersonalizes the hosts of the heavens, equating them with those on earth, mineral and vegetable as well as animal, in the summary of Gen 2:1 (cf. Exod 7:4; 12:41); yet this program passage

---

[44] H. B. Huffmon, *Amorite Personal Names in the Mari Texts* (Baltimore: Johns Hopkins University Press, 1965); cf. H.-P. Müller, "Der Jahwename und seine Deutung: Ex 3:14 im Licht der Textpublikationen aus Ebla," *Bib* 62 (1981): 305–27.

[45] For an exception in central Syria, see Stephanie Dalley, "Yahweh in Hamath in the 8th Century BC: Cuneiform Material and Historical Deductions," *VT* 40 (1990): 21–32.

[46] Cross, *Canaanite Myth,* 68–75; also W. H. Brownlee, "The Ineffable Name of God," *BASOR* 226 (1977): 39–46, both with bibliography.

characterizes the hosts as YHWH's creation, what he caused to be. The fuller "cultic" phrase occurs in Samuel, but it is not attested in the earliest poetry, which prefers *not* to attach an object to YHWH.[47] In sum, it is innovative in the monarchic period. It was especially popular in the Jerusalem court (it is widespread first among the eighth-century literary prophets), where it must efficiently have served an ideological purpose, perhaps having to do with cosmogony.

Another phrase emerges from texts, especially the J source—generally certain to date from the tenth to eighth centuries—as in Gen 2–3. This is יהוה אלהים, AV "LORD God." Were one to take the phrase on the analogy of יהוה צבאות, the meaning would be, "He causes the pantheon to be"; the name targets the same reference as יהוה צבאות.

Tryggve Mettinger has consolidated the position that יהוה צבאות is a compound, DN + adjectival genitive. This is syntactically unlikely, especially in view of the parallels explored here. Conversely, an appositional interpretation of יהוה אלהים is supported by D. R. Hillers based on the Palmyrene usage, DN *'lh'*.[48] Adducing 1 Chr 22:1, 19; 2 Chr 32:16 as parallels, Hillers equates this with occurrences of יהוה אלהים in Chronicles[49] (11x, but 3 of them, cited above, with the article between the two terms). Outside of the J Eden story (20x), this name appears nine other times, once in the Pentateuch (J, Exod 9:30). יהוה אלהים is appositional in Chronicles; the pattern passages, in the start of the account of Solomon's and the climax of Hezekiah's reign, program the work's reader. It is nevertheless a late interpretation, justifying no conclusion as to the traditional character of the name; Chronicles sees YHWH as a proper name, without verbal force, so that the only possible relationships are appositional or genitival. The choice of apposition is telling: the same problem motivates the expansion, יהוה אלהי הצבאות, which heavily influences Mettinger. However, Hillers rightly observes, the Palmyrene appositives are in the "emphatic" or determined state—like Elephantine *'lh'*, and Palmyrene *'štr'* and the plural *'lhy'*; this parallels usage in other Northwest Semitic languages, especially Hebrew, where the apposition is always RN המלך, RN the king, never RN מלך, RN, king. Thus, we never find the formulation, YHWH (of) Israel or YHWH (of) PN (contrast the distribution of Elohim), though the genitive of

[47] For the epithets of early poetry, D. N. Freedman, *Pottery, Prophecy and Poetry* (Winona Lake, Ind.: Eisenbrauns, 1980), 77–109.

[48] See Hillers, "Palmyrene Aramaic Inscriptions and the Bible"; Tryggve Mettinger, *In Search of God* (Philadelphia: Fortress, 1988), 135, 155–56.

[49] Citing Sara Japhet, *The Ideology of the Book of Chronicles and its Place in Biblical Thought* (BEATAJ 9; Frankfurt: Peter Lang, 1989), 37–41. The usages in Chronicles follow, but do not duplicate, those in 2 Sam 6–7, in which both יהוה צבאות and יהוה אלהים occur.

location (//Ishtar of Arbela) does occur at Kuntillet ʾAjrud (YHWH of Samaria, of Teman). Moreover, our concern here is with יהוה צבאות, J's יהוה אלהים (neither with an article before the second term), and (below) with E's explanation of the name; in E, the name is verbal. The embryonic and the late meanings are irrelevant to the theologies of the Iron Age. Moreover, the genitival understanding is attested only late and is possibly derivative from comparison with geographical genitives or gods abroad (the Carian Zeus of Hosts!); P, for example, makes YHWH's host Israel, although in the context (Gen 2:1) of a view of the name as implying creation, and the distribution of "YHWH, god of Hosts" seems to start with its dominance in Amos (1 Kgs 19:10, 14; Jer 5:14, 16; 35:17; 38:17; 44:7; Hos 12:6; Zeph 2:9; Ps 89:9; Am 3:13; 5:14–16, 27; 6:8, 14; but not 9:5). A peculiar usage, יהוה אלהים צבאות, in Pss 59:6; 80:5, 20; 84:9 (cf. 12!) combines J's term as appositive with further apposition. Still, this must be taken as archaizing, and the genitival analysis makes better grammatical sense than the appositional. It is worth noting that the claim, יהוה הוא האלהים in 1 Kgs 18:39 = 24 and the expression יהוה האלהים ה־, followed by an adjective (1 Sam 6:20; Neh 8:6; 9:7), in fact predicate the equivalence expressed more economically by apposition, but must do so with an article on the common noun (but cf. Jer 10:10).

The verbal interpretation, natural to a personal name prefixed with י- (like the patriarchal names), should have an object: "He is" (present) (as Mettinger) would be awkward (the onomastic equivalent is יש, but cf. Akk. *ibašši* + DN). Another, unmooted, option is "He is" Sebaoth/Elohim. The third explanation of the name YHWH (Exod 3:14) falls into this category. It derives from an author different from P (who reveals the name in Exod 6)[50] and from J (who introduces the usage in Gen 4:26). E's work was combined with J's before the two were conjoined with P (but possibly after JE was stitched to Deuteronomy).[51] It was known to P and to the author of the D document. It

---

50 See W. R. Garr, "The Grammar and Interpretation of Exodus 6:3," *JBL* 111 (1992): 385–408.

51 For E's dating, R. E. Friedman, *Who Wrote the Bible?* (New York: Summit, 1987). P reformulates the combined JE (Friedman, *The Exile and Biblical Narrative* [HSM 23. Chico, Calif.: Scholars Press, 1981]); and P was interleaved with them more conservatively than was E with J, on which see my *A History of Israel in Her Land,* in progress. For a different approach, see Erhard Blum, *Studien zur Komposition des Pentateuch* (BZAW 189; Berlin: de Gruyter, 1990), positing an Engnellian D-work overlain by a P-work, with important qualification in Eckart Otto, "Kritik der Pentateuchkomposition," *TRu* 60 (May 1995): 163–91, esp. 171–72 on the Holiness Code's dependence on the Covenant Code and D. Otto, however, assigns the Covenant Code to P and the writing of the Holiness Code to R-JEPD. Whether or not this is correct, his understanding of the harmonistic character of the pentateuchal assembly is certainly on track, though R was less prolix than he

also shows signs of revising J. So the written E probably originates after J's codification and before P and D. This places it in the ninth to seventh century, probably about 775–650 (the dates can be raised some fifty years, but not lowered).[52] It is often regarded as northern because of "northern" references. These may, however, represent a Judahite strategy for renationalizing a petty kingdom through co-option of an Israel with which elements of a rivanchist south could identify, especially non-Aaronide priests or those allied with them.

Regardless, E's definition of YHWH is now the central theological statement of the Pentateuch and Former Prophets, an effect not lost on these documents' editors. This is the programmatic Israelite explanation of the divine name, its formal introduction despite anterior use by J. Here it is given an etymology, explicated. P's doublet is subordinated for literary reasons (Moses already knows the name if the P version precedes E's presentation of YHWH's invention and revelation of it). It is here that the name is *invented*. Not dissimilar is an old skit: Will Rogers applies for the dole; asked for his birth certificate, he stammers, "But ... I must have been born. I'm here!" Likewise, E's YHWH checks his wallet for identification and can only stammer, אהיה אשר אהיה.

The coinage comes with a folk etymology. The neologism "YHWH" is "(he who) is what (or: who) he is," AV "I AM THAT I AM." That the text originally read, "I cause what I cause" is doubtful. Neither biblical nor other texts attest the causative formation of הוי, "to be," in Hebrew in any historical period. E has thus updated the semantic content of the name based on its formal unfamiliarity; there is no causative of הוי in early Aramaic that sounds like YHWH as the Israelites inflected it as /yahu/ or /yaw/; (for the "*w*" in Aramaic הוי is consonantal, not vocalic). Even in Hebrew, other verbs C*wy* (קוי, חוי, אוי, דוי, לוי, סוי, עוי, צוי, רוי, שוי, תוי) make Piels or Qals; those with causatives never end in /û/ (contrast * ישתחו), but in /i/ > /e/ (is the root * חוו?). Nor, indeed, is the -*ו- of היה visible in the Qal. Even if the Qal of היה was realized phonetically as *yahe,* the name could at best have been felt to be a biform. In any case, E's X אשר X demands a verb after the relative, so the identical X's are verbs. This confirms that צבאות and אלהים are either predicates or objects, at least as E understands the syntax. E, however, *broadens the verb's governance* to include all things acted upon by, or all manners of being, the god's הוי.

YHWH is he who is in E, יהוה אלהים in J, יהוה צבאות in the cult, and יהוה + שלום, נסי, שמרון, or תמן, (who) will provide/appear (יראה) in mani-

---

supposes. For a recent attempt to eliminate E, see C. Levin, *Der Jahwist* (FRLANT 157; Göttingen: Vandenhoeck & Ruprecht, 1993).

52 This and the following *obiter dicta* are based on observations too complex for summary here. Who in any case plays chess with someone who explains his every move in excruciating detail?

festations near shrines (some in J narratives). Here, too, is a key—the combination of the name with a word is more and more frequent the later our literature. Thus, E's theology contradicts expectations; YHWH is what is, the absolute quality of being, haecceity, a quality in comparison to the character of which human life is mere reflection, in the Platonic taxonomy of forms—reason in contrast to knowledge, the instance inferred from the manifest resemblance to, but contrasted with the ideal. But YHWH is not what causes, for E, or so it would seem at first glance.

Still, wherever the name appears with an object, YHWH is "he causes," even if the causation is taken to be identity ("he is the pantheon" < "he causes the pantheon [to be, act]"). Israelite authors alive to the content rather than the mere denomination define him through his action; he is a *verb.* One knows this god more intimately than any other god, because one sees his effects pantheistically, in the sense in which Spinoza is a true monotheist. YHWH is manifest in history, in what he determines that is. He is not just what *He* is, He is What *IS;* he is history itself. This god, who causes the gods to be, the author of Henry Ward Beecher's globe, controls and recreates the universe. He is the universe, he is, as E says in a more indirect, sophisticated fashion, what is. What really is.

In 1973, Thorkild Jacobsen explained the passage of the *Enuma Elish* in which, at Marduk's command, a *lumāšu* is created, then destroyed. "If I say to you," he began, "'There is a policeman outside the door,' then in your mind there arises the image of a policeman, in uniform and cap, standing outside the door to this room. If Marduk says, 'There is a policeman outside the door,' then there is a policeman outside the door." That is, in "Being," YHWH generates, at a remove less real than he, all other existence, which is his nimbus; "the fulness of the whole earth is his 'glory.'"[53] Reality is the perceptible if not perspicuous manifestation of YHWH's even more real existence, a theology P endorses rather than rejects, even when inexplicit about the numinous character of the relationship, when seeming to demystify it.[54]

[53] See Halpern, "Brisker Pipes." Moshe Greenberg observes that Isa 6:3, cited here, may merely compare the size of YHWH's nimbus to the world; the equivalence is theologically charged in any case. I want to thank my friend and, in the best sense, elder, Professor Greenberg, for sharing many insights in discussion with me over the last twenty years on this subject.

[54] Like E, P and D avoid using the name with an object. This relates to the rejection of the host in Deuteronomy and their marginalization to the shadows in P. But P does *explain* יהוה צבאות as YHWH (creator!) of the "hosts" of creation and of Israel (his invocation of the "hosts" of creation in Gen 2 is meant to mirror and explicate or correct the use of יהוה אלהים in J's creation account). Oddly, Jeremiah, even in LXX, is not shy about the epithet, despite a heightened consciousness of monotheism's logical implications. Ezekiel does not use it. With Jeremiah, both

The same principle obtains in E as in the "law of the prophet." One learns the god's will through prophets. But what distinguishes true from false prophecy is what comes to pass. One can know god, god's will, only through events, through the nature of the cosmos; the three are indistinguishable, the changing river ever the same. YHWH, in effect, may be described as Fate, but known fate. The god defined by his deeds, as they are manifest in the natural and cosmic worlds, is History. In devoting itself thus to a cosmic personal god who rules the universe, Israel worships Fate. Israel accepts history as judge; like Margaret Fuller, Israel accepts, in the theology of E (and of DtrH) the Universe. Carlisle's gleeful retort, "Gad, she'd better!" turns out to be the oversimplification of a man who could not even begin to understand the revolutionary intent of the remark, revolutionary in its abjuration of wish fulfilment, of afterlife, of the *Unreal*.

Another dimension of elite religion should not be omitted. From J through postexilic literature, "the covenant," already mentioned, contains articulations of the god's will. Forests have been clear-cut to construct scholarly edifices around "the covenant." One of the most secure conclusions is that the law rests on the foundation of YHWH's benefices. Because he "brought Israel out" from Egypt and gave (or promised) them a land and nationhood, Israel must acknowledge YHWH's sovereignty. Because YHWH configured the cosmos, from creation to re-creation, Israel is subject to his law.

The legislation of Exodus through Deuteronomy systematically regulates society. To take familiar material, it provides against the abrogation of obligations assumed under oath, murder, adultery, theft, perjury, and similar crimes. It sets up two relationships: between Israel as a social corporation and YHWH; and, among component elements of Israel herself. If one embraces Israelite identity, if one embraces YHWH's sovereignty, one undertakes obedience to these ordinances. The ordinances in turn furnish coherence for the society.

The laws express Israel's self-understanding. YHWH, the laws' guarantor, is the contractual partner, by the time of Deuteronomy explicitly. Modern society vests in its legal articulation, or government, a monopoly on the legitimate use of force. It theoretically deploys this monopoly to

DtrH and postexilic literature make widespread use of the name. This pattern of relationships yields a date for E as the source of the exegesis, and two schools of thought agreeing with different elements of Deuteronomy. The isoglosses of the pentateuchal sources make a fascinating study, which remains to be pursued systematically on the model of text-critical research. This evidence also indicates the integrity if not of the words, then of the sentiments of our sources from their earliest to their latest recensions, though values assigned to particular epithets do not imply a defect of critical scholarship.

compel individuals (in Israel, kinship communities) to respect rules. This is the individual's contractual relation to the national corporation: should he or she jaywalk, sleep under bridges, or cross the sights of an attorney, force is brought to bear. In Israelite theory, YHWH was vested with the monopoly on the legitimate use of force. An obedient Israel would prosper, a refractory one suffer. Thus, where Americans might speak of "society" or "the people" condoning necrophilia, Israel would speak of YHWH doing so. YHWH is the fictitious incorporation of Israelite society.[55]

Again, Israel certainly worshiped YHWH as a god, and even accorded to subsidiary deities the devotion accruing to gods in most religions, including "monotheistic" ones. There was probably no time when YHWH's minions were not closely attended by the population, as distinct from a philosophically monotheistic elite, or when the mythic character of divine action was attenuated. This is most clearly attested in the reinfusion of myth into postexilic prophecy and the developed angelology of traditional Judaism. At the same time, the quantitative concentration of historical power in YHWH's hands, coupled with the idea of a covenant that tied those hands, effected a qualitative difference in the elite conceptualization of Israel's gods.

If one conceives of one's god as a YHWH, as a prime puppeteer, a causer, the universe ceases to be an impenetrable thicket of gods, perverse and whimsical in their emotions. History ceases to be the synthesis of numerous numinous wills acting now in conflict, now in synergy to produce a result that is the aim of none (as Erra). Fate is not random or unpredictable, the sum of a series of individually rational, but collectively chaotic intellects. It is the reasoned elaboration of a single, sentient will. Here one learns from experience. What works is good; what fails is evil. YHWH does not reward the Israelite who repeatedly draws to an inside straight.

To bind such a god by agreement and by legal revelation is to predetermine events. Again, observance or abrogation of the law has predictable consequences. And the illogical inference is the converse: if Israel suffers, the cause is her sin; if she prospers, she is right. This is the ideological fabric of the Prophets, against which the book of Job lodges an adolescent protest. Affirming responsibility for her fate, Israel claims to command destiny itself.[56]

---

55 This point is clearly understood by Mendenhall and especially Gottwald, who by projecting the *legal* incorporation into the premonarchic era make of it a revolution against Canaanite kingship, that perpetual *bête noire* of historical commentators ideologically unemancipated from their debt-slavery to Deuteronomistic theology. In our sources, all monarchically transmitted, the legal incorporation is of the monarchic regime.

56 Levin's *Jahwist* (JE) only blesses Israel and attacks her foes. Because the literary premise is future fidelity, an inference as to the relative dating of J and

This conclusion contradicts the constructs of the "liberation theologians." True, the basic impulse behind the theology is liberation from the petty gods of the heavenly bureaucracy. Israel directs sacrificial payment, rather, to a single, central authority. The world, then, is simplified, rationalized. On a historiographic level, it is no coincidence that the concomitant credo is of liberation from "bondage," from Egypt or from later "oppressors." Liberation is the pillar of the laws and of Israel's exaltation of YHWH. Even more, Israel is freed, in all codes, from unremitting labor and affirms an obligation to refrain from work one day each week. Labor, the primal curse (Gen 3:16–19), bondage to others, even to other gods—all of these are compulsions from which the theology frees the Israelite.

Yet amid the liberation, Israel affirms responsibility for herself. Sin engenders suffering; obedience, success. The people, the kinship community, the individual (in the late seventh century) all assume responsibility for their own fate. History, the Israelite theologian asserts, is just; it is god's will. Israel declares, "I am right or wrong, and the consequences indicate which."

Israel's god is more than the causer, more than the consequences. It is no coincidence that the first commandments in J, E, P, and D (Exod 34:12–17; 20:23; 20:3–5; Deut 4:16–28 < 5:7–9) are those of exclusivism and aniconism, or something approaching it. The god who liberates Israel insists, "You shall have no other gods." Yet the god will not be represented. This intangible deity—fate, history, the causer—places destiny in his worshipers' hands. In that sense, YHWH consecrates the status quo, not revolution; he is a god, like many others, whose worship is that of the universe as it is. So as Israel's vision is of unchanging reality—a perpetual covenant with the sun or the seasons or with existence never again to be threatened by flood—its god is Eleatic. And yet he incorporates an element of Heracleitan flux, which emerges especially in the brilliant but inevitable recognition, especially of Second Isaiah, that the god who controls the cosmos is responsible for what is evil as well as for what is good.

Responsible for evil, placing destiny in the worshipers' hands, YHWH, or the theologians who took him in charge, abdicates divinity. Here, as in the injunctions against his representation, he is the negation of gods. He teaches only the Pavlovian lesson that one must learn from experience, as a rat in a maze. He enjoins Israel from imagining the cause of that experience, so that even the name is sacralized; one should not inquire diligently after it, even in early stories of Jacob's wrestling or Samson's birth (Gen 32:30; Judg 13:6, 17–18), though the former is part of YHWH's reluctance to define himself before Moses. The god who claims exclusive loyalty casts his own mantle of responsibility for events onto the mortals' shoulders.

---

literary prophecy fails. This attempt at comparison across genres is of apples and oranges. In any case, J, too, provides for punishment in cases of sin.

In this measure, Israel's monotheistic impulse is an atheistic impulse. By killing off, eventually (cf. Judg 13:16), all the gods but one, by relegating other gods to a subordinate status, Israel liberated herself neither from social obligations nor from sacral and certainly never from the material world, but from gods, altogether. Israel assumed the responsibility for her condition, which hinged on the proper array of her society.

Remarkable is the optimism all this expresses. To affirm responsibility, to concede one's culpability, to accept the judgment of history is to accept absolutely one's own moral agency. The emphasis here is on behavior, not intent; only the result, the tangible outcome, counts. And in this scheme, God is virtually no factor; he mediates responsibility, but almost mechanically, until the great breakdown of Israelite schemes of causality in the postexilic period, when Job repudiated the notion of a god responding only to human stimuli, personal or ancestral, in the immediate present, and Qohelet, with Job, denied the relationship of merit to divine favor. Here, in ancient equivalents, the deism of apocalyptic leads to the atheism of the Enlightenment. In the most basic impulses of Israelite monotheistic theology, it is as though no god ever existed. Perhaps this is the essential seed from which charges of deicide, pagan in their emotional origins, sprouted.

Friedrich Nietzsche once quipped, "All the gods died laughing when one of them stood up and said, 'I am the only god.'" As is often the case, Nietzsche might be understood here to have confused careful thought with the *bon mot*. And yet, the expression is more precise than most of his readers have dreamed; "*all* the gods died laughing." Had Nietzsche read his Agatha Christie Mallowan, he might have added, "And then there were none."

Part 2:

Textual Perspectives

Section 1:

The Exodus Story

Liberation Theology and the Exodus[1]

Jon D. Levenson

The Exodus from Egypt As Political Revolution

However much the Bible may have lost its power to inspire and direct public discourse, one of its phrases has resounded in recent decades with impressive force: "Let my people go!" Whether in the American civil rights movement or in the campaigns to allow Jews to leave the Soviet Union or Ethiopia, Moses' demand upon Pharaoh forges an instantaneous connection between the ancient archetype and a modern situation, thus providing enormous moral force to those identified with Moses and Israel against those identified with Pharaoh and his house of bondage.

Over the past twenty years, a more sustained and systematic use of the exodus has been made by liberation theologians seeking to enlist the biblical story in support of social reform or even quasi-Marxist revolution. One of them, J. Severino Croatto, a Latin American biblical scholar, argues that "we are enjoined to prolong the Exodus event because it was not an event solely for the Hebrews but rather the manifestation of a liberative plan of God for all peoples ... an unfinished historical project."[2]

Surveying the literature of liberation theology as it stood in 1978, Robert McAfee Brown concluded that the greatness of the exodus story for this school of thought is that it describes a "God who takes sides, intervening to free the poor and oppressed." But from whom does he free them? Just who are the Pharaohs of our time? "The rich and powerful from other nations," Brown informs us, "who keep national oligarchies in power, thereby becoming complicit in the ongoing exploitation of the poor."[3] The practical implication is clear: one continues and advances Croatto's "unfinished historical project" by acting

[1] This article was originally published in *Reflections* (Spring 1991): 2–12. It is an abbreviated and revised form of the Bonnie Pedrotti Kittel Memorial Lecture delivered at Yale Divinity School on February 23, 1989. It appeared also in the October 1989 issue of *Midstream*.

[2] J. Severino Croatto, *Exodus: A Hermeneutics of Freedom* (Maryknoll, N.Y.: Orbis Books, 1981), 15.

[3] Robert McAfee Brown, *Theology in a New Key: Responding to Liberation Themes* (Philadelphia: Westminster, 1978), 88, 90.

against the rich and powerful of the North Atlantic world who bear a major burden of responsibility for the dire economic straits in which Latin America finds itself. As the archetype becomes antitype, Pharaoh becomes the First World, and the people Israel turns into the impoverished masses of Latin America.

But liberation theology does not always restrict its use of the exodus to the elaboration of the obvious analogy between Israel in Egypt and those who are exploited and impoverished today. If it did, the movement would be far less suspect, for, whatever one may think of its political and economic theories, its use of the Bible would fall within recognizable limits of homiletic license. In fact, however, some liberationists go beyond the *analogy* between Israel and the oppressed and construct a *historical* scenario in which the defining characteristic of the beneficiaries of the exodus was not ethnic identity but political victimization. The clearest example of this is the recent commentary on the book of Exodus by George (or Jorge) Pixley, a Baptist minister and biblical scholar born in Chicago but raised in Nicaragua.[4]

Pixley reconstructs a four-stage development of the exodus story from the time of the events themselves until the book came to assume the shape it has now.[5] The first stage corresponds to historical fact: "a heterogeneous group of peasants in Egypt, accompanied by a nucleus of immigrants from regions to the east" escaped from Egypt under the leadership of "the Levite Moses"; it was this heterogeneous underclass who were the original Levites, and the Levites, so understood, who actually came out of the house of bondage. In the second stage, these Levites joined an alliance of rebellious Canaanite peasants known as "Israel," so that the exodus "was then read as the experience of a struggle against exploitation at the hands of an illegitimate royal apparatus." In Pixley's third stage, when Israel had become a monarchy, the exodus was again reconceived, this time as "a national liberation struggle—no longer a class struggle [but] a struggle between two peoples: Israel and Egypt." Finally, in the Second Temple period, long after the Israelite and Judean monarchies had fallen, the exodus was converted into the foundation story for a Jewish community in which religion tried to fill the void left by the loss of political autonomy, and priesthood became the central religious institution. This time the ancient story served as a justification for Israel's religious obligations to YHWH, their God, to whom the deliverance from Egypt was now exclusively attributed. "It is obvious," writes Pixley, "that the sacerdotal revision is an 'interested' reading of Exodus. It is the ideo-

---

[4] George V. Pixley, *On Exodus: A Liberation Perspective* (Maryknoll, N.Y.: Orbis Books, 1987).

[5] Ibid., xviii–xx.

logical product of a class that seeks to have people place religion at the center of its life."[6]

As Pixley reconstructs the historical development of the exodus story, the overall movement is thus one from religion that is intensely political to religion that is ostensibly apolitical, piety having taken the place of activism. But the apolitical character of the latter stages is a mirage, for the piety is really only a cover for the maintenance of the political status quo. Those texts that speak of God's initiative or credit an action exclusively to him fall, according to Pixley,[7] in the category of "ideology, in the pejorative sense of camouflage and mystification." Their ideological function is to render the populace helpless, impotent, and thus dependent upon the "dominant class, monarchical or priestly." This ideologization of the exodus begins rather early in Pixley's view; already by the third stage in the development of the story, nation-state and monarchy had become the dominating facts of social life. The major literary product of this stage supports "an ideological indoctrination that would sustain the new national consensus, and counteract revolutionary or antimonarchical tendencies."[8] And in both the third and the fourth stage, which is marked by a concern for priest and cult, "the account of the plagues serves to fill the vacuum left by the obliteration of the popular struggles against the Egyptian tyrant," a vacuum now filled by the struggle between YHWH and Pharaoh.[9]

The implication of Pixley's analysis is that the book of Exodus is an artful but ultimately unsuccessful effort to disguise the reality of the exodus event as a class struggle and social revolution. This implication puts the commentator in the unusual situation of having to argue against the sacred text he has chosen to expound. He must argue not only that the historicity of the events narrated is questionable, a point that many biblical scholars readily concede, but that the very mode of consciousness that informs the text is false, a matter of "camouflage and mystification." Were Pixley an orthodox Marxist, this situation would not be problematic, for in that case he could consistently hold that the Bible, like religion in general, works to the advantage of the ruling class, forestalling revolutionary action by offering the victims an anodyne, Marx's "opiate of the masses." But Pixley, though obviously sympathetic to the Communist tradition, is not an orthodox Marxist. In fact, he defines the intention of his commentary by a word that many would place at the opposite pole from Marxism—"evangelical," a term that has for him two senses. The first refers to the belief of some Protestant churches that "it is in the Bible that the highest authority

[6] Ibid., 39.

[7] Ibid., 25.

[8] Ibid., xix.

[9] Ibid., 37.

for their faith is to be found." The second, which he judges "the more important sense," derives from the New Testament term *euangelion,* which means "good news" (it has traditionally been translated "gospel"). Given that Pixley's commentary is "dedicated to the heroic struggle of the Salvadoran people," it is no surprise that he sees this good news as inextricably associated with what he calls "the liberation of oppressed individuals and peoples."[10]

It is precisely here that the contradiction in Pixley's liberation theology becomes apparent. For by his own account the Bible that is "the highest authority for ... faith" has almost entirely suppressed the identity of the exodus and the ensuing conquest of Canaan as a popular insurrection and class struggle, replacing this with an "ideology" in the Marxist sense: a system of belief that works to preserve the oppression and alienation of the masses and the privileges of the ruling class. The choice for Pixley comes to this: should he expound the *counter-revolutionary* Bible or the reconstructed *revolutionary history* that has been alleged to lie at the origin of Israelite tradition? If the Bible is really "the highest authority," as he avers in his first definition of "evangelical," then the answer is obvious, and if his own sociopolitical analysis is sound, Pixley will have to become the theological equivalent of a *contra.* If, on the other hand, the underlying history is sovereign over the text, there is room to wonder why *biblical* history deserves such attention, since it has to be reconstructed from sources produced by self-interested ideologues whose chief accomplishment seems to have been the concealment of their nation's origins in a revolution that has been rediscovered only in our own generation. Nor can there be any doubt as to what sort of revolution Pixley thinks lies at the base of Israel's identity. "Perhaps we could understand Moses' special role," he writes, in commenting upon the prophet's lack of a successor in his own mold, "by comparing it with the special role of revolutionary figures such as Lenin, Tito, Mao, Ho Chi Minh, and Castro."[11] But other revolutionaries also lacked successors in the same mold as themselves—George Washington, for example. What actually joins the five figures to whom Pixley likens Moses is their allegiance to some form of Communism, and this, in turn, is suggested by his belief that early Israel, Israel in its state of grace before it was corrupted by self-interest, was "a classless society, a society of primitive communism."[12]

In light of the analogy with Marxist revolutions, it is strange that Pixley's bibliography does not include a book by the American muckraker Lincoln Steffens, *Moses in Red: The Revolt of Israel As a Typical Revolution,*

---

[10] Ibid., xiv.

[11] Ibid., 121.

[12] Ibid., 81.

published in 1926, before anyone ever heard of liberation theology and when almost all Christians and almost all Marxists still saw the two perspectives as mutually exclusive. "Let Jehovah personify and speak for Nature," suggested Steffens, "think of Moses as the uncompromising Bolshevik; Aaron as the more political Menshevik; take Pharaoh as the ruler who stands for the Right (the conservative 'evolutionist') and the Children of Israel as the people—any people; read the Books of Moses thus and they will appear as a revolutionary classic." But just as ten out of the twelve spies that Moses sent to reconnoiter the promised land counseled against trying to take it, so, wrote Steffens, "minds as scientific as those of Bertrand Russell and H.G. Wells, and spirits as bold and revolutionary as Emma Goldman, reported against the Promised Land of Russia; they preferred England and the United States."[13] Now, having written only nine years after Lenin's revolution, Steffens can perhaps be forgiven for thinking of Russia as the promised land (and England and the United States presumably as Egypt). Perhaps he would have changed his assessment had he lived to hear Jews shout Moses' demand "Let my people go!" not at Thatcher and Reagan, but at Brezhnev and Gorbachev, and to see death-defying rebels again escaping across perilous seas, only this time in crude boats launched from "liberated" Vietnam or from Castro's Cuba, crowded with people fleeing those promised lands in hopes of coming to the United States. Soviet Jewish émigrés, Vietnamese boat-people, and Cuban refugees might indeed find their experience in the book of Exodus, just as Pixley wants, except that they would see in his Communist revolutionaries not Moses but Pharaoh. An elementary acquaintance with the bloody history of Marxist regimes in the six decades since Steffens wrote *Moses in Red* ought to have prompted Pixley to question the identification of that tradition with true liberation. What is curious, but also depressing, is that the hermeneutics of suspicion that Pixley applies to the biblical text—at least when it fails to endorse his social ideal—is never applied to the ideal itself and to the political tradition that has tried the hardest to implement it. Were the Communist tradition to be subjected to the same sort of scrutiny, the result might suggest that those nonegalitarian biblical texts have a wisdom beyond the capacity of Pixley's liberationism even to recognize.

Is the Bible Really against Slavery?

Perhaps the greatest understatement in the long history of biblical interpretation occurs when Pixley comments upon the law of the Hebrew

---

[13] Lincoln Steffens, *Moses in Red: The Revolt of Israel As a Typical Revolution* (Philadelphia: Dorrance, 1936), 21, 28.

slave in Exod 21:2–6. "We are surprised," he writes, "to discover that there were slaves in the new revolutionary society."[14] Surprise on the part of interpreters usually indicates an error in their preconception of the text. In this case, the error is the image of early Israel as a classless society exemplifying primitive communism. In truth, the code in which the law of the Hebrew slave first appears, the book of the covenant (Exod 20:22–23:33), paints a very different picture throughout. It is a picture of a society that knows of property rights; recognizes a distinction between chiefs, freemen, and slaves; differentiates sharply between men and women; and, though it shows no knowledge of a priestly caste, does require hefty offerings for the support of the sacrificial cultus—in short, a portrait of a society that is hardly egalitarian or communistic.

In Pixley's native country in the nineteenth century, another set of politically engaged theologians would not have found the law of the Hebrew slave at all surprising. These were the Christians in the American South who sought theological warrants for their region's "peculiar institution." Like today's liberation theologians, these men tried to show that the social and political order that claimed their allegiance had already been announced and even mandated in holy writ. James Smylie of Mississippi, for example, writing in 1836, noted that slavery, far from being just some piece of superseded Jewish law, is mentioned twice in the Decalogue itself and without censure. "If God foresaw, or intended, that servitude should expire with the Mosaic ritual," wrote Smylie, "the authority of masters would, probably, not be recognized in a law, intended to be perpetual; nor would there have been, as is the fact, a recognition made of servants, as property." Frederick A. Ross, a Presbyterian minister from Huntsville, Alabama, went even further. Noting on the eve of the Civil War that the King James Version of Lev 25:44–46 uses the verb "shall" rather than "may" in speaking of the acquisition of Gentiles to be lifetime slaves, Ross held that "God *commanded* [the Israelites] to be slave-holders. He *made* it the law of their social state." Nor did the New Testament speak against the "peculiar institution." John England, the Roman Catholic bishop of Charleston, South Carolina, pointed out that Jesus made use of the master-slave relationship without once condemning the institution.[15] In fact, one of the passages of which the pro-slavery preachers were fondest is this verse from Eph 6:5: "Slaves, obey your earthly masters with fear and trembling, single-mindedly, as serving Christ." Another favorite of theirs, 1 Pet 2:18–19, goes even further: "Servants, accept the authority of your masters with all due submission, not only when they are kind and

---

[14] Pixley, *On Exodus,* 169.

[15] H. Shelton Smith, *In His Image, But: Racism in Southern Religion, 1780–1910* (Durham, N.C.: Duke University Press, 1972), 132–33.

considerate, but even when they are perverse. For it is a fine thing if a man endures the pain of undeserved suffering because God is in his thoughts."[16]

To arguments like these, Christian abolitionists had their answers ready. In his great tract *The Bible against Slavery* (published in 1839, reprinted in 1864), Theodore Dwight Weld pointed out the differences between slavery in biblical Israel and in the American South. In the Bible, "servants who were 'bought' *sold themselves* as a way of discharging their debts";[17] they were not kidnapped, as were the African ancestors of the American slaves. In fact, biblical law expressly forbids kidnapping a person to sell into slavery (Exod 21:16)—the very basis of what was to become the South's "peculiar institution." Furthermore, Weld argued, those unfortunates who did sell themselves into debt slavery were paid for their labor and, as Lev 25:49 makes clear, when they had accumulated sufficient capital, they could redeem themselves, that is, buy themselves out of slavery, as the American blacks could not, since they were defined as property themselves.[18] Even the period for which one was a slave was scarcely one of continuous hard labor, according to Weld. Adding up all the Sabbaths and other holy days, together with the Sabbatical and Jubilee Years, during which the fields lay fallow, he found that Old Testament slaves were actually free from labor for over twenty-three years out of every fifty.[19] Finally, given the vast differences between the biblical and the American institutions, Weld felt justified in going so far as to claim that the Hebrew term עבד should be translated not as "slave" but as "servant," for the Hebrew language, like Hebrew society, was unfamiliar with the institution of slavery, for which Weld's opponents mistakenly thought they had found biblical authorization.[20]

In retrospect, it is apparent that both the pro-slavery and the abolitionist theologians yielded to what can be termed the temptation of selective attention. Both saw part of the picture—the part that provided biblical support for their own position—but failed to do justice to the remainder.

---

16 See Eugene D. Genovese, *Roll, Jordan, Roll* (New York: Pantheon, 1974), 208. In this essay, all quotations from the Hebrew Bible are taken from *Tanakh* (Philadelphia: Jewish Publication Society of America, 5746/1985) and those from the New Testament from *The New English Bible* (n.p.: Oxford University and Cambridge University, 1970).

17 Theodore Dwight Weld, *The Bible against Slavery* (Pittsburgh: United Presbyterian Board of Education, 1864; repr., Detroit: Negro History Press, 1970), 38. The tract was originally published in the *Anti-Slavery Quarterly Magazine* (1839).

18 Ibid., 22–30.

19 Ibid., 44.

20 Ibid., 106.

Weld, for example, correctly perceived the importance of what liberation theologians call "the preferential option for the poor," the enormous concern in the Hebrew Bible for those who are weak and vulnerable. It is within this framework that we are to understand the limitations that biblical law placed upon the institution of slavery and its elaborate efforts to prevent or mitigate the impoverishment that often led to enslavement. Weld failed, however, to reckon adequately with a point of which some of his opponents made much: many of those limitations and safeguards applied only to *Israelite* slaves. For example, biblical law requires the master to offer his "Hebrew slave" manumission after six years of servitude, but not his Gentile slave, and Lev 25:44–46 expressly excludes slaves taken from the "nations around about you" and those who are "the children of aliens resident among you" from the general amnesty proclaimed every fifty years. These non-Israelites may be kept as slaves "for all time." It is only fellow Israelites who may not be treated "ruthlessly," using the term that Exod 1:13 employs to describe the way that Egyptians worked Israel in Egypt. To be sure, there is throughout the Hebrew Bible a passionate concern to avert the victimization of the "stranger" (גר). Most memorable and most germane to our discussion is Exod 23:9—"You shall not oppress a stranger, for you know the feelings of a stranger, having yourselves been strangers in the land of Egypt." But the stranger in question is not necessarily a foreigner at all, and even if he is, the Hebrew Bible does not seem to have regarded his enslavement as inevitably an instance of the oppression prohibited in verses like this one.

In an odd way, then, the difference between the two sets of pre–Civil War theologians comes down to a question depressingly familiar in contemporary Jewish life, "Who is a Jew?" In applying the Hebrew Bible's humanitarian legislation about slavery to contemporary blacks, Weld assumed that the black person in the antebellum South was analogous to the Hebrew slave in ancient Israel and thus eligible for the more humane set of norms. Ross's use of Lev 25:44–46 shows that he assumed the opposite—that blacks in America were analogous to Gentiles in Israel and thus excluded from the emancipatory dynamics of the Jubilee Year and similar institutions. If, as Christian tradition had long taught, the church is the "new Israel," then in the case of black slaves who had accepted Christianity, it was Weld who had the better argument: these slaves were no more Gentile than were their Christian masters and should thus be treated according to the more humanitarian norms. But this point is hardly a vindication of Weld's argument in *The Bible against Slavery,* for it speaks only for the reform of slavery, not for its abolition, and even then it holds out the unwelcome possibility that those black slaves who declined baptism could legitimately be subjected to the harsher form of servitude.

Who Benefited from the Exodus?

The controversy between the abolitionist and the pro-slavery theologians in antebellum America shows how misleading it is to speak of the Bible's message as "liberation" without serious qualifications. No collection of books so generally tolerant of slavery as are both the Hebrew Bible and the New Testament can be said to be decisively on the side of liberation in the social and political sense intended by liberation theologians. More importantly, "the preferential option for poor," though it is hardly in danger of over-emphasis today, is in some tension with another ubiquitous and all-important theological tenet of the Hebrew Bible, the chosenness of the people Israel. And this is a tenet that in a democratic and egalitarian age like ours is in decided danger of *under-emphasis* on the part of interpreters of the Hebrew Bible.

If the exodus were an expression of only "the preferential option for the poor," the story would be rather different from the one we know from the Bible. First, *all* the slaves and oppressed of Egypt, indeed of the entire world, would be released, not just the Israelites. Second, the newly freed would remain in the countries in which they had been enslaved, only under a new social and political system that, if not exactly primitive communism, would represent something very different from the *ancien régime,* now dismantled.

In fact, however, the book of Exodus tells of the emancipation only of the people Israel (the obscure term ערב רב in Exod 12:38, which describes those who went out of Egypt with the Israelites and is traditionally rendered "a mixed multitude," probably refers to mixed-blooded people; see Neh 13:3; Ezra 9:2; and Lev 24:10–23). Gentile slaves in Egypt and elsewhere undergo no such change. And the emancipated people do not stay in Egypt but leave for the land of Canaan. There is no indication that the oppressive social system of Egypt would not go on as before. The reason for these troubling features is given in Exod 2:23–25:

> A long time after that, the king of Egypt died. The Israelites were groaning under the bondage and cried out, and their cry for help from the bondage rose up to God. God heard their moaning, and God remembered His covenant with Abraham and Isaac and Jacob. God looked upon the Israelites, and God took notice of them.

If God's hearing the groaning, crying, and moaning of the afflicted slaves reflects "the preferential option for the poor," His remembering the covenant with Abraham, Isaac, and Jacob reflects the chosenness of Israel. Of the two concepts, chosenness is in this narrative the more important, for only it accounts for the identity of those freed in the exodus and for their leaving Egypt rather than staying: they are the descendants of Abraham, Isaac, and Jacob, and they leave in order to participate in God's fulfillment of his promise to give them the land of Canaan.

The centrality of the land-promise to the exodus accounts for another feature ignored when the event is presented exclusively as an instance of liberation or emancipation. Most of the references to the exodus in the Hebrew Bible make no mention of slavery. A surprisingly large proportion of them speak of the God who took Israel out of Egypt without the appositive so familiar from the Decalogue, "the house of bondage." This suggests that the emancipation of slaves may be less important to the exodus than the repatriation of aliens, exile more than slavery being in that case the condition for which a remedy is provided. This, in turn, accounts for the fact that, in Michael Walzer's words, "the memory of the Exodus is more often invoked on behalf of aliens than on behalf of slaves."[21] If the exodus is more a matter of repatriation than of emancipation, then we see again how inappropriate it is to liken Moses to Lenin, Tito, Mao, Ho Chi Minh, and Castro, as Pixley does. For what Moses effects is not a domestic revolution, Marxist or other, but the return of an exiled people to their native and promised land. A more apposite comparison would be with the Zionist heroes Herzl, Weizmann, and Ben-Gurion. The absence of these names in Pixley's book is conspicuous.

As Pixley reconstructs the exodus, there is no need to take account of the tension between "the preferential option for the poor" and the chosenness of Israel, for those who left Egypt were not Israelites at all, but a "heterogeneous group of peasants in Egypt, accompanied by a nucleus of immigrants from regions to the east." Only later did these escapees meet up with Israel, but the Israel with whom they met up was still not a kin-group (like the Jews), but a political coalition made up of Canaanite peasants in rebellion against their rulers. Whatever the probability of the particular theory of Israelite origins upon which Pixley builds, the redefinition of biblical Israel as something other than a kin-group has a ring to the Jewish ear that should be as alarming as it is familiar. For the theory follows on a long tradition of Christian supersessionism, in which Jewish ethnicity is denied theological meaning and replaced with some other basis of association. Probably the first example of this venerable tendency in Christian theology is Paul's argument in Galatians that faith, not birth, endows one with the status of descent from Abraham (Gal 4:21–5:1). This type of thinking, extended perhaps further than Paul meant it to go, led Christian theologians to portray Jewish identity as obsolete, as the "old Israel," or, in Paul's terms, "Israel according to the flesh" (1 Cor 10:18) gave way in the new dispensation to the "new Israel," that is, the church itself. This dichotomy is associated with others that equally conduce to the disadvantage of the Jews.

---

[21] Michael Walzer, *Exodus and Revolution* (New York: Basic Books, 1985), 31.

Judaism is defined as the letter in opposition to the spirit, for example, or as law in opposition to faith, grace, or love, and the Hebrew Bible becomes only an "Old Testament," whose main purpose is to point to a new one.

Whereas in Judaism the operative dichotomy is Jew and Gentile and in Christianity it is the church and the world (or those in Christ and those outside Christ), in Pixley's liberation theology it is the poor and oppressed as opposed to everyone else (though each of the three systems has a universal dimension, none represents an unqualified universalism). The politicization of Israelite identity in Pixley's and other liberation theologies is thus not to be equated with the Christian spiritualization of the Jewish people. Nonetheless, the two have a tangent in their eagerness to substitute some other group for the people Israel, and even to hear a reference to the other group when the Hebrew Bible speaks of the family of Abraham, Isaac, and Jacob. Given Pixley's evident sympathy for the Communist tradition, it bears mention that Karl Marx's historical prognosis has certain affinities with classic Christian eschatology. The author of his own particular brand of supersessionism, Marx expected the disappearance of the Jews not after the second coming, but after the revolution. Now it is true that he considered religion to be an epiphenomenon upon the true motive force of history, which is economic, and therefore *all* religions, like all class divisions, were to disappear together with the alienation that they reflect but cannot cure. But it is also the case that Marx saw in Judaism the epitome of capitalism and the bourgeoisie. In fact, the Israeli historian Jacob Katz points out that Marx "initially presented his historical diagnosis, which became the kernel of his socialist thought, as a sequel to a polemic on the Jewish question."[22] Katz's quotation from Marx's early essay, "Zur Judenfrage" ("On the Jewish Question," 1844) shows his image of capitalist society as a partial generalization of anti-Jewish stereotypes:

> What is the worldly basis of Judaism?
> *Practical* need, *self-interest*.
> What is the worldly cult of the Jew?
> *Haggling*.
> What is his worldly god? *Money*. Very well! Emancipation from haggling and money, that is from the practical and tangible Judaism, might well be the self-emancipation of our age.[23]

In liberation theology of the sort represented by Pixley's commentary on Exodus, we find an odd confluence of these two currents of anti-Jewish

---

[22] Jacob Katz, *From Prejudice to Destruction* (Cambridge: Harvard University Press, 1980), 173.

[23] Ibid.

thinking, the Christian and the Communist. The Christian current is seen in the tendency to minimize the chosenness of Israel in the Hebrew Bible, replacing peoplehood with another form of identity. The Communist current is seen in the nature of that identity: not a churchlike spiritual sodality, but a political movement impelled mostly by issues of class. For Marx, the Jews represented capitalism; for Pixley, they represent its heroic victims, the poor and oppressed engaged in class struggle.[24] Neither sees them as the Hebrew Bible and the rabbinic tradition see them: as a kin-group providentially constituted for the service of God and his mysterious purposes (and, in the case of postbiblical tradition, a kin-group with procedures for the absorption of outsiders). However odd the intersection of Christianity and Marxism in liberation theology may seem from some perspectives, on the questions of the Jews, Judaism, and Zionism, it is unremarkable. For each system presents an image of liberation in which it is the Jews who represent the negative pole—that from which humanity must be liberated. That the apocalyptic systems of those two baptized Jews, Paul of Tarsus and Karl of Trier, have now formed a symbiosis is less surprising than it at first seems.

Liberation for Service

The Protestant theologian, John Howard Yoder, points out that in the kind of liberation that the exodus represents, "*what for* matters more than *what from*."[25] That from which God liberates Israel is the condition of exile in Egypt and the dehumanizing enslavement to Pharaoh. That *for* which he liberates them is life in the promised land and the ennobling and sanctifying service of himself that is its precondition. The people Israel perform that service by obeying the commandments that God has given them; the commandments, in turn, point back to the exodus in order to justify God's claim upon Israel. "When, in time to come, your children ask you, 'What mean the decrees, laws, and rules that the LORD our God has enjoined upon you?'" reads Deut 6:20–21, "You shall say to your children, 'We were slaves to Pharaoh in Egypt and the LORD freed us from Egypt with a mighty hand.'" The movement represented by the exodus is not one from slavery to freedom in the sense of individual autonomy or even national self-determination. Instead, it is a movement from one form of servitude to another,

[24] On the reappearance of classic Christian anti-Semitism in some ranking liberationists, see John T. Pawlikowski, *Christ in the Light of the Christian-Jewish Dialogue* (New York: Paulist, 1982), 59–73; and John P. Meier, "The Bible As a Source for Theology," *Proceedings of the Catholic Theological Society of America* 43 (1988): 1–14.

[25] John Howard Yoder, "Probing the Meaning of Liberation," *Sojourners* 5 (September 1976): 28.

from the service of a brutal, self-interested tyrant to the service of a kind, loving, and generous monarch, YHWH, God of Israel. Though this latter type of service involves the end of alienation and oppression, it is founded upon an act of submission to God on the part of the human community that is not exhausted by the mutual submission of individuals in a just and loving community.

Earlier, we had occasion to note that Lev 25 forbids one Israelite to subject another to the sort of slavery inflicted upon the entire nation by Pharaoh. It might be thought that the reason for this humanitarian provision is that, having been redeemed from Egypt, Israel is to be free. The truth, however, is almost the opposite, as we see from the great summary statement of that chapter:

> For it is to Me that the Israelites are servants [עבדים = "slaves"]: they are My servants, whom I freed from the land of Egypt, I the LORD your God. (Lev 25:55)

The limitation on Israelite slavery is owing to YHWH's prior claim upon them: he, and none other, is their master, and the "jealous God" will share their service with no one else. To speak of this subtle and paradoxical theology as one of "liberation" is to miss the paradox that lies at the heart of the exodus: Israel's *liberation* from degrading bondage is a function of their *subjugation* to YHWH their God. The exodus is not only a road out of Egypt; it is also a road to Mount Sinai. To speak of exodus/liberation apart from Sinai/subjugation is to miss the profound interconnection of the two that lies at the foundation of the Jewish religious vision. In the words of the midrash, God took Israel "from the yoke of iron to the yoke of Torah, from slavery to freedom" (*Exod. Rab.* 15:11). Torah, the rabbis tell us over and over, equals freedom.

Honesty in Confronting Embarrassing Scriptures

To the plight of the Gentile slave, whom the Hebrew Bible expressly excludes from the humanitarian dynamics of exodus and Sinai, the Jewish tradition has not proven insensitive. An attempt at a remedy can be seen in the concluding section of the laws of slavery in the *Mishneh Torah* of Maimonides (1138–1204):

> It is permitted to work a gentile slave harshly. And although such is the law, kindness and wisdom dictate that a man be merciful, pursue justice, and not make his yoke on his slave too heavy or afflict him.... Thus, in reference to the attributes of the Holy One (blessed be He), which He commanded us to imitate, the Bible says, "and His mercy is upon all His works" [Ps 145:9], and upon all who are merciful God is merciful.

Maimonides begins with a blunt and unqualified statement of the law as he has received it. He goes on, however, to bring every piece of support from within the biblical and rabbinic traditions and his own philosophy to bear against the implementation of that very law. For a Jewish master to brutalize his Gentile slave, he tells us, is to act unkindly, foolishly, and unjustly, to ignore the precedent of the rabbis themselves, to disregard biblical affirmations of the fatherhood of God and the brotherhood of man, to be like an idolator, to act against self-interest, and to fail to observe the commandment to imitate God, which for Maimonides means to imitate the divine attributes, which are merciful and not severe. Having honestly acknowledged the law in his first sentence, Maimonides succeeds in showing that it is ethically unconscionable and theologically unsound to avail oneself of it. Indeed, his heavy emphasis upon mercy and justice comes close to casting the entire institution of slavery into grave theological doubt.

What Maimonides's approach to the law of the Gentile slave loses in simplicity it gains in honesty and fidelity to the tradition. For although the offending feature is transcended, it is not denied, disguised, ignored, or explained away. The beauty of this way of handling the problem is that it allows for the full implementation of "the preferential option for the poor"—indeed, demands it—without eradicating the chosenness of Israel. In this, it is to be preferred to Pixley's liberationist approach, which uses a recent theory about Israelite origins to replace the Israel of the text with a heterogeneous underclass involved in insurrection and class warfare.

So little is known about the origins of Israel that any historical reconstruction, even one that merely paraphrases the biblical narrative, will perforce be speculative in the extreme. The particular theory that Pixley endorses emerged in the United States in the 1960s, a period whose tone it unmistakably reflects. Though the theory has its learned proponents, in recent years it has also come in for harsh criticism by some historians and archaeologists.[26] Its popularity in religion departments and liberal Christian seminaries is owing less to the evidence in its favor, of which there is necessarily little, than to the fact, amply demonstrated in recent statistical surveys,[27] that professors in the

---

26 See Baruch Halpern, *The Emergence of Israel in Canaan* (SBLMS 29; Chico, Calif: Scholars Press, 1983), esp. 239–61; and Israel Finkelstein, *The Archaeology of the Israelite Settlement* (Jerusalem: Israel Exploration Society, 1988). Finkelstein's empirical findings are particularly devastating to the peasant-revolt model of Israelite origins.

27 See, e.g., Everett Carl Ladd Jr. and Seymour Martin Lipset, *The Divided Academy* (New York: McGraw-Hill, 1975); and Stanley Rothman and S. Robert Lichter, *Roots of Radicalism* (New York: Oxford University Press, 1982). "Despite the conservative turn of public opinion in the 1970s and early 1980s, then," Rothman and Lichter wrote, "a predominantly liberal or progressive professoriate continues to nourish critical and reformist tendencies among college youth" (392).

humanities and social sciences now generally incline markedly to the left side of the political spectrum. When academics wish to maintain fidelity to a tradition based upon the Bible, the biblical texts that speak against the common political agenda of the academy can become an acute embarrassment to them. The liberation hermeneutic saves them from this embarrassment by enabling them to brand the offending texts as only an ideological camouflaging of the historical reality. And if the historical reality is still unclear or inconvenient, it can always be "reconstructed" so as to reflect a golden age in which the politics advocated today were already a potent reality. Pixley's liberation perspective on Exodus recalls a disturbing comment of Edward Shils's about the current state of the humanities. "Through this collaboration of 'theory' with a frivolous flaunting of a smattering of Marxism and political antinomianism," Shils wrote, "the study of the humanities is now being ravaged. Much of what now passes for humanistic study is little more than radical political propaganda."[28]

The painless coincidence of Scripture and the desired politics that we have seen in Pixley's liberationist commentary on Exodus is not unique to the left. Indeed, it is in plentiful evidence also among those Christian fundamentalists who, after much prayerful and spirit-filled scrutiny of the holy writ, conclude that God is, like themselves, a conservative Republican. The difference is that, unlike fundamentalists, the university world and the liberal denominations have traditionally prided themselves on their openness to the historical-critical method of biblical studies, a method that promises (and threatens) to recover a Bible very different from the one familiar from tradition and contemporary usage—in other words, to widen the gap between past and present in the name of an uncompromising historical honesty. This honesty is the first casualty when political commitments of whatever stripe are allowed to govern the encounter with the text. If lib-

---

The point has been made more impressionistically but also more pungently by Professor Werner Dannhauser of Cornell University in "Allan Bloom and the Critics," *The American Spectator* 21:10 (October 1988): 18. "[S]how me a professor," wrote Dannhauser, "and I'll show you someone who mocks Ronald Reagan."

[28] Edward Shils, "The Sad State of Humanities in America," *Wall Street Journal* (July 3, 1989): 5. The felt need of many professors of religion to address nonacademic constituencies makes them particularly vulnerable to the trends that Shils decries. The urge to sermonize is the mother of much politicized scholarship, and politicized scholarship is now the mother of many wrongheaded sermons.

The politicization of scholarship in religion that has taken place over the last two decades is an academic manifestation of a larger shift in American religious life, as the fault lines have moved from theological to political axes. On the nature—and danger—of this shift, see Wilfred M. McClay, "Religion in Politics; Politics in Religion," *Commentary* 86 (October 1988): 43–49, and, more broadly, Robert Wuthnow, *The Restructuring of American Religion* (Princeton, N.J.: Princeton University Press, 1988).

eration theology is now threatening to become the fundamentalism of the religious left, the present moral and intellectual condition of the academic world suggests that this threat will not be so easily averted as the threat from the religious right. If so, this does not bode well for the future of the university as a place of critical, dispassionate inquiry, in which all commitments—religious, political, and others—are subjected to a hard-headed scrutiny. And the erosion of the university has implications that go far beyond the subject of the present essay.

When the sort of Latin American liberation theology exemplified by Pixley is translated into the context of the contemporary North American university, the effect is an act of accommodation not only to the dominant leftist ethos of the academy, but also to its pervasive secularism.[29] When class is so much better known and respected than covenant and revolution than redemption, the pressure to regard the politically embarrassing theological affirmations as only so much "camouflage and mystification" (to use Pixley's terms) can become unbearable. By treating theological affirmations as primarily political, academic liberation theologians can avoid the embarrassment of being in a cognitive minority, all the while presenting themselves as courageously standing in solidarity with minorities and the marginalized. The irony is that a strategy of cultural accommodation now lays claim to the cachet of prophetic protest. In the case of George Pixley's commentary on the book of Exodus, there is a greater irony: under the pretext of allowing the book of Exodus to be heard anew today, the book is actually being muzzled, as its delicate message of redemption and service is forced into a mold in which it cannot fit.

---

[29] On the secularity of the American professoriate, see the illuminating chart in Ladd and Lipset, *Divided Academy,* 345. Note also the interesting older data on pp. 135–36.

History and Particularity in Reading the Hebrew Bible: A Response to Jon D. Levenson

Jorge V. Pixley

In Jon D. Levenson's 1991 article, "Liberation Theology and the Exodus,"[1] he raises some issues that still merit consideration today. Thus, although my response is out of season, it seems justified in the light of the continuing pertinence of some of the issues raised by Professor Levenson. I wish to address three of them: (1) the use of historical reconstruction or the lack thereof in appropriating Scripture as an authoritative text; (2) the question of the preservation of particular cultural values in the struggle for the defense of universal human values associated with modernity; and (3) the need for a language for political struggle that preserves the tolerance for differing views without which academic life is impossible and social coexistence difficult.

These are all issues central to Levenson's challenge to liberation theology and particularly to my reading of the exodus, and they are related to each other. I would like to proceed in reverse order, since the first matter is the most basic one for biblical scholarship, but the other two deal with the climate necessary for any productive scholarly endeavor, indeed for any fully human life together in some form of community.

A Climate of Respectful Political Debate

Levenson challenges me for including in my Exodus commentary[2] a list of contemporary irreplaceable revolutionary figures like Moses that includes only persons with "allegiance to some form of Communism" and not others such as George Washington and, he might have added, Simón Bolívar or Giuseppe Garibaldi. My list, "Lenin, Tito, Mao, Ho Chi Minh, and Castro," obviously reflects the political tradition within which my commitment has developed. Levenson's objections to my reading of the exodus from this political tradition are clearly set in the equally exclusive tradition

---

[1] Jon D. Levenson, "Liberation Theology and the Exodus," in *Reflections* (Spring 1991): 2–12, reprinted in this volume, pp. 215–30. All references are to the latter.

[2] Jorge Pixley, *On Exodus: A Liberation Perspective* (Maryknoll, N.Y.: Orbis Books, 1987).

of anti-Communism. Levenson's quote from Edward Shils about "a frivolous flaunting of a smattering of Marxism and political antinomianism" with which the humanities are being "ravaged"[3] sets Levenson on the low road of political confrontation.

Now, according to note 1 of the article, this "essay is an abbreviated and revised form of the Bonnie Pedrotti Kittel Memorial Lecture delivered at Yale Divinity School on Februrary 23, 1989,"[4] in other words, almost a year before the destruction of the Berlin Wall and the dramatic sequel of events that followed! My Exodus commentary appeared in the original Mexican edition in 1983, during the early years of the Sandinista popular revolution with which I was (and still am) identified. Both Levenson and I were caught up in the confrontational style of the Cold War. The one-sidedness of my list of revolutionaries and the extremism of Levenson's political statements have something to do with this setting, when we were trying to "win" what we thought was a war for the salvation of humanity.

Now, the Cold War is over, and there is no reason to attempt to revive it. Although Jewish refugees will no doubt continue to leave the Ukraine and Christians to leave Cuba and Nicaragua, they can no longer blame their flight on Communism. The problems of human society that led to the efforts at revolutionary social engineering in Mexico, the Soviet Union, China, and other countries are still with us and advancing at a frightening pace. Thousands of infants die every day from lack of adequate nutrition and medical attention. Hundreds of thousands of adults die every month from hunger. Deserts advance, forests are declining, the ozone layer is reducing our protection from ultraviolet rays, and there is global increase in temperatures. With the increase in the canyon separating the beneficiaries of modern conveniences from those left out, there is a dramatic increase in personal insecurity. But no one wants to return to the Cold War, with its witch hunts of Communists in unions and university faculties and its execution of counter-revolutionaries as traitors to humanity.

Nevertheless, the danger of political intolerance did not begin with the Cold War, nor, sadly, will it end with the Cold War. Today we have some who feel that the lesson of the collapse of the Soviet Union is that the free market is the salvation of humanity; they are, some of them, convinced missionaries of the market economy. On the other hand, some of us feel that the real war is and always was between those who have and the increasing number of have-nots, that these poor people typically from the South have increasingly become a threat to the rich, and that the only real salvation for humanity is in an increase in planning to limit the damages of an uncontrolled market.

---

[3] Levenson, "Liberation Theology and the Exodus," 229.

[4] Ibid., 215 n. 1.

In spite of these differing perspectives, the Cold War is over, thank God! Let us try to make our competition for the political side of human salvation one that recognizes the common humanity of all. We are all children of God, even the market apologists and the convinced socialists. At least in the church and synagogue, in the university and the editorial pages of the newspapers, let us try to build an inclusive community. In these spaces, and others we hope to promote, let Marxists and classical economists, ecologists and promoters of industrial development, live and pray together and debate their differences in the search for common solutions.

These remarks are not intended as criticisms of Professor Levenson, whose present political perspective I do not know. They are a self-criticism of some of the political language of my Exodus commentary and a criticism of Levenson's article first published in 1989. We both allowed our language to get sucked into the confrontational style that did us all much damage. It is likely that, should we meet, Levenson and I (or another liberation theologian) would find that our proposals to get out of the present destructive global situation would prove radically different. Let us hope that we would be able to talk about them without disqualifying each other. So, the substance of this first section of my article is a call to a culture of peace, to the search for generally acceptable political solutions, whether these be market-oriented or socialist or, what seems more likely, some combination of social planning with a limited market.

Modern Universality and Traditional Particularity

Professor Levenson accuses liberation theology, and my Exodus commentary in particular, of "the redefinition of biblical Israel as something other than a kin-group [which] has a ring to the Jewish ear that should be as alarming as it is familiar. . . . Jewish ethnicity is denied theological meaning and replaced with some other basis of association."[5] That liberation theologians' preferred theory of Israelite origins has this alarming ring to Jewish ears I take to be a statement of fact coming from a sensitive observant Jewish professor of Hebrew Bible. And it is alarming to us that this should be so.

Let me assure Professor Levenson that it is not my (our) intention to deny theological meaning to Jewish ethnicity, although, obviously, my main concern is to read the exodus narrative as something other than a story about ethnicity. Contemporary reading theory allows for alternative readings of any significant text; to read the exodus as the liberation of poor peasants is not to deny that it can also be read as the story of the return to Canaan of the children of Israel. I would contend that both of these

[5] Levenson, "Liberation Theology and the Exodus," 224.

readings are legitimate readings, and in my commentary both are somehow present, though I related them to the different layers of tradition that I postulated as present in the text. The opening sentence of my commentary stated, "In this introduction to the book of Exodus, the most important character in the book comes on the scene: the 'sons of Israel,' the offspring of Israel (Jacob) and their families."[6]

The fact that I read the text from the perspective of the poor, and that many of the poor of Latin America identify with the enslaved people who left Egypt under Moses' leadership, need not be a rejection of the reading of the narrative by a Jewish people who defines itself as a kin-group. In fact, insofar as the Jewish people feel oppressed in dominantly Christian societies, they can also identify with this "liberationist reading." My commentary was an effort to assist those Christian communities who read the Bible as the book of the God of the poor. This is an aggressive reading, if you like, not against the Jewish people or any oppressed people, but against the economic system, capitalism, that these communities interpret as the equivalent today of what Pharoah was for the children of Israel in the exodus narrative.

Nevertheless, even though I reject the legitimacy of an anti-Jewish reading of my commentary, I cannot deny the alarming ring it has, according to our Jewish colleague, to the Jewish ear. I take this to be a statement of fact, and it is a matter of concern to me. In Latin America, and especially in Central America, we Christians are not much aware of Jews because their number is so small among us. Still, the question of ethnic particularity is an important issue that was neglected until rather recently. It is the issue raised by the Zapatistas in Chiapas with their utopian slogan, "*por una sociedad donde quepan todos,*" (towards a society in which all have a place). The Zapatistas represent a new leftist guerrilla that is not struggling to take power in Mexico but to transform Mexico into a democracy where all peoples will be respected *as peoples*.

Mexico has a very instructive history of the acceptance of Native American peoples as a national trophy for tourists and the rejection of the measures that would support the existence of these peoples as peoples. The laws are made for citizens, and in the tradition of modern democracies all citizens are individuals with equal rights. At the origin of the system is the struggle against a Christian Catholic colonial society that had a dual legislation, for Spaniards and their descendants, on the one hand, and for native peoples on the other. The heart of the legal system was the recognition of the territorial rights of the native communities *as peoples*. There were also other privileges and obligations (like voluntary labor for the Spanish cities), which were also incumbent on the communities as communities (and not on individuals as citizens).

---

[6] Pixley, *On Exodus,* 1.

It was the honored liberal president, Benito Juárez, who in the 1850s and 1860s carried out the national transformation known in Mexico as the Reform, which made full citizens of the native people and also stripped them of the protection of the laws protecting their rights as peoples. They now became, individually, Mexicans, and their communal lands became subject to laws of private property. President Juárez was himself not of Spanish descent nor of mixed descent; he was a Zapoteco and prided himself in this fact. But he had become a lawyer and then a judge and believed that the liberalizing of the laws so that they applied equally to all citizens was in the best interests of all. It took a major revolution at the beginning of this century to reinstitute in Mexican law the protection of the "*ejido*" property of the native peoples of Mexico!

The commemoration of five-hundred years of resistance against foreign colonialization in 1992 was a major awakening of the Left in Latin America to the need for any future revolutionary democracy to make the participation of numerous peoples and movements (various Native American nations and African nations, feminist movements, ecologists, peasants, etc.) a permanent feature. The class and anti-imperialist groupings that were dominant in our struggles in the 1960s and 1970s are still valid, but they are only part of the story. Political scientists of the stature of Jorge Castaneda in Mexico and Helio Gallardo in Costa Rica have called for a fluid coalition of "leftist" groups (i.e., those committed to people's welfare above all) that would be in a continuous state of redefining their alliance. A common program will last only as long as it represents the interests of the various groups making up the coalition.

This seems to be the net effect of putting into political terms the slogan of the Zapatistas. The rights of the various peoples (not "Indians," but Tojolobales, Mazahuas, Miskitos, and also Yorubas, Ibos, etc.) can hardly be assured in any permanent program, but can only be constantly renegotiated in an open society where workers are only one group. It seems to me that the issue of Jewish kinship and its rights over against a homogenizing modernity is the issue that among us has been posed by the "movement of indigenous, Black and popular organizations" which grew out of the 1992 conmemorations.

It would be a mistake, in my opinion, to ignore the virtues of modernity's universal human rights in our concern for the rights of peoples. In a local community that denigrates women or exposes deformed children to cruel treatment, the universal rights may prove a liberating factor to transform the people's culture. In a traditional society where kings have absolute rights, modernity may prove liberating to persons who find their own customs intolerable. Yet, we have learned that the survival of peoples with their particularities is a human value and certainly a value for the people involved. And peoples don't survive without the recognition of their rights as peoples. We would all be poorer without the presence of the Jewish people—and also without the tzoltziles or the cakchiqueles. If rights of emigration are fundamental for the protection of the Jewish people, communal lands are basic for the latter peoples. We do indeed require societies in which "all can find a place."

Part of Jewish identity is reading the Hebrew Bible as the foundation of a kinship group. The fact that we as Christians struggling for liberation read it differently should not imply a denial of the legitimacy of that Jewish reading as also a possibility. For the last fifteen years, at least, we have been engaged in Latin America in trying to read the Hebrew Bible with Yorubas in Northeast Brazil, with Kunas in the Panamanian Caribbean, and with Aymaras in the Bolivian altiplano, peoples who have a resistance to dominant Christian readings as strong, though not as well known, as that of the Jewish people.

Is the Authority of the Bible in the History or in the Text?

Levenson raises the question whether the authority of the Bible is in the text or in the history that lies behind the text, which is necessarily hypothetical, and he opts for the former while arguing that my opting for the latter disallows my claim to stand in the evangelical tradition of biblical authority. In order to respond in a manageable way, let me set aside the degree to which my reading of the exodus as a revolutionary liberation is plausible by admitting that this is a debatable issue that will be debated for some time still. Perhaps it will be disproved; that is a possibility I can contemplate, though I do not believe that will happen. Apart from any particular reconstruction of the history, let us address the necessity and legitimacy of history and historical reconstruction in making real the authority of Scripture.

I wish to argue that history is an integral part of the biblical record and that all history is today a matter for scholarly debate. Even more, given the interested use of history by dominant classes and by oppressed peoples, there is no "objective" history. The Bible itself records the conflict of interpretations.

Take the prophecies of the Second Isaiah as an example of the need for historical reconstruction, if we are not to fall into the hands of privileged sectors who leave their concerns on the surface of the biblical text. Deutero-Isaiah calls for the return of the exiles to Jerusalem. In order to understand the implications of this call it is indispensable to remember that the exiled community was only a fraction of the people of Judah and that the returnees, should Deutero-Isaiah's prophecy be heeded, would again be a fraction of the inhabitants of Judah. What the prophet omits, the fate of the people who reside in Judah and who authored the book of

Lamentations, is as significant as what he includes. Unless we imagine/reconstruct that situation we will never fully understand the significance of his message. The biblical text with its silence calls for a historical reconstruction to situate it, because it is about a historical project, and historical projects are always the projects of particular people. Unless we can establish or hypothesize about the group that Deutero-Isaiah is addressing, we will not be able to understand all the historical dimensions of his message.

The sacred text at times is rather direct about its demands to situate it historically and about its containing "ideological" elements, in the sense of the interest of particular groups that claim to represent the interests of the whole. A good example is the cycle about the selection of Saul as king (or prince). It is well known that here we have a debate about kingship, probably reflected in the incorporation of pro- and antimonarchical sources into a unified account that includes the tension within itself. How are we to understand that our divinely authorized text takes up within itself the conflicts of the nation Israel, without resolving them? The Uruguayan theologian Juan Luis Segundo argued that God is teaching the readers of the sacred text to discern. Scripture does this by forcing us to face the textual conflict that reflects the living conflict of different groups within one society. In this way the Hebrew Bible teaches us to deal with our contemporary world in which the conflicts of peoples and of movements and classes of persons have to be faced and addressed.

In fact, to read the Bible as an ahistorical text means to fail as believing people to engage in historical projects. To enter into history, let us say, to defend the rights of the Jewish people or the survival of the Afro-Ecuadorians of Esperanza or to recover the lands of the Sutiavas in Nicaragua, we must know the enemies and their interests. We must learn to read our own present history critically. To read the history of the tribes of Israel and the nations of Judah and Israel critically is a discipline that will bear fruit in our present history. If we fail to read the Bible historically, we will probably fail to see anything sacred in the historical struggles of our own time. This is the most important aspect of the theology of the Hebrew Bible. Even though Professor Levenson may be able with his kinship-oriented reading of the Hebrew Bible to defend Jewish survival, the struggles of less-established groups also require historical criticism of the ancient text and the contemporary situation to support their claims. This is what is at stake in defending a historical-critical reading of the Hebrew Bible!

The Perils of Engaged Scholarship: A Rejoinder to Jorge Pixley

Jon. D. Levenson

Activism or Theology?

To take a scholar's argument seriously is to do him high honor, all the more so when one's own position is its principal target. In the case of Jorge Pixley's response to my essay on "Liberation Theology and the Exodus," I am impressed not only by its author's courtesy but also by the humanity of his evident and deep-felt concern for the Indian tribes of South America and his eagerness to prevent their further exploitation and the disappearance of their cultures. However much we disagree on the method and substance of biblical interpretation (my major concern in the essay) or on political and economic issues (at best a peripheral matter therein, as I shall show), I remain an admirer of his humanitarian motivation and the religious tradition from which it springs.

The religious root of Pixley's humanitarianism is the theology and social policy that liberation theologians have termed "the preferential option for the poor," which in my essay I glossed as "the enormous concern ... for those who are weak and vulnerable" and interpreted as the "framework ... [for] the limitations that biblical law placed upon the institution of slavery and its elaborate efforts to prevent or mitigate the impoverishment that often led to enslavement."[1] I also wrote of the positive influence of this undeniable and indispensable feature of biblical theology in modern reform movements, such as Anglo-American abolitionism. In the longer form of the same essay, I wrote about more recent manifestations of the same theology, offering the thought of Martin Luther King Jr. as a more defensible application of it than Pixley's liberationism.[2]

In both forms of the essay, however, I pointed out that in the biblical story of the exodus, more than just the "preferential option for the poor"

---

[1] Jon D. Levenson, "Liberation Theology and the Exodus," 215–30 in this volume. This quote appears on p. 222.

[2] Jon D. Levenson, "Exodus and Liberation," in *The Hebrew Bible, the Old Testament, and Historical Criticism: Jews and Christians in Biblical Studies* (Louisville: Westminster/John Knox, 1993), 156–57.

is at work. Otherwise, in that narrative, all slaves would have been released from bondage, and the now-free people would have "remain[ed] in the countries in which they had been enslaved, only under a new social and political system," in which slavery would have been a thing of the past.[3] To read the interpretations of the exodus by Pixley and other liberationists, one would think that this is, in fact, the transformation that the book of Exodus narrates. But, in actuality, it speaks of the manumission only of the descendants of Abraham, Isaac, and Jacob—that is, of the chosen people, defined as a kin-group (Exod 2:23–25)—their future repatriation to the land promised to their ancestors at the expense of its Caananite inhabitants (13:3–5), and the revelation to them of a legal system that does not abolish slavery but only mitigates it—and that only for the "Hebrew slave" (21:2–6). Embarrassing to the liberationist reading, these pervasive and stubborn features of the biblical text represent a different aspect of biblical theology, which I called "the chosenness of Israel."

I remain convinced that no biblical theology, and certainly no theology of the book of Exodus, can succeed if it fails "to take account of the tension between 'the preferential option for the poor' and the chosenness of Israel."[4] Neglecting one or the other of these points of theology doubtless makes for a cleaner, simpler interpretation and may help preachers or social activists correct an imbalance in their hearers' attitude and practice. Needless to say, this includes those who preach and otherwise work for justice to Indians.

But, as I see it, biblical theologians have another assignment, not necessarily better or higher, but certainly different from that of the homilist and activist. They also have another accountability—to the text in its wholeness and its complexity. This does not exempt them from accountability to particular communities and the postbiblical books and traditions that are authoritative for them, but it does require biblical theologians to cast a cold eye on the passions and causes of the moment and to step back and exercise a "preferential option" for the features of the text that are currently not being heard or deemed useful. So doing, biblical theologians will offer a more complex interpretation than many preachers and most activists will find serviceable, and, as a result, they will experience a temptation to simplify the biblical message by suppressing the discordant features in the name of social relevance and immediate application. If they yield (as many do), they win a following (as some do) but lose a discipline and a vocation. I hope it need not be said, but I shall say it anyway: it is no derogation of preachers and activists to point out that they are not biblical theologians and that their characteristic use of the Bible may obscure as much of its message as it illumines. The pursuit of relevance to the moment is essential to the vitality of religious communities,

[3] See Levenson, "Liberation Theology and the Exodus," 223.

[4] Ibid., 224.

but it comes at a price, and one of the tasks of those with a longer and larger view is to point out the notes in the text that practitioners of engaged scholarship are not currently hearing. Ironically, this very restoration of the repressed can lay the groundwork for new practical applications and relevance to new moments as times change—and for the next correction as well.

Let me parry one objection that in this era of postmodernism I can already hear coming. In pointing out these limitations on the practice of engaged scholarship, I am not adhering to the equally simplistic notion that human beings can realize total objectivity. Since all scholars stand at a particular historical location and not at some Archemedian point, claims of "objective history" are, as Pixley points out, to be greeted with intense skepticism. This does not mean, however, that we are incapable of attending to the discordant and unpalatable notes in the text and its underlying history or that those who do so must be motivated by class interest, or the like.[5] I once heard the philosopher Stephen Toulmin put it in words like these: "The fact that total antisepsis is not possible does not give us license to do surgery in a sewer." In other words, perfect objectivity is not realizable, but the *pursuit* of perfect objectivity is worthwhile and productive of valuable insights.[6] It is also an element indispensable to historical criticism and a point of differentiation between that activity, on the one hand, and homiletics and religiously inspired activism, on the other.

Pixley is able to avoid reckoning with the key biblical doctrine of the chosenness of Israel because he concentrates not on the biblical texts

---

[5] Note Pixley's powerful interest in my political commitments, or what he perceives to be my political commitments (Jorge V. Pixley, "History and Particularity in Reading the Hebrew Bible: A Response to Jon D. Levenson," 231–32, 233). His assumption throughout seems to be that one's exegesis is governed by one's politics, or perhaps even the cynical notion that exegesis is just politics pursued through other means. My own view is that it is eminently possible for people to recognize that their own political, social, and economic ideals are not those of the Bible. Though Pixley thinks that we both "were caught up in the confrontational style of the Cold War" (232), I should point out that I have never thought that categories like Communism and capitalism have much relevance to the social and economic situation of ancient Israel. It is simplistic and destructive to regard the Bible as a book of answers to the various social and political questions of our time. One of the functions of historical-critical study is to problematicize that notion.

[6] See my comments in my response to Edward L. Greenstein in *The State of Jewish Studies* (ed. Shaye J. D. Cohen and Edward L. Greenstein; Detroit: Wayne State University Press, 1990), 53, where I distinguish between two very similar statements: "We all have biases" and "All we have is biases." The first is true; the second is false. One of the saddest phenomena in contemporary intellectual life is the false assumption that the first statement entails the second. Most of the arguments against objectivity that one hears today are actually only arguments against *perfect* objectivity.

about the exodus but on the historical event itself. He accepts a controversial reconstruction of that event as an insurrection of "a heterogeneous group of peasants in Egypt" who then made alliance with a group of Caananite peasants, known as "Israel," who were challenging the monarchical traditions of their homeland.[7] Let us leave aside the weighty critiques of that reconstruction to which I referred in my article[8] and focus, instead, on the hermeneutical issue. Against my charge that he makes "the underlying history … sovereign over the text," Pixley argues that "[t]he biblical text with its silence calls for a historical reconstruction to situate it, because it is about a historical project, and historical projects are always the projects of particular people."[9] This, however, begs the question I posed: why should we *privilege* the reconstructed history *over* the manifest text of Scripture? Situating a biblical text is one thing; disqualifying its *theology* because of the historical situation is quite another. All the situating in the world cannot validate Pixley's claim that texts that speak of God's initiative belong to the category of "ideology, in the pejorative [Marxist] sense of camouflage and mystification."[10] Nor can it validate his preference for the putative earlier stage in which "Israel" referred to a Caananite underclass over the biblical texts in which "Israel" means the descendants of Abraham, Isaac, and Jacob. Whatever the grounds for that preference in Pixley's case—I believe they lie in his political activism—they do not derive from exegesis or a historical-critical reading of the Bible. This is not to say that one may not have a preference that contradicts the biblical text. The point, rather, is that the statement of the preference should not be disguised as exegesis. And I still find it odd that Pixley applies the term "evangelical" to a theology that is so at odds with the Bible itself.

Chosenness Is More Than Particularism

If I read Pixley correctly, his response to my critique backs away from the intense concentration on class and revolution that one finds in his commentary and moves toward a greater recognition of the role of ethnic particularity in the theology of the Hebrew Bible. His observation that "peoples don't survive without recognition of their rights as peoples"[11] grants a measure of value to collective national identities that Karl Marx and his Enlightenment predecessors would not have accepted. In this,

---

[7] George V. Pixley, *On Exodus: A Liberation Perspective* (Maryknoll, N.Y.: Orbis Books, 1987), xviii–xx.

[8] See Levenson, "Liberation Theology and the Exodus," 228 n.26.

[9] Pixley, "History and Particularity," 237.

[10] Pixley, *On Exodus,* 25.

[11] Pixley, "History and Particularity," 235–36.

Pixley seems to be laying the foundation for an interpretation of the Hebrew Bible that is true to the text—one, that is, that recognizes both the preferential option for the poor and the chosenness of Israel. When, however, he goes on to write that "[w]e would all be poorer without the presence of the Jewish people—and also without the tzoltziles or the cakchiqueles,"[12] he demonstrates that there is less here than meets the eye. For the biblical idea of the chosenness of Israel is very different from a celebration of human diversity. For, in this vision, Israel "is a people that dwells apart, / Not reckoned among the nations" (Num 23:9). "Indeed, all the earth is Mine," the God of Israel thus announces at Sinai, "but you shall be to Me a kingdom of priests and a holy nation" (Exod 19:5–6).

A dichotomy of particularism and universalism cannot do justice to the theological perspective from which these verses are written (and there is a plethora of others).[13] Like a particularism, this theology affirms the ultimate importance of a subgroup of humanity, a subgroup that is, in fact, a natural family and not, for example, a voluntary association based on common beliefs, experiences, values, or whatever. But like a universalism, the theology of Israelite chosenness poses a challenge to human diversity. For the ultimate importance of the kin-group that is Israel derives from the act of the universal God, who rules over all nations, brooks no rivals, and demands the submission of everyone, from Pharaoh on his throne to the lowliest Caananite peasant in revolt against his feudal lord. In short, though the Hebrew Bible conceives of Israel as an ethnic group, its very existence is a standing reproach to ethnicity and, for understandable reasons, arouses the hostility of the unchosen (הגוים, τὰ ἔθνη). Within this theological perspective, the loss of Israel (were such even conceivable) would be vastly more catastrophic than the disappearance of the tzoltziles or the cakchiqueles.

It bears mention that in neither form of my essay do I identify the chosen people of the Hebrew Bible with the modern Jews. In the longer form, I am at pains to point out that "[w]ho is or is not a member of the people Israel has seldom, if ever, been self-evident, at least since the close of the biblical period itself."[14] Because historical criticism cannot answer the question as to the identity of the chosen people, I recognize that my own identification of it with the Jews (i.e., those born of a Jewish mother or converted according to rabbinic law) rests on an act of faith, and I respect those whose faith impels them in a different direction, toward an identification of the chosen people with the church, for example. But Christian faith does not

---

[12] Ibid., 236.

[13] I lay this out in greater detail in Jon D. Levenson, "The Universal Horizon of Biblical Particularism," in *Ethnicity and the Bible* (ed. Mark G. Brett; Leiden: Brill, 1996), 143–69.

[14] Levenson, "Exodus and Liberation," 155.

exempt one from the obligation to acknowledge that the Hebrew Bible itself sees Israel as a kin-group, and not a church or, for that matter, a social or political grouping. Traditionally, Christians *have* acknowledged that and, as a consequence, deemed the Hebrew Bible to represent an inferior revelation, and the Jewish people ("Israel according to the flesh," "carnal Israel") to be only a prototype of the higher, spiritual Israel, the church. To a committed Jew, this is, of course, grossly wrongheaded, but compared to the liberationist reading of Israel in the Hebrew Bible as a social or political grouping, it has the merit of recognizing the ultimate importance of the natural family and the kin-group within that set of books.

For this reason, as moving and impressive as the recognition of Jewish sensitivities in Pixley's response is, it does not speak to the gravamen of my critique. He still fails to see that the Hebrew Bible, even in an early and relatively egalitarian corpus like the Covenant Code (Exod 21–23), conceives Israel as a socially stratified and economically diverse kin-group. And when Pixley writes that "insofar as the Jewish people feel oppressed in dominantly Christian societies, they can also identify with this 'liberationist reading,'"[15] all he does is to allow that the Jews, too, might benefit from the preferential option for the poor; he does not move even an inch toward reclaiming the chosenness of Israel as a theological resource or even toward recognizing the possibility of a tension between this idea and the preferential option for the poor. Both of these ideas, I repeat, are essential aspects of biblical theology and of the message of Exodus as well. They cannot be collapsed one into the other. When Pixley writes of my "kinship-oriented reading of the Hebrew Bible," he thus tells a half-truth, missing my emphasis on the special solicitude of the God of Israel for the poor and oppressed. And when he writes that I adopt that reading in order "to defend Jewish survival,"[16] he misses the point that the nature of Israel in the Hebrew Bible as a kin-group is independent of the choice to identify them with their modern Jewish descendants.

Marxism or Open Debate?

As one would expect from a practitioner of engaged scholarship, Pixley casts much of his disagreement with me as a disagreement about politics. In fact, the disagreement is deeper than that, for I have been at pains to insist that honest exegetes, especially those involved in historical criticism, can (and must) recognize dimensions of the text that are at odds with their own commitments. In "Liberation Theology and the Exodus," for example, I pointed out that modern claims that the Hebrew Bible and the New

[15] Pixley, "History and Particularity," 234.

[16] Ibid., 237.

Testament oppose slavery are much exaggerated and misleading. Yet I personally have no respect for slavery, obviously, and this means I must wrestle with my Scripture in ways that are not pleasant. One of my objections to Pixley's liberationist reading of Exodus is that, by redefining the exodus as an egalitarian revolution, he lets himself off the hook and exempts himself from the wrestling that we more disengaged scholars must endure.

It is hard to fault Pixley's "hope that we would be able to talk about [our proposals to get out of the present destructive global situation] without disqualifying each other."[17] This hope, however, grows out of a very different political tradition from the one "within which [his] commitment has developed," the tradition of "Lenin, Tito, Mao, Ho Chi Minh, and Castro."[18] Whatever else one may wish to say about them, none of those five Communist dictators encouraged open and respectful dialogue, and in some and perhaps all their cases, they disqualified thousands upon thousands of dissidents in blood. Unlike Pixley himself, none of the heroes of his political tradition saw those who doubt the benefits of Communism as "children of God" who should "live and pray together and debate their differences in the search for common solutions."[19] The tradition out of which that noble view developed is the tradition of liberalism and liberal Christianity. It stands in stark contrast to the Marxist notion that the nonrevolutionary masses are afflicted with "false consciousness" and that the non-Communist political traditions are, to quote Pixley again in a different context, "ideology, in the pejorative sense of camouflage and mystification." In short, if Pixley sustains his liberal belief in courteous and open debate, he will have to move very far from his Marxist commitment, both in theory and in exegetical practice. He can still argue that the rest of us are wrong, but he can no longer argue that our ideas are only a cover for power.

This difference between the political theories of Marxism and of liberalism calls into question Pixley's assertion that my "objections to [his] reading of the exodus ... are clearly set in the equally exclusive tradition of anti-Communism."[20] Anti-Communism can be a dimension of a wide spectrum of political traditions, for, defined as it is by a negative, the term has little meaning. Fascists have been anti-Communist, but so have liberals, theocrats, social democrats, monarchists, and democratic capitalists. In the case of some of these (the liberals, social democrats, and democratic

[17] Ibid., 233. Pixley's assumption that biblical scholars and preachers have more to contribute to the resolution of global issues than the average person is doubtful and elitist.

[18] Ibid., 231.

[19] As Pixley recommends, ibid., 233.

[20] Ibid., 231–32.

capitalists), the commitment allows and may even encourage a diversity of opinion and competition among political parties. To say that these traditions and the tradition that speaks warmly of Lenin, Tito, Mao, Ho Chi Minh, and Castro are "equally exclusive" is irresponsible in the extreme. And that last sentence could be underlined in blood.

The Exodus and Biblical Theology[1]

John J. Collins

The book of Exodus occupies a pivotal place in any attempt to construct a theology of the Hebrew Bible or First Testament. While the Bible encompasses several strands of tradition, and attempts to relate everything to a "center" of biblical theology are invariably reductive, the exodus stands out as the most influential story of the origin of Israel and as the setting for the authoritative Mosaic law. In the foundational importance assigned to it within the Bible, it is rivaled only by the theme of creation and the complex of material associated with David and Zion.

But how should Exodus be interpreted? The story has a "history-like" character, but nowhere in the biblical corpus has "the collapse of history" been more painfully obvious in this generation.[2] While some evangelical scholars[3] and liberation theologians[4] still speak naively of the exodus as something that "actually happened," the credibility of such assertions has been irreparably undermined in academic biblical scholarship. On the one hand, archaeological work, to which biblical theologians of the mid-twentieth century looked for confirmation, has cast severe doubts on the entire biblical account of Israel's early history.[5] On the other hand, the amalgam of literary genres found in the book of Exodus inspires no confidence in their value as historical sources. The Song of the Sea, widely regarded as the oldest witness to the central event of the exodus, is a hymn, which at least in its present form encompasses the conquest as well

---

[1] Unlike Jorge V. Pixley ("History and Particularity in Reading the Hebrew Bible: A Response to Jon D. Levenson," pp. 231–37 in this volume), who engages Levenson's "Liberation Theology and the Exodus" (pp. 215–30 in this volume), Collins is responding to a slightly fuller version of the same basic argument not printed in this volume ("Exodus and Liberation").

[2] Leo G. Perdue, *The Collapse of History: Reconstructing Old Testament Theology* (Minneapolis: Fortress, 1994), 17–68.

[3] See K. A. Kitchen, "The Exodus," *ABD* 2:700–8.

[4] See A. Fierro, "Exodus Event and Interpretation," in *The Bible and Liberation* (ed. Norman K. Gottwald; New York: Orbis Books, 1983), 474.

[5] See N. P. Lemche, "Israel: History of (Premonarchic Period)," *ABD* 3:526–45; and W. G. Dever, "Archaeology and the Israelite 'Conquest,'" *ABD* 3:545–58.

as the exodus.[6] Attempts to reconstruct history from such material are dubious at best. Even if one is inclined, as I am, to grant that a story of national origins that begins with a state of slavery is likely to have some historical nucleus, we are very far from being able to reconstruct what happened with any confidence.

It is no wonder, then, that biblical theologians have increasingly substituted the category "story" for "history" in speaking of the exodus.[7] A story may include historical elements. It can also make use of myth and legend. Its truth is not measured by its correspondence with verifiable fact. It is a work of imagination whose value lies in the degree to which it captures something typical about life in concrete detail. No doubt, many people find a story such as the exodus more compelling if they believe it is rooted in historical fact. Such an "aura of factuality" is often held to be especially important in religious texts.[8] But in the case of the exodus, the historical evidence is too scanty and controverted, and so we shall have to make do without the aura of factuality.

To say that the exodus is a story, however, does not resolve the problems of interpretation; it only helps to frame them. If this is a classic religious text, as it surely is, with the power to shape people's lives,[9] then the shape of the story becomes crucially important. In fact, the major theological debates about Exodus in the past century have been concerned primarily with the shape of the story, or, more precisely, with the relation between the narrative that occupies the first part of the book and the laws that dominate the second half. One such debate centered on Gerhard von Rad's thesis that the traditions about the exodus from Egypt and those about the giving of the law at Mount Sinai were originally distinct. A second, more recent, debate has centered on the use of the exodus in Latin American liberation theology.

The Separation of Exodus and Sinai

Von Rad argued that it was only at a comparatively late date that the complex of tradition relating to the giving of the law on Mount Sinai was

---

[6] See F. M. Cross, *Canaanite Myth and Hebrew Epic* (Cambridge: Harvard University Press, 1973), 112–44; J. Day; *God's Conflict with the Dragon and the Sea* (Cambridge: Cambridge University Press, 1985), 97–101; and B. F. Batto, *Slaying the Dragon: Mythmaking in the Biblical Tradition* (Louisville: Westminster/John Knox, 1992), 102–27.

[7] See Perdue, *The Collapse of History,* 231–47; and James Barr, "Story and History in Biblical Theology," *JR* 56 (1976): 1–17.

[8] Clifford Geertz, *The Interpretation of Cultures* (New York: Basic Books, 1973), 90.

[9] David Tracy, *The Analogical Imagination* (New York: Crossroad, 1981), 99–229.

inserted into the canonical picture of the saving history.[10] His argument was twofold. First, the great block of Sinai traditions that stretches from Exod 19:1 to Num 10:10 is both preceded and followed immediately by traditions about Israel at Kadesh. This point had been vigorously argued by Wellhausen.[11] Second, he noted that the various poetic recitations of Israelite history that he dubbed the "credo" make no mention of the events at Sinai.

This thesis has been criticized on various grounds. The identification of Kadesh traditions before and after the Sinai complex is open to dispute. Ernest Nicholson argues, for example, that "what we have in Exod 15:22–18:27 is a rather loosely connected series of originally self-contained stories,"[12] only one of which (Exod 17:1–7) can be associated with Kadesh. The "credos," which von Rad believed to be the oldest nucleus of biblical narrative, are now widely regarded as Deuteronomic summaries.[13] The separation of exodus and Sinai seemed to be definitively refuted by George Mendenhall's discovery of parallels between the Sinai covenant and Hittite suzerainty treaties,[14] although Mendenhall's theory was far from commanding universal assent.[15] In the treaties, history was used to provide a prologue to the stipulations at the heart of the document. On this analogy, the historical narrative of the exodus was only the prelude to the giving of the law and meaningless without it, a point made most lucidly by J. D. Levenson.[16]

As far as the history of traditions is concerned, von Rad's thesis had considerable merit, even if his own arguments were not decisive. The oldest references to Sinai regard it as the abode from which Yahweh issues

---

[10] Gerhard von Rad, "The Form-Critical Problem of the Hexateuch," in *The Problem of the Hexateuch and Other Essays* (London: SCM, 1966), 1–78; idem, *Old Testament Theology* (trans. D. M. G. Stalker; 2 vols.; New York: Harper & Row, 1962), 1:187–88.

[11] Julius Wellhausen, *Prolegomena to the History of Israel* (1878; repr. Atlanta: Scholars Press, 1994), 342–44.

[12] Ernest W. Nicholson, *Exodus and Sinai in History and Tradition* (Atlanta: John Knox, 1978), 26.

[13] D. A. Knight, "The Pentateuch," in *The Hebrew Bible and Its Modern Interpreters* (ed. D. A. Knight and G. M. Tucker; Philadelphia: Fortress, 1985), 268.

[14] G. E. Mendenhall, *Law and Covenant in Israel and the Ancient Near East* (Pittsburgh: Biblical Colloquium, 1955).

[15] See D. J. McCarthy, *Old Testament Covenant: A Survey of Current Opinions* (Richmond: John Knox, 1973).

[16] Jon D. Levenson, *Sinai and Zion: An Entry into the Jewish Bible* (Minneapolis: Winston, 1985), 42–45.

forth as divine warrior to lead his people to the promised land.[17] Von Rad thought the giving of the law at Mount Sinai was already incorporated in the Yahwist narrative in the tenth century. Recent scholarship has cast great doubt on the antiquity of the J source and entertained the notion that the continuous pentateuchal narrative was first strung together no earlier than the exile.[18] Mendenhall's covenant form is not exemplified in the Sinai narrative in Exodus. The best parallels are found in Deuteronomy, and so the suspicion arises that Assyrian treaties may be more immediately relevant to the biblical covenant than the older Hittite ones.[19] Recently, Thomas Dozeman has argued that Sinai came to be identified as the mountain of the revelation of the law only by priestly redactors in the exilic or early postexilic periods.[20] Whether such a late date is justified or not, there is good reason to regard the association of Sinai with the giving of the law as secondary and to think that the oldest recitations of Israel's foundational history did not include the giving of the law.

The theological issues raised by von Rad's thesis, however, went far beyond the history of traditions. The implication of the thesis was that a separation could be made between exodus and Sinai, as between gospel and law. The Lutheran overtones of this position were unmistakable. Wellhausen, who was notoriously prejudiced against the Jewish law, had held essentially the same thesis. Yet, whatever the prejudices of these scholars, they raised a fundamental question for biblical theology. Where is the locus of authority to be situated? Does it lie in the oldest traditions, or are these superseded by the canonical biblical text? Is a biblical theologian bound by the canonical text in its fullness, or are we at liberty to build our theologies on some traditions and disregard others? These questions inevitably arise in Christian theology that attempts to appropriate the First Testament without undertaking the full "yoke of the law," especially in its Levitical form. Essentially the same question arises in the case of liberation theology, where there is no reason to suspect any Lutheran bias.

---

[17] Wellhausen, *Prolegomena,* 343–44; Cross, *Canaanite Myth,* 99–105; and Moshe Weinfeld, "The Tribal League at Sinai," in *Ancient Israelite Religion: Essays in Honor of Frank Moore Cross* (ed. P. D. Miller Jr., P. D. Hanson, and S. D. McBride; Philadelphia, Fortress, 1987), 303–14.

[18] See E. Blum, *Studien zur Komposition des Pentateuch* (BZAW 189; Berlin: de Gruyter, 1990).

[19] So especially D. J. McCarthy, *Treaty and Covenant* (AnBib 21; Rome: Pontifical Biblical Institute, 1963).

[20] See Thomas Dozeman, *God and the Mountain* (SBLMS 37; Atlanta: Scholars Press, 1989), 120–26.

Liberation Theology

Although liberation theologians frequently appeal to the exodus, they have made very few attempts to exegete the text in detail (although we do have the study by Gottwald[21] and the volume edited by van Iersel and Weiler[22]). Gustavo Gutierrez devotes only a few pages to the exodus in *A Theology of Liberation* but articulates some basic principles of liberation exegesis. First, he insists that creation, not the exodus, is the first salvific act in the Bible. The exodus, then, is to be viewed in the context of creation, so its significance transcends the historical people of ancient Israel. Second, it is fundamental that exodus is viewed as a social and political event: "The Exodus is the long march towards the promised land in which Israel can establish a society free from misery and alienation. Throughout the whole process, the religious event is not set apart."[23] Finally, "The Exodus experience is paradigmatic. It remains vital and contemporary due to similar historical experiences which the People of God undergo."[24] Gutierrez grounds the paradigmatic understanding of the exodus by placing it in the context of creation. The historical particularity of the event is not denied, but it must also be transcended if the text is to speak to people in other historical locations. The grounding in creation is not strictly necessary. As Walter Brueggemann has observed, "the most convincing warrant for such a usage is the undeniable fact that it is so used, that its adherents find it to 'work.'"[25]

In a similar vein, J. Severino Croatto interprets the exodus as a sociopolitical event that remains revelatory for contemporary Latin America, just as it was for ancient Israel.

> We are enjoined to prolong the Exodus event because it was not an event solely for the Hebrews but rather the manifestation of a liberative plan of God for all peoples. According to a hermeneutical line of thinking, it is perfectly possible that we might understand ourselves *from* the perspective of the biblical Exodus and, above all, that we might understand the

---

21 Norman K. Gottwald, "The Exodus As Event and Process: A Test Case in the Biblical Grounding of Liberation Theology," in *The Future of Liberation Theology: Essays in Honor of Gustavo Gutierrez* (ed. M. H. Ellis and O. Maduro; Maryknoll, N.Y.: Orbis Books, 1983).

22 B. van Iersel and A. Weiler, eds. *Exodus: A Lasting Paradigm* (Concilium 189; Edinburgh: T&T Clark, 1987).

23 Gustavo Gutierrez, *A Theology of Liberation* (Maryknoll, N.Y.: Orbis Books, 1973), 157.

24 Ibid., 159; cf. Norbert Lohfink, *Option for the Poor: The Basic Principle of Liberation Theology in the Light of the Bible* (Berkeley: Bibal, 1987), 27–52.

25 Walter Brueggemann, "Pharaoh As Vassal: A Study of a Political Metaphor," *CBQ* 57 (1995): 27.

Exodus *from* the vantage point of our situation as peoples in economic, political, social, or cultural "bondage."[26]

The liberationist understanding of the exodus has recently been subjected to a sharp critique by Jon Levenson.[27] The critique is somewhat distorted by the fact that it is based on the work of George Pixley, who has offered a Marxist critique of Israelite society that goes far beyond the more typical liberationist views of Gutierrez or Croatto.[28] Levenson's basic criticisms do apply, however, to the entire liberationist project; they concern "the categories in which the Exodus should be conceived."[29] In the case of the exodus, we are told, "*what for* matters more than *what from*."[30] Levenson notes that slavery is not mentioned in the Song of the Sea. Instead, the Song celebrates the kingship of Yahweh. The exodus constitutes the basis for the covenant: "Then the Lord commanded us to observe all these statutes..." (Deut 6:24). One form of servitude is replaced by another: "For it is to me that the Israelites are servants: they are my servants whom I freed from the land of Egypt" (Lev 25:55). There is no intrinsic objection to slavery, as can be seen from the book of the covenant, which provides for slavery in its very first law. At most, there is an objection to excessive cruelty and harsh treatment, but "the question may be asked whether God would have freed Pharaoh's slaves at all if they had not happened to be the descendants of Abraham, Isaac, and Jacob, to whom God had promised a land of their own."[31] "The point is not that it is Israel's *suffering* that brings about the exodus, but that it is *Israel* that suffers...."[32] Levenson grants that a "preferential option for the poor" can be found in the biblical text, but he insists that it must always be balanced with acknowledgment of the election of Israel.

Now, there is reason to doubt that Levenson has done justice here to the liberation theologians. Even though slavery is not mentioned in the

---

[26] J. S. Croatto, *Exodus: A Hermeneutics of Freedom* (Maryknoll, N.Y.: Orbis Books, 1978), 15.

[27] Jon D. Levenson, *The Hebrew Bible, The Old Testament, and Historical Criticism* (Louisville: Westminster/John Knox, 1993), 127–59. A shorter version of the critique is on pp. 215–30 of this volume.

[28] Jorge (George) V. Pixley, *On Exodus: A Liberation Perspective* (Maryknoll, N.Y.: Orbis Books, 1987). Levenson's criticism of Pixley for substituting a dubious and hypothetical history for the biblical text does not seem to me to apply to the work of Gutierrez or Croatto.

[29] Levenson, *Hebrew Bible,* 140.

[30] Ibid., 145–46, citing John Howard Yoder; cf. p. 226 above.

[31] Levenson, *Hebrew Bible,* 152.

[32] Ibid., 151.

Song of the Sea, the book of Exodus leaves no room for doubt about the occasion of the exodus: "I have observed the misery of my people who are in Egypt; I have heard their cry on account of their taskmasters. Indeed I know their sufferings, and I have come down to deliver them from the Egyptians and to bring them up out of that land to a good and broad land, a land flowing with milk and honey" (Exod 3:7–8). The liberationists are quite right that exodus is first of all liberation from slavery and oppression.

Moreover, I see no reason why a liberationist should deny that the goal of the exodus is the kingdom of God, or even servitude to God. As Brueggemann observes: "No one I know imagines that the Exodus results in autonomous independence."[33] The point is that this involves a new social order. While the social order described in the book of the covenant is not as egalitarian as some Marxist liberationists, such as Pixley, would have it, it is light years away from the regime of Pharaoh in Egypt. The liberationists do not deny that the exodus leads to a covenant or that it brings obligations with it, but they see those obligations in social and political terms, as "the beginning of the construction of a just and fraternal society."[34] Levenson is grossly misleading when he compares the liberationists with the Anglo-Israelite movement in the nineteenth century, which held that the British were the true Jews.

The real point at issue here is whether a theology of the exodus must embrace the particularity of the election of Israel, rather than see the exodus as a metaphor for the liberation of all peoples, and whether it must accord equal validity to all the laws, Leviticus as well as Deuteronomy, simply because they are commanded and not only because of their humanitarian character. Levenson is strangely inconsistent when he endorses the use of the exodus paradigm by Martin Luther King Jr. while rejecting the similar analogical use by the liberation theologians. The fact that Pixley adopts a questionable and hypothetical reconstruction of Israelite origins does not invalidate the basic liberationist analogy between the slaves in Egypt and the poor in Latin America. While liberation theology does not necessarily require a separation of history and law, such as von Rad's tradition-history implied, it does require the freedom to depart from the particularity of the laws found in the Torah and to be selective about the kind of laws that retain paradigmatic significance.

---

33 Brueggemann, "Pharaoh As Vassal," 28.

34 Gutierrez, *Theology of Liberation,* 155. There is a long tradition, independent of liberation theology, that sees the exodus as a paradigm for political action; see M. Waltzer, *Exodus and Revolution* (New York: Basic Books, 1985).

Tradition and Canon

The conflict of interpretations between liberation theology and its critics brings us back to the question of the locus of authority in biblical theology, or—to put it another way—the manner in which the biblical text should be construed for theological purposes. In recent biblical theology there have been two principal ways of addressing this question. On the one hand, there is the traditio-historical approach, which is associated especially with von Rad, but which admits of several variations.[35] On the other, there is the emphasis on "canonical shape" championed by Brevard Childs and recently endorsed by Jon Levenson.[36] To be sure, these are not the only possible ways in which the biblical text can be construed. Much biblical theology in the past century has been preoccupied with the search for a "center" around which the rest of the biblical material can be organized.[37] I believe that this quest has proven futile. Many of the prominent issues in biblical theology, however, such as the relation between the Testaments or the problem of history, can be viewed in various ways depending on whether the basic vantage point is provided by a synchronic canonical perspective or by a diachronic traditio-historical approach.

The particular form of tradition-history practiced by von Rad is now dated, in the sense that its shortcomings have been exposed.[38] Even if one were to grant the antiquity of the so-called "historical credos," as few now would, they cannot bear the weight that von Rad laid on them in his *Old Testament Theology*. To his credit, von Rad tried to pay more attention to other aspects of the biblical text, notably the wisdom literature, in his later work. There are also vestiges of traditional Christian typology in von Rad's work, which are problematic in the context of an ecumenical theology.[39] The tradition-history approach, however, can be adapted in ways that avoid these shortcomings.

---

[35] See D. A. Knight, ed., *Tradition and Theology in the Old Testament* (Philadelphia: Fortress, 1977); P. D. Hanson, *Dynamic Transcendence* (Philadelphia: Fortress, 1978); Walter Brueggemann, *Old Testament Theology: Essays on Structure, Theme, and Text* (Minneapolis: Fortress, 1992); and R. Gnuse, "New Directions in Biblical Theology," *JAAR* 62 (1994): 893–918.

[36] See Brevard S. Childs, *Introduction to the Old Testament As Scripture* (Philadelphia: Fortress, 1979); idem, *Old Testament Theology in a Canonical Context* (Philadelphia: Fortress, 1985); idem, *Biblical Theology of the Old and New Testaments* (Minneapolis: Fortress, 1993); see Levenson, *Hebrew Bible*.

[37] See G. F. Hasel, *Old Testament Theology: Basic Issues in the Current Debate* (4th ed.; Grand Rapids: Eerdmans, 1991), 117–47.

[38] See Perdue, *The Collapse of History*.

[39] See Jon D. Levenson, "Why Jews Are Not Interested in Biblical Theology," *Hebrew Bible,* 56–61.

One model of post–von Radian tradition-based theology has been provided by James A. Sanders, although he speaks of a "canonical process" rather than of tradition.[40] Sanders views "canon" not from the perspective of divine revelation, but with a view to its function in the human community:

> Canon functions, for the most part, to provide indications of the identity as well as the life-style of the on-going community which reads it. The history of the biblical concept of canon started with the earliest need to repeat a common or community story precisely because it functioned to inform them who they were and what they were to do even in their later situation.[41]

While Sanders puts the primary emphasis on "story," much the same could be said for laws, hymns, oracles, or proverbs. This material was passed on from generation to generation because it spoke to the needs of the people and was adaptable enough to address changing situations. This process was not concluded either with the Second Testament or with the closing of the biblical canon but continues in various ways down to the present: "Each generation reads its authoritative tradition in the light of its own place in life, its own questions, its own necessary hermeneutics. This is inevitable."[42]

In a somewhat similar vein, but from a distinctly Jewish perspective, Michael Fishbane has written on how the traditions of Israel "could also have turned into a closed and lifeless inheritance without the courage of the tradents of biblical teachings to seize the *traditum* and turn it over and over again, making *traditio* the arbiter and midwife of a revitalized *traditum*."[43] He notes that this ongoing process is both constructive and deconstructive, as it both affirms the authority of the received text and simultaneously implies its insufficiency for the needs of the present.[44] Sanders's model has been criticized for lacking theological criteria, and the criticism is justified if one is looking for a contemporary normative theology.[45] As a description

---

[40] See esp. J. A. Sanders, "Adaptable for Life: The Nature and Function of Canon," *Magnalia Dei: The Mighty Acts of God* (ed. F. M. Cross, W. Lemke, and P. D. Miller Jr.; Garden City, N.Y.: Doubleday, 1976), 531–60; cf. idem, *Canon and Community* (Philadelphia: Fortress, 1984).

[41] Sanders, "Adaptable for Life," 537.

[42] Ibid., 551.

[43] Michael Fishbane, *Biblical Interpretation in Ancient Israel* (Oxford: Clarendon, 1985), 18.

[44] Michael Fishbane, "Revelation and Tradition: Aspects of Inner-Biblical Exegesis," *JBL* 99 (1980): 361.

[45] See James Barr's review of James Sanders, *From Sacred Story to Sacred Text: Canon As Paradigm*, *CRBR* (Atlanta: Scholars Press, 1988), 137–41.

of the way in which tradition is actually transmitted, however, his account is cogent. If our question concerns the fidelity of a biblical theology to the biblical text, there is much to be said for Sanders's model as a framework for the discussion.

Brevard Childs is as keenly aware as Sanders is of the multiplicity of traditions encompassed in the biblical text, but he denies that the prehistory of the text has theological significance: "The history of the canonical process does not seem to be an avenue through which one can greatly illuminate the present canonical text."[46] His approach is concisely described as follows by his former student Gerald Sheppard:

> Childs prefers to speak of a "canonical approach," highlighting how the "canonical shape" of a biblical book established possibilities and limits to its interpretation as a part of Jewish and Christian scripture. He starts with "the final text" of scripture, without uncritically accepting the *textus receptus,* and makes observations about how diverse, even contradictory, traditions share a canonical context together. Rather than allowing the reader to pick and choose what elements of traditions seem the most appealing, this canonical context deepened the demand for interpretation in specific ways and in certain significant theological directions.[47]

Levenson's critique of the liberationist interpretation of Exodus is based on essentially the same premises. The liberationists do not read Exodus in its "canonical context," where the liberation from Egypt culminates in the giving of the full Mosaic law, but are selective in their emphasis on social and political liberation.

I do not dispute that Levenson's understanding of the exodus is in accordance with the biblical text, embracing the full Torah with both its Priestly and its Deuteronomic components. I want to suggest, however, that there may be other ways of reading the text that can also claim to be authentically biblical in their theology. Neither the Bible itself nor Jewish nor Christian tradition requires that the text be always read in the holistic way that Childs prescribes. Childs's notion of canonical shape must be seen in the context of the "New Criticism" that was much in vogue in literary circles in the recent past, even though he himself rejects the association.[48] This is not to deny that attention to "canonical shape" may be helpful, just as attention to historical context can be beneficial, but only to deny that there is any theological imperative in the matter.

---

[46] Brevard S. Childs, *Introduction to the Old Testament As Scripture,* 67.

[47] G. T. Sheppard, "Canonical Criticism," *ABD* 1:863.

[48] See J. Barton, *Reading the Old Testament* (Philadelphia: Westminster, 1984), 153–54.

The Use of the Exodus in the Prophets

By way of renewing the case for tradition criticism as a context for biblical theology, I propose to direct attention to the way the exodus is used and interpreted within the Hebrew Bible itself. First, it may not be amiss to dwell on the obvious: the exodus is never treated simply as a matter of ancient history. Already in Deuteronomy, the Israelites are told that the covenant was not just for that generation but for all generations to come: "It is not with you only that I make this covenant and this oath, but also with those who stand with us this day before Yahweh, our God, as well as with those who are not here with us today."[49] The repetition of the exodus story in the Passover to this day enjoins that each person should look on herself or himself as if she or he came forth from Egypt. The exodus, as Gutierrez pointed out, is paradigmatic.[50] Within the biblical corpus, the paradigmatic use is inevitably associated with the history of Israel and the chosen people, but it is never stipulated that no one else may think of herself or himself as having been a slave in the land of Egypt. The classic quality of the story lies precisely in its adaptability and in its ability to transcend its original historical and ethnic setting.

The oldest witness that we have to the exodus tradition within the Bible is the eighth-century prophet Amos. There are three references to the exodus in the book of Amos, at 2:10; 3:1; and 9:7. The first two of these may well be secondary, Deuteronomic, additions but are no less part of the exodus tradition for that.[51] The third passage, however, has the unmistakable ring of the iconoclastic prophet: "Are you not like the Cushites, to me, sons of Israel? says the Lord. Did I not bring Israel up from the land of Egypt and the Philistines from Caphtor and Aram from Kir? Hence the eyes of the Lord are against the sinful kingdom. I shall destroy it from the face of the earth." (R. Coote is exceptional if not unique in arguing that this is an exilic addition.[52]) It is clear from this passage that the exodus from Egypt was commemorated in the cult at Bethel, against which Amos directed much of his preaching. Amos does not question the exodus itself, but he radically relativizes it by suggesting that other peoples have parallel experiences.[53]

---

[49] Deut 29:14–15; cf. 5:2–3; and von Rad, *Old Testament Theology,* 2:99–112.

[50] Gutierrez, *Theology of Liberation,* 159.

[51] See H. W. Wolff, *Joel and Amos* (Hermeneia; Philadelphia: Fortress, 1977), 169–70 (on Amos 2:10) and 175 (on 3:1). See, however, the objections of S. Paul (*Amos* [Hermeneia; Minneapolis: Fortress, 1991], 90, 100), who allows that there is an editorial expansion at 3:1.

[52] R. Coote, *Amos among the Prophets* (Philadelphia: Fortress, 1981), 117–20.

[53] Cf. Paul, *Amos,* 284, who maintains that the exodus as such is not a unique event and grants its participants no special priority or immunity.

Amos, then, lends no support to particularist Israelite interpretations of the exodus. His God is the God of all peoples and is responsible for everything that happens in history (cf. 3:6: "Does disaster befall a city unless the Lord has done it?").

The fact that Amos threatens that the sinful kingdom will be wiped off the face of the earth points to another crucial aspect of his understanding of the exodus: it entails responsibility. It is much disputed whether the notion of a covenant, wherein there is an intrinsic link between the exodus and the laws of Sinai, was already part of Israelite religion in the eighth century.[54] The worshipers at Bethel do not appear to have made such a connection between history and law. But Amos certainly made such a connection. In this respect, the two "secondary" references to the exodus are faithful to the thought of the prophet. Amos 2:10 berates the Israelites for trampling the poor into the dust of the earth, even though "I brought you up from the land of Egypt and led you forty years in the wilderness." Amos 3:1–2 is more concise: "You alone have I known of all the families of the earth. Therefore I will punish you for all your iniquities." It is not apparent that the moral obligations arise from the exodus. Amos holds other peoples responsible for their iniquities, too.[55] But insofar as the exodus confers any distinction on Israel, it is a distinction in responsibility, not in privilege. The iniquities in question, the matters for which Israel is especially accountable because of the exodus, are primarily related to social justice. Some of the crimes mentioned can be construed as issues of purity or ritual (e.g., 2:7, "father and son go in to the same girl"), but sacrificial observance is pointedly dismissed ("Did you offer me sacrifices and offerings the forty years in the wilderness, O house of Israel?" 5:25). Amos most probably did not know the laws of Leviticus, but his understanding of the moral requirements of the exodus could scarcely accommodate them.

The moral obligations entailed by the exodus tradition are also at the heart of the "covenant-lawsuit" of Mic 6.[56] Speaking in God's name, the prophet recites all that God has done for Israel. Then he switches to the persona of the worshiper. "With what shall I come before the Lord?" Various kinds of sacrificial offering, including the human firstborn, are con-

---

[54] See especially L. Perlitt, *Bundestheologie im Alten Testament* (Neukirchen-Vluyn: Neukirchener Verlag, 1969).

[55] J. Barton, *Oracles against the Nations: A Study of Amos 1,3–2,5* (Cambridge: Cambridge University Press, 1980).

[56] See M. De Roche, "Yahweh's *rîb* against Israel: A Reassessment of the So-Called 'Prophetic Lawsuit' in the Preexilic Prophets," *JBL* 102 (1983): 563–74; on the authenticity of Mic 6, see J. Blenkinsopp, *A History of Prophecy in Israel* (Philadelphia: Westminster, 1983), 120.

sidered, before the oracle concludes: "He has told you, O mortal, what is good; and what does the Lord require of you but to do justice, and to love kindness, and to walk humbly with your God" (Mic 6:8). The notion that some commandments are greater than others and capture the essence of biblical morality was neither original nor peculiar to Jesus of Nazareth (Matt 22:34–40; Mark 12:28–34; Luke 10:25–28). The reduction of the law to two main principles, of duty to God and to human beings, is especially characteristic of Hellenistic Judaism.[57]

The socially oriented preaching of Amos is not the only lens through which the exodus may be read, but Amos is a biblical, Israelite author. His reading of the exodus cannot be dismissed as either Christian confessionalism or Marxist ideology. A theology that treats the exodus in a manner similar to Amos is surely within the bounds of biblical legitimacy.

Implicit in Amos's critique of the way the exodus was used in his time is the belief that the God of Israel is also the creator who controls the affairs of all peoples. Creation is prior to exodus in the narrative of the Bible and provides the backdrop against which the exodus must be seen.[58] The association of exodus and creation can be seen most vividly in Second Isaiah.[59] The anonymous prophet of the exile uses the exodus as the paradigm for understanding the liberation of the Jewish exiles from Babylon in his own day. He reminds his listeners how the Lord "makes a way in the sea, a path in the mighty waters" (43:16), but goes on to bid them, "Do not remember the former things, or consider the things of old. I am about to do a new thing" (43:18–19). The emphasis is not on the past, but on the reenactment of the exodus in the present. The paradigmatic, mythic character of the exodus is more apparent in Isa 51:9–11, where it is juxtaposed not only with the new exodus from Babylon but also with the primordial battle of creation:

> Was it not you who cut Rahab in pieces, who pierced the dragon?
> Was it not you who dried up the sea, the waters of the great deep?
> Who made the depths of the sea a way for the redeemed to pass over?

The juxtaposition suggests that the two events are alike, if not identical. The power manifested in the exodus is the same power manifested in

---

57 See Philo, *On the Special Laws* 2.282; K. Berge, *Die Gesetzauslegung Jesu* (Neukirchen-Vluyn: Neukirchener Verlag, 1972), 137–76.

58 This point is emphasized by Gutierrez, *Theology of Liberation,* 154–57.

59 See B. W. Anderson, "Exodus Typology in Second Isaiah," *Israel's Prophetic Heritage* (ed. Bernhard Anderson and Walter Harrelson; New York: Harper, 1962), 177–95; C. Stuhlmueller, *Creative Redemption in Deuteuro-Isaiah* (AnBib 43; Rome: Pontifical Biblical Institute, 1970), 59–98; and B. F. Batto, "The Motif of Exodus in Deutero-Isaiah," unpublished paper.

creation. While the paradigm is applied here to the deliverance of the Jewish people from Babylon, it is cosmic in principle and so potentially applicable in other times and places.

The universal implications of the creation story are most fully realized in the Wisdom of Solomon, which is not part of the Hebrew Bible but is nonetheless a pre-Christian Jewish work. The wisdom tradition was slow to address the specific history of Israel. The first attempt at a sapiential hermeneutic of the Torah is found in Ben Sira, in the early second century B.C.E. The Wisdom of Solomon, however, addresses the subject more systematically. It is characteristic of Wisdom's treatment of history that no names are mentioned. Instead, we read of "an unrighteous man" (Cain) or "a righteous man" (Noah). Wisdom is interested, not in historical specificity, but in typical examples.[60] The exodus is described as follows:

> A holy people and blameless race wisdom delivered from a nation of oppressors. She entered the soul of a servant of the Lord and withstood dread kings with wonders and signs. She gave to holy people the reward of their labors; she guided them along a marvelous way, and became a shelter to them by day and a starry flame through the night. She brought them over the Red Sea and led them through deep waters; but she drowned their enemies and cast them up from the depth of the sea. (Wis 10:15–18)

In this sapiential hermeneutic, the emphasis is neither on Israel nor on oppression, but on the notion of a holy people. The author assumes that Israel is the holy people par excellence, but nonetheless the people are delivered qua holy people, not because God had a covenant with their ancestors. Wisdom's reading of the exodus is not without its problems. The implication that deliverance was "the reward of their labors" is hard to justify from the text of Exodus. But the book provides an ancient and venerable precedent for reading Exodus as a paradigm that transcends the historical specificity of Israel. The liberation theologians then have good biblical warrants for arguing that the exodus paradigm is not the exclusive property of Israel or Judaism.

Constants and Constraints

It is not our purpose here to rehearse the whole history of the exodus tradition within the biblical corpus.[61] The examples cited, however, sup-

---

[60] B. Mack, "Imitatio Mosis: Patterns of Cosmology and Soteriology in the Hellenistic Synagogue," *Studia Philonica* 1 (1972): 27–55.

[61] Aspects of such a review can be found in S. E. Loewenstamm, *The Evolution of the Exodus Tradition* (Jerusalem: Magnes, 1992).

port Sanders's contention that "each generation reads its authoritative tradition in the light of its own place in life, its own questions, its own necessary hermeneutics." There is, then, no single normative way to read the exodus story, or, to put it another way, the exodus is not only a *traditum,* but also a *traditio*.[62]

There are, however, some parameters within which the exodus story is read in the biblical tradition. First, it is assumed that the Israelites are the slaves. No biblical author reads the story from the perspective of Pharaoh. It is highly probable that the cult at Bethel, which drew down the wrath of Amos, celebrated the exodus in a triumphalistic way. Such a celebration is never sanctioned in the biblical text. Rather, the typical appeal to the tradition is to remind the Israelites that they were slaves in the land of Egypt.

Second, the biblical authors insist that the exodus carries moral obligations with it. The nature of these obligations is spelled out in various ways, from Micah's terse command to do justice and love kindness to the full complex of pentateuchal law. Several prophets dispense with (or were unaware of) the ritual and purity laws of Leviticus. Nobody, however, can dispense with the demand for justice and kindness. Some commandments occupy a more central place in the tradition than others.

Nonetheless, we should be wary of attempts to identify biblical theology too narrowly with any one normative kerygma. The Latin American emphasis on the theme of liberation is well grounded in the biblical texts, and the analogical application of this theme to other settings is entirely legitimate. But the recognition of the theme of liberation as central does not arise inevitably from the biblical text. Rather, it arises from the conjunction of the text with the political situation of the interpreters and from a set of values that is informed by a wide range of sources, including but not confined to the Bible.[63] The same could be said of any normative biblical theology, Jewish or Christian. There are limits to the range of valid interpretations, but there is also a legitimate diversity of ways in which the Bible can be read. No one has a monopoly on biblical authority.

---

[62] Fishbane, *Biblical Interpretation in Ancient Israel,* 6.

[63] For a sober and balanced discussion of this issue, see James Gustfason, "The Place of Scripture in Christian Ethics: A Methodological Study," *Int* 24 (1970): 430–55.

The Exodus and Biblical Theology: A Rejoinder to John J. Collins[1]

Jon D. Levenson

In my essay on "Exodus and Liberation,"[2] I point out that "it is essential to avoid two extremes, each of which oversimplifies the issue, as extremes are wont to do." One extreme I term "universalistic." It "ignores . . . the chosenness of Israel, altogether and subtly universalizes the exodus story, as if all Egypt's slaves were manumitted in the exodus, if not all the world's slaves." The other extreme that I identified "ignores the universalistic dimension of the exodus, the connection of the exodus with the character of the God who brings it about, as if only the Patriarchal Covenant enabled him to be moved by the pain and suffering of those in great affliction." A theology adequate to the *biblical* texts themselves (and not simply to our own values and immediate situations)—that is to say, a *biblical* theology—"must," I wrote, "reckon both with the chosenness of Israel and with what the liberation theologians tend to call the preferential option for the poor."[3]

Each extreme perceives a dimension of the exodus story that must be honored if the fullness of the text is to be done justice. The universalists, I pointed out, can justly point to examples like invocation of the exodus in support of the humane treatment of Hebrew slaves and the obligation to redeem the impoverished kinsman and to make interest-free loans to fellow Israelites—all of which point to an event that is paradigmatic and is seen as giving birth to an ethic.[4] The particularists, on the other hand, can justly point to aspects of the exodus story and of the social practices that it author-

---

[1] In this article Levenson responds to Collins's critique (pp. 247–61 above) of his "Exodus and Liberation" as well as to another shorter piece by Collins not included in this volume ("Historical Criticism and the State of Biblical Theology," *ChrCent* 110 [July 28–Aug 4, 1993]: 743–47). In this latter piece, Collins takes Levenson to task for mischaracterizing historical criticism and for privileging certain confessional approaches.

[2] Jon D. Levenson, "Exodus and Liberation," in *The Hebrew Bible, the Old Testament, and Historical Criticism: Jews and Christians in Biblical Studies* (Louisville: Westminster/John Knox Press, 1993), 127–59.

[3] Ibid., 151. The same idea is expressed in slightly different words on pp. 223–24 in this volume.

[4] Ibid., 150.

izes that the universalists vainly wish were not there. "Gentile slaves," for example, "unlike their Israelite coworkers, did not have to be released in their seventh year of service or in the jubilee";[5] the laws about redemption are inextricably embedded in a clan structure and are explicitly particularistic in their phrasing; Israelites are quite free to lend at interest to outsiders; only Israelites are freed in the exodus, and even then the law that they are given is not described as a charter of freedom (*pace* rabbinic Judaism) but allows for slavery and other forms of what we know to be oppression.[6] Most important, only the interpretation that I have been calling "particularistic" "reckon[s] sufficiently with the cold fact that the biblical criteria for inclusion among those who benefit from the exodus are not poverty, oppression, suffering, or anything of the kind" but only "descent from a common ancestor, Jacob/Israel son of Isaac son of Abraham."[7]

Given the misunderstandings that the terminology of "universalistic" and "particularistic" can engender, I now prefer for reasons of clarity to call these two dimensions the "social-ethical" and the "familial-national," respectively. In my essay, I noted that most modem appropriations of the exodus have stressed one dimension at the expense of the other, so much so that we might never have suspected that the suppressed dimension existed, were it not for the nasty habit of the biblical texts themselves to survive all their modem (and premodern) retellings. The example of a modern appropriation of the social-ethical dimension of the exodus upon which I concentrated was that of liberation theology, whereas the familial-national dimension was represented, though only briefly, by the Anglo-Israelite movement of the nineteenth century.[8] In his latest critique of my book in which that essay appears, John J. Collins, an old friend who is among those to whom the book is dedicated, writes that "Levenson is grossly misleading when he compares the liberationists with the Anglo-Israelite movement in the nineteenth century, which held that the British were the true Jews."[9] When I first read this sentence, I expected to see it followed by an argument that denied the point of comparison, namely, that the two groups identify one particular group (the poor and the British, respectively) with biblical Israel, at the expense of the dimension better represented by the other group. I also expected Professor Collins to qualify his use of the verb *compares* by noting that I immediately *contrasted*

[5] Ibid., 136.

[6] E.g., ibid., 133–38, 151–53.

[7] Ibid., 152–53. The same sentiment is expressed in slightly different words on pp. 223–24 in this volume.

[8] Ibid., 127–40, 155–57.

[9] John J. Collins, "The Exodus and Biblical Theology," *BTB* 25.4 (1995): 154; cf. p. 253 in this volume.

the Anglo-Israelite movement with the Reverend Martin Luther King Jr.'s use of the exodus on the grounds that the latter "does not project his own group into the past; he *brings the past, the story of Israel, to bear upon the present*" by developing "the obvious analogy of the American black experience of slavery and emancipation and the experience of ancient Israel." Indeed, I contrasted the liberationists, too, with King by noting the same "all-important difference between *projection* and *appropriation*."[10]

My expectations of Collins were, alas, disappointed, for he follows the sentence quoted above with the remark that "[t]he real point at issue here is whether a theology of the Exodus must embrace the particularity of the election of Israel, rather than see the Exodus as a metaphor for the liberation of all peoples, and whether it must accord equal validity to all laws, Leviticus as well as Deuteronomy, simply because they are commanded and not only because of their humanitarian character."[11] Collins is illogical here: one cannot invalidate a comparison between two perspectives by simply stating a preference for one of them. One does not undermine a comparison of two movements on the basis of their employment of anachronism and retrojection by pronouncing one of them to be normatively acceptable. Even if it is legitimate to view the election of Israel as a metaphor (does Collins think it is only a metaphor in the Hebrew Bible?), the comparison with the selective reading given by the Anglo-Israelites still stands. Collins then goes on the say that "Levenson is strangely inconsistent when he endorses the use of the Exodus paradigm by Martin Luther King Jr., while rejecting the similar analogical use by the liberation theologians."[12] But merely by noting the words italicized in the quotes from my essay in the previous paragraph (also italicized in the original), Collins could have seen the *dis*similarity of the two uses and the conceptual sloppiness of terming them both "analogical." Perhaps I should have put those words in capitals as well.

Part of the confusion here is Collins's apparent misperception that I have somehow denied the availability of the exodus story for use by Gentiles. He writes, for example, of "its adaptability and ... its ability to transcend its original and ethnic setting" and concludes that "[t]he liberation theologians then have good biblical warrants for arguing that the Exodus paradigm is not the exclusive property of Israel or Judaism,"[13] as if I had said that only "Israel or Judaism" could lay claim to the paradigm. In point of fact, my discussion of Martin Luther King Jr.'s use of it is only one of

---

[10] Levenson, *Hebrew Bible,* 156–57.

[11] Collins, "The Exodus and Biblical Theology," *BTB,* 154; cf. 253 in this volume.

[12] Ibid.

[13] Collins, "The Exodus and Biblical Theology," *BTB,* 156–57; cf. 260 in this volume.

several indications that I made no such argument. Another is my judgment that Pauline Christianity "shows itself a worthy heir of the tradition at whose foundation lies the exodus from Egypt."[14] But the most important is my discussion of the crucial question of just who "Israel" is. Allow me to quote:

> Who is or is not a member of the people Israel has seldom, if ever, been self-evident, at least since the close of the biblical period. For eighteen and a half centuries the rabbinic tradition has followed the biblical precedent in respecting the natural, familial definition, though with a matrilineal criterion: a Jew is a person born of a Jewish mother or converted according to Jewish law and with a commitment to observe it. Christianity, not surprisingly, has identified Israel with the church, with the mystical body of Christ.[15]

Whether I was correct that the matrilineal principle is a Tannaitic innovation,[16] my words put it beyond all doubt that I believe that neither today's Jews nor any other group can make a claim to be the "Israel" of the Hebrew Bible simply by a historical or exegetical argument. Collins has not challenged my point that a "natural, familial definition" of Israel is carried on by rabbinic Judaism or that classical Christian supersessionism has historically weakened the readiness of Christian interpreters to recognize the importance of the familial-national identity of Israel in the Hebrew Bible.[17] Instead, obviously thinking of this kind of identity as something backward, he repeatedly speaks of "transcend[ing]" it and raises the possibility of our being "at liberty to build our theologies on some traditions and disregard others."[18]

In holding this negative view of the familial-national dimension of the exodus, Collins aligns himself squarely with the Christian and against the Jewish appropriation of the story. In so doing, he sets himself in sharp contrast with my own position about the pluralistic possibilities for reappropriation. This is an exquisite irony, since in his earlier critique of my book in which "Exodus and Liberation" appears, he tried valiantly to paint me as a quasi-fundamentalist, a confessionalist, and a practitioner of "theological apartheid" (as well as "coitus interruptus"), "privileg[ing] certain positions and exempt[ing] them from the requirement of supporting arguments"

---

[14] Levenson, *Hebrew Bible,* 149.

[15] Ibid., 155.

[16] For the opposite view, see Mayer I. Gruber, "Matrilinear Determination of Jewishness: Biblical and Near Eastern Roots," in *Pomegranates and Golden Bells* (ed. David P. Wright et al.; Winona Lake, Ind.: Eisenbrauns, 1995), 437-43.

[17] Collins, "The Exodus and Biblical Theology," *BTB,* 157–58.

[18] Ibid., *BTB,* 156, 153; cf. 251, 250 in this volume.

and thus "tak[ing] biblical theology out of the public discussion" and out of the university as well.[19]

In my judgment, *every* reappropriation and recontextualization inevitably involves some recombining and reweighting. This is true not only of Judaism and Christianity in all their immense variety, but also of historical criticism, a point that renders Collins's dichotomy of "confessional approach" versus "public discussion"[20] philosophically naive. That upon which historical criticism insists, however, is that anachronism is illicit, and when descent from Abraham, Isaac, and Jacob is seen as a "metaphor"—or, even worse, when it is "disregarded"—an anachronism has occurred. The resulting interpretation can, in my view, be quite legitimate and situationally appropriate, but not according to the canons of historical criticism. For a discussion informed either by historical criticism or by the *sensus literalis* requires interpreters to bracket their own commitments and to attend patiently to the entire content of the manifest text. To put the point differently: within these modes of interpretation, there is no place for interpreting away or ignoring the elements we find ourselves unable to affirm. Instead, to do that we must move into another mode, one that gives freer reign to selectivity and analogy (as opposed to retrojection), such as that employed by King in the speech I quoted. Of course, this move is available only to those willing to relativize historical criticism and to resist the erroneous notion that doing so involves a retreat from "public discussion" or a relationship of "coitus interruptus" with historical criticism.

In defense of his accusation of "theological apartheid," Collins cited this sentence of mine:

> In insisting that the supreme document of revelation is the whole Pentateuch and that the whole Pentateuch must ultimately (but not immediately or always) be correlated with the oral Torah of the rabbis, Jewish thinkers will separate themselves not only from those who absolutize the historical-critical perspective but also from their Christian colleagues in the field of biblical theology.[21]

Unfortunately, Collins began the sentence only with "Jewish thinkers" but accidentally omitted the three dots that indicate an ellipsis. If one restores the omitted opening phrase, my sentence shows that what he calls "theological apartheid" is really only the recognition of the inevitable difference that one's religious tradition makes for the way one interprets the

---

[19] Collins, "Historical Criticism," 747.

[20] Ibid.

[21] John J. Collins, Untitled reply, *ChrCent* 110 (October 13, 1993): 998; Levenson, *Hebrew Bible,* 81.

Bible and even for one's identification of a given set of books as a "Bible" in the first place. As I point out in numerous places in my book, especially in its title essay,[22] the rough functional equivalent in Christianity for the Oral Torah of Judaism is the New Testament. Just as a biblical theology that is authentic to rabbinic Judaism must "ultimately (but not immediately or always)" reckon with the Oral Torah (and the axiological priority of the Pentateuch), so must a biblical theology authentic to Christianity ultimately reckon with the New Testament. Though Collins claims that he "find[s my] attempts to prescribe what Christians must believe rather presumptuous,"[23] the idea that a Christian biblical theology ought to take account of the New Testament strikes me as neither daringly innovative on my part nor generally controversial among Christians. What is innovative, though on Collins's part, is his statement in this new critique, that "[t]hese questions [of the locus of authority] inevitably arise in Christian theology that attempts to appropriate the First Testament without undertaking the full 'yoke of the Law,' especially in its Levitical form."[24] With this I am in total agreement, but does posing the problem this way not fall under the rubric of "theological apartheid" as Collins defines it? Will not those who develop this particular "Christian theology" inevitably separate themselves not only from those who absolutize the historical-critical perspective but also from their Jewish colleagues, and would it really be fair to label their so doing a retreat from "public discussion" into a "confessional approach" that the modern university somehow cannot accommodate?

Because Collins gives the impression that I think the canonical context is binding on all forms of biblical theological work, I am compelled to note that in the same book, I explicitly point out the existence of a stream of Christianity that "does not vest scripture uniformly with divine authority and, in this ... does smooth the way for ... liberationism."[25]

The point at issue, then, is not whether selectivity is warranted. It is to some extent made inevitable by the very nature of reappropriation and recontextualization. The point, rather, is whether an intellectually honest exegesis of a biblical text may legitimately disregard the points that are not appropriated or consistently interpret them against their plain sense and without regard for the plain sense. That sermons and activist addresses may do so is quite arguable, but can scholars informed by historical criticism and centuries of pursuit of the *sensus literalis* do likewise? In light of this question, I believe Collins has unfairly criticized my choice of the work

---

[22] Levenson, *Hebrew Bible,* 1–32.

[23] Collins, "Historical Criticism," 746.

[24] Collins,"The Exodus and Biblical Theology," *BTB,* 153; cf. 250 in this volume.

[25] Levenson, *Hebrew Bible,* 73.

of George (Jorge) V. Pixley as an example of the liberationist interpretation of the exodus.[26] For, as I pointed out in the essay that he now attacks, "Pixley's commentary does not rest content with sporadic homiletical flourishes [about the exodus as a paradigm of universal liberation] but continually and systematically engages critical scholarship on the book of Exodus."[27] Given Collins's totalistic (and, I believe, uncritical) endorsement of historical criticism in his earlier critique,[28] I would have expected him to have more sympathy with Pixley than with the other liberation theologians whom he now cites.

Collins's charge that Pixley is atypical would have been immeasurably strengthened had he cited even one self-identified liberation theologian who does not equate the Israel of the biblical exodus with the poor and the oppressed but instead acknowledges and ungrudgingly upholds the familial-national dimension of the biblical story alongside the social-ethical. But the citations from Gutierrez and Croatto that he provides move in exactly the opposite direction, immediately subsuming the exodus into creation or otherwise ignoring the biblical definition of Israel as a kin-group.[29] In this respect, Pixley is actually more faithful to the biblical text, since he believes that at a certain stage in the historical evolution of the exodus story, what was originally a revolt of peasants came to be redefined as "a national liberation struggle ... between two peoples: Israel and Egypt."[30] Though in good Marxist fashion he subordinates ethnicity to class, he does acknowledge the importance of the familial-national dimension in the manifest text of the book of Exodus. But this then impels him to transfer the locus of authority from the text to the reconstructed underlying history, so that he, too, finally dissolves the familial-national dimension of the exodus into the social-ethical. Though Marxism is one justification for this move, one does not have to be a Marxist to make it, as Gutierrez, Croatto, and Collins demonstrate.

It must be noted that upholding the familial-national dimension of the exodus does not require us to subordinate the social-ethical to it (though it suggests that those who want a less complicated affirmation of the preferential option for the poor might be better advised to choose another text). In my essay, I tried to keep both dimensions continually in play,

[26] Collins, "The Exodus and Biblical Theology," *BTB*, 154; 251–52 in this volume.

[27] Levenson, *Hebrew Bible*, 128.

[28] Collins, "Historical Criticism and the State of Biblical Theology."

[29] Collins, "The Exodus and Biblical Theology," *BTB*, 153–54; 250–51 in this volume. I cited the same two liberation theologians, in addition to Pixley (Levenson, *Hebrew Bible*, 127, 180 n. 4).

[30] George (Jorge) V. Pixley, *On Exodus: A Liberation Perspective* (Maryknoll, N.Y.: Orbis Books, 1987), xix.

though without equating them.[31] Thus, when Collins writes that "Levenson *grants* that 'a preferential option for the poor' can be found in the biblical text, but he insists that it must always be balanced with acknowledgment of the election of Israel,"[32] I find the italicized verb inappropriate because it implies a concession. I do not *concede* the existence of the social-ethical aspect of the exodus at all; I affirm it as crucial to many biblical presentations of the story and an idea of inestimable import throughout the Hebrew Bible as well as postbiblical Judaism and Christianity.

Similarly, when Walter Brueggemann writes that "Levenson acknowledges that while enactment of liberation pertains primarily to Israel, 'the pain of any slave can evoke sympathy in God; slaves need not be members of the covenantal community for God to be affected by their plea,'"[33] he tells only half the story. The other half is that in Brueggemann's own discussion of my essay, he never acknowledges the familial-national dimension but only affirms the exodus as "paradigmatic [and thus able] to hold together precisely the particular and the universal, so that the universal may be discerned in other, non-Israelite particularities."[34] This misses the key point that not every particularity is familial-national in character. Affirming particularism is not the same as upholding descent from a common ancestor as the criterion for inclusion in the community of those redeemed from Egypt, who, as I pointed out in the essay,[35] are not always thought of as having been slaves anyway.

The Familial-National Dimension outside the Pentateuch

A constant in both of Collins's critiques is his identification of me with the canonical method of Brevard Childs, which in the second critique he says I have "recently endorsed" in *The Hebrew Bible, The Old Testament, and Historical Criticism*.[36] Since Collins provides no page reference for my alleged endorsement, I had to look up all the references to Childs in that volume. In the process, I have found statements that Childs's concept of canon is a "rather Protestant formulation," that his method is founded upon "a certain variety of Christian faith," represents "a revision of Calvinist scripturalism"

---

[31] E.g., Levenson, *Hebrew Bible,* 151–53.

[32] Collins, "The Exodus and Biblical Theology," *BTB,* 154; 252 in this volume; italics added.

[33] Walter Brueggemann, "Pharaoh As Vassal: A Study of a Political Metaphor," *CBQ* 57 (1995): 30, citing Levenson, *Hebrew Bible,* 152.

[34] Brueggemann, "Pharaoh As Vassal," 31.

[35] Levenson, *Hebrew Bible,* 140–41.

[36] Collins, "The Exodus and Biblical Theology," *BTB,* 155 (his date for my volume is erroneous there; it was published in 1993, not 1994); cf. 256 in this volume.

(though with broader implications), and stands in need of "a pluralistic reconstruction"[37]—not exactly a ringing endorsement from the pen of a non-Christian. The closest thing to Collins's putative endorsement is this sentence:

> The form of biblical scholarship that would incorporate these reflections is one like that of Brevard Childs, which, in the words of James L. Mays, "holds a series of moments [in the history of the biblical text] in perspective, primarily the original situation, the final literary setting, and the context of the canon."[38]

Collins has a different reading of Childs. He holds that the latter "denies that the pre-history of the text has theological significance."[39] Though some of Childs's formulations do indeed lend themselves to this interpretation, I believe Collins drastically underestimates the importance of the diachronic dimension in Childs's theology and misses the dialectic of the part and the whole in his conception of the text. But if Collins's interpretation is, in fact, right, then Mays's is wrong, and my endorsement of Mays cannot be simultaneously an endorsement of Childs.

Nowhere in "Exodus and Liberation" do I maintain that an assessment of the theological significance of the story of the exodus should ignore the prehistory of the text to the advantage of its canonical shape. On the contrary, my practice is quite the opposite. I point out, for example, that the Song of the Sea (Exod 15:1–21) is an enthronement hymn, informed by Mesopotamian and Canaanite cosmogony, in which "neither slavery nor freedom is so much as mentioned."[40] In rebuttal, Collins acknowledges that this poem is "widely regarded as the oldest witness to the central event of the Exodus" but then writes that "[e]ven though slavery is not mentioned in the Song of the Sea, the Book of Exodus leaves no room for doubt about the occasion of the exodus."[41] Andy Warhol spoke of every person's fifteen minutes of fame. This is John Collins's fifteen seconds of the canonical method, as he defines it.

The problems go even deeper. The truth is that slavery is conspicuous for its absence in a number of other biblical texts about the exodus, includ-

---

37 Levenson, *Hebrew Bible,* 81, 120, 122, 172 n. 39.

38 Ibid., 79, quoting James L. Mays, "Historical and Canonical: Recent Discussions about the Old Testament and Christian Faith," *Magnalia Dei: The Mighty Acts of God* (ed. F. M. Cross, W. Lemke, and P. D. Miller Jr.; Festschrift G. E. Wright; Garden City, N.Y.: Doubleday, 1976), 524. The brackets are in Levenson.

39 Collins, "The Exodus and Biblical Theology," *BTB,* 155; cf. 256 in this volume.

40 Levenson, *Hebrew Bible,* 140–42.

41 Collins, "The Exodus and Biblical Theology," *BTB,* 152, 154; cf. 247, 252–53 in this volume.

ing every citation from Amos that Collins adduces in support of his "case for tradition criticism as a context for biblical theology."[42] Indeed, had we only Amos, or even Hosea, for whom the exodus is more central (e.g., Hos 2:17; 8:13; 11:1; 12:14; 13:4), we should never have suspected that the story of the deliverance from Egypt involved liberation from slavery as well. This is also true for the longest reminiscence of the condition of Israel in Egypt outside the book of Exodus itself, Ezek 20, in which the exodus appears as a transition not from slavery to freedom, but from idolatry to proper worship, the latter defined as the observance of YHWH's laws and rules, especially the Sabbath (Ezek 20:10–12, 18–20). Some might speculate that the exodus story once circulated apart from the account of the enslavement and served as an alternate account of Israel's foreign origins that had not yet been harmonized with the more familiar account of the nation's beginnings in Mesopotamia. Whether this historical reconstruction be valid or not, any theology based on the use of the exodus in the prophets will have to relativize the idea of liberation from slavery and set other interpretations alongside (though not in place of) the one that emphasizes emancipation. A theology of this sort may have less homiletic usefulness than one that concentrates on only one tradition, since not every major element in the tradition possesses equal situational relevance. But it will also be a more pluralistic theology and one more reflective of the variety of the traditions in the Bible itself.

Collins turns to Amos for two reasons: to demonstrate that the exodus could be appropriated without "the laws of Leviticus," and to show that the prophet "lends no support to particularist Israelite interpretations of the Exodus."[43] The first is a point that I did not dispute in my essay and do not dispute now, so long as it is properly contextualized and not imagined to govern how all postbiblical religious traditions should view the relationship of the exodus to Toraitic law. The second point is more problematic. Here Collins's text is Amos 9:7, which compares God's bringing Israel out of Egypt with his bringing the Philistines from Caphtor and Aram from Kir. Note, however, that even this text shows no awareness of enslavement in Egypt but even goes so far as to compare Israel to nations that were never in bondage. Furthermore, in categorizing the exodus as a national migration, Amos makes use of the familial-national dimension of the exodus that liberation theologians (and Collins) tend to disregard or "transcend." But, most important, can we be confident that Amos's telling the Israelites that they are (or have become) like other nations is not yet another of his verbal assaults upon them? Elsewhere in the Hebrew Bible, when Israelites become like other nations, they are seen to be failing in their divinely

[42] Ibid., *BTB,* 156; 257 in this volume.

[43] Ibid., *BTB,* 156; 258 in this volume.

assigned mission (e.g., 1 Sam 8:4–22). Here, too, Amos may be telling his Israelite audience that they are no different from other nations (including the odious Philistines) who have benefited from YHWH's universal superintendence of history and yet fail to recognize him and to honor his moral claims upon them. This is the interpretation that fits best with the intense particularism of another passage that Collins quotes, Amos 3:1–2: "You alone have I known of all the families of the earth. Therefore, I will punish you for all your iniquities." His comment that these verses show that "insofar as the Exodus confers any distinction on Israel, it is a distinction in responsibility, not in privilege"[44] is overstated. For, though the verses do indeed affirm Israel's unique degree of responsibility and accountability, the use of the verb ידע ("to know") suggests a covenantal context[45] and thus implies that Israel's special degree of responsibility is grounded in YHWH's prior benefactions.[46] Amos dwells on one such benefaction in 2:9–10:

> 9 Yet I destroyed the Amorites from before them,
> Who were as tall as cedars,
> And as sturdy as oaks.
> I destroyed their fruit above,
> And their roots below.
> 10 I brought you up from the land of Egypt,
> And led you through the wilderness forty years,
> To take possession of the land of the Amorites.

Try telling the Amorites that the exodus conferred no distinction in privilege on Israel.

The Egyptian Social Order or the Wickedness of the Second Pharaoh?

Finally, allow me to make a comment about the social-ethical dimension of the exodus traditions in the Hebrew Bible. In "Exodus and Liberation," I argued that the acceptance of slavery in the Bible and the exemption of non-Israelites from certain constraints upon it are points that call into question a modern concept of "liberation" as the message of the exodus and require more careful definition of what the biblical writers would have considered to be true liberation.[47] In rebuttal, Collins writes

---

[44] Ibid., *BTB,* 156; cf. 258 in this volume.

[45] See Herbert B. Huffmon, "The Treaty Background of Hebrew *Yādaʿ*," *BASOR* 181 (1966): 31–37; and Herbert B. Huffmon and Simon B. Parker, "A Further Note on the Treaty Background of Hebrew *Yādaʿ*" *BASOR* 184 (1966): 36–38.

[46] See Jon D. Levenson, *Sinai and Zion: An Entry into the Jewish Bible* (Minneapolis: Winston, 1985), 23–42.

[47] Levenson, *Hebrew Bible,* 133–38, 145–51.

that "[w]hile the social order described in the Book of the Covenant is not as egalitarian as some Marxist liberationists, such as Pixley, would have it, it is light years away from the regime of Pharaoh in Egypt."[48] Whether or not this is a conclusion that critical historians can accept, it is itself light years away from the biblical ways of thinking. The book of Exodus does not compare social orders and then endorse YHWH's because it conforms to an independent criterion of egalitarianism. Instead, as I pointed out,[49] the narrative in Exodus is structured around a contest of two masters, Pharaoh and YHWH, with the latter finally besting his powerful opponent and earning the right to define the normative regime. The difference between social orders is secondary to the difference between the two contestants for the prize of ultimate power and the corollary right to command. Indeed, it is doubtful that the biblical authors condemned the Egyptian social order at all. The problem, rather, is the new pharaoh "who knew not [i.e., recognized no obligation to] Joseph" (Exod 1:8). Under the old pharaoh, Joseph succeeded in enslaving all of Egypt to his master, a grossly inegalitarian act that the narrator does not condemn and may actually enjoy (Gen 47:13–26). What differentiates the bad pharaoh from the good is, thus, not the social order at all, but the treatment of the Israelites. That pesky familial-national dimension: every time we think we have succeeded in disregarding or transcending it, it pops back up!

Collins's remark about the difference in social orders seems to imply that there exists a religion-free position from which to assess their relative worth. Even if this be so, the Hebrew Bible does not seem to have known about it. Thus, when Collins seconds Brueggemann's point that "[n]o one I know imagines that the Exodus results in autonomous independence" and adds that "[t]he liberationists . . . see those obligations [associated with the exodus] in social and political terms,"[50] I have no objection to enter, only a caution. The social obligations that the Hebrew Bible associates with the exodus are never subordinated therein to any autonomous ethic of egalitarianism, and the identification of justice with equality is not native to Israelite culture.[51] That is why the legal corpora and prophetic preachings alike can combine the most thoroughly egalitarian and the most grossly inegalitarian elements without a problem. If the liberationists have a problem with this, it is because they have projected a certain theory of justice into texts that do not share it.

---

[48] Collins, "The Exodus and Biblical Theology," *BTB,* 154; cf. 253 in this volume.

[49] Levenson, *Hebrew Bible,* 150–51.

[50] Collins, "The Exodus and Biblical Theology," *BTB,* 154; 253 in this volume; Brueggemann, "Pharaoh As Vassal," 28.

[51] See Jon D. Levenson, "The Universal Horizon of Biblical Particularism," in *Ethnicity and the Bible* (ed. Mark G. Brett; Leiden: Brill, 1996), 165–68.

Biblical theologians need not, in my view, accept all that they find in the text, but they are obligated to listen patiently to it and to acknowledge the existence of what they cannot accept and its relationship with the remainder. Whether the text is biblical or scholarly, unhurried reading and careful attention to context are indispensable if error is to be avoided.

Part 2:

Textual Perspectives

Section 2:

Pivotal Passages

Which Blessing Does Isaac Give Jacob?

Terence E. Fretheim

This theological study works with the final form of Genesis and with the literary unit 26:34–28:9, bracketed as it is with the issue of Esau's wives.[1] The text is commonly thought to be an interweaving of Yahwistic (27:1–45) and Priestly (26:34–35; 27:46–28:9) strands. Isaac's blessing of Jacob is usually considered to be the heart of both texts, with the blessing in 27:27–29 (J) paralleled by that in 28:3–4 (P).[2] In the context of considering various theological themes in this text, I will claim that the latter is part of a farewell blessing wherein Isaac commends Jacob to God regarding "the blessing of Abraham" (28:4), which God proceeds to grant (28:13–15; 35:10–12). Isaac's blessing in chapter 27, on the other hand, is a blessing gained by deception, which does not position Jacob for the Abrahamic blessing.[3] Isaac's blessing of Jacob in chapter 27 does not make God's blessing of Jacob necessary. Moreover, God's oracle to Rebecca (25:23), parallel in many ways to Isaac's blessing of 27:27–29 and with no reference to "the blessing of Abraham," constitutes no predetermination of

---

[1] See Gordon Wenham, *Genesis 12–50* (Waco, Tex.: Word, 1994), 202–4.

[2] In the present form of the text, several scholars speak of 28:3–4 as a supplement or complement to 27:27–29, adding the elements of nationhood and land. See Nahum M. Sarna, *The JPS Torah Commentary: Genesis* (Philadelphia: Jewish Publication Society of America, 1989), 196. Wenham, *Genesis 12–50,* 214, considers the blessing of 28:3–4 to be "very different" from that of 27:27–29 and is "the first time that Jacob has been designated heir of the Abrahamic promises."

[3] For the rationale for the source-critical divisions, together with a proposal regarding their relationship, see David Carr, *Reading the Fractures of Genesis: Historical and Literary Approaches* (Louisville: Westminster/John Knox, 1996), 85–88. Carr understands that Isaac actually does give Jacob the blessing in 28:3–4 and that it is parallel to Isaac's blessing in 27:27–29. I argue that they are not parallel, at least in the present form of the text. It is difficult to relate the various references to Isaac's blessings of Jacob. In 27:41, the reference to Esau's observation regarding the blessing is clearly to 27:27–29; a comparable reference to Esau's observation is located in 28:6. This could have the same reference as 27:41. More likely, it refers to Isaac's blessing in 28:1, which is a blessing for the upcoming journey. Verses 3–4 are part of this departure blessing, but it is a commendation of Jacob to God, not an actual transmission of "the blessing of Abraham."

the matter.[4] God's free choice of Jacob as the recipient of the blessing of Abraham is not certainly in place until it is actually made in the theophany (28:13–15).[5]

Genesis 26:34–28:9 presents several interrelated theological themes, especially blessing, election, promise, and the place of the human in the divine purpose. These themes are not new to this story; they are deeply rooted in prior narratives wherein divine actions decisively shape the unfolding story. These actions include God's election of certain individuals, including Noah, Abraham, and Isaac; the giving of promises to these individuals and their families; and the ongoing bestowal of blessings on these families (and various "unchosen" folk). The connection of Genesis 26:34–28:9 to prior divine activity is especially evident in God's oracle to Rebecca (25:23), which announces a future wherein Esau will serve the younger Jacob. And so, though God neither speaks nor acts in Genesis 26:34–28:9, divine speaking and acting provide the deep background for the story and the most basic frame of reference for much of the human activity.

These linkages demonstrate that theological interests inform this chapter in decisive ways. At the same time, God's actions do not absolutely determine human decisions or life directions. Indeed, human initiatives and activities prove to be very important in the development of the Genesis narrative, not least in 26:34–28:9. Yet, for all this, it is God's speaking, choosing, and acting that initiate various relationships and commitments, elicit varying human responses, and create both conflict and new possibilities for life in the midst of that conflict. It is important to set this theological stage in greater detail before considering Genesis 26:34–28:9 in particular.

A Universal Frame of Reference

As with any effective literary work, the way in which Genesis begins is important for a proper interpretation of all that follows. Genesis begins, not with Israel, but with the creation of the universe and the ordering of families and nations. These opening chapters (1–11) catch the reader up in a universal frame of reference.[6] They provide one

---

[4] The most important demonstration of this point is that of Laurence A. Turner, *Announcements of Plot in Genesis* (JSOTSup 96; Sheffield: Sheffield Academic Press, 1990), 115–41. I consider various details below and seek to give even broader support for the point.

[5] For an earlier assessment of these texts, see my "The Book of Genesis," in *NIB* 1:537 where I note that 28:3–4 "does not transmit the promises formally, but anticipates God's own speaking."

[6] For detail, see Terence Fretheim, *The Pentateuch* (Nashville: Abingdon, 1996), 39–53.

essential backdrop for understanding what God is about in this story. This universal framework includes the following claims that impact Genesis 26:34–28:9.

Blessing

God is active for good in the lives of all creatures, not just among the Israelites. Genesis 26:34–28:9 (and the story more generally) assumes that God is active for good in the lives, not only of Jacob, but also of Esau and his descendants (witness Esau's prosperity in chs. 33; 36). Divine election does not include a corner on participation in the goodness of God's creation. God's creative activity is ongoing and, through acts of blessing, provides a life-giving, life-enhancing context for all creatures. Blessing is a gift of God that issues in life and well-being within every sphere of existence. It is given creation-wide scope from the beginning (1:22, 28) and continues in the post-sin, pre-Abrahamic world (9:1).[7]

Inasmuch as blessing belongs primarily to the sphere of creation, the nonelect peoples are not dependent upon the elect for many forms of blessing. Thus it rains on the just as well as the unjust, and families continue to thrive. The genealogies of the nonelect, two of which bracket the story of Jacob, demonstrate this point. Various human and nonhuman agents mediate these blessings from God. Indeed, the nonelect may even mediate blessing to the elect, a point stated in general terms (12:3; 27:29) and illustrated several times in the larger narrative (12:16; 20:14; 26:12–14).

Blessing becomes a catchall word throughout Genesis to encompass two realities: (1) God's specific, constitutive promises to the elect family, initially through Abraham (son, land, many descendants, nationhood; 12:1–3, 7; 13:14–18; 15:4–5, 18–21), and not mediated by the nonelect. I call them "constitutive" because they are community-creating, without which Israel would not have come to be. These promises are called "the blessing of Abraham" in 28:4 and repeated to Isaac (26:3–4, 24) and Jacob (28:13–14; 35:10–12). (2) The general, creational realities such as fertility, various forms of prosperity, and success in the sociopolitical sphere, which all of God's creatures can mediate and experience independent of their knowledge of God. This distinction is important for our text. The blessing Isaac extends to Jacob in 27:27–29 consists only of the latter; the

[7] Generally, see Claus Westermann, *Blessing in the Bible and the Life of the Church* (Philadelphia: Fortress, 1978). Westermann divides God's activity in the world into categories of saving and blessing. This is a useful distinction, but it should not be understood too strictly, for God's saving activity is also described in terms of blessing. One should not translate these categories into a creation/redemption distinction or, for that matter, into a law/gospel distinction.

former is commended by Isaac to God (28:3–4), who gives it to Jacob (28:13–15).[8]

The creational blessings are life-enabling and life-enhancing, but they are finally not sufficient for the fullest possible life. The constitutive blessings mediated through the elect bring focus and intensity to the blessings of creation, make them more abundant, and decisively give new shape to both the human self and the larger community. Through relationships with this family, life for individuals and communities will become even more correspondent to God's will for goodness and well-being in creation. The larger issue at stake in these divine choices is a universal one: the reclamation of the entire creation in view of sin and its deleterious effects upon life.[9]

The identity of the son who is to be positioned to receive the constitutive blessings (and related responsibilities) becomes the bone of contention between Jacob and Esau and their parents. Before considering this point further, several other aspects of the universal frame of reference need attention.

Election

God's electing activity does not begin with Jacob (or with Abraham). Genesis understands electing in universal terms as a fundamental way in which God chooses to work in the world. Hence, God chooses the offering of the younger brother (Abel) rather than that of the older (Cain), for undisclosed reasons, as God will choose the younger Isaac rather than Ishmael and the younger Jacob rather than Esau, also for undisclosed reasons. Moreover, God chooses Noah (and his family and the animals) to be saved from the flood. In this instance, God's electing is not an end in itself but a means to preserve the creation. God's choice of the family of Abraham has a comparable life-giving purpose.

God's purposes in the world are cosmic in scope, and God's choice of Israel's ancestors serves those comprehensive purposes. Israel comes on the scene only within the context of all the "families/nations" of the earth (Gen 10:5, 18, 20, 31, 32). God's choice of Jacob is specifically related to the blessing of these "families" as his family "spreads abroad" throughout the earth

---

8 One might also distinguish between communal promises (e.g., 28:13–14) and personal promises (28:15). Turner, *Announcements of Plot,* 116, is right to criticize the distinction between "religious" promises and "earthly" promises (see Walter Brueggemann, *Genesis* [IBC; Atlanta: John Knox, 1982], 206–7). The last two phrases of 27:29 do refer to 12:3, but this is the only time they are recalled in Genesis and hence not integral to the "blessing of Abraham." It may be a more personal reference (cf. 28:15).

9 For detail, see Terence Fretheim, "The Reclamation of Creation: Redemption and Law in Exodus," *Int* 45 (1991): 354–65.

(Gen 28:14; cf. 12:3; 18:18; 22:18; 26:4). As with God's election of Noah, God's exclusive moves with Israel's ancestors are for the sake of a maximally inclusive end, including all human families, indeed the entire creation.

Promise

Regarding promises in particular, God has a promissory relationship with the universe before any covenants are made with the progenitors of Israel. God makes a covenant with Noah and his descendants, indeed with all creatures (Gen 9:8–17; cf. 8:21–22); this promise that life will be preserved come what may makes all subsequent promises with Israel possible and reveals that their scope has universal implications. With the promise to Noah and "all flesh" God is committed to the future life of the world; without this promise the creation would not be preserved in the wake of continued human wickedness. Moreover, this universal covenant is revealing of God's most basic way of relating to a post-sin world—from within a committed relationship, in patience, and in mercy. The covenant promises that God makes with Abraham, Isaac, and Jacob are as firm and good as the universal promises God has made, and they have a comparable purpose, namely, to serve and preserve life for all.

Given that the God who makes such commitments is faithful, Isaac can speak with some confidence that God will continue to see to the promises and will pass the constitutive blessings on to his son. But he can finally only commend Jacob to God (28:3–4). It is important to note that he does not claim or imply that his prior blessing of Jacob (27:27–29) has tied God down to extending the special blessing to Jacob. It remains to be seen whether God will in fact finally choose Jacob as the recipient. It would appear that the human principals have gotten all the pins lined up for just such a divine decision (birthright, paternal blessing). It would seem to be even clearer that God's word to Rebecca has committed the divine self to just such a move. But that divine oracle is sufficiently ambiguous with respect to its relationship to the constitutive blessing that one cannot be sure. Besides, God's oracles do not necessarily cast the future into concrete, and in the narrative development Esau does not serve Jacob as the oracle states. Matters might indeed be tipped toward Jacob as he leaves Canaan (28:10), but with this God one cannot finally be certain about the choice until it has been made. Yet, the family of the text (and readers) can be confident of the continuation of the promise.

The Place of the Human

God's entrusting of human beings with significant responsibilities in God's creation is a universal claim. This high role given to the human is evident throughout Genesis, from the assignment of dominion (1:28) to the role that Joseph plays in the world (41:57). Divine activity does not entail human passivity in working toward God's purposes for the creation. Human sin successfully resists the will of God (evident, e.g., in Gen 2:16–17) and has disastrous consequences for the life of the world. But this reality does not occasion a divine pulling back of the high role given to human beings (e.g., Gen 3:23–24 exhibits no change in the divine commission of 2:15; cf. 9:1, 7; Ps 8).

Importantly, God does not perfect people before deciding to work in and through them. This means that God's work in the world will always be associated with realities such as deception or patriarchy, which to one degree or another will frustrate the divine purposes and issue in mixed results. The faithfulness of individuals is important for the effectiveness of God's work in the world (see Gen 22:15–18; 26:3–5). At the same time, these individuals are both finite and sinful and will make mistakes and violate relationships. Yet, God will remain committed to promises made and will work through their failures to bring about life and well-being for as many as possible.

This more general understanding of the human is important in assessing the characters in this story. One scholarly tendency has been to demonize some of the characters[10] or to whitewash them or to agonize over the moral issues. The narrator, however, seems to have no particular interest in this direction of thought. God does not measure morality before making choices; in fact, that the initial choice occurs before the boys are born indicates that the divine choice is "disengaged" from Jacob's later behaviors.[11] While that choice is not finally put into place until the blessing of Abraham has been conveyed to Jacob, a firm direction has been set. That Isaac proceeds to commend Jacob without qualification even after the deception is another sign of this disinterest. God works in and through people of all sorts, people who have both gifts and character deficiencies. At the same time, this way of working reveals a deep divine vulnerability, for it links God with people whose reputations are not stellar and opens God's ways in the world to sharp criticism.

The Jacob-Esau Relationship

Three texts focus on the Jacob-Esau relationship: 25:23–34; 26:34–28:9; 33:1–17. We focus first on God's oracle to Rebecca (25:23) and move through the others. God's oracle to Rebecca about the future relationship of the two brothers certainly has efficacy, but how one states that effectiveness theologically is important.

For one thing, God's oracle creates conflict in this family. Initially, it is important to recall that God's oracle interprets an already-existing struggle in

---

[10] For example, Gerhard von Rad (*Genesis* [rev. ed.; Philadelphia: Westminster, 1972], 275) describes Esau as "a coarse, butchering, Edomite hunter."

[11] So Sarna, *Genesis,* 179.

Rebecca's womb. Yet God's speaking propels this struggle forward. At the same time, that divine action does not necessitate the human conflict that follows. The way in which the human characters respond to the oracle, or act more generally, contributes to the shape of their futures. Jacob's trickery with respect to the birthright (25:29–34)—which focuses on matters of inheritance—is one such instance. Though he acts without apparent knowledge of the oracle, parental preferences may have shaped such behaviors (e.g., 25:21–28), for Rebecca was certainly influenced by the oracle. In any case, the theological reality of the divine oracle means that the familial conflict cannot be reduced to an issue of family systems or to psychological categories. God's oracle does not excuse personal behaviors, which have their own efficacy, but God's speaking has generated certain levels of the conflict.

From another perspective, while God's oracle gives shape to the future relationship between the two brothers, that future remains open to some degree. Many scholars, however, consider God's oracle to be, in effect, the last word on the subject of Jacob's election; it sets the future course of relationship between Jacob and Esau in stone. Jacob will be the recipient of the constitutive blessing, "the blessing of Abraham" (28:4), come what may; all that follows is only "the actualization of a predetermined fate."[12] Such a viewpoint, however, functions with the unexamined assumption that divine oracles put the future firmly in place regardless of how people respond. Such claims, on the part of both Jewish and Christian scholars, seem to be dependent upon theistic models that stem more from, say, Hellenistic philosophy than the biblical narrative itself (see below). More generally, open-endedness is true of divine pronouncements about the future (e.g., 2 Kgs 20:1–7), at least those that do not entail a divine promise. These utterances express the future as God sees it (or would like it to occur). The divine will can be frustrated by human behaviors (e.g., sin). Moreover, God's knowledge of future human behaviors is not absolute (as shown in 22:12; cf. the divine "if" in 18:20–21),[13] so this is a genuine venture for God as well, with all of the attendant risks.

---

[12] Michael Fishbane, *Text and Texture: Close Readings of Selected Biblical Texts* (New York: Schocken Books, 1964), 62. J. P. Fokkelman tries to have it both ways. The divine oracle to Rebecca "predestines" Jacob and Esau to the future God has specified, but all characters act "freely" and "independently" (*Narrative Art in Genesis: Specimens of Stylistic and Structural Analysis* [2d ed.; Sheffield: JSOT Press, 1991], 115–21). But, in addition to the lack of correspondence between oracle and "fulfillment," this effort severs God's activity completely from the ongoing sphere of human activity, a view simply not consonant with any biblical perspective, and brings them together only at the point of fulfillment.

[13] For further detail on God's foreknowledge being less than absolute, see Terence Fretheim, *The Suffering of God: An Old Testament Perspective* (Philadelphia: Fortress, 1984), 45–59.

The narrative itself demonstrates that God's oracle does not set the future of Jacob or Esau into concrete.[14] How the various principals work through the divine choices and promises shapes the future of both family and God. From 26:3–5 (cf. vv. 24–26; 22:15–18) we have learned that Abraham's faithfulness has been crucial for the transmission of the promise to the next generation. Both divine and human faithfulness makes a difference with respect to the future of this family.

Take Rebecca. Rebecca's actions demonstrate that she does not understand the divine oracle to have absolutely determined her sons' futures. She acts in ways that she thinks will contribute to the future of which God has spoken. God probably recognized an ally in Rebecca, one who would pursue the divine will, a will that would not be irresistible (evident in human sin) and could be frustrated. In addition, it is noteworthy that God is not described as the agent in the oracle to Rebecca, and the reader is invited to consider how Rebecca might respond to open-ended issues of agency. The oft-suggested idea that Rebecca is unfaithful by pursuing such activities, that she seeks to take the divine word and will into her own hands, is a docetic view of the way in which God works in the world.[15] God always works in and through human or nonhuman agents and, as noted above, does not perfect them first.

Rebecca could conceivably have pursued other, less deceptive options, such as informing Isaac about God's oracle. Yet, she had to consider various matters that might have made such a straightforward move deeply problematic for Jacob's future. Note the following: Isaac's special relationship to Esau (25:28); the secondary means she has to use to discover what goes on in the family (27:5, 42); the care used in approaching Isaac about Jacob's predicament (27:46); the revealing of Isaac's temperament in 27:33 at finding out what had happened (because his authority had been undercut?); how Isaac might have responded when finding out that God's oracle had been given to his wife rather than to him. At the same time, she is willing to suffer the consequences should the ruse be found out (27:13).

---

[14] Again, see Turner, *Announcements of Plot,* 115–41. Turner demonstrates his point, not by an analysis of oracles and blessings more generally, but through a consideration of the subsequent narrative. See also David Clines, *What Does Eve Do To Help? And Other Readerly Questions to the Old Testament* (JSOTSup 94; Sheffield: Sheffield Academic Press, 1990), 59–62.

[15] The conclusions of Turner (*Announcements of Plot,* 179–80) move in this direction when he states the following formula: "human attempts to frustrate the Announcements tend to fulfil them; human attempts to fulfil the Announcements tend to frustrate them.... the implication of all of this is that the Announcements would have had a better chance of fulfilment if the human characters had done less to attempt to fulfil them and allowed Yahweh to do more."

She is open to suffering, perhaps even death, on behalf of her son and the divine purpose she understands herself to be serving.[16] Hugh White is probably right to claim that her deception is justified in her attempt to open a closed system.

> Deception and desire may now have positive roles to play so long as they are subservient to the contingency of the promissory Word and faith, rather than serving the interest of symbiotic personal behavior and structures of power.[17]

In the face of the powerlessness patriarchy engenders, manipulation often remains the only route open to God's promised future.[18] Yet the deception of Rebecca/Jacob is probably more ambiguous here, given that the blessing Jacob receives from Isaac is not the blessing of Abraham. Moreover, the negative effects Jacob experiences have a "what goes around comes around" sense (see 29:25–26; 37:31–33).

A "fixed" understanding of words about the future is also evident in comments made about Jacob's blessing in 27:27–29. For example, Wenham calls the blessing "a prophecy whose fulfillment is certain," while for Westermann, "the blessing of the father ... inexorably determined destiny."[19] A response can be made to this view that is comparable to that regarding God's oracle to Rebecca, but further considerations are in order.

It is often noted that God's oracle to Rebecca and Isaac's blessing seem to contradict Jacob's later serving Esau and bowing down to him (32:4–5, 18, 20; 33:3, 8, 11, 13–15). Moreover, in no instance does Esau "bow down" or "serve" Jacob. But these texts should occasion no such difficulty, for neither God's oracle nor Jacob's blessing is understood to have set the future in concrete or in detail in the first place. The texts from chapters 32–33 are one more indication that God's oracle and Isaac's blessing do not do what some have claimed for them. Indeed, such a lack of "fulfillment" is what readers should be prepared to find following a divine oracle or a human

---

[16] See Sharon Pace Jeansonne, *The Women of Genesis: From Sarah to Potiphar's Wife* (Minneapolis: Fortress, 1990), 53–69. Brueggemann (*Genesis*) overstates the situation when he states that "there are no hints in the entire narrative that she [Rebecca] knows what she is doing" (235).

[17] Hugh White, *Narration and Discourse in the Book of Genesis* (Cambridge: Cambridge University Press, 1991), 225.

[18] Note that the deception of Tamar and the midwives in comparably oppressive situations is commended (Gen 38:26; Exod 1:20).

[19] Wenham, *Genesis 12–50,* 216; Claus Westermann, *Genesis 12–36* (CC; Minneapolis: Augsburg, 1985), 442.

blessing! Even if the blessing cannot be revoked, this does not mean its content will inevitably be realized (see below). Rebecca acts to prevent Esau from killing Jacob, understanding that Isaac's blessing does not inevitably protect Jacob.

This consideration brings up the understanding of word, often thought to be crucial in interpreting this text. Scholarly perspectives on Isaac's blessing have often been rooted in a dynamistic understanding of word.[20] But such words (or words in general) are not effective because of some inherent, independent power in the words themselves. Certain words produce effects because of societal understandings regarding the function of such speech-acts. The words must be spoken in a particular situation by the appropriate person in the proper form to be so effective; in fact, if these factors are not present the words may have the opposite effect intended (even blessings and curses, Prov 27:14).

The blessing of Jacob in Gen 27 is not a magical transfer of power by means of words. The blessing reflects cultural understandings of the effectiveness and legally nonrescindable character of such testaments. The fact that modern legally attested oaths would be comparably understood is illustrative of the fact that Israel's understanding of word was not particularly unique. Both in ancient and modern societies certain words immediately produce effects because they are spoken by individuals exercising authority in certain conventional or institutional situations.[21]

One integral part of Isaac's blessing is the meal; Isaac cites this ritualistic element as a reason for not retracting the blessing (v. 33).[22] This may be an important factor in the convention, but, generally, if Isaac could not revoke the blessing, it was because no convention was available for its revocation. If such a convention did exist, Isaac chooses not to make use of it. It is notable that Rebecca apparently believes that the curse could be transferred (27:12–13). Esau, in asking for another blessing, appears to believe that no such convention exists (unless Jacob is killed?) but that Isaac should have other blessings to give (perhaps because deathbed blessings are usually given to all children; see ch. 49). And Isaac does have another blessing to give. In fact, Isaac's blessing of Esau (27:39–40) demonstrates that words can be spoken that qualify the impact of a blessing already spoken (v. 40; cf., e.g., Ps 137). Note also that, at a later point

[20] An important discussion of the power of words is that of Anthony Thiselton, "Supposed Power of Words in the Biblical Writings," *JTS* (1974): 283–299. This article stands as a corrective to many studies of "word" by biblical scholars, including Gerhard von Rad (*Old Testament Theology* [trans. D. M. G. Stalker; 2 vols.; New York: Harper & Row, 1962], 2:80–98).

[21] For detail, see Terence Fretheim, "Word of God," *ABD* 6:961–68.

[22] For detail, see Westermann, *Genesis 12–36,* 439.

in the narrative, Jacob understands that he can give his father's blessing over to Esau or at least include Esau within its sphere (33:11; NRSV "gift"). This gesture shows that Isaac's blessing of Jacob does not include "the blessing of Abraham."

A case could be made that Isaac actually wants Jacob, rather than Esau, to have "the blessing of Abraham." Isaac refers to the planned blessing of Esau as a "personal" (נפשי, 27:4) blessing. This could mean that in giving the blessing to Jacob (as Esau) in 27:27–29 Isaac is reserving the Abrahamic blessing. This may be shown further in the fact that its language is only minimally correspondent to the Abrahamic blessing (unlike 28:3–4, 13–14).[23] As Gerhard von Rad notes, "the blessing is strangely independent of the otherwise uniformly formulated patriarchal promises"[24] This is the case, I would claim, because Isaac's blessing of Jacob as Esau is not counted as such a promise, either by Isaac or the narrator! From another angle, a case could be made that this blessing comes to fruition for Esau rather than Jacob, at least in terms of the subsequent narrative (see above).

Whether Isaac mediates a blessing to Esau upon his request is a matter of dispute (27:38–40). The suggestion that Isaac is ambiguous in his reply may be correct (the מי prefix can mean either "away (far) from" or "of"), but with either use of the particle Isaac's word to Esau still has a blessing component.[25] Isaac's word to Esau includes the gift of life and at least occasional freedom from oppression. In any case, Isaac's word is a blessing from the narrator's perspective, for Esau interprets Isaac's word as a blessing (27:41). Even more, in the larger context the narrator resolves any ambiguity, for Esau receives blessings in abundance (33:1, 9, 15; 36:6–8 and the entire genealogy). If in fact Isaac gives an "antiblessing," the subsequent narrative shows that his word is not effective to that end. God will be at work in Esau's life so that he prospers, and in a way not too different from those blessings promised Jacob in 27:27–29. This is testimony to a God who is at work beyond the specific promise to the elect family on behalf of life and well-being for all peoples.

There is a kind of irony in Isaac's blessing of Jacob (as Esau), and a key point of the story may lie precisely here. If Jacob thought that through this ruse he was going to be the recipient of the Abrahamic promises, he was mistaken. His deception did not bring him "the blessing of Abraham." In

---

[23] See Wenham, *Genesis 12–50,* 210. The last two clauses of v. 29 are linked to 12:3 (the only such instance in Genesis), but they differ in several respects in what is a more impersonal word, e.g., passive participles; numerous enemies; reversal of cursing and blessing.

[24] See von Rad, *Genesis,* 278.

[25] See Westermann, *Genesis 12–36,* 443. See also J. G. Janzen, *Genesis 12–50: Abraham and All the Families of the Earth* (Grand Rapids: Eerdmans, 1993).

other words, even if the deception had not been attempted and Isaac had actually blessed Esau, that act would not have foreclosed what God did in chapter 28. Isaac's blessing of Esau would not have constituted a continuation of God's promises to Abraham and himself. That happens only later after Isaac commends him to God. If Isaac were reserving the constitutive blessing for Jacob all along, that would help explain why he commends Jacob to God without any reference to the deception. Isaac's experience was that God rather than his father or grandfather had transmitted the blessing. Nothing indicates that Isaac now thought that this was to be a human rather than a divine task. The positioning of chapter 26, with its repeated reference to the blessing of Isaac by God, reinforces this interpretation.

And so, in the present form of the text,[26] Isaac cannot himself transmit the "blessing of Abraham" (28:4); all that Isaac can do is commend Jacob to God (28:3–4). Westermann correctly notes that the "blessing" in 28:3–4 is no longer an effectual word spoken by the father; it has been changed into an optative. The "blessing" takes "the form of a wish," or is "reworked into a wish or prayer."[27] This language, I would claim, reveals Isaac's understanding that God must transmit the promised blessing to Jacob, as God had done with both Abraham and himself (12:1–3; 22:17–18; 26:2–5, 24). Note that Abraham's name is specifically mentioned in each case wherein God transmits the blessing to Isaac and Jacob (26:3–5, 24; 28:13–15; 35:10–12), as is the case here. God proceeds to do this in an appearance to Jacob at Bethel (28:10–22; reaffirmed later at Bethel, 35:9–12). One might claim that Isaac does prepare the way for God's own speaking by elevating Jacob to the premier family position, but that act does not make God's action necessary. The surprising thing is that God chooses Jacob at all, that the deception and manipulation do not disqualify Jacob. This divine move helps readers escape the trap of placing Esau and Jacob on a "fitness" scale, as if God's choices were determined by measuring morality (see Deut 7:7–8; 9:4–7). This narrative, with God's choice of a deceiver to be the recipient of the Abrahamic promise, demonstrates that Israel's God is not a moralist and confounds those who think that questionable morality should disqualify individuals for such a blessing (see 1 Cor 1:26–31).

---

[26] Another effort to read the text in its present form focuses on the issue of the marriages of Esau and Jacob (see the discussion in Carr, *Reading the Fractures of Genesis,* 321). Esau's exogamous marriages are decisive for the decision to pass the blessing on through Jacob. Carr speaks against such an emphasis, stressing that the focus of the final form of the text is not on marriage but on still further machinations of Rebecca to save Jacob from Esau. In any case, moral fitness is not the grounds for the divine decision to transmit the blessing of Abraham to Jacob.

[27] Westermann, *Genesis 12–36,* 447–48.

We close with a word about Jacob himself. Divine decisions and actions make life very difficult for him, though his own behaviors intensify the negative effects. His life is endangered, he becomes a fugitive, he endures years of hard labor and waiting in a foreign land, and he has to struggle with a God who may at times go on the attack. The "blessing, surely intended for good, has become a source of heavy anxiety. The blessing so passionately sought is a burden."[28] Divine election and the vocation that goes with it may entail, perhaps more often than not, both blessing and danger. This portrayal of Jacob in the present form of the text was probably directed to an exilic audience, who could read their identity, failures, difficult experiences with God, and an uncertain future off the pages of this one named as they were—Israel. Finally, the exiles could only rest back in the theological reality that God had chosen them and promised them that they would be recipients of God's blessing with its attendant responsibilities.

---

[28] Brueggemann, *Genesis,* 227.

Traditional Jewish Responses to the Question of Deceit in Genesis 27

David Marcus

The main theme of Gen 27 is Jacob deceiving his father Isaac for his brother's blessing. The story is familiar. Isaac, nearing death,[1] makes a request of his favorite son Esau for a meal of venison after which he is promised a blessing. Rebecca, overhearing Isaac's promise,[2] persuades her favorite son Jacob to camouflage himself, impersonate Esau, and obtain the blessing in his stead. After some initial protest Jacob agrees, and he is clothed with lambskins to simulate Esau's hairy skin and with Esau's clothes to simulate Esau's look and smell. Instead of venison Jacob brings a meal of lambstew, bread, and wine,[3] all specially prepared by Rebecca. Isaac, after much demurring and questioning, seems to be persuaded that the figure in front of him is Esau and so blesses Jacob. When Esau returns he discovers that his father's blessing has already been given and cannot be revoked.[4] When he asks for an alternate blessing he is given one that can be interpreted as antithetical to Jacob's blessing.[5] What is most note-

---

[1] Though another tradition has Isaac remaining alive until after Jacob returns from Haran (Gen 35:28).

[2] Rebecca, like Sarah before her (ושרה שמעת, 18:10), is described in v. 5 with the same formulation (ורבקה שמעת) as listening in the wings to fateful news.

[3] The cultic nature of Isaac's meal and Jacob's use of skins has been noted by various commentators, including Ronald S. Hendel, *The Epic of the Patriarch: The Jacob Cycle and the Narrative Tradition of Canaan and Israel* (HSM 42; Atlanta: Scholars Press, 1987), 83–86; and Susan Ackerman, "The Deception of Isaac, Jacob's Dream at Bethel, and Incubation on an Animal Skin," in *Priesthood and Cult in Ancient Israel* (ed. Gary A. Anderson and Saul M. Olyan; JSOTSup 125; Sheffield: Sheffield Academic Press, 1990), 107–8.

[4] David Daube (*Studies in Biblical Law* [New York: Ktav, 1969], 191–93, 198) has pointed out that even though given under questionable circumstances based on an error of identity the blessing is valid and irrevocable. Another instance of Jacob extracting a blessing under duress is in the incident with the man of God in Gen 32. Here too the blessing was valid despite its being given under duress (193).

[5] Note the exact correspondences between the phrases מטל השמים "of the dew of heaven" and משמני הארץ, "of the fat of the earth" (vv. 28, 39). If one interprets the

worthy about these blessings is that they are different both in form and content from the standard patriarchal blessings previously given to Abraham and Isaac and that subsequently will be given to Jacob by Isaac himself (Gen 28:1–4) and by God (28:13–15).

The major difference between the standard patriarchal blessing and Isaac's blessing in Gen 27 is that, whereas the former blessing is consistently one of land and progeny,[6] the latter is one of material prosperity and of superiority of one brother over another. Jacob is promised superiority over Esau. To him it is declared: "be master over your brothers" (v. 29), whereas to Esau: "and you shall serve your brother" (v. 40). This biblical story with its elevation of one brother over another can be seen as the personification of two different ways of life, namely, that of the shepherd and that of the hunter,[7] or of a civilized and outlaw society.[8] This sibling rivalry between Jacob and Esau can also be seen as a reflection of the later historical relations between the two nations Israel and Edom.[9] In postbiblical times the conflict of Jacob with Esau became archetypal symbols of the conflict between Jewry and Rome.[10] In the fourth century when the Christian church was established as the religion of the empire Jewish homilists extended the name of Edom to Christendom, thus midrashically contrasting Jacob/Israel and Judaism with Esau/Edom and Christianity.[11]

---

preposition" מן in v. 39 as partitive, then the meaning will be that Esau will live "away from the dew of heaven and away from the fat of the earth."

[6] See 12:1–3; 13:14–16; 22:17; 26:24; 28:3, 13–15; etc.

[7] Cf. Hermann Gunkel, *Genesis* (Macon, Ga.: Mercer University Press, 1997), 308.

[8] Hendel, *The Epic of the Patriarch,* 128; Meir Malul, "*ʿAqeb* 'Heel' and *ʿAqab* 'To Supplant,' and the Concept of Succession in the Jacob-Esau Narratives," *VT* 46 (1996): 206–7.

[9] Edom was subjected by David (2 Sam 8:12–14), but in Solomon's time it acquired independence (1 Kgs 11:11–22, 25).

[10] See Gerson D. Cohen, "Esau As Symbol in Early Medieval Thought," in *Jewish Medieval and Renaissance Studies* (ed. Alexander Altmann; Cambridge: Harvard University Press, 1967), 19–48.

[11] For their part medieval Christianity used this same typology in reverse. Jacob or Israel represented the church, whereas the synagogue was the incarnation of Esau or Edom. Irenaeus, for example, in the latter part of the second century held that "Jacob-Israel-Christendom had supplanted Esau-Jewry in birthright and blessing, the 'younger' destined to freedom and victory, the 'older' to eternal rejection and servitude" (ibid., 33). At first this typology was simply an allegorical interpretation used by Christians to illustrate a distinction between "Jews" and "Israel" (Christianity). However, when the church became the official religion of the empire, this theoretical exegesis became political theory and laid the foundations for many anti-Jewish restrictions. Both the oracle of Gen 25:23 ("the older [Esau =

Notwithstanding the symbolism of these connections, devout interpreters were faced with the embarrassing problem of how to explain the inconvenient fact that this blessing granted to their ancestral father was acquired through an obvious deception. It is the intention of this paper to delineate the traditional Jewish responses to this problem.[12]

Over the years two major traditional Jewish responses have emerged, one holding that the deception was not justified while the other held that it was. Those who acknowledged that the deception was wrong offered a moral interpretation or attempted to shift the blame from Jacob to Rebecca or even to Isaac himself. Those who celebrated the deception justified it in various ways, by means of legal niceties or by theological explanations.

The first response took a moral view of the problem. Jacob did deceive his father, but he was punished for his deception later on in his life. Indeed, it has often been pointed out by many modern scholars that this moral critique of Jacob's actions is built into the Jacob cycle of stories itself.[13] The biblical text alludes to Jacob's deceitful conduct. When Jacob complained to Laban, ולמה רמיתני, "why did you deceive me" (29:25),[14] Laban replied that "it is not the practice in our place to marry off the younger [הצעירה] before the elder [הבכירה]" (29:26), a clear allusion to

---

the Jews] shall serve the younger [Jacob = the church]") and the blessings of Gen 27 ("and you [Esau = the Jews] shall serve your brother [Jacob = the church]") were implemented by law (ibid., 35, 37).

[12] By "traditional Jewish" I mean rabbinic exegesis that extends from the Targumim through the midrashim to the medieval Jewish commentators (Rashi, Rashbam, Ibn Ezra, David Kimchi) up to nineteenth-century commentators such as Malbim (Meir Loeb Ben-Yechiel Michael, 1809–1879). It should be noted that earlier Jewish writers such as the author of *Jubilees,* Philo, and Josephus attempted to tone down Jacob's deception. See Louis H. Feldman, "Josephus' Portrait of Jacob," in *The Jews in the Hellenistic-Roman World: Studies in Memory of Menahem Stern* (ed. I. M. Gagni et al.; Jerusalem: Zalman Shazar Center for Jewish History/ Historical Society of Israel, 1996), 1141; and James H. Charlesworth, ed., *The Old Testament Pseudepigrapha* (2 vols.; Garden City, N.Y.: Doubleday, 1983, 1985), 2:106.

[13] This moral point of view is popular with modern Jewish scholars; see Benno Jacob, *Das Erste Buch der Tora: Genesis* (Berlin: Schocken Books, 1934), 564; E. A. Speiser, *Genesis* (AB 1; Garden City, N.Y.: Doubleday, 1964), 211; Nahum M. Sarna, *The JPS Torah Commentary: Genesis* (Philadelphia: Jewish Publication Society of America, 1989), 397–98; Nehama Leibowitz, *New Studies in Bereshit (Genesis)* (Jerusalem: Dept. for Torah Education and Culture in the Diaspora, 1995), 266–67; Michael Fishbane, "Composition and Structure in the Jacob Cycle (Gen. 25:19–35:22)" *JJS* 26 (1975): 16; Yair Zakovitch, "Through the Looking Glass: Reflections/Inversions of Genesis Stories in the Bible," *BibInt* 1.2 (1993): 140.

[14] Note the same root רמה occurs in our chapter in the form במרמה (v. 35).

Jacob being the צעיר (25:23) and Esau the בכור (27:19). The implication is that "it may be the custom in your home to deprive the older child of his or her rights, but not in ours."[15] Jacob's acts are also evaluated negatively in some later biblical traditions. Hosea mentions that "The Lord once indicted Judah and punished Jacob for his conduct, requited him for his deeds" (Hos 12:3), and Jacob's underhanded conduct is also remembered by Jeremiah: "For every brother takes advantage [עקוב יעקב], every friend is base in his dealings" (Jer 9:3).

Similarly, many rabbinic writers noted that there was a poetic quality in Jacob's punishment, one seemingly meted out according to the principle of מדה כנגד מדה, "measure for measure."[16] Just as Jacob deceived Isaac by an error of identity for the firstborn blessing, so Laban deceived him with an error of identity with his firstborn daughter Leah; just as Jacob took advantage of his father's blindness, so Laban took advantage of the darkness of the night on his wedding night and replaced his younger daughter Rachel with the elder one Leah.[17] *Genesis Rabbah* imagines the following morning-after conversation between Jacob and Leah:

> The whole of that night he called her "Rachel," and she answered him. In the morning, however, "behold it was Leah" (Gen 29:25). Said he to her: "You are a deceiver and the daughter of a deceiver!" She retorted: "Is there a teacher without pupils; did not your father call you 'Esau,' and you answered him! So did you too call me and I answered you!"[18]

From the time of Josephus[19] to the present[20] another means of defending Jacob's honor emerged to shift the blame for the deception to

---

[15] Zakovitch, "Through the Looking Glass," 15.

[16] Cf. Daube (*Studies in Biblical Law,* 192): "It is safe to assume that the original audience did connect the two stories and enjoy so striking an instance of exact retaliation. They may well have chuckled even over such details as that whilst Jacob's stratagem was to act his elder brother, he in his turn was deceived by Leah's acting her younger sister."

[17] On the symmetry of the two stories, see Yair Zakovitch, "Jacob's Cunning," *Sefer Baruch Ben-Yehudah* (in Hebrew) (ed. B. Z. Luria; Tel-Aviv: Israel SBL, 1981), 121–44.

[18] Julius Theodor and Chanokh Albeck, *Bereschit Rabba* (in Hebrew) (Jerusalem: Wahrmann Books, 1965), 70:19 (819).

[19] Feldman, "Josephus' Portrait of Jacob," 115.

[20] Cf. Claus Westermann (*Genesis 12–36* [Minneapolis: Augsburg, 1985], 438): "The author's intention is to attribute this deliberately calculated initiative entirely to Rebekah; one cannot therefore entitle the chapter, 'Jacob cheats Esau of the blessing of the firstborn.' The motive must be sought with Rebekah, not with

others and in particular to Rebecca. Rebecca's motivation is explained on the grounds that she was simply making sure that God's plan would not be frustrated and that Jacob would receive the blessing promised to him in the womb (Gen 25:23).[21] Rebecca, knowing her husband, who was no stranger to performing a deceptive act himself,[22] knew what was required to be done and prepared Jacob accordingly. The text itself offers much supporting evidence for this point of view. Rebecca is in fact the initiator of the deception (v. 8)[23] and takes full responsibility for anything that might go wrong by offering to take the curse upon herself should things go awry (v. 13). She knows how to treat goats as "false" game[24] and is able to prepare Jacob for any feeling, smelling, and taste tests he may have to undergo.[25] She issues commands to Jacob (vv. 8–10) and is involved not only in the planning but also in the execution of the plan (she prepared a dish; she took Esau's best clothes and clothed Jacob; she covered his hands; and she literally puts into his hand the dish and the bread, vv. 14–17). That Jacob was the passive partner in the preparations is clearly noted by *Genesis Rabbah,* the fifth-century haggadic or homiletical midrash on the book of Genesis: "he went and took and brought to his mother under duress, bent and weeping."[26] The twelfth to thirteenth-century Provence exegete David Kimchi (1160–1235) observed that Jacob had to go along with the deception because of his mother's command: "Furthermore, it was a command of his mother and it is written: 'you shall each revere his mother and his father.'"[27] Finally, Rebecca's suggestion

---

Jacob." Among modern Jewish commentators holding this view are Samson Raphael Hirsch (*The Pentateuch, 1: Genesis* [London: L. Honig & Sons, 1959], 441); Speiser (*Genesis,* 211); and Zakovitch ("Jacob's Cunning," 130–31).

21 W. Gunther Plaut, "The Strange Blessing: A Modern Midrash on Genesis 27," *CCAR Journal* (June 1960): 30.

22 Isaac, just like his father Abraham before him, had deceived Abimelech of Gerar by stating that Rebecca was his sister, not his wife (Gen 26:7).

23 Susan Niditch ("Genesis," *The Women's Bible Commentary* [ed. Carol A. Newsom and Sharon H. Ringe; Louisville: Westminster/John Knox, 1992], 19–20) calls Rebecca "the trickster heroine."

24 Gunkel, *Genesis,* 303.

25 "The extent of Rebekah's cunning is thus fully revealed: one might have wondered why Jacob needed his brother's garments to appear before a father incapable of seeing them—now we realize she has anticipated the possibility that Isaac would try to smell Jacob: it is Esau's smell that he detects in Esau's clothing" (Robert Alter, *Genesis* [New York: Norton, 1996], 140).

26 *Gen. Rab.* 65:14.

27 Moshe Kamelhar, *Rabbi David Kimhi's Commentary on the Pentateuch* (in Hebrew) (Jerusalem: Mossad Harav Kook, 1970), 145.

to Isaac that Jacob be sent away because of the danger of intermarriage may be considered to be another deception on her part "since she has just advised Jacob to flee for other reasons, namely to save his life from Esau."[28]

But Rebecca was not the only one to be blamed for the deception. Some biblical scholars held that Isaac himself was complicit in the affair. In his commentary on the book of Genesis, Rashbam (Samuel ben Meir, 1085–1174) hinted at this possibility: "Isaac furthermore realized that Jacob had done everything at Rebecca's suggestion."[29] If he was complicit, then a number of questions in the text might be explained.

1. Why did he allow Rebecca to listen to his conversation with Esau (v. 5) to alert her of his intentions?[30]

2. Why did he pretend not to be able to recognize Jacob? After all, how could Isaac really have confused the brothers?[31] He was able to tell their voices apart. He was able to recognize Esau just from his one word response הנני when he first called him in (v. 1)[32] and he did recognize Jacob's voice: "the voice is the voice of Jacob" (v. 22).

3. Why did he pretend to be able to recognize Esau's skin? For in feeling Jacob's arms, how could Isaac have mistaken the texture of goat skin for human skin?

4. Why did he pretend not to notice the switch of domesticated meat for game?[33] How could he have accepted the taste of lamb, no matter how expertly prepared, for the taste of venison?[34]

---

[28] Fishbane, "Composition and Structure in the Jacob Cycle," 26.

[29] Comment on v. 33, see David Razin, *Commentary on the Torah by Samuel Ben Meir (Rashbam 1085–1174)* (in Hebrew) (1882; repr., New York: Om, 1949), 33. Rashbam's surmise has been revived recently by some modern Jewish writers: W. Gunther Plaut, "The Strange Blessing," 30–34; Adrien Janis Bledstein, "Binder, Trickster, Heel and Hairy-Man: Rereading Genesis 27 As a Trickster Tale Told by a Woman," in *A Feminist Companion to Genesis* (ed. Athalya Brenner; FCB 2; Sheffield: JSOT Press, 1993), 282–95; Burton L. Visotzky, *The Genesis of Ethics* (New York: Crown, 1996), 152.

[30] Bledstein ("Binder, Trickster, Heel and Hairy-Man," 287) suggested that Isaac was acting as a trickster trying to decide which of his two sons is clever enough to receive his blessing. According to *Midr. Tanḥ.* (Sholomo Buber, *Midrash Tanḥuma to the Pentateuch* [in Hebrew] [New York: Sefer, 1946], 71) Isaac intended also to bless Jacob but started with the older brother first.

[31] See Visotzky, *The Genesis of Ethics,* 152.

[32] Plaut, "The Strange Blessing," 32.

[33] Ibid., 33. Visotzky, *The Genesis of Ethics,* 152.

[34] But Rashi (on v. 10) was of the opinion that goat meat can be made to taste like venison.

5. Why did he refrain from blessing Jacob with the Abrahamic blessing of progeny and land?[35] Was this departure from the traditional blessing Isaac's way of demonstrating to Rebecca that he was aware all along of her plans?[36]

6. Why did he tremble with fear when Esau entered (v. 33)? David Kimchi suggested that Isaac's fear was not genuine. He was just feigning the fear because "he did not want Esau to think that Isaac had blessed Jacob intentionally."[37] He could offer as an excuse that he was duped. Blessing Jacob was not Isaac's fault because Jacob came במרמה, "deceitfully."[38]

This reading would suggest that Isaac intended in advance to bless Jacob but needed an excuse to mollify Esau such as that he, Isaac, had been the victim of deceit.[39] If Isaac was complicit then this would also explain why Isaac can later bless Jacob without reprimand despite the deception recently played upon him.[40]

A more popular variant of the attempt to shift the blame for the deception from Jacob to Isaac is the one that holds that Isaac misled himself. This point of view was championed by both the rabbis and the church fathers.[41] Those parts of the story where it is thought that Jacob lied have been misunderstood. The two verses in which Jacob appears to make straightforward declarations to Isaac that he is in fact Esau have to be interpreted differently. When this is done one will see that there is actually no lie in the text. In verse 19 Isaac asks Jacob: מי אתה בני, "Who are you my son?" and Jacob replies: אנכי עשׂו בכרך, "I am Esau your firstborn." The key is that Jacob's reply has to be taken as two independent declarative statements, the first being אנכי, "I," and the second being עשׂו בכרך,

---

[35] See above p. 294.

[36] Cf. Bledstein, "Binder, Trickster, Heel and Hairy-Man," 289.

[37] Kamelhar, *Rabbi David Kimhi's Commentary,* 146.

[38] Cf. Plaut, "The Strange Blessing," 33.

[39] Ibid., 34. Similarly Visotzky, *The Genesis of Ethics,* 151–52.

[40] It should be noted that the general consensus of critics is that Gen 27 is to be ascribed to J, whereas Gen 28 is to be ascribed to P so that the Isaac of Gen 28 is not necessarily aware of events occurring in Gen 27. However, even in a diachronic reading one would have to wonder why a later editor would have put these two narratives together if it was really believed that Isaac had been deceived by Jacob.

[41] From Théodoret (fourth century) to Thomas Aquinas (1225–1274), see Roland de Vaux, *La Genèse* (Paris: Cerf, 1951), 125–26. In his revision of the Douay Rheims Latin translation from the Vulgate, Bishop Richard Challoner (eighteenth century) noted that St. Augustine (354–430, *Contra mendacium,* ch. 10) excuses Jacob from a lie. He himself comments that "if there were any lie in the case, it could be no more than an officious and venial one" (*The Holy Bible: Douay Rheims Version* [Rockford, Ill: Tan Books, 1971], 32).

"Esau is your firstborn." The *Midrash Tanḥuma* (dating from the eighth to tenth centuries) explains: "You might think that Jacob lied, but he did not lie for Balaam said 'there is no iniquity in Jacob' (Num 23:21). But in fact what happened was he made two statements: 'He said "I am Jacob" and "Esau is your firstborn."'"[42] This interpretation was popularized by Rashi, (Solomon ben Isaac, 1040–1105), the most famous and most widely quoted of the Jewish medieval commentators. He connected the first sentence with Jacob's mission of bringing food to his father: "One might think that this statement indicates that Jacob was lying, but in fact this phrase ought to be understood as two, the first being 'I am the one who is bringing you (food)' and the second being 'and Esau is your firstborn.'" The significance in Jacob's use of the personal pronoun אנכי (rather than אני) was noted by Judah Loew ben Bezalel (1525–1609),[43] who observed that when Jacob introduced himself to his father he used אנכי, but Esau, when he introduced himself, used אני (v. 32). Judah Loew believed that there was a distinction between the two pronouns, that אנכי is disjunctive and can stand alone, but אני is conjunctive and must be joined to what follows. Hence, Esau said "I am your son, Esau, your first born" using אני, but Jacob avoided using אני, using instead אנכי, which can stand by itself. According to Judah Loew, the text (of Scripture) thus proves that Jacob did not lie.[44]

Others interpreted the specific choice of pronoun used by Jacob more homiletically. In *Genesis Rabbah* a connection was made between Jacob's use of the pronoun אנכי and the fact that this pronoun is the same one with which the Ten Commandments start (Exod 20:2; Deut 5:6): "Rabbi Levi said, אנכי means: 'I am the one (who will in the future) receive the Ten

---

[42] Buber, *Midrash Tanḥuma,* 66. Similarly the twelfth-century northern French biblical exegete Bechor Shor (Joseph ben Isaac): "He did not lie to his father but when he was asked 'who are you?' answered 'I' that was the normal way to respond, then he added 'Esau is your firstborn'" (Yehoshua Navo, *Commentary on the Torah by Joseph Bekor Shor* [in Hebrew] [Jerusalem: Mossad Harav Kook, 1994], 46) and the eleventh- to twelfth-century Spanish biblical commentator Ibn Ezra (Abraham Ibn Ezra, 1092–1167): "Some say, Heaven forbid that a prophet should lie. We must therefore interpret Jacob's words to his father as follows: 'I am who I am' and 'Esau is thy first born'" (H. N. Strickman and A. M. Silver, *Ibn Ezra's Commentary on the Pentateuch: Genesis (Bereshit)* [New York: Menorah Publishing Company, 1988], 262).

[43] Judah Loew, also known as the Maharal from Prague, was one of Rashi's supercommentators; that is, he wrote a commentary on Rashi's commentary.

[44] Joshua David Hartman, *The Complete Gur Aryeh (Judah Loew Ben Bezalel [1525–1609]) on the Pentateuch,* vol. 2, *Toldot–Wayehi* (in Hebrew) (Jerusalem: Machon Jerusalem, 1990), 38.

Commandments' but עשו בכרך, 'Esau is your firstborn.'"[45] By linguistically associating Jacob with the Ten Commandments the midrash attempts "to dissociate him from blatant falsehood."[46]

The same type of reason was applied to the second verse thought to be another indication of Jacob's deception. In verse 24 Isaac asks Jacob, אתה זה בני עשו, "Are you really my son Esau?" to which Jacob answers simply אָנִי, "I am." The disjunctive force of אָנִי is emphasized by Rashi, who implies that Jacob did not actually lie: "He did not say, I am Esau' (אֲנִי עשו), but 'I am' (אָנִי)."[47] Because there is no interrogative ה before אתה some exegetes took the phrase as declarative:[48] "You are indeed my son Esau." Thus Rashbam (Samuel ben Meir, 1085–1174) comments that the meaning of the phrase is: "you appear to be my son, Esau."[49] Likewise, the seventeenth to eighteenth-century kabbalist Hayyim ibn Attar (Or Hachayim, 1696–1743), comments: "the verse is not a question. Jacob's reaction was a simple 'I' (confirming that Isaac was correct, of course)."[50] Interpreting the phrase in this manner would not make Jacob culpable because he is simply affirming Isaac's statement.

The second major Jewish traditional response to Jacob's deception was to justify it. One way of doing that was to claim that at the time of the blessing Jacob was the legal Esau. The sale of the birthright by Esau to Jacob in the pottage episode (Gen 25:27–34) justified any later deception by Jacob of his father. Jacob had already acquired the rights of the firstborn. Since Esau had sold him these rights *Jacob was now the legal Esau,* hence he could legitimately respond to his father's question in verse 19 "Who are you?" with "I am Esau your firstborn." This opinion is found in the commentary of Abrabanel (Isaac ben Judah 1437–1508), who wrote: "After Jacob bought the birthright from Esau who had sold it freely, he was entitled to say to his father 'I am Esau your firstborn' ... because he had

[45] Theodor and Albeck, *Bereschit Rabba,* 730. So also in *Yalqut Shimoni,* a thirtheenth- to fourteenth-century midrashic compilation (Isaac Shiloni, *Yalqut Shimoni. Book of Genesis* [in Hebrew] [Jerusalem: Mossad Harav Kook, 1973], 547–48.

[46] So Moshe Aryeh Mirkin, *Bereshit Rabbah* (in Hebrew) (Tel-Aviv: Yavneh, 1958), 47.

[47] Similarly, Bechor Shor (see Navo, *Commentary on the Torah,* 46).

[48] This grammatical detail was pointed out by David Kimchi: "despite the absence of the interrogative ה, it is a question" (Kamelhar, *Rabbi David Kimhi's Commentary,* 145).

[49] Razin, *Commentary on the Torah,* 32, and Martin Lockshin, *Rabbi Samuel Ben Meir's Commentary on Genesis (Rashbam)* (Lewiston, N.Y.: Mellen, 1989), 155 n. 3.

[50] Eliyahu Munk, *Or Hachayim: Commentary on the Torah by Rabbi Chayim Ben Attar,* vol. 1, *Genesis* (Jerusalem: Eliyahu Munk, 1995), 225.

the legal right of the firstborn."[51] Simililarly, Hayyim ibn Attar observed: "Jacob meant that seeing he had purchased the birthright from Esau, he was now the legal Esau."[52]

On the other hand, other commentators looked on the deception in theological terms. Justification for Jacob's conduct was based on the fact that the blessing had already been prenatally promised by God to Jacob when Rebecca consulted the oracle: "two nations are in your womb, two separate peoples shall issue from your body; one people shall be mightier than the other, and the older shall serve the younger" (Gen 25:23). Since Jacob was destined to be the beneficiary of the divine promise, Jacob was only taking what was rightfully his. That Jacob was divinely chosen over Esau is reinforced by the postexilic prophet Malachi: "The Lord says, 'Esau is Jacob's brother, is he not? Yet I have loved Jacob'" (1:2). Jacob's deception was thus necessary because without it the divine plan might have been thwarted. Yes, Jacob deceived his father, but it was necessary because "the goal justifies the means."[53] David Kimchi expressed this point of view as follows:

> How is it possible that Jacob a righteous and God-fearing man could deceive? Because Jacob knew that he was more fitting than his brother for the blessing of his brother ... and deception in circumstances like this is not a matter of shame or disrepute to a righteous person. A similar deception was initiated by God himself with Samuel when he was commanded to: "take a heifer and say 'I have come to sacrifice to the Lord'" (1 Sam 16:2). Likewise, Abraham and Isaac said that their wives were their sisters and this was not considered deception because they were fearful of their lives.[54]

The same reasoning is found in the commentaries of Ibn Ezra (Abraham Ibn Ezra, 1092–1167) and in that of Hezekiah ben Manoah, the thirteenth-century French biblical exegete. They pointed to other examples of this principle where biblical characters found it necessary to engage in

---

[51] Isaac Abravanel, *Commentary on the Pentateuch* (in Hebrew) (Jerusalem: Bnei Arbael, 1964), 309.

[52] Munk, *Or Hachayim,* 224–25. Cf. also the commentary of the nineteenth-century East European rabbi and biblical exegete Malbim (Meir Loeb Ben Jechiel Michael, 1809–1879): "Yet, he was not lying; he was saying: 'I am Esau in that I am your first born; although I am actually Jacob, buying the birthright of Esau rendered me, in this respect, not Jacob but Esau'" (Zvi Faier, *Malbim. Commentary on the Torah by Meir Leibus Ben Yechiel Michel [1809–1879]* [Jerusalem: Hillel, 1979], 2:371).

[53] M. Malul, "*ʿAqeb* 'Heel' and *ʿAqab* 'To Supplant,'" 211.

[54] Kamelhar, *Rabbi David Kimhi's Commentary,* 145.

deception where the "goal justifies the means." Thus David "perverted the truth" with Ahimelech when he said that the vessels of the young men were consecrated (1 Sam 21:6). Also the prophet Elisha did not speak the truth when he said to Hazael to tell Ben Hadad that he would recover (2 Kgs 8:10) because he knew he would die from his illness. Similarly Abraham said to Abimelech that Sarah was his sister (Gen 20:12) and lied to his young men, saying that "The boy and I will go up there; we will worship and we will return to you" (Gen 22:5) when he knew that he intended to offer Isaac as a burnt offering.[55]

But if "the goal justifies the means" then Jacob, in doing what he had to do, was acting not deceitfully but adroitly. Rabbinic commentators generally interpret במרמה (v. 35) as בחוכמה "wisely," "cunningly," or "cleverly."[56] *Targum Neofiti* adds בסוגי חכמתא "with good cunning"[57] and *Genesis Rabbah,* בחכמת תורתו "with the wisdom of his law."[58] *Midrash Tanḥuma* observes: "Can it be said that the righteous man (Jacob) acted with deceit (במרמה), God forbid! but he came with trickery (ברמיות)."[59] Here "trickery," רמיות, has the connotation of outsmarting—a sort of legal deception.[60] Likewise, at verse 36 in Esau's derogatory explication of Jacob's name, ויעקבני זה פעמים, he has supplanted[61] me twice," *Targum Onqelos* reads וחכמני, "he has outsmarted me"[62] and Rashi נתחכם לי "he outwitted me."[63]

---

[55] Moseh Charaz, *Commentary of Ibn Ezra [1092–1167] on the Pentateuch,* vol. 1, *Genesis* (in Hebrew) (Jerusalem: Chamad, 1983), 190. Chayim David Shavel, *Hizekuni: Commentary on the Torah by Rabbi Hezekiah Ben Manoah* (in Hebrew) (Jerusalem: Mossad Harav Kook, 1981), 105.

[56] See Moses Aberbach and B. Grossfeld, *Targum Onkelos to Genesis* (Hoboken, N.J.: Ktav, 1982), 165; and Rashi.

[57] A. Diez Macho, ed., *Targum Palestinense in Pentateuchum* (Biblia Polyglotta Matritensia Series; Madrid: Consejo Superior de Investigaciones Cientificas, 1980), 1:xxx.

[58] Theodor and Albeck, *Bereschit Rabba,* 758; cf. Shiloni, *Yalqut Shimoni,* 562. "This means that wisdom gained in lofty pursuits can be utilised for ignoble ends also" (*Midrash Rabbah: Genesis* [trans. H. Freedman; London: Soncino, 1939], 609 n. 2).

[59] Buber, *Midrash Tanhuma,* 72.

[60] Aberbach and Grossfeld, *Targum Onkelos to Genesis,* 165 n. 11.

[61] Or "deceived." For the apparent semantic shift of the root עקב from "to supplant" to "to cheat," see Malul, "*ʿAqeb* 'Heel' and *ʿAqab* 'To Supplant,'" 211–12.

[62] Aberbach and Grossfeld, *Targum Onkelos to Genesis,* 166. Rashi cites another *Tg. Onq.* variant וכמני, "he lied in wait for me." But *Tg. Neof.* reads עקב יתי, "he has supplanted me."

[63] But other rabbinic commentators interpret ויעקבני, "he deceived me," e.g. *Tg. Ps.-J.* ושקר, and Ibn Ezra, כמו מרמה "like deceit" (Charaz, *Commentary of Ibn Ezra,*

With these interpretations the rabbis anticipated those modern scholars who maintain that in biblical times deception and lying by hero figures was considered highly laudatory and that shrewd opportunism of a clever trickster was much appreciated.[64] In this view, our story is one of an ancestral hero who employs classic trickster techniques to outdo his rival. Examples of trickster-type material may be found throughout the ancient Near East and the classical world,[65] and it is quite clear that in our story Jacob does seem to fit the part of the trickster.[66] In fact, he calls himself by that very term (מתעתע, "trickster," v. 12) when he voices concern to Rebecca that the scheme might not work and he be thought of as a bad trickster. He is not so much worried about deceiving his father, only that he would be found out.[67] As it happens Jacob meets all the tests that Isaac puts to him. He is able to give him adequate answers about his identity (vv. 18, 24) and how he succeeded so quickly (v. 20). Thanks to Rebecca's preparations he also succeeds with three of the nonverbal tests: the feel-

---

192). Note David Kimchi's rendering "because he made his hands hairy" (Kamelhar, *Rabbi David Kimhi's Commentary,* 146).

[64] Cf. Gunkel (*Genesis,* 301): "Since in the figure of 'Jacob,' hearers and narrators discern themselves. It is entire impossible that the successors of Jacob would have recounted something shameful of their hero or ancestor. Rather they were originally recounted in praise of the hero and his successor. One cannot have seen sin and shame in these deceits, but only amusing, successful pranks." Some of the scholars who have developed this theme in recent years are Kathleen A. Farmer, "The Trickster Genre in the Old Testament" (Ph.D. diss; Southern Methodist University, 1978; Ann Arbor: University Microfilms, 1978); David Marcus, "David the Deceiver and David the Dupe," *Prooftexts* 6 (1986): 163–71; and Susan Niditch, *Underdog and Tricksters: A Prelude to Biblical Folklore* (San Francisco: Harper & Row, 1987).

[65] For example in the Epic of Gilgamesh (Ea), Story of Adapa (Ea), Descent of Ishtar (Ea), Poor Man of Nippur (poor man), The Tale of Aqhat (Anat), Contest of Horus and Seth (Seth/Isis), Myth of Illuyankas (Inaras), The Odyssey (Athena/Odysseus), etc. See also Cyrus H. Gordon, "Homer and Bible: The Origin and Character of East Mediterranean Literature," *HUCA* 26 (1955): 74; and Hendel, *The Epic of the Patriarch,* 122–28.

[66] Hendel (*The Epic of the Patriarch,* 113) points out another episode where Jacob is seen playing his role as the trickster and where he is also a participant involving a change of blessings from a firstborn to a youngest son. In Gen 48, in a scene that resonates with the one in Gen 27, instead of the blind father being deceived by his youngest son, the blind grandfather (Jacob/Israel) deceives the father (Joseph) by bestowing the blessing of the firstborn (Manasseh) onto the youngest son (Ephraim).

[67] Cf. Alter (*Genesis,* 139): "It is surely noteworthy that Jacob expresses no compunction, only fear of getting caught."

ing test (vv. 21–22), the taste test (v. 25), and the smell test (v. 27). But he does not succeed with the voice test, since Isaac realizes that "the voice is the voice of Jacob" (v. 22).

To sum up we can say that there were basically two traditional Jewish responses to the question of deceit in Gen 27, a moral one and an amoral one. The moral one acknowledged that the deception was wrong and is the reason why Jacob suffered later in life. But attempts are also made to exculpate Jacob as much as possible by trying to shift the blame of the deceit to Rebecca or even to Isaac himself. The amoral approach in effect sees nothing wrong with Jacob's conduct. It was justified either because at the time of the blessing Jacob considered himself "the legal Esau" or that, ironically for an amoral approach, the deception was necessary to accomplish God's will. The results of this theological approach where "the goal justifies the means" curiously coincide with many modern views of the narrative that sees Jacob as an ancestral hero employing classic trickster techniques to outdo his rival.

A Jewish-Feminist Reading of Exodus 1–2

Esther Fuchs

Reading Ourselves

When I first read Exod 1–2, I was a student at the elementary school for girls, "Dizengoff," in Tel Aviv. My favorite teacher, Mrs. Shechter, commented on the courage of the midwives, Shiphrah and Puah, and challenged us to explain their names. It was in the early sixties, when Nasser, the Egyptian president delivered fiery proclamations against Israel and vowed to throw the Jews into the sea. I cannot recall whether any explicit analogy was drawn between the contemporary Egyptian ruler and the ancient pharaoh, but I, for one, was well aware that then, as now, the Jews were exposed to mortal danger from Egypt. We were asked if we, the girls, would dare risk our lives to save the lives of (male) babies as did the midwives. Without hesitation my hand flew up. There was general jubilation when we read about the plagues that were visited on the Egyptians and the military losses they suffered. Each Passover the story would be retold, though less emphasis was placed on the midwives.

Years later, as a high school student at "Tichon Ironi Hei," I made the point that the midwives were politically shrewd. They fought the Egyptian leader by participating in a campaign to increase the birth rate. It was in the mid 1960s, as the growing recognition of the demographic disparity between Jews and Arabs became a national obsession. A campaign was mounted by Prime Minister David Ben-Gurion to promote Jewish births. Large families were promised tax breaks and other benefits. National survival depended on the cooperation of mothers. I was considered something of a prodigy in Tanak. My comment regarding the political aspect of the midwives' activities won praise from my much-admired teacher, Mrs. Yaeger.

But as an Israeli Jew I encountered the story of Exodus not just in school, but also in the annual celebration of Passover. As I reread the haggadah year after year it became apparent to me that subsequent persecutions of Jews in Europe bore the imprint of the very first genocidal attempt against the Jews in Egypt. The haggadah was a story of liberation and a story of triumph, the triumph of the weak over the strong, and the good over evil. The annual celebration of the exodus from Egypt was the context that permitted the celebrants to think about other historical tragedies, the persecutions and expulsions of Jews from medieval Europe, the pogroms in eastern Russia in the nineteenth century, the Holocaust, the distress of Soviet Jews in the 1950s. Egypt became a metaphor for the Diaspora. The ritual of the Seder transformed the bitterness of the back-breaking labor of the Israelites in Egypt into the pleasant bitterness of the maror, while the mortar the slaves used for bricks had the inviting taste of the haroset. The Seder was all about order, four questions, four answers, four sons, four cups of wine. The Seder, which means order, imposed coherence and logic, meaning and significance on what may otherwise seem chaotic and terrifying. The Seder was the scene that permitted the very young to be initiated into an inexorable genealogy whose progenitors were heroic men of great repute, such as Moses, who overcame the mighty Egyptian king. No one, including myself, noticed that in the retelling of the story of the exodus, the midwives, the mother and the sister of Moses, as well as the pharaoh's daughter all but disappeared. No one noticed that the four children for which the story of the exodus was meant were male, and no one noticed that the haroset and the maror were prepared by women, while the men led the Seder year after year. After all, women too recited from the haggadah, women too ate the meals, and women too drank four cups. Again, women had a double role, that of Jews and that of women; the same but different, equal but complementary, subject and object, independent yet peripheral.

In the early 1980s I began to publish feminist criticism of contemporary Hebrew male-authored fiction. I called attention to the exclusions and distortions of women in Israeli mythogynies, or myths about women.[1] In a secular modern culture, why should women be stereotyped as confined, male-related characters? Furthermore, why were women so often presented as sinister national enemies, as the enemy within? How did the national ethos come to be figured as male-centered? I began to realize that the disruption of modernity, notably the Enlightenment and secularism, was a transference rather than a revolution. It transferred the locus of meaning from a male deity to a male human subject. Women in both scenarios remained excluded. If the new context was national, then women had to be excluded from national meaning. Women were allowed to live on the periphery. Like the midwives, like the mother and sister of Moses, they were necessary, but they were a means to an end. The biblical women were exceptions, and in subsequent retellings they could be ignored without causing any structural damage to the male edifice. Similarly, women in modern Israel—Henrietta Szold, Sarah Aharonson, Hannah Senesh, Rachel, Golda

---

[1] Esther Fuchs, *Israeli Mythogynies: Women in Contemporary Hebrew Fiction* (Albany, N.Y.: State University of New York Press, 1987).

Meir—were exceptions. They were means to a greater end, the end of national sovereignty and victory. They could be dismissed or ignored in subsequent retellings. Their omission did not dismantle the master's house. The national house was a house built with male arms, and male muscles, for male children. In other words, modern secular national constructions of identity continued the biblical logic of ambivalent inclusion. In times of crisis women are permitted to figure as rescuers. But as soon as the crisis is over, the women disappear. Women are not completely suppressed; they are allowed to fulfill certain roles, within certain limits, in certain contexts. But in essence, this role is secondary.

When women read male-constructed texts what do they do? Patrocinio Schweickart suggests that female readers automatically obliterate their subject position and begin to imagine themselves as the male-constructed women acting out male-constructed myths, or "mythogynies."[2] In Schweickart's words, "The process of immasculation is latent in the text, but it finds its actualization only through the reader's activity. In effect, the woman reader is the agent of her own immasculation."[3] In other words, when women read male-authored texts, they absorb them as if the female readers were in the male position; they identify with the masculinist ideology of the text, they become immasculated, they look at themselves and at the world as men. When I read the Hebrew Bible as an Israeli/Jewish adult woman I am not only already immasculated but also nationalized and Judaized, as it were. To the extent that the process of immasculation puts me at war with my own gender, this process is harmful to my growth and development as a person and as a reader. When I call attention to the ideological constructions of women in the Hebrew biblical text, I am ultimately reading myself; I am seeking to undo my own past immasculations, my own co-opting by a masculinist ideology.

The following reading of Exod 1–2 is an attempt at deconstructing the immasculating process as it unfolds in the text and as it already has come to construct me as a reader. The immasculating process constructs me as female as less of an Israeli and less of a Jew. It constructs me as an "Other" in my own cultural text. By questioning this process and by uncovering its procedures I seek to question the relationship of Jewish national identity formation and gender. Regina Schwartz has recently writ-

---

[2] Patrocinio P. Schweickart, "Reading Ourselves: Toward a Feminist Theory of Reading," in *Gender and Reading: Essays on Readers, Texts and Contexts* (ed. Elizabeth A. Flynn and Patrocinio P. Schweickart; Baltimore: Johns Hopkins University Press, 1986), 31–62. "Mythogynies" is a term I coined for practical purposes, to refer briefly to male-narrated or male-written stories (or narratives) about women. This term is defined and used broadly in my book *Israeli Mythogynies*.

[3] "Reading Ourselves," 49.

ten about the fictional constructions of national identity in the Hebrew Bible.[4] I agree with Schwartz that the biblical narrative offers us fictions of identity and that these fictions are based in a conception of scarcity and therefore the need for violence. Schwartz argues that the Bible accommodates various ideologies in conflict with each other. I, however, do not believe that biblical patriarchalism is at war with itself. I do not believe that in the Hebrew Bible we find both female and male voices.[5] What we find are prevarications, distortions, suppressions, and repressions of female voices. In this essay I argue that the suppression of the female voice is one of the necessary methods through which biblical national identity structures itself. The violent process of immasculation is in progress in the text, because it is one of the necessary features of the formation of the national fiction of identity.

Rereading Exodus 1–2

The first chapters of Exodus present us with three groups of women. Each group is variously tied to the character of Moses. The first two groups may be categorized as mother-figures, the third group as wife-figures. The first two groups consist of women who function in one way or another as enablers; they enable the safe birth of a male child. The third group consists of wife-figures in the sense that they function as potential brides for a male hero. As we shall see, the first two groups of women are characterized as active, eloquent, and intelligent. They are affirmed. The third group of the potential wives emerges as passive, lacking in initiative and not terribly alert. The collective wife-figure is ambiguated. This corresponds to a general pattern in the Hebrew Bible, which I discussed in several articles published in the mid and late 1980s.[6] Mothers in the Hebrew Bible give birth to male babies and go all out to preserve their sons' lives and protect their interests (Rebecca, Bathsheba). Women are valorized in their maternal roles as long as they ensure a patrilineal genealogy (e.g., Tamar, Judah's daughter-in-law; Ruth). In the book of Genesis, a succession of barren wives become mothers through the intervention of a male

---

[4] Regina M. Schwartz, *The Curse of Cain: The Violent Legacy of Monotheism* (Chicago: University of Chicago Press, 1997).

[5] That the Hebrew Bible is composed of female poetic texts as well as male texts is a thesis proposed by Athalya Brenner and Fokkelien van Dijk-Hemmes in *On Gendering Texts: Female and Male Voices in the Hebrew Bible* (Leiden: Brill, 1993).

[6] See, for example, "The Literary Characterization of Mothers and Sexual Politics in the Hebrew Bible," in *Feminist Perspectives on Biblical Scholarship* (ed. Adela Yarbro Collins; Atlanta: Scholars Press, 1985), 117–36. See also "Structure and Patriarchal Functions in the Biblical Betrothal Type-Scene: Some Preliminary Notes," *JFSR* 3 (Spring 1987): 7–14.

deity, YHWH, who intends to reward the righteousness of their husbands. As soon as their maternal role is completed, these women disappear from the narrative, which is subsequently taken over by their husbands or sons. The recognition that the text is inspired by a patriarchal ideology that constructs mothers as "good" is what drove Cheryl Exum to move from an appreciative description of the role of women in the first two chapters of Exodus to a critical analysis of their marginalization and fragmentation.[7]

In what follows I would like to extend Exum's second analysis. The mother-figures who are further from the male object of concern are presented in more positive terms than the mother-figures who are closer and more directly involved in his rescue. While it may have been safe to credit the quasi-mothers, the midwives, with strength, faith, and resourcefulness, it may not have been so safe to credit the actual mother or even the sister with such qualities. In other words, there is a process of affirmation and ambiguation at work in the characterization of both groups, but ambiguation is more prominent in the characterization of those mother-figures who are presented as directly responsible for the survival and preservation of the male baby. The biblical narrator both promotes and undercuts the status of mother-figures; they are valued, but they must not emerge as too important. The very multiplicity of women in various maternal roles ensures that not one of them should be privileged as having secured the life of Israel's leader and redeemer. The complementarity of their roles displays their mutual dependence. The biological mother could never have secured the life of her male baby without the crucial assistance of the midwives, the sister, and Pharaoh's daughter.

The Midwives

Exodus 1 describes in some detail the hard labor the pharaoh inflicts on the Israelites in order to prevent an insurrection (Exod 1:10). But the Israelites seem to multiply in number (Exod 1:12). This does not please the Egyptian monarch, though presumably he could make use of a large workforce. The monarch decides to embark on a genocidal plan. But instead of sending his oppressed slaves to fight a dangerous battle, he opts for an especially cowardly and cruel plan. He turns to two Hebrew midwives, whose names he seems to know. The mighty Egyptian ruler turns to women in an attempt to deal with a perceived political threat. He asks them to kill the Hebrew male babies on the birthing stool, before their mothers have a

---

[7] See Cheryl Exum, "You Shall Let Every Daughter Live: A Study of Exodus 1:8–2:10," in *A Feminist Companion to Exodus to Deuteronomy* (ed. Athalya Brenner; FCB 6; Sheffield: Sheffield Academic Press, 1994), 37–61; idem, "Second Thoughts about Secondary Characters: Women in Exodus 1:8–2:10," in *A Feminist Companion,* 75–87.

chance to see them. The ruler of Egypt is out to deceive Israelite mothers and to kill Israelite babies: "if it is a boy, kill him; but if it is a girl, she shall live" (Exod 1:16). Shiphrah and Puah do not obey the pharaoh. The midwives have what the pharaoh lacks: the fear of God (v. 17). They do not do as they are told. Instead, they let the children, ילדים (rather than "sons"—בנים), live. When called to task by the irate monarch, the midwives use deception to defend their actions. They tell the pharaoh that the Hebrew mothers are too quick to give birth, that they give birth even before they have a chance to help with the delivery (Exod 1:19). This monarch learns the names of Hebrew midwives, rather than knowing the name of Joseph, his predecessor's chief assistant (Exod 1:8). He is prejudiced enough to believe that Hebrew women are physiologically different from Egyptian women. He is stupid enough to turn to Hebrew women and ask them to deceive and kill their own people. This pharaoh is so stupid he does not even bribe the midwives or reward them. It is God who is said to make houses for them (Exod 1:24). Frustrated and confused, the pharaoh orders his entire people to throw every single newborn son into the Nile and to let every daughter live. This new instruction does not even specify that the newborn male baby must be Hebrew. That all male babies should be drowned in the Nile is indeed an edict that only a fool or a madman could issue.

The juxtaposition of the God-fearing, poor, courageous, and resourceful midwives with the mighty but cowardly and stupid king uses gender to undercut the antagonist. The Israelite story uses Shiphrah and Puah—women who have never been mentioned before and who will never be heard from again—as a satiric weapon against Israel's prototypical enemy. The scene of defeat is not the battlefield but rather the female-dominated realm replete with terms referring to conception and delivery, birthstools, and babies. The story pokes fun at the enemy by presenting his demise at the hands of women.[8] The midwives are valorized, even idealized at the expense of the pharaoh. The dialogue and action confront the gullible enemy with resourceful midwives. He is rejected, while they are endorsed. The midwives participate in the production of a national ethos. And yet they are permitted to play a crucial role on the boundary that is constructed between Israelites and Egyptians. They are privileged, named, and said to be rewarded by God, but only in their capacity as the pharaoh's antagonists. But as the national story continues to unfold, they soon are submerged in a narrative gap, as it were. They become casualties of a narratological ending. They are not valorized in their capacity as the saviors of Moses. In fact there is a break between their story and the story of the birth of Moses. It is not too clear whether and to what extent the midwives

---

[8] The possibility of being killed by a woman is presented as a source of great shame in the case of Abimelech, son of Jerubbaal, in the book of Judges.

played any role in Moses' birth. My argument is that it is the ambiguity of the relationship between the midwives and Moses that allows them to emerge as valorized.

Mother, Sister, Surrogate Mother

Chapter 2 begins with a reference to an anonymous man from the house of Levi who takes the daughter of Levi (Exod 2:1). This nameless woman gives birth to a son (Exod 2:2). What follows may strike us as a bit odd: "and as she saw him that he was good, she hid him for three months."[9] Does the verse indicate that had the baby not been "good," that his mother may have thrown him out into the Nile? The predicate "and she saw him" suggests that he was good-looking, that what the woman values is the exterior features of the baby, that she is pleased with his physical features. There is no insight here into something deeper or more momentous. The next verse is similar in both affirming and ambiguating the mother. The verse declares, but fails to explain, why the mother can no longer hide the baby. It then goes on to tell us that she made an ark of bulrushes, daubed it with slime and pitch. Is this a fitting and safe enclosure for a baby?[10] Why did the mother not hide the baby in a more secure environment? Why did she end up putting the ark by the bank of the river? If she felt compassion for the child, she surely was not terribly effective. Considering the previous story of the midwives, who fearlessly challenged the pharaoh, who came up with excuses, who did not hesitate to deceive and to con the monarch himself, the nameless mother emerges as unimaginative at best. She both obeys and disobeys the edict to throw every male baby into the Nile. She both protects the baby but at the same time exposes him to possible danger. The narrator then credits the mother with the physiological birth, but the preservation of the baby is a credit shared by two other nameless women, his sister and the pharaoh's daughter. Her ability to later suckle the baby is a reward of sorts, but it is a temporary one, and she is paid for this service. God does not intervene to reward the mother, as he is said to do in the previous story. Neither is the mother said to be particularly God-fearing, as the midwives are said to be. There is in fact nothing particularly striking about her. She is attached to a string of actions and to practically no adjectives that might give us an illusion of interiority or subjectivity. The mother is capable of seeing a nice-looking or healthy baby. She can only see an exterior façade. The mother then is reduced to a physiological function that is cut down and reduced by her subsequent actions. The narrative

[9] Rashi, who must have noticed this, explains that as soon as Moses was born, the entire house began to shine.

[10] Again Rashi explains that the pitch was smeared on the outside as insulating matter, so as not to expose the righteous man to the malodorous material.

makes it clear that without the intervention of the baby's sister, the inept mother may have risked her own baby's life.

But the sister is ambiguated as well. She too is nameless. Her connection to her mother is not clear. Was she told to stand guard and watch over the baby, or did she do so independently? The sister is said to stand from afar (v. 4). Was the sister afraid to stand closer by the river, closer to the ark? What did the sister expect at this point? The text explains that the sister stands watch in order to find out what would be done to him. The text then attributes to the sister a will to know, curiosity. But the text stops here. It does not ascribe to the sister any adjectives, any emotional descriptors. The nameless and ageless sister—it is not clear if she is a girl or a grown woman, perhaps a mother herself—jumps into action when it is safe to do so. After the pharaoh's daughter finds the ark and recognizes the baby as a Hebrew child, she is quoted as saying to the princess: "Shall I go and fetch you a woman wetnurse from among the Hebrews?" (v. 7). The sister is resourceful and clever no doubt, but one assumes that the princess could have just as easily found another wetnurse. An Egyptian woman could probably have done as well. A woman of the status of the princess could surely hire the best wetnurses. Her brief response to the sister, "go," indicates a measure of impatience. The sister then serves as the link between the biological mother and the surrogate mother, but her action is not as crucial to the baby's survival as the actions of the others. Nevertheless the sister is mentioned in this story. In subsequent interpretations she will be identified as Miriam, but the text itself does not confirm this possibility.

The surrogate mother who saves the infant's life is not a biological relative. She is a foreigner. She shares neither family nor national kinship with the future savior of the Israelites. She is the pharaoh's own daughter. Once again the narrative pokes fun at the Egyptian ruler by aligning his own daughter with the Israelite cause.[11] When the princess opens the ark and sees the child, she notices a young boy crying and consequently has compassion on him.[12] The pharaoh's daughter is the only female subject who is characterized by an affective verb that explains motivation. The verb to see, ראה, is ascribed twice to the princess. But like the nameless mother, the pharaoh's daughter is moved by what most women would be moved, a crying baby. Neither woman sees more than her eyes show her. The princess then plays a crucial role in saving the baby, but she remains obliv-

---

[11] The trope of the foreign woman who sides with the Israelites appears in Josh 2 in the character of Rahab the Canaanite and later in the character of Jael the Kenite (Judg 4).

[12] Rashi explains the distinction in this verse between "the child" (ילד) and the "young boy (נער) as follows: the baby was crying with the voice of a young adult.

ious to the meaning of her actions. She pays the baby's mother for suckling him, not knowing who she is (v. 9). The princess adopts the baby; she thus effectively replaces both the mother and the sister. Finally the princess names the baby, claiming credit for saving his life: "for I drew him out of the water"; in other words, I saved his life (v. 10).

David Gunn and Danna Fewell argue for a recognition of the princess's national significance: "Where would Moses be, where would the people Israel be, where the divine promise, if not for the mothering of this foreign woman?"[13] And yet, is this not the point of the narrative? Is not the point to shift the credit of the birth of the national redeemer from mother to foreign princess? Is not the point precisely to fragment the power of motherhood among several figures and to balance them against each other? The princess is a foreigner. As such she cannot compete with the future redeemer for recognition. She is safe because she is outside the national boundary as constructed by the text. But the sister, on the other hand, is not safe. She cannot be credited with having saved his life, because she may later claim a share in the divine promise.

The women who are directly related to Moses are nameless and somewhat ambiguated. They all have a share in the preservation of his life. In fact they all depend upon each other to complete the task of preserving his life. The maternal task is fragmented, to be sure, it is splintered among five women. The women who are most directly related to Moses remain nameless. Those whose relationship is not clear are named. It is easy to see that Moses' mother, had she had to save him single-handedly from the trials and tribulations imposed upon her by a tyrant like the Egyptian pharaoh, might have emerged from the story as a heroine in her own right.

The Wife-Figures

Yet, much as they are ambiguated and constricted, the mother-figures are allowed to emerge as resourceful, collaborative, and perspicacious. This is more than we can say in regard to the wife-figures, the seven maidens who go down to the well to draw water for their father's flock.[14] The daughters of the Midianite priest are nameless.[15] More important, they are

---

[13] See Danna Nolan Fewell and David M. Gunn, *Gender, Power, and Promise: The Subject of the Bible's First Story* (Nashville: Abingdon, 1993), 93.

[14] On the trope of the well and its connection to the betrothal type-scene, see my article, "Structure and Patriarchal Functions in the Biblical Betrothal Scene."

[15] Drorah O'Donnell Setel in her article on "Exodus," in *The Women's Bible Commentary* (ed. Carol A. Newsom and Sharon H. Ringe; Louisville: Westminster/John Knox, 1992), 26–35, suggests that Zipporah may have been a priestess in her own right, that there is some allusion here to a cultic role of women in ancient

hardly distinguishable from each other. They are interchangeable. Their duty is to fill up the troughs and to water the flock. This relatively simple task is rendered impossible by the Midianite shepherds who chase them away from the well (v. 17). It is Moses who, like Jacob before him, unblocks the access to the well for a girl who will later become his wife. Zipporah, however, is only one of seven sisters. And it is not too clear what eventually singles her out as Moses' intended wife. In verse 21, "and Moses was content to dwell with the man; and he gave Moses Zipporah his daughter," the narrator does not even specify that Zipporah is "given" to Moses as a wife.

The girls who are redeemed by Moses fail to thank their benefactor, whom they take to be an Egyptian. Upon their return home, they report to their father that "an Egyptian man" watered their flock (Exod 2:19). Their father consequently rebukes them for their failure to reward the stranger for his efforts (Exod 2:20). The girls are exhorted by their father to return to the well and to invite the stranger for a meal (v. 20). The Midianite girls are told by their father what to do. They are redeemed by Moses, who proceeds to water their flock. They are weak and dependent, unlike the mother-figures in the first two groups. Even Zipporah is treated merely as a direct object who is transferred from her father to Moses. When she gave birth to a son, "he [Moses] called his name Gershom, for he said, I have been a stranger in a foreign land" (Exod 2:22).

More than anything the last group serves as a collective catalyst, as a means of enhancing the heroic features of our protagonist. They are the victims whom Moses helps out. If as mother figures women are permitted to emerge as independent and active agents, as wife-figures they are helpless and vulnerable. They are in need of male assistance. They are in effect controlled by a male authority. The wife-figures are contained within an economy of water drawing, domestic chores, that at worst pitted up against male shepherds. This conflict lacks the moral and national significance of Moses' conflict with the Egyptian taskmaster and later with the Hebrew thug. The scene at the well is preceded by two episodes that explain why Moses will later become an Israelite leader. Moses is said to rescue a man who is beaten by an Egyptian taskmaster (Exod 2:11). Later he intervenes on behalf of an Israelite who is attacked by a fellow Hebrew man (Exod 2:13). Moses' interventions on behalf of the oppressed are the actions of a future national leader. His actions in fact expose him to mortal danger at the hands of the pharaoh, who is said to want to "kill Moses" (v. 15). Moses must seek political asylum. He therefore flees to Midian. What a far cry between Moses' world of political intrigue, conflicts with oppressive

---

Israel. If this is indeed the case, then the text goes out of its way to suppress this and to cover it up.

authorities, narrow escapes, and acts of intervention on behalf of political victims and the world of women. Both the mother-figures and the wife-figures are restricted to reproductive activities (birthing, suckling) or to other physical activities such as bathing, or to domestic activities such as water drawing. In a few strokes the narrator constructs for us the male world of public action and the female world of private familial affairs.

Cheryl Exum suggests that "Exodus 1:8–2:10 serves as a kind of compensation for the fact that women are not given a role in the bulk of the account of exodus and wanderings."[16] I would like to argue that the first chapters of Exodus set the scene for the exclusion of women from any meaningful action in the story of the religious and national construction of the Israelites. These chapters justify the suppression of women in the story of the exodus and the wanderings by associating women with procreative and domestic roles. By presenting women as either mother- or wife-figures, as sisters and as daughters, they contain women within familial boundaries. The very definition of femaleness is inexorably connected to marriage, procreation, and the preservation of male lives. The first chapters of Exodus naturalize and legitimize what is in fact a fictional construction fueled by a self-serving ideology: that public meaning belongs to men. These chapters validate the subsequent exclusion of women from most of the significant narratives about the religious relationship of the people to God and the national promise of deliverance and redemption.

The construction of national identity in the first chapters of Exodus hinges on its fundamental association with masculinity. For one thing, the opening verses of Exod 1 list male names exclusively. This male genealogy lists the names of the sons of Jacob. Dinah is naturally not mentioned here. There is no explanation for the omission of Dinah. We are expected to understand that only sons can become tribal collectivities, the foundation blocks of the future national edifice; daughters do not qualify.

To some degree, the first chapters of Exodus suggest that the important functions of marriage and procreation, women's recognized preserve, may be fulfilled both by Israelite and by non-Israelite women. After all, was not Moses rescued by an Egyptian princess? Foreign women could also serve as adequate substitutes for Israelite wives. After all, did not Moses marry a Midianite wife? Indeed when Miriam is said to protest against Moses' interest in a Cushite woman in Num 12:1–2, she is struck down with leprosy and confined outside the camp. Miriam is punished as much for challenging her brother's authority as for questioning the privileging of the foreign woman. While the national identity of the Israelites is constructed by stories of conflict with powerful male foreigners, female foreigners are perceived not only as nonthreatening but also as necessary allies in the people's struggle

[16] Exum, "Second Thoughts about Secondary Characters," 85.

for survival. Thus, we will encounter in the book of Joshua Rahab the Canaanite prostitute, who offers crucial assistance to Joshua's spies, and in Judges we will meet Jael the Kenite, who is said to have killed the fearsome Sisera. We do not encounter any stories about male foreigners who rescue the Israelites. This construction is unthinkable, because the national "Other" must be male, just as the national "Subject" is male. Because women are defined as peripheral Israelites, both insiders and outsiders, because women are an integral part of the national story, they figure as both Israelite and foreign. Indeed Israelite women are permitted to figure as rescuers and leaders. In our story, the midwives are credited with rescuing many Israelite infants, but they are mentioned once. Miriam is mentioned in Exod 15 as a prophetess and the sister of Aaron. Exodus 15:20–21 introduces Miriam as a singer and a dancer who leads other women in celebrations of the national redemption. If Carol Meyers is right to posit the singing and dancing women as an ancient Israelite institution, then the story of Exodus is skillful in its ability to reinterpret the historical record in ways that diminish, distort and obliterate the national and public significance of women's roles.[17] If, similarly, Drorah Setel is right to posit that the story of the exodus is alluding to women's cultic functions as prophets and priestesses, then again, the story is very effective in its fictional reinterpretation of women as strictly and exclusively male-dependent and male-related entities.[18]

The Suppression of the Wife

It has been suggested that Zipporah, who reemerges in Exod 4:25–26, joins the other female characters in Exod 1–2 in asserting female supremacy and power. Ilana Pardes argues that Zipporah in Exod 4 stands up to YHWH himself and outwits him, in much the same way that the midwives and Moses' sister and mother outwit the pharaoh.

> The triumph of the female saviors over the mighty Pharaoh in the opening chapters of Exodus is truly wondrous and astounding, but it is still far more palatable than Zipporah's uncanny victory in "The Bridegroom of Blood." Zipporah's opponent is not merely an august father figure, but the Father Himself! By warding off YHWH, Zipporah endangers monotheistic tenets, as well as patriarchal ones.[19]

While the ambiguous text describing Zipporah's circumcision of her son and the cryptic phrase she utters have indeed mystified commentators, it

[17] See Carol Meyers, "Miriam the Musician," *A Feminist Companion,* 207–30.

[18] See Setel, "Exodus."

[19] Ilana Pardes, *Countertraditions in the Bible: A Feminist Approach* (Cambridge: Harvard University Press, 1992), 88.

is, I would argue, a bit of a stretch to extrapolate from two textually difficult verses that Zipporah outwits YHWH. After all, Zipporah is said to take a "flint" and to cut off the foreskin of her son. She thus sanctions the entrance of her son into the covenantal relationship with YHWH. She herself is not party to this covenant, because as a Midianite and a woman she cannot participate in the exclusive community of Israel.[20] The biblical narrator attributes to the woman an act of consensual collaboration with the masculine covenant cut in the male phallus. As it does in the case of polygyny, the biblical narrator would have us believe that the woman is invested in the patriarchal arrangement that patently excludes her from sites of meaning and power. Thus we are told that Sarai was behind Abram's decision to take another wife. We are told that polygyny was a woman's invention. In a similar fashion, Exod 4 would have us believe that the cutting of the covenant in male flesh, the transition of the penis from the status of a biological/functional organ to a symbol of religious and national identity, is a transition sanctioned and enabled by the wife-mother. By cutting off her son's foreskin, Zipporah cuts herself off, willingly as it were from the special covenant Moses and his son will henceforth have with YHWH.

The text attributes to Zipporah incomprehensible incantations regarding a bridegroom of blood. I would like to argue that the incomprehensibility of Zipporah's incantations reinforces on the level of discourse her national "Otherness," her Midianite identity. She understands the circumcision in terms of her own foreign national and religious culture. These terms have something to do with blood and marriage. The strangeness of her utterances point to a possible Midianite ritual or myth. The obfuscation, the inaccessibility of Zipporah's words, is part of her general characterization as an outsider. So, though Zipporah appears to deal with the divine will properly, she remains nevertheless an "Other" and a stranger. This extraordinary tale, which admits a female character into the inner sanctum of the scene of covenantal circumcision, also explains why it is the only one that does so. I would like to argue that the textual obfuscation of verses 25–26 reveals the author's attempt to suppress the wife-figure. The incident is being expressed and suppressed, traced and erased at the same time. The textual ambiguity is part of the patriarchal message.

Even if we were to agree with Pardes that the ambiguous verses are polytheistic vestiges alluding to Isis, the Egyptian goddess who hovers over the body of her husband Osiris—especially over his genitals—in an attempt to revive him, even if we were to accept that these verses are an unmediated disruption of the monotheistic text, would not the ambiguity of the text also suggest an attempt to obscure and suppress these vestiges?

---

[20] On the violent metaphor of circumcision and its relationship to the creation of national identity, see Schwartz, *The Curse of Cain,* 15–38.

In other words, to suggest that the biblical text reveals patriarchal thinking as much as it reveals disruptions, or, as Pardes calls them, "countertraditions," leaves open the question of the final editing.

My point is that the alleged "countertraditions" reveal the hand of a patriarchal editor as much as they reveal the contours of an alleged goddess. The Freudian analysis of ruptures can be used to detect ideological displacement and suppression. On the one hand, Pardes argues that Zipporah incarnates the powerful goddess Isis, but on the other hand she herself contends that the figuration of Isis as protective of her husband is in many ways a patriarchal figuration.[21] This suggests that Zipporah is not necessarily an expression of a female-centered "countertradition" at all, but rather of a patriarchal Egyptian myth. In this case, shorn of the flutter of Isis's wings, what is left of Zipporah? We are told that she cuts off her son's foreskin and that she touches it to "his" feet. Whether "his" refers to Moses, her son, or YHWH, there is nothing in this gesture to suggest female superiority.

Howard Eilberg-Schwartz suggests that Zipporah's role in the conventionally male-centered scene of the circumcision is part of the larger theme of the metaphoric emasculation, or feminization, of Israel in recent critical discourse.[22] Eilberg-Schwartz represents a larger trend in Jewish theology to co-opt feminist criticism by what Elaine Showalter defined in another context as "critical cross-dressing."[23] To him, the male gender of God should first and foremost be studied in terms of its implications for the identity of Jewish men. YHWH's attack on Moses is according to Eilberg-Schwartz an attack on his masculinity. The fundamental fear in ancient Israel is seen in this context not as gynophobia but as homophobia. It is the homophobic impulse that explains why Moses, like Jacob before him, must be emasculated. But the incident reported in Exod 4 speaks of the circumcision of Moses' son, and there is little to suggest that Moses himself becomes emasculated in this context. If circumcision implies a symbolic emasculation, why does YHWH attack Moses, who is supposedly already circumcised? Eilberg-Schwartz conflates the father and the son without explanation. Like Pardes, Eilberg-Schwartz also struggles with the meaning of Zipporah's oracular expressions. He suggests that Zipporah addresses both Moses and YHWH as a bridegroom. She tells both that she is their bride. Zipporah is presented here as a jealous woman, fearful of losing her man to another man, fearful of losing Moses to YHWH.

---

21 See Pardes, *Countertraditions in the Bible,* 94–95.

22 See Howard Eilberg-Schwartz, *God's Phallus and Other Problems for Men and Monotheism* (Boston: Beacon, 1994), 142–74.

23 Elaine Showalter, "Critical Cross-Dressing: Male Feminists and the Woman of the Year," in *Men in Feminism* (ed. Alice Jardine and Paul Smith; New York: Methuen, 1987), 116–32.

Zipporah presents "an ideal image of the Israelite woman. Israelite women are in danger of losing their men to God."[24] Eilberg-Schwartz does not explain how Zipporah, a Midianite woman, serves as the ideal image of the Israelite woman. More important, he does not question the idealization of woman as someone fearful of losing her husband. Who is doing the idealization, the patriarchal narrator who may be exemplifying Gen 3:16, or Eilberg-Schwartz? According to Eilberg-Schwartz, Zipporah is a willing participant in the male scene of triangular bonding (YHWH, Moses, his son), because she perfers to sacrifice her husband's masculinity to God, she prefers the loss of masculinity to the complete loss of the man she loves. In other words, Eilberg-Schwartz does not see Zipporah as a product of patriarchal desire but rather as a female agent, the "ideal woman" who acts in her best interests, and her best interests are to be married and stay married to her man.

To reveal and conceal Zipporah's intervention on Moses' behalf is part of the general presentation of Zipporah: it is sporadic, intermittent, partial, and ambiguous. On the one hand, she is shown to have saved her husband's life; on the other hand, we do not understand her motives, her reasoning, her words. She appears again in Exod 18, "Then Jethro, Moses' father-in-law took Zipporah, Moses' wife, after he had sent her back" (Exod 18:2). The text does not explain why Moses sent her back; it is not too clear what "sent her back" means in this context, whether it was a temporary separation agreed on by both parties or one imposed on Zipporah by Moses. The presentation of the biblical wife in general tends to be ambiguous. We are left with the impression that she does not matter as much, unless she is involved in an act that requires some kind of intervention on behalf of her husband.

Female Infanticide: A Hypothesis

But what if the story of Exodus is a fictional interpretation of a more serious historical circumstance, one that was unavoidable given the valuation of male babies? What if the first two chapters suppress the historical necessity in ancient Israel, and perhaps the ancient Near East in general, to get rid of female babies? What if the emphasis on male genealogy produced such pressure on young mothers that they had to hide the birth of their daughters, even to kill them? What if there circulated a story in ancient Israel about a woman who felt compelled to hide her baby daughter in an ark, because loath to drown her, she chose to make the baby available for adoption by a wealthy foreign person, who perhaps did not have children? Shiphrah and Puah are describing the Hebrew women as חיות, which may mean "animals" or "lively." Either way, they are portrayed

[24] Eilberg-Schwartz, *God's Phallus,* 161.

as having numerous male babies, numerous enough to create anxiety in as mighty a ruler as the pharaoh. Did women bear male babies more frequently than they bore daughters? Is the silence about daughters in the Bible connected in some fashion to the suppressed knowledge about the fate of so many female girls who were drowned or otherwise destroyed by their own mothers? Is it possible that the mothers told their husbands that their babies died on the birthing stool, so as not to reveal the painful fact that they had baby daughters rather than sons? Is it possible, then, that the story of Exodus displaces and represses a female story by exchanging male identity for female?

Ilona Rashkow suggests that several narratives in the book of Genesis reverse, displace, and repress stories about female abuse and oppression by projecting onto women the desire to be victimized or the desire to inflict this very abuse on men.[25] The story of Exod 1–2 is just such a story. It tells us about the palpable threat to the lives of male infants. It endows this threat with religious and national meaning. God himself is working behind the scene to avert this threat. The future of the Israelite nation depends on averting this threat. The story reverses and displaces the gender of the more likely victim. It is the male baby we are told who was unwanted. Female infants were safe. Their lives were not endangered. The threat to male infants is shown to mobilize several women characters, and indeed to the extent that they avert this threat they are affirmed.

The story of Exodus, which focuses our attention on the destruction of male babies as a national tragedy of the first degree, presents the survival of female babies as irrelevant to the story of national struggle and survival. The fact that the national "Other," Pharaoh, instructs his people to kill Hebrew male babies and to spare the lives of female babies indicates that female babies are of no concern, of no significance from a political point of view. Women cannot ever endanger the enemy. They are too weak or marginal or insignificant. The death of male babies thus emerges as a political catastrophe. The death of female babies emerges as a historical impossibility. And yet, as I suggested, there is more reason to believe that infanticide was practiced on girls rather than boys. By shifting the focus from baby girls to baby boys, by constructing a story about their demise, and by endowing this demise with national and political significance, the first chapters of Exodus suppress or hide the oppression of women and project it instead on men. Indeed even if the historical record may bear out the story of the Israelites' enslavement by the pharaoh, it is unlikely that the Egyptian monarch should put to death the slaves who build mighty cities for him. It is unlikely that any dictator who respects himself should

[25] See Ilona N. Rashkow, *The Phallacy of Genesis: A Feminist Psychoanalytic Approach* (Louisville: Westminster/John Knox, 1993).

resort to killing his own workforce. After all, the Hebrew slaves offered the monarch endless economic resources. They could be exploited endlessly as an oppressed minority. Even if they multiplied as the story suggests, the Israelites could only benefit the Egyptian masters and increase their wealth. Genocide under such circumstances would be tantamount to political suicide. As I noted before, the Egyptian monarch could use the Israelites as a military buffer against mightier enemies.

If female infanticide was indeed common in ancient Israel, then this would explain why men like Moses may have had to resort to marrying non-Israelite women. There may have been a shortage of marriageable women at a certain point in history, which made it necessary for Israelite men to marry non-Israelite women.

In the prelude to this paper I suggested that in reading biblical narratives critically, we attempt to reread the stories that have constructed our consciousness of ourselves as agents and subjects. For a woman to realize that her understanding of herself as secondary is the product of her own collaborative identification with patriarchy is a first step in a process of liberation. Rereading ourselves is a liberationist praxis as much as it is a literary critical approach. To consider the stories of both the Israelite and the Egyptian women as forged by a phallocentric desire to co-opt and subsume female agency is to consider the many incidents in which we as women have collaborated with male exploitation believing that it is something else.

In her critique of postmodernist theory, Teresa L. Ebert points up the collusion of allegedly playful, plural, multivocality with hegemonic hierarchies and orders of oppression, including patriarchy.[26] By giving up a coherent theory, feminist postmodernists subscribe to current discourses that are not necessarily inspired by a concern for gender equality. The distinction between masculinity and femininity is treated as a false binary opposition, and the transition from one to another—a matter of playful transvestism. The bending of the category of gender in putatively playful directions, giving primacy to desire and language, threatens to depoliticize feminist criticism.[27] This is not to reject the critical space opened out by postmodernism, but rather to question the validity of an idealistic and utopian trend in recent biblical feminist scholarship, a trend that Ebert identifies in feminist theory in general and terms "Ludic Feminism." The radical relativism of ludic feminism, which tends to emphasize the multiplicity of codes and perspectives, refuses the kind of knowledge of social

[26] Teresa L. Ebert, *Ludic Feminism and After: Postmodernism, Desire, and Labor in Late Capitalism* (Ann Arbor: University of Michigan Press, 1996).

[27] Elaine Showalter, "Feminism and Literature," in *Literary Theory Today* (ed. Peter Collier and Helga Geyer-Ryan; Ithaca, N.Y.: Cornell University Press, 1990), 179–202.

totality "that can enable us to change the actually existing world."[28] Ludic feminism refuses to accept the possibility of our access to truth, encouraging us instead to adjust to the social order as it is. This recapitulation to the status quo plays into the hands of those who would have us believe that the Bible is itself a multiple and irreducibly multifocal text in which heterogeneous ideologies and discourses constantly clash and jostle together.[29] From here it is merely a step away from the argument that the Bible is in the eyes of the beholder and that it has not shaped our national, racial, or gender identities. We should let another kind of postmodernism, a resistance postmodernism, flourish alongside the ludic brand that currently dominates biblical feminist criticism. In affirming the oppositional space as a productive site in which a collectivity of critique can thrive and flourish, I seek to encourage a continued exploration of feminist theory as an emancipatory praxis.

This emancipatory praxis seeks to relativize the biblical narrative, to question its authority, and by so doing also to relativize subsequent narratives and paradigms that are based on its tropologies and gyniconologies.[30] My feminist critique of the Bible questions not only a specific text but also the national(ist) narrative it authorizes. The modern Zionist attempt to secularize Judaism launched multiple projects of interpretation that sought to substitute nationalist for religious authority. God was replaced by "national will." The authority of the prophet was translated as the cultural authority of the (male) poet; Jewish law was replaced by self-realization through immigration to Palestine. "This set of substitutions was the foundation of the Zionist transvaluation of values."[31] The modernization and secularization of Judaism did not, however, reject the centrality of the male subject. Equality and social justice were general ethical principles that were not

---

[28] Ebert, *Ludic Feminism and After,* 17.

[29] The most influential practitioner of ludic feminism is Mieke Bal, who did important work in criticizing traditional biblical scholarship on the book of Judges, as in *Death and Dissymmetry: The Politics of Coherence in the Book of Judges* (Chicago: University of Chicago Press, 1988), but who offers a multiplicity of methodological and theoretical approaches, of which feminist criticism is one of several in her other books, e.g., *Murder and Difference: Gender, Genre and Scholarship on Sisera's Death* (Bloomington: Indiana University Press, 1988) and *Lethal Love: Feminist Literary Readings of Biblical Love Stories* (Bloomington: Indiana University Press, 1987).

[30] Tropology refers to the collectivity of tropes and paradigms based on power-determined hierarchies. Gyniconology refers to stereotypic representations of women. See Fuchs, *Israeli Mythogynies.*

[31] See Eliezer Schweid, *Judaism and Secular Culture* (in Hebrew) (Hakibbutz Hameuchad, 1981).

necessarily applied to gender issues. As women of the second Aliya (1911–1917) testify, gender was not considered a priority in Labor Zionism, and women often had to form their own groups to fight the general tendency to confine them to domestic chores.[32] The Bible is central to Zionism because it continues to nurture the national dream of uniqueness and historical continuity, if not eternality. Current events in modern Israel are often interpreted by reference to biblical texts, which often sanction right-wing policies as preordained and predetermined.

For me, then, as a young student of the Bible growing up in Israel, Exod 1–2 exemplified the brutality of the national enemy, the Arabs. The collective representation of the Arabs was the pharaoh. I was asked to identify with the oppressed Israelites embodied by Moses. I projected into the future my possible role as a mother of soldiers and fighters who would take on the enemy some day and bring justice and peace to the land. My real role was to become a mother, in full compliance with the natalist policies of David Ben-Gurion, and the age-old natural truth that was implied by the biblical text.[33]

Whether consciously or subconsciously, modern national master narratives draw on biblical paradigms, which lend an aura of natural and eternal veracity to their claims. A Jewish-feminist approach to the Bible does not seek to repudiate Judaism but to question misogynous ideas that are incompatible with the search for equality.[34] Feminist criticism enables modern Jewish women to hear the double message conveyed to them since the late 1880s, namely, that they are both equal members in a national renewal movement and that they are also less than equal, because their contribution depends primarily on their biology. As Yael Yishai points out, Jewish women in Israel have typically been torn between their allegiance to "the banner" of their own interests as a gendered group and the national demands made on them by "the flag."[35] National demands have typically labeled feminist activism as selfish and trivial. By focusing on the origin of

---

[32] See Deborah S. Bernstein, ed., *Pioneers and Homemakers in Pre-State Israel* (Albany: State University of New York Press, 1992).

[33] "Any Jewish woman who, as far as it depends on her, does not bring into the world at least four healthy children is shirking her duty to the nation, like a soldier who evades military service" (David Ben-Gurion, *Israel: A Personal History* [New York: Funk & Wagnalls, 1971], 36). Needless to add, Ben-Gurion was not a right-wing leader.

[34] In this sense this critique continues such classic critical assessments of Judaism as Judith Plaskow's *Standing Again at Sinai: Judaism from a Feminist Perspective* (San Francisco: Harper & Row, 1990).

[35] See Yael Yishai, *Between the Flag and the Banner: Women in Israeli Politics* (Albany: State University of New York Press, 1997).

the myth, we set in motion a continuous process of challenging subsequent master texts, including modern nationalist texts. By reading against the grain of Exod 1–2, I am rereading myself as the product of a modern Jewish national ethos that implicitly marginalizes me by virtue of my gender. This rereading is intended to question not only the exclusion of women from the national master narrative; it questions above all the assumptions of the national paradigm as such. The feminist struggle for equality and the critique of academic discourses has begun to penetrate public consciousness in Israel only in the last decade. More often than not this struggle is allied with the effort to expose the suppression of other voices in Israeli society, of Arab-Israeli, Palestinian, and Mizrahi women.[36] Though ludic postmodern discourses have begun to infiltrate Israeli academic feminism as well, the dominant drive is toward a commitment to social and political change. To forego the clarity and coherence of this theoretical direction in the name of a supposedly more refined and more complex or multiple antitheory is to give up an explanatory model for historical process. This is quite a loss, I would argue, and one not worth risking.

---

[36] See Barbara Swirski and Marilyn P. Safir, eds., *Calling the Equality Bluff: Women in Israel* (New York: Pergamon, 1991).

Exodus 19 and Its Christian Appropriation

Brooks Schramm

Exodus 19 records the arrival of the Israelites at Mount Sinai on the first day of the third month after their exodus from Egypt, the offer and acceptance of a covenant of mutual obligation, a theophany, and various preparations undertaken by the people on both sides of the theophany, all of which leads directly into the "giving of the Torah" in Exod 20:1–17.[1] That which Exod 19 introduces has a radically different theological function for Jews and Christians, and there is perhaps no greater disparity between the two religions than our respective evaluations of the significance of Sinai. Though there are dissenting voices among the rabbis to the effect that God *forced* the Torah on Israel, by far the dominant stream, molded in the spirit of Ps 119, identifies Sinai with the language of romance, marriage, life, and above all freedom.[2] Christian traditions on the other hand, particularly those molded in the spirit of Galatians and Romans, tend to identify Sinai with slavery and even death. One Jewish writer has described this stark disparity as follows: "in the Pentateuch Mount Sinai is the first great *destination* of those freed in the exodus (Exod 3:12), in Paul's Gospel Mount Sinai is the point of *departure* for the exodus, the equivalent of the house of bondage."[3]

---

[1] Unless otherwise noted, Old Testament quotations are from Everett Fox, *The Five Books of Moses* (New York: Schocken Books, 1995), and New Testament quotations are from the NRSV. I regret that I came across the following works too late to include them in the composition of this work: Christoph Dohmen, "Der Sinaibund als Neuer Bund nach Ex 19-34," in *Der Neue Bund Im Alten: Studien zur Bundestheologie der Beiden* (ed. Erich Zenger; QD 146; Freiburg: Herder, 1993), 51–83; Rolf Rendtorff, *Die Bundesformel: Eine Exegetisch-theologisch Untersuchung* (SBS 160; Stuttgart: Katholisches Bibelwerk, 1995), English: *The Covenant Formula: An Exegetical and Theological Investigation* (trans. Margaret Kohl; OTS; Edinburgh: T&T Clark, 1998); idem, "Nehemiah 9: An Important Witness of Theological Reflection," in *Tehillah le-Moshe: Biblical and Judaic Studies in Honor of Moshe Greenberg* (ed. Mordechai Cogan, Barry L. Eichler, and Jeffrey H. Tigay; Winona Lake, Ind.: Eisenbrauns, 1997), 111–17.

[2] See, e.g., *b. ʿErub.* 54a: "Read not חרות but חירות.

[3] Jon D. Levenson, *The Death and Resurrection of the Beloved Son* (New Haven: Yale University Press, 1993), 215.

Conscious of the nature of the volume in which this article appears, I will treat Exod 19 as a springboard for a closer examination of basic theological issues undergirding the disparity just described. The first two sections will investigate Exod 19 within the context of the Old Testament[4] itself, with special attention given to the concept of covenant. The third section will focus on the problematic character of the Sinaitic covenant within New Testament traditions, especially Paul, and examine how these New Testament claims impact Christian understanding of the theological significance of Sinai.[5]

Exodus 19

The events recorded in the Pentateuch span a period of some 2,706 years.[6] Although the stay at Sinai accounts for slightly less than one year of this total, in terms of the literary structure of the Pentateuch the Sinai pericope encompasses approximately one-third of the entire Pentateuch,[7] extending from Exod 19:1 through Num 10:10.[8] This structural feature suggests that the Sinai pericope occupies prime position within the central document of Judaism, the Pentateuch or Torah. Exodus 19, which serves to introduce the Sinai pericope, exhibits a deep awareness of the theological gravitas of what is to come, and this awareness becomes

---

[4] The title, "Old Testament," will be utilized throughout this article. I have nothing new to add to this hotly debated issue, only to say that my sentiments are consistent with the arguments put forward by Christopher R. Seitz, "Old Testament or Hebrew Bible?" *Word without End: The Old Testament As Abiding Theological Witness* (Grand Rapids: Eerdmans, 1998), 61-74.

[5] While certain theological assumptions and certain forms of theological expression may be readily recognized as generically or typically Christian, the denominational affiliation of a Christian interpreter is by no means inconsequential. This is never more true than when it comes to the question of how Old Testament texts are to be appropriated theologically. The Lutheran theological instincts of the present writer are fully acknowledged.

[6] Joseph Blenkinsopp, *The Pentateuch: An Introduction to the First Five Books of the Bible* (ABRL; New York: Doubleday, 1992), 48.

[7] Gen 1:1–Exod 18:27 = 2,028 verses; Exod 19:1–Num 10:10 = 1,972 verses; Num 10:11–Deut 34:12 = 1,849 verses.

[8] Modern critics have long suspected that this textual unit has all of the characteristics of a massive insertion into the pentateuchal narrative. Cf. Julius Wellhausen, *Prolegomena to the History of Ancient Israel* (1878; repr. Gloucester, Mass: Peter Smith, 1983), 342; Blenkinsopp, *The Pentateuch*, 138; idem, "Structure and Meaning in the Sinai-Horeb Narrative," in *A Biblical Itinerary: In Search of Method, Form and Content: Essays in Honor of George W. Coats* (ed. Eugene E. Carpenter; JSOTSup 240; Sheffield: Sheffield Academic Press, 1997), 109.

manifest in the encounter with the acute literary density that characterizes the chapter.[9]

Literary Density

Although few scholars today would accept Wellhausen's judgment that Exod 19, together with the larger Sinai pericope to which it belongs, is well-nigh incomprehensible, there is virtual scholarly unanimity to the effect that the text of Exod 19 has been worked over many times on the way to its final, canonical form. This unanimity, however, basically goes no further. For well over a century scholars have struggled to describe the history of the text's growth. Creative new studies continue to appear, but as yet no single hypothesis has emerged as a clear front-runner.[10] Nevertheless certain commonalities can be discerned in the newer studies. One is a heightened appreciation of and sensitivity to the roles and accomplishments of the redactors of this material. This attitudinal shift is connected to a growing conviction that the manifold decisions that went into the shaping of the material were in themselves theological in nature and not merely mechanical. The second commonality is a tendency to date the various materials that make up the chapter, particularly those traditionally ascribed to J, E, or JE, later and later, even as late as the exilic period.[11] Connected to this shift in dating is an unwillingness to equate literary "lateness" with theological inferiority or theological atrophy.

But can the chapter as it stands be read? It certainly cannot be read in isolation because it is not a self-contained unit; it functions rather as the introduction to a larger unit. Though the extent to which the chapter pre-

---

[9] A significant component of this literary density is the fact that several different genres are interwoven within the space of a mere twenty-five verses: e.g., cosmic mountain, prophetic oracle, covenant making, ritual instructions, and theophany. This lends support to the claim that the chapter is clearly aware of the profundity of what it introduces.

[10] See, for example, the following recent studies: Thomas B. Dozeman, *God on the Mountain: A Study of Redaction, Theology and Canon in Exodus 19–24* (SBLMS 37; Atlanta: Scholars Press, 1989); Erhard Blum, *Studien zur Komposition des Pentateuch* (BZAW 189; Berlin: de Gruyter, 1990); John Van Seters, *The Life of Moses: The Yahwist As Historian in Exodus–Numbers* (Louisville: Westminster/John Knox, 1994); Wolfgang Oswald, *Israel am Gottesberg: Eine Untersuchung zur Literargeschichte der vorderen Sinaiperikope Ex 19–24 und deren historischem Hintergrund* (OBO 159; Freiburg: Universitätsverlag, 1998).

[11] For example Dozeman, *God on the Mountain,* argues that three levels of tradition can be isolated in Exod 19: a preexilic Mountain of God/Zion tradition, a late preexilic/exilic Deuteronomic/Horeb tradition, and an exilic/postexilic Priestly/Sinai tradition. Van Seters, *Life of Moses,* argues for two literary sources in the chapter: an exilic (post-Deuteronomic) J source and a postexilic P source.

supposes material in Exod 1–18 is still debated,[12] there is no question but that it is an integral part of a unit extending at least from Exod 19–24, and likely from Exod 19–34. Whatever is said of Exod 19 applies to a large extent to this wider unit. In terms of Exod 19 itself, there is broad agreement that reading this chapter is difficult in the extreme, not so much for textual or lexical or grammatical reasons, but for literary reasons. The general parameters of the narrative are clear. The geographical features are the mountain and the camp located opposite the mountain. The characters are God, Moses and the people. God is on the mountain, the people are in the camp, and Moses moves back and forth between the two. But beyond these basic features ambiguity reigns.[13] Basic questions such as who is where and when, who can go where and why and on what terms, who hears what when and where, are deceptively difficult to ascertain. A few examples must suffice. God is variously described as already at the mountain (19:3, 8), as coming to the mountain (19:9), as descending upon the mountain (19:11, 18), and as descending upon the peak of the mountain (19:20). The movement of Moses is variously described as ascending and descending (19:3, 14, 20, 21, 24, 25), as going and coming (19:7, 10), as ascending higher (19:20), while at other times the nature of the movement is not expressly stated (19:8, 9). Strict separation of the people from the mountain is prescribed (19:12–13a, 20–25), and yet an ascent of the people is expected (19:13b). Priests appear in the narrative although the priesthood has not yet been instituted (19:22, 24). The whole is apparently designed to lead into the giving of the laws in 20:1–17, and yet the transition from 19:25 to 20:1 is especially difficult.

The result of this literary ambiguity is a profound sense of disorientation on the part of the reader; one is repeatedly plagued by the feeling that one has missed something. The more one reads the narrative the more sympathy one has for the judgment of incomprehensibility. A fascinating alternative, however, is to reconceive our understanding of the nature of the narrative material before us. Thomas Dozeman has proposed that the ambiguity and disorientation experienced by the reader of Exod 19 is actually characteristic of the broader Sinai narrative that stretches from Exod 19–34. He argues that the numerous trips by Moses up and down the mountain create problems of chronology and causality for the reader; the repeated ascents and descents of

---

[12] See Rendtorff, "Der Text in seiner Endgestalt: Überlegungen zu Exodus 19," in *Ernten was man sät: Festschrift für Klaus Koch zu seinem 65. Geburtstag* (ed. Dwight R. Daniels et al.; Neukirchen-Vluyn: Neukirchener Verlag, 1991), 459–70.

[13] Much, not all, of the ambiguity can be removed by excising portions of the text. Van Seters's reconstructed J runs from 19:2–11 to 13b–19 to 20:18–26 and makes for a tolerably clear narrative. Read in this fashion it is the insertion of the P material (19:1, 12–13a, 20–25; 20:1–17) that creates the problems.

Moses "make it difficult for the reader to maintain any chronological framework for the narrated events," and at certain key points in the narrative, action is all but halted. These twin features of the Sinai narrative Dozeman describes as a "problem of temporal sequence."[14] Drawing on the work of Mickelsen, Smitten, and Daghistany,[15] he goes on to describe this problem of temporal sequence as a typical effect of narratives that employ "spatial-form devices." These devices are "techniques that subvert the chronological sequence inherent in narrative," and where they are employed temporal sequence is minimized so as "to suspend the forward momentum of the story." Narratives that employ such techniques are not predicated on temporal sequence, for example, the movement from a to b to c; rather, "characterization and setting predominate over chronology and plot."

> The resulting structure of narrative in which spatial-form devices predominate has been likened to an orange. Like an orange, such a narrative is structured into individual pieces—similar segments of equal value—in which the movement is circular, focused on the single subject, the core. Scenes, therefore, are often juxtaposed to each other to provide a different perspective on the same core event, with the result that temporal sequence is often replaced by characterization, slow pace, lack of resolution, and repetition. Thus, when spatial-form devices predominate in narrative, the reader is forced "to project not so much forward (what happens next) as backward or sideways" in order to uncover the progression of the narrative.[16]

Reconceiving Exod 19 (and the Sinai narrative in general) as primarily "orange-like" and circular in character rather than sequential raises interesting possibilities about how the chapter can be most fruitfully read. Dozeman proposes that Exod 19 introduces the reader to a strange new world, the world of Sinai. It is a world in which time is virtually suspended and the sequence of and the relation between events is ambiguous. In the midst of this ambiguity Mount Sinai emerges as the central element in the story, and the various ways in which the characters—God, Moses, and Israel—interrelate become the story's primary focus. Although the terminology is different, Dozeman's proposal is similar to that of Moshe Greenberg. He argues that the narrative complexity of Exod 19–20

> is best explained as the result of the interweaving of parallel narrations; the author appears to have been reluctant to exclude any scrap of data

---

[14] Thomas B. Dozeman, "Spatial Form in Exod 19:1–8a and in the Larger Sinai Narrative," *Semeia* 46 (1989): 87–101.

[15] Jeffrey R. Smitten and Ann Daghistany, eds., *Spatial Form in Narrative* (Ithaca, N.Y.: Cornell University Press, 1981).

[16] Dozeman, "Spatial Form in Exodus 19:1–8a," 88.

> relevant to this momentous occasion. The consequent looseness and obscurity of the story can hardly have escaped his notice, and may well have been intended as a literary reflex of the multivalence of the event.[17]

The degree to which the literary effects of Exod 19 were *intended* by the final author of the chapter is of course debatable, but the possibility that this is the case should not be automatically dismissed. That these effects nevertheless do occur is more readily granted. But what is the theological significance of the latter? There is a sense in which the ambiguous and disorienting character of the chapter, its literary "looseness and obscurity," its evasiveness, all work together to ensure the central theological status of the larger pericope to which it serves as an introduction. This can be illustrated in different ways: (1) The chapter both invites and deflects; it brings near and drives away. On the one hand it seems to cry out for "unraveling"; on the other it has proven staunchly resistant to unraveling. Regardless of the reading strategy adopted, one never feels quite confident that one has fully grasped what one has just read. For example, the chapter announces the coming of God to meet his people, but just when this meeting is starting to take place and readerly expectations are high, action is deflected (19:20–25) and the nature of God's presence is all but obscured; the description of the theophany recedes behind further warnings regarding separation. (2) The chapter therefore does not lend itself to rapid reading. Not only does the reader encounter various problems of "temporal sequence," these encounters also have the simultaneous effect of causing the reader to slow down the reading process. (3) This retarding effect in the reading process leads naturally into the desire to reread, to start all over again from the beginning.

To be sure, similar things could be said about other texts in the Old Testament. But the heightened concentration of these characteristics in Exod 19 and throughout the larger Sinai narrative sets this material apart as unique. Exodus 19 is a chapter in which understanding is elusive, where reading is slow, careful, and meticulous, and rereading is virtually guaranteed. This is significant theologically because the material to which the reader is beckoned to return again and again is precisely that which introduces the core elements of Judaism: Mount Sinai, the coming of God and the inauguration of an exclusive relationship between God and the people Israel, Moses as the sole intermediary between God and Israel, and preparations for the giving of commandments expressive of the will of God for his people. *In terms of Old Testament theology, all of this suggests that the Sinai event is not just one link in the chain, equal in significance to all others; rather, it has a qualitatively different status.* The fact that just at this

[17] Moshe Greenberg, "Exodus, Book of," *EncJud* 6:1056.

crucial point in the pentateuchal narrative, namely, the arrival of Israel at Sinai, things become so excruciatingly difficult literarily is a canonical signal that a datum of pressing theological significance is at hand.

Israel's "Yes" to God

The book of Exodus is suffused with the conviction that the God who is at work therein is blatantly partial to a particular group of people, the people Israel. This partiality is expressed in diverse ways. The special status of the relationship between the God of Exodus and the people Israel is emphatically underscored in the words that Moses is to carry to Pharaoh:

> Thus says YHWH: My son, my firstborn, is Israel! I said to you: Send free my son, that he may serve me. (Exod 4:22–23a)

That Israel in fact actually belongs to God is emphasized through the repeated occurrences of the phrase, "my people,"[18] and the polemical character of this designation can be seen in those passages that contain the word הפלה, for example,

> But against all the Children of Israel, no dog shall even sharpen its tongue, against either man or beast, in order that you may know that YHWH makes a distinction [הפלה] between Egypt and Israel.[19] (Exod 11:7)

While the exclusive character of the relationship between God and Israel is a clear theme running throughout Exod 1–18, Exod 19 serves as an intensification of this theme. As can be seen from Exod 19:4–6, not only does God make a distinction between Israel and Egypt, the distinction extends to all nations of the world as well:

> You have seen what I did to Egypt, how I bore you on eagles' wings and brought you to me. And now, if you will hearken, yes, hearken to my voice and keep my covenant, you shall be to me a special-treasure from among all peoples. Indeed, all the world is mine, but you, you shall be to me a kingdom of priests, a holy nation.

Terence Fretheim has recently criticized the view that what is distinctive about Exod 19:4–6 is that it refers to the "election" of Israel as the people of God. He argues that this view is true neither of Exod 19:4–6 nor of the book of Exodus as a whole. In actuality, the election of Israel is nowhere described in Exodus for the simple fact that it is presupposed

---

[18] Exod 3:7; 5:1; 7:4, 16, 26; 8:16, 17, 18, 19; 9:1, 13, 17; 10:3, 4; cf 6:7; 15:16; 18:1.

[19] Cf. Exod 8:18, 19 (with LXX and Peshitta); 9:4.

throughout. Israel is already the people of God even prior to their arrival at Sinai.[20] The significance of this point should not be overlooked. While the preexilic prophets know little or nothing of any promises to the patriarchs prior to Egypt,[21] Exodus in its final, canonical form presupposes the covenant with Abraham-Isaac-Jacob; indeed it is precisely this covenant that motivates God to intervene, after some 430 years of inactivity, on behalf of suffering Israel.[22] For Exodus, then, God's partiality toward Israel in Egypt is directly attributable to God's prior partiality toward Abraham. In terms of the self-understanding of Exodus there is therefore no inherent contradiction between the covenant of Exod 19 and the covenant with Abraham. In fact, as Fretheim argues, the language of "two covenants" is itself misleading. A more accurate description would be to speak of a covenant within a covenant, because "the covenant of Sinai, whatever its tradition history, has here been drawn into the same orbit as the covenant with Abraham."[23]

This, however, still leaves open the question of what is peculiar about Exod 19:4–6, or, put differently, what does Exod 19:4–6 add to, or subtract from, the equation? Christian theologians have often regarded the covenant with Abraham as theologically superior to the covenant of Sinai, arguing that the former is based on sheer, prevenient grace while the latter is a conditional covenant, based on obedience. And there is in fact something to be said for such a distinction. Within the ancient Near East there were covenants (i.e., grants) based solely on the self-imposed obligation of one of the two parties involved and others (i.e., compacts) based on mutual obligations agreed to by both parties.[24] But the problem is whether the covenant with Abraham and the covenant of Sinai fall neatly into either of these two categories, because there are strong elements of obedience in the former and strong elements of grace in the latter. As the much underutilized Gen 22:15–18 demonstrates, the obedience of the human partner is clearly conceived as constituent of the Abrahamic covenant:

> Now YHWH's messenger called to Avraham a second time from heaven and said: By myself I swear—YHWH's utterance—indeed, because you

---

[20] Terence E. Fretheim, *Exodus* (IBC; Louisville: John Knox, 1991), 208.

[21] See Van Seters, "Confessional Reformulation in the Exilic Period," *VT* 22 (1972): 448–59.

[22] Exod 2:24; cf 6:2–7.

[23] Fretheim, *Exodus,* 209.

[24] Moshe Weinfeld, "The Covenant of Grant in the Old Testament and in the Ancient Near East," *JAOS* 90 (1970): 184–203; Jeffrey H. Tigay, *The JPS Torah Commentary: Deuteronomy* (Philadelphia: Jewish Publication Society of America, 1996), 48.

> have done this thing, have not withheld your son, your only-one, indeed, I will bless you, bless you, I will make your seed many, yes, many, like the stars of the heavens and like the sand that is on the shore of the sea; your seed shall inherit the gate of their enemies, all the nations of the earth shall enjoy blessing through your seed, in consequence of your hearkening to my voice.[25]

While the promissory nature of the Abrahamic covenant is unmistakable, this text adds that Abraham's action, his obedience, serves as it were to justify God's prior confidence in him. What is more, Abraham's action becomes the foundation on which the future blessings for Israel and for all nations are predicated. In the covenant of Sinai, too, grace and obedience are tightly interwoven. The obedience required of the people in Exod 19:5a is anchored in God's prior liberating act on Israel's behalf in 19:4. But a more pressing question is whether the covenant now inaugurated could somehow be nullified through Israel's subsequent disobedience. Stated differently, just how "conditional" is this covenant understood to be? The answer to this question is not immediately clear, and on this point the text is provocatively silent. Could it be that this silence is intentional? Scholars have long puzzled over why it is that in a text that contains all of the broad outlines of covenant making, the list of covenant curses is missing; that is, there is no "but if you do not. . . . " This lacuna may conceal a partial answer to our question. Omission of the covenant curses allows all of the emphasis in the passage to fall on the benefits of Israel's obedience and makes that the central focus, while the weighty and unavoidable question of Israel's possible disobedience and the consequences thereof is put off until a later time. In other words, this omission functions as a kind of delaying mechanism, one that builds tension, for only after the reader has read twelve more chapters will this question finally be taken up.

If obedience as such is not the distinguishing characteristic of the covenant of Exod 19, what is? A possible answer is suggested by Exod 19:8a:

> And all the people answered together, they said:
> All that YHWH has spoken, we will do.[26]

---

[25] Cf. the repetition of the very same idea in Gen 26:1–5. For a full discussion of the significance of Abraham's obedience, see Levenson, *The Death and Resurrection of the Beloved Son,* 125–42.

[26] It is difficult to know how much significance should be attached to the fact of Israel's saying yes to covenantal stipulations that have not yet been promulgated. Walter Brueggemann (*Theology of the Old Testament: Testimony, Dispute, Advocacy* [Minneapolis: Fortress, 1997], 183) sees Israel here signing "a blank check of obedience." Jon D. Levenson (*Sinai and Zion: An Entry into the Jewish Bible* [Minneapolis: Winston, 1985], 30) draws on Rashi to Exod 19:11 and argues that the stipulations

All the people said, "Yes, we will obey." But what kind of a "yes" is this? It is the "yes" of a specific, liberated people. It is the "yes" of a people who have themselves experienced liberation and who, on that basis, submit themselves to the will of their liberator. Neither God's demand for Israel's obedience nor Israel's affirmative response to this demand takes place in a vacuum. In this regard, the midrash is absolutely correct in terms of canonical logic:

> Why were the Ten Commandments not said at the beginning of the Torah? They give a parable. To what may this be compared? To the following: A king who entered a province said to the people: May I be your king? But the people said to him: Have you done anything good for us that you should rule over us? What did he do then? He built the city wall for them, he brought in the water supply for them, and he fought their battles. Then when he said to them: May I be your king? They said to him: Yes, yes. Likewise, God. He brought the Israelites out of Egypt, divided the sea for them, sent down the manna for them, brought up the well for them, brought the quails for them, he fought for them the battle with Amalek. Then He said to them: I am to be your king. And they said to Him: Yes, yes.[27]

Though the midrash is dealing specifically with Exod 20:1–17, the argument that it puts forward works equally well for 19:4–5a. Israel's "yes" to God in terms of a vow of obedience is forever and inseparably linked to God's prior act of liberation on Israel's part.[28]

Throughout Exod 1–18 Israel has been God's people. Exodus 19, however, emphasizes that it is here that God becomes Israel's אלהינו, Israel's מלכנו. The distinctive character of Exod 19:4–8 does not consist in the election of Israel, much less in the promulgation of a qualitatively different covenant conditioned on obedience rather than grace. It consists rather in Israel's "coming of age" as a people[29] and the henceforth mutual identifi-

are presupposed and finds in this oddity an indication that the present text is not in its original location. Fretheim (*Exodus*), noting that Exod 15:26 is already able to speak of Israel's obedience to God prior to their arrival at Sinai, sees here "a recognition that to obey the voice of God entails more than obeying the laws given at Sinai" (211). Rendtorff ("Der Text in seiner Endgestalt," 467) argues that Exod 19:8a is intended to be read together with 24:3, 7 so that the latter twofold affirmation, which takes place in full knowledge of God's will, serves to confirm and strengthen the prior affirmation.

[27] *Mekilta Baḥodesh* 5. The translation is that of Jacob Z. Lauterbach, *Mekilta de-Rabbi Ishmael* (3 vols.; Philadelphia: Jewish Publication Society of America, 1933, 1935), 2:229–30.

[28] On the reciprocal nature of liberation and obedience, grace and commandment, in Exodus, see Brueggemann, *Theology of the Old Testament,* 182–83.

[29] Israel is pictured as helpless and childlike in Exod 19:4, whereas in 19:5 Israel is faced with a very adult choice.

cation of this liberating God and this particular liberated people, for the sake of the world.[30] The narrowing of focus in the canonical narrative, begun in Gen 12, has now reached its apex. God's partiality toward Abraham is sealed by the making of a covenant with Israel and Israel alone out of all of the peoples of the world. Particularism within a universal perspective has thus become concretely the lens through which reality is viewed. Israel's "yes" to God is far from an incidental matter. Rather, as subsequent Old Testament and rabbinic reflection would be at pains to demonstrate, it marks for Israel a point after which there can be no return.[31]

"Conditional" Covenant?

Israel's Disobedience

Having argued that the obedience promised by Israel in Exod 19 should always be seen in direct relationship to God's prior liberating act, it must also be clear that the utter necessity of Israel's obedience is emphatically emphasized there: Israel must "keep" the covenant in order to realize its status as "priestly kingdom" and "holy nation." There are in the text of Exod 19 no grounds for casting aspersions on Israel's sincerity, that is, on the genuineness of Israel's desire to do the will of God. But we do know from the portrait of the people in the first eighteen chapters of the book that a rather precarious situation is being set up here, because these chapters have made no attempt to idealize the people but rather present them in a straightforward, balanced, and realistic light. When oppressed they groan and cry out (Exod 2:23); but when they hear the news that God has sent them a deliverer and when this message is accompanied by the performance of signs, they believe and they worship (4:30–31). When an impossible task (bricks without straw) is laid upon them the officers of the people complain bitterly (5:1–23); but throughout the long series of plagues when their deliverance is delayed time and again, scarcely a word of complaint is heard from the people (6:28–12:36). When they are trapped at the sea, they cry out against Moses, "Better red than dead";[32] but when they are rescued and the enemy is destroyed they fear YHWH and believe in YHWH and Moses, and they sing a triumphant hymn of praise (14:30–31; 15:1–21). When hungry or thirsty, they grumble and desire to

---

[30] Though the implications are by no means spelled out, the language of "priestly kingdom" and "holy nation" indicates that Israel does not simply exist for its own sake.

[31] See Moshe Greenberg, *Ezekiel 1–20* (AB 22; Garden City, N. Y.: Doubleday, 1983), 386.

[32] Exod 14:10–12. Note that 14:12 implies that the people had been skeptical of the whole enterprise from the beginning.

return to Egypt (16:3; 17:3); in the incident of the manna a minority disobeys the Sabbath regulations while the majority obeys (16:1–36). In contrast to certain prophetic perspectives on Israel's early history that portray the people in a completely negative light,[33] in Exod 1–18 the people come off as exhibiting a broad range of characteristics. They are capable of obedience and disobedience, of faith and mistrust, of endurance and pettiness, and the like. The ambiguity in Israel's character is thus no more or no less than what is typically human. But this is precisely what accounts for the tenuous nature of Israel's commitment in Exod 19, because the history of the people to this point in the story would seem to imply that the people can, as it were, go either way.

Any assessment of Israel's potential obedience, therefore, cannot help but be constrained by the looming shadow of Exod 32.[34] There, in a chapter containing obvious echoes of Exod 19,[35] something tantamount to an act of adultery committed on a honeymoon takes place: Israel worships a molten calf. The egregiousness of this act and the gravity of the situation is such that Israel is described as mirroring the situation of humanity just prior to the flood:

> Now the earth had gone to ruin [תשחת] before God, the earth was filled with wrongdoing. God saw the earth, and here: it had gone to ruin [נשחתה], for all flesh had ruined [השחית] its way [דרכו] upon the earth. (Gen 6:11–12)

> YHWH said to Moshe: Go, down! for your people whom you brought up from the land of Egypt has wrought ruin [שחת]! They have been quick to turn aside from the way [הדרך] that I commanded them. (Exod 32:7–8a)

Just as at that time God had moved to destroy humanity and start over with Noah, so now God moves to destroy Israel and start over with Moses:

> Now YHWH saw that great was humankind's evildoing [רעת האדם] on earth and every form of their heart's planning was only evil [רע] all the day. Then YHWH was sorry [וינחם] that he had made humankind on earth, and it pained his heart. YHWH said: I will blot out [אמחה] humankind, whom I have created, from the face of the soil, from man to beast, to crawling thing and to the fowl of the heavens, for I am sorry [נחמתי] that I made them. But Noah found favor in the eyes of YHWH. (Gen 6:5–8)

> And YHWH said to Moshe: I see this people—and here, it is a hard-necked [קשה ערף][36] people! So now, let me be, that my anger may flare

[33] See especially Ezek 16; 20; 23.

[34] Josephus omits any reference to this story!

[35] E.g., כל העם (19:8; 32:3), לך רד (19:24; 32:7).

[36] This is the first time in Exodus that Israel is described in this manner.

> against them and I may destroy them [ואכלם]—but you I will make into a great nation! (Exod 32:9–10)

But there is one important difference. Unlike Noah,[37] Moses refuses to become the new father of the nation; instead, he intercedes on behalf of the people:

> Moses soothed the face of YHWH his God, he said: For-what-reason, O YHWH, should your anger flare against your people whom you brought out of the land of Egypt with great power, with a strong hand? For-what-reason should the Egyptians (be able to) say, yes, say: With evil intent [ברעה] he brought them out, to kill them in the mountains, to destroy them from the face of the soil? Turn away from your flaming anger, be sorry [והנחם] for the evil [הרעה] (intended) against your people! Recall Avraham, Yitzhak and Yisrael your servants, to whom you swore by yourself when you spoke to them: I will make your seed many as the stars of the heavens, and all this land which I have promised, I will give to your seed, that they may inherit (it) for the ages! And YHWH let himself be sorry [וינחם] concerning the evil [הרעה] that he had spoken of doing to his people. (Exod 32:11–14)

Moses' intercession thus has the effect of averting for Israel the fate of the flood generation. In Gen 6:5–12, God was sorry (וינחם) that he had made humankind because of its evil (רע), but in Exod 32:11–14, God was sorry (וינחם) for the evil (הרעה) he intended to do to his hard-necked people.[38]

These similarities cannot be coincidental, and, in fact, they extend even further. Rolf Rendtorff has argued persuasively that "the primeval history in Genesis 1–11 and the Sinai story in Exodus 19–34 show a parallel structure."[39] This parallel structure can be diagramed as follows:

Humanity	Creation (Gen 1)	Human Sin	Noah	Massive Destruction	Covenant (Gen 9)
Israel	Covenant (Exod 19)	Golden Calf	Moses	Partial Destruction	Covenant (Exod 34)

---

37 "From beginning to end of the Flood narrative, Noah says not a word" (Avivah Gottlieb Zornberg, *Genesis: The Beginning of Desire* [Philadelphia: Jewish Publication Society of America, 1995], 58).

38 Moses actually engages in a second intercession in Exod 32:30–35, and this text contains a striking parallel to Gen 6 as well: "Erase me [מחני נא] from your book" (32:32) recalls "I will erase [אמחה]" (Gen 6:7; cf 7:23).

39 Rolf Rendtorff, "'Covenant' As a Structuring Concept in Genesis and Exodus," in *Canon and Theology: Overtures to an Old Testament Theology* (Minneapolis: Fortress, 1993), 134; cf. 125–34.

Just as in the former, God's intention for creation was spoiled by human sin, so in the latter, God's intention for Israel was spoiled by Israel's sin. In addition, both narratives emphasize that the sinful nature of the human characters involved remains the same as before. Humanity is described with identical language before and after the flood: their inclination is evil (רע, Gen 6:5; 8:21). Israel too is described with identical language before and after its partial destruction: the people are hard-necked (קשה ערף, Exod 32:9; 33:3, 5; 34:9). In both narratives, that which assures the future existence of sinful humanity and of sinful, hard-necked Israel is the establishment or the reestablishment of a covenant.

It is also interesting to note the basis upon which the institution of these two respective covenants is founded, because herein resides a subtle but crucial difference. It can be argued that both stories focus on the central role played by an individual, Noah and Moses, and that the turning point in each story has to do with the relationship between this individual and God's "memory." In the flood story God "remembers" (ויזכר) Noah, and then the waters begin to recede (Gen 8:1). In the story of the calf Moses beseeches God, "Remember (זכר) Abraham, Isaac, and Israel" (Exod 32:13), and then God desists from his intention to destroy his people. The subtle difference here has to do with the object of God's memory. God does not remember *Moses,* but rather Moses beseeches God to remember *Abraham!* Thus the condition for the possibility of the renewed covenant in Exod 34 is regarded as lying outside the structure of the Sinai narrative itself.

What might this mean theologically? With its unabashed stress on the radicality of Israel's disobedience, Exod 32 calls into question a *sine qua non* of the covenant of Exod 19. A primary function, therefore, of the golden calf episode is to emphasize that the covenant of Exod 19 does not and cannot stand on its own: were it not for Moses' invocation of God's prior promise to Abraham, Israel would have been destroyed then and there. This linking, in Exod 32, of the Abrahamic and Sinaitic covenants can be seen to contain a double theological claim: (1) Israel's radical disobedience cannot ultimately thwart God's grace and mercy toward Israel through Abraham; (2) God's grace and mercy toward Israel through Abraham do not and cannot ensure Israel's obedience. The outcome of the golden calf narrative, thus, results in a kind of oddity. In Exod 34, a covenant, strongly reminiscent of Exod 19, demanding obedience to specific commandments, is reestablished with a people who have proven themselves radically disobedient. This would seem to imply two things as well: (1) the Abrahamic covenant does not displace the Sinaitic, for God still demands obedience from Israel even after the golden calf incident; (2) the covenant of Exod 19 is renewed/reestablished, but things are not simply put back to the way they were before. The parties involved now know one another in a dramatically different way. For God, Israel is no longer simply עמי; rather, they are עם קשה ערף. And for Israel, God is no longer simply אלהינו who brought us up out of Egypt and on that basis demands our obedience; rather, God is now known as:

> יהוה יהוה אל, showing-mercy, showing-favor, long-suffering in anger, abundant in loyalty and faithfulness, keeping loyalty to the thousandth (generation), bearing iniquity, rebellion and sin, yet not clearing, clearing (the guilty), calling-to-account the iniquity of the fathers upon the sons and upon sons' sons, to the third and fourth (generation)! (Exod 34:6–7)

Abraham does not displace Sinai, but he does serve as a bulwark against the frailty and tenuousness of Sinai.

The One Enduring Covenant

In his famous essay of some sixty years ago, Gerhard von Rad pointed to the pivotal significance of Neh 9 for understanding the growth of the pentateuchal/hexateuchal traditions.[40] There, for the first time, all of the basic traditions that make up the pentateuchal/hexateuchal story are drawn together in one place.[41] Though it would be too bold to assert that Neh 9 presupposes the Pentateuch/Hexateuch in its final, canonical form, it can be stated with some confidence that Neh 9 does presuppose something very close to it. This penitential prayer in the form of a historical recital describes Israel's history from creation to the restoration period. The following items are treated in sequence: creation, Abraham, the exodus from Egypt, the rescue at the sea, Mount Sinai and the giving of the commandments through Moses, the molten calf, forty years in the wilderness, the conquest of both sides of the Jordan, the handing over of the people into the power of the peoples of the lands, and the dire straits in which the community finds itself during the restoration period; the persistent rebellion of the people is repeatedly noted from the calf incident onward. The important thing about Neh 9 is not just that it provides such a list but that it also comments theologically on the elements that make up the list. Neh 9 represents a wholistic reading of Israel's history, and in so doing it functions as an invaluable resource for helping us understand how, during the restoration period when they were approaching their final, canonical form, the diverse traditions that make up this history were understood to cohere theologically. For our purposes, the noteworthy item is the manner in which Neh 9 construes the relationship between Abraham and Sinai.

---

[40] Gerhard von Rad, "The Form-Critical Problem of the Hexateuch," in *The Problem of the Hexateuch and Other Essays* (London: SCM, 1984), 1–78.

[41] Contrast Neh 9 with Exod 15; Deut 6:20–24; 26:5b–9; Josh 24:2b–13; 1 Sam 12:8; Pss 78; 105; 106; 135; 136.

The historical recital presents Israel's history in terms of a cyclical repetition of three themes: God's grace and mercy, Israel's persistent failure to obey the commandments, and God's unwillingness to abandon his people. Within this recital, the concept of "covenant" plays the central role, both structurally and theologically. At the beginning of the relationship between God and Israel stands God's choice of Abraham and the covenant that God made with him (וכרות עמו הברית, Neh 9:7–8). At the end of the prayer, the God who "keeps the covenant" (שומר הברית) is invoked as Israel's only source of hope for the future (v. 32). God's unfailing grace and mercy toward Israel are therefore to be seen as a predication of God's covenant keeping. What is especially striking, however, is the fact that Neh 9 knows only one covenant. "The covenant" (הברית) that God is said to keep is precisely "the covenant" (הברית) with Abraham. But what then does this imply about the covenant of Sinai? It is unlikely that this can be taken as evidence that Sinai has somehow lost its covenantal character. More unlikely still is the possibility that the Abrahamic has somehow displaced the Sinaitic covenant. What is apparently the case is that Sinai is regarded rather as a constituent element *within* the one covenant.

Such a reading gains support from Neh 10. Having participated in the corporate confession of sins on the twenty-fourth day of the seventh month, the people then join together and take

> an oath with sanctions to follow the Teaching of God, given through Moses the servant of God, and to observe [לשמור] carefully all the commandments of the LORD our God, His rules and laws. (Neh 10:30 NJPS)

Israel's response to the God who keeps (שמר) the covenant is an oath to keep (לשמור) the commandments of God. The internal logic of Neh 9–10 is something like this: God made a covenant with Abraham, a covenant that God faithfully keeps in spite of Israel's persistent disobedience, but Israel's access to this covenant is only through Sinai, through the observance of commandments. The Abrahamic and the Sinaitic are therefore conceived as one covenant. The Abrahamic aspect of the covenant ensures its endurance, while the Sinaitic aspect is that which "energizes" it.

In terms of the "conditionality" of the covenant, one must concede that there is something of the "conditional" here. But any use of such language must be carefully nuanced. As a flat statement spoken without qualification it does violence to the intricate manner in which the Abrahamic and Sinaitic aspects of the covenant are interwoven. The possibility of Israel's realization of God's promises to Abraham is assumed to be constantly available through obedience, but the indispensable flipside of this statement is that Israel's disobedience can in no sense be said to void the covenant. It is this conviction that permeates the prayer in Neh 9. The prayer fully acknowledges Israel's repeated failure to observe the commandments while at the same time containing no hint whatsoever that the covenant is somehow no longer in effect.[42] On the one hand Neh 9, with its emphasis on the God who keeps the covenant, is thus a particularly fine example in support of Rendtorff's argument that

> Israel can break the covenant, and will break it many times, as the Hebrew Bible tells us. Nevertheless, the covenant itself will never be broken because God has promised to keep it.... This is true for the Hebrew Bible in general, where it is never said that God has broken or ever will break his covenant, no matter how often Israel might break it.[43]

On the other hand Neh 10, with its emphasis on the indispensable role of Israel's observance of the commandments, demonstrates that Israel throughout its subsequent generations is called time and again to assume the position of its forebears who stood at the foot of the mountain in Exod 19.[44]

The New Testament and Sinai in Tension

Sinai in the New Testament and Beyond

What the Old Testament in its final, canonical form has bound so inextricably together, namely the Abrahamic and Sinaitic aspects of the covenant, is severed in the theology of the Apostle Paul. As alluded to briefly in the introduction, it is in the theology of Paul that "a hard wedge" is driven "between the Abrahamic and the Sinaitic moments in the history of redemption."[45] For Paul, Mount Sinai has a distinctly negative theological function. It would be mistaken, however, to think that it is only in Paul that Sinai is cast in a negative light. In fact, the negative portrayal of Sinai can be discerned in large portions of the New Testament.

Brevard Childs has argued that in the New Testament two primary views of Exod 19 and the covenant inaugurated therein are in evidence,[46] and to a large extent these two New Testament views persist throughout Christian history. The first is that the covenant of Sinai is "inadequate" and

---

[42] Cf. Lev 26:40–45; Deut 4:30–31; 9:4–5.

[43] Rendtorff, "'Covenant' As a Structuring Concept," 131.

[44] On the significance of Neh 9–10 in terms of its relationship to Exod 19, Halivni has argued that the "return to Sinai" enacted in Neh 9–10 is evidence that "the giving and receiving of the Torah, according to the Bible itself, were not one and the same event" (David Weiss Halivni, *Peshat and Derash: Plain and Applied Meaning in Rabbinic Exegesis* [New York: Oxford University Press, 1998], vi).

[45] Levenson, *The Death and Resurrection of the Beloved Son,* 218.

[46] Brevard S. Childs, *The Book of Exodus: A Critical, Theological Commentary* (OTL; Philadelphia: Westminster, 1974), 375–78.

has been replaced by a new one,[47] while the second "stresses the continuity between the Old Testament promise and the New Testament church."[48] Actually Childs is too charitable on this issue. Regarding the first view, the language of "inadequacy" is itself inadequate to capture the full force and radicality of the New Testament claims. Both Paul and the writer of Hebrews assert not simply that the covenant of Sinai is inadequate but rather that it has failed or miscarried due to a fatal flaw and that it now stands in virtual diametric opposition to the new covenant. Thus the writer of Hebrews can assert:

> For if that first covenant had been faultless, there would have been no need to look for a second one.... In speaking of "a new covenant," he has made the first one obsolete. And what is obsolete and growing old will soon disappear. (Heb 8:7, 13)

Regarding the second view, that some New Testament texts stress a certain continuity between Sinai and the church, further explication is warranted. In a sense, one could argue that the New Testament (whole and entire) presupposes some kind of continuity between Israel as constituted at Sinai and the church and that historical Israel is a prerequisite for the existence of the church. But this continuity must be seen in the light of New Testament claims that the church is not merely an extension or further development of historical Israel; rather, it represents something fundamentally and qualitatively new.[49] If we have learned anything from the Jewish participants in Jewish-Christian dialogue it is that the language of "continuity" is a primary vehicle for supersessionist thought, and from a Jewish perspective it is perhaps the most insidious vehicle. When Jews are faced with the Christian language of continuity, the obvious question arises: continuity at what cost? Put differently, the continuity that exists between Sinai and the church is a Christian and not a Jewish perception. Thus, rather than using Childs's language of "inadequacy" and "continuity," it may be more helpful to see in the New Testament an oscillation between a position that views the covenant of Sinai as inherently negative and one

---

47 Cf. Matt 26:28 // Mark 14:24 // Luke 22:20 // 1 Cor 11:25; Acts 7:35–43; Gal 3:19–29; 4:21–31; Heb 8:8–13; 10:16–17 (quoting Jer 31:31–34); Heb 12:18–29.

48 Childs acknowledges that this second position is "not completely without some negative overtones" (*The Book of Exodus,* 375–76). Cf. 1 Pet 2:9; Rev 1:6; 5:9–10; 14.

49 Thus, the church is a new creation (2 Cor 5:17). "Precisely when the principal accent falls on continuity in the schema of promise and fulfillment, the antithetical undertone still cannot be ignored: the provisional is overcome, the final has come" (Gerhard Ebeling, *The Study of Theology* [Philadelphia: Fortress, 1978], 28).

that views it as negative but only in the light of the *novum* that is subsequent to it.

New Testament aversion to Sinai continues to be strongly in evidence and even to intensify in the writings of the early church fathers, examples of which can be multiplied at will.[50] As a rule, Christian writers take for granted the Pauline claim that once the new has come, the old has passed away (2 Cor 5:17); in other words, with the coming of Christ and the formation of the church the covenant of Sinai has been abrogated. At least one writer, however, takes matters to an extreme. This is the second-century *Epistle of Barnabas,* which, drawing on the episode of the golden calf and its immediate aftermath, essentially argues that the covenant of Sinai was so flawed that it was doomed even before it got started.[51] *Barnabas* "maintains the thesis that there never was an efficacious covenant between God and his people."[52] Though the argument of *Barnabas* may appear to have gone completely overboard, the seeds of this very notion can already be found in 2 Cor 3. Unlike *Barnabas,* Paul is willing to acknowledge the remaking of the covenant after the golden calf incident, but his midrash on the significance of the veil of Moses makes the point that this remade covenant is a very strange covenant indeed. For the human participants in the covenant are ones whose "minds have been hardened," whose "hearts are veiled," and who, as a result, are unable to understand the covenant (2 Cor 3:14–15). Theologically speaking, it is a short step from 2 Cor 3 to *Barnabas.*

The issue here is certainly not to present Gentile Christianity as some kind of monolith, but it is an attempt to highlight certain inescapable realities in the early history of Christian thought. It is a mistake of Protestantism to make a hard and fast theological distinction between the

---

50 See Hans von Campenhausen, *The Formation of the Christian Bible* (Philadelphia: Fortress, 1972), esp. 21–102.

51 *Barnabas* 4:7–8: "It [i.e., the covenant] is ours: but in this way did they finally lose it when Moses had just received it, for the Scripture says: 'And Moses was in the mount fasting forty days and forty nights, and he received the covenant from the Lord, tables of stone written with the finger of the hand of the Lord.' But they turned to idols and lost it. For thus saith the Lord: 'Moses, Moses, go down quickly, for the people, whom thou broughtest forth out of the land of Egypt, have broken the Law.' And Moses understood and cast the two tables out of his hands, and their covenant was broken, in order that the covenant of Jesus the Beloved should be sealed in our hearts in hope of his faith" (the translation is that of Kirsopp Lake in *The Apostolic Fathers* [2 vols; LCL; Cambridge: Harvard University Press, 1977], 1:351, brackets added).

52 Peter von der Osten-Sacken, *Christian-Jewish Dialogue: Theological Foundations* (Philadelphia: Fortress, 1986), 151.

New Testament on the one hand and early Christian literature on the other, and argue that although the New Testament "got it right" in all matters theological, things quickly went wrong. What one often finds in early Christian literature is instead a profound and sustained working out of the theological trajectories that are either overt or latent in that collection of writings that were soon to become the New Testament. In terms of early Christian theology, though there are different levels of negativity, one simply has to reckon with the fact that the overwhelming tendency is for Sinai to function negatively, and this tendency is directly attributable to the New Testament itself.[53]

The degree to which the negative portrait of Sinai persists in the subsequent history of Christian thought is conspicuous in that it is only quite recently that Christians have seriously begun to entertain the notion that, at least for Jews, Sinai is still in effect. This new development is linked with the growing conviction that the ongoing existence of the Jewish people is a datum of the highest significance for Christian theology. There are several key elements apart from which the current situation cannot be understood: (1) historical-Jesus studies and the "rediscovery" of the Jewishness of Jesus; (2) a new-found interest in Rom 9–11 and a reevaluation of its significance for Pauline theology; (3) an explosion of research into Second Temple Judaism and the related phenomenon of early Jewish Christianity; (4) the slow but growing interest of Christian scholars in a critical engagement with the texts of postbiblical Judaism. The fact that, with the exception of historical-Jesus studies, these are primarily post–World War II phenomena raises the possibility that but for the Shoah this reappraisal would not yet be upon us.[54]

In terms of the theological interpretation of the Sinai pericope as a whole or any of the parts thereof, a Christian who in some sense wants to stand within the broad parameters of traditional Christian thought cannot help but be affected by the deep-seated aversion, and even animosity, to

[53] One is reminded in this regard of the case mounted by von Harnack to the effect that the theology of the oft-castigated Marcion "did not come as a bolt out of the blue" and that Paul, in certain key respects, would have regarded Marcion as his genuine student (*sein echter Schuler*) (Adolf von Harnack, *Marcion: The Gospel of the Alien God* [trans. J. E. Steely and L. D. Bierma; Durham, N.C.: Labyrinth, 1990], 127, 124; orig. *Marcion: Das Evangelium vom fremden Gott* [Darmstadt: Wissenschaftliche Buchgesellschaft, 1960], 206, 199). To be sure, von Harnack qualifies this assertion to some extent and is fully aware that Paul could never have accepted certain elements of Marcionite theology. Nevertheless his overarching contention is that Marcionism "grew out of Paulinism or out of an extension of it."

[54] See Kornelis H. Miskotte, *When the Gods are Silent* (New York: Harper & Row, 1967), 313.

Sinai that has so saturated Christian theology. It cannot simply be ignored or jettisoned.

The attempt by Christians to read the Old Testament as if the New Testament does not exist is, as well, no solution at all. Not only does such an approach tend to arouse understandable suspicions on the part of Jewish interpreters,[55] it also begs the larger question of the ultimate usefulness of such an approach for modern Christian theology. This is not in any way to argue for a return to a situation in which the Old Testament is held theologically captive to the New. The Reformation discovery of the distinctive character of the Tanak, the Bible in Hebrew, as over against the Greek New Testament should not be compromised.[56] And Christians must acknowledge that the Old Testament as such has a distinctive theological integrity of its own. But it does not have exclusive theological integrity. The Christian interpreter can and should seek to read the Old Testament on its own terms, but not exclusively on its own terms. To do so would be to concede the notion that in the final analysis the potential contribution of the New Testament and its subsequent interpretation to a modern Christian appropriation of the Old Testament is tangential at best. The very structure of the Christian Bible makes the theological claim that the Old Testament can be read in a broader literary and theological context,[57] and the deeply held conviction that the Christian Bible in its bipartite structure is not theologically incoherent accounts to a large extent for the history of the discipline of Old Testament theology. One possible model that does justice to the theological claim inherent in the structure of the Christian Bible is one in which the two volumes are construed as both mutually informative and mutually correcting. Such an approach allows for reading to take place in two directions.[58] This is by no means a neat and tidy business. It is fraught with pitfalls, and such Christian handling of the Old

---

[55] As I understand it, Jewish critiques of the discipline of Christian Old Testament theology have nothing to do with the "rights" of Christians to read the Old Testament with Christian presuppositions, much less that doing so may be an extremely fruitful enterprise for *Christians*. The critiques focus rather on *unacknowledged* Christian presuppositions (masking themselves under so-called objective, scientific historical criticism), and also on implied claims that the Old Testament can *only* be correctly understood in a Christian manner.

[56] See Rolf Rendtorff, "Toward a Common Jewish-Christian Reading of the Hebrew Bible," in *Canon and Theology*, 38.

[57] The assumptions underlying the structure of the Christian Bible, of course, make stronger theological claims than this.

[58] "The test of the justification of the Christian incorporation of the Old Testament lies in the capacity of this affirmation of a connection to move in the other direction" (Ebeling, *The Study of Theology*, 28).

Testament will inevitably stand in some tension with Judaism. But pursuing such an approach makes it possible to speak, in a meaningful sense, of a "Christian" interpretation of the Old Testament.[59]

Paul, the Covenant of Sinai, and the Gentiles

Given the theological stature of Sinai within the canonical Pentateuch and thus within the Old Testament as a whole, and given the pronounced early Christian aversion to Sinai, it is no small wonder that the church continued to regard the Old Testament as sacred Scripture. The fact that the question of the binding character of Sinaitic law on Christians was so hotly contested in the first decades of the church's existence suggests that Jesus himself likely took no definitive stand on the issue or that his own position was ambiguous.[60] It appears rather that Sinaitic law becomes problematic for the early Christian movement for the first time as a practical issue within the context of the Gentile mission.[61] Because the starting point of Christian proclamation was not the law but Jesus Christ, very early on the church was able to make a decision, based on the practical demands of the mission context, not to require observance of the commandments by converts. As it encountered the Gentile world with its message of freedom in Christ, the church effectively relinquished the law in practice, thus ensuring that the church would not remain solely a movement within Judaism. This practice, however, had the simultaneous effect of placing the Old Testament into a precarious position. How could the Old Testament continue to be received as sacred Scripture when its concrete demands were all but ignored?[62] The answer to this question is the unique contribution of Paul. Not content with any *de facto* explanations of Christian practice, Paul provided a deep theological rationale to undergird it and in so doing claimed the Old Testament for the church. Von Campenhausen has stated the issue concisely:

> For it was not the defense and preservation of the Law, but its nullification which in the end made it possible for the Church to regard the whole

---

[59] I am in full agreement with Seitz in his call "for a reconnection of Old Testament and New Testament studies, for that is where theological combustion occurs" ("The Old Testament As Abiding Theological Witness," *Word without End,* 11).

[60] Arguing that Jesus explicitly opposed the law "may make hostility towards Jesus easier to account for, but it makes the controversies in the early church incomprehensible" (E. P. Sanders, *Jesus and Judaism* [Philadelphia: Fortress, 1985], 246).

[61] Von Campenhausen, *Formation of the Christian Bible,* 21–24.

[62] Ibid., 23.

> Old Testament, including the Torah, as God's word, to understand it in a Christian sense, and to keep it as part of her own Canon.[63]

But Paul's contribution extends even further. His meditations on the law essentially proposed a "definite, concrete distinction between the epochs," that of the law and that of Christ. In so doing,

> Paul created the presuppositions which made it possible to take over the ancient Scriptures, and to set a "New" Testament alongside the "Old" but clearly distinct from it.... it is a sheer historical fact that the permanent basic assumption of the Christian Bible is a Pauline conception, or at least one inaugurated by Paul, and to that extent the Christian Bible is inconceivable without him.[64]

Christian theological approaches to the Sinaitic covenant, therefore, cannot help but go through Paul. His is not the only New Testament voice on the matter,[65] but sooner or later he must be reckoned with.

Anyone with even a cursory knowledge of rabbinic literature is quick to realize that there is a vast chasm between what Sinai represents for the rabbis and what it represents for Paul. The chasm is so great that it is almost as if they are not talking about the same thing. And yet they are. Some have seen a consistency between Paul's critique of the law and the scathing judgments spoken by Israel's prophets, but the radicality of Paul's position ultimately goes beyond anything envisioned in the Old Testament. A crucial aspect of Paul's thought regarding the law occurs in Rom 7:7–13, where he argues that the law is a kind of tool of sin. Though he struggles mightily not to equate the law with sin, he does argue that the law is vulnerable to sin in a peculiar manner, that in fact sin is worse with the law than without it. In the midst of this discussion, he makes the extraordinary statement: "the very commandment that promised life, proved to be death for me" (Rom 7:10b; cf. Ezek 20:25). Fierce debates continue to be waged over the question of the centrality of Rom 7 within the overall Pauline discussion of the law and over the question of the autobiographical character of the chapter.[66] But in spite of the complexity of the issue, a case can be made that Rom 7 is at least not an aberration in Paul's thought, if for no other reason than that the position he adopts there coheres to a marked extent with a key element of his life and ministry.

---

63 Ibid.

64 Ibid., 36–37.

65 See especially the Sermon on the Mount and James.

66 A helpful discussion of the issues is contained in E. P. Sanders, *Paul, the Law, and the Jewish People* (Philadelphia: Fortress, 1983), esp. 70–86.

Two times and in two different letters Paul makes reference to his pre-"Christian" life in a manner that expressly links his persecution of the church with his zeal for the Torah:

> You have heard, no doubt, of my earlier life in Judaism. I was violently persecuting the church of God and was trying to destroy it. I advanced in Judaism beyond many among my people of the same age, for I was far more zealous for the traditions of my ancestors.[67] (Gal 1:13–14)

> If anyone else has reason to be confident in the flesh, I have more: circumcised on the eighth day, a member of the people of Israel, of the tribe of Benjamin, a Hebrew born of Hebrews; as to the law, a Pharisee; as to zeal, a persecutor of the church; as to righteousness under the law, blameless. (Phil 3:4b–6)

On a third occasion, he mentions his persecution of the church yet again, and this time he regards it as the reason for his low stature among the apostles:

> For I am the least of the apostles, unfit to be called an apostle, because I persecuted the church of God. (1 Cor 15:9)

We shall probably never know the exact details surrounding Paul's "conversion experience," but we do know that what followed in its wake was a profound reevaluation, on his part, of the meaning of his persecution of the church.[68] When one looks at the above quoted passages in their broader context, it is striking how Paul presents his persecution of the church as a logical extension of his Torah zeal. He never backs away from this. Even after his conversion he continues to regard his persecution of the church as a superlative in terms of "righteousness under the law," an example of faithful obedience. He never so much as hints, for example, that his role as persecutor just might have been a perversion of Torah zeal rather than proof of it. The conclusion that he draws is instead that it was precisely his obedience to the law that led him to work against the very God whom he was trying to honor. The extent to which this reevaluation affected his subsequent understanding of the law is difficult to know with certainty, but any treatment of Paul and the law has to take this with utter seriousness because it was clearly of great significance for Paul himself. Paul never says that the problem with the law is that it cannot be fulfilled.

---

[67] Regarding "the traditions of my ancestors" as a reference to the Torah, see Hans Dieter Betz, *Galatians* (Hermeneia; Philadelphia: Fortress, 1979), 68.

[68] All three references in Acts to Paul's conversion emphasize his persecution of the church as the central feature: 9:4–5; 22:7–8; 26:14–15.

The problem rather is that even when it is fulfilled it cannot give life (Gal 3:21). The reason it cannot, according to Paul, is because sin is stronger than God's law and has always been so (Rom 8:3). Paul's lasting contribution to Christian theology emerges from his penetrating meditation on the power of sin to corrupt and distort that which is holy and righteous and good, even the law of God.

What happens, then, when Christians turn to Exod 19 with Rom 7 ringing in their ears? Perhaps at this point more than any other it is imperative to remember, and to insist, that Paul was a Jew and that what he has bequeathed to Christian posterity is to a large extent the product of an internal Jewish debate. During the New Testament period, Sinai was problematic within Judaism. Paul's solutions are indeed peculiar in the extreme from the perspective of anyone standing in the tradition of rabbinic Judaism, but his genius is that he was able to prevent the negative *function* of the Sinaitic covenant from evolving into its *negation* or annihilation. This is evident when one examines his statements about the relationship between the "new" and the "old." Why is it that the coming of the "new" inexorably implies the passing away of the "old"? Why could not the *novum* that Paul proclaims simply have left the "old" untouched? Why could he not have simply ignored it? Ironically, the polemical character of Paul's covenantal theology flows directly from the deeply held conviction that what has taken place in Jesus Christ is in no sense irrelevant or tangential to the people Israel. Though the covenant is "new," it is conceived through and through as the work of the God of Israel, and it is for this reason that for Paul the "new covenant" must have powerful implications for the status of the "old." To leave the "old" untouched and simply move off in a completely different direction would be tantamount to saying that what has taken place in Jesus Christ is unrelated to God's history with Israel. For Paul the Jew, this was an unthinkable option. However peculiar his Jewishness may have been, God's history with the people Israel was an element that Paul could not sacrifice, because what is ultimately at stake in the "new covenant" is the identity of the God who is at work in it.

The dilemma for Christian readers of Paul is that written texts are able to transcend the immediate contexts in which they were produced and thus take on a life of their own. This is an inevitable aspect of all written texts. But the particular problem with which Paul was faced involved his walking a very fine line, and a fundamental concern of his was to preserve the identity of the God who was at work through the gospel among the Gentiles. Once that concern is no longer recognized, the integral connection between the "new" and the "old" is lost as well, and negativity easily evolves into negation. This has always been the test for the church, because negation has direct consequences for the identity of God. To its credit, the church has consistently recognized this danger and for the most part has strongly resisted those movements that wanted to make the "new covenant" (and later, the New Testament) self-sufficient. The church preserves the Old Testament as Scripture not that it might function as a foil for the New but rather to ensure that the readers of the New are absolutely clear about the identity of the God whom Christians are privileged to call "our Father." In terms of how all of this relates to the Christian appropriation of Exod 19, one would be hard-pressed to say it better than Childs:

> The new covenant is not a substitution of a friendly God for the terror of Sinai, but rather a gracious message of an open access to the same God whose presence still calls forth awe and reverence.[69]

---

[69] Childs, *Exodus,* 384.

The Many Faces of God in Exodus 19

Marc Zvi Brettler

Even the classical rabbis realized that Exod 19 lacks uniformity. The *Pesiqta de Rab Kahana,* a fifth-century Palestinian midrashic work that contains collections of discourses for various special Sabbaths,[1] contains the following sermon for the Sabbath of Shavuot, the Feast of Weeks, when according to tradition Exod 19–20 are read to commemorate the giving of the Torah:

> R. Ḥanina bar Papa said: The Holy One appeared to Israel with a stern face, with an equanimous face, with a friendly face,[2] with a joyous face .... Therefore the Holy One said to them: Though you see Me in all these guises, [I am still One]—*I am the Lord thy God.*

> R. Levi said: The Holy One appeared to them as though He were a statue with faces on every side, so that though a thousand men might be looking at the statue, they would be led to believe that it was looking at each one of them.... [This is followed by a set of prooftexts concerning the manna, which according to rabbinic tradition, had the similar ability to have a "customized" taste, palatable to each individual. The *Pesiqta* continues:] Thus David said: "The voice of the Lord is in its strength" (Ps 29:4)—not "The voice of the Lord is in His strength," but "The voice of the Lord is in its strength"—that is, in its strength to make itself heard and understood according to the capacity of each and every person who listens to the Divine Word. Therefore the Holy One said: Do not be misled because you hear many voices. Know ye that I am He who is one and the same: *I am the Lord thy God.*[3]

---

[1] On this work, its likely date, and its provenience, see Hermann Strack and Günter Stemberger, *Introduction to the Talmud and Midrash* (trans. Markus Bockmuehl; Edinburgh: T&T Clark, 1991), 317–22.

[2] It is probably not coincidental that four faces are depicted here, following the tradition of Ezek 1:6, which is part of the larger ancient Near Eastern tradition; cf. Moshe Greenberg, *Ezekiel 1–20* (AB 22A; Garden City, N.Y.: Doubleday, 1993), 55, and the illustration (of Marduk?) in Thorkild Jacobsen, *The Treasures of Darkness: A History of Mesopotamian Religion* (New Haven: Yale University Press, 1976), 166.

[3] *Pesikta de-Rav Kahana: R. Kahana's Discourses of Sabbath and Festal Days* (trans. W. G. Braude and I. J. Kapstein; Philadelphia: Jewish Publication Society of

Certainly, the rabbis of the *Pesiqta* would not have accepted any one of the source-critical models that divide today's biblical scholars. Yet, evidence is evidence, and the evidence that the Bible, a text that in some places is obsessed with unity, does not present a single, consistent view of divine revelation, is incontrovertible. This is not only true for the contents of the revelation, where the differences between the Exodus and Deuteronomy versions of the Decalogue are plain and visible,[4] but in the narrative material that surrounds the Decalogue and the Covenant Collection.[5] This is why the *Pesiqta* could suggest that God is simultaneously stern, equanimous, friendly, and joyous, or that God was perceived in many different ways on Sinai, and that these different perceptions might be responsible for the current shape of the narrative material that attempts to describe that event.

In fact, Exod 19 remains one of the most intractable chapters in the entirety of the Pentateuch in terms of source-critical analysis.[6] It is quite literally a dizzying chapter, most especially for those who are afraid of heights or don't like hiking up and down mountains repeatedly: Moses is commanded to descend in verses 21 and 24, and commanded to ascend in verse 24, and possibly verse 9; he ascends the mountain in verses 3 and 20, and descends in verses 14 and 25. Much of this ascending and descending is done alone. In verse 24 only, Aaron may accompany Moses, while verse 13b, seemingly a fragment that does not fit with any other part of this chapter, suggests "When the ram's horn sounds a long blast, they [all Israel] may go up on the mountain."[7] More to the point of the midrash, which is focused on God's face, God is indeed multifaceted. In verses 1–8, nothing remarkable is narrated about God's appearance. In verse 9, YHWH is manifest through "a thick cloud." In verse 16, he is characterized by a

---

America, 1975), 249–50. For the Hebrew text, see Bernard Mandelbaum, ed., *Pesikta de Rav Kahana* (New York: Jewish Theological Seminary of America, 1962), 1:223–24.

[4] In English, see the convenient chart in Moshe Greenberg, "The Decalogue Tradition Critically Examined," in *The Ten Commandments in History and Tradition* (ed. Ben-Zion Segal; Jerusalem: Magnes, 1985), 92–93. For the typical rabbinic solution to these differences, see Jacob Z. Lauterbach, *Mekilta de-Rabbi Ishmael* (Philadelphia: Jewish Publication Society of America, 1976), 2:252.

[5] I refer specifically to Exod. 20:18–21 and to ch. 24.

[6] See esp. the literature cited in Joseph Blenkinsopp, "Structure and Meaning in the Sinai-Horeb Narrative," in *A Biblical Itinerary: In Search of Method, Form and Content: Essays in Honor of George W. Coats* (ed. Eugene E. Carpenter; JSOTSup 240; Sheffield: Sheffield Academic Press, 1997), 111 n. 5. The comparative chart in Erich Zenger, *Die Sinaitheophanie: Untersuchungen zum jahwistischen und elohistischen Geschichtswerk* (Würzburg: Echter, 1971), 207–10, is also quite instructive.

[7] All translations are from the NJPS.

thunderstorm, while in verse 18, YHWH has "come down upon it in fire; the smoke rose like the smoke of a kiln, and the whole mountain trembled violently," reminiscent of a volcano. The latter descriptions represent the danger of revelation; a more extensive look at revelation, which would go beyond chapter 19 and would encompass Exod 24 as well, would surely contrast these depictions to Exod 24:9-11, where Moses, Aaron, Nadab, and Abihu, along with seventy elders "saw the God of Israel" (v. 10) while they, in a quite everyday manner, ate and drank. Looking more broadly at the complex depiction of revelation in Deuteronomy would muddy the picture still more,[8] but it is already plenty muddy when confined "just" to Exod 19.

The standard source-critical analysis of this chapter may be found, for example, in Driver's Exodus commentary.[9] This division fails the basic tests of source criticism: it does not yield two largely parallel, largely complete, largely self-sufficient, largely nonredundant sources. For example, according to the "standard" picture, in verse 9, from J, YHWH tells Moses that he will appear "in a thick cloud" (בעב הענן), but there is no fulfillment of this anywhere in the chapter, in material attributed to J (or in any other material). Instead, in the continuation of the reconstructed J document (v. 18), "Now Mount Sinai was all in smoke, for the LORD had come down upon it in fire; the smoke rose like the smoke of a kiln, and the whole mountain trembled violently." Although the juxtaposed images might not be very jarring for the English reader, the conflict between the obscuring cloud (ענן) of verse 9 and the volcanic imagery of verse 18 is striking, and it seems impossible that they both share the same source. Such examples of "sources" that do not quite tell the same story, of verses that seem to have no connection to any other part of the chapter (e.g., 19:13b), could be multiplied.

It then becomes tempting to either give up, offering one of the various synchronic readings of the chapter,[10] or to attempt a new, nonstandard analysis of the chapter. Yet, I do not believe that the evidence is available to allow for a new source-critical analysis of the chapter that would not rely on the standard sources. The chapter is too short to serve as the sole

---

[8] See esp. Stephen A. Geller, *Sacred Enigma: Literary Religion in the Hebrew Bible* (London: Routledge, 1996), 30–61.

[9] This is delineated quite conveniently in S. R. Driver, *The Book of Exodus* (CBC; Cambridge: Cambridge University Press, 1918), 169–75; for a summary of more recent views, see Brevard Childs, *The Book of Exodus: A Critical, Theological Commentary* (OTL; Philadelphia: Westminster, 1974), 344–47; and the chart of Zenger (see above, n. 6).

[10] See, for example, Umberto Cassuto, *A Commentary on the Book of Exodus* (trans. Israel Abrahams; Jerusalem: Magnes, 1967), 223–35. A good survey of various synchronic methods currently used in biblical studies is Gale A. Yee, ed., *Judges and Method: New Approaches in Biblical Studies* (Minneapolis: Fortress, 1995).

piece of evidence for a source-critical analysis, and it is interconnected in extremely complex ways with the material at the conclusion of chapter 20 and in chapter 24. Source-critical analysis is possible in "regular" chapters because it is easy to divide them into a small number of pieces that fit together and then to fit these larger pieces together into greater wholes that may be allied to other units using vocabulary, style, and ideology as criteria—this is impossible for this chapter. Finally, I must confess that I feel that a basic question that must be answered before attempting an "independent" source-critical analysis of Exod 19 has not been adequately addressed by scholars: How much variation in style, content, or theology may a unit have before we decide that it is composite? And, to complicate the issue, how do we know if it is composite on the written, source-critical level, or if some unevenness is the result of a source integrating preexistent (oral) traditions?[11] Until these issues are further studied, as they must be, perhaps using the type of "empirical models" used by Tigay and others,[12] it will simply be impossible to offer a detailed, "scientific" examination of the sources for Exod 19 or similar chapters with multiple strands. I fully concur with Childs's observation on Exod 19: "The point of this criticism is not to suggest that there are no literary tensions in the text, but rather that the traditional source division is unable to cope with them in this chapter."[13]

Although no detailed source analysis will be provided, various differences between sections will be pointed to—it is unimportant for this analysis whether they represent different "sources" in the classical sense, or are fragments in the sense used by the old fragmentary hypothesis,[14] or are traditions that may have been integrated into what contemporary scholars consider one of the pentateuchal sources. To some extent, this type of examination, interested in a vague type of sources, rather than Sources, has been completed on this material by Jacob Licht, who isolates fifteen different conceptions of the Sinaitic revelation.[15] Following Licht, I will not attempt to isolate the exact extent of the narrow sources themselves but will concentrate on understanding the multiple ideologies represented in

[11] On this issue, see Susan Niditch, *Oral World and Written Word: Ancient Israelite Literature* (Library of Ancient Israel; Louisville: Westminster/John Knox, 1996), esp. 99–130.

[12] Jeffrey H. Tigay, ed., *Empirical Models for Biblical Criticism* (Philadelphia: University of Pennsylvania Press, 1985).

[13] Childs, *Exodus,* 349.

[14] For a description of this hypothesis, see Otto Eissfeldt, *The Old Testament: An Introduction* (trans. P. R. Ackroyd; New York: Harper & Row, 1965), 178–80.

[15] Jacob Licht, "The Sinai Theophany" (in Hebrew), in *Studies in Bible and the Ancient Near East Presented to Samuel E. Loewenstamm on His Seventieth Birthday*

the chapter, in discerning ancient Israel's understanding of the *Pesiqta's* "faces of God." We must remember that source criticism, no matter how it is accomplished, is a tool rather than an end in itself—in fact, part of the current crisis of biblical studies is that too many scholars have forgotten that tools are tools and have confused them with exegesis or interpretation, leading to dull results with little utility.

Before examining the ideology of various components of Exod 19, it is necessary to examine why the chapter is not accommodated by standard source-critical models. It is one of a small number of passages that I have elsewhere labeled "magnet texts," because they attract more than the usual number of traditions.[16] For example, 2 Kgs 17, which attempts to understand why the northern kingdom was exiled, is one such text—the question was so weighty that many different answers were ultimately incorporated into the chapter.[17] This has been noted, in a different way, by Moshe Greenberg, concerning Exod 19: "The extraordinary complexity is best explained as the result of the interweaving of parallel narrations; the author appears to have been reluctant to exclude any scrap of data relevant to this momentous occasion."[18]

It is not, however, at first glance obvious why the revelation at Sinai should be considered such a "momentous occasion." Internal biblical and external Near Eastern evidence coalesce nicely to explain this. Deuteronomy 4:1–40, which is usually characterized as an exilic sermon,[19] notes toward its conclusion (vv. 32–36):

(ed. Yitschak Avishur and Joshua Blau; Jerusalem: E. Rubenstein's Publishing House, 1978), 251–67 [English summary in non-Hebrew volume, 201–2].

[16] See my "The Composition of 1 Samuel 1–2," *JBL* 116 (1997): 601–12 and "Interpretation and Prayer: Notes on the Composition of 1 Kings 8.15–53," in *Minḥah le-Naḥum: Biblical and Other Studies Presented to Nahum M. Sarna in Honour of his 70th Birthday* (ed. Marc Brettler and Michael Fishbane; JSOTSup 154; Sheffield: Sheffield Academic Press, 1993), 17–35, esp. 34.

[17] See my *The Creation of History in Ancient Israel* (London: Routledge, 1995), 112–34.

[18] Moshe Greenberg, "Exodus, Book of," *EncJuc* 6:1056. Cf. the earlier comments of Martin Noth: "it is easily understandable that the important, central section of the tradition of the theophany on Sinai should frequently have been worked over and provided with expansion" (*Exodus* [trans. J. S. Bowden; OTL; Philadelphia: Westminster, 1962], 154).

[19] I am uncomfortable with the term *sermon* but continue to use it as a scholarly convention; see my comments in "Predestination in Deuteronomy 30.1–10," in *Those Elusive Deuteronomists: The Pheonomonon of Pan-Deuteronomism* (ed. Linda Schearing and Steven McKenzie; JSOTSup 268; Sheffield: Sheffield Academic

> (32) You have but to inquire about bygone ages that came before you, ever since God created man on earth, from one end of heaven to the other: has anything as grand as this ever happened, or has its like ever been known? (33) Has any people heard the voice of a god speaking out of a fire, as you have, and survived? (34) Or has any god ventured to go and take for himself one nation from the midst of another by prodigious acts, by signs and portents, by war, by a mighty hand and an outstretched arm and awesome power, as the LORD your God did for you in Egypt before your very eyes? (35) It has been clearly demonstrated to you that the LORD alone is God; there is none beside Him. (36) From the heavens He let you hear His voice to discipline you; on earth He let you see His great fire; and from amidst that fire you heard His words.

The "demonstration" (v. 35) of the correctness of radical monotheism,[20] arguably the central concern of the exilic Deuteronomist, has two parts: YHWH's power as a redeemer from Egypt, and his ability to effectively and closely communicate with Israel, without Israel being harmed (vv. 33 and 36). Yet, other biblical texts suggest that this first "proof," God as sole liberator, is no proof at all; in the words of Amos 9:7:

> To me, O Israelites, you are just like the Ethiopians—declares the LORD. True, I brought Israel up from the land of Egypt, but also the Philistines from Caphtor and the Arameans from Kir.

The second proof, however, "stands" the test of biblical and extrabiblical evidence. Nowhere does the Bible suggest that any nation other than Israel was the recipient of divine law. In fact, the standard ancient Near Eastern pattern was for the kings to give the law to their people.[21] The relief atop the Code of Hammurabi illustrates this; it does *not* show, as some had earlier thought, Hammurabi getting the law "code" from the

---

Press, 1999), 171–88. On Deut 4, see esp. A. D. H. Mayes, "Deuteronomy 4 and the Literary Criticism of Deuteronomy," in *A Song of Power and the Power of Song: Essays on the Book of Deuteronomy* (ed. Duane L. Christensen; Sources for Biblical and Theological Study 3; Winona Lake, Ind.: Eisenbrauns, 1993), 195–224; Jon D. Levenson, "Who Inserted the Book of the Torah?" *HTR* 68 (1975): 203–33; Alexander Rofé, "The Monotheistic Argument in Deuteronomy iv 32–40: Contents, Composition and Text," *VT* 35 (1985): 434–45; and Geller, *Sacred Enigma,* 30–61.

[20] This term is borrowed from Tikva Frymer-Kensky, *In the Wake of the Goddesses: Women, Culture, and the Biblical Transformation of Pagan Myth* (New York: Free Press, 1992).

[21] This is clearest in Mesopotamia; see the evidence collected in Martha T. Roth, *Law Collections from Mesopotamia and Asia Minor* (SBLWAW 6; Atlanta: Scholars Press, 1995), 4–5.

god, but illustrates Hammurabi, who had composed the "code" so the gods would be happy, in a position of worship, as the god Shamash gives him the scepter and ring of kingship.[22] The conclusion of the prologue to the laws of Hammurabi illustrates unambiguously what the relationship between the king and god was: "When the god Marduk commanded me to provide just ways for the people of the land (in order to attain) appropriate behavior, I established truth and justice as the declaration of the land, I enhanced the well-being of the people. At that time: [law one follows]."[23]

Stated differently, since the turn of the century biblical scholarship has been deeply interested in the connection between Israel and its neighbors, whether this was in the form of what some have called "parallelomania"[24] or in sweeping attempts to discern "The Common Theology of the Ancient Near East."[25] This extensive research, however, has indicated no other case in the ancient Near Eastern world where the law was attributed to divine revelation. As with Hammurabi, a deity might "request" that a king establish law; there might be a general expectation that kings should establish justice in the land,[26] but nowhere else is a body of law "revealed" to either a king or to the population as a whole.

---

[22] For a photo of the relief, see *The Ancient Near East in Pictures Relating to the Old Testament* (ed. James B. Pritchard; 2d ed. with suppl.; Princeton: Princeton University Press, 1969), 175 (photo no. 515). See the discussion of the relief in Moshe Greenberg, "Some Postulates of Biblical Criminal Law," in *The Jewish Expression* (ed. Judah Goldin, 1960; repr., New Haven: Yale University Press, 1976), 35 n. 10; also repr. in Moshe Greenberg, *Studies in the Bible and Jewish Thought* (Philadelphia: Jewish Publication Society of America, 1995), 39 n. 10.

[23] Roth, *Law Collections from Mesopotamia and Asia Minor,* 80–81.

[24] Samuel Sandmel, "Parallelomania," *JBL* 81 (1962): 1–13.

[25] This is the title of an essay by Morton Smith appearing in *JBL* 71 (1952): 135–47. If anything, further study has substantiated Smith's claim, finding small differences between Israel and its neighbors but emphasizing that much of what was thought to be uniquely Israelite was shared between Israel and its neighbors. See, for example, Bertil Albrektson, *History and the Gods: An Essay on the Idea of Historical Events as Divine Manifestations in the Ancient Near East and Israel* (ConBOT 1; Lund: Gleerup, 1967); H. W. F. Saggs, *The Encounter with the Divine in Mesopotamia and Israel* (London: Athlone, 1978); Karel van der Toorn, *Sin and Sanction in Israel and Mesopotamia: A Comparative Study* (SSN 22; Assen: Van Gorcum, 1985); idem, *Family Religion in Babylonia, Ugarit and Israel: Continuity and Changes in the Forms of Religious Life* (Leiden: Brill, 1996); and idem, *The Image and the Book: Iconic Cults, Aniconism, and the Rise of Book Religion in Israel and the Ancient Near East* (Leuven: Uitgeverij Peeters, 1997).

[26] See n. 21 above and Moshe Weinfeld, *Social Justice in Ancient Israel and in the Ancient Near East* (Jerusalem: Magnes, 1995), 45–56.

Latecomer cultures[27] like Israel typically absorbed different practices from the surrounding nations, ultimately creating a new religion. It is easy to see what they absorbed and, in the process, might have changed somewhat to fit the surrounding cultural norms,[28] but it seems impossible to reconstruct why at certain points fundamentally new ideas developed in Israel or in any other culture. Thus, it is very difficult to understand, as a historian of religions, how, why, and precisely when monotheism developed in ancient Israel;[29] it is much easier, for example, to understand how Gen 1, which is at points clearly related to the Mesopotamian myth *Enuma Elish,* developed within ancient Israel. This means that when some ancient Israelites tried to envision what the act of a divinely given law might look like, there were no direct models to follow. This uniqueness by itself fueled diverse and multiple speculation, which ultimately resulted in the many views exhibited in Exod 19, in other biblical texts, and ultimately in later speculative and philosophical traditions.[30] Stated differently, when an Israelite tried to imagine how the world was created, the standard myths of the surrounding cultures influenced the results; in the case of "imagining" the revelation of law, no such prestigious external legacy held sway.

This does not mean that the specifics of various concepts of revelation were invented *de novo,* without any influences from other material. Various trajectories may be traced through biblical literature (not just the Torah!) that align various pieces of Exod 19 with other biblical literature. The two most obvious axes for looking at these concepts are the role of Moses versus the role of the people and the physical description of God.

---

[27] I do not mean to suggest that I am sympathetic to the new school that suggests that Israel is an exilic creation; all I mean is that compared to the great civilizations of Egypt and Mesopotamia, Israel was a latecomer. Those of us who focus on Israel tend to forget this important fact.

[28] The clearest exposition of this is J. J. Finkelstein, *The Ox That Gored* (TAPS 71.2; Philadelphia: American Philosophical Society, 1981).

[29] Othmar Keel, ed., *Monotheismus im alten Israel und seiner Umwelt* (BibB 14; Stuttgart: Katholisches Bibelwerk, 1980); Walter Dietrich and Martin A. Klopfenstein, eds., *Ein Gott Allein? JHWH-Verehrung und biblischer Monotheismus im Kontext der Israelitischen und altorientalischen Religiongeschichte* (OBO 139; Frieburg: Universitatsverlag, 1994); the discussion in Hershel Shanks and Jack Meinhardt, eds., *Aspects of Monotheism: How God Is One* (Washington, D.C.: Biblical Archaeology Society, 1997); and Robert Karl Gnuse, *No Other Gods: Emergent Monotheism in Israel* (JSOTSup 241; Sheffield: Sheffield Academic Press, 1997).

[30] On the continuity between the biblical and postbiblical views, see the comments of Licht, "The Sinai Theophany," 266, and Arie Toeg, *Lawgiving at Sinai* (in Hebrew) (Jerusalem: Magnes, 1977), 162.

Without any question, Moses plays a central role in this chapter.[31] In verse 3, he ascends to God. In verse 7 (having descended, at least in the redacted version), he speaks YHWH's words to the people. In verse 8, he returns to God. In verse 9, YHWH again speaks to Moses, and Moses relays this information to the people. In verses 10–13, Moses is given instructions in preparation for the revelation. In verses 14–15, Moses descends from the mountain and prepares the people. In verse 17, Moses leads the people out toward God. In verse 19, Moses is in dialogue with God. In verse 20b, YHWH calls to Moses, who ascends. In verses 21–22, Moses is given a (new) commandment for the people, so they might avoid death. In verses 23–24, Moses speaks to YHWH, who responds, and Moses is told to descend, which he finally does in verse 25. This summary reflects the importance of Moses in this narrative; indeed, his name appears fourteen times in the chapter.

Moses is not only privileged in terms of the number of times he is mentioned but in terms of his function. In most of the chapter, he is the one who has the special relationship with YHWH, to the exclusion of all others. He goes up to God (vv. 3, 20). He relays messages to the community or to the elders, who represent the community (vv. 3, 7, 9, 15, 25). He directly conveys the people's response to YHWH (v. 9). The beginning of verse 9 is even more remarkable: "And the LORD said to Moses, 'I will come to you in a thick cloud, in order that the people may hear when I speak with you and so trust you ever after.'" Part of the purpose of revelation is that Moses be trusted forever! He is directly responsible for preserving the life of the community, by assuring that they will be ritually pure and will keep their distance (vv. 10–15, 21–24), a role that elsewhere the *entire* Levite clan would have.[32] He leads the people out toward God (v. 17). He initiates a conversation with God, and God responds (v. 19).

These details together certainly fit well with the main image of Moses presented in the Torah and elsewhere as *the* central figure, as the covenant mediator.[33] They recall the remarkable verse of the previous pericope

[31] For a broader description of the role of Moses in the Sinai pericope, see Toeg, *Lawgiving at Sinai,* 48–51.

[32] See Jacob Milgrom, *Studies in Levitical Terminology,* vol. 1: *The Encroacher and the Levite, The Term ʿAboda* (University of California Publications, Near Eastern Studies 14; Berkeley and Los Angeles: University of California Press, 1971).

[33] See the discussion in Childs, *Exodus,* 347–60, and concerning parts of the chapter, James Muilenburg, "The Form and Structure of the Covenantal Formulations," *VT* 9 (1959): 347–65; and Thomas B. Dozeman, *God on the Mountain: A Study of Redaction, Theology and Canon in Exodus 19–24* (SBLMS 37; Atlanta: Scholars Press, 1989), 39–45. This whole depiction is now complicated by the redating of various biblical texts and the greater hesitation of scholars to find the idea of covenant in texts that do not explicitly contain the term. See the

(Exod 14:31): "And when Israel saw the wondrous power which the LORD had wielded against the Egyptians, the people feared the LORD; they had faith in the LORD and His servant Moses." They are also reminiscent of Num 12:8: "With him I speak mouth to mouth, plainly and not in riddles, and he beholds the likeness of the LORD. How then did you not shrink from speaking against My servant Moses!" It even recalls his remarkable death and burial by YHWH (Deut 34:6)[34] and the concluding verses of the Torah, which do not focus on YHWH but on Moses (Deut 34:10–12):

> (10) Never again did there arise in Israel a prophet like Moses—whom the LORD singled out, face to face, (11) for the various signs and portents that the LORD sent him to display in the land of Egypt, against Pharaoh and all his courtiers and his whole country, (12) and for all the great might and awesome power that Moses displayed before all Israel.

This image is of course well known and continued to develop throughout biblical literature, as Moses became YHWH's servant par excellence (e.g. 1 Kgs 8:56; Mal 3:22; Neh 1:7; 2 Chr 24:6); the Torah was so closely associated with him that it was called Moses' Torah (e.g., Josh 8:31; 1 Kgs 2:3; Mal 3:22; Dan 9:13; Ezra 3:2; Neh 8:1) or the Book of Moses (Neh 13:1; 2 Chr 25:4; 35:12; cf. Ezra 6:18 [Aramaic]). Seeing this development, the centrality of Moses is in many senses "normal," especially if we concede that the majority of Exod 19 within its wider context has "covenant" as its background, in which case Moses is falling into the "expected" role of covenant mediator. The remarkable texts become those that do *not* focus solely on Moses.

Exodus 19 provides us with two such texts: verses 13b and 24. As noted above, verse 13b, which states, "When the ram's horn sounds a long blast, they [the nation as a whole] may go up on the mountain," is quite unusual. It is most likely a preserved fragment of a larger, quite different description of the revelation, which was much more democratic. Moses did not play the same central role and, as in other exceptional cases (Judg 6:22; 13:22), a regular individual, or in this case the entire community of individuals, could directly experience YHWH without dying. Although this idea has no other parallels in this chapter, it is reflected in other revelation material, most clearly in certain sections of Deuteronomy's depiction of the revelation (Deut 4:10–13, 33, 36a; 5:4, 22–24; these sections are largely a

---

discussion of Ernest W. Nicholson, *God and His People: Covenant and Theology in the Old Testament* (Oxford: Clarendon, 1986).

[34] See Samuel E. Loewenstamm, "The Death of Moses," in *From Babylon to Canaan: Studies in the Bible and its Oriental Background* (Jerusalem: Magnes, 1992), 136–66.

reinterpretation of Exod 20:19–20).[35] Similar "democratic" ideals are reflected in the story concerning Eldad and Medad prophesying after the prophetic spirit had descended on the seventy elders (Num 11:16–30),[36] where Moses says to Joshua (v. 29): "Are you wrought up on my account? Would that all the LORD's people were prophets, that the LORD put His spirit upon them!" However, this type of democratization of prophecy could lead to confusion and anarchy, as no one would be sure who the "true" prophet was;[37] for this reason, such texts, which allow the entire nation to partake of the prophetic spirit or to hear YHWH's word in an unmediated fashion, are few and far between.[38]

Exodus 19:24 seems to suggest that Aaron could partake in the revelation to the same extent as Moses. This fits in clearly with a certain Aaronide priestly bias that is found in sections of the Bible, especially in Priestly literature.[39] Given the role of Aaron as high priest and as founder of the priestly clan, it is not surprising that some group would "insist" that Aaron be included in the revelation to the same extent as Moses. The verse may then be seen as legitimating both prophecy and priesthood as institutions. Finally, the verse need not be Priestly in the narrow sense of the word; Ps 77:21, "You led Your people like a flock in the care of Moses and Aaron," among other texts, offers an example of Aaron playing as prominent a role as Moses.

The predominant image of this chapter is without any question one that privileges Moses. Given the centrality of Moses within the Pentateuch, which ultimately becomes the Torah of Moses, this is hardly surprising. What is surprising, however, is that other images do compete in this chapter with these Moses-centered views.[40] The verse that puts Aaron on par

---

35 I do not agree with the revisionist position of John Van Seters, "'Comparing Scripture with Scripture:' Some Observations on the Sinai Pericope of Exodus 19–24," in *Canon, Theology, and Old Testament Interpretation: Essays in Honor of Brevard S. Childs* (ed. Gene M. Tucker et al.; Philadelphia: Fortress, 1988), 111–30.

36 Exod 24:9–10 similarly reflects a type of "representational democracy" where the representatives of the people, not just Moses, receive the highest level of revelation.

37 The recognition that prophecy could be a destabilizing influence on society is one of the major contributions of the sociological approach to biblical prophecy; see, for example, Robert R. Wilson, *Prophecy and Society in Ancient Israel* (Philadelphia: Fortress, 1980).

38 For a broader description of these democratizing texts in the Sinai pericope, see Toeg, *Lawgiving at Sinai,* 51–59.

39 For a summary, see John R. Spencer, "Aaron," *ABD* 1:1–6; and Merlin D. Rehm, "Levites and Priests," *ABD* 4:297–310.

40 I use "views" in the plural to emphasize that not all of the verses that depict Moses in this central role derive from the same source—it is not the case that we

with Moses fits a different set of ideological motives, legitimating Aaron. The fragment that democratizes the process, allowing all of Israel to ascend, is more surprising, until we recall the various indications throughout the Bible, such as the rebellions of Korah, and of Dathan and Abiram (Num 16), and the various texts that are deeply suspicious of kingship (e.g., 1 Sam 8), that suggest that within Israel there were people who were deeply suspicious of centralized authority, favoring instead a more democratic type of social organization. Alternatively, this group may have been suspicious of any type of mediated covenant, since that opened the possibility of saying that the mediator was not accurately reflecting the wishes of the suzerain. A similar idea seems to stand behind Deut 5:3–4: "It was not with our fathers that the LORD made this covenant, but with us, the living, every one of us who is here today. Face to face the LORD spoke to you on the mountain out of the fire."[41]

As noted earlier, Exod 19 may also be connected to various trajectories in terms of the way YHWH is depicted. The first manifestation of YHWH is in verse 9, where he says: "I will come to you in a thick cloud."[42] Clouds are elsewhere associated with YHWH's theophany (e.g., Judg 5:4; Ps 18:12 [par. 2 Sam 22:12], 13). Exodus 19:9 may be partaking of that tradition, but most other theophany texts are much richer, describing the power of YHWH as associated with the storm, so this is unlikely to be the main reason that YHWH is manifest here as a thick cloud. Instead, the function of the cloud here is likely to obscure YHWH, so that the people need not worry about seeing YHWH and dying.[43] It is crucial to note that this verse emphasizes that the nation must *hear* YHWH rather than see him. This verse, then, in a nutshell, expresses the theology that stands behind much of Deut 4:1–40: Hearing (and not seeing!) is believing.[44] It is therefore not surprising that Deut 4 describes YHWH as being obscured as well, in that case by (v. 11): "dark with densest clouds." In non-Sinai traditions, a similar idea is expressed in the ritual for the Day of Atonement, where a cloud of incense smoke must cover the *kapporet* so that the high

---

can neatly divide the chapter into a Moses source, a Moses and Aaron source, and an "all Israel" source. The chapter is much more complicated than that because the Moses sections do not form a unity.

[41] The relationship of v. 5 to vv. 3–4 need not concern us here.

[42] The Hebrew is a case of synonymous constructs; see Yitshak Avishur, *Stylistic Studies of Word-Pairs in Biblical and Ancient Semitic Literature* (AOAT 210; Kevelar: Butzon & Bercker, 1984), 173.

[43] On the fear of seeing God and dying, see above, 362.

[44] See Geller, *Sacred Enigma,* 30–61. Note esp. vv. 35–36, which says "see" and "hear" twice. However, YHWH is never seen directly, though he is heard. Cf. Deut 4:12, 15.

priest will not die (Lev 16:13), presumably as a result of seeing the enthroned deity.[45]

The cloud of verse 9 is thus different from the cloud of verse 16, which notes: "On the third day, as morning dawned, there was thunder, and lightning, and a dense cloud upon the mountain, and a very loud blast of the horn; and all the people who were in the camp trembled." This cloud expresses YHWH's great power and, as many scholars have shown, is a primary part of many theophany scenes (e.g. Judg 5:4; Hab 3:10; Ps 77:19); it is most likely borrowed from depictions of Baal as a Canaanite storm god.[46] It contrasts with the cloud of verse 9—the former does not strike fear in the nation—indeed, it facilitates their ability to apprehend YHWH, while this is a *storm* cloud, with its accompanying thunder and lightning, that causes the people to tremble.

The lightning of verse 16 is quite different from the fire of verse 18, though they may evoke the same reaction[47]—fire is not typically part of the imagery of a storm. It can represent YHWH's destructive nature (cf., e.g., Deut 4:24; 9:3; Isa 30:30; 66:15; Zeph 1:18; Lam 4:11), which explains the fear at the end of the verse.[48] Fire is central as well to Deut 5:22–26, which has most likely borrowed the image from here. However, Deuteronomy omits the image of smoke that is such a central part of Exod 19:18. Perhaps Deuteronomy sensed that a volcano stood behind the image of its source in Exod 19, which depicted a fire, smoke, and a trembling mountain;[49] Deuteronomy did not like this naturalistic interpretation of fire and removed the volcano so that the image of fire would fit more comfortably with the Deuteronomic understanding of the revelation as absolutely *sui generis*. Exodus, on the other hand, subsumed the image of fire into that of a volcano, one of the great manifestations of YHWH's power.[50]

Thus, in a way, the various images of YHWH coalesce, since they are all connected to clouds or darkness. But the images are fundamentally different; we must distinguish between the cloud that obscures (v. 9), the cloud of the thunderstorm (v. 16), and the dark smoke of the volcano (v. 18). Despite the

---

[45] See the discussion in Jacob Milgrom, *Leviticus 1–16* (AB; New York: Doubleday, 1991), 1028–31.

[46] See the summary in Mark S. Smith, *The Early History of God: Yahweh and the Other Deities in Ancient Israel* (San Francisco: Harper & Row, 1990), 49–55.

[47] See the commentaries and John William Wevers, *Notes on the Greek Text of Exodus* (SBLSCS 30; Atlanta: Scholars Press, 1990), 304, concerning the text-critical issues of MT's reading ההר.

[48] אש, "fire," also found in this verse, is used by YHWH for punishment and may evoke fear (cf., e.g., Deut 29:19; Pss 18:9; 74:1).

[49] So MT; see n. 47 above.

[50] Note how the volcano is the climactic image of Ps 104:32.

similarities of image, which may have helped the fragments coalesce, they represent fundamentally different ideas, different "faces (or voices) of God." They should not be collapsed together, at least when dealing with an interpretation of the chapter that is sensitive to its history of composition.

Much of this essay could be characterized as "weakly" source critical, in the sense that various traditions or fragments have been discerned, though for reasons outlined above, exact sources were not delineated. It was natural for these various ideas to come together as the Bible went through the canonical *process,*[51] as individuals and groups attempted to understand the unique process of revelation. I will conclude with some brief observations concerning the final product. These will be from a weak redaction-criticism perspective—"weak" because we do not know the exact sources, so we cannot outline precisely how they came together and exactly how the redactor proceeded with the work.[52] In this age, we can no longer accept Wellhausen's idea that the Sinai pericope is an "improvised unity,"[53] and some more meaningful examination of how the finished whole might have been put together should be attempted.

One thing is obvious about Exod 19: in its redacted form, it is a mess, telling a very confusing, ambiguous story. Moshe Greenberg has observed: "The consequent looseness and obscurity of the story can hardly have escaped his [the redactor's] notice, and may well have been intended as a literary reflex of the multivalence of the event."[54] This structure, or lack of structure, of chapter 19 stands in marked contrast to chapter 24, which is almost as complicated in terms of its history of composition as chapter 19 but is a much "neater" chapter in its final form. There the redactor has assembled sources to create a picture of what might be called progressive revelation, where Moses alone is on top of the mountain, with other individuals or groups camping at various points on the mountain, in areas that reflect their perceived importance—Joshua toward the top (v. 13); the elders, Aaron, Nadab, Abihu, and the seventy elders below him (vv. 1, 9); and the nation further below (v. 2). Surely, a similar structure could have been created in chapter 19, or a different type of more satisfying, unitary depiction of how YHWH was manifest could have been created there. Yet this was not done.

---

[51] Philip R. Davies, *Scribes and Schools: The Canonization of the Hebrew Scriptures* (Library of Ancient Israel; Louisville: Westminster/John Knox, 1998) constructively emphasizes the extent to which the formation of the Bible was a "process," with many different agendas and groups behind it.

[52] Contrast the approach to redaction and its purpose in Thomas B. Dozeman, "Spatial Form in Exod 19:1–8a."

[53] See the discussion of this idea in Dozeman, *God on the Mountain,* 3.

[54] Greenberg, "Exodus, Book of," 1056.

Exodus 19 and 24, in their redacted form, thus represent two polar visions of religion. Chapter 19 is redacted to heighten the mysterious aspect of religion, with a God who does not quite fit together, with revelation as a singular, not fully intelligible event.[55] It is inclusive, highlighting the many faces and voices of YHWH, even if, or perhaps particularly if, this creates a paradox. Chapter 24 is redacted in a more rationalistic vein, bringing together various sources and traditions so they would make sense, so revelation would be relatively straightforward. To scholars, trained in rationalistic, scientific methodologies, the redaction of Exod 19 should be instructive; it must remind us that we are interpreting religious texts, which have elements of both rationality and mystery within them.[56]

---

[55] Compare Greenberg, *Ezekiel,* 52, 58, who emphasizes that the chariot vision in the initial chapters of Ezekiel does not quite fit together. In contrast to much of German scholarship, which uses the LXX and conjectural emendations to rewrite the chapter so that it reads more smoothly, Greenberg prefers to retain the MT, with its ambiguities, lack of clarity, and contradictions that highlight the mysterious in the vision.

[56] See Geller, *Sacred Enigmas,* esp. 168–94. I would like to thank Sarah Shectman and Alan Lenzi, who assisted me with this article.

For Aloysius Fitzgerald, F.S.C.

Habakkuk 2:4b: Intertextuality and Hermeneutics

Alice Ogden Bellis

Biblical authors often cite passages in other parts of the Bible as they develop their own arguments and rhetoric. This intertextuality creates a rich and complex web of relationships among biblical texts. Understanding how authors use the cited material is crucial to the interpretation of their work. This paper focuses on Hab 2:4b and its citation in Rom 1:16–17; Gal 3:11; and Heb 10:37–38. The implications of the New Testament apropriations of Hab 2:4b for how we may properly appropriate biblical material today—an important aspect of biblical theology—will then be considered.

Habakkuk 2:4b, literally, "the righteous shall live by his (its or my) faithfulness," has been and continues to be a pivotal text for Protestant Christianity, even though most Christians have little awareness of the ways in which the New Testament authors have lifted it from its original context and dramatically reinterpreted it for use in a different theological world. Neither do they recognize the ways in which popular Protestant theology has radically reinterpreted these New Testament appropriations of the Hebrew Bible for a yet different religious world. As bold as the New Testament reinterpretations of Hab 2:4b seem at first glance, they are not a complete reversal of the original; neither the meaning of the original nor that of its appropriations are as one-dimensional as often thought, nor are they as different from each other as they first appear in the Hebrew and Greek. Both include the notions of faith in the sense of trust in God and faithfulness, living according to God's law in response to God's faithfulness.[1] The popular Protestant reappropriation of the New Testament appropriations of Hab 2:4b is another matter.

Several passages in the New Testament are based, at least in part, on Hab 2:4b. Romans 1:16–17 reads:

---

[1] On the inseparability of faith and faithfulness (works), see Jas 2:14–26. James may have been responding to those who had misconstrued Paul as minimizing the importance of righteous living. See Cain Hope Felder, "James," in *The International Bible Commentary* (ed. William R. Farmer; Collegeville, Minn.: Liturgical Press, 1998), 1796.

> For I am not ashamed of the gospel; it is the power of God for salvation to everyone who has faith, to the Jew first and also the Greek. For in it the righteousness of God is revealed through faith for faith; as it is written, "The one who is righteous will live by faith."[2]

Similarly, Gal 3:11 states that "it is evident that no one is justified before God by the law; for 'The one who is righteous will live by faith.'" Finally, we find in Heb 10:37–38a:

> For yet "in a very little while,
> the one who is coming will come and will not delay;
> but my righteous one will live by faith. . . . "

Each of these passages cites and interprets Hab 2:4b, and the last one includes Hab 2:3b as well, though the initial words "in a very little while" do not come from Hab 2:3b but from Isa 26:20. These interpretations read Hab 2:4b in a new religious context and put a new spin on it. This "spinning" is most evident in the way Heb 10:37–38a handles Hab 2:3b. In the original, what is coming and will not delay is either a vision of the end or, more likely, the end itself, that is, the fulfillment of the vision. Habakkuk 2:3 encourages the Judahites who are downcast after the untimely death of Josiah and the rise of a new force on the international scene, the Babylonians:

> For there is still a vision for the appointed time;
> it speaks of the end and does not lie.
> If it seems to tarry, wait for it;
> it will surely come; it will not delay.

The writer of the letter to the Hebrews reinterprets the latter part of this verse to refer to the second coming of Jesus rather than the demise of the Babylonians.[3] In both cases what is expected to come is understood to save the day.

Habakkuk 2:3–4 has clearly been taken out of its original context and appropriated in a new situation. Such appropriation in the New Testament has often disturbed Christian seminary students in their introductory Bible classes because in a modern context this kind of approach to an ancient biblical text has often been denounced as proof-texting. It is considered a misuse or even abuse of Scripture. Yet the Hebrew Bible is full of exam-

---

[2] Biblical citations are from the NRSV unless otherwise indicated.

[3] See Harold W. Attridge, *The Epistle to the Hebrews* (Hermeneia; Philadelphia: Fortress, 1989), 300–1; George Wesley Buchanan, *To the Hebrews* (AB; New York: Doubleday, 1972), 175.

ples of creative reinterpretations of earlier material,[4] and New Testament examples of such reinterpretation are not always as alien to the spirit of the original text as it might first appear.

One example of creative reinterpretation within the Hebrew canon will suffice to support the first part of that last statement. In Jer 6:22–24, Jeremiah prophesies that an unnamed enemy from the north will rise up against Judah:

> Thus says the LORD:
> See a people is coming from the land of the north,
> a great nation is stirring from the farthest parts of the earth.
> They grasp the bow and the javelin,
> they are cruel and have no mercy,
> their sound is like the roaring sea;
> they ride on horses
> equipped like a warrior for battle,
> against you, O daughter Zion!
> "We have heard news of them,
> our hands fall helpless;
> anguish has taken hold of us,
> pain as of a woman in labor."

A later author living during the Babylonian exile takes up Jeremiah's words, reworks them, and applies them not to Judah, but to the Babylonians:

> Look, a people is coming from the north;
> a mighty nation and many kings
> are stirring from the farthest parts of the earth.
> They wield bow and spear,
> they are cruel and have no mercy.
> The sound of them is like the roaring sea;
> they ride upon horses,
> set in array as a warrior for battle,
> against you, O daughter Babylon!
> The king of Babylon heard news of them
> and his hands fell helpless;
> anguish seized him,
> pain like that of a woman in labor. (Jer 50:41–43)

The author of this latter prophecy was surely aware of what he was doing, as presumably was his audience. They must have experienced a delicious sense of irony at the thought of the Babylonians receiving the same

---

[4] Michael Fishbane, *Biblical Interpretation in Ancient Israel* (New York: Oxford University Press, 1985).

treatment that the Babylonians had previously perpetrated on Judah. The reinterpretation is, in one sense, a complete reversal of the original prophecy, though it is not clear whether Jeremiah had the Babylonians in mind as the enemy from the north at the time this prophecy was uttered. In effect, the author of Jer 50:41–43 was suggesting that although the original Jeremian prophecy had been fulfilled when the Babylonians sacked Jerusalem, that was not the end of the story. God would now punish the Babylonians whom God had previously used as a divine instrument. Jeremiah might well have been surprised to hear his words directed against the enemies of Judah rather than against Judah itself, but he might also have concurred with the revised version of his prophecy if he had been alive at the time.[5] It does not negate his point but instead makes a new point—not inconsistent with the original one, even if in a sense it is a reversal.[6] The New Testament appropriations of Hab 2:4b are cut out of similar cloth.

Habakkuk 2:4b

In the Habakkuk text, Habakkuk has had a conversation, more like an argument, with God. At the beginning of the dialogue Habakkuk complains to God about all the violence in the world that God is allowing to go unchecked (Hab 1:1–4). God responds that the violent Babylonians are being aroused to deal with the situation (1:5–11). At this point Habakkuk responds sarcastically, questioning God's judgment, asking why people who are more wicked than the Judahites should be used to punish them (1:12–17). God does not reply to Habakkuk's harangue. But Habakkuk, not willing to take silence for an answer, even from God, refuses to slink away in defeat. Reminiscent of some twentieth-century hunger strikers, he boldly waits for God to respond, with no apparent plans to move until God has indeed spoken (2:1). In spite of what may seem to some modern readers as incredible chutzpah on Habakkuk's part, God does respond to Habakkuk's complaint. God tells Habakkuk that God has everything under control and that events will unfold at exactly the right moment in history, even if God's timing may seem painfully slow to those who are waiting (2:2–3).

---

[5] The material in Jer 50 and 51 is best dated to between 562 and 550. See my *The Structure and Composition of Jeremiah 50:2–51:58* (Lewiston, N.Y.: Mellen Biblical Press, 1995), 15–17. Assuming that Jeremiah was born around 645 (rejecting William Holladay's later date of 627 as stretching the meaning of the words in Jer 1:2 [*Jeremiah 2: A Commentary on the Book of the Prophet Jeremiah, Chapters 26–52* [Minneapolis: Fortress, 1986], 1), Jeremiah would have been over ninety years old at the time the poems in Jer 50–51 were composed.

[6] See my "Poetic Structure and Intertextual Logic in Jeremiah 50," in *Troubling Jeremiah* (ed. A. R. Pete Diamond, Kathleen M. O'Connor, and Louis Stulman; JSOTSup 260; Sheffield: Sheffield Academic Press, 1999), 179–89.

What follows is best understood as the "vision" in which God explains to Habakkuk how things will turn out (Hab 2:4–20). The final prayer in Hab 3 is a prayer urging God to get a move on the plan (3:1–17); at the same time the end of the prayer reveals a change of attitude on the speaker's part (3:18–19). Habakkuk beautifully confesses his total confidence in God, to the point of being able to imagine himself rejoicing in God even in the midst of a total famine.

The focal verse in this paper, Hab 2:4b, is part of the introduction to the vision, Hab 2:4. The second word in Hab 2:4a, עֻפְּלָה, is difficult but may refer either to those who do not heed the law or those who are puffed up, that is, arrogant. The two meanings are not inconsistent. Indeed, it is possible that both meanings were intended. Such double entendres were used on a number of occasions by biblical authors.[7] In any case, the reference is probably to certain Judahites who think they know better than God how God ought to act (although perhaps the prophet is also hinting at the recklessness/arrogance of the Babylonians). They recklessly ignore the law because they arrogantly believe they know better than God what is right. These are contrasted with the righteous, law-abiding (Judahites) who will live—in the sense of physically withstanding the national crisis brought on by the Babylonians. (After the fact "living" could have taken on the additional meaning of surviving the crisis of religious identity ensuing from the Babylonian destruction of Jerusalem and the temple.)

The righteous are able to outlast the crisis because of **אמונתו**, rendered in many Christian translations simply as "his or their faith," but sometimes with a footnote suggesting the alternative "his or their faithfulness." The Hebrew term as it is vocalized in the Masoretic Text is indeed better translated as "faithfulness."

Yet it is possible that another double entendre is lurking here. The root **אמן** includes the meaning of believing or trusting in God. The noun **אֵמֻן**, occurring only in Deut 32:20, is perhaps best understood primarily as faith.[8] Perhaps Habakkuk had Isaiah's words (Isa 7:9) challenging King Ahaz to have faith (תַאֲמִינוּ) in God in the Syro-Ephraimite crisis or else be unable to stand at all (תֵאָמֵנוּ).[9] In Deut 32:18, God has complained that the people have forgotten the one who gave them birth. In other words they

---

[7] Another example of such a double entendre is found in Jer 50:7, where מקוה means both "pool" and "hope." See my *The Structure and Composition of Jeremiah 50:2–51:58,* 23–24. On word play in the Hebrew Bible, see I. Casanowicz, *Paronomasia in the Old Testament* (Boston: Norwood, 1894).

[8] See *HALOT,* 62. Contra BDB, which reads אֱמוּנִים as the plural of אֵמוּן. *HALOT* reads these forms as plurals of אֱמוּנָה.

[9] See also Isa 28:16. I am grateful to my colleague Gene Rice for pointing out Habakkuk's probable dependence on Isaiah of Jerusalem.

have lost faith in God. They no longer trust God. In verse 19 God declares his jealousy that has led to the divine children being spurned. Then in verse 20 we read the divine announcement that God's face will be hidden from them because they are perverse and there is no אֵמֻן in them. In the following verses God then catalogues the sins flowing from the lack of faith, primarily worshiping other gods. Lack of faith thus leads to faithlessness, but the accent in verse 20 is on the latter.

The word אֵמֻן sounds a lot like אֱמוּנָה. Without the *matres lectionis* and pointing the two words would be indistinguishable. Could this be another case of double entendre? Before this question can be answered, an additional issue must be addressed. The masculine singular pronoun in אמונתו is presumed by many Christian readers to refer to the righteous, because this is the way it is interpreted in the New Testament. In the context of the Habakkuk prophecy, however, it might be better understood as referring to God. The proud and reckless folks who implicitly rely on their own unsound spirits are contrasted with the righteous who survive difficult times through God's faithfulness. One might expect a first-person pronoun, since God is the speaker—"The righteous will live through my faithfulness"—but the text sometimes uses third person pronouns in reference to the deity even when God is the speaker, probably because the actual speaker is the prophet for whom referring to God in the third person is quite natural.

Although an argument can be made for the consonant ו being the original reading, the best manuscripts of the Septuagint read πίστεως μου, "my faithfulness."[10] Indeed the similar-looking Hebrew consonants ו and י are sometimes accidentally interchanged. Thus, "my faithfulness" could be the original reading. On the other hand, if what will make it possible for the righteous to survive is both God's faithfulness and the individual's trust or faith in God's faithfulness, then the third masculine singular pronoun would be correct because this pronoun can refer both to the individual and to God.

Interestingly the Qumran *Pesher Habakkuk* interprets אמונה as both doing the law and having faith in the Teacher of Righteousness.[11] This faith apparently involved acknowledging his divinely appointed role as teacher of the community and trusting his teaching as correct and authoritative.[12] The object of faith has shifted at Qumran from God to the Teacher of Righteousness, though even here God is implicitly in the picture since it is God's law that is being obeyed and it is God who sent the Teacher of Righteousness. The subject of אמונה, the one who is having faith or being faithful, is here understood

[10] Joseph A. Fitzmyer, *Romans* (AB; New York: Doubleday, 1993), 264–65.

[11] William H. Brownlee, *The Midrash Pesher of Habakkuk* (SBLMS 24; Missoula, Mont.: Scholars Press, 1979), 125.

[12] Ibid., 30.

to be the human individual. The possible double meaning in the original prophecy involving both God's faithfulness and human faith(fulness) is eliminated. Nevertheless the dual interpretation of אמונה as both faith and faithfulness adds weight to the argument that the term was originally intended to be understood in both senses. Although there is no way to be certain what the original poet had in mind, this reading is certainly possible and its rich complexity in line with Hebrew rhetoric.

Romans 1:17

Paul's quotation of Hab 2:4b in Rom 1:17 is neither from the Hebrew Masoretic Text nor the best manuscripts of the Septuagint,[13] or else Paul has freely rendered his source.[14] Paul (or his Greek source) drops the pronoun altogether. πίστεως, the Greek rendering of אמונתו, can mean either "faithfulness" or "faith," just as I have argued the Hebrew term might have been understood. Although Paul is generally assumed to have used the term with only the meaning of "faith" in mind, this assumption has recently been challenged. Mark Nanos suggests that πίστεως for Paul was "a seamless blending of trust and commitment as it defines the obedient character of the one who trusts in God."[15]

Citing the Jewish context of the Gentile Christian audience to whom Paul writes, he argues that the concern of Romans is not so much with Judaizers as with "Gentilizers." These Gentilizers' problem was the reverse of that of the Jewish Christians addressed in Galatians. The Galatians advocated Gentiles being circumcised and thus becoming full members of the Jewish people as a prerequisite to becoming Christians. The Roman Gentile Christians, on the other hand and perhaps partly in response to those who unsuccessfully pressured them into becoming Jews, seemed to think that Jews who continued to feel bound by the Torah could not be good Christians. Paul argues in Romans that everyone is justified by faith/faithfulness, trust in God that results in faithful living. Otherwise, Paul's concern with the lawlessness of the Gentiles would not make sense.[16]

---

[13] One LXX manuscript (263) reads the same as Rom 1:17, but this may be as a result of the copyist's harmonization of the text with the Pauline reading and thus this manuscript is regarded as secondary in the LXX tradition. See Fitzmyer, *Romans,* 265.

[14] I do not mean to suggest by this that Paul has done violence to whatever text he was using. If Paul understood the multiple meanings of the text, his rendering could have been his way of capturing the multivalence of אמונתו/πίστεως αὐτοῦ (μου).

[15] See Mark D. Nanos, *The Mystery of Romans: The Jewish Context of Paul's Letter* (Minneapolis: Fortress, 1996), 223.

[16] Mark D. Nanos, "The Jewish Context of the Gentile Audience Addressed in Paul's Letter to the Romans," *CBQ* 61 (1999): 283–304.

In Rom 1:17 Paul does not explicitly specify the object of human faith. Clearly Jesus is in the picture, and it may be that in a manner similar to the Qumran reinterpretation of Hab 2:4b, he believed that Jesus was divinely appointed to bring God's message of salvation and that through trusting or having faith in Jesus as divinely commissioned, one would be trusting and believing in God. On the other hand, the fact that Paul later in his extended argument for the priority of faith cites Abraham's exemplary faith in God (Rom 4:3) suggests that in Rom 1:17 the primary object of faith is God and that the gospel is the catalyst (cf. Rom 1:16).

This is not so far off the point of Hab 2:4b as is often thought, though of course Jesus is certainly not in view. God is responding to Habakkuk's complaint that God isn't dealing with the problems of the world adequately. God tells Habakkuk that even though divine action may seem slow, he and those who listen to his words should wait for it, trust in it, have faith in it or more accurately in the God who will save the people from their enemies. In my reading it is God's faithfulness that will save the day, but the people should trust in God's faithfulness if they are going to survive the crisis as a people. Indeed, God does not physically save the people from the Babylonians, but God does stay with them, bring them back, and ultimately punish the Babylonians. Those who trust in the trustworthiness of God will come out with their religious identity intact.

Galatians 3:11

In Gal 3:11 Paul quotes from Hab 2:4b using exactly the same form as used in Rom 1:17, again leaving out the pronoun and understanding the individual human as the "subject" of πίστεως, rather than God. Here, however, Paul is contrasting the individual's faith/trust in God[17] as a means of salvation with fulfilling the requirements of Torah. He suggests that no one can be justified or saved, in other words become spiritually whole, merely by doing what the law requires. His concern, however, is not really with Jews who lived by the law in response to God's grace instead of as a means of self-justification. Rather, it may be argued that Paul's conflict was with those Jews who used the law as a tool of ethnocentric exclusivism that denied non-Jews equal access to God's mercy.[18] This concern involves a greater stretch from the original meaning of Hab 2:4b than Rom 1:17 requires. Not only is human trust in God praised, which I argue is an

---

[17] On the question of the object of faith (God or Jesus), see Hans Dieter Betz, *Galatians* (Hermeneia; Philadelphia: Fortress, 1979), 147, and the literature cited there.

[18] Nanos, *Mystery of Romans,* 9. Nanos's focus is on Romans, but the problem of the Judaizers in Galatians is in the picture as well.

element of the meaning of Hab 2:4b; human misuse of the Torah is condemned. It must be emphasized that it is not the law itself that is condemned, but humans who used the law as a tool of exclusion. God gave the Torah as a gracious gift, as a guide for living, not as an excuse for human arrogance. Admittedly, the Hebrew Scriptures were interpreted by some as exclusionary. Others apparently disagreed.

That brings us back to Hab 2:4a and Habakkuk's condemnation of the heedless/proud people whose spirits are not right. They are puffed up with self-importance, believing themselves to know better than God God's proper course. They are not interested in hearing God's plan or heeding God's counsel. They only follow their own foolish understanding, in effect substituting it for God's. They neither love God nor follow God's teaching. The attitude to which Paul is reacting is not exactly the same one to which Habakkuk was responding. Paul is concerned with a different kind of self-righteousness that uses or interprets the law in such a way as to provide a cover, a rationale, a justification for excluding non-Jews. Paul's complaint, however, is related indirectly to Habakkuk's and is not without precedent in the Tanak.

In the postexilic period, the exclusive and repressive aspects of the law, or its interpretation, were especially disturbing to some. After the Deuteronomic law with its provisions excluding foreigners and eunuchs (Deut 23:1–3) had become part of the community's legal system, a number of biblical authors protested. The exclusion of foreigners and sexual oddities, though intended to protect the purity of the community, was believed by the protesters in reality to endanger the community. Inherent in the exclusivistic policies, the challengers believed, was an ethnic arrogance, fueled by fear and buttressed and justified by the religious establishment's misuse of the law.

Third Isaiah counseled against the rules outlawing foreigners and eunuchs (Isa 56:1–8). It is likely that he did so in the context of a community wrestling with whom to blame for the exile. Foreigners and eunuchs were easy targets. Ultimately, the negative attitudes toward these groups led to Ezra and Nehemiah's exclusionary policies, which even went so far in Ezra's case as to sanction the exile of foreign wives of Jewish husbands along with their half-breed children (Ezra 10; Neh 13:23–27). Although Third Isaiah does not explicitly condemn the law and/or call those who uphold it arrogant, his opening remarks suggest an assessment of it, or at least its human understanding, as inadequate: "Maintain justice, and do what is right, for soon my salvation will come, and my deliverance be revealed" (Isa 56:1). Implicit in these words is his conviction that those who uphold the provisions of the law but exclude foreigners and sexual minorities are missing an important element of what God requires.

The following line might lead the reader to believe that all Third Isaiah is calling for is fulfillment of the obligations of the law: "Happy is the mortal who does this, the one who holds it fast, who keeps the sabbath, not profaning it, and refrains from doing any evil" (Isa 56:2). The antecedent of "it" is not clear. Although one might well expect the Torah to be the antecedent, the primary candidates in the preceding line, where antecedents are usually found, are "justice" and "what is right." "It" could also refer forward to the Sabbath. In poetry, unlike prose, the referent can follow the pronoun. If this is correct, then the line sounds like an ordinary injunction to obey the commandment to keep the Sabbath. Could "refrain from doing any evil," however, suggest that one must go beyond the written regulations and exercise judgment? Such judgment is typically exercised by someone whose goal is not simply to live up to the requirements of the law, but whose spirit is sound, who is in right relationship with God, who in response to God's goodness genuinely desires to follow God's law in the most profound sense of the term.

The fact that the following verses challenge Deuteronomic law lends credence to this position. Why would the prophet urge people to live up to the law for the sake of fulfilling all its requirements and then turn around and denounce some of the provisions? It is true, of course, that the speaker urges the inclusion of eunuchs who keep the Sabbath (Isa 56:4), which provides a reason for having extolled those who keep the Sabbath (Isa 56:2); nevertheless, it is ironic that the prophet counsels the Jewish community to disregard one law in order to include people who keep another law, albeit a very central one.

Throughout this passage the speaker praises those who "are joined to the LORD" (Isa 56:3), "who choose the things that please me" (Isa 56:4) "and hold fast my covenant" (Isa 56:4, 6), and "who join themselves to the LORD, to minister to him, to love the name of the LORD and to be his servants" (Isa 56:6). The emphasis is on a relationship with God that results in doing the right thing. Nowhere is the Torah mentioned explicitly, even where we might expect to find it. Is this omission intentional? It is difficult to be certain, but it seems possible, even probable.

The book of Ruth also can be read as protest literature against the Jerusalem establishment who in order to save the community attempted, and may have succeeded though we do not know the outcome, to send foreign wives of Jewish men away, along with their mongrel children (Ezra 10).[19] A Moabite woman is the hero of the book of Ruth, through whose initiative is born King David, who ultimately consolidates the nation and makes it strong. The story may subtly express the conviction that the sal-

[19] See André LaCocque, "Ruth," in *The Feminine Unconventional: Four Subversive Figures in Israel's History* (OBT; Minneapolis: Fortress, 1990), 84–116.

vation of the community comes not from rigidly following the requirements of the Torah but rather by thoughtfully and faithfully responding to God's leading, which at times may suggest changes in the law or at least resistance to it.[20] In other words it is not enough to follow the requirements of the written law in a rote fashion. חסד, courageous, thoughtful, loving, even risk-taking loyalty to God and God's people, exemplified by Ruth (Ruth 3:10), is the most important quality required of humans.

Similarly, the book of Esther may be read as a story lampooning the rigidity of Jewish law in general and the inadvisability of an individual law in particular. By ridiculing the irrevocability of Persian law that resulted in the absurdity of the Persian king not being able to reverse a law he had stupidly promulgated, a law mandating the death of the Jews, the author may have been making a veiled comment on Jewish law in general, or at least those who were in charge of interpreting it (cf. Jer 8:8), as well as with the particular law forbidding marriage to foreigners. When Esther, a Jewish woman married to a foreigner, acts in such a courageous and thoughtful way that she saves the Jewish community from destruction, the implication is that the law against marriage to foreigners was wrong. Indeed, her marriage to the foreign king is critical to her success! Such things could not be said directly, but they could be implied through an entertaining story.[21]

Paul's attitude toward the law in Gal 3:11 and the surrounding passage may seem harsh and anti-Jewish. A case can be made, however, that his general perspective on law was part of a trajectory that traced back at least to the eighth century B.C.E. Well before the postexilic period when the antiforeign attitude apparently reached its zenith, many of the prophets expressed their conviction that observation of the law without the concomitant appropriate attitude toward other people and God was not pleasing to God.

Amos denounced those who brought sacrificial offerings but who did not live justly: "Let justice roll down like waters and righteousness like an ever-flowing stream" (Amos 5:24). Probably engaging in hyperbole, Hosea declared: "I desire mercy [חסד] and not sacrifice, the knowledge of God rather than burnt offerings" (Hos 6:6). (The book of Ruth with its attribution of חסד to Ruth could be, in part, a midrash on this passage.) Micah expressed a similar conviction when he asked the rhetorical question of

---

[20] It is possible that the debate in the book of Ruth is not with the exclusionary laws per se but rather with an interpretation that extended these laws to cover not only men, but women as well. In any case the author seems to have been involved in a community debate about the advisability of excluding certain types of people from the Jewish community.

[21] See LaCocque, "Esther," 49–83.

what God requires of us. He rejects even the most valuable sacrifices in preference for justice, mercy (חסד), and walking humbly with God (Mic 6:8). Examples could be multiplied.

The Jewish-Gentile issue in the early Christian community pushed Paul to articulate something that was always a part of the Jewish tradition, but never so explicit as it became in Paul's letters. The crisis that challenged him forced him to take another look at his own tradition and mine it for perspectives that he could use to support his convictions about God's inclusive love. He may have pushed the logic of the Jewish position to its limits, but he did not take as giant a step away from his tradition as is sometimes supposed, at least not in his use of Hab 2:4b.

Hebrews 10:37–38

The final quotation of Hab 2:4b in the New Testament is in the book of Hebrews. Its use here is not like that in Romans, where Paul is trying to show that both Gentiles and Jews are justified on the same basis, or like that in Galatians, where Paul, again dealing with the Jewish-Gentile issue, is advocating the priority of relationship with God over fulfilling the requirements of the law. In Hebrews the context is eschatological. The Messiah is expected to return imminently.

The author is using a different Septuagint manuscript from the one used by Paul in Romans and Galatians. The manuscript used by the author of Hebrews transposes the pronoun from אמונה/πίστεως to צדיק/δίκαιος, from "faithfulness/faith" to "the righteous," resulting in the reading "but my righteous one will live by faith/faithfulness" (Heb 10:38a). Just as Paul did, the author interprets πίστεως primarily as faith. The point being made in the Hebrews passage is that in the interim period before the risen Christ returns to earth, the righteous one will hang on by means of faith, that is by trusting in God's promises, by trusting in the trustworthiness of God, by not allowing the delay to create a panic. Such faith will, however, be accompanied by faithfulness, living faithfully in the interim. Although the context is different and the crisis is different, Hab 2:4b has not been ripped out of its original context with no awareness of nor concern for its meaning; rather, its meaning has been reapplied to a new situation.

Reflections

At the turn of the millennium, it is commonplace to acknowledge that theology is biography. Biography certainly affects biblical scholarship. Having received my M.Div. degree from Howard University's School of Religion, where I have now served for ten years on the faculty in its reincarnation as the School of Divinity, I have come to appreciate the creative reappropriation of Scriptures from both Testaments, through which preachers find new meanings in ancient texts, yet meanings that are often connected at some level with the original. Having spent almost ten years of my academic life studying Jer 50–51 to complete my doctoral dissertation at the Catholic University of America, I was forced to give up the Bible Belt literalist approach to Scripture with which I was brought up and to embrace a more nuanced understanding of the ways in which biblical authors creatively reused earlier materials. Even as I have come to appreciate the richness of such creative work, new questions emerge, especially as I find myself engaged with Jewish biblical scholars.

What are the limits of such revisions, if any, and when does or how can such reinterpretation become oppressive, and who has the authority to decide such questions? The story is told, I believe by Howard Thurman though I have been unable to locate the quotation, of a woman who read Paul's mandate to put on the new man (Eph 4:24) as an injunction to get a new husband. Most would immediately agree that this is an irresponsible, if humorous, reappropriation of Paul. Depending on the circumstances of the woman, however, this first impression might be wrong. What if the interpretation helped her find the courage to leave an abusive marriage?

Another story may be helpful. Lawrence Jones, the Dean Emeritus of Howard University School of Divinity, once quipped that new students seemed to think that the faculty had taken their Jesus and laid him they knew not where, an allusion to John 20:2. He was, of course, being cleverly funny, but he was also making a serious point—that contrary to some students' opinion, the faculty was not out to steal their Jesus, even if they did want to help students develop a more nuanced theology. His point did not have much to do with John 20:2, but it worked. He drew an analogy from the text that did not violate the spirit of the text, even as he exercised considerable liberty in his appropriation of it.

These anecdotes suggest that clear-cut answers to the questions posed above are not easy to find. Scripture may be appropriated in virtually infinite ways and directions as long as the person doing the appropriation does it sensitively, thoughtfully, and responsibly. If the new interpretation later becomes problematic, that is hardly the fault of the originator of the new reading or grounds for avoiding such reinterpretation. There is no tribunal to which we can turn to tell us what is acceptable or not, nor a set of simple guidelines to follow.

Historically, the problems of interpretations becoming oppressive have usually arisen when the original context of the appropriation has been forgotten. We lose sight of the fact that Paul was a Jew involved in an intrareligious debate, not a Christian in the modern sense of the word fighting against Jews. The only antidote to such problems is understanding the original context and educating those affected, both the perpetrators and the victims of the oppressive use of the readings.

One issue worth revisiting is the matter of supersessionism. Because of the ways in which Christians have historically viewed the New Testament as, in many respects, superseding the Old Testament and the reprehensible ways in which they have behaved toward Jews, this word has become a very dirty one in some circles. Yet if we consider this term in other contexts, it is clear that supersession is not inherently evil. In secular law, new cases sometimes overturn old rulings, thus superseding them. In this way important flexibility is built into the legal system of the United States and other countries with similar legal systems. The system is not superseded, but particular provisions are. If at some point in the future a better system is invented and we abandon the old one, the new one will supersede the old system. If the new system is in fact better than the old one, the supersession will be judged a good thing. Yet, Paul's use of Hab 2:4b is not precisely supersessionist; it appropriates and reinterprets; it does not quite supersede.

Biblical interpreters have typically taken two opposite courses when dealing with contradictions found in the Bible. One is to find ways of harmonizing the differences. This sometimes has led to rather amazing mental gymnastics. The other is to understand later perspectives that contradict earlier ones as superseding them, as in many modern legal systems. Following this principle, the challenges to the exclusion of foreigners and eunuchs found in Third Isaiah, Ruth, and Esther—assuming that these books are all postexilic—supersede the presumably earlier Deuteronomic law that prohibits the inclusion of such people in the people of Israel. The problem with this approach, however, is that the people who were responsible for canonizing the collection may have included these late books, not to overturn earlier material, but rather simply because these books had become "family" to the Jews (the original battles of which they were a part may have been forgotten) or possibly to provide an honest record of the theological and legal struggles that had forged the community. In addition, the combination of the disparate parts has created a theological and ethical whole that is greater than the sum of its parts, even though the parts are in tension with one another. Picking a part we like over a part we dislike, regardless of the principle guiding our choice, may not be the most responsible way to proceed.

We are thus faced with a question for which the Hebrew Bible alone does not provide obvious answers. Yet it is evident that the self-understanding of the Jewish community (as well as the Christian community and all other religious communities), including its theology and law, evolved over time, with newer perspectives in effect superseding older ones. When agreement could not be reached, subgroups developed in which the evolutionary process continued, often in opposing directions. Occasionally, the process involves doubling back and sometimes even mergers of groups that once separated. At any moment in time, however, each religious community operates with a self-understanding that supersedes all earlier ones. There is nothing sinister about this.

What can be sinister is the arrogance of some religious communities who assume that they have the only truth or are the only ones who have the whole truth or the like. It is natural for religious communities to believe in what they believe; it is also necessary that they have sufficient humility to recognize that they don't know it all. At the same time, the kind of tolerance advocated here has its own limits. These limits appear when religious tolerance butts up against convictions relating, for example, to humanitarian concerns.

If a religious community's values include a passionate devotion to the sanctity of human life, they may not be able in good conscience simply to tolerate those who in the name of their own different religious values, no matter how sincerely held, perpetrate child abuse. They must humbly admit that their understanding of what constitutes child abuse may be faulty or that their conviction that such abuse is a violation of the principle of the sanctity of human life may be ill-conceived; nevertheless, this humility should not prevent them from intervening on behalf of a child who they believe is being abused, even if the abuser believes what he or she is doing is divinely sanctioned. Neither should they desist from challenging the values of a religious community that advocates such behavior. Naturally the appropriateness of the means has to be considered.

Religious values are not simply other-worldly philosophical ideas that have no impact on practical, everyday life. And of course for some people, both past and present, other-worldly matters matter(ed) even more than matters in this transient world. It is true that many religious battles have been fought in part as much for reasons of arrogance and greed as for the healthy motives of sacred convictions. This does not negate the historical reality that many people have struggled passionately over religious ideas, hated each other vehemently, and persecuted each other terribly because of ideas that they believed mattered very much—not to their egos and pocketbooks, but to their concern for the health and happiness of the world. They may not always have been right, but they frequently were more sincere than we like to admit. This fact is quite uncomfortable for those moderns who are quick to condemn, even ironically demonize, the people they accuse of demonizing others!

Having said this, however, I want to suggest that fighting is usually the result of lapsed or faulty communication. With the tremendous technological advances in communication we have experienced in the twentieth century, it is incumbent upon us in religious communities, and especially those of us who are scholars of a shared sacred text that has been appropriated in different ways, including a history of Christians persecuting Jews, to learn all we can from each other and about each other. If we truly believe that no one person or even one community has a corner on the truth, then the divergent streams of Judaism and Christianity may have much to teach each other.

Studying the New Testament appropriations of Hab 2:4b and knowing the subsequent history of Christian and particularly Protestant theology, both official and popular, has helped me to recognize the arrogance and accompanying lawlessness within my own Protestant tradition and the tendency within all religious communities to become arrogant and lawless in various ways. The irony is that Protestantism has touted individual salvation by God's grace through faith, in part as a way of excluding others from its camp while congratulating itself on its righteousness! Paul must be turning over in his grave.

This false pride has in turn led many Christians into the notion that the New Testament is a book of grace without law and the Old Testament one of law without grace. This false dichotomy then leads to a kind of anti-nomianism and a disregard for most moral laws other than those that are easy to keep and those that agree with the believers' prejudices, especially those that deal with sexuality. Why else would the issue of homosexuality, which is not a temptation for the majority of Christians, loom so large in much of the Christian community? This preoccupation is particularly strange when arguably more (or at least equally) fundamental matters like economic and racial justice, which do affect many people, are of such minimal practical concern—even among those who claim to be concerned.

In addition, popular Protestantism has created a new kind of pseudo-law by misconstruing faith as credulity rather than trust. In other words, unquestioning belief in ideas that would otherwise be unbelievable (e.g., Jesus is literally God or Lord) is substituted for trust in God. This new "law" is made the touchstone of acceptance into the religious community and is considered essential for salvation, even as it condemns Jews for their devotion to the law! What would Paul say if he walked among us today? A new epistle would be required, not terribly different from the ones he wrote in the first century.

Both Habakkuk on the one hand and Paul and the author of Hebrews on the other understood that faith in the sense of trust in God's faithfulness and human faithfulness—living to the best of our abilities in harmony with God's eternal law—are two inextricably bound parts of a whole. We may dissect them for purposes of discussion, we may argue about their order of priority like the perennial chicken and egg debate, but in real life the two are Siamese twins; you can't have one without the other.

This perception was not the issue in Habakkuk's work, however, as it was in Paul's. Habakkuk's concern was with surviving the crisis created by the rise of the Babylonians. Yet, different as the problems facing the two men were, dissimilar as the questions that presented themselves to them, Paul's appropriation of Habakkuk to deal with a new conundrum is not inconsistent with Habakkuk's prophecy, though it is certainly a creative reinterpretation.

In some ways the author of Hebrews and Habakkuk had more in common than Habakkuk and Paul, in that both were facing crises caused by God's slowness to act. Here again, the New Testament author has freely reread Habakkuk, but not in a way that fundamentally violates Habakkuk's theology. Of course Jesus was not an issue for Habakkuk and he was for the author of Hebrews, but that does not mean that the New Testament authors have misused Habakkuk in applying his work in a new theological context. As radical as the New Testament appropriation of Habakkuk at first seems, it is in line with Jewish methods of interpretation at the time and its inner logic makes sense.

On the other hand, the popular Christian reappropriation of Paul's appropriations of Hab 2:4b does violence to both Habakkuk and Paul. They are a misreading of Paul and indirectly of Habakkuk. They amount to superstition, and arrogant, dangerous superstition at that. They should not be confused with Paul's own much more subtle handling of his tradition.

Habakkuk 2:4b, its New Testament appropriation, and its modern reappropriation by some Christians have certainly played an important role in the sad history of Jewish-Christian relations. That history cannot be undone. It can be understood, and, we may hope, understanding will lead to mutual respect and even friendship.

It is not enough, of course, simply to look at one text. The New Testament appropriations of the Hebrew Scriptures must be considered text by text in light of emerging perspectives. Ultimately, these studies will mutually shape each other as scholars seek to understand the complexities of the New Testament authors' use of their Scriptures. This article is simply one small piece of a fascinating and profoundly important puzzle.[22]

---

[22] I would like to thank my colleagues at Howard University School of Divinity, Gene Rice and Cain Hope Felder, and my colleagues in this project, Joel Kaminsky and Brooks Schramm, for their thoughtful reading of this paper and their helpful suggestions.

Bibliography of Primary Sources

Aberbach, Moses, and B. Grossfeld, trans. *Targum Onkelos to Genesis.* Hoboken, N.J.: Ktav, 1982.

Abravanel, Isaac. *Commentary on the Pentateuch* (in Hebrew). Jerusalem: Bnei Arbael, 1964.

Attar, Hayim ben Moses. *Or Hachayim: Commentary on the Torah by Rabbi Chayim Ben Attar.* Vol. 1, *Genesis* (in Hebrew). Edited by Eliyahu Munk. Jerusalem: Eliyahu Munk, 1995.

Bechor Shor (Joseph ben Isaac). *Commentary on the Torah by Joseph Bekor Shor* (in Hebrew). Edited by Yehoshua Navo. Jerusalem: Mossad Harav Kook, 1994.

Braude, William G., trans. *The Midrash on Psalms.* Vol. 2. Yale Judaica Series 13. New Haven: Yale University Press, 1959.

Braude, William G., and I. J. Kapstein, trans. *Pesikta de-Rab Kahana: R. Kahana's Discourses of Sabbath and Festal Days.* Philadelphia: Jewish Publication Society of America, 1975.

———. *Tanna Debe Eliyyahu.* Philadelphia: Jewish Publication Society of America, 1981.

Buber, Sholomo, ed. *Midrash Tanḥuma to the Pentateuch* (in Hebrew). New York: Sefer, 1946.

Charlesworth, James H., ed. *The Old Testament Pseudepigrapha.* 2 vols. Garden City, N.Y.: Doubleday, 1983, 1985.

Cohen, A., trans. *Midrash Rabbah, Ecclesiastes.* 3d ed. London: Soncino, 1983.

Diez Macho, Alejandro, ed. *Targum Palestinense in Pentateuchum* (in Aramaic). Vol. 1. Biblia Polyglotta Matritensia Series. Madrid: Consejo Superior de Investiga-ciones Cientificas, 1980.

Finkelstein, Louis, ed. *Sifre on Deuteronomy* (in Hebrew). New York: Jewish Theological Seminary of America, 1993.

Freedman, H., trans. *The Babylonian Talmud, Tractate Shabbath.* Vol. 2. London: Soncino, 1972.

———. *Midrash Rabbah: Genesis*. London: Soncino, 1939.

Friedlander, Gerald, trans. *Pirke de Rabbi Eliezer*. 1916. Repr., New York: Sepher Hermon, 1981.

Gregory of Nyssa. *The Life of Moses*. Translated by Abraham Malherbe and Everett Ferguson. New York: Paulist, 1978.

Hammer, Reuven, trans. *Sifre: A Tannaitic Commentary on the Book of Deuteronomy*. Yale Judaica Series 24. New Haven: Yale University Press, 1986.

Hezekiah Ben Manoah. *Hizekuni: Commentary on the Torah by Rabbi Hezekiah Ben Manoah* (in Hebrew). Edited by Chayim David Shavel. Jerusalem: Mossad Harav Kook, 1981.

Ibn Ezra, Abraham ben Meir. *Commentary of Ibn Ezra [1092–1167] on the Pentateuch*. Vol. 1, *Genesis* (in Hebrew). Edited by Moseh Charaz. Jerusalem: Chamad, 1983.

———. *Ibn Ezra's Commentary on the Pentateuch: Genesis (Bereshit)*. Translated by H. N. Strickman and A. M. Silver. New York: Menorah Publishing Company, 1988.

Jellinek, Adolph, ed. *Bet ha-Midrash* (in Hebrew). 3d ed. 1872. Repr., Jerusalem: Wahrmann Books, 1967.

Judah Loew ben Bezalel. *The Complete Gur Aryeh (Judah Loew Ben Bezalel [1525–1609]) on the Pentateuch*, Vol. 2, *Toldot– Wayehi* (in Hebrew). Edited by Joshua David Hartman. Jerusalem: Machon Jerusalem, 1990.

Kimchi, David. *Rabbi David Kimhi's Commentary on the Pentateuch* (in Hebrew). Edited by Moshe Kamelhar. Jerusalem: Mossad Harav Kook, 1970.

Lauterbach, Jacob Z., trans. *Mekilta de-Rabbi Ishmael*. 3 vols. Philadelphia: Jewish Publication Society of America, 1933, 1935.

Lehrman, S. M., trans. *Midrash Rabbah: Exodus*. London: Soncino, 1939.

Mandelbaum, Bernard, ed. *Pesikta de Rav Kahana* (in Hebrew). New York: Jewish Theological Seminary of America, 1962.

Margulies, M., ed. *Midrash Vayyikra Rabbah: A Critical Edition Based on Manuscripts and Genizah Fragments with Variants and Notes* (in Hebrew). 5 vols. Jerusalem: American Academy of Jewish Research, 1953–1960.

McNamara, Martin, trans. *Targum Neofiti 1: Genesis*. Collegeville, Minn.: Liturgical Press, 1992.

Meir Loeb ben Jechiel Michael. *Malbim. Commentary on the Torah by Meir Leibus Ben Yechiel Michel [1809–1879]* (in Hebrew). Edited by Zvi Faier. Jerusalem: Hillel, 1979.

Mirkin, Moshe Aryeh, ed. *Bereshit Rabbah* (in Hebrew). Tel-Aviv: Yavneh, 1958.

Origen. *The Song of Songs: Commentary and Homilies*. Translated by R. P. Lawson. Westminster, Md.: Newman, 1957.

Samuel ben Meir. *Commentary on the Torah by Samuel Ben Meir (Rashbam 1085–1174)* (in Hebrew). Edited by David Razin. 1882. Repr., New York: Om, 1949.

———. *Rabbi Samuel Ben Meir's Commentary on Genesis (Rashbam)*. Translated by Martin Lockshin. Lewiston, N.Y.: Mellen, 1989.

Shiloni, Isaac, ed. *Yalqut Shimoni: Book of Genesis* (in Hebrew). Jerusalem: Mossad Harav Kook, 1973.

Slotki, Judah J., trans. *Midrash Rabbah, Leviticus*. 3d ed. London: Soncino, 1983.

Theodor, Julius, and Chanokh Albeck, eds. *Bereschit Rabba* (in Hebrew). Jerusalem: Wahrmann Books, 1965.

Weinstock, Moshe, ed. *Seder Olam Rabbah Ha-shalem* (in Hebrew). Jerusalem: Torat Hesed, 1961.

Bibliography of Modern Authors

Ackerman, Susan. "The Deception of Isaac, Jacob's Dream at Bethel, and Incubation on an Animal Skin." Pages 92–120 in *Priesthood and Cult in Ancient Israel*. Edited by Gary A. Anderson and Saul M. Olyan. JSOTSup 125. Sheffield: Sheffield Academic Press, 1990.

Ahituv, Samuel. *Joshua: Introduction and Commentary*. Jerusalem: Magnes, 1995.

Ahlström, G. W. *The History of Ancient Palestine*. JSOTSup 146. Sheffield: JSOT Press, 1993.

Albrektson, Bertil. *History and the Gods: An Essay on the Idea of Historical Events As Divine Manifestations in the Ancient Near East and Israel*. ConBOT 1. Lund: Gleerup, 1967.

Alt, Albrecht. *Der Gott der Väter*. Stuttgart: Kohlhammer, 1929.

Alter, Robert. *Genesis*. New York: Norton, 1996.

Anderson, Bernhard. W. "Esther. Introduction and Exegesis." *IB*, 3:821–74.

———. "Exodus Typology in Second Isaiah," Pages 177–95 in *Israel's Prophetic Heritage*. Edited by Bernhard W. Anderson and Walter Harrelson. New York: Harper, 1962.

Anderson, Bernhard. W., with Steven Bishop. *Contours of Old Testament Theology*. Minneapolis: Fortress, 1999.

Anderson, Gary. "The Cosmic Mountain: Eden and Its Early Interpreters in Syriac Christianity." Pages 187–224 in *Genesis 1–3 in the History of Exegesis: Intrigue in the Garden*. Edited by Gregory Allen Robbins. Lewiston, N.Y.: Mellen, 1988.

———. "The Garments of Skin in Apocryphal Narrative and Biblical Commentary." Pages 101–43 in *Studies in Ancient Midrash*. Edited by James Kugel. Cambridge: Harvard University Press, 2000.

Attridge, Harold W. *The Epistle to the Hebrews*. Hermeneia. Philadelphia: Fortress, 1989.

Auerbach, Elias. *Moses*. Detroit: Wayne State University Press, 1975.

Avishur, Yitshak. *Stylistic Studies of Word-Pairs in Biblical and Ancient Semitic Literature.* AOAT 210. Kevelar: Butzon & Bercker, 1984.

Bal, Mieke. *Death and Dissymmetry: The Politics of Coherence in the Book of Judges.* Chicago: University of Chicago Press, 1988.

———. *Lethal Love: Feminist Literary Readings of Biblical Love Stories.* Bloomington: Indiana University Press, 1987.

———. *Murder and Difference: Gender, Genre and Scholarship on Sisera's Death.* Bloomington: Indiana University Press, 1988.

Balthasar, Hans Urs von. *Mysterium Paschale: The Mystery of Easter.* Edinburgh: T&T Clark, 1990.

Barr, James. *The Garden of Eden and the Hope for Immortality.* Minneapolis: Fortress, 1992.

———. Review of James Sanders, *From Sacred Story to Sacred Text: Canon As Paradigm.* Pages 137–41 in *CRBR*. Atlanta: Scholars Press, 1988.

———. *The Scope and Authority of the Bible.* Philadelphia: Westminster, 1980.

———. "Story and History in Biblical Theology." *JR* 56 (1976): 1–17. Reprinted in J. Barr. *The Scope and Authority of the Bible.* Philadelphia: Westminster, 1980, 1–17.

Barstad, Hans. "The Understanding of the Prophets in Deuteronomy," *SJT* 8 (1994): 236–51.

Barton, John. *Amos's Oracles against the Nations: A Study of Amos 1:3–2:5.* Cambridge: Cambridge University Press, 1980.

———. *Reading the Old Testament.* Philadelphia: Westminster, 1984.

Batto, Bernard F. "The Motif of Exodus in Deutero-Isaiah." Unpublished.

———. *Slaying the Dragon: Mythmaking in the Biblical Tradition.* Louisville: Westminster/John Knox, 1992.

Bauer, U. F. W. "Anti-Jewish Interpretations of Psalm 1 in Luther and in Modern German Protestantism." *Journal of Hebrew Scriptures* (Electronic) 2 (1998): 1–27.

Bauman, Zygmunt. *Modernity and the Holocaust.* Ithaca, N.Y.: Cornell University Press, 1989.

Beaulieu, P. A. "An Episode in the Fall of Babylon to the Persians." *JNES* 54 (1993): 241–61.

Bellis, Alice Ogden. "Poetic Structure and Intertextual Logic in Jeremiah 50." Pages 179–89 in *Troubling Jeremiah*. Edited by A. R. Pete Diamond, Kathleen M. O'Connor, and Louis Stulman. JSOTSup 260. Sheffield: Sheffield Academic Press, 1999.

———. *The Structure and Composition of Jeremiah 50:2–51:58*. Lewiston, N.Y.: Mellen Biblical Press, 1995.

Ben-Gurion, David. *Israel: A Personal History*. New York: Funk & Wagnalls, 1971.

Berge, K. *Die Gesetzauslegung Jesu*. Neukirchen-Vluyn: Neukirchener Verlag, 1972.

Berkovitz, Eliezer. *Faith after the Holocaust*. New York: Ktav, 1973.

Bernstein, Deborah S., ed. *Pioneers and Homemakers in Pre-State Israel*. Albany: State University of New York Press, 1992.

Betz, Hans Dieter. *Galatians*. Hermeneia. Philadelphia: Fortress, 1979.

Bledstein, Adrien Janis. "Binder, Trickster, Heel and Hairy-Man: Rereading Genesis 27 As a Trickster Tale Told by a Woman." Pages 282–95 in *A Feminist Companion to Genesis*. FCB 2. Edited by Athalya Brenner. Sheffield: JSOT Press, 1993.

Blenkinsopp, Joseph. *A History of Prophecy in Israel*. Philadelphia: Westminster, 1983.

———. "The Mission of Udjahorresnet and Those of Ezra and Nehemiah." *JBL* 106 (1987): 409–21.

———. "Old Testament Theology and the Jewish-Christian Connection." *JSOT* 28 (1984): 3–15.

———. "Structure and Meaning in the Sinai-Horeb Narrative." Pages 109–25 in *A Biblical Itinerary: In Search of Method, Form and Content: Essays in Honor of George W. Coats*. Edited by Eugene E. Carpenter. JSOTSup 240. Sheffield: Sheffield Academic Press, 1997.

Blum, Erhard. *Studien zur Komposition des Pentateuch*. BZAW 189. Berlin: de Gruyter, 1990.

Blumenthal, David R. *Facing the Abusing God: A Theology of Protest*. Louisville: Westminster/John Knox, 1993.

Boadt, Lawrence, Helga B. Croner, and Leon Klenicki, eds. *Biblical Studies: Meeting Ground for Jews and Christians*. Mahwah, N.J.: Paulist, 1980.

Boesak, Allan A. *Farewell to Innocence: A Socio-Ethical Study on Black Theology and Power.* Maryknoll, N.Y.: Orbis Books, 1977.

Bonhoeffer, Dietrich. *No Rusty Swords: Letters, Lectures and Notes 1928–1936.* London: Collins, 1965.

Booth, Wayne. *The Company We Keep: An Ethics of Fiction.* Berkeley and Los Angeles: University of California Press, 1988.

Brenner, Athalya, and Fokkelien van Dijk-Hemmes. *On Gendering Texts: Female and Male Voices in the Hebrew Bible.* Leiden: Brill, 1993.

Brettler, Marc. "The Composition of 1 Samuel 1–2." *JBL* 116 (1997): 601–12.

———. *The Creation of History in Ancient Israel.* London: Routledge, 1995.

———. "Interpretation and Prayer: Notes on the Composition of 1 Kings 8.15–53." Pages 17–35 in *Minḥah le-Naḥum: Biblical and Other Studies Presented to Nahum M. Sarna in Honour of his 70th Birthday.* Edited by Marc Brettler and Michael Fishbane. JSOTSup 154. Sheffield: Sheffield Academic Press, 1993.

———. "Predestination in Deuteronomy 30.1–10." In *Those Elusive Deuteronomists: The Phenomenon of Pan-Deuteronomism.* Edited by Linda Schearing and Steven McKenzie. JSOTSup 268. Sheffield: Sheffield Academic, 1999.

Brock, Rita Nakashima. "Dusting the Bible on the Floor: A Hermeneutics of Wisdom." Pages 64–75 in *Searching the Scriptures: A Feminist Introduction.* Edited by Elisabeth Schüssler Fiorenza. New York: Crossroad, 1993.

Brooks, Roger, and John J. Collins, eds. *Hebrew Bible or Old Testament? Studying the Bible in Judaism and Christianity.* Christianity and Judaism in Antiquity 5. Notre Dame: University of Notre Dame Press, 1990.

Brown, Robert McAfee. *Theology in a New Key: Responding to Liberation Themes.* Philadelphia: Westminster, 1978.

Brownlee, William H. "The Ineffable Name of God." *BASOR* 226 (1977): 39–46.

———. *The Midrash Pesher of Habakkuk.* SBLMS 24. Missoula, Mont.: Scholars Press, 1979.

Brueggemann, Walter. "A Convergence in Recent Old Testament Theologies." *JSOT* 18 (1980): 2–18.

———. "The Crisis and Promise of Presence in Israel." *HBT* 1 (1979): 47–86.

———. *Genesis.* Atlanta: John Knox, 1982.

———. *In Man We Trust.* Richmond: John Knox, 1972.

———. *Old Testament Theology: Essays on Structure, Theme, and Text.* Minneapolis: Fortress, 1992.

———. "Pharaoh As Vassal: A Study of a Political Metaphor." *CBQ* 57 (1995): 27–51.

———. "Praise and the Psalms: A Politics of Glad Abandonment." Pages 112-32 in *Psalms and the Life of Faith.* Minneapolis: Fortress, 1995.

———. Review of Carl E. Braaten and Robert W. Jenson, eds., *Reclaiming the Bible for the Church. Theology Today* 53 (1996): 349–53.

———. "A Shape for Old Testament Theology, I: Structure Legitimation." *CBQ* 47 (1985) 28-46.

———. *Texts under Negotiation: The Bible and Postmodern Imagination.* Minneapolis: Fortress, 1993.

———. *Theology of the Old Testament: Testimony, Dispute, Advocacy.* Minneapolis: Fortress, 1997.

———. "Trajectories in Old Testament Literature and the Sociology of Ancient Israel." *JBL* 98 (1979): 161–85.

Buber, Martin. *Moses: The Revelation and the Covenant.* New York: Harper & Row, 1958.

———. "On Word Choice in Translating the Bible: In Memoriam Franz Rosenzweig." Pages 79–89 in *Scripture and Translation: Martin Buber and Franz Rosenzweig.* Translated by Lawrence Rosenwald with Everett Fox. 1930. Repr., Bloomington: Indiana University Press, 1994.

Buber, Martin, and Franz Rosenzweig. *Die fünf Bücher der Weisung: Fünf Bücher des Moses.* Cologne: Jacob Hegner, 1968.

Buchanan, George Wesley. *To the Hebrews.* AB. New York: Doubleday, 1972.

Budd, Philip J. *Numbers.* WBC 5. Waco, Tex.: Word Books, 1984.

Calvin, John. *Commentaries on the Four Last Books of Moses: Arranged in the Form of a Harmony by John Calvin.* Grand Rapids: Eerdmans, 1950.

Campenhausen, Hans von. *The Formation of the Christian Bible.* Philadelphia: Fortress, 1972.

Caputo, John D. *Demythologizing Heidegger.* Bloomington: Indiana University Press, 1993.

Carr, David. *Reading the Fractures of Genesis: Historical and Literary Approaches.* Louisville: Westminster/John Knox, 1996.

Casanowicz, I. *Paronomasia in the Old Testament.* Boston: Norwood, 1894.

Cassuto, Umberto. *A Commentary on the Book of Exodus.* Translated by Israel Abrahams. Jerusalem: Magnes, 1967.

Chaney, Marvin. "Ancient Palestinian Peasant Movements and the Formation of Premonarchic Israel." Pages 39–90 in *Palestine in Transition: The Emergence of Ancient Israel.* Edited by D. N. Freedman and D. F. Graf. SWBA 2. Sheffield: Almond Press, 1983.

Childs, Brevard S. *Biblical Theology of the Old and New Testaments: Theological Reflection on the Christian Bible.* Minneapolis: Fortress, 1992.

———. *The Book of Exodus: A Critical, Theological Commentary.* OTL. Philadelphia: Westminster, 1974.

———. *Introduction to the Old Testament As Scripture.* London: SCM Press, 1979.

———. *Old Testament Theology in a Canonical Context.* Philadelphia: Fortress, 1986.

Clements, Ronald E. *Abraham and David: Genesis XV and Its Meaning for Israelite Tradition.* SBT 2/5. London: SCM Press, 1967.

———, ed. *The World of Ancient Israel: Sociological, Anthropological, and Political Perspectives.* Cambridge: Cambridge University Press, 1989.

Clifford, R. J. *The Cosmic Mountain in Canaan and the Old Testament.* HSM 4. Cambridge: Harvard University Press, 1972.

Clines, David J. A. *What Does Eve Do To Help? And Other Readerly Questions to the Old Testament.* Sheffield: Sheffield Academic Press, 1990.

———. "Yahweh and the God of Christian Theology." *Theology* 83 (1980): 323–30.

Cohen, Gerson D. "Esau As Symbol in Early Medieval Thought." Pages 19–48 in *Jewish Medieval and Renaissance Studies.* Edited by Alexander Altmann. Cambridge: Harvard University Press, 1967.

Cohen, Jeremy, ed. *Essential Papers on Judaism and Christianity in Conflict: From Late Antiquity to the Reformation.* New York: New York University Press, 1991.

Coleridge, Mark. "Life in the Crypt or Why Bother with Biblical Studies." *Biblical Interpretation* 2 (1994): 139–51.

Collins, John J. "The Exodus and Biblical Theology." *BTB* 25 (1995): 152–60.

———. "Historical Criticism and the State of Biblical Theology." *ChrCent* 110 (July 28–Aug 4, 1993): 743–47.

———. "Is a Critical Biblical Theology Possible?" Pages 1-17 in *The Hebrew Bible and Its Interpreters.* Edited by W. H. Propp, Baruch Halpern, and D. N. Freedman. Winona Lake, Ind.: Eisenbrauns, 1990.

———. *Jewish Wisdom in the Hellenistic Age.* OTL. Louisville: Westminster/John Knox, 1997.

———. Untitled reply. *ChrCent* 110 (October 13, 1993) 997–98.

———. "Wisdom, Apocalypticism and the Dead Sea Scrolls." Pages 19–32 in *Jedes Ding Hat seine Zeit. . .* Edited by Anja Diesel et al. Berlin: de Gruyter, 1996.

Constas, Nicholas. "The *Conceptio per Aurem* in Late Antiquity: Observations on Eve, the Serpent, and Mary's Ear." Forthcoming.

Cooper, A. M., and Bernard Goldstein. "The Cult of the Dead and the Theme of Entry into the Land." *Biblical Interpretation* 1 (1993): 285–303.

———. "Exodus and Matsot in History and Tradition." *Maarav* 8 (1992) 15–37.

———. "The Festivals of Israel and Judah and the Literary History of the Pentateuch." *JAOS* 110 (1990) 19-31.

Coote, R. *Amos among the Prophets.* Philadelphia: Fortress, 1981.

Croatto, J. Severino. *Exodus: A Hermeneutics of Freedom.* Maryknoll, N.Y.: Orbis Books, 1981.

Cross, F. M. *Canaanite Myth and Hebrew Epic.* Cambridge: Harvard University Press, 1973.

Crüsemann, Frank. *The Torah.* Philadelphia: Fortress, 1996.

Cunningham, David S. "On Translating the Divine Name." *TS* 56 (1995): 414–40.

Dalley, Stephanie. "Yahweh in Hamath in the 8th Century BC: Cuneiform Material and Historical Deductions." *VT* 40 (1990): 21–32.

Daube, David. *Studies in Biblical Law*. New York: Ktav, 1969

Davies, Philip R. *In Search of Ancient Israel*. JSOTSup 148. Sheffield: JSOT Press, 1992.

———. *Scribes and Schools: The Canonization of the Hebrew Scriptures*. Library of Ancient Israel. Louisville: Westminster/John Knox, 1998.

Davis, Ellen. *Proverbs, Ecclesiastes, the Song of Songs*. Westminster Bible Commentary. Louisville: Westminster/John Knox, 2000.

Dawidowicz, Lucy S. *The War against the Jews 1933–1945*. New York: Holt, Rinehart & Winston, 1975.

Day, John. *God's Conflict with the Dragon and the Sea*. Cambridge: Cambridge University Press, 1985.

De Roche, M. "Yahweh's *rîb* against Israel: A Reassessment of the So-Called 'Prophetic Lawsuit' in the Preexilic Prophets." *JBL* 102 (1983): 563–74.

Dearman, J. A. *Property Rights in the Eighth Century Prophets*. SBLDS 106. Atlanta: Scholars Press, 1988.

Delling, Gerhard. "πληρόω." *TDNT*, 6:286–98.

Dever, W. G. "Archaeology and the Israelite 'Conquest.'" *ABD*, 3:545–58.

Dietrich,Walter, and Martin A. Klopfenstein, eds. *Ein Gott Allein? JHWH-Verehrung und biblischer Monotheismus im Kontext der Israelitischen un altorientalischen Religiongeschichte*. OBO 139. Frieburg. Universitatsverlag, 1994.

Dimant, Devorah. "Pesharim, Qumran." *ABD*, 5:244–51.

Dinnerstein, Leonard. *Anti-Semitism in America*. New York: Oxford University Press, 1994.

Dohmen, Christophe. "Der Sinaibund als Neuer Bund nach Ex 19-34." Pages 51–83 in *Der Neue Bund Im Alten: Studien zur Bundestheologie der Beiden*. Edited by Erich Zenger. QD 146. Freiburg: Herder, 1993.

Dozeman, Thomas B. *God on the Mountain: A Study of Redaction, Theology and Canon in Exodus 19–24*. SBLMS 37. Atlanta: Scholars Press, 1989.

———. "Spatial Form in Exod 19:1–8a and in the Larger Sinai Narrative." *Semeia* 46 (1989): 87–101.

Driver, G. R. "The Original Form of the Name Yahweh: Evidences and Conclusions." *ZAW* 46 (1928): 7–25.

Driver, S. R. *The Book of Exodus*. CBC. Cambridge: Cambridge University Press, 1918.

Ebeling, Gerhard. "The Meaning of 'Biblical Theology.'" Pages 79–97 in *Word and Faith*. Philadelphia: Fortress, 1963.

———. *The Study of Theology*. Philadelphia: Fortress, 1978.

Ebert, Teresa L. *Ludic Feminism and After: Postmodernism, Desire, and Labor in Late Capitalism*. Ann Arbor: University of Michigan Press, 1996.

Eerdmans, B. D. "The Name Jahu." *Oudtestamentische Studiën* 5 (1948): 2–29.

Eichrodt, Walther. *Theology of the Old Testament*. Translated by J. A. Baker. 2 vols. Philadelphia: Westminster, 1961–1967.

Eilberg-Schwartz, Howard. *God's Phallus and Other Problems for Men and Monotheism*. Boston: Beacon Press, 1994.

Eisenstadt, S. N. *Jewish Civilization: The Jewish Historical Experience in a Comparative Perspective*. Albany: State University of New York Press, 1992.

Eissfeldt, Otto. "El and Yahweh." *JSS* 1 (1956): 25–37.

———. *The Old Testament: An Introduction*. Translated by Peter R. Ackroyd. New York: Harper & Row, 1965.

Exum, Cheryl. "Second Thoughts about Secondary Characters: Women in Exodus 1:8–2:10." Pages 75–87 in *A Feminist Companion to Exodus to Deuteronomy*. Edited by Athalya Brenner. FCB 6. Sheffield: Sheffield Academic Press, 1994.

———. "You Shall Let Every Daughter Live: A Study of Exodus 1:8–2:10." Pages 37–61 in *A Feminist Companion to Exodus to Deuteronomy*. Edited by Athalya Brenner. FCB 6. Sheffield: Sheffield Academic Press, 1994.

Fackenheim, Emil L. *The Jewish Bible after the Holocaust: A Re-reading*. Bloomington: Indiana University Press, 1990.

Farmer, Kathleen A. "The Trickster Genre in the Old Testament." Ph.D. diss. Southern Methodist University, 1978. Ann Arbor: University Microfilms, 1978.

Felder, Cain Hope. "James." Pages 1786–1800 in *The International Bible Commentary*. Edited by William R. Farmer. Collegeville, Minn.: Liturgical Press, l998.

Feldman, Louis H. "Josephus' Portrait of Jacob." *JQR* 79 (1988–1989): 101–51.

Fewell, Donna Nolan, and David M. Gunn. *Gender, Power, and Promise: The Subject of the Bible's First Story*. Nashville: Abingdon, 1993.

Fierro, A. "Exodus Event and Interpretation." In *The Bible and Liberation*. Edited by N. K. Gottwald. New York: Orbis Books, 1983.

Finkelstein, Israel. *The Archaeology of the Israelite Settlement*. Jerusalem: Israel Exploration Society, 1988.

Finkelstein, J. J. *The Ox That Gored*. TAPS 71/2. Philadelphia: American Philosophical Society, 1981.

Fish, Stanley. *Is There a Text for this Class? The Authority of Interpretive Communities*. Cambridge: Harvard University Press, 1980.

Fishbane, Michael. *Biblical Interpretation in Ancient Israel*. New York: Oxford University Press, 1985.

———. "Composition and Structure in the Jacob Cycle (Gen. 25:19–35:22)." *JJS* 26 (1975): 15-38.

———. "The 'Eden' Motif/The Landscape of Spatial Renewal." Pages 111–20 in *Text and Texture*. 1964. Repr., New York: Schocken Books, 1979.

———. "Revelation and Tradition: Aspects of Inner-Biblical Exegesis." *JBL* 99 (1980): 343–61.

Fitzmyer, Joseph A. *Romans*. AB. New York: Doubleday, 1993.

Flusser, David. *Judaism and the Origins of Christianity*. Jerusalem: Magnes, 1990.

Fohrer, Georg. *Theologische Grundstrukturen des Alten Testaments*. Berlin: de Gruyter, 1972.

Fokkelman, J. P. *Narrative Art in Genesis: Specimens of Stylistic and Structural Analysis*. 2d ed. Sheffield: JSOT Press, 1991.

Fox, Everett. *The Five Books of Moses*. New York: Schocken Books, 1995.

Fraade, Steven D. *Enosh and His Generation: Pre-Israelite Hero and History in Postbiblical Interpretation*. SBLMS 30. Chico, Calif.: Scholars Press, 1984.

Freedman, D. N. "Headings in the Books of the Eighth-Century Prophets." *AUSS* 25 (1987): 9–26.

———. "The Name of the God of Moses." *JBL* 79 (1960): 151–56.

———. *Pottery, Prophecy and Poetry*. Winona Lake, Ind.: Eisenbrauns, 1980.

Freedman, D. N., and M. P. O'Connor. "יהוה (YHWH)." *TDOT,* 5:500–21.

Frerichs, E. S. "Introduction: The Jewish School of Biblical Studies." Pages 1–6 in *Judaic Perspectives on Ancient Israel*. Edited by Jacob Neusner, B. A. Levine, and E. S. Frerichs. Philadelphia: Fortress, 1987.

Fretheim, Terence E. "The Book of Genesis." In vol. 1 of *The New Interpreter's Bible*. Nashville: Abingdon, 1994.

———. *Exodus*. Interpretation. Louisville: John Knox, 1991.

———. *The Pentateuch*. Nashville: Abingdon, 1996.

———. "The Reclamation of Creation: Redemption and Law in Exodus." *Int* 45 (1991): 354–65.

———. *The Suffering of God: An Old Testament Perspective*. Philadelphia: Fortress, 1984.

———. "Word of God." *ABD,* 6:961–68.

Friedman, R. E. *The Exile and Biblical Narrative*. HSM 23. Chico, Calif.: Scholars Press, 1981.

———. *Who Wrote the Bible?* New York: Summit, 1987.

Friedman, Shamma. "Holy Scriptures Defile the Hands." Pages 117–32 in *Minḥah le-Naḥum: Biblical and Other Studies Presented to Nahum M. Sarna in Honour of his 70th Birthday*. Edited by Marc Brettler et al. JSOTSup 154. Sheffield: Sheffield Academic Press, 1993.

Frymer-Kensky, Tikva. *In the Wake of the Goddesses: Women, Culture, and the Biblical Transformation of Pagan Myth*. New York: Free Press, 1992.

Fuchs, Esther. *Israeli Mythogynies: Women in Contemporary Hebrew Fiction*. Albany: State University of New York Press, 1987.

———. "The Literary Characterization of Mothers and Sexual Politics in the Hebrew Bible." Pages 117–36 in *Feminist Perspectives on Biblical Scholarship*. Edited by Adela Yarbro Collins. Chico, Calif.: Scholars Press, 1985.

———. "Structure and Patriarchal Functions in the Biblical Betrothal Scene: Some Preliminary Notes." *JFSR* 3 (Spring 1987): 7–14.

Gallardo, Helio. "Perspectivas para una izquierda política en la América Latina de la década del noventa." *XILOTL* 12/13 (1994) (Managua): 79–128.

Galli, Barbara E. "Rosenzweig and the Name for God." *Modern Judaism* 14 (1994): 63–85.

Gamble, Henry. "Canon, New Testament." *ABD,* 1:852–61.

Gammie, John G. *Holiness in Israel.* OBT. Minneapolis: Fortress, 1989.

Garber, Zev, and Bruce Zuckerman. "Why Do We Call the Holocaust 'The Holocaust?' An Inquiry into the Psychology of Labels." *Modern Judaism* 9 (1989): 197–211; repr. pages 51–66 in Zev Garber, *Shoah: The Paradigmatic Genocide.* Studies in the Shoah 8. Lanham, Md.: University Press of America, 1994.

Garr, W. R. "The Grammar and Interpretation of Exodus 6:3." *JBL* 111 (1992): 385–408.

Geertz, Clifford. *The Interpretation of Cultures.* New York: Basic Books, 1973.

Geller, Stephen A. *Sacred Enigma: Literary Religion in the Hebrew Bible.* London: Routledge, 1996.

Genovese, Eugene D. *Roll, Jordan, Roll.* New York: Pantheon, 1974.

Gezelle, Guido. "Het Schrijverke (Gyrinus Natans)." In *Een Nieuwe Bundel (vierde deel) Bloemlezing van Nederlandse Poëzie: Achtiende en Negentiende Eeuw.* Edited by K. H. de Raaf and J. J. Griss; rev. by F. W. van Herikhuizen. Rotterdam: W. L. & J. Brusse Uitgevers-maatschappij, 1958.

Ginsberg, H. L. *The Writings of Ugarit* (in Hebrew). Jerusalem: Bialik, 1936.

Ginsburg, Elliot K. *The Sabbath in the Classical Kabbalah.* Albany: State University of New York Press, 1989.

Ginzburg, Louis. *The Legends of the Jews.* 7 vols. Philadelphia: Jewish Publication Society of America, 1913–1938.

Gnuse, Robert Karl. "New Directions in Biblical Theology." *JAAR* 62 (1994): 893–918.

———. *No Other Gods: Emergent Monotheism in Israel.* JSOTSup 241. Sheffield: Sheffield Academic Press, 1997.

Goldhagen, Daniel Jonah. *Hitler's Willing Executioners: Ordinary Germans and the Holocaust.* New York: Alfred A. Knopf, 1996.

Goldingay, John. *Theological Diversity and the Authority of the Old Testament.* Grand Rapids: Eerdmans, 1987.

Gordon, Cyrus H. "Homer and Bible: The Origin and Character of East Mediterranean Literature." *HUCA* 26 (1955): 43–108.

Goshen-Gottstein, M. H. "Christianity, Judaism and Modern Bible Study." Pages 69–88 in *Congress Volume Edinburgh 1974*. Edited by G. W. Anderson. VTSup 28. Leiden: Brill, 1975.

———. "Tanakh Theology: The Religion of the Old Testament and the Place of Jewish Biblical Theology." Pages 617–44 in *Ancient Israelite Religion: Essays in Honor of Frank Moore Cross*. Edited by P. D. Miller Jr., P. D. Hanson, and S. D. McBride. Philadelphia: Fortress, 1987.

Gottwald, Norman K. "The Exodus As Event and Process: A Test Case in the Biblical Grounding of Liberation Theology." In *The Future of Liberation Theology: Essays in Honor of Gustavo Gutierrez*. Edited by M. H. Ellis and O. Maduro. Maryknoll, N.Y.: Orbis Books, 1983.

———. *The Hebrew Bible: A Socio-Literary Introduction*. Philadelphia: Fortress, 1985.

———. "The Participation of Free Agrarians in the Introduction of Monarchy to Ancient Israel: An Application of H. A. Landsberger's Framework for the Analysis of Peasant Movements." *Semeia* 37 (1986): 77–106.

———. *The Tribes of Yahweh*. New York: Orbis Books, 1979.

Greenberg, Moshe. "The Decalogue Tradition Critically Examined." Pages 83–119 in *The Ten Commandments in History and Tradition*. Edited by Ben-Zion Segal. Jerusalem: Magnes, 1985.

———. "Exodus, Book of." Page 1056 in vol. 6 of *Encyclopedia Judaica*. 16 vols. Jerusalem, 1972.

———. *Ezekiel 1-20*. AB 22A. Garden City, N.Y.: Doubleday, 1983.

———. "Some Postulates of Biblical Criminal Law." Pages 18–37 in *The Jewish Expression*. Edited by Judah Goldin. 1960. Repr., New Haven: Yale University Press, 1976; repr. pages 25–41 in Moshe Greenberg, *Studies in the Bible and Jewish Thought*. Philadelphia: Jewish Publication Society of America, 1995.

Greenstein, Edward L. "Kirta." Pages 9–48 in *Ugaritic Narrative Poetry*. Edited by Simon B. Parker. SBLWAW Atlanta: Scholars Press, 1997.

Gruber, Mayer I. "Matrilinear Determination of Jewishness: Biblical and Near Eastern Roots." In *Pomegranates and Golden Bells*. Edited by David P. Wright et al. Winona Lake, Ind.: Eisenbrauns, 1995.

Gruenwald, Itamar. "Midrash and the 'Midrashic Condition': Preliminary Considerations." Pages 6–22 in *The Midrashic Imagination*. Edited by Michael Fishbane. Albany: State University of New York Press, 1993.

Gunkel, Hermann. *Genesis.* 1910. Repr. Macon, Ga.: Mercer University Press, 1997.

Gunneweg, A. H. J. *Biblische Theologie des Alten Testament: Eine Religionsgeschichte Israels in biblisch-theologischer Sicht.* Stuttgart: Kohlhammer, 1993.

Gustfason, James. "The Place of Scripture in Christian Ethics: A Methodological Study." *Int* 24 (1970): 430–55.

Gutierrez, Gustavo. *A Theology of Liberation.* Maryknoll, N.Y.: Orbis Books, 1973.

Halivni, David Weiss. "From Midrash to Mishnah: Theological Repercussions and Further Clarifications of 'chate'u yisrael.'" Pages 23–44 in *The Midrashic Imagination.* Edited by Michael Fishbane. Albany: State University of New York Press, 1993.

———. *Peshat and Derash: Plain and Applied Meaning in Rabbinic Exegesis.* New York: Oxford University Press, 1998.

———. "Reflections on Classical Jewish Hermeneutics," *PAAJR* 62 (1996): 21–127.

Halpern, Baruch. "The Baal (and the Asherah) in Seventh-Century Judah: Yhwh's Retainers Retired." Pages 115–54 in *Konsequente Traditionsgeschichte. Festschrift für Klaus Baltzer.* Edited by Rüdiger Barthelmus, Thomas Krüger, and Helmut Utzschneider. OBO 126. Freiburg: Universitätsverlag, 1993.

———. "Brisker Pipes Than Poetry: The Development of Israelite Monotheism." Pages 77–115 in *Judaic Perspectives on Ancient Israel.* Edited by Jacob Neusner, Baruch Levine, and E. S. Frerichs. Philadelphia: Fortress, 1987.

———. "Center and Sentry." In *Megiddo III.* Edited by Israel Finkelstein, David Ussishkin, and Baruch Halpern. Tel Aviv: Institute of Archaeology, 1999.

———. *Constitution of the Monarchy in Israel.* HSM 25. Chico Calif.: Scholars Press, 1981.

———. *The Emergence of Israel in Canaan.* SBLMS 29. Chico, Calif.: Scholars Press, 1983.

———. "A Historiographic Commentary on Ezra 1–6: Achronological Narrative and Dual Chronology in Israelite Historiography." Pages 81–142 in *The Hebrew Bible and its Interpreters.* Edited by W. H. Propp, Baruch Halpern, and D. N. Freedman. Biblical and Judaic

Studies from the University of California, San Diego. Winona Lake, Ind: Eisenbrauns, 1990.

———. *A History of Israel in Her Land*. In Progress.

———. "How Golden Is the Marshaltown, How Holey the Scripture?" *JQR* 87 (1997) 1–16.

———. "Jerusalem and the Lineages in the 8th–7th Centuries BCE: Kinship and the Rise of Individual Moral Liability." Pages 11–107 in *Law and Ideology in Monarchic Israel*. Edited by Baruch Halpern and D. W. Hobson. JSOTSup 124. Sheffield: Sheffield Academic Press, 1991.

———. "The New Name of Isaiah 62:4: Jeremiah's Reception in the Restoration and the Politics of 'Third Isaiah.'" *JBL* 117 (1998): 623–43.

———. "Sociological Comparativism and the Theological Imagination: The Case of the Conquest." Pages 53–67 in *"Sha'arei Talmon": Studies in the Bible, Qumran, and the Ancient Near East Presented to Shemaryahu Talmon*. Edited by Michael Fishbane and Emanuel Tov. Winona Lake, Ind.: Eisenbrauns, 1992.

———. "Sybil, or the Two Nations? Archaism, Kinship, Alienation and the Elite Redefinition of Traditional Culture in Judah in the 8th–7th Centuries B.C.E." Pages 291–338 in *The Study of the Ancient Near East in the 21st Century: The William Foxwell Albright Centennial Conference*. Edited by Jerrold S. Cooper and Glenn M. Schwartz. Winona Lake, Ind.: Eisenbrauns, 1996.

Hanson, A. "John's Citation of Psalm LXXXII." *NTS* 11 (1964–1965): 158–62.

Hanson, P. D. *The Diversity of Structure: A Theological Interpretation*. Philadelphia: Fortress, 1982.

———. *Dynamic Transcendence*. Philadelphia: Fortress, 1978.

Harnack, Adolf von. *Marcion: The Gospel of the Alien God*. Translated by John E. Steely and Lyle D. Bierma. Durham, N.C.: Labyrinth, 1990. German original: *Marcion: Das Evangelium vom fremden Gott*. Darmstadt: Wissenschaftliche Buchgesellschaft, 1960.

Harris, R. Laird. "The Pronunciation of the Tetragram." Pages 215–24 in *The Law and the Prophets: Old Testament Studies Prepared in Honor of Oswald Thompson Allis*. Edited by John H. Skilton. Nutley, N.J.: Presbyterian & Reformed, 1974.

Hasel, Gerhard. *Old Testament Theology: Basic Issues in the Current Debate*. 4th ed. Grand Rapids: Eerdmans, 1991.

Hendel, Ronald S. *The Epic of the Patriarch: The Jacob Cycle and the Narrative Tradition of Canaan and Israel.* HSM 42. Atlanta: Scholars Press, 1987.

Heschel, Abraham Joshua. *God in Search of Man.* 1955. Repr. Cleveland: World Publishing/Jewish Publication Society of America, 1963.

Hillers, D. R. "Palmyrene Aramaic Inscriptions and the Bible." Forthcoming in *ZAH.*

Hirsch, Samson Raphael. *The Pentateuch.* Vol 1, *Genesis.* London: L. Honig & Sons, 1959.

Hirshman, Marc. *A Rivalry of Genius: Jewish and Christian Biblical Interpretation in Antiquity.* Translated by B. Stein. Albany: State University of New York Press, 1996.

Hoglund, Kenneth G. *Achaemenid Imperial Administration in Syria-Palestine and the Missions of Ezra and Nehemiah.* Atlanta: Scholars Press, 1992.

Holladay, J. S. "Religion in Israel and Judah under the Monarchy: An Explicitly Archaeological Approach." Pages 249–99 in *Ancient Israelite Religion: Essays in Honor of Frank Moore Cross.* Edited by P. D. Miller Jr., P. D. Hanson, and S. D. McBride. Philadelphia: Fortress, 1987.

Holladay, William. *Jeremiah 2: A Commentary on the Book of the Prophet Jeremiah, Chapters 26–52.* Hermeneia. Minneapolis: Fortress, 1986.

Howard, George. "The Tetragram and the New Testament." *JBL* 96 (1977): 63–83.

Huffmon, Herbert B. *Amorite Personal Names in the Mari Texts.* Baltimore: Johns Hopkins University Press, 1965.

———. "The Treaty Background of Hebrew *Yādaᶜ.*" *BASOR* 181 (1966) 31–37.

Huffmon, Herbert B., and Simon B. Parker. "A Further Note on the Treaty Background of Hebrew *Yādaᶜ.*" *BASOR* 184 (1966): 36–38.

Hull, Robert F., Jr. Review of Reidar Hvalvik, *The Struggle for Scripture and Covenant: The Purpose of the* Epistle of Barnabas *and Jewish-Christian Competition in the Second Century. JECS* 6 (1998): 325–27.

Hurvitz, Avi. "On the Borderline between Biblical Criticism and Hebrew Linguistics: The Emergence of the Term ספר־משה." Pages 37–44 (Hebrew section) in *Tehillah le-Moshe: Biblical and Judaic Studies in Honor of Moshe Greenberg.* Edited by Mordecai Cogan, Barry L. Eichler and Jeffrey H. Tigay. Winona Lake, Ind.: Eisenbrauns, 1997.

Hvalvik, Reidar. *The Struggle for Scripture and Covenant: The Purpose of the* Epistle of Barnabas *and Jewish-Christian Competition in the Second Century*. Tübingen: Mohr Siebeck, 1996.

Idel, Moshe. "Midrashic versus Other Forms of Jewish Hermeneutic: Some Comparative Reflections." Pages 45–58 in *The Midrashic Imagination*. Edited by Michael Fishbane. Albany: State University of New York Press, 1993.

Iersel, B. van, and A. Weiler, eds. *Exodus: A Lasting Paradigm*. Concilium 189. Edinburgh: T&T Clark, 1987.

Jacob, Benno. *Das Erste Buch der Tora: Genesis*. Berlin: Schocken Books, 1934.

Jacob, Edmond. *Theology of the Old Testament*. London: Hodder & Stoughton, 1958.

Jacobsen, Thorkild. *The Treasures of Darkness: A History of Mesopotamian Religion*. New Haven: Yale University Press, 1976.

Janzen, J. G. *Genesis 12–50: Abraham and All the Families of the Earth*. Grand Rapids: Eerdmans, 1993.

Japhet, Sara. *The Ideology of the Book of Chronicles and Its Place in Biblical Thought*. BEATAJ 9. Frankfurt: Peter Lang, 1989.

Jeansonne, Sharon Pace. *The Women of Genesis: From Sarah to Potiphar's Wife*. Minneapolis: Fortress, 1990.

Jeppesen, Knud. "Is Deuteronomy Hostile Toward Prophets?" *SJT* 8 (1994): 252–56.

Johnson, Elizabeth A. *She Who Is: The Mystery of God in Feminist Theological Discourse*. New York: Crossroad, 1992.

Jüngel, Eberhard. *God As the Mystery of the World: On the Foundation of the Crucified in the Dispute Between Theism and Atheism*. Grand Rapids: Eerdmans, 1983.

Kaiser, Otto. *Der Gott des Alten Testaments. Theologie des Alten Testaments*. Vol. 1, *Grundlegung*. Göttingen: Vandenhoeck & Ruprecht, 1993.

Katz, Jacob. *From Prejudice to Destruction*. Cambridge: Harvard University Press, 1980.

Kaufmann, Yehezkel. *The Religion of Israel: From Its Beginnings to the Babylonian Exile*. New York: Schocken Books, 1960.

Keel, Othmar, ed. *Monotheismus im alten Israel und seiner Umwelt*. Biblische Beiträge 14. Stuttgart: Katholisches Bibelwerk, 1980.

Kellenbach, Katharina von. *Anti-Judaism in Feminist Religious Writings.* American Academy of Religion Cultural Criticism Series 1. Atlanta: Scholars Press, 1994.

Kitchen, K. A. "The Exodus." *ABD,* 2:700–8.

Knierim, Rolf P. "On Gabler." Pages 495–556 in *The Task of Old Testament Theology: Substance, Method, and Cases.* Grand Rapids: Eerdmans, 1995.

———. "The Task of Old Testament Theology." *HBT* 6 (1984): 25–57. Rev. ed., pages 1–20 in *The Task of Old Testament Theology: Substance, Method and Cases.* Grand Rapids: Eerdmans, 1995.

Knight, D. A. "The Pentateuch." Pages 263–96 in *The Hebrew Bible and Its Modern Interpreters.* Edited by D. A. Knight and G. M. Tucker. Philadelphia: Fortress, 1985.

———, ed. *Tradition and Theology in the Old Testament.* Philadelphia: Fortress, 1977.

Knudtzon, J. A. *Die El-Amarna-Tafeln.* Vorderasiatische Bibliothek. Aalen: Otto Zeller, 1964.

Köhler, Ludwig. *Old Testament Theology.* London: Lutterworth, 1957.

Kraus, Hans-Joachim. *Psalms 60-150: A Commentary.* Translated by Hilton C. Oswald. Minneapolis: Augsburg, 1989.

Kugel, James L. *The Bible As It Was.* Cambridge: Harvard University Press, 1997.

Kugel, James L., and Rowan A. Greer, eds. *Early Biblical Interpretation.* Philadelphia: Westminster, 1986.

LaCocque, André. *The Feminine Unconventional: Four Subversive Figures in Israel's History.* OBT. Minneapolis: Fortress, 1990.

Ladd, Everett Carl, Jr., and Seymour Martin Lipset. *The Divided Academy.* New York: McGraw-Hill, 1975.

Lambden, Stephen N. "From Fig Leaves to Fingernails: Some Notes on the Garments of Adam and Eve in the Hebrew Bible and Select Early Postbiblical Jewish Writings." Pages 74–90 in *A Walk in the Garden: Biblical, Iconographical and Literary Images of Eden.* Edited by Paul Morris and Deborah Sawyer. JSOTSup 136. Sheffield: JSOT Press, 1992.

Lambert, W. G. *Babylonian Wisdom Literature.* London: Oxford University Press, 1960.

Lambert, W. G., and A. R. Millard. *Atra-ḫasīs*. London: Oxford University Press, 1969.

Leibowitz, Nehama. *New Studies in Bereshit (Genesis)*. Jerusalem: Dept. for Torah Education and Culture in the Diaspora, 1995.

Leiman, Shneur Zalman. *The Canonization of the Hebrew Scriptures*. Hamden: Archon, 1976.

Lemche, N. P. "Israel: History of (Premonarchic Period)." *ABD*, 3:526–45.

Levenson, David. "Different Texts or Different Quests? The Contexts of Biblical Studies." Pages 153–64 in *Hebrew Bible or Old Testament? Studying the Bible in Judaism and Christianity*. Edited by Roger Brooks and John J. Collins. Christianity and Judaism in Antiquity 5. Notre Dame: University of Notre Dame Press, 1990.

Levenson, Jon D. *Creation and the Persistence of Evil: The Jewish Drama of Divine Omnipotence*. San Francisco: Harper & Row, 1988.

———. *The Death and Resurrection of the Beloved Son: The Transformation of Child Sacrifice in Judaism and Christianity*. New Haven: Yale University Press, 1993.

———. "The Eighth Principle of Judaism and the Literary Simultaneity of Scripture." Pages 62–81 in *The Hebrew Bible, the Old Testament, and Historical Criticism*. Louisville: Westminster/John Knox, 1993.

———. *Esther: A Commentary*. OTL. Louisville: Westminster/John Knox, 1997.

———. "Exodus and Liberation." Pages 127–59 in *The Hebrew Bible, the Old Testament, and Historical Criticism*. Louisville: Westminster/John Knox, 1993.

———. "The Jerusalem Temple in Devotional and Visionary Experience." Pages 32–61 in *Jewish Spirituality: From the Bible through the Middle Ages*. Edited by A. Green. New York: Crossroad, 1988.

———. "Response to Edward L. Greenstein." Pages 47–54 in *The State of Jewish Studies*. Edited by Shaye J. D. Cohen and Edward L. Greenstein. Detroit: Wayne State University Press, 1990.

———. *Sinai and Zion: An Entry into the Jewish Bible*. New York: Winston, 1985.

———. "The Temple and the World." *JR* 64 (1984): 275–98.

———. "Theological Consensus or Historicist Evasion? Jews and Christians in Biblical Studies." Pages 109–45 in *Hebrew Bible or Old Testament?*

Studying the Bible in Judaism and Christianity. Edited by Roger Brooks and John J. Collins. Christianity and Judaism in Antiquity 5. Notre Dame: University of Notre Dame Press, 1990.

———. *Theology of the Program of Restoration of Ezekiel 40–48.* HSM 10. Missoula, Mont.: Scholars Press, 1976.

———. "The Universal Horizon of Biblical Particularism." Pages 143–69 in *Ethnicity and the Bible.* Edited by Mark G. Brett. Leiden: Brill, 1996.

———. "Who Inserted the Book of the Torah?" *HTR* 68 (1975): 203–33.

———. "Why Jews Are Not Interested in Biblical Theology." Pages 281–307 in *Judaic Perspectives on Ancient Israel.* Edited by Jacob Neusner, Baruch A. Levine, and Ernest S. Frerichs. Philadelphia: Fortress, 1987; repr. pages 33–61 in *The Hebrew Bible, the Old Testament, and Historical Criticism.* Louisville: Westminster/John Knox, 1993.

Levin, C. *Der Jahwist.* FRLANT 157. Göttingen: Vandenhoeck & Ruprecht, 1993.

Levine, Baruch. *The JPS Torah Commentary: Leviticus.* Philadelphia: Jewish Publication Society of America, 5749/1989.

Levison, Jack. "A Contextual Analysis of Sir 25:24." *CBQ* 47 (1985): 617–23.

Lewis, C. S. *An Experiment in Criticism.* Cambridge: Cambridge University Press, 1961.

Licht, Jacob. "The Sinai Theophany" (in Hebrew). Pages 251–67 in the Hebrew volume of *Studies in Bible and the Ancient Near East Presented to Samuel E. Loewenstamm on His Seventieth Birthday.* Edited by Yitschak Avishur and Joshua Blau. 2 vols. Jerusalem: E. Rubenstein, 1978. (English summary in non-Hebrew volume, 200–1)

Lieberman, Saul. *Hellenism in Jewish Palestine.* New York: Jewish Theological Seminary of America, 1950.

Lieberman, Stephen. "A Mesopotamian Background for the So-Called Aggadic 'Measures' of Biblical Hermeneutics?" *HUCA* 58 (1987): 157–225.

Lightstone, Jack. "The Formation of the Biblical Canon in Judaism of Late Antiquity: Prolegomenon to a General Reassessment." *Studies in Religion* 8 (1979): 135–42.

Loewenstamm, Samuel E. "The Death of Moses." Pages 136–66 in *From Babylon to Canaan: Studies in the Bible and its Oriental Background.* Jerusalem: Magnes, 1992.

———. *The Evolution of the Exodus Tradition*. Jerusalem: Magnes, 1992.

Lohfink, Norbert. "Bund als Vertrag im Deuteronomium." *ZAW* 107 (1995): 215–39.

———. *Das Jüdische am Christentum: Die verlorene Dimension*. Freiburg: Herder, 1987.

———. *Option for the Poor: The Basic Principle of Liberation Theology in the Light of the Bible*. Berkeley: Bibal, 1987.

Lowrie, Walter. "The Proper Name of God." *AThR* 41 (1959): 245–52.

Machinist, Peter. "The Question of Distinctiveness in Ancient Israel: An Essay." Pages 196–212 in *Ah, Assyria. . . : Studies in Assyrian History and Ancient Near Eastern Historiography Presented to Hayim Tadmor*. Edited by Mordechai Cogan and Israel Ephᶜal. ScrHier 33. Jerusalem: Magnes, 1991.

Mack, B. L. "Imitatio Mosis: Patterns of Cosmology and Soteriology in the Hellenistic Synagogue." *Studia Philonica* 1 (1972): 27–55.

Malul, Meir. "*ᶜAqeb* 'Heel' and *ᶜAqab* 'To Supplant' and the Concept of Succession in the Jacob-Esau Narratives." *VT* 46 (1996): 190–212.

Mandelbaum, Irving. "Tannaitic Exegesis of the Golden Calf Episode." Pages 207–23 in *A Tribute to Geza Vermes*. Edited by Philip R. Davies and Richard White. JSOTSup 100. Sheffield: JSOT Press, 1990.

Marcus, David. "David the Deceiver and David the Dupe." *Prooftexts* 6 (1986): 163–71.

———. *From Balaam to Jonah: Anti-Prophetic Satire in the Hebrew Bible*. Atlanta: Scholars Press, 1995.

———. "Is Nehemiah a Translation from Aramaic?" In *Boundaries of the Ancient Near Eastern World: A Tribute to Cyrus H. Gordon*. Edited by Meir Lubetski et al. JSOTSup 273. Sheffield: Sheffield Academic Press, 1998.

Marmorstein, Arthur. "Judaism and Christianity in the Middle of the Third Century." Pages 179–224 in *Studies in Jewish Theology*. Edited by J. Rabbinowitz and M. S. Lew. London: Oxford University Press, 1950.

Mayes, A. D. H. "Deuteronomy 4 and the Literary Criticism of Deuteronomy." Pages 195–224 in *A Song of Power and the Power of Song: Essays on the Book of Deuteronomy*. Edited by Duane L. Christensen. Sources for Biblical and Theological Study 3. Winona Lake, Ind.: Eisenbrauns, 1993.

Mays, James L. *Amos: A Commentary*. OTL. Philadelphia: Westminster, 1969.

———. "Historical and Canonical: Recent Discussions about the Old Testament and Christian Faith." In *Magnalia Dei: The Mighty Acts of God*. Edited by F. M. Cross, W. Lemke, and P. D. Miller Jr. Festschrift G. E. Wright. Garden City, N.Y.: Doubleday, 1976.

McCarthy, D. J. *Old Testament Covenant: A Survey of Current Opinions*. Richmond: John Knox, 1973.

———. *Treaty and Covenant*. AnBib 21. Rome: Pontifical Biblical Institute, 1963.

McClay, Wilfred M. "Religion in Politics. Politics in Religion." *Commentary* 86:4 (October 1988): 43–49.

McKenzie, John L. *A Theology of the Old Testament*. Garden City, N.Y.: Doubleday, 1974.

Meier, John P. "The Bible As a Source for Theology." *Proceedings of the Catholic Theological Society of America* 43 (1988): 1–14.

Mendenhall, G. E. "Ancient Israel's Hyphenated History." Pages 91–103 in *Palestine in Transition: The Emergence of Ancient Israel*. Edited by D. N. Freedman and D. F. Graf. SWBA 2. Sheffield: Almond Press, 1983.

———. "Ancient Oriental and Biblical Law." *BA* 17 (1954): 26-46.

———. "Biblical History in Transition." Pages 27–58 in *The Bible and the Ancient Near East: Essays in Honor of William Foxwell Albright*. Edited by G. E. Wright. Garden City, N.Y.: Doubleday, 1965.

———. "Covenant Forms in Israelite Tradition." *BA* 17 (1954): 49–76.

———. "The Hebrew Conquest of Palestine." *BA* 25 (1962): 66–87.

———. *Law and Covenant in Israel and the Ancient Near East*. Pittsburgh: Biblical Colloquium, 1955.

———. *The Tenth Generation*. Baltimore: Johns Hopkins University Press, 1973.

Mettinger, Tryggve. *The Dethronement of Sabaoth: Studies in the Shem and Kabod Theologies*. ConBOT 18. Lund: Gleerup, 1982.

———. *In Search of God*. Philadelphia: Fortress, 1988.

Meyers, Carol. "Miriam the Musician." Pages 207–30 in *A Feminist Companion to Exodus to Deuteronomy*. Edited by Athalya Brenner. FCB 6. Sheffield: Sheffield Academic Press, 1994.

Miles, Jack. *God: A Biography*. New York: Knopf, 1995.

Milgrom, Jacob. *Leviticus 1–16*. AB. New York: Doubleday, 1991.

———. *Studies in Levitical Terminology 1: The Encroacher and the Levite, The Term* ʿAboda. University of California Publications, Near Eastern Studies 14. Berkeley and Los Angeles: University of California Press, 1971.

Miller, Patrick D., Jr. "Creation and Covenant." Pages 155–68 in *Biblical Theology: Problems and Perspectives*. Edited by Steven J. Kraftchick et. al. Nashville: Abingdon, 1995.

———. *They Cried to the Lord: The Form and Theology of Biblical Prayer*. Minneapolis: Fortress, 1994.

Miskotte, Kornelis H. *When the Gods Are Silent*. New York: Harper & Row, 1967.

Moberly, R. W. L. *At the Mountain of God: Story and Theology in Exodus 32–34*. JSOTSup 22. Sheffield: JSOT Press, 1983.

Montgomery, James A. *Aramaic Incantation Texts from Nippur*. Philadelphia: University Museum, 1913.

Moore, Carey A. *Esther*. AB 7b. Garden City, N.Y.: Doubleday, 1971.

———. "Esther, Book of." *ABD*, 2:633–43.

Morgan, Robert, and John Barton. *Biblical Interpretation*. The Oxford Bible Series. Oxford: Oxford University Press, 1988.

Morris, Paul. "Exiled from Eden: Jewish Interpretations of Genesis." Pages 117–66 in *A Walk in the Garden: Biblical, Iconographical and Literary Images of Eden*. Edited by Paul Morris and Deborah Sawyer. JSOTSup 136. Sheffield: JSOT Press, 1992.

Moule, Charles. "Fulfill." *IDB*, 2:327–38.

Mowinckel, Sigmund. *Der achtundsechzigste Psalm*. Oslo: Jacob Dybwad, 1953.

———. "The Name of the God of Moses." *HUCA* 32 (1961): 121–33.

———. *The Psalms in Israel's Worship*. New York: Abingdon, 1962.

Muffs, Yochanan. *Love and Joy*. New York: Jewish Theological Seminary of America, 1992.

Muilenburg, James. "The Form and Structure of the Covenantal Formulations." *VT* 9 (1959): 347–65.

Müller, H.-P. "Der Jahwename und seine Deutung, Ex 3:14 im Licht der Textpublikationen aus Ebla." *Bib* 62 (1981): 305–27.

Müller, K. F. *Das assyrische Ritual I. Texte zum assyrischen Königsritual.* Leipzig: Hinrichs, 1937.

Murphy, Roland O. "Tanakh—Canon and Interpretation." Pages 11–29 in *Hebrew Bible or Old Testament? Studying the Bible in Judaism and Christianity.* Edited by Roger Brooks and John J. Collins. Christianity and Judaism in Antiquity 5. Notre Dame: University of Notre Dame Press, 1990.

Nanos, Mark D. "The Jewish Context of the Gentile Audience Addressed in Paul's Letter to the Romans." *CBQ* 61 (1999): 283–304.

———. *The Mystery of Romans: The Jewish Context of Paul's Letter.* Minneapolis: Fortress, 1996.

Nelson, Richard D. *Raising Up a Faithful Priest: Community and Priesthood in Biblical Theology.* Louisville: Westminster/John Knox, 1993.

Nicholson, Ernest W. *Exodus and Sinai in History and Tradition.* Richmond: John Knox, 1973.

———. *God and His People: Covenant and Theology in the Old Testament.* Oxford: Clarendon, 1986.

Niditch, Susan. "Genesis." Pages 10–25 in *The Women's Bible Commentary.* Edited by Carol A. Newsom and Sharon H. Ringe. Louisville: Westminster/John Knox, 1992.

———. *Oral World and Written Word: Ancient Israelite Literature.* Library of Ancient Israel. Louisville: Westminster/John Knox, 1996.

———. *Underdogs and Tricksters: A Prelude to Biblical Folklore.* San Francisco: Harper & Row, 1987.

Noth, Martin. *Exodus.* Translated by J. S. Bowden. OTL. Philadelphia: Westminster, 1962.

Ollenburger, Ben C., E. A. Martens, and G. F. Hasel, eds. *The Flowering of Old Testament Theology: A Reader in Twentieth-Century Old Testament Theology, 1930–1990.* Winona Lake, Ind.: Eisenbrauns, 1992.

Osten-Sacken, Peter von der. *Christian-Jewish Dialogue: Theological Foundations.* Philadelphia: Fortress, 1986.

Oswald, Wolfgang. *Israel am Gottesberg: Eine Untersuchung zur Literargeschichte der vorderen Sinaiperikope Ex 19–24 und deren historischem Hintergrund.* OBO 159. Freiburg: Universitätsverlag, 1998.

Otto, Eckart. "Kritik der Pentateuchkomposition." *TRu* 60 (1995): 163–91.

———. "Die Tora in Israels Rechtsgeschichte." *TLZ* 118 (1993): 903–10.

———. "Treueid und Gesetz: Die Ursprünge des Deuteronomiums im Horizont neuassyrischen Vertragsrechts." *Zeitschrift für Altorientalische und Biblische Rechtsgeschichte* 2 (1996): 1–52.

Padel, Ruth. *Whom the Gods Destroy*. Princeton, N. J.: Princeton University Press, 1995.

Pardes, Ilana. *Countertraditions in the Bible: A Feminist Approach*. Cambridge: Harvard University Press, 1992.

Parke-Taylor, G. H. "יהוה." Pages 79–96 in *Yahweh: The Divine Name in the Bible*. Waterloo, Ontario: Wilfrid Laurier University Press, 1975.

Paul, Shalom. *Amos*. Hermeneia. Minneapolis: Fortress, 1991.

Pawlikowski, John T. *Christ in the Light of the Christian-Jewish Dialogue*. New York: Paulist, 1982.

———. "Christology, Anti-Semitism, and Christian-Jewish Bonding." Pages 245–68 in *Reconstructing Christian Theology*. Edited by R. S. Chopp and M. L. Taylor. Minneapolis: Fortress, 1994.

Perdue, Leo G. *The Collapse of History: Reconstructing Old Testament Theology*. OBT. Minneapolis: Fortress, 1994.

Perlitt, L. *Bundestheologie im Alten Testament*. Neukirchen-Vluyn: Neukirchener Verlag, 1969.

Perry, Marvin, and Frederick M. Schweitzer, eds. *Jewish-Christian Encounters over the Centuries: Symbiosis, Prejudice, Holocaust, Dialogue*. New York: Peter Lang, 1994.

Pfeiffer, Robert H. "Hebrew and Greek Sense of Tragedy." Pages 54–64 in *The Joshua Bloch Memorial Volume*. Edited by Abraham Berger et al. New York: The New York Public Library, 1960.

Pixley, Jorge (George) V. *On Exodus: A Liberation Perspective*. Maryknoll, N.Y.: Orbis Books, 1987.

Plaskow, Judith. *Standing Again at Sinai: Judaism from a Feminist Perspective*. San Francisco: Harper & Row, 1990.

Plaut, W. Gunther. "The Strange Blessing: A Modern Midrash on Genesis 27." *CCAR Journal* (June 1960): 30–34.

Preuß, Horst Dietrich. *Old Testament Theology*. 2 vols. Louisville: Westminster/John Knox, 1995–1996.

Quell, Gottfried. "κύριος." *TDNT*, 3:1058–81.

Rad, Gerhard von. "The Form-Critical Problem of the Hexateuch." Pages 1–78 in *The Problem of the Hexateuch and Other Essays*. London: SCM Press, 1984.

———. *Old Testament Theology*. Translated by D. M. G. Stalker. 2 vols. New York: Harper & Row, 1962.

———. *Wisdom in Israel*. Nashville: Abingdon, 1972.

Rashkow, Ilona N. *The Phallacy of Genesis: A Feminist Psychoanalytic Approach*. Louisville: Westminster/John Knox Press, 1993.

Redford, D. B. *Akhenaten, the Heretic King*. Princeton, N.J.: Princeton University Press, 1994.

Rehm, Merlin D. "Levites and Priests." *ABD*, 4:297–310.

Reitlinger, Gerald. *The Final Solution: The Attempt to Exterminate the Jews of Europe 1939–1945*. Northvale, N.J.: Aronson, 1987.

Rendtorff, Rolf. *Die Bundesformel: Eine Exegetisch-theologisch Untersuchung*. SBS 160; Stuttgart: Katholisches Bibelwerk, 1995. Eng.: *The Covenant Formula: An Exegetical and Theological Investigation*. Translated by Margaret Kohl. OTS. Edinburgh: T&T Clark, 1998.

———. "'Covenant' As a Structuring Concept in Genesis and Exodus." Pages 125–34 in *Canon and Theology: Overtures to an Old Testament Theology*. OBT. Minneapolis: Fortress, 1993.

———. "The Impact of the Holocaust Shoah on German Protestant Theology." *HBT* 15 (1993): 154–67.

———. "Nehemiah 9: An Important Witness of Theological Reflection." Pages 111–17 in *Tehillah le-Moshe: Biblical and Judaic Studies in Honor of Moshe Greenberg*. Edited by Mordechai Cogan, Barry L. Eichler, and Jeffrey H. Tigay. Winona Lake, Ind.: Eisenbrauns, 1997.

———. *The Old Testament: An Introduction*. Translated by J. Bowden. Philadelphia: Fortress, 1986.

———. "Recent German Old Testament Theologies." *JR* 76 (1996): 328–37.

———. "Der Text in seiner Endgestalt: Überlegungen zu Exodus 19." Pages 459–70 in *Ernten was man sät: Festschrift für Klaus Koch zu seinem 65. Geburtstag*. Edited by Dwight R. Daniels et al. Neukirchen-Vluyn: Neukirchener Verlag, 1991.

———. "Toward a Common Jewish-Christian Reading of the Hebrew Bible." Pages 89–108 in *Hebrew Bible or Old Testament? Studying the Bible in Judaism and Christianity*. Edited by Roger Brooks and J. J.

Collins. Christianity and Judaism in Antiquity 5. Notre Dame: University of Notre Dame Press, 1990; rev. and repr. in pages 31–45 of idem, *Canon and Theology*. OBT. Minneapolis: Fortress, 1993.

Roberts, J. J. M. "Does God Lie? Divine Deceit As a Theological Problem in Israelite Prophetic Literature," Pages 211–20 in *Congress Volume: Jerusalem 1986*. Edited by J. A. Emerton. VTSup 40. Leiden: Brill, 1988.

———. "Myth *versus* History." *CBQ* 38 (1976): 1–13.

Rofé, Alexander. "How Is the Word Fulfilled? Isaiah 55:6–11 within the Theological Debate of Its Time." In *Canon, Theology and Old Testament Interpretation: Essays in Honor of Brevard S. Childs*. Edited by Gene Tucker et al. Philadelphia: Fortress, 1988.

———. *Introduction to the Prophetic Literature*. Jerusalem: Academon, 1992.

———. "The Monotheistic Argument in Deuteronomy IV 32–40: Contents, Composition and Text." *VT* 35 (1985): 434–45.

Rose, Paul Lawrence. *Revolutionary Antisemitism in Germany from Kant to Wagner*. Princeton, N.J.: Princeton University Press, 1990.

Rosenzweig, Franz. "Der Ewige: Mendelssohn und der Gottesname." Pages 801–15 in *Gesammelte Schriften. Zweistromland: Kleinere Schriften zu Glauben und Denken*. Dordrecht, 1984. Eng.: "'The Eternal': Mendelssohn and the Name of God:" Pages 99-113 in *Scripture and Translation: Martin Buber and Franz Rosenzweig*. Translated by Lawrence Rosenwald with Everett Fox. Bloomington: Indiana University Press, 1994.

Roth, Martha T. *Law Collections from Mesopotamia and Asia Minor*. SBLWAW 6. Atlanta: Scholars Press, 1995.

Rothman, Stanley, and S. Robert Lichter. *Roots of Radicalism*. New York: Oxford University Press, 1982.

Ruether, Rosemary Radford. *Faith and Fratricide: The Theological Roots of Anti-Semitism*. New York: Seabury, 1974.

Saggs, H. W. F. *The Encounter with the Divine in Mesopotamia and Israel*. London: Athlone Press, 1978.

Sanders, E. P. *Jesus and Judaism*. Philadelphia: Fortress, 1985.

———. *Paul, the Law, and the Jewish People*. Philadelphia: Fortress, 1983.

Sanders, James A. "Adaptable for Life: The Nature and Function of Canon." Pages 531–60 in *Magnalia Dei: The Mighty Acts of God*. Edited by

F. M. Cross, W. Lemke, and P. D. Miller, Jr. Festschrift G. E. Wright. Garden City, N.Y.: Doubleday, 1976. Repr. in pages 9–39 of idem, *From Sacred Story to Sacred Text*. Philadelphia: Fortress, 1987.

———. "Canon, Hebrew Bible." *ABD,* 1:837–52.

———. *Canon and Community*. Philadelphia: Fortress, 1984.

Sandmel, Samuel. "Parallelomania." *JBL* 81 (1962): 1–13.

Sarna, Nahum M. *The JPS Torah Commentary: Genesis*. Philadelphia: Jewish Publication Society of America, 1989.

Sasson, Jack M. "On Choosing Models for Recreating Israelite Pre-Monarchic History." *JSOT* 21 (1981): 3–24.

Schechter, Solomon. *Aspects of Rabbinic Theology*. 1909. Repr., New York: Schocken Books, 1961.

Schmidt, W. H. *Alttestamentlicher Glaube*. Neukirchen-Vluyn: Neukirchener Verlag, 1996.

Scholem, Gershom. "Toward an Understanding of the Messianic Idea in Judaism." Pages 1–36 in *The Messianic Idea in Judaism*. New York: Schocken Books, 1971.

Schreiner, Josef. *Theologie des Alten Testaments*. Würzburg: Echter, 1995.

Schwartz, Regina M. *The Curse of Cain: The Violent Legacy of Monotheism*. Chicago: Chicago University Press, 1997.

Schweickart, Patrocinio P. "Reading Ourselves: Toward a Feminist Theory of Reading." Pages 31–62 in *Gender and Reading: Essays on Readers, Texts and Contexts*. Edited by Elizabeth A. Flynn and Patrocinio P. Schweickart. Baltimore: Johns Hopkins University Press, 1986.

Schweid, Eliezer. *Judaism and Secular Culture* (in Hebrew). Hakibbutz Hameuchad, 1981.

Seeligmann, I. L. "The Understanding of Prophecy in Deuteronomistic and Chronistic History." Pages 205–28 in *I. L. Seeligmann Studies in Biblical Literature*. Edited by Avi Hurvitz et al. Jerusalem: Magnes, 1992.

Segal, Alan. *Rebecca's Children*. Cambridge: Harvard University Press, 1986.

Segundo, Juan Luis. *El dogma que libera*. Santander: Sal Terrae, 1989.

Seitz, Christopher R. "The Old Testament As Abiding Theological Witness." Pages 3–12 in *Word without End: The Old Testament As Abiding Theological Witness*. Grand Rapids: Eerdmans, 1998.

———. "Old Testament or Hebrew Bible?" Pages 61–74 in *Word without End: The Old Testament As Abiding Theological Witness.* Grand Rapids: Eerdmans, 1998.

Setel, Drorah O'Donnell. "Exodus." Pages 26–35 in *The Women's Bible Commentary.* Edited by Carol A. Newsom and Sharon H. Ringe. Louisville: Westminster/John Knox, 1992.

Shanks, Hershel, and Jack Meinhardt, eds. *Aspects of Monotheism: How God Is One.* Washington, D.C.: Biblical Archaeology Society, 1997.

Sheppard, G. T. "Canonical Criticism," *ABD,* 1:863.

Shermis, Michael. *Jewish-Christian Relations: An Annotated Bibliography and Resource Guide.* Bloomington: Indiana University Press, 1988.

Showalter, Elaine. "Critical Cross-Dressing: Male Feminists and the Woman of the Year." Pages 116–32 in *Men in Feminism.* Edited by Alice Jardine and Paul Smith. New York: Methuen, 1987.

———. "Feminism and Literature." Pages 179–202 in *Literary Theory Today.* Edited by Peter Collier and Helga Geyer-Ryan. Ithaca, N.Y.: Cornell University Press, 1990.

Silver, Abba Hillel. *Where Judaism Differed: An Inquiry into the Distinctiveness of Judaism.* Philadelphia: Jewish Publication Society of America, 1957.

Smend, Rudolph. *Die Entstehung des Alten Testaments.* 1978. Repr., Stuttgart: Kohlhammer, 1989.

Smith, H. Shelton. *In His Image, But: Racism in Southern Religion 1780–1910.* Durham, N.C.: Duke University Press, 1972.

Smith, Mark S. *The Early History of God: Yahweh and the Other Deities in Ancient Israel.* San Francisco: Harper & Row, 1990.

Smith, Morton. "The Common Theology of the Ancient Near East." *JBL* 71 (1952): 135–47.

———. "The Image of God." *BJRL* 40 (1958): 473–512.

Smitten, Jeffrey R. and Ann Daghistany, eds. *Spatial Form in Narrative.* Ithaca, N.Y.: Cornell University Press, 1981.

Smolar, Leivy, and Moshe Aberbach. "The Golden Calf Episode in Postbiblical Jewish Literature." *HUCA* 39 (1968): 91–116.

Solomon, Norman. "The Christian Churches on Israel and the Jews." Pages 141–54 in *Anti-Zionism and Anti-Semitism in the Contemporary World.*

Edited by Robert S. Wistrich. New York: New York University Press, 1990.

Soulen, R. Kendall. *The God of Israel and Christian Theology*. Minneapolis: Fortress, 1996.

Speiser, Ephraim A. "Ancient Mesopotamia." Pages 35–76 in *The Idea of History in the Ancient Near East*. Edited by Robert C. Dentan. New Haven: Yale University Press, 1955.

———. *Genesis*. AB 1. Garden City, N.Y.: Doubleday, 1964.

Spencer, John R. "Aaron." *ABD,* 1:1–6.

Sperling, S. David. "An Arslan Tash Incantation: Interpretations and Implications." *HUCA* 53 (1982): 1–10.

———. "Israel's Religion in the Ancient Near East." Pages 5–31 in *Jewish Spirituality: From the Bible through the Middle Ages*. Edited by Arthur Green. New York: Crossroad, 1986.

———. *The Original Torah: The Political Intent of the Bible's Writers*. New York: New York University Press, 1998.

Spieckermann, Hermann. "Die Verbindlichkeit des Alten Testaments: Unzeitgemäße Betrachtungen zu einem ungeliebten Thema." *Jahrbuch für Biblische Theologie* 12 (1997); pages 25–51 in *Hermeneutik*. Neukirchen-Vluyn: Neukirchener, 1998.

Stanton, G. "Matthew." Pages 205–19 in *It Is Written—Scripture Citing Scripture: Essays in Honour of Barnabas Lindars, SSF.* Edited by D. A. Carson and H. G. M. Williamson. Cambridge: Cambridge University Press, 1988.

Steiner, George. *After Babel: Aspects of Language and Translation*. London: Oxford University Press, 1975.

———. "On Difficulty." Pages 18–47 in *On Difficulty and Other Essays*. New York: Oxford University Press, 1987.

———. *Real Presences*. Chicago: University of Chicago Press, 1989.

Stendahl, Krister. "Judaism and Christianity II: A Plea for a New Relationship." *Harvard Divinity Bulletin* New Series 1 (1967): 2–9. Repr. pages 217–32 in K. Stendahl, *Meanings: The Bible As Document and As Guide*. Philadelphia: Fortress, 1984.

Steffens, Lincoln. *Moses in Red: The Revolt of Israel As a Typical Revolution*. Philadelphia: Dorrance, 1936.

Strack, Hermann, and Günter Stemberger. *Introduction to the Talmud and Midrash*. Translated by Markus Bockmuehl. Edinburgh: T&T Clark, 1991.

Stuhlmueller, Carroll. *Creative Redemption in Deutero-Isaiah*. AnBib 43. Rome: Pontifical Biblical Institute, 1970.

Sulzberger, Mayer. *The Status of Labor in Ancient Israel*. Philadelphia: Dropsie College Press, 1923.

Sweeney, Marvin A. "Absence of G-d and Human Responsibility in the Book of Esther." In *Reading the Hebrew Bible for a New Millinnium: Form, Concept, and Theological Perspective*. Vol. 1, *Theological and Hermeneutical Studies*. Edited by Deborah Ellens et al. Harrisburg, Penn.: Trinity Press International, 2000.

———. "The Book of Isaiah As Prophetic Torah." Pages 50–67 in *New Visions of Isaiah*. Edited by R. F. Melugin and Marvin A. Sweeney. JSOTSup 214. Sheffield: JSOT Press, 1996.

———. "Form Criticism." Pages 58–89 in *To Each Its Own Meaning: An Introduction to Biblical Criticisms and Their Application*. Edited by Steven L. McKenzie and Stephen R. Haynes. Rev. ed. Louisville: Westminster/John Knox, 1999.

———. "Formation and Form in Prophetic Literature." Pages 113–26 in *Old Testament Interpretation: Past, Present, and Future*. Edited by J. L. Mays, D. L. Petersen, and K. H. Richards. Festschrift G. M. Tucker. Nashville: Abingdon, 1995.

———. "Tanakh versus Old Testament: Concerning the Foundation for a Jewish Theology of the Bible." Pages 353–72 in *Problems in Biblical Theology*. Edited by H. T. C. Sun et al. Festschrift Rolf P. Knierim. Grand Rapids: Eerdmans, 1997.

———. "Why Jews Should Be Interested in Biblical Theology." *CCAR Journal* 44 (Winter 1997): 67–75.

Swirski, Barbara, and Marilyn P. Safir, eds. *Calling the Equality Bluff: Women in Israel*. New York: Pergamon Press, 1991.

Talmon, Shemaryahu. "*Har* and *Midbār*. An Antithetical Pair of Biblical Motifs." Pages 117–42 in *Figurative Language in the Ancient Near East*. Edited by M. Mindlin, M. J. Geller, and J. E. Wansbrough. London: University of London School of Oriental and African Studies, 1987.

———. "Literary Motifs and Speculative Thought in the Hebrew Bible." *Hebrew University Studies in Literature and the Arts* 16 (1988): 150–68.

Tec, Nechama. *When Light Pierced the Darkness: Christian Rescue of Jews in Nazi-Occupied Poland.* New York: Oxford University Press, 1986.

Terrien, Samuel. *The Elusive Presence: Toward a New Biblical Theology.* New York: Harper & Row, 1978.

Thiselton, Anthony. "The Supposed Power of Words in the Biblical Writings." *JTS* (1974): 283–99.

Thompson, Thomas L. *Early History of the Israelite People: From Written and Archaeological Sources.* Leiden: Brill, 1992.

Thureau-Dangin, Francois. *Rituels accadiens.* Osbarück: Otto Zeller, 1975.

Tigay, Jeffrey H. *The JPS Torah Commentary: Deuteronomy.* Philadelphia: Jewish Publication Society of America, 1996.

———. "The Significance of the End of Deuteronomy (Deuteronomy 34:10–12)." Pages 137–43 in *Texts, Temples, and Traditions: A Tribute to Menahem Haran.* Edited by Michael Fox et al. Winona Lake, Ind.: Eisenbrauns.

———, ed. *Empirical Models for Biblical Criticism.* Philadelphia: University of Pennsylvania Press, 1985.

Toeg, Arie. *Lawgiving at Sinai* (in Hebrew). Jerusalem: Magnes, 1977.

Toorn, Karel van der. *Family Religion in Babylonia, Ugarit, and Israel: Continuity and Changes in the Forms of Religious Life.* Leiden: Brill, 1996.

———. *The Image and the Book: Iconic Cults, Aniconism, and the Rise of Book Religion in Israel and the Ancient Near East.* Leuven: Uitgeverij Peeters, 1997.

———. *Sin and Sanction in Israel and Mesopotamia: A Comparative Study.* SSN 22. Assen: Van Gorcum, 1985.

Tov, Emanuel. "The Septuagint." Pages 161–88 in *Mikra: Text, Translation, Reading and Interpretation of the Hebrew Bible in Ancient Judaism and Early Christianity.* Edited by M. J. Mulder. CRINT 2.1. Assen: Van Gorcum; Philadelphia: Fortress, 1988.

Tracy, David. *The Analogical Imagination.* New York: Crossroad, 1981.

Trible, Phyllis. *God and the Rhetoric of Sexuality.* Philadelphia: Fortress, 1978.

Tsevat, Matitiahu. "God and the Gods in Assembly: An Interpretation of Psalm 82." Pages 131–47 in *The Meaning of the Book of Job and Other Biblical Studies: Essays on the Literature and Religion of the Hebrew Bible.* New York: Ktav, 1980.

Tucker, Gene, "Exegesis." *IDBSup,* 296–303.

Turner, Laurence A. *Announcements of Plot in Genesis.* JSOTSup 96. Sheffield: Sheffield Academic Press, 1990.

Van Buren, Paul M. *A Christian Theology of the People Israel 2: A Theology of the Jewish-Christian Reality.* New York: Seabury, 1983.

———. "On Reading Someone Else's Mail: The Church and Israel's Scriptures." Pages 595–606 in *Die Hebräische Bibel und ihre zweifache Nachgeschichte.* Edited by E. Blum, C. Macholz, and E. W. Stegemann. Festschrift Rolf Rendtorff. Neukirchen-Vluyn: Neukirchener Verlag, 1990.

Van Seters, John. "Comparing Scripture with Scripture: Some Observations on the Sinai Pericope of Exodus 19–24." Pages 111–30 in *Canon, Theology, and Old Testament Interpretation: Essays in Honor of Brevard S. Childs.* Edited by Gene M. Tucker et al. Philadelphia: Fortress, 1988.

———. "Confessional Reformulation in the Exilic Period." *VT* 22 (1972): 448–59.

———. *The Life of Moses: The Yahwist As Historian in Exodus–Numbers.* Louisville: Westminster/John Knox, 1994.

Vaux, Roland de. *The Early History of Israel.* Philadelphia: Westminster, 1978.

———. *La Genèse.* Paris: Cerf, 1951.

Visotzky, Burton L. *The Genesis of Ethics.* New York: Crown, 1996.

Vriezen, Th. C. *An Outline of Old Testament Theology.* Oxford: Blackwell, 1958, 1970.

Walfish, Barry Dov. *Esther in Medieval Garb: Jewish Interpretation of Esther in the Middle Ages.* Albany: State University of New York Press, 1993.

Wallace, Howard N. *The Eden Narrative.* HSM 32. Atlanta: Scholars Press, 1985.

Walzer, Michael. *Exodus and Revolution.* New York: Basic Books, 1985.

Weinfeld, Moshe. "The Covenant of Grant in the Old Testament and in the Ancient Near East." *JAOS* 90 (1970): 184–203.

———. *Deuteronomy 1-11.* AB. New York: Doubleday, 1991.

———. “דיק, עין, שׂכל: A Semantic Analysis.” Pages 101–6 (Hebrew section) in *Tehillah le-Moshe: Biblical and Judaic Studies in Honor of Moshe Greenberg*. Edited by Mordechai Cogan, Barry L. Eichler, and Jeffrey H. Tigay. Winona Lake, Ind.: Eisenbrauns, 1997.

———. *Social Justice in Ancient Israel and in the Ancient Near East*. Jerusalem: Magnes, 1995.

———. “Tithe.” Pages 1156–62 in vol. 15 of *Encyclopedia Judaica*. 16 vols. Jerusalem, 1972.

———. “The Tribal League at Sinai.” Pages 303–14 in *Ancient Israelite Religion: Essays in Honor of Frank Moore Cross*. Edited by P. D. Miller Jr., P. D. Hanson, and S. D. McBride. Philadelphia: Fortress, 1987.

Weiss-Rosmarin, Trude. *Judaism and Christianity: The Differences*. 1943. Repr., New York: Jonathan David, 1972.

Weld, Theodore Dwight. *The Bible against Slavery*. Pittsburgh: United Presbyterian Board of Education, 1864. Repr., Detroit: Negro History Press, 1970. First published in the *Anti-Slavery Quarterly Magazine* (1839).

Wellhausen, Julius. *Prolegomena to the History of Ancient Israel*. 1878. Repr., Atlanta: Scholars Press, 1994.

Wenham, Gordon. *Genesis 12–50*. WBC. Waco, Tex.: Word Books, 1994.

Westenholz, J. G. *Legends of the Kings of Akkade: The Texts*. Mesopotamian Civilizations 7. Winona Lake, Ind.: Eisenbrauns, 1997.

Westermann, Claus. *Blessing in the Bible and the Life of the Church*. Philadelphia: Fortress, 1978.

———. *Elements of Old Testament Theology*. Atlanta: John Knox, 1982.

———. *Genesis 12–36*. Minneapolis: Augsburg, 1985.

Wevers, John William. *Notes on the Greek Text of Exodus*. SBLSCS 30. Atlanta: Scholars Press, 1990.

White, Hugh. *Narration and Discourse in the Book of Genesis*. Cambridge: Cambridge University Press, 1991.

Wiesel, Elie. *Memoirs: All Rivers Run to the Sea*. New York: Knopf, 1995.

Wijk-Bos, Johanna W. H. van. *Reimagining God: The Case for Scriptural Diversity*. Louisville: Westminster/John Knox, 1995.

Williamson, Clark M. *A Guest in the House of Israel: Post Holocaust Church Theology*. Louisville: Westminster/John Knox, 1993.

Williamson, H. G. M. *Ezra, Nehemiah*. WBC 16. Waco, Tex.: Word Books, 1985.

———. "History." Pages 25–38 in *It Is Written—Scripture Citing Scripture: Essays in Honour of Barnabas Lindars, SSF.* Edited by D. A. Carson and H. G. M. Williamson. Cambridge: Cambridge University Press, 1988.

Willoughby, B. E. "Amos, Book of." *ABD,* 1:203–12.

Wilson, Robert R. *Prophecy and Society in Ancient Israel.* Philadelphia: Fortress, 1980.

Wolff, Hans Walter. *Joel and Amos*. Hermeneia. Philadelphia: Fortress, 1977.

Wright, G. E. *God Who Acts: Biblical Theology As Recital.* London: SCM Press, 1952.

Wuthnow, Robert. *The Restructuring of American Religion*. Princeton, N.J.: Princeton University Press, 1988.

Wyman, David S. *The Abandonment of the Jews: America and the Holocaust, 1941–1945*. New York: Pantheon, 1984.

Yahil, Leni. *The Rescue of Danish Jewry: Test of Democracy*. Philadelphia: Jewish Publication Society of America, 1969.

Yaron, Reuven. "Social Problems and Policies in the Ancient Near East." Pages 19–41 in *Law, Politics and Society in the Ancient Mediterranean World*. Edited by Baruch Halpern and D. W. Hobson. Sheffield: Sheffield Academic Press, 1993.

Yee, Gale A., ed. *Judges and Method: New Approaches in Biblical Studies*. Minneapolis: Fortress, 1995.

Yerushalmi, Yosef Hayim. *Zakhor: Jewish History and Jewish Memory*. Seattle: University of Washington Press, 1982.

Yishai, Yael. *Between the Flag and the Banner: Women in Israeli Politics*. Albany: State University of New York Press, 1997.

Yoder, John Howard. "Probing the Meaning of Liberation." *Sojourners* 5.7 (September 1976): 26–29.

Zakovitch, Yair. "Jacob's Cunning." Pages 121–44 in *Sefer Baruch Ben-Yehudah* (in Hebrew). Edited by B. Z. Luria. Tel-Aviv: Israel SBL, 1981.

———. "Through the Looking Glass: Reflections/Inversions of Genesis Stories in the Bible." *Biblical Interpretation* 1 (1993): 139–52.

Zenger, Erich. *Die Sinaitheophanie: Untersuchungen zum jahwistischen und elohistischen Geschichtswerk*. Würzburg: Echter, 1971.

Zenger, Erich, et al. *Einleitung in das Alte Testament*. Stuttgart: Kohlhammer, 1998.

Zimmerli, Walter. *Old Testament Theology in Outline*. Atlanta: John Knox, 1978.

Zornberg, Avivah Gottlieb. *Genesis: The Beginning of Desire*. Philadelphia: Jewish Publication Society of America, 1995.

Contributors

Alice Ogden Bellis, Howard University Divinity School

Marc Zvi Brettler, Department of Near Eastern and Judaic Studies, Brandeis University

Walter Brueggemann, Columbia Theological Seminary

John J. Collins, Yale University, Divinity School

Ellen F. Davis, Virginia Theological Seminary

Terence E. Fretheim, Luther Seminary

Tikva Frymer-Kensky, The Divinity School, The University of Chicago

Esther Fuchs, Department of Judaic Studies, University of Arizona

Baruch Halpern, History Department, Pennsylvania State University

Joel S. Kaminsky, Department of Religion and Biblical Literature, Smith College

Jon D. Levenson, Albert A. List Professor of Jewish Studies at Harvard University Divinity School

Murray H. Lichtenstein, Department of Classical and Oriental Studies, Hunter College, S.U.N.Y

David Marcus, The Jewish Theological Seminary of America

Rolf Rendtorff, Professor Emeritus, University of Heidelberg

Brooks Schramm, Lutheran Theological Seminary at Gettysburg

S. David Sperling, Hebrew Union College-Jewish Institute of Religion

Marvin A. Sweeney, Claremont School of Theology and Claremont Graduate University

Johanna W. H. van Wijk-Bos, Louisville Presbyterian Theological Seminary

Acknowledgments

Davis, Ellen F., forthcoming article in *Pro Ecclesia*

Levenson, Jon D. "Liberation Theology and the Exodus," reprinted from *Reflections* (Spring 1991): 2–12.

Sweeney, Marvin F., reprinted from *Biblical Interpretation* 6 (1998): 142–61. E. J. Brill, publishers

Three articles from *Biblical Theology Bulletin* (Levenson, Collins, Brueggemann)

Index of Primary Sources

Hebrew Scriptures

Apocrypha, Pseudepigrapha, and Dead Sea Scrolls

Targums

New Testament

Mishnah, Tosefta, and Talmud

Other Classical Jewish Sources

Greek and Latin Authors

Medieval Commentators

Index of Modern Authors